You Live Where?

Interesting and Unusual Facts About Where We Live

George E. Thompson

iUniverse, Inc.
New York Bloomington

You Live Where?
Interesting and Unusual Facts About Where We Live

Copyright © 2009 by George E. Thompson.

All rights reserved. No part of this book may be used or reproduced by any means, graphic, electronic, or mechanical, including photocopying, recording, taping or by any information storage retrieval system without the written permission of the publisher except in the case of brief quotations embodied in critical articles and reviews.

The views expressed in this work are solely those of the author and do not necessarily reflect the views of the publisher, and the publisher hereby disclaims any responsibility for them.

iUniverse books may be ordered through booksellers or by contacting:

iUniverse
1663 Liberty Drive
Bloomington, IN 47403
www.iuniverse.com
1-800-Authors (1-800-288-4677)

Because of the dynamic nature of the Internet, any Web addresses or links contained in this book may have changed since publication and may no longer be valid.

ISBN: 978-1-4401-3421-0 (pbk)
ISBN: 978-1-4401-3422-7 (ebk)

Printed in the United States of America

iUniverse rev. date: 7/14/2009

YOU LIVE WHERE?

Twenty-seven states are named from Native American languages

[ ] = suburb of this city   ( ) = interesting fact

ALABAMA – Choctaw word meaning "tribal town." Statehood was 1819; seceded 1861; readmitted 1868. The unofficial state nickname is "Heart of Dixie." It has the second largest inland waterway system in the nation. A natural wonder is Natural Bridge, the longest land bridge span east of the Mississippi River. Mobile is the name of an Indian tribe. The phrase, "The Heart of Dixie" is required by state law to be included on standard state vehicle license plates. As of 2006, Alabama also provides an alternative "God Bless America" license plate at no additional charge.

Famous Alabamians include:
- Henry Lewis "Hammerin' Hank" Aaron (1934–), Mobile; played professional baseball from 1952–1976
- Nat King Cole (1919–1965), Montgomery; born Nathaniel Adams Coles; nickname taken from the nursery rhyme "Old King Cole;" formed his first jazz band while in high school
- W. C. Handy (1873–1958), Florence; known as "Father of the Blues;" wife Elizabeth was from Henderson (Henderson County), KY; over 150,000 people attended his funeral
- Helen Keller (1880–1968), Tuscumbia; the first deaf-blind person to graduate from college; she met every U.S. president from Grover Cleveland to Lyndon B. Johnson who awarded her the Presidential Medal of Freedom
- George "Goober" Lindsey (1935–), Jasper; served in the Air Force; graduated from Kemper Military School and Florence State College with a Bachelor of Bioscience
- Jim "Gomer Pyle" Nabors (1930–), Sylacauga; graduated from University of Alabama; first job in New York was a typist for the United Nations; started in television on *The Steve Allen Show*; recorded twenty-eight albums and several singles; has five gold records and one platinum record
- Condoleezza Rice (1954–), Birmingham; name is from Italian musical term *con dolcezza*, meaning "with sweetness;" played piano for the Queen of England, December, 2008
- Hank Williams (1923–1953), Mount Olive; singer-songwriter, musician; "I Saw the Light," 1948
- Pat Garrett (1850–1908), Cusseta; an Old West lawman, bartender, and customs agent who is best known for killing Billy the Kid; also sheriff of Lincoln County, New Mexico; he was personal friends with President Theodore Roosevelt

Interesting names include: Active; Adams; Addison (Pat Buttram); Alexandria; Aliceville; Allen; Almond; Alpine; America; Anderson; Apple Grove; Arab; Arkadelphia; Ashland; Athens; Axle; Ballplay; Bangor; Bath Springs; Battery Hill; Battleground; Beacon; Bean Rock; Beans Mill; Bear Creek; Beaver Town; Beechwood; Beehive; Bell; Bell Factory; Berlin; Berry; Big Ridge; Billy Goat Hill; Birdeye; Birdsong; Black; Black Bottom;

Black Cat; Black Creek; Black Rock; Blooming Grove; Blueberry Hill; Blue Ford Landing; Blue Mountain; Blue Pond; Blue Ridge; Blue Springs; Blue Springs Park; Boar Tush; Bobo; Boiling Springs; Boot Hill; Boston; Boyd; Bradley; Bravo; Bright Star; Brilliant; Brooklyn; Brooksville; Brownsville; Bucksnort; Buena Vista; Bull City; Burnt Corn; Bush; Butler; Caldwell; Calhoun; Camp Hill; Camp Spring; Campbell; Canoe; Carlisle; Carpenter; Carson; Casey; Catherine; Cave Spring; Cedar Grove; Cedar Plains; Cedar Springs; Cedar Valley; Center Hill; Central; Central City; Chance; Cherrytree; Chestnut; Chestnut Grove; Chigger Hill; China; China Grove; Chrysler; Churchill Downs; Clark; Clay; Cleveland; Clinton; Coal City; Coal Fire; Coaling; Coffee Springs; Coffeeville; Cold Springs; Coldwater; Commerce; Concord; Congo; Cool Springs; Copper Springs; Cornerstone; Cornhouse; Cornwall Furnace; Cottage Grove; Cotton; Cotton Hill; Cotton Valley; Cottonton; Cottontown; Cottonville; Cottonwood; Council Bluff; County Line; Crooked Oak; Crystal Springs; Cuba; Cypress; Daisey City; Dallas; Daniel Boone; Dart; Dayton; Deposit; Derby; Detroit; Dime; Dixie; Dixieland; Dodge City; Dog Town; Dogwood; D'Olive; Dollar; Double Bridges; Double Springs; Doublehead; Douglas; Douglasville; Dove; Dripping Springs; Dry Forks; Dry Valley; Dublin; Duck Springs; Dundee; Eagle; Eagle Creek; Echo; Eclectic; Edna; Egypt; Eight Mile; Equality; Eureka; Evergreen; Fair Oaks; Fairfield (George Lindsey); Fairlane; Fairview; Falls City; Farmersville; Fayette; Fayetteville; Fig Tree; Fishpond; Fishtrap; Five Forks; Five Points; Flat Rock; Flat Top; Floral Crest; Florence; Floyd; Four Mile; Fourmile; Franklin; Freetown; French Hill; French Mill; Fridays Crossing; Friendship; Frog Eye; Fulton; Gamble; Garland; Gary Springs; Geneva; Georgetown; Georgia; German Crossing; Gipsy; Glasgow; Glasgow Corner; Glass; Gobblers Crossing; Gold Hill; Gold Mine; Gold Ridge; Goldbranch; Golddust; Goldville; Gonce; Good Springs; Goodsprings; Goodwater; Goodwins Mill; Gordon Landing; Gordonsville; Grace; Grant; Gravel Hill; Grayson; Green Hill; Green Street; Greenville; Guest; Gulf Crest; Gulf Shores; Gulfcrest; Gum Spring; Gu-Win; Half Acre; Half Chance; Hamburg; Happy Hill; Harmony; Harper Hill; Harpersville; Harvest; Hatchet; Havana; Hawk; Hawk Pride; Hawthorn; Hawthorne; Headland; Healing Springs; Henderson; Hickory Flat; Hickory Grove; High Level; High Pine; Highland Home; Highnote; Hill Number 1; Hill Top; Hoboken; Hog Jaw; Holland Gin; Holly Hills; Holly Springs; Hollytree; Hollywood; Homewood; Hooks; Hopeful; Houston; Hurricane; Idaho; Incline; Indian Springs; Industry; Ino; Institute; Intercourse; Iron City; Ironville; Ivy Creek; Jackson; Jefferson; Jet; Johnson; Johnson Crossroads; Jones Crossroads; Jumbo; Kansas; Kendall Crossroads; Kennedy; Kentuck; Knoxville; Lawrence; Leatherwood; Lebanon; Lee; Letcher; Level Plains; Levelroad; Lewis; Lexington; Liberty; Liberty City; Liberty Hill; Libertyville; Light; Lime; Lime Kiln; Lime Rock; Lincoln; Lindsey; Little New York; Little Oak; Little Rock; Little Texas; Little Warrior; Live Oak; Livingston; Lizzieville; Locust Fork; Lofty; Logan; London; Louisville; Love Hill; Lower Peach Tree; McKenzie; Madison; Madrid; Magnolia; Manchester; Maple Forks; Maple Grove; Maple Hill; Maplesville; Margaret; Marigold; Marion; Mars Hill; Marshall; Martin; Mary; Matthews; Mechanicsville; Memphis; Mercury; Midway; Milk Springs; Miller; Mint Spring; Montgomery (Nat King Cole); Moontown; Morgan; Morris; Morris Mill; Moscow; Mt Sterling; Mt Vernon; Mountain Home; Mountain View; Muck City; Mud Creek; Muscle Shoals; Natural Bridge; Nectar; Needmore; Nelson; New Castle; New Moon;

Nicholsville; Nitrate City; Nix; Normal; Nothing; Oak Grove; Oak Level; Oak Ridge; Oak Village; Oaky Grove; Octagon; Old Harmony; Old Texas; Old Town; Ollie; Opine; Opp; Orange; Our Town; Overlook; Owenton [Birmingham]; Ozark; Paint Rock; Paragon; Partridge Crossroads; Pea Ridge; Pea Ridge Crossroads; Peaceburg; Peach Tree Hills; Peacock; Pennsylvania; Perry Store; Persimmon Grove; Philadelphia; Pigeye; Pikeville; Pilgrims Rest; Pine Apple; Pine Flat; Pine Grove; Pine Haven; Pine Hill; Pine Level; Pine Mountain; Pine Needles; Pine Orchard; Pine Springs; Pineville; Pioneer; Pleasant Grove; Pleasant Groves; Pleasant Hill; Pleasant Home; Pleasant Plains; Pleasant Ridge; Pleasant Site; Pleasant Valley; Pleasant View; Plum Springs; Pogo; Polk; Ponderosa; Pope; Poplar Creek; Poplar Ridge; Poplar Springs; Poplar Springs Branch; Possum Trot; Powell; Prairie; Pratts; Pronto; Prospect; Providence; Pull Tight; Pumpkin Center; Pushmataha; Rabbit Town; Rabbittown; Rabbityard; Rainbow; Rainbow City; Ralph; Rash; Red Bank; Red Bay; Red Hill; Red Level; Red Oak; Red Rock; Red Springs; Red Star; Redbud; Redstone Arsenal; Reform; Refuge; Riddle; Ridge; Ripley; River Bend; River Ridge; Rock City; Rock Creek; Rock Fence; Rock Springs; Rocky Head; Rocky Mount; Rome; Rosebud; Roundhill; Rural; Russell; Salt Well; Samson; Sand Mountain; Sand Rock; Scant City; Scotland; Scratch Ankle; Screamer; Section; Seven Pines; Shady Grove; Shelby; Shorter; Silver Springs; Simpson; Six Mile; Six Way; Sky Ball; Skyline; Slapout; Sledge; Slicklizzard; Smoke Rise; Smuteye; Snow Hill; Social Town; Society Hill; Somerset; South; Speed; Spencer Store; Spring Hill; Spring Valley; Springfield; Spruce Pine; Stage Coach Woods; Stamp; Standard; Stanton; State Line; Straight Mountain; Strawberry; Sugar Creek; Sugarville; Sulphur Springs; Summit; Suncrest; Sunflower; Sunlight; Sunny Home; Sunny South; Sunshine; Sweet Home; Sweet Water; Swift Ford; Sycamore; Sylaucuga (Jim Nabors); Tanner; Taylor; Texas; Texasville; The Bottle; The Village; Thompson; Three Forks; Three Notch; Toadville; Toadvine; Town Creek; Trade; Travelers Rest; Trickem; Trimble; Trio; Tunnel Springs; Tuscumbia (Helen Keller); Twin; Tyler; Uniform; Union Grove; Union Hill; Valley Head; Verbena; Vienna; Viewpoint; Village Number 1; Vinegar Bend; Vine Hill; Vineland; Vocation; Walnut Hill; Warrior; Warsaw; Wateroak; Weathers; Wenonah; White House Springs; White Oak; White Plains; Whitehouse; Whiteoak; Williamsburg; Williamstown; Willow Springs; Winterboro; Wolf Creek; Wolf Springs; Wren; Yelling Settlement; Yellow Pine; Yucca; Zip City

ALASKA – Eskimo word (Aleut) for "great land." Statehood was January 3, 1959. The state nickname is "Last Frontier." It is the largest in land mass but ranks forty-seventh in population. Alaska covers 656,000 square miles while Rhode Island covers 1,500 square miles. Alaska has a ratio of one person per square mile. It is the only state whose capital city is accessible only by boat or air since there are no roads leading in or out of Juneau. If a map of Alaska were laid over a map of the lower forty-eight states, it would stretch north and south from the southern tip of Texas to the Canadian border; the east and west tips would reach from San Francisco to Chicago. The highest recorded temperature in Alaska was 100° on June 27, 1915, and the coldest was -80° on January 23, 1971. The state flag was designed by a thirteen-year-old Alaska native who won a $1,000 scholarship and a watch. Anchorage has never recorded a temperature of 90°. At 400 miles north of the Arctic Circle, Barrow is America's northernmost town and subject to some of the longest stretches of daylight and darkness in the world. In a typical year, the sun rises on about May 10, and does not set again until August 2, creating eighty-four days of daylight. The sun sets in Barrow at about 12:50 PM., on November 18, and is not seen again until January 24, which creates sixty-six days of darkness.

Interesting names include: Alaktak; Ambler; Anderson; Arctic Village; Barrow; Bear River; Beaver; Bell Island Hot Springs; Big Delta; Broad Pass; Campbell; Candle; Central; Chena Hot Springs; Chicago Creek; Chicken; Christian; Circle; Circle Hot Springs; Clam Gulch; Cold Bay; Cold Feet; Coldfoot; Colorado; Comet; Cottonwood; Council; Crystal Fall; Crystal Falls; Dairy; Dead Horse; Diamond; Divide; Douglas; Eagle; Eagle River; Eagle Village; Edna Bay; Eek; Eureka; Excursion Inlet; False Pass; Flat; Folger; Glacier; Goodnews Bay; Happy Valley; Hawk Inlet; Hog Landing; Houston; Humpy Creek; Hurricne; Iditarod; Igloo; Indian; Iron Creek; Johnson; Juneau; Ketchikan; King Salmon; Kodiak; Krik; Lefthand Bay; Lignite; Lime Village; Long; Marshall; Martin; Meyers Chuck; Minto (six miles from) Minto; Montana; Mountain Village; Mud Bay; New Igloo; Nightmute; Nome; North Pole; Old Camp; Old Rampart; Orca; Pelican; Perryville; Platinum; Point Hope; Poorman; Porcupine; Port Protection; Primrose; Rowan Bay; Salt Chuck; Sand Point; Silvertip; Stevens Village; Summit; Sunnyside; Sunshine; Taylor; Tenmile Post; The Harbor; Tin City; Todd; Unalaska; Valdez; Vanderbilt Hill; Washington; West Juneau; White Eye; White Mountain

ARIZONA – Aztec word for "silver bearing." Statehood was February 14, 1912, the last contiguous state admitted to the Union. The state nickname is "Grand Canyon State." The Grand Canyon is one of the seven natural wonders of the world. Arizona is home to the largest and best-preserved meteorite site in the world. The crater is nearly one mile wide and 570 feet deep. During World War II, German and Italian prisoner of war camps were set up in Arizona. Walmart is the state's largest private employer with 17,000 employees (in 2003). Much of the popular Route 66 is now I-40. Tucson has a visibility of 10 miles or more 99% of the time.

Famous Arizonans include:
- Barry Goldwater (1909–1998), Phoenix; served in the Army Air Force in World War II; served five terms in the U.S. Senate; defeated by Lyndon Johnson for president
- Linda Ronstadt (1946–), Tucson
- Lynda Carter (Wonder Woman), (1951–), Phoenix; cast as *Wonder Woman* in 1976

One of the youngest mayors elected in America was twenty-two-year-old Marco Lopez, Nogales, Santa Cruz County.

Interesting names include: Alpine; Anderson; Apex; Apron Crossing; Arizona; Arizona City; Arizona Village; Ash Fork; Asher; Aztec; Baby Rock; Bagdad; Bear; Beaver Dam; Bell; Big Fields; Big Horn; Big Park; Big Springs; Bitter Springs; Black Bear Spring; Black Canyon City; Black Diamond; Black Gap; Blackwater; Blue; Blue Gap; Blue Vista;

Bluewater; Boneyard; Boone; Bootlegger Crossing; Bowie; Brenda; Briggs; Buckeye; Buckeye Mill; Bullhead City; Bumble Bee; Burnt Water; Cactus Flat; Cane; Cane Beds; Carefree; Casa Blanca; Castle Hot Springs; Catfish Paradise; Cave Creek; Cedar; Cedar Creek; Cedar Mill; Cedar Ridge; Centennial; Charleston; Cherry; Chloride; Christmas; Coal Mine Mesa; Colorado City; Columbia; Congress; Constellation; Continental; Copper Creek; Copper Mine; Copper Mines; Cork; Cornfields; Cornville; Cotton Center; Cottonwood; Cow Springs; Coyote Field; Coyote Springs; Crash-up Mountain; Crown King; Cyclopic; Dagger; Date; Date Creek; Desert Wells; Diamond Fields; Dixie; Douglas; Dry Beaver Creek; Earp; Eden; Eleven Mile Corner; Fair Oaks; Fish Creek; Flagstaff (Andy Devine, Jingles); Flat Rock; Floss; Forest Lakes; Fox; Franklin; Gallups; Glendale (Marty Robbins); Globe; Gold Camp; Gold Canyon; Golden Valley; Goobertown; Goodwin; Goodyear; Government Hill; Grand Canyon Village; Grand View; Granite; Granite Dells; Grapevine; Grasshopper; Gray Mountain; Green Valley; Gunsight; Hackberry; Happy Jack; Hayden; Headquarters; Highjinks; Highland Park; Highland Pines; Hillside; Hilltop; Hope; Horse Mesa; House Rock; Hunters Point; Indian Hot Springs; Indian Pine; Indian Wells; Inspiration; Jackrabbit; Johnson; Kansas Settlement; Klondyke; Lebanon; Liberty; Lincoln; Little Spring; Little Tucson; Lost Eden; Love; Low Mountain; Lower Miami; Lower Wheatfields; Magma; Many Farms; Marked Tree; Maverick; Mexican Town; Mexican Water; Miami (Jack Elam); Midway; Milkwater; Minnehaha; Mint; Moccasin; Monkey Run; Monkeys Eyebrow; Montezuma; Morning Star; Mountain Fork; Mountain Meadow; Mountain View; Mule Crossing; Nelson; North Rim; Nothing; Oak Creek; Oak Grove; Oak Springs; Oak Wells; Oatman; Octave; Old Glory; One Mile; Owl; Page; Paradise; Paradise Valley; Parsons Grove; Partridge; Penzance; Peridot; Picture Rocks; Pine; Pine Springs; Pinetop; Pink Arrow; Pioneer; Planet; Point of Pines; Potato Patch; Powell; Punkin Center; Quartzsite; Queen Valley; Rainbow Mines; Rainbow Valley; Rare Metals; Red Lake; Red Mesa; Red Rock; Rim Rock; Robbers Roost; Rock Point; Rocky Point; Rose Well; Rosebud; Rough Rock; Round Rock; Saddle; Sand Springs; Santa Claus; Sawmill; Second Mesa; Show Low; Sierra Vista; Silver Creek; Skull Valley; Smelter Town; Smoke Signal; Snowflake; Soldier Camp; Star Valley; Steamboat; Strawberry; Strayhorse; Strong; Summerhaven; Summit; Sun City (59% females); Sun Valley; Sundad; Sunflower; Sunizona; Sunnyside; Sunrise; Sunset; Sunshine; Suntree [Phoenix]; Sunview; Superior; Surprise; Sweetwater; Swift Trail Junction; Sycamore; Tanner Springs; Taylor; The Gap; Three Forks; Three Way; Three-Way Corner; Tin House; Tombstone; Tonto Village; Top-of-the-World; Tuba City; Twin Falls; Two Guns; Upper Wheatfields; Valentine; Walnut Grove; Washington; Washington Camp; Wheatfields; Whetstone; Whispering Pines; White Cone; Whiteriver; Why; Wide Ruins; Willow Beach; Willow Springs; Window Rock; Winona; Winslow; Winslow West; Wintersburg; Wood Springs; Wood Trap; Yellow Hammer Mill; Yellville; York

ARKANSAS – Indian term meaning "downstream people." From the same root as Kansas. Statehood was June 25, 1836. The state nickname is "Natural State." The first European to arrive in Arkansas was Hernando de Soto in the 1500s. It is one of several states formed from the territory purchased from Napolean Bonaparte as part of the Louisiana Purchase in 1803. Arkansas refused to join the Confederate States of America until after President

Abraham Lincoln called for troops to respond to the provoked attack of Fort Sumter by Confederate forces in South Carolina. Arkansas seceded from the Union on May 6, 1861.

Famous Arkansans include:
- Glen Campbell (1936–), Delight; received his first guitar at age four
- Johnny Cash (1932–2003), Kingsland; enlisted in the Air Force during the Korean War
- William Jefferson Clinton (1946–), Hope; forty-second president of the United States
- John Grisham (1955–), Jonesboro; earned a law degree from University of Mississippi; novelist
- Alan Ladd (1913–1964), Hot Springs; actor; stood 5' 5" tall
- Dick Powell (1904–1963), Mountain View; singer, actor, producer, director
- Charlie Rich (1932–1995), Colt; served in the U.S. Air Force; country music singer-musician
- Paul "Bear" Bryant (1913–1983), Moro Bottom
- Sonny Liston (1928–1971), Sand Slough, Johnson Township; the twelth of thirteen children born to a sharecropper; at 6' 0½" tall his reach of eighty-four inches was matched only by boxers 6' 4" and taller; for many years his fifteen-inch fists were the largest in heavyweight history
- Mark Martin (1959–), Batesville; NASCAR driver
- Scottie Pippen (1965–), Hamburg; 6' 8", 228 lbs; Chicago Bulls and Houston Rockets; worked at a McDonald's Restaurant to help support himself through college
- Brooks Robinson (1937–), Little Rock; third baseman for Baltimore Orioles from 1955–1977; won sixteen consecutive Gold glove Awards and was elected to the Baseball Hall of Fame, 1983
- General Douglas McArthur (1880–1964), Little Rock; officially accepted Japan's surrender September 2, 1945; credited for implementing far-reaching democratic reforms in Japan; in 1951, was removed from command by President Harry S. Truman for publicly disagreeing with his Korean War Policy
- Jerome Hanna "Dizzy" Dean (1910–1974), Lucas; pitcher for Chicago Cubs and St. Louis Cardinals; in game four of the 1934 World Series against the Detroit Tigers, Dean was sent to first base as a pinch runner. The next batter hit a ground ball that that looked like a sure double play. Intent on avoiding the twin killing, Dean threw himself in front of the throw to first. The ball struck him on the head, knocking him unconscious. Although the Tigers went on to win the game, Dean recovered in time to pitch in games five and seven and won the series for the Cardinals.

Two of the youngest mayors elected in America were twenty-one-year old Charles Taylor, 1885, of Van Buren, Crawford County, who killed a man while in office; and twenty-one-year-old Joe Sullivan, 1911, of Imboden, Lawrence County. Sullivan was physically unable to walk, so he relied on a goat-driven cart for transportation.

Interesting names include: Aberdeen; Acorn; Advance; Alabam; Alamo; Albert; Almond; Alpine; Amateur; Antimony; Apt; Arbor Grove; Arkadelphia; Arkansas City; Assumption; Atlanta; Avon; Back Gate; Bald Knob; Ballard; Banner; Barcelona; Bardstown; Bass; Bauxite; Bear; Bear Creek; Bear Creek Springs; Beaver; Bee Branch; Beech Creek; Beech Creek Crossing; Beechwood; Belfast; Bell City; Ben Gay; Berea; Berlin; Berryville; Beverage Town; Bexar; Big Creek Corner; Big Flat; Big Fork; Biggers; Big Hill; Big Lake; Big Rock; Big Spring Mill; Big Springs; Birdeye; Birdsong; Birdtown; Bismarck; Black Diamond; Blackfish; Black Fork; Blackfoot; Black Jack; Blackjack Corner; Black Oak; Black Rock; Black Springs; Bloomer; Blue Bayou; Blue Eye; Blue Springs; Blytheville; Boiling Springs; Boone; Booster; Boston; Bothersome; Bovine; Box Springs; Boyd; Bradley; Briggsville; Bright; Bright Star; Brightwater; Brownsville; Buck Knob; Buck Snort; Buckeye; Buena Vista; Buffalo; Buffalo City; Buffo; Bulltown; Burg; Burnt Cane; Burnt Hill; Burnville; Butler; Butter Creek; Buttermilk; Cache Lake; Calamine; Caldwell; Calico Neck; Calico Rock; Calls; Calmer; Campbell; Cane Creek; Cane Island; Canehill; Caney; Caney Valley; Cannon Creek; Carbon City; Carlisle; Carrollton; Carson Lake; Casey; Cash; Catalpa; Cave; Cave City; Cave Creek; Cave Spring; Cave Springs; Cedar Creek; Cedar Glade; Cedar Grove; Center; Center Grove; Center Hill; Center Point; Centerville; Central; Central City; Chant; Charleston; Charlotte; Checks Corner; Cherry Hill; Chicken; Chimes; Cincinnati; Clear Lake; Clear Spring; Clearwater; Clinton; Clover Bend; Coal Hill; Coffeeville; Coin; Cold Springs; College City; College Hill; Collegeville; Combs; Comet; Concord; Cornhill; Cotton Belt; Cotton Town; Cottonwood Corner; County Line; Cove; Cow Mound; Coy; Cozahome; Credit; Crest; Crittenden; Crockett; Crocketts Bluff; Cross Roads; Crossroad; Crossroads; Crow Creek; Crown; Crystal Springs; Cumberland; Current View; Cypress; Cypress Corner; Daisy; Danville (Jerry Van Dyke); Davenport; Deep Elm; Deer; Defiance; Delaware; Delight (Glen Campbell); Democrat; Denmark; Diamond Cave; Diamond City; Diamond Grove; Dimple; Dixie; Dodge City; Dogpatch; Dogwood; Double Wells; Douglas; Driftwood; Driver; Dryfork; Dub; Dublin; Duff; Dug Hill; Dutch Mills; Eagle Corner; Echo; Economy; Edmonson; Edna; Edwards; Egypt; El Dorado; El Paso; Elevenpoint; Elizabeth; Elk Ranch; Elliott; Elm; Elm Grove; Elm Park; Elm Springs; Elm Store; Elmwood; Empire; England; Enterprise; Estes; Eureka Springs; Evansville; Evening Shade; Evening Star; Experiment; Fairbanks; Fairplay; Fairview; Fairwell; Falcon; Fayetteville; Fender; Fern; Fidelity; Fifty-Six; Figure Five; Finch; Fisher; Fivemile; Flag; Flat; Flatwoods; Fleming; Flint; Flint Springs; Floodway; Floral; Floss; Floyd; Fly Gap; Forest Grove; Formosa; Fort Douglas; Fortune; Forty Four; Forum; Fountain Lake; Four Groves; Four Gums; Fox; Franklin; Free Hope; French; Frenchmans Bayou; Fresno; Friendship; Fulton; Furlow; Gallatin; Garland; Garland City; Garlandville; Gate; Geneva; George; Georges Creek; Georgetown; Gepp; Gid; Gin City; Gobbler; Goobertown; Good Hope; Goodwin; Grapevine; Graphic; Gravel Junction; Grayson; Greasy Corner; Green Forest; Green High; Greene High; Greenland; Greenville; Greenway; Gregory; Gum Grove; Gum Springs; Gum Tree; Half Moon; Halfway; Hamburg; Hamlet; Hancock; Hand; Hand Valley; Happy Corners; Hardin; Hardy; Harmony; Harp; Harriet; Harrison; Hart; Hartford; Hasty; Havana; Healing Springs; Health; Heart; Heelstring; Heifer Landing; Henderson; Henry; Hickman; Hickory Flat; Hickory Grove; Hickory Valley; Hicksville; High; High Fill; Hill Top; Hillside;

Hogeye; Hog Jaw; Holland; Holly Grove; Holly Island; Hollywood; Hope; Hopewell; Horsehead; Horseshoe; Hot Springs; Houston; Hunt; Hunter; Hurricane Grove; Index; Indian; Indian Bay; Ink; Iron Springs; Iron Stob Corner; Island; Island Town; Jasmine; Jaybird; Jefferson; Johnson; Jonquil; Jumbo; Kalamazoo; Kansas; Kay; Kentucky; King; Knob; Knob Creek; Knoxville; Kokomo; LaGrange; Lake City; Lancaster; Larue; Lauratown; Lead Hill; Lebanon; Lee; Leslie; Lewis; Liberty; Liberty Springs; Lick Branch; Lignite; Limedale; Limestone; Lincoln; Lindsey; Little Arkansaw; Little Buffalo; Little Flock; Little Italy; Little Red; Little River; Little Rock; Little Texas; Loafer; Logan; London; Lone Elm; Lone Pine; Lone Rock; Lone Star; Lone Valley; Long; Longwill; Lost Cane; Lost Corner; Love; Love Place; Low Gap; Lucerne; Lumber; Madison; Magazine; Magnet; Magnet Cove; Magnolia; Mammoth Spring; Manila; Many Island; Maple Grove; Maple Springs; Marble; Marion; Marked Tree; Marmaduke; Marshall; Mars Hill; Martha; Martin Box; Maysville; Melbourne; Menifee; Midway; Midway Corner; Miller; Mineral; Mineral Springs; Mistletoe; Mock; Monarch; Monkey Run; Monroe; Monticello; Morgan; Morning Star; Morris; Moscow; Mounds; Mt Holly; Mt Pleasant; Mount Adams; Mount Pleasant; Mount Vernon; Mountain Fork; Mountain Grove; Mountain Home; Mountain Pine; Mountain Springs; Mountain Top; Mountain Valley; Mountain View (Dick Powell); Mountainburg; Mozart; Mulberry; Murray; Nail; Natural Dam; Natural Steps; Nebraska; Needmore; New Moon; New Thompson; Newark; Nogo; Northern Ohio; Nuckles; Number Nine; Oak Forest; Oak Grove; Oak Hill; Oak Ridge; Oakwood; O'Conee; Oil Trough; Okay; O'Kean; Okean; Old Alabam; Old Buffalo; Old Cove; Old Joe; Old Lexington; Old Liberty; Old Thompson; Omaha; Omega; One Horse Store; Oneida; Onyx; Opal; Optimus; Orchard; Ozark; Ozone; Paepcke; Pansy; Paradise View; Paris; Park Place; Parks; Parthenon; Peace; Peach Orchard; Pea Ridge; Peak; Peanut; Pecan Grove; Pecan Point; Pee Dee; Peel; Pencil Bluff; Pendleton; Perry; Perryville; Philadelphia; Pickles Gap; Piggott; Pilgrims Rest; Pine Bluff; Pine City; Pine Ridge; Pine Top; Pinetree; Pineville; Plainview; Plant; Pleasant Grove; Pleasant Hill; Pleasant Home; Pleasant Plains; Pleasant Ridge; Pleasant Valley; Pleasant View; Plum Bayou; Poindexter; Point Cedar; Polo; Ponders; Poplar Ridge; Possum Grape; Post Oak; Potash Sulphur Springs; Poughkeepsie; Powell; Prague; Prairie Creek; Prairie Grove; Prairie Union; Prairie View; Pratt; Prattsville; Princeton; Promised Land; Prosperity; Provo; Pulaski [Little Rock]; Pump Springs; Pumpkin Bend; Rainbow Island; Rally Hill; Ralph; Raspberry; Ratio; Red Bank; Red Bluff; Red Hill; Red Leaf; Red Oak; Red Rock; Red Star; Red Wing; Redbird; Redfield; Reform; Rendezvous; Riceville; Rich; Rivervale; Rock; Rock Hill; Rocky Comfort; Rocky Hill; Rocky Mound; Rockhouse; Roe; Romance; Rome City; Rose City; Roseville; Round Hill; Round Pond; Rover; Royal; Rule; Rushing; Russell; Ruth; St Charles; St Joe; Saddle; Sage; Saginaw; Salesville; Saline; Sand Ridge; Sandtown; Sandy; Sandy Bend; Sandy Land; Scotland; Scott; Scranton; Self; Sellers Store; Sensation; Settlement; Shady; Shady Grove; Shark; Shelbyville; Shell Lake; Shirley; Sidney; Silver; Silver Hill; Simpson; Skylight; Slicker; Smackover; Smithland; Snow; Snow Hill; Snow Lake; Snowball; Social Hill; Spring Creek; Spring Hill; Springfield; Stacy; Stamps; Standard Umpstead; Stanford; Star; State Line; Sterling Spring; Sterling Springs; Stillwater; Stinking Bay; Stonewall; Stop; Strawberry; Stringtown; Strong; Stumptoe; Sturgis; Stuttgart; Success; Sulphur City; Sulphur Rock; Sulphur Springs; Summit; Sunnyside; Sunrise; Sunset; Sunshine; Supply;

Sutherland Crossroads; Swan Lake; Sweden; Sweet Home; Sweethome; Sycamore; Sycamore Spring; Tall Trees; Tannenbaum; Tax; Taylor; Temperanceville; Tennessee; Texarcana; The Basin; The Pines; The Quarry; Thompson; Three Brothers; Three Creeks; Three States; Three Way; Toledo; Tomahawk; Topaz; Trident; Trigg; Tulip; Tumbling Shoals; Turkey; Turkey Creek; Turkey Scratch; Turnip; Twentythree; Twin Bridges; Twin Creek; Twist; Two Mile; Tyler; Umpire; Union; Union Hill; Uniontown; Uno; Valentine; Valley Ridge; Valley Springs; Valley View; Van Buren; Venus; Viney Grove; Viola; Violet Hill; Walnut; Walnut Corner; Walnut Grove; Walnut Grove Corner; Walnut Hill; Walnut Ridge; Walnut Springs; War Eagle; Warm Springs; Washington; Watervalley; Weathers; Weeks; Weiner; Welcome; West Liberty; Whisp; Whispering Springs; Whistleville; White Bluff; White Cliffs; Whitehall; White Oak; White Oak Bluff; White Rock; Wild Cherry; Williams Gulf; Willow; Wing; Winona Springs; Winslow; Wolf Bayou; Wolquarry; Wooden Hills; Woodland Hills; Wyanoke; Y City; Yellow Banks; Yellow Bayou; Yellville; Yukon; Zinc

CALIFORNIA – Spanish for "paradise." Statehood was September 9, 1950, after Mexico ceded California to the United States. The state nickname is "Golden State." It is the most populous state in the United States. It has fifty-eight counties (Kentucky has 120). California is home to:

- the largest living organisms on earth–the Giant Sequoia
- the highest point in the lower forty-eight states–Mount Whitney
- the tallest living things on Earth–the giant redwoods
- the lowest and hottest place in the Western Hemisphere–Death Valley (282 feet below sea level)
- the highest temperature ever recorded in the U.S. is 134° Fahrenheit on July 10, 1913. The highest and lowest places in America are less than 200 miles apart.
- bristlecone pines in the White Mountains are the oldest known trees in the world; one is estimated to be 4,700 years old

Famous Californians include:

- General George Smith Patton (1885–1945), San Gabriel; "Only two defining forces have ever offered to die for you, Jesus Christ and the American soldier. One died for your soul; the other for your freedom."
- Shelley Fabares (1944–), Santa Monica; born Michele Anne Marie Fabares; played the role of the daughter on the television series *The Donna Reed Show;* she and Annette Funicello have been close friends since they were teenagers

As the twentieth century came to a close, 40% of all Buddhists in America lived in southern California. California has fifteen major professional sports league franchises, far more than any other state. The richest place in America, with a population of one thousand or more, is Belvedere whose per capita income is $113,600. Numbers two, three, and four are also in California. Willow Creek is the "Bigfoot Capital of the World." Fruit cocktail was invented in Campbell.

Interesting names include: Aberdeen; Academy; Advance; Afton; Alabama Hill; Alamo; Albany; Alleghany; Allen; Alliance; Alpine; Ampere; Amsterdam; Anchor Bay; Anderson; Angels Camp; Annapolis; Antelope; Antlers; Apex; Apple Valley; Arcade; Aromas; Arrowhead Springs; Ash Hill; Aspen Valley; Asylum; Athens; Atlanta; Atlas; Avocado; Avon; Azalea; Badger; Badwater; Bagdad; Balance Rock; Ballard; Bangor; Barber City; Basin; Bath; Bear Creek; Bear Valley; Beegum; Bee Rock; Bell; Bell Springs; Bend; Ben Hur; Berry Creek; Beverly Glen; Beverly Hills; Big Bear City; Big Bend; Big Bunch; Big Chief; Big Creek; Big Oak Flat; Big Pine; Big River; Big Sur; Big Trees; Bird Rock; Birds Landing; Bitterwater; Bivalve; Blackhawk; Blue Jay; Blunt; Bonnie Bell; Booneville; Bootjack; Boston Ravine; Boulder Creek; Boulder Oaks; Boys Republic; Bradley; Bridge House; Bridgeport; Bridgeville; Briggs Terrace; Brownsville; Bruceville; Buchanan; Buckeye; Buckhorn; Bucktown; Buena Vista; Buffalo Hill; Bull Creek; Bully Hill; Bumblebee; Bummerville; Bunker Hill; Burnt Ranch; Bush; Butler; Buttonwillow; Cabbage Patch; Cabin Cove; Cactus; Cactus City; Cadiz; Cain Rock; Calexico; California City; California Hot Springs; Camden; Camp Eighteen; Campbell (eBay); Canebrake; Cannery Row; Canyon City; Canyon Dam; Cape Horn; Capetown; Capital Hill; Carbondale; Caribou; Carmel; Carmel-by-the-Sea; Carson; Cascade; Castle Rock Springs; Cave City; Cedar Crossing; Cedar Flat; Cedar Glen; Cedar Grove; Cedar Ridge; Cedar Slope; Cedar Springs; Centerville; Central; Central Valley; Challenge; Cheeseville; Cherry Valley; Chicago Park; Childs Meadows; Chinese Camp; Chiquita; Chloride City; Chrome; Citrus; Clear Creek; Clearing House; Clinton; Clover Flat; Clovis; Coarsegold; Cockatoo Grove; Coffee Creek; Cold Fork; Cold Springs; College City; Collegeville; Commerce; Concord; Confederate Corners; Confidence; Consume; Consumme; Convict Lake; Cooks Valley; Cool; Copper City; Copperopolis; Corporal; Cottage Corners; Cottage Grove; Cottage Springs; Cotton Center; Cottonwood; Cow Creek; Coyote Wells; Crater; Crescent City; Crest; Crestview; Crittenden; Crockett; Cypress; Cypress Grove; Dairyland; Danville; Date City; Dates; Davenport; Day; Deadwood; Death Valley; Deep Park; Deep Springs; Deer Creek; Deer Creek Crossing; Deer Crossing; Deer View; Derby Acres; Desert; Desert Camp; Desert Center; Desert Hills; Desert Hot Springs; Desert Lake; Desert View; Dew Drop; Diamond Bar; Diamond Springs; Diamond Valley; Ditch Camp Five; Dixie; Dixieland; Dogtown; Dollar Point; Douglas City; Douglas Flat; Dove Canyon; Dry Valley; Drytown; Dublin; Dunes; Dunmovin; Dutch Flat; Eagle Mountain; Eagle Tree; Eagleville; Earp; Edwards; Eel Rock; Elk Creek; Elk Grove; Emigrant Gap; Engineer Springs; English Town; Enterprise; Erie, Eucalpytus Hills; Eureka; Everglade; Ewing; Fair Oaks; Fair Play; Fairbanks; Fairport; Fall River Mills; Fallen Leaf; Fawnskin; Fayette; Feather Falls; Fern; Fernwood; Fiddletown; Field; Fig Orchard; Fillmore; Fine Gold; Fire Mountain; Firebrick; Fish Camp; Fish Rock; Fish Springs; Fisher; Five Mile Terrace; Five Points; Flea Valley; Flower Pot; Floyd; Forest; Forest Falls; Forest Home; Forest Meadows; Forest Ranch; Forest Springs; Foresthill; Forks of Salmon; Fountain Springs; Fountain Valley; Four Corners; Four Pines; Fourth Crossing; Franklin; Fredericksburg; French Camp; French Gulch; Fresh Pond; Freshwater Corners; Frying Pan; Fulton; Garden Grove; Garden Valley; Gardenland; Gas Point; Gasoline Alley; Gazelle; Geneva; Georgetown; Giant; Glasgow; Globe; Goat Rock; Gold Flat; Gold Hill; Gold River; Gold Run; Golden Hills; Goldstone; Grabtown; Grand; Grandview; Granite Bay;

Granite Springs; Graniteville; Grant; Grapeland; Grapevine; Grass Flat; Grass Lake; Grass Valley; Grays Flat; Grayson; Greekstore; Greendale; Greenfield; Greenhorn; Green Valley; Greenville; Greenwater; Grizzly Flats; Grove; Grover Beach; Groverland; Gum; Half Moon Bay; Halfway House; Hallelujah Junction; Hambone; Hamburg; Happy Camp; Happy Valley; Hardy; Harlem; Harmony; Harp; Harper; Harpertown; Harriet; Harrisburg; Hart; Hat Creek; Hayden; Hayden Hill; Hayfield; Hayfork; Haystack; Helltown; Henderson; Henry; Hercules; Hershey; Hetch Hetchy Junction; Hickman; Highway City; Highway Highlands; Hollydale; Hollywood; Home Gardens; Homeland; Home Valley; Honeydew; Hood; Hope Valley; Hop Yard; Horse Creek; Horse Lake; Hot Springs; Hub; Hunter-Liggett; Huron; Iceland; Igo; Incline; Independence; Indian Falls; Indian Gulch; Indian Hill; Indian Springs; Indian Wells; Ingot; Interlaken; Iowa Hill; Iris; Irish Town; Iron Horse; Irvine; Island Mountain; Ivanhoe; Jackson; Jamestown; Java; Jefferson [LA]; Jimtown; Johannesburg; Joshua Tree; June Lake; Juniper Springs; Jupiter; Keddie; Keg; Kennedy [Stockton]; Kensington; Kentucky House; Keystone; Kid; Kilowatt; King City; King Salmon; Kit Carson; Klondike; Knoxville; La Grange; Lake Alpine; Lake City; Lake of the Woods; Last Chance; Laurel; Lawrence; Laws; Lemon Cove; Levee; Liberty; Likely; Lincoln; Lincoln Village; Little Lake; Little Norway; Little Paradise; Little Penny; Little River; Littlerock; Little Valley; Live Oak; Livingston; Logan; Logandale; Loganville; London; Lone Pine; Lone Star; Lone Wolf Colony; Long Beach; Long Valley; Lookout; Los Angeles (Jackie Cooper, *Our Gang Comedy, The People's* Choice); Lost City; Lost Hills; Lotus; Lovelock; Lucerne; Mad River; Madison; Maglolia; Mammoth; Mammoth Lakes; Manhattan Beach; Manila; Maple Grove; Marsh Mill; Marshall; Marysville; Matthews Mill; Meadow Brook; Melbourne; Menifee; Mercuryville; Meridian; Merryman; Mesquite Oasis; Michigan Bluff; Midas; Midway; Midway City; Mile High; Miles; Mill City; Miller; Mineral; Mineral King; Minnesota; Minnesota Flat; Miracle Hot Springs; Missouri Triangle; Moccasin; Monroe [Santa Rosa]; Montezuma; Montgomery; Moonstone; Morgan Hill; Morgan Springs; Motion; Motor City; Mt Washington; Mt Wilson; Mount Baldy; Mountain Center; Mountain Pass; Mountain Ranch; Mountain Top Junction; Mountain View; Mudrock Crossing; Murray; Mystic; Naples; Nashville; Need; Needles; Nelson; Nevada City; Newark; Nice; Ninetynine Oaks; North Star; Nut Tree; Oak Bottom; Oak Glen; Oak Grove; Oak Hills; Oakhurst; Oak Knoll; Oakland (Eddie Anderson, *Rochester*); Oak Park; Oak Run; Oak Valley; Oak View; Oakville; Oasis; Ocean Roar; Old River; Old Station; Olympic Valley; Omega; Onehundred Palms; One Hundred Palms; Ono; Ontario; Onyx; Orange; Orange Cove; Orangevale; Oregon City; Oregon House; Overlook; Pacific; Pacific House; Palmdale; Palm Desert; Palmetto; Palm Grove; Palm Springs; Palm Wells; Panama; Paradise; Paradise City; Paradise Springs; Paris; Patch; Peaceful Pines; Peachton; Peachtree Crossing; Peanut; Peavine; Penney; Pennys Corner; Pepper Corner; Pepperwood; Perry [Los Angeles]; Pierce; Pike; Pinecrest; Pine Flat; Pine Grove; Pine Hills; Pineridge; Pine Valley; Pinewood; Pinnacles; Pioneer; Pioneertown; Pioneer Point; Pismo Beach (from *Dragnet*); Pittsburg; Plantation; Plaster City; Pleasant Grove; Pleasant Hill; Pleasant Valley; Pleasant View; Point Arena; Point Pleasant; Poker Flat; Pole Garden; Polk Springs; Pond; Pondosa; Posts; Poverty Hill; Prattville; Priest; Princeton; Prospect; Prunedale; Pumpkin Center; Quail; Quail Valley; Quaker Meadow; Quality; Quartz Hill; Queen City; Rail Road Flat; Rainbow;

Rainbow Spring; Rainbow Wells; Raisin City; Rawhide; Red Apple; Red Bank; Redbanks; Red Bluff; Redcrest; Red Dog; Red Hill; Redlands; Redman; Red Rock; Red Top; Redway; Redwood City; Redwood Corral; Redwood Grove; Redwoods; Redwood Valley; Relief; Rescue; Retreat; Reward; Rice; Rich; Richmond; Ridge; Rimrock; Ripley; Riverbank; Riverbend; River Oaks; River Pines; Riverside; Riverside Park; Roads End; Robbers Creek; Robert; Rochester; Rock City; Rock Creek; Rock Haven; Rodeo; Rosedale; Rose Place; Roseville; Rough and Ready; Round Mountain; Round Valley; Running Springs; Russell; Ruth; Sabre City; Saddle; Sage Hen; Sageland; Saint Louis; Salt Creek; Salvia; Salyer; Samoa; San Andreas; Sands; San Francisco (Sen Yung, *Hop Sing on "Bonanza"* who was, in fact, a great cook); San Gabriel (General George Patton); San Leandro (Harold Peary, *The Great Gildersleeve*); Sarasota Springs; Sargent; Savercool Place; Sawmill Flat; Scales; Scissors Crossing; Scotland; Scranton; Seabright; Seacliff; Seal Beach; Secret Town; Selma; Seven Oaks; Seven Pines; Seven Trees; Shadow Hills; Shady Glen; Sheepranch; Sheepshead; Shingletown; Shoulder; Shrub; Siberia; Sierra City; Sierraville; Signal Hill; Silverado; Silver City; Singing Springs; Skull Valley; Skyforest; Sky High; Skyhigh; Skytop; Sky Valley; Sleepy Hollow; Sleepytown; Sleepy Valley; Smartville; Snow Bend; Snow Creek; Snowflake; Soapweed; Soda Bay; Soda Springs; Somerset; Spanish Flat; Spanish Ranch; Spring Garden; Spring Valley; Springville; Squabbletown; Squaw Valley (Stu Erwin); Stacy; Stallion Springs; Stanford; Stanton; Stateline; Steam; Steelhead; Stevens; Stone; Stone Place; Stovepipe; Stovepipe Wells; Strawberry; Strawberry Valley; Sudden; Sugarfield; Sugar Pine; Summer Home; Summertown; Summit; Sun City; Suncrest; Sundad; Sunkist; Sunland; Sunnybrook; Sunnyside; Sunnyslope; Sunnyvale; Sunrise; Sunrise Vista; Sunset; Sunsweet; Surf; Surfside; Surprise Station; Susanville; Sweetbriar; Sweetland; Sycamore Flat; Sycamore Springs; Table Bluff; Tan Oak Park; Tarzana; Taylor; Taylor Crossing; Taylorsville; Teakettle Junction; Telegraph City; Tennant; Tent City; The Cedars; The City; The Crossing; The Forks; The Oaks; The Pines; The Willows; Thermal; Thompson; Thompson Place; Thousand Oaks; Thousand Palms; Three Arch Bay; Three Crossing; Three Points; Three Rivers; Three Rocks; Tiger Lily; Timbuktoo; Toadtown; Tollhouse; Topaz; Top of the World; Tranquility; Twain; Twentynine Palms; Twin Bridges; Twin Creeks; Twin Lakes; Twin Oaks; Twin Pines; Two Rivers; Union City; Union Hill; Union Mills; Upper Lake; Upper Town; Vacation Beach; Valley Ranch; Valley Springs; Vine Hill; Virginiatown; Volcano; Volcanoville; Walnut; Walnut Creek; Walnut Grove; Washington; Weaverville; Weed; Weeds Point; Weedpatch; West Carson; Wheatland; Whispering Pines; White River; White Spot; White Wolf; Whitehawk; Whitehorn; Wildflower; Wildrose; Wildwood; Willow Brook; Willow Creek; Willow Creek Crossing; Willow Point; Willow Springs; Willow Valley; Willows; Wilson Corner; Wilson Grove; Wimp; Winchester; Winter Gardens; Winters; Winterhaven; Witch Creek; Wolf; Woodford; Woodland; Woodleaf; Woodside; Woodville; Yorba Linda (Richard Nixon); You Bet; Yosemite Forks; Yosemite Village; Youngstown; Yreka; Yucca Grove; Yucca Inn; Yucca Valley; Zurich; Zzyzx;

COLORADO – The Colorado Territory was named by Congress in 1861, by taking the name from the Colorado River (Rio Colorado), a Spanish term meaning red or reddish.

Statehood was August 1, 1876, giving it the nickname "Centennial State." It is the only state whose elevation does not go below 3,315. Pikes Peak is 14,115 and can be seen from near the Kansas border on clear days. Colorado has fifty-four mountain peaks that are at least fourteen thousand feet in elevation; they are known as "fourteeners." It is one of the leading states in deaths due to lightning. The highest temperature ever recorded in Colorado was 118° Fahernheight, while the lowest recorded temperature was -61° Fahernheight. It is the only state to refuse the opportunity to host the Olympics. The Denver metropolitan area is home to half the state's population.

Famous Coloradoans include:
- Lon Chaney Sr (1883–1930), Colorado Springs; as a child of deaf parents he became skilled in pantomime; known as "The Man of a Thousand Faces"; *Phantom of the Opera, The Hunchback of Notre Dame*
- Ralph Edwards (1913–2005), Merino; in 1940, he created *Truth or Consequences* which aired for thirty-eight years on radio and television; in 1956 Edwards enlisted Bob Barker to emcee *Truth or Consequences*; hosted *This Is Your Life*
- Jack Dempsey (1895–1983), Manassa; born William Harrison Dempsey; World Heavyweight Boxing Champion from 1910–1926

Interesting names include: Able; Agate; Akron; Alamo; Alice; Allen; Alpine; American City; Americus; Anaconda; Angora; Antelope Springs; Antlers; Anvil Points; Apex; Applewood; Arrowhead; Aspen; Aspen Park; Atlanta; Aurora; Austin; Avon; Azure; Bachelor; Basalt; Basin; Beartown; Beaver Creek; Beaver Point; Bedrock; Beetland; Beta; Beverly Grove; Beverly Hills; Big Elk Meadows; Bighorn; Bijou; Birdseye; Black Eagle Mill; Black Forest; Black Hawk; Bloom; Blue Mountain; Blue River; Blue Valley; Boone; Boulder; Bountiful; Bridgeport; Briggsdale; Brimstone Corner; Bristol; Brook Forest; Brush; Buchanan; Buckeye; Buckeye Crossroads; Buckskin Joe; Buena Vista; Buffalo Creek; Buick; Burlington; Burnt Mill; Cabin Creek; Calhoun; Cameo; Camp Bird; Capitol City; Carbonate; Cardinal; Carracas; Carson; Carterville; Cascade; Castle Pines; Castle Rock; Cathedral; Catherine; Cattle Creek; Cedar Creek; Cedar Crest; Cedar Grove; Cedar Point; Cedaredge; Centennial; Center; Central City; Chance; Chattanooga; Cherry Ridge; Cheyenne Wells; Chimney Rock; Cimarron; Clark; Clay; Coal Creek; Coalmont; Cold Spring; Colorado City; Colorado Springs; Columbine; Columbine Hills; Columbine Valley; Columbus; Commerce City; Concrete; Conifer; Continental; Cope; Copper Mountain; Cozy Corner; Crescent; Cripple Creek; Crook; Dallas; De Beque; Deer Tail; Delta; Derby; Derby Junction; Dinosaur; Divide; Dome Rock; Dominion; Dove Creek; Dover; Eagle; Eagles Nest; Echo; Echo House; Echo Lake; Eden; Edler (one mile from) Elder; Edwards; Elephant Park; Elizabeth; Elk Park; Elk River; Elk Springs; Elkhead; Elkton; Empire; Erie; Estes Park; Evanston; Evergreen; Fairplay; Fairview; Falcon; Farmers; Fayette; Ferncliff; Fink; Fir; Fire Clay; Firestone; First View; Flager; Flat; Fleming; Florence; Florida; Ford; Fort Carson; Fort Garland; Fort Morgan; Fountain; Four Corners Crossing; Fox Creek; Foxfield; Freeland; Frick; Frost; Fruitvale; Futurity; Garden City; Garland City; Gary; Gateview; Gateway; Gem Village; Georgetown; Gladstone; Golden; Goodnight; Goodpasture; Goodrich; Graft; Granite; Grant; Grate; Greely (Ted

Mack); Greenhorn; Greenland; Green Mountain Falls; Green Mountain Village; Grizzly; Grover; Gunbarrel; Gypsum; Happy Canyon; Hardin; Hasty; Heartstrong; Henderson; Henry; Hillside; Holly; Hollywood; Hot Sulphur Springs; Hygiene; Idaho Creek; Idaho Springs; Independence; Indian Hills; Indian Meadows; Iris; Iron City; Irondale; Ironton; Jack Springs; Jefferson; Joes; Johnson; Juniper Hot Springs; Keyhole; Keystone; Kit Carson; Knob Hill; Kokomo; Lake City; Lake George; Larkspur; Las Animas (Ken Curtis, *Festus Haggen*); Last Chance; Lay; Leader; Lebanon; Lewis; Liberty; Liberty Bell; Liggett; Lime; Lincoln; Lincoln Hills; Lincoln Park; Little Dam; Living Springs; Logan; Log Lane Village; Logtown; Lone; Lone Oak; Lone Star; Lonetree; Lone Tree; Lonetree; Louisville; Lucerne; Mad Creek; Madrid; Magnolia; Manhattan; Manila; Marble; Marigold; Marshall; Marvel; Mayday; Maysville; McCoy; Meeker; Meridian; Midland; Midway; Mineral Hot Springs; Minnehaha; Mirage; Model; Monarch; Montezuma; Monument; Moonridge; Morgan; Morning Glory; Mountain View; Mt Lincoln; Muleshoe; Narrows; Nelson; Nevadaville; New Castle; Nighthawk; Noel; No Name; Norfolk; Oak Creek; Ohio; Ohio City; Old Roach; Old Wells; Orchard; Orchard City; Orchard Corner; Orchard Park; Owl Canyon; Oxyoke; Pagoda; Palisade; Parachute; Paradise Hills; Paradox; Pea Green Corner; Pearl; Pear Park; Peoria; Phoenix; Pieplant Mill; Pierce; Pine; Pine Nook; Pinewood Springs; Pittsburg; Placerville; Plainview; Planter; Plastic; Plateau City; Pleasant View; Plumbs; Portland; Powderhorn; Powder Wash; Powell; Princeton; Prospect; Punkin Center; Puritan; Quartzville; Radium; Ragged Mountain; Range; Red Cliff; Redlands; Red Lion; Red Mountain; Redstone; Redvale; Rifle; River Bend; Riverview; Rock Creek Park; Rockvale; Rocky; Rocky Ford; Roe; Romeo; Rosedale; Roundup Junction; Rugby; Russell; Rustic; Rye; St Charles; Salt Creek; Sample; San Antonio; San Francisco; Sargents; Sawpit; Security; Selma; Seven Lakes; Severance; Shamrock; Sheephorn; Silt; Silver Cliff; Silverdale; Silver Heights; Silver Plume; Silver Springs; Silver Spruce; Silverthorne; Silverton; Simpson; Skinners; Sky Village; Skyway; Slick Rock; Smeltertown; Snowball gap; Snowmass; Snowmass Village; Snow Water Springs; Somerset; Spanish Village; Sparks; Spencer; Spike Buck; Springfield; Spruce; Sprucedale; Sprucewood; Stage; State Bridge; St Charles; Steamboat; Steamboat Springs; Sterling Place; Stonewall; Strasburg; Sublette; Sugar; Sugar City; Sugar Junction; Sugarloaf; Summitville; Sunbeam; Sunnyside; Sunset City; Sunshine; Superior; Swallows Nest; Switzerland Village; Tacoma; Texas Creek; The Pinery; Thistledown; Three Forks; Tin Cup; Tiny Town; Tomboy; Trapper; Treasure; Trimble; Trinidad; Troublesome; Troutdale; Trump; Tungsten; Turret; Twelve-mile Corner; Twin Cedars; Twin Crossing; Twin Forks; Twin Mills; Twin Spruce; Una; Uncompahgre; Union; Utah Junction; Valdez; Vigil; Vineland; Viola; Vulcan; Wagon Wheel Gap; Wallstreet; Washington; Wauneta; Weaver; Wheat Ridge; White River City; Whitehorn; Whitepine; Whitewater; Wild Cat; Wild Horse; Wiley; Williamsburg; Will-O-The-Wisp; Wilson Junction; Winter Park; Woody Creek; Xenia; Yampa; Yarmony; Yellow Jacket; Yuma

CONNECTICUT – The name originates from the Mohican word for the Connecticut River, *quinnitukqut,* "long tidal river." Statehood was January 9, 1788. The state nicknames is "Constitution State," and unofficially "The Nutmeg State." It is the fifth of the original Thirteen Colonies. A Resident of Connecticut is a Connecticuter. The first

English settlers in the area were Puritans in 1633. Connecticut has the most million-dollar homes in the northeast with four percent of homes valued at over $1 million. Nationwide it ranks second to California. The state manufactures helicopters, aircraft parts, and nuclear submarines. The state officially recognizes aircraft designer Gustav Whitehead as "Father of Connecticut Aviation" for his research into powered flight in 1901, two years before the Wright Brothers flew their plane at Kitty Hawk. Connecticut is home of Yale, one of the world's richest universities. Only eight percent of incoming freshman applicants are accepted. Manero's Steakhouse in Greenwich offers to any baby born in the restaurant free meals for life.

Television shows that were set in Connecticut include *Bewitched, Who's the Boss, Gilmore Girls, The Luci-Desi Comedy Hour,* and *Judging Amy.*

Signers of the Declaration of Independence from Connecticut include: Samuel Huntington, Roger Sherman, William Williams, and Oliver Wolcott.

Famous Connecticuters include:
- Benedict Arnold (1741–1801), Norwich; an American general who originally fought for the Americans in the Revolutionary War but later switched to the British Empire; was considered by most to be the best and most accomplished leader in the Continental Army
- Nathan Hale (1755–1776), Coventry; at age thirteen his brother sent him to Yale College; graduating with honors in 1773, he became a teacher; after the Revolutionary War began in 1775, he joined the Connecticut militia as a first lieutenant; just before being hanged, said, "I regret that I have but one life to lose for my country"
- Harriet Beecher Stowe (1811–1896), Litchfield; in the novel, *Uncle Tom's Cabin,* she attacked the cruelty of slavery; her brother was Henry Ward Beecher
- Henry Ward Beecher (1813–1887), Litchfield; Protestant clergyman and abolitionist
- George W. Bush (1946–), New Haven; 43rd president of the United States
- Bob Crane (1928–1978), Waterbury; in 1946, he enlisted in the Army Reserve; played the role of Colonen Hogan on the television series *Hogan's Heroes* from 1965—1971; he also played the role of Dr. Dave Kelsey on *The Donna Reed Show*

Interesting names include: Aspetuck; Avon; Beacon Falls; Beaverbrook; Bedlam; Bedlam Corner; Berlin; Bethel (P.T. Barnum); Birch Groves; Birchwood; Birdland; Black Rock; Blue Hills; Bradleyville; Branchville; Breakneck; Bridgeport; Bridgewater; Bristol; Broad Brook; Brooklyn; Buckland; Bull Run Corner; Bulls Bridge; Bunker Hill; Burnt Hill; Calhoun Corners; Campville; Candlewood Orchards; Candlewood Pines; Candlewood Point; Candlewood Springs; Canterbury; Canton; Canton Center; Canton Valley; Cedar Land; Central Village; Cherry Park; Cheshire; Chester; Clayville; Clinton; Cobalt; Cobalt Landing; Columbia; Cornwall; Cornwall Bridge; Cornwall Center; Cornwall Hollow; Cos Cob; Cottage Grove; Crystal Run; Deep River; Derby; Durham; Eagleville; East Morris;

East Thompson; Ebbs Corner; Elmdale; Elm Hill; Falls; Falls Village; Farmers Mills; Field Corners; Firetown; Five Points; Floydville; Forestville; Four Corners; Fox Den; Franklin; Georgetown; Germantown; Giants Neck; Gildersleeve; Glasgo; Goodrichville; Graniteville; Greenfield Hill; Green Hill; Greenville; Grosvendor Dale; Hamburg; Hammertown; Happyland; Hartford (Katherine Hepburn); Hayden; Hazardville; Headquarters; Hickory Haven; Hollywile Park; Honeypot Glen; Hope Valley; Hopeville; Hopewell; Horse Heaven; Hotchkissville; Hungary; Ivoryton; Kensington; Kent Furnace; Lake Bungee; Laurel Glen; Lebanon; Liberty Hill; Lime Rock; Litchfield; Little City; Long Hill; Lordship; Madison; Manchester; Mansfield Four Corners; Marble Dale; Marion; Mayberry Village; Mechanicsville; Middlefield; Middletown; Midway; Milestone Corner; Millstone; Minortown; Miry Brook; Mixville; Monroe; Moosup; Morningside; Morris; Murray; Mystic; Norfolk; North Thompsonville; Nut Plains; Oakland; Oakland Gardens; Oakville; Obtuse Hill; Old Mystic; Orange; Orcutts; Orcuttsville; Ore Hill; Overlook; Ox Hill; Perkins Center; Perkins Corner; Phoenixville; Pilgrim Corners; Pine Bridge; Pine Grove; Pine Hill; Pine Meadow; Pineville; Plainfield; Podunk; Pond Meadow; Portland; Presidential; Prospect; Puddle Town; Quaddick; Quaker Hill; Quakertown; Quarryville; Quebec; Quinebaug; Rainbow; Ridgewood; Rising Corner; River Glen; Riversville; Robertsville; Rockfall; Rockville; Rocky Glen; Rocky Hill; Salem; Salem Four Corners; Salmon Brook; Sandy Hook; Scotland; Shady Harbor; Spring Hill; Sterling; Sterling Hill; Stetson Corner; Stevenson; Stony Ford; Tariffville; Taylor Corners; The Cedars; Thompson; Thompsonville; Town Hill; Town Plot Hill; Trumbull; Turkey Cobble; Twin Lakes; Union City; Unionville; Vernon; Vernon Center; Vernon Rockville; Versailles; Village Hill; Warehouse Point; Warren; Washington; Washington Depot; Watertown; West Thompson; Whigville; Whipstick; Wilson; Wilsonville; Winchester; Woodbridge; Woodstick; Woodville; Yelping Hill

DELAWARE – Named after Lord De La Warr. Statehood was December 7, 1787. It is one of the original Thirteen Colonies and is known as the "First State," officially referring to the fact that it was the first to ratify the United States Constitution. Delaware is the second-smallest state, next to Rhode Island. Before Delaware was settled by the Europeans, the area was home to the Eastern Algonquian tribes. Dover Air Force Base, one of the largest in the country, is located in Delaware's state Capital.

Signers of the Declaration of Independence include: Thomas McKean, George Read, and Caeser Rodney.

Notable Delawarans include:
- Eleuthere Irenee (E.I.) du Pont (1771–1834), Paris, France; migrated to U.S. in 1799, and founded the gunpowder manufacturer E. I. du Pont

Interesting names include: Afton; Ashland; Atlanta; Augustine; Bacon; Bear; Bear Valley; Beech Haven; Bell; Belltown; Berrytown; Big Oak Corners; Big Stone Beach; Birds Corner; Blackwater; Blades; Blue Ball; Breezewood; Briar Park; Brick Store;

Bridgeville; Broad Creek; Brookside; Camden; Camden-Wyoming; Canterbury; Carpenter; Carpenters Corner; Cave Colony; Centerville; Cocked Hat; College Park; Colony Hills; Columbia; Cool Spring; Cottage Mill; Covered Bridge; Cripple Creek; Deer Creek; Deerwood; Delaware City; Derby Shores; Dover; Drawbridge; Dublin Hill; Eagles Nest Landing; Fairwinds; Federalsburg; Fern Hook; Five Points; Fleming Corners; Forest; Forest Park; Four Seasons; Fox Hall; Fox Hollow; Georgetown; Glasgow; Glasgow Pines; Goose Point; Gordon Heights; Gravel Hill; Green Briar; Green Hill; Greenville; Gulls Nest; Gumboro; Gumwood; Hares Corner; Harlemtown; Hedgerow Hollow; Henry Clay; Hickman; Hickory Hill; Hickory Ridge; Hilldale; Hillendale; Holiday Pines; Hollandsville; Holly Knoll; Hollymount; Holly Oak; Hollyville; Hopkins Corner; Hourglass; Houston; Iron Hill; Ivy Ridge; Johnson; Kenton; Laurel; Lebanon; Liberty; Lincoln; Little Creek; Little Heaven; Locustville; London Village; Long Neck; Lords Corner; Loveville; Magnolia; Marshallton; Marydel; Meadowbrook; Meadowood; Mechanicsville; Meeting House Hill; Melody Meadows; Mermaid; Middletown; Mill Creek; Mockingbird Hills; Mount Cuba; Mount Pleasant; Nassau; New Castle; Nooseneck; North Star; Oak Forest; Oak Grove; Ocean View; Overbrook; Owls Nest; Oyster Rocks; Packing House Corner; Peacock Corners; Penny Hill; Pepper; Pepperbox; Philadelphia; Pike Creek; Pilottown; Pinetown; Pine Tree Corners; Pleasant Hill; Pleasant Hills; Pleasantville; Quaker Heights; Quaker Hill; Quakertown; Quarryville; Ralphs; Red Lion; Rising Sun; Riverside; Riverview; Rockland; Roseville; Sand Hill; Sandtown; Savannah Place; Schoolview; Scrap Town Crossroads; Seven Hickories; Shady Grove; Shelbyville; Sherwood Forest; Shortly; Silverside; Six Forks; Spring Hill; Spring Valley; Stanton; Star Hill; St George; St Georges; Summit Bridge; Susan Beach Corner; Swallow Hill; Sweet Briar; Sycamore; Taylors Bridge; Taylors Corner; Taylortown; Tent; The Timbers; Thompsonville; Three Seasons; Turnkey; Twin Oaks; Valley View; Viola; Walnut Hill; Walnut Ridge; White Hall; Whitehall Crossroads; Williamsburg; Williamsville; Willow Grove; Willow Run; Wooddale; Woodenhawk; Woodland; Woods Haven; Woodshaven; Wyoming

FLORIDA – Spanish for "flowers." Statehood was March 3, 1845. Seceded from the Union on January 10, 1861; readmitted January 25, 1868. The state nickname is "Sunshine State." It was named by Juan Ponce de Leon who landed in St. Augustine in 1513, during Pascua Florida, the Spanish term for "Easter Flowery." Ponce de Leon encountered at least one native Indian who could speak Spanish. Florida became a state in 1845. In 1861, just before the formal breakout of the Civil War, Florida seceded from the Union. Ten days later, it became a founding member of the Confederate States of America. Before the Civil War, when slavery was legal, and during the Reconstruction period following the Civil War, blacks made up nearly one-half of the state's population.

The highest elevation is 345 feet. The hottest temperature ever recorded in the state was 109° Ferenheight set on June 29, 1931. The coldest temperature on record, -2° Ferenheight, was set just twenty-five miles away on February 13, 1899. It is the only time the temperature ever went below zero. At that time, snow fell as far south as Tampa Bay. In January, 1977, snow flurries were seen at Miami Beach for the only time in recorded history. Central Florida is known as the lightning capital of the world since it experiences more lightning strikes than anywhere else in the country. Hurricane Andrew (1992) was the second costliest weather disaster in American history, costing $25 billion. Tourism is the state's greatest cash crop followed by citrus. Florida produces about sixty-five percent of all the citrus grown in America. Nearly 95% of all oranges grown in Florida will be used to make juice. NASA arrived on Merritt Island in 1962. Century (Escambia County) is fifty miles north of Stokesville (Charlton County), Georgia.

Notable Floridians include:
- Bobby Goldsboro (1941–), Marianna; played guitar for Roy Orbison 1962–1964 before going out on his own; he was on a plane that was hijacked to Cuba; biggest hit was "Honey" in 1968

One of the youngest mayors elected in America was twenty-three-year-old Willie Logan, Opa-locka, Miami-Dade County.

Interesting names include: Aberdeen; Acres of Diamonds; Adams; Alpine; Atlantic Beach; Atlantis; Avon Park; Azalea Park; Bagdad; Bahama Beach; Barberville; Battle Ground Forks; Bayonet Point; Bayou George; Beachville; Bean City; Bear Hollow; Beaver Creek; Beech Creek; Beechwood; Bee Ridge; Beetree Ford; Belgium; Bell; Bellville; Benton; Berrydale; Beverly Beach; Beverly Hills; Big Pine; Big Scrub; Bimini; Black Creek; Black Diamond; Blackman; Black Point; Blacks Ford; Bland; Blowing Rocks; Bluefield; Blue Gulf Beach; Blue Lake; Blue Mountain Beach; Blue Springs; Bluff Springs; Bon Ami; Bowling Green; Boyd; Bridges; Bridgeport; Briny Breezes; Brooksville; Browns Still; Brownsville [Pensacola]; Bruce; Bruceville; Buchanan; Buckhead Ridge; Buckhorn; Buckville; Buena Vista; Buffalo Bluff; Bunker Donation; Bunker Hill; Burbank; Cabbage Grove; Cadillac; Callaway; Campbell; Campton; Caney Creek; Cannon Town; Carol City; Cedar Creek; Cedar Grove; Cedar Key; Celebration; Centerville; Central City; Century; Cherry Lake; Chosen; Christmas; Citrus Center; Citrus Park; Citrus Springs; City Point; Clark; Clay Sink; Clear Springs; Clearwater; Cleveland; Cloud Lake; Cocoa; Cocoa Beach; Coconut; Coconut Creek; College Park; College Station; Concord; Cook; Corckscrew; Cottage Hill; Country Walk; Covington; Cow Creek; Crackertown; Crescent City; Crestview; Crystal River; Crystal Springs; Cypress; Cypress Creek; Cypress Gardens; Cypress Harbor; Cypress Lake; Cypress Point; Dallas; Danville; Davenport; Day; Deep Lake; Deerland; Deer Park; De Soto City; Dixie; Dixietown; Dogtown; Douglas City; Douglas Crossroads; Duck Key; Eagle Island; Eagle Lake; Early; Eden; Edgewater; Elfers; Elkton; Eureka; Everglades City; Evergreen; Fairview; Fairview Shores; Falmouth; Farm Hill; Fawn Ford; Feather Sound; Federal Point; Fiddlesticks; Fidelis; Fisher Corner; Fish Hawk; Five Points; Flamingo Bay; Floral City; Florence; Florida Beach; Florida City; Florida Garden; Floridale; Florida Ridge; Floridatown; Flowersville; Fluffy Landing; Forest City; Fortymile Bend; Fountain; Franklin; Freeport; Frog City; Frostproof; Fruit Cove; Fruitland; Fruitville; Fulton; Garden City; Garden Grove; Gardenville; Gardner; Geneva; Georgetown; Glass; Golden Beach; Golden Gate; Golden Glades; Goldenrod; Goodbys; Good Hope; Gopher Ridge; Gordon; Gordonville;

Graceville; Grand Island; Grand Ridge; Grand View; Grant; Green Bay; Greenhead; Green Pond; Greensboro; Greenville; Grocery Place; Gross; Groverland; Gulf City; Gulf Hammock; Gulfport; Gulf Stream; Half Moon; Hamburg; Hancock; Happy Valley; Harbor Oaks; Harbor View; Harlem; Harp; Harper; Harrisburg; Harrison; Havana; Hen Scratch; Hero; High Springs; Hill and Dale; Hog Valley; Holiday; Holland; Holly Hill; Holly Point; Hollywood; Homestead; Homestead Ridge; Honey-in-the-Hills; Hopewell; Hornsville; Horseshoe; Horseshoe Beach; Houston; Howey-in-the-Hills; Huntington; Hypoluxo; Indian Ford; Indian River City; Indian Rocks Beach; Indian Shores; Indiantown; Intercession City; Interlochen; Iowa City; Irvine; Italia; Jacksonville (Pat Boone); Jay; Jay Jay; Jessamine; Johnson; Juniper; Jupiter; Jupiter Island; Kathleen; Kennedy Still; Kensington; Keystone; Key West; Kilarney Shores; La Crosse; Lake Bird; Lake City; Lake Placid; Land O' Lakes; Laurel; Laurel Grove; Laurel Hill; Lebanon; Lee; Leisure City; Lemon Bluff; Lemon Grove; Lewis; Liberty; Limestone; Limestone Creek; Lincoln City; Little Lake City; Little Torch Key; Live Oak; Loch Lommond; Long Beach; Long Hammock; Long Key; Lorida; Madison; Magnolia Beach; Magnolia Springs; Mango; Manhattan; Marion; Mason; Mayo; McAllister Landing; McDavid; Meadow Woods; Melbourne; Memphis; Mercer; Meridian; Midway; Miller; Mineral Springs; Molasses Junction; Monarch; Monticello; Morgantown; Mosquito Landing; Moss Bluff; Mossy Head; Mount Pleasant; Muddy Ford; Mud Hole; Naples; Nassau; Nassauville; Needmore; Neptune Beach; New York; Niceville; Nichols; Ninemile Bend; Nixon; Oak Grove; Oak Hill; Oakland; Oak Ridge; Old Bay View; Old Town; Orange; Orange Blossom; Orange Blossom Hills; Orange City; Orangedale; Orange Hill; Orange Home; Orange Lake; Orange Mills; Orange Mountain; Orange Park; Orange Springs; Orangetree; Orchid; Orient Park; Osprey; Otter Creek; Pace; Padlock; Painters Hill; Palm Bay; Palm Beach; Palm Beach Gardens; Palm City; Palm Coast; Palmdale; Palmeto; Palm Harbor; Palm Shadows; Palm Shores; Palm Springs; Panacea; Panama City; Panama City Beach; Paradise; Pass Station; Peach Orchard; Pecan; Peck; Penney Farms; Perry; Picnic; Pine Barren; Pine Bluff; Pine Castle; Pinecrest; Pine Forest; Pine Grove; Pine Hills; Pine Island; Pine Island Ridge; Pineland; Pine Level; Pine Log; Pine Mount; Pine Ridge; Piney Grove; Pirates Cove; Pittsburg; Plantation Key; Plant City; Pleasant Grove; Plum Orchard; Point Pleasant; Ponce de Leon; Pond Creek; Poplar Head; Port Lonesome; Port Orange; Powell; Pretty Bayou; Princeton; Prosperity; Providence; Rainbow Falls; Redbay; Red Head; Redland; Red Level; Relay; Rice Creek; Rideout; Riverside; Roach; Rock Bluff; Rock Creek; Rock Hill;Rockledge; Rock Ridge; Rocksprings; Rocky Point; Roeville; Rosedale; Roseland; Rosewood; Royal; Russell; Saint George; Saint Nicholas; Salt Springs; Sampson; Sampson City; San Antonio; Sand Cut; Sand Hill; Sandy Hills; Sandy Point; Santa Fe; Sargent; Sawdust; Scotland; Seaside; Seven Springs; Seville; Shadeville; Shady; Shady Grove; Shady Rest; Shamrock; Shell Bluff; Shiny Town; Silver Palm; Silver Springs; Silver Springs Shores; Sink Creek; Sixmile Bend; Sixmile Creek; Snow Hill; Snows Corner; Sopchoppy; Spray; Spring Creek; Springfield; Spring Hill; Springville; Spuds; Stanton; Stockade; Sugarloaf Shores; Sugarmill Woods; Sun City; Sun Garden; Sunnyside; Sunset; Sunset Beach; Sunset Corners; Sunset Harbor; Sunset Point; Sunshine Beach; Sun Valley; Surfside; Suwannee; Suwannee Springs; Suwannee Valley; Sweetwater; Switzerland; Sycamore; Tampa (Butterfly McQueen, *Prissy* and *Beulah*); Tangerine; Tarpon;

Tarpon Springs; Taylor; Thompson; Three Oaks; Tidewater; Tiger Bay; Tobacco Patch Landing; Trailtown; Treasure Island; Turkey Creek; Turkey Foot; Twentymile; Twentymile Bend; Two Eggs; Tyler; Union; Up the Grove Beach; Usher; Utopia; Valpariso; Venice; Venus; Vicksburg; Wagon Wheel; Walnut Hill; Warm Mineral Springs; Watertown; Welcome; Whisper Walk; White Beach; Whitehouse; White Oak Landing; White Springs; Wildwood; Williamsburg; Willow Oak; Winter Beach; Winter Garden; Winter Haven; Winter Park; Winter Springs; Woodville; Yankeetown; Yeehaw; Yellow Bluff; Yellow Water

GEORGIA – Named after King George, II. Statehood was January 2, 1788. The state nickname is "Peach State." It was the last of the original Thirteen Colonies and the fourth state to ratify the U.S. Constitution. It seceded from the Union January 21, 1861, and was readmitted July 15, 1870. It was one of the seven original Confederate States of America. In December, 1864, a large swath of land from Atlanta to Savannah was destroyed during General Sherman's infamous March to the Sea. This event served as the historical background for the 1936 novel, *Gone with the Wind*, which was followed by the film in 1939. In 1870, five years after the end of the Civil War, Georgia was the last Confederate State to be readmitted back into the Union.

Although agriculture is the leading economic standard, it is aided by ten military installations throughout Georgia. Aflac, Arby's, BellSouth, Chic-Fil-A, Coca-Cola, Delta Airlines, Home Depot, and UPS have their business headquarters in Atlanta.

The state song is "Georgia on My Mind," by Hoagie Carmichael. The song was originally written about a woman by that name, but after Georgia native Ray Charles recorded it, the state legislature voted it the state song on April 24, 1979. Ray Charles sang it on the legislative floor the day the bill was passed. Georgia not only has a state song, it also has a state possum: Pogo Possum (the comic strip character). Native Ted Turner founded TBS, TNT, TCM, Cartoon Network, CNN, and Headline News. The Weather Channel's headquarters are in Smyrna, a metropolitan area of Atlanta, but in the next county.

In 1969, seven years before Jimmy Carter was elected president, he reported seeing a UFO. During the 1976 presidential campaign, Carter reported that it was one of the most amazing things he had ever seen. He described it as being very large, very bright, and that it changed colors. He reported that it was watched for ten minutes, but no one could determine exactly what it was. Carter is reported to have said that he will never again make fun of people who say they have seen a UFO.

Signers of the Declaration of independence include: Button Guinette, Lyman Hall, and George Walton.

Notable Georgians include:

- Jimmy Carter (1924–), Plains; thirty-ninth president of the United States; first U.S. president born in a hospital; taught Sunday school for most of his adult life
- Oliver Hardy (1892–1957), Milledgeville; his father, a Confederate soldier, was wounded in the Battle of Antietam; Hardy's career with Stan Laurel lasted 40 years
- Sterling Holloway (1905–1992), Cedartown; voice of *Winnie the Poo* and other Disney characters; appeared on *Superman* as the squeaky-voiced Uncle Oscar, the eccentric inventor; also appeared on *The Life of Riley; Hazel; Gilligan's Island; F-Troop; The Andy Griffith Show*; and several movies
- Martin Luther King Jr. (1929–1968), Atlanta; youngest person to receive Nobel Peace Prize; sang with his church choir at the 1939 Atlanta premiere of the movie *Gone with the Wind*
- Brenda Lee (1944–), Atlanta; born Brenda May Tarpley; at age two she could whistle a tune heard on the radio; by age ten she was the primary breadwinner for the family; she began her recording career at age twelve
- Little Richard (1932–), Macon; born Richard Wayne Penniman; helped lay the foundation for rock and roll music in the mid 1950s with such songs as "Tutte Frutti," "Lucille," and "Long Tall Sally;" on a 1963 tour of Europe, The Beatles opened for Little Richard; in 1957, he became a born-again Christian and recorded only gospel music until the early 1960s
- Jackie Robinson (1919–1972), Cairo; the Army transferred Lieutenant Robinson to Camp Breckinridge, Morganfield (Union County), KY where he served as an athletics coach; was first African-American to integrate major league baseball, 1947; played for the Brooklyn Dodgers 1947–1956; played in the World Series six times; inducted into the Baseball Hall of Fame 1962
- Ray Charles (1930–2004), Albany; born Ray Charles Robinson; name changed to avoid confusion with boxer Sugar Ray Robinson; when the Georgia state legislature adopted "Georgia on My Mind" as the state song, Ray Charles sang the song in front of the entire body of legislators

Interesting names include: Aberdeen; Acorn Pond; Adel; Aerial; Afton; Agricola; Airline; Alamo; Albany (Ray Charles); Alley; Alpine; Alps; Americus; Apple Valley; Arborville; Archery; Argyle; Athens; Ball Ground; Barbers; Bath; Beech Hill; Beechwood; Belfast; Bell; Benefit; Benevolence; Benton; Berlin; Bermuda; Berryville; Between; Beverly; Beverly Hills; Big Creek; Big Oak; Big Springs; Birds; Birdsong Crossroads; Birdsville; Birmingham; Blackjack; Blackwood; Bloodtown; Blowing Spring; Blue Ridge; Blue Springs; Bogart; Bold Springs; Boston; Box Ankle; Box Springs; Briarcliff; Brick Store; Bridges Crossroad; Bridgetown; Broad; Bronco; Brooklyn; Brook Springs; Brooksville; Brownsand; Brownsville; Brownwood; Buchanan; Buckhead; Buena Vista; Bullhead Bluff; Burning Bush; Burnside; Burnt Creek; Burnt Fort; Butler; Cairo; Calhoun; Callaway; Campton; Cane Creek; Carrollton; Cavalry Hill; Cave Spring; Cedar Cliff; Cedar Crossing; Cedar Grove; Cedar Rock; Cedar Springs; Cedar Valley; Centennial; Center; Center Hill; Center Point; Centerville; Charles; Cheddar; Cherry Log; Chestnutflat; Chestnut Mountain; China Hill; Clearview; Clearwater Springs; Cleaton; Cleveland;

Clinton; Cloudland; Clover; Coal Mountain; Coffee; Coffee Bluff; Coldbrook; College Park; Columbus; Commerce; Commissary Hill; Concord; Cool Springs; Corbin; Cork; Cottle; Cotton Hill; County Line; Covington; Crabapple; Crane Eater; Credit Hill; Crescent; Cross Roads; Crossroads; Crystal Springs; Cuba; Cutcane; Daisy; Dallas; Danville; Dasher; David; Debruce; Deepstep; Denmark; Denver; Deposit; Dewy Rose; Diamond; Diamond Hill; District Path; Divide; Dixie; Doctortown; Dog Crossing; Double Run; Douglas; Douglasville; Dove Creek; Dresden; Dry Branch; Dry Pond; Dublin; Ducker; Ducktown; Dugdown; Dug Hill; Duluth; Eagle Grove; Early; Eden; Edna; Egypt; Eightmile Still; Elmview; Empire; English Eddy; Enigma; Enterprise; Excelsior; Experiment; Faceville; Fair Oaks; Fairplay; Fairview; Falling Rocks; Fantasy Hills; Fargo; Farmdale; Farmersville; Farmville; Fashion; Fayetteville; Fields; Fighting Pine; Fish; Fish Creek; Five Forks; Fivemile Still; Five Points; Five Springs; Flat Ford; Flat Rock; Flat Shoals; Fleming; Flint; Flint Hill; Flintstone; Floral Hill; Flowery Branch; Floyd; Forest Glen; Fort Gordon; Fort McAllister; Four Points; Franklin; Free Home; Friendship; Fruitland; Fulton [Atlanta]; Gamma; Garden City; Garden Valley; Gary; Geneva; Georgetown; Germany; Glasgow; Goat Town; Gobblers Hill; Goldmine; Good Hope; Gordon; Gordon Springs; Grandview; Granite Hill; Graves; Grayson; Greensboro; Greens Cut; Greenville; Gregory; Grove Level; Gumbranch; Gum Branch; Gumlog; Halfmoon Landing; Handy; Happy Landing; Hard Cash; Harding; Harlem (Oliver Hardy, *Laurel and Hardy*); Harmony; Harp; Harper; Harrisburg; Harrison; Hart; Hartford; Harvest; Hazard; Head River; Helena; Hemp; Henderson; Henderson Still; Hentown; Hephzibah; Hickory Bluff; Hickory Flat; Hickory Level; High Falls; High Point; High Shoals; Hill City; Hillman; Hills; Hilltop; Hobby; Hoboken; Hog Hammock; Hog Mountain; Holland; Holly Spring; Holly Springs; Homerville; Homestead; Hood; Hopeful; Hopeulikeit; Hopewell; Hopkins; Hothouse; Houston; Ideal; Imperial; Indian Springs; Industrial City; Iron City; Irondale; Iron Stab; Ivylog; Jackson; Jacksonville; Jamaica; Jamestown; Jay Bird Springs; Jefferson; Jersey; Jewelville; Jinks; Jot Em Down; Julia; Junction City; Juniper; Kansas; Kensington; Kite; Klondike; Knott; Knoxville; K'Ville; LaGrange; Lake City; Lake Creek; Lebanon; Leslie; Level Land; Lewis; Lexington; Liberty; Lily Pond; Limerick; Lincoln Landing; Lincolnton; Little Hope; Little River; Livingston; Loco; Locust Grove; Logan; Loganville; Log Landing; Logtown; Lone Oak; Long Cane; Lookout Mountain; Louisville; Love Hill; Loving; Lumber City; Madison; Magnet; Magnolia; Major; Manassas; Manchester; Marble Hill; Marion; Marshall; Marshallville; Mars Hill; Martin; Mason; Match; Mayday; Mayfield; Maysville; McKee; Meadow; Mechanic Hill; Mechanicsville; Meridian; Mexico Crossing; Miami Valley; Midway; Mineral Bluff; Mize; Monroe; Montezuma; Montgomery; Monticello; Moons; Morgan; Morningside; Morris; Mosquito Crossing; Moss Oak; Mossy Creek; Mountainbrook; Mountain City; Mountain Hill; Mountain Park; Mountain Scene; Mountain Springs; Mountain View; Mount Airy; Mt Berry; Mt Vernon; Mulberry; Mulberry Grove; Nashville; Needmore; Nelson; Newborn; New England; Newport; Nicholasville; Nixon; Noble; Noonday; Note; Oakfield; Oak Grove; Oak Hill; Oakland; Oak Mountain; Oak Park; Oakwood; Okay; Old Town; Omaha; Omega; Orange; Orchard Hill; Orchard Hills; Owen; Owensboro; Owltown; Panhandle; Park City; Peachtree City; Peacocks Crossing; Pecan; Pecan City; Percale;Perennial; Perry; Persimmon; Phoenix; Piddleville; Pineboro; Pinefield Crossroads; Pine Grove; Pine Hill;

Pinehurst; Pine Lake; Pineland; Pine Log; Pine Mountain; Pine Mountain Valley; Pine Park; Pine Ridge; Pine Valley; Pineview; Piney Grove; Pink; Pin Point; Pittsburg; Plainfield; Plains; Plainview; Pleasant Grove; Pleasant Hill; Pleasant Valley; Poetry Tulip; Pomona; Ponderosa; Pond Spring; Poplar Grove; Poplar Springs; Portal; Portland; Powder Springs; Prairie View; Presidential; Pretoria; Priest; Primrose; Princeton; Prior; Prosperity; Pulaski; Quality; Queensland; Quitman; Rabbit Hill; Radio Springs; Raleigh; Ranger; Raytown; Rebecca; Recovery; Red Bluff; Redbone Crossroads; Redbud; Red Clay; Red Hill; Red Rock; Red Stone; Red Wine; Register; Relay; Reno; Rest Haven; Retreat; Ripley; Rising Fawn; Rivers End; Riverside; Rivertown; Rock Branch; Rock Hill; Rockledge; Rockridge; Rock Spring; Rockville; Rocky Creek; Rocky Face; Rocky Ford; Rocky Hammock Landing; Rocky Mount; Rocky Plains; Rome; Roosterville; Rosebud; Rosedale; Rose Hill; Round Oak; Roundtop; Rover; Royal; Russell; Russellville; Saginaw; Sale City; Sand Bend; Sand Hill; Sandtown; Sandy; Sandy Bottom; Sandy Point; Sandy Springs; Santa Claus; Sarah; Sargent; Sautee; Sawdust; Scarlet; Scenic Hills; Scotland; Scott; Scuffletown; Sells; Seville; Shady Dale; Shady Grove; Shake Rag; Sharpsburg; Sharp Top; Shell Bluff; Sherwood Forest; Shoal Creek; Shoals; Shoulderbone; Silk Hope; Silk Mills; Silver City; Silver Creek; Silver Hill; Silver Pines; Silvertown; Simpson; Six Mile; Sky Valley; Snake Nation; Snapfinger; Snapping Shoals; Snows Mill; Snow Springs; Soapstick; Social Circle; South Thompson; Southward; Spain; Sparta; Split Silk; Spooner; Spring Bluff; Spring Branch; Springfield; Spring Place; Star Point; St Charles; Stephens; Stephensville; Sterling; Stevens Crossing; St Louis; Stocks; Stone Mountain; Stonewall; Stoney Point; Stop; Sugar Creek; Sugar Hill; Sugartown; Sugar Valley; Sumac; Summertown; Summerville; Summit Hill; Sunbury; Sun Hill; Sunny Side; Sunnyside; Sunset Village; Sunsweet; Suwanee; Sweden; Sweet Gum; Swords; Tails Creek; Talking Rock; Tax Crossroads; Taylors Mill; Taylorsville; Temperance; Texas; The Rock; Thirteen Forks; Thompson Crossroad; Thompsons Mill; Thompsonville; Three Forks; Three Points; Thunderbolt; Tidings; Tiger; Toledo; Toonerville; Torreys Landing; Traders Hill; Trenton; Trimble; Truckers; Tunnel Hill; Twin City; Ty Ty; Union; Union City; Union Hill; Union Point; Unionville; Valley View; Veribest; Vienna; View; Vineyard Crossroads; Waco; Wagon Wheel; Walnut Grove; Warfield; Warm Springs; Warsaw; Washington; Wax; Wayback; Waycross (Pernell Roberts *Adam Cartwright; Trapper John, M.D.*); Wayside; Weaver; Welcome Hill; Wenona; Whispering Pines; Whistleville; White; White Bluff; White City; White Hall; White Oak; White Path; White Plains; Whitesburg; Whitestone; White Sulphur; White Sulphur Springs; Whitesville; Wildwood; Wiley; Williamson; Wilsonville; Winchester; Winder; Winterville; Wire Bridge; Woodville; Workmore; Wrens; Yellowdirt; Yoemans; Yonkers; York; Youth; Ypsilanti

HAWAII – A possible translation is "homeland." Statehood was August 21, 1959. The state nickname is "Aloha State." The fiftieth state was added to the Union August 21, 1959, and signed by President Eisenhower. The state is made up of several islands each rising out of the Pacific Ocean due to many years of volcanic activity. Although generally considered our westernmost state, Alaska actually extends farther west than Hawaii. Some believe that the Hawaiian race did not come from the South Pacific islands but from Alaska. The theory is that a chieftain, his wife, their three sons, and their wives traveled by canoe from the Alaska area and landed on Hawaii. They were the first Hiwaiians, according to the theory. However, more believe the first humans arrived from other South Pacific islands. In 1898, Congress voted to annex Hawaii but the legality of that act continues to be debated because it was a United States government resolution, not a treaty of cession or conquest as required by international law. Though several attempts were made to achieve statehood, Hawaii remained a territory for sixty years due largely to the plantation owners who enjoyed cheap labor.

Today, 24% of the state's economy is from tourism. Only the city and county of Honolulu are incorporated. All other municipal governments are administered at the county level. There are four federal highways in Hawaii, all on the island of Oahu and all part of the Interstate Highway System. Other state-maintained roads exist but they are not plentiful. The Cathedral of Our Lady of Peace is the oldest Roman Catholic cathedral in continuous use today in the United States. 'lolani Palace is the only official royal residence on United States land. The Royal Hawaiian Hotel was the Western White House of President Franklin D. Roosevelt. The Shirley Temple cocktail was invented in one of its bars. Hawaii does not observe Daylight Savings Time (nor does Arizona). Hawaii does not have a state police force nor a department of motor vehicles. Driver's licenses are issued by the four counties. The eruption of Kilauea Volcano that began in 1983, continues to produce lava from thirty-five miles below the earth's surface.

The fish with the longest name in the world, the Humuhumunukunukuapuaa (also known as the Queen Tiggerfish), is Hawaii's state fish. The literal translation of this Hawaiian word is "the tigger fish that grunts like a pig."

Famous Hiwaiians include:
- Barack Obama, (1941–); Honolulu; forty-fourth president of the United States and the only president from Hawaii
- Duke Kahanamoku (1890–1968), Waikiki; Olympic gold medal winner who popularized surfing
- Don Ho (1930–2007), Honolulu; born Donald TaiLoy Ho; musician and entertainer

Interesting names include: Airport Village; Alabama Village; Captain Cook; Crater Village; Happy Valley; Hawaiian-Spanish Village; Honolulu (Brack Obama); Iroquois Point; Japanese Village One; Kaaawa; Kokomo; Lanai City; Lower Village Three; Middle Village Three; Mountain View; Pearl City; Pearl Harbor; Princeville; Russian Village; Salt Lake; Sam Sing Village; School Village; St Louis Heights; Store Village; Sunset Beach; Thompson Corner; Village Five; Village Four; Village Six; Village Thirteen; Village Two; Volcano

IDAHO – Apache for "Comanche." Statehood was July 3, 1890. The state nickname is "Gem State." Idaho is a Rocky Mountains state with snow-capped mountain ranges, rapids, placid lakes, and steep canyons. The Snake River runs through Hells Canyon, deepest canyon in U.S. Shoshone Falls is higher than Niagara Falls. Science and technology produces over 25% of the state's revenue, more than mining, agriculture, and forestry combined. Idaho produces one-third of all the potatoes grown in America. By using one's imagination, one may see the silhouette of President Nixon on the Montana-Idaho border facing in a southwesterly direction.

Notable Idahoans include:
- Gutzon Borglum (1871–1941), a sculptor famous for creating the monumental Presidents' heads at Mount Rushmore, South Dakota

Interesting names include: Aberdeen; Adair; Alpha; Alpine; American Falls; Amsterdam; Anderson; Apple Valley; Arrow; Artesian City; Asbestos Point; Atlanta; Atlas; Atomic City; Avon; Banks; Barber; Basin; Bayhorse; Bayview; Beaches Corner; Bear; Bear Lake Hot Springs; Beaver Head; Bedstead Corner; Beetville; Bench; Bernice; Best Corner; Big Cedar; Big Creek; Big Eddy; Big George; Big Springs; Black Canyon; Black Cloud; Black Pine; Blackrock; Blacktail; Bliss; Blue Dome; Bone; Boulder; Box Canyon; Bradley; Bridge; Bronx; Bruce Eddy; Budge; Burley; Cable Car Crossing; Cache; Caldwell; Calendar; Canyon; Carbonate; Carbon Center; Caribou City; Cascade; Castleford; Castle Rocks; Cathedral Pines; Cedar; Cedar Creek; Centerville; Central; Central Cove; Chalk Cut; Cherry Creek; Cherrylane; Cherryville; Chilly; China Hill; Clark Tree; Clearwater; Cleft; Cleveland; Clicks; Cliffs; Clover; Cobalt; Coffee Point; Concrete; Copperville; Corral; Cottonwood; Council; Cow Creek; Crabtree; Cream Can Junction; Crescent; Crouch; Crystal; Culdesac; Dairy Creek; Dayton; Dead Dog Creek; Deep Creek; Delta; Democrat; Dent; Denver; Diamond; Dixie; Dover; Eagle; Eagle Nest; Eddyville; Eden; Edwardsburg; Egypt; Eighteenmile; Elk City; Elkhorn Village; Elk River; Elk Summit; Emerald Creek; Era; Estes; Evergreen; Fairfield; Fairylawn; Falcon; Fall Creek; Falls City; Featherville; Felt; Fernwood; Fish Haven; Five Corners; Five Points; Flat Creek; Flint; Florence; Forest; Fort Wilson; Four Corners; Fourway Junction; Fox Creek; France; Franklin; Freedom; French Corner; French Creek; Fruitland; Fruitvale; Garden City; Garden Valley; Gem; Geneva; Georgetown; German Settlement; Giveout; Goldburg; Gold Creek; Golden; Gold Point; Good Grief; Goodrich; Grace; Grainville; Grandjean; Grand Junction; Grand View; Grandview; Granite; Grant; Green; Greencreek; Greenleaf; Gross; Harlem; Harrisburg; Harrison; Hart; Haycrop; Hayden; Headquarters; Helena; Hellhole; Henry; Hill City; Hollywood; Homedale; Hope; Horsecamp; Horseshoe Bend; Hot Springs; Houston; Hunt; Idaho City; Idaho Falls; Idahome; Indian Cove; Indian Grove; Indian Head Rock; Indian Valley; Ireland Springs; Jackson; Jacques; Judge; Judge Town; Juniper; Ketchum; Lake Fork; Lakeview; Lamb Creek; Lane; Last Chance; Lava Hot Springs; Leadore; Leadville; Leslie; Liberty; Lightfoot; Lightning; Lincoln; Little Rock; Little Sugarloaf; Lone Pine; Lone Rock; Lost River; Lotus; Madison; Magic; Magic City; Marble Creek; Marion; Marsh Valley; Marysville; Mayfield; Meadow Creek; Meadows; Meridian; Meteor; Midas; Midnight; Midway; Mineral; Mink Creek; Montpelier; Moose City; Morgan; Moscow;

Mound Valley; Mountain Home; Mozart; Mt Idaho; Mud Springs; Murray; Musselshell; Naples; North Pole; Oakley; Obsidian; Old Beaver; Old Golden; Omega; Orchard; Oxbow; Palisades; Palisades Corner; Paradise Hot Springs; Paris; Park; Pearl; Pebble; Peck; Pedee; Piano; Pierce; Pine; Pine Creek; Pinehurst; Pine Ridge; Pineview; Pioneerville; Pleasant Valley; Pleasant Valley Place; Pleasantview; Pleasant View; Pocatello; Pocono; Poplar; Post Falls; Potlatch; Prairie; Princeton; Punkin Corner; Quartzburg; Raft River; Rebecca; Reclamation Village; Red River Hot Springs; Red Rock Junction; Reno; Reverse; Riddle; Ridgedale; Rising River; Ritz; Riverside; Robin; Rockaway Beach; Rockland; Rocky Bar; Rookstool Corner; Roseberry; Rose Lake; Rubicon; Ruby; Salmon; Sand Hollow; Sandpoint; Santa; Sawtooth City; Seabree; Seaburg; Setters; Silver Beach; Silver City; Silverton; Skeleton Creek; Slacks Corner; Slate Creek; Slickpoo; Small; Smelterville; Smokehouse; Soda Springs; Soldier; Spanish Town; Spencer; Springfield; Squirrel; Stanford; Star; State Line; St Charles; Steamboat Rock; Sterling; Stetson; Stevens; Stone; Sucker; Sugar City; Sunbeam; Sunbelt; Sunnydell; Sunnyside; Sunnyslope; Sun Valley; Swan Falls; Swanlake; Swan Valley; Sweet; Sweetwater; Tahoe; Taylor; Taylorville; Teepee Creek; Telegraph Hill; The Cedars; Three Creek; Three Forks (ten miles from) Three Forks; Threemile Corner; Threemile Crossing; Tipperary Corner; Topaz; Torreys; Town; Tramway; Treasureton; Trestle Creek; Triangle; Triumph; Trout; Turnpike; Twin Beaches; Twin Falls; Twin Forks (one mile north of) Two Forks; Twinlow; Twin Springs; Ulysses; Upper Crossing; View; Viola; Virginia; Warm Lake; Warm River; Warren; Wayland; Whipsaw Saddle; White Bird; Winchester; Windy Gap; Winona; Wolf Lodge; Wolverine; Wood; Woodland; Yellowjacket; Yellow Pine; York

ILLINOIS – The state is named for the French adaptation of an Algonquin phrase for "warrior" or "he speaks normally." Statehood was December 3, 1818. The state nickname is "Land of Lincoln." The word for Chicago is based on an Algonquin phrase for "the place where wild onions grow." About 2,000 Native American hunters and a small number of French villagers inhabited the area during the time of the American Revolution. American settlers began arriving from Kentucky in the early 1800s. Illinois received statehood in 1818. Yankees arrived a little later and dominated the northern part of the state, founding the area of present-day Chicago by the 1830s. The coming of the railroads in the 1850s, made the rich prairie farmland profitable, attracting a large number of immigrant farmers from Germany and Sweden. By 1900, factories were being built in the northern cities and coal mines in central and southern Illinois began to flourish.

The winter of 1830–1831, is called the "Winter of the Deep Snow." A sudden, deep snowfall blanketed the state, making travel impossible for the remainder of the winter. Many travelers perished. Several severe winters followed, including the "Winter of the Sudden Freeze." On December 20, 1836, a fast-moving cold front passed through freezing puddles in minutes and killing many travelers who could not reach shelter. The adverse weather caused crop failure in the northern part of the state. The southern part of the state shipped food north which may have contributed to its name, "Little Egypt," after the biblical story of Joseph in Egypt supplying grain to his brothers.

During a routine flight while he was governor of California, Ronald Reagan reported seeing a bright, white light zigzagging through the sky. After his plane gave chase for a few minutes, Reagan reported that the object went straight up and out of sight.

Famous Illinoisans include:

- Julius Rosenwald (1862–1932), Springfield; born and raised a few blocks from President Lincoln's home; he and Aaron Nussbaum bought out Roebuck's share in 1889 for $75,000
- Ronald Reagan (1911–2004), Tampico [120 miles west of Chicago]; fortieth president of the United States
- Frederick Maytag (1857–1937), Elgin; in 1907, Maytag manufactured the washing machine; first electric model was introduced in 1911; a gasoline-powered model was introduced in 1914
- George Gobel (1919–1991), Chicago; initially a country music singer; during WWII he served as a flight instructor on AT-9 aircraft at Altus Air Base, Altus, OK and later on the B-26 aircraft at Frederick, OK; in 1954, he received his own network TV show as an alternative to Milton Berle; his show popularized several catch phrases, such as, "Well, then there now," "Well, I'll be a dirty bird," and "You don't hardly get those anymore;" he described himself as "Lonesome George;" in 1957, three B-52 Stratofortresses made their first non-stop, round-the-world flight by turbojet aircraft; one of the aircraft was christened "Lonesome George;" the crew of that plane appeared on his TV show to recount the flight
- Sandy Allen (1955–2008), Chicago; reared in Shelbyville, IN; up to the time of her death she was the tallest living woman in America (7 feet 7 ¼ inches); in the 5th grade she was 6 feet 3 inches tall
- "Wild Bill" Hickock (1837–1876), Homer (later changed name to Troy Grove); born James Butler Hickock; his father's farm was one of the stops on the Underground Railroad; at age eighteen he met twelve-year-old William Cody (later known as Buffalo Bill); came to the west as a stage coach driver then became a lawman in the territories of Kansas and Nebraska; fought in the Union Army during the Civil War; sometimes was a scout for General Custer's 7th Cavalry; his favorite guns were a pair of cap-and-ball Colt 1851 .36 Navy Model pistols which he wore until his death
- Edgar Bergen (1903–1978), Chicago; at age eleven he taught himself ventriloquism from a pamphlet; a few years later he commissioned a Chicago woodcarver to sculpt the likeness of a rascally Irish newspaper boy he knew; the head went on a puppet named Charlie McCarthy; they were on the air from 1937 to 1956
- Buddy Ebsen (1908–2003), Belleville; born Christian Rudolph Ebsen, Jr.; served as an officer in the Coast Guard during World War II; learned to dance at a dance studio operated by his father; in 1935, he signed a contract with MGM for $1,500 per week; Walt Disney chose Ebsen to be filmed dancing in front of a grid as an aid in animating Mickey Mouse dancing in *Silly Symphonies*; played the role of Jed Clampett on *The Beverly Hillbillies* from 1962 to 1971

Interesting names include: Adair; Advance; Akron; Albany; Aliceville; Allen; Alpha; America; Anchor; Anderson; Annapolis; Apple River; Argyle; Ashland; Athens; Atlanta; Atlas; Augusta; Aurora; Avon; Bath; Beaver Creek; Bedford; Bee Creek; Belgium; Bell; Belleville (Buddy Ebsen); Benton; Ben Town; Benville; Berlin; Berry; Beverly; Beverly Hills; Big Bay; Big Foot; Big Rock; Birch Island; Birds; Birmingham; Blackberry Woods; Blackhawk; Blackhawk Island; Blackstone; Bloomington; Blue Island; Blue Mound; Blue Point; Blue Ridge; Bluff City; Bluff Hail; Bluffs; Bogota; Bolivia; Boulder; Bourbon; Boyd; Boyle; Bradley; Breckenridge; Briar Bluff; Bridgeport; Bristol; Brooklyn; Brownsville; Bruce; Brussels; Buckhorn; Bucks; Buena Vista; Buffalo; Buffalo Grove; Buffalo Prairie; Bull Valley; Bungay; Bunker Hill; Bureau; Burksville; Burlington; Burnside; Burnt Prairie; Burt; Bush; Butler; Cache; Cadiz; Cairo (K-row); Caldwell; Calhoun; Calloway; Camargo; Camden; Campbell; Camp Logan; Campus; Canton; Carbon Hill; Carlock; Carol Stream; Carrollton; Carterville; Cascade; Casey; Cave-in-Rock; Cedar Brook; Centerville; Central; Central City; Centralia; Central Park; Cereal; Champaign; Charleston; Chautauqua; Cherry; Cherry Point; Cherry Valley; Chestnut; Chicago (Clayton Moore, *The Lone Ranger*); Chili; Chillicothe; Chinatown; Christian; Cincinatti Landing; Clark; Clay City; Clear Lake; Cleveland; Clinch; Clinton; Coal City; Coal Hollow; Coal Valley; Coldbrook; Columbus; Concord; Confidence; Coral; Cornland; Cottonwood; Council Hill; Covington; Crab Orchard; Crescent; Crisp; Crossroads; Cuba; Cypress; Dakota; Dale; Dallas City; Danville; Dayton; Deer Creek; Deerfield; Deer Grove; Deer Park; Deers; Delhi; Democrat Spring; Denmark; Denver; Derby; Detroit; Diamond; Diamond City; Divide; Divine; Dog Walk; Douglas; Dover; Dry Hill; Dundee; Eagle Lake; Eagle Point; Eddyville; Edinburg; Edwards; Edwardsville; Elizabeth; Elizabethtown; Elkhart; Elkhorn Grove; Elkton; Elkville; Elliott; El Paso; Embarrass (EM-brah); Empire; Energy; Equality; Erie; Eureka; Evanston; Evergreen Park; Ewing; Fairbanks; Fairview; Fall Creek; Falling Springs; Falmouth; Fancher; Fancy Prairie; Farmer City; Farmersville; Farm Ridge; Fayette; Fayetteville; Fayville; Ferndale; Fidelity; Fillmore; Findlay; Fisher; Fishhook; Five Points; Flat Rock; Flatwoods; Florence; Forest City; Forest River; Formosa Junction; Fountain; Fountain Creek; Fountain Gap; Fountain Green; Four Corners; Fox; Fox Lake; Frankfort; Franklin; Friendsville; Frog City; Frogtown; Fruit; Fulton; Future City; Garden of Eden; Garden Prairie; Garland; Garrett; Geneva; Georgetown; Germantown; German Valley; Ginger Hill; Glasgow; Golden; Golden Eagle; Golden Gate; Golf; Good Hope; Goodrich; Goofy Ridge; Gordons; Grand Detour; Grandview; Granite City; Grass Lake; Green Brier; Green Creek; Greendale; Greenfield; Greenoak; Green Oaks; Greenpond; Green River; Green Rock; Greenup; Green Valley; Greenview; Greenville; Gross; Half Day; Hamburg; Hamilton; Hammond; Hampshire; Hardin; Harding; Harlem; Harmony; Harper; Harriet; Harrison; Havana; Haypress; Henderson; Henpeck; Henry; Hickman; Hickory Corners; Hickory Grove; Hill Top; Holiday Hills; Holland; Hometown; Honey Creek; Hoosier; Hope; Hopewell; Hop Hollow; Houston; Hunter; Huntsville; Hurricane; Ideal; Illinois City; Independence; Indian Creek; Industry; Island Grove; Jackson; Jacksonville; Jamaica; Jamestown; Jenkins; Jimtown; Justice; Kankakee (Fred MacMurray); Kansas; Kendall Hills; Kennedy [Chicago]; Kensington; Kentucky; Kildeer; Klondike; Knox; Knoxville; La Crosse; La Grange; Lake City; Lamb; Lane; Lansing; Lawrence; Lawrenceville; Lebanon; Lee; Lehigh; Lexington; Liberty;

Libertyville; Lick Creek; Lightsville; Lily Lake; Lima; Limerick; Lincoln; Lisbon; Litchfield; Little Egypt; Little Indian; Little Oklahoma; Little Rock; Little York; Liverpool; Livingston; Logan; Logan Square; Long Branch; Long Creek; Longview; Loogootee; Lost Nation; Louisville; Love; Loves Corner; Loves Park; Low Point; Mackinaw; Macon; Madison; Magnet; Magnolia; Manchester; Manhattan; Mansfield; Maple; Maple Grove; Marblehead; Marigold; Marine; Marion; Marquette; Marshall; Marydale; Maryland; Maryville; Mason; Matthews; Mayberry; McLean; Meadows; Mechanicsburg; Melody; Mercer; Metcalf; Metropolis; Michigan Beach; Mid City; Middle Creek; Middletown; Midland City; Midway; Milan; Miller; Miller City; Millersburg; Mineral; Moccasin; Montezuma; Montgomery; Monticello; Moonshine; Morris; Morristown; Moscow; Mound City; Mt Morris; Mt Pleasant; Mt Pulaski; Mt Sterling; Muddy; Mulberry Grove; Muncie; Naples; Nashville; National City; Needmore; Nelson; Nevada; Newark; New City; New Delhi; New Design; New Douglas; New Philadelphia; Normal; Normandy; Norway; Oakford; Oak Grove; Oakland; Oak Park (Betty White); Oak Ridge; Oakwood; Obed; Oblong; Ogden; Ogle; Ohio; Oil Center; Oilfield; Oil Grove; Old Mill Creek; Old Pearl; Old Ripley; Oldtown; Olive Branch; Omaha; Oneida; Ontario; Orange; Orangemans Hall; Orange Prairie; Orangeville; Orchardville; Oregon; Orient; Ottowa; Owen; Oxville; Ozark; Palisades; Palm Beach; Panama; Paradise; Paris (Carl "Alfalfa" Switzer); Parkersburg; Passport; Paw Paw; Pearl; Pearl City; Perks; Perry; Perryville; Peru; Philadelphia; Phoenix; Piety Hill; Pike; Pine Grove; Pinkstaff; Pitchin; Pittsburg; Pleasant Plains; Pleasant Valley; Pleasantview; Plum Hill; Polk; Pomona; Pond; Poplar Grove; Poplar Ridge; Portland; Posey; Post Oak; Potomac; Prairie City; Prairie Grove; Prairie Hall; Prairie Home; Prairietown; Prairie View; Princeton; Prospect; Pulaski; Pyramid; Quaker; Quincy; Raleigh; Rapids City; Red Bud; Red Oak; Reno; Rice; Richmond; Riddle Hill; Ring Neck; Ripley; Rising Sun; Riverstream; Roachtown; Roanoke; Rochester; Rock; Rockbridge; Rock City; Rock Creek; Rock Falls; Rockford; Rock Grove; Rock Island (Eddie Albert); Rockport; Rockton; Rohrer; Rome; Rosebud; Rosedale; Rose Hill; Roseville; Round Knob; Round Prairie; Royalton; Ruby; Russell; Russellville; Rust; Sacramento; Sag Bridge; Sailor Springs; Saline; Sand Ridge; Sands; Sandusky; Sandwich; San Jose; Savage; Savanna; Scales Mound; Scotland; Seehorn; Shady Beach; Shakerag; Shamrock; Shanghi City; Sharpsburg; Shelbyville; Sidney; Signal Hill; Simpson; Somerset; South Park (Bob Newhart); Spencer; Springfield; Spring Garden; Spring Grove; Spring Hill; Spring Valley; Standard City; Stanford; St Charles; St David; Steel City; St George; Stonefort; Strasburg; Stringtown; Sublette; Sugar Grove; Sugar Island; Summer Hill; Summerville; Summit; Sunbeam; Sunbury; Sunfield; Sunnyland; Sunnyside; Swan Creek; Sweetwater; Sycamore; Table Grove; Tampico (Ronald Reagan); Taylor; Taylor Hill; Taylor Ridge; Taylor Springs; Taylorville; Tennessee; Texas City; Texico; Thayer; The Burg; Thompson; Thompsonville; Three States; Timber Ridge; Time; Timewell; Toledo; Tomahawk Bluff; Topeka; Toronto; Trimble; Triumph; Trow Grove (Wild Bill Hickok); Tunnel Hill; Twelvemile Corner; Union; Union Hill; Union Town; Uniontown; Unionville; Unity; University; Urbana; Ustick; Utah; Valley City; Valley View; Vandalia; Vermillion; Vermont; Versailles; Vienna; Viola; Virginia; Walla Walla; Walnut; Walnut Grove; Walnut Hill; Walnut Prairie; Warren; Warsaw; Washington; Water Valley; Wayland; Weaver; Webster; Wenonah; West Liberty; Wheeling; White City;

White Hall; White Hearth; White Oak; White Rock; Whitewash; Wildwood; Williamsburg; Willow; Willowbrook; Willow Hill; Willow Springs; Wilmington; Wilsonville; Winchester; Winslow; Wolf Creek; Wolf Lake; Woodford; Woodland; Woodside; Woodville; Woodyard; Wyoming; Xenia; Yellow Banks; Yellow Creek; York; Youngstown; Zanesville

INDIANA - "Land of the Indians." Statehood was December 11, 1816. The state nickname is "Hoosier State." Since slavery was not allowed, settlers from Kentucky and Ohio began moving there, including Abraham Lincoln's family. The population in 1820 was 150,000; ten years later it had more than doubled to 350,000. Initially, the town of Santa Claus went nameless for a number of years, being called the "no name village." In 1856, a meeting was called at a local church to resolve the issue of a name. When no solution could be reached, it happened that a stranger came to the door of the church in a sleigh. At once the village children cried, "Santa Claus." America's biggest clock is in Clarksville, Indiana but those desiring to get a better look at it must cross the Ohio River into Louisville which affords a better view since the clock sits on the banks of the Ohio River facing south. Colgate-Polmolive bought the building that was a former state prison in 1921 and converted it into a factory for making soap. Plans were to close the plant in 2008. The tallest woman in America, Sandy Allen (7' 71/4"), lived in Indianapolis. She died in 2008.

Notable Indianans include:
- Larry Bird (1956–), French Lick; "The Hick from French Lick;" played for Indiana State University, Terre Haute and the Boston Celtics
- Hoagy Carmichael (1899–1981), Bloomington; started playing the piano at age six; earned a law degree from Indiana University School of Law; wrote "Stardust"
- Jim Davis (1945–), Fairmount; created cartoon characters Garfield and Odie
- Don Mattingly (1961–), Evansville; drafted after high school graduation by New York Yankees; played from 1982-1995
- Cole Porter (1891–1964), Peru; started his musical training at age five; mother changed his birth year to 1893 to make him appear more precocious
- Ernie Pyle (1900–1945), Dana; joined Naval Reserves prior to his eighteenth birthday; he was a war correspondent during WW II; Pyle was killed by machine gun fire on Okinawa
- Orville Redenbacher (1907–1995), Brazil; joined 4-H as a child where his goal was to develop the perfect popcorn; after trying tens of thousands of popcorn strains he and parter Charles Bowman reached their goal; he stumped the panel on *To Tell the Truth*
- Colonel Harland Sanders (1890–1980), Henryville; after the death of his father (1896) he helped with cooking at home; dropped out of school in seventh grade; was given the title "Kentucky Colonel" in 1935 by Governor Ruby Laffoon
- John Wooden (1910–), Martinsville; first person to be inducted into the Basketball Hall of Fame both as a player and a coach; coached two seasons at Dayton (Campbell County), KY where his first season was his only losing season in his coaching career; coached at UCLA 1945–1975

31

- Fuzzy Zoeller (1951–), New Albany; he is one of three golfers to have won The Masters in his first appearance; he won the 1984 U.S. Open
- Benjamin Harrison (1833–1901), North Bend, Ohio; twenty-third president of the United States; served in the U.S. Senate; brigadier general in the Civil War; resided in Indiana at time of his election making him the only president from Indiana

Interesting names include: Aberdeen; Adams; Advance; Africa; Akron; Albany; Alexandria; Algiers; Alpine; Americus; Anderson; Aroma; Ash Iron Springs; Ashland; Athens; Atlanta; Avon; Azalia; Bacon; Badger Grove; Bald Knobs; Barbersville; Bath; Battle Ground; Bean Blossom; Bear Branch; Bear Lake; Bear Wallow; Beaver City; Bedford; Beech Grove; Beehunter; Bee Ridge; Bengal; Bentonville; Beverly Hill; Beverly Shores; Big Springs; Billville; Birds Eye; Birdseye; Birmingham; Black Oak; Black Point; Blooming Grove; Bloomington; Bluegrass; Blue Lick; Blue Ridge; Bobo; Bobtown; Boston; Boundary City; Bourbon; Bowling Green; Boyd; Bracken; Bramble; Brazil; Breckenridge; Briggs; Bright; Bristol; Brook; Brooklyn; Broom Hill; Brown Jug Corner; Brownsville; Bruce Lake Station; Bruceville; Buchanan; Buck Creek; Buckeye; Buckskin; Bucktown; Bud; Buena Vista; Buffalo; Buffaloville; Bunker Hill; Burlington; Burr Oak; Butler; Buttermilk Point; Cadiz; Camden; Campbellsburg; Cannelburg; Canteloupe; Carbon; Carbondale; Carefree; Carlisle; Carrollton; Cedar; Cedar Grove; Cedar Lake; Cedar Point; Centenary; Centennial; Center Valley; Centerville; Charlestown; Cherry Grove; Chestnut Ridge; Chili; China; Chinatown; Cincinnati; Circleville; Clarksville; Clay City; Clear Creek; Clear Lake; Cleveland; Clinton; Coal City; Coal Creek; Coke Oven Hollow; Cold Springs; College City; College Corner; Columbia; Columbia City; Columbus; Concord; Cornstalk; Correct; Cottage Hill; Covington; Crane; Crete; Crumb Corner; Crystal; Cuba; Cumberland; Cyclone; Cynthiana; Cypress; Daisy Hill; Dale (Florence Henderson); Danville; Dayton; Dead Mans Crossing; Deep River; Deer Creek; Deerfield; Deer Park; Deer Mill; Delaware; Denver; Deputy; Derby; Dewberry; Diamond; Dinwiddie; Dixie; Domestic; Douglas; Dublin; Duff; Eagle Point; Eagletown; Eagle Village; Early Station; East Chicago; Economy; Edinburgh; Edna Mills; Egg Harbor; Egypt; Elizabethtown; Elizaville; Elkhart; Elliott; Elmdale; Elm Tree Crossroads; English; Eureka; Evanston; Ewing; Exchange; Fair Oaks; Fairview; Falmouth; Farmers; Farmers Retreat; Farmland; Fayette; Fickle; Fillmore; Fish Lake; Five Points; Five Points Corner; Fleming; Florence; Florida; Ford; Forest; Forest Hill; Formosa Junction; Fountain; Fountain City; Fountain Park; Fountaintown; Four Corners; Four Presidents Corners; Fox; Fox Hill; Fox Lake; Frankfort; Franklin; Free; French; French Lick (Larry Bird); Frenchtown; Friendly Corner; Friendship; Fulton; Furnace; Galveston; Garden Village; Garrett; Gary; Gas City; Gem; Geneva; George Town; Georgetown; Georgia; Globe; Gnaw Bone; Goldsmith; Goodland; Grandview; Grass Creek; Gravel Hill; Greenbrier; Greencastle; Green Center; Greenfield; Green Hill; Green Meadows; Greenoak; Greensboro; Greentown; Greenville; Greetingville; Grovertown; Guy; Hamburg; Hamilton; Handy; Hanging Grove; Hardinsburg; Hardscrabble; Harlan; Harlansburg; Harmony; Harper; Harrisburg; Harrodsburg; Hartford; Hartford City; Hayden; Hemlock; Henderson; Henry; Hickory Corner; Hickory Ridge; Hillcrest; Hogtown; Holland; Hollandsburg; Honduras; Honey Creek; Honeyville; Hoosierville; Hope; Houston; Huber;

Huntington; Huntsville; Illinoi; Independence; Indian Springs; Indian Village; Ireland; Ironton; Island City; Ivy Hills; Jackson; Jacksonville; Jamestown; Jasonville; Jefferson; Jimtown; Jockey; Johnson; Kankakee; Kendallville; Keystone; Klondyke; Knox; Kokomo; La Crosse; Lagrange; Lake Bruce; Lamb; Lancaster; Lapel; Lapland; Largo; Laura; Laurel; Lawrence; Lawrenceburg; Leatherwood; Leavenworth; Lebanon; Lee; Lewis; Lewisburg; Lexington; Liberal; Liberty; Liberty Center; Liggett; Limedale; Lincoln; Lincoln City; Lincolnville; Lisbon; Little Charlie; Little Rock; Little St Louis; Little York; Liverpool; Locust Grove; Logan; Logansport; Log Cabin Crossroads; London; Lone Tree; Long Beach; Long Lake; Loogootee; Lookout; Loon Lake; Lost River; Lotus; Lucerne; Madison; Magnet; Magnolia; Manchester; Manhattan; Manilla; Maple Ridge; Maples; Maple Valley; Maplewood; Marion; Marshall; Maryville; Maysville Crossing; Meadowbrook; Mecca; Mechanicsburg; Melody Hill; Memphis; Mexico; Miami; Miami Bend; Michigan City; Michigantown; Middlebury; Middlefork; Middlesboro; Middletown; Midway; Miller [Gary]; Millersburg; Mineral City; Monitor; Monroe; Monroeville; Montezuma; Montgomery; Monticello; Montpelier; Morgantown; Morningside; Morocco; Morris; Moscow; Mt Healthy; Mt Olympus; Mt Pleasant; Mt Sterling; Mt Vernon; Mulberry; Murray; Nashville; Natchez; Needmore; Nevada; Nevada Mills; Newburgh; New Castle; New Philadelphia; Newport; Ninemile; Normal; Norway; Oaktown; Oak Tree Crossroads; Oakville; Oakwood; Octagon; Old Halfway; Old St Louis; Old Town; Olive; Omega; Onward; Orange; Orangeville; Orchard Grove; Organ Springs; Orleans; Otter Lake; Owen; Page; Panama; Paradise; Paragon; Paris Crossing; Parkersburg; Patriot; Pendleton; Pennyville; Peppertown; Perrysburg; Peru (Cole Porter); Petroleum; Philadelphia; Phlox; Phoenix; Pigeon; Pike; Pikeville; Pimento; Pinch; Pine; Pine Valley; Pine Village; Pinhook; Pittsburg; Pleasant Lake; Pleasant Mills; Pleasant Plain; Pleasant Ridge; Pleasant View; Pleasantville; Pleasure Valley; Plum Tree; Poland; Pony; Popcorn; Poseyville; Poundstone Corner; Prairie City; Prairie Creek; Princeton; Prince William; Progress; Prosperity; Providence; Pueblo; Pulaski; Pumpkin Center; Quaker; Quakertown; Queensville; Quercus Grove; Raccoon; Radioville; Rainsville; Raintown; Raleigh; Ranger; Rapture; Reagan; Reno; Riceville; Richmond; Riddle; Ridgeville; Ripley; Rising Sun; River Ridge; Riverside; River Vale; Riverwood; Roanoke; Rochester; Rock Creek; Rockfield; Rockford; Rock Hill; Rockville; Rocky Ford; Roll; Rome; Rome City; Rosebud; Rosedale; Roseland; Round Grove; Royalton; Rural; Russellville; Russiaville; Sand Ridge; Sandy Beach; Sandy Hook; Sandy Nook; Sandytown; Santa Claus; Santa Fe; Sassafras; Saturn; Scircleville; Scott; Selma; Seven Springs; Shady Banks; Shamrock Lake; Sharpsville; Shelby; Shelbyville; Shepherd; Shipshewana; Shoals; Sidney; Silver Lake; Silver Point; Silverwood; Simpson; Skelton; Smithland; Smoke Corner; Snow Hill; Solitude; Somerset; South Bend; Spades; Speed; Spencer; Spiceland; Spraytown; Springfield; Spring Grove; Spring Lake; Springtown; Springville; Stanford; Star City; State Line; State Line City; St Bernice; St Croix; Steam Corner; St Louis Crossing; St Marys; Stone; Stonebluff; Stones Crossing; Stony Creek; Strawtown; Stringtown; Stubenville; Sugar Creek; Sulphur; Sulphur Spring; Sulphur Springs; Summit; Summit Grove; Summitville; Sun Down; Sunrise Beach; Sunview; Swan; Sweet Gum; Sweetser; Sycamore; Sycamore Corner; Syndicate; Syracuse; Taylor Corner; Taylors; Taylorsville; Taylorville; Teegarden; Tell City; Texas; Tippecanoe; Toledo; Topeka; Toto;

Town Hill; Town of Pines; Trails End; Treaty; Tree Spring; Trenton; Turkey Creek; Twelve Mile; Union Center; Union City; Union Mills; Uniontown; Unionville; Universal; Upland; Urbana; Utah; Valentine; Valparaiso; Van Buren; Vandalia; Versailles; Vienna; Vincennes (Red Skelton); Wall Lake; Walnut; Walnut Corners; Walnut Grove; Walnut Ridge; Warren; Warsaw; Washington; Weaver; Webster; West Liberty; Wheatfield; Wheatland; Wheeling; White Cloud; Whiteoak; White Rose; White Sulphur Springs; Whitewater; Wickliffe; Williamsburg; Williamstown; Willow Branch; Willow Valley; Wilson; Winchester (Dinah Shore); Windfall; Winslow; Wolflake; Yankeetown; Yankee Town; Yellowbanks; Yoeman; Yorktown; Young America; Youngstown; Zanesville; Zulu

IOWA - "Beautiful Land." Statehood was December 28, 1846. The state nickname is "Hawkeye State." The official name of the state is "State of Iowa" named for the Native American Iowa people. During the 1835 Dragoon expedition to survey and map central Iowa, many dragoons became lost in the prairie grass which was over their heads, even on horseback. One of the commanders was Nathan Boone, Daniel's youngest son. During the Civil War, more than seventy-five thousand Iowans (nearly 60% of eligible men) fought, thirteen thousand of whom died, mostly from disease. Iowa had a higher percentage of soldiers serve in the Civil War per capita than any other state in the Union.

Notble Iowans include:
- William Frederick "Buffalo Bill" Cody (1846–1917), near Le Claire; contracted with the Kansas Pacific Railroad to supply meat to the workers; killed over four thousand buffaloes in eighteen months; first job was at age eleven as an ox team driver; became a Pony Express rider at age fourteen; served in various capacities in the Civil War; Annie Oakley performed in Buffalo Bill's Wild West Show
- Johnny Carson (1925–2005), Corning; in the early 1950s Carson was a writer for Red Skelton; an hour before a show, Skelton knocked himself unconscious; Carson filled in for him; *The Tonight Show Starring Johnny Carson* ran from 1962–1992
- Mamie Eisenhower (1896–1979), Boone; her birthplace was established as an historic site; only Mrs. John Adams shares that honor
- Herbert Hoover (1874–1964), West Branch; thirty-first president of the United States; first president born west of the Mississippi River; an orphan by age nine; earned a degree in geology; helped organize food distribution to Europeans after World War I; helped in the development and regulation of radio broadcasting, projects for navigation, irrigation of farm land, electrical power, flood control, aviation codes and regulations, promoted health education in schools and communities, addressed the growing number of traffic deaths; often said that the difference between a dictatorship and a democracy is that dictators organize from the top down, democracies from the bottom up
- Glenn Miller (1904–1944), Clarinda; about age eleven was given his first trombone; as a high school senior, Miller became interested in a new style of music called "dance band music;" was one of the best-selling recording artists from 1939 to 1942; the traditional Glenn Miller sound is a clarinet playing over four saxophones; although he was not the first to try that combination, he was the first to

refine it to a pleasing sound; his recording of "Tuxedo Junction," sold 115,000 copies the first week; on December 15, 1944, while flying from the United Kingdom to Paris to play for the soldiers who liberated Paris, his plane, a UC-64 Norseman, USAAF serial 44-70285, disappeared over the English Channel; at his death, 20% of the music played on juke boxes was his

- Donna Reed (1921–), Denison; born Donna Belle Mullenger; the movie *It's a Wonderful Life* was a failure when it was released but Reed's performance was noticed; *The Donna Reed Show* aired from 1958 to 1966; for twenty-four episodes, 1984–1986, she played the part of "Miss Ellie" on *Dallas*
- George Reeves (1914–1959), Woolstock; born George Keefer Brewer; his birth certificate mistakenly lists Kentucky as his birthplace; his first acting role was in *Gone with the Wind* (1939) portraying him as one of the red-headed Tarlton twins during the opening scenes; the *Adventures of Superman* aired from 1952–1958; in 1956, he sang on the *Tony Bennet* show and briefly appeared in character on *I Love Lucy*; he died in 1959
- Joseph, Francis, Albert, Madison, and George Sullivan, Waterloo; all five siblings died when their submarine, the USS Juneau (CL-52), was attacked in WW II. As a result of their deaths, the U.S. War Department adopted the Sole Survivor Policy
- Billy Sunday (1862–1935), near Ames; his father was a Union soldier in the Civil War; played professional baseball for the Chicago White Stockings; one Sunday afternoon he heard a team from the Pacific Garden Mission, Chicago, preaching and was subsequently saved; by 1910, his revival meetings would last a month or more; the term "hit the sawdust trail" seems to have emerged from his meetings; it is estimated that he preached to over one hundred million persons; from 1896– 1935, he preached an average of forty-two sermons each month; from 1908–1920, he earned over $1 million, despite the fact that he gave away large sums to charities
- John Wayne (1907–1979), Winterset; born Marion Robert Morrison; parents changed name to Marion Michael when they decided to have another son to be named Robert; after family moved to Glendale, CA a local firefighter called him "Little Duke" because as Wayne passed by the fire station on his way to school he was usually accompanied by the family Airedale Terrier; he prefered the nickname Duke to his real name Marion; first starring role was in 1930
- Clyde Cessna (1879–1954), Hawthorne; built his first airplane and flew it successfully 1911; Cessna Aircraft Corporation was established in 1927
- Howard Andrew "Andy" Williams, (1927–), Wall Lake; recorded eighteen gold and three platinum albums; in 1955, an appearance on *The Steve Allen Show* gave him his first national exposure

One of the youngest mayors elected in America was eighteen-year-old Sam Juhl, Roland, Story County. He was a high school student at the time of his election.

Interesting names include: Adair; Adams; Afton; Agency; Akron; Albany; Alexander; Alice; Allen; Alpha; Amish; Anderson; Angus; Argyle; Artesian; Atlantic; Badger; Baltimore; Bangor; Battle Creek; Beaver; Bedford; Beech; Belfast; Berea; Beverly Depot;

Big Spring; Birmingham; Blackhawk; Blessing; Bloomfield; Blue Grass; Bluff Creek; Boone; Booneville; Boyd; Brazil; Brooklyn; Brownsville; Brucewell; Buck Creek; Buckeye; Buck Grove; Buckhorn; Buena Vista; Buffalo; Burlington (William Frawley); Burnside; Burr Oak; Burt; Business Corners; Calhoun; Campbell; Canoe; Carbon; Carlisle; Carroll; Carrollton; Carson; Cartersville; Cascade; Casey; Castle Grove; Cedar; Cedar Bluff; Cedar City; Cedar Falls; Cedar Grove; Cedar Rapids (Don DeFore, *Hazel*); Cedar Valley; Center Grove; Center Point; Centerville; Central City; Charles City; Charter Oak; Chautauqua; Chillicothe; Cincinnati; Clarinda (Glenn Miller); Clark; Clear Lake; Climbing Hill; Clinton; Cloud; Coal Creek; Coal Valley; Coalville; Coin; College Springs; Columbia; Columbus City; Commerce; Confidence; Coon Rapids; Correctionville; Cottonville; Council Bluffs; Crab Town; Creamery; Crescent; Crisp; Crystal Lake; Cumberland; Cylinder; Dakota City; Dale; Danville; Davenport; Dayton; Daytonville; Deep River; Deer Creek; Deerfield; Defiance; Delaware; Delhi; Delta; Denison (Donna Reed); Denmark; Denver; Derby; Des Moines (Harriet Nelson); Diagonal; Diamond; Dixie; Douglass; Dover; Dresden; Dundee; Dutchtown; Eagle Center; Eagle City; Eagle Grove; Eagle Point; Early; Echo; Eddyville; Edenville; Edinburg; Edna; Elkhart; Elk Horn; Elkport; Elkton; Elliott; Enterprise; Eureka; Evanston; Fairview; Fairville; Fallow; Farmersburg; Fayette; Fern; Fertile; Fillmore; Five Points; Florence; Florenceville; Floyd; Floyd Crossing; Floyd School; Ford; Forest City; Four Corners; Frankfort; Franklin; Fredonia; French Creek; Fruitland; Fulton; Garden City; Garden Grove; Gardner; Garland; Geneva; George; Germantown; German Valley; Glade; Glasgow; Golden; Goldfield; Goose Lake; Grace Hill; Grand Mound; Grand River; Grandview; Granite; Grant; Gravil Pit; Gravity; Great Oaks; Green Bay; Green Brier; Green Castle; Green Center; Green Island; Green Mountain; Greenville; Hamburg; Hancock; Hardin; Hard Scratch; Hardy; Harlan; Harper; Harpers Ferry; Hart; Hartford; Hawkeye; Hayfield; Henderson; Hickory Group; Hickory Grove; High Creek; High Point; Hills; Holland; Holstein; Homestead; Honey Creek; Hope; Hopeville; Hull; Huntington; Illinois Grove; Independence; Indiana; Indianapolis; Indiantown; Ion; Iowa City; Iowa Falls; Iron Hills; Ivy; Jackson; Jacksonville; Jamaica; Jamestown; Jefferson; Jeffersonville; Juniata; Kendallville; Kennedy; Keystone; Key West; Kirkman (Lew Anderson, third person to play Clarabell); Klondike; Knoxville; Lakewood Corner; Lambs Grove; Lancaster; Lansing; Laurel; Lawrenceburg; Lebanon; Le Claire (William Frederick "Buffalo Bill" Cody); Lee; Leslie; Lewis; Lexington; Liberty; Lima; Lime City; Lime Springs; Lincoln; Lisbon; Little Cedar; Little Groves; Littleport; Little Rock; Little Turkey; Livingston; Lizard; Locust; Logan; Logansport; Lone Rock; Lone Tree; Lost Nation; Luxemburg; Luzerne; Madison; Madrid; Magnolia; Maine; Mallard; Manchester; Manilla; Manly; Maple River; Mapleside; Marble Rock; Marion; Marquette; Marshall; Marshalltown; Mary Hill; Marysville; Maryville; Maysville; Mechanicsville; Melbourne; Mercer; Middleburg; Middle River; Middletown; Midland; Midway; Miller; Millersburg; Miner; Missouri Valley; Monroe; Montezuma; Montgomery; Monticello; Montpelier; Morgan; Morning Sun; Moscow; Motor; Mt Pleasant; Mt Sterling; Mt Vernon; Murray; Mystic; Nashville; National; Neptune; Nevada; New York; Nichols; Noel; Norway; Oakland; Oakwood; Ogden; Old Peru; Old Town; Old Tripoli; Oneida; Orange; Orange City; Orchard; Orient; Orleans; Otter Creek; Otterville; Ottumwa (*Radar O'Reilly's* hometown); Owen; Pacific City; Painted Rock; Panama;

Panther; Paris; Perry; Persia; Pigeon; Pioneer; Pittsburg; Plainfield; Plainview; Pleasant Creek; Pleasant Grove; Pleasant Hill; Pleasant Plain; Pleasant Valley; Pleasant View; Pleasantville; Poplar; Portland; Portsmouth; Prairiebell; Prairie City; Prairie Grove; Primrose; Princeton; Promise City; Prussia; Pulaski; Quarry; Quick; Racine; Radcliffe; Rake; Raleigh; Red Line; Redman; Red Oak; Republic; Riceville; Richmond; Ricketts; Ridgeway; Rising Sun; Riverside; Robertson; Robins; Rochester; Rock Creek; Rock Falls; Rockford; Rock Rapids; Rock Valley; Rockville; Rome; Rose Hill; Rowan; Royal; Russell; Russellville; Sac City; Sand Springs; Sandyville; Santiago; Savannah; Scarville; Scott; Scranton; Sedan; Selection; Sergeant Bluff; Shady Grove; Shady Oak; Sharpsburg; Shelby; Shell Rock; Shenandoah; Siam; Sidney; Silver City; Silver Lake; Sioux City (Jerry Mathers); Six Mile; Sixteen; Skunk River; Smithland; Soldier; Somber; Spencer; Spring Branch; Springbrook; Spring Fountain; Spring Grove; Spring Hill; Spring Valley; Springville; Springwater; Stacyville Junction; Stanton; State Center; St Charles; Steamboat Rock; Sterling; Stevens; St Marys; Storm Lake; Story City; Strawberry Point; Stringtown; Sugar Creek; Sulphur Springs; Summit; Sunbury; Sunshine; Superior; Sutherland; Swan; Swisher; Taylor; Taylorsville; Ten Mile; Tennant; Thayer; Thirty; Thompson; Tingley; Tioga; Tipperary; Toledo; Toronto; Tripoli; Turkey River; Twin Springs; Union; Union Burg; Union Center; Union Mills; Unionville; Unique; Urbana; Van Buren; Vandalia; Vincennes; Viola; Vista; Wall Lake (Andy Williams); Walnut; Walnut City; Walnut Grove; Washington; Washington Prairie; Waterville; Wayland; Webster; West Branch (Herbert Hoover); West Liberty; What Cheer; Wheatland; Whitebreast; White Cloud; White Oak; Wichita; Williamsburg; Williamstown; Winchester; Winterset (John Wayne); Wise; Wolf; Woolstock (George Reeves, *Superman*); Wren; Wyoming; Xenia; Yellow River; Yoemans

KANSAS – Sioux for "south wind people." Statehood was January 29, 1861. The state nickname is "Sunflower State." It was named after the river that runs through it and after the Kansa Indian tribe who lived there. Residents are called Kansans. When the territory was being settled in the 1850s, both abolitionists from New England and pro-slavery settlers from Missouri rushed to the territory to help determine if Kansas would be a free state or a slave state. Because of that, the area became a hot bed of violence and earned the nickname Bleeding Kansas. After the Civil War, the population exploded as waves of immigrants turned the prairie into productive farm land.

From 1821 to 1880, the Santa Fe Trail went from Kansas to Mexico transporting manufactured goods from Missouri and silver and furs from Santa Fe. Wagon ruts from the trail are still visible. In 1827, Fort Leavenworth became the first permanent settlement in the Missouri territory. Wild Bill Hickok was a deputy marshal at Fort Riley and a marshal at Hays and Abeline, TX. In one year alone, eight million heads of cattle were driven from Texas to board trains in Dodge City bound for the east, earning Dodge the nickname, "Queen of the Cowtowns." Wyatt Earp (who lived in Ohio County, KY) and Bat Masterson were both lawmen in Dodge City. Kansas became the first U.S. state to adopt a Constitution amendment prohibiting all alcoholic beverages. This was partly due to the violence from the cowboys.

Notable Kansans include:

- Buster Keaton (1895–1966), Piqua; he served furing World War I during which his hearing became impaired; at the age of three, Buster began performing with his parents
- Amelia Earhart (1897–missing in 1937, decleared dead 1939), Atchison; when she was ten years old, she saw her first aircraft show at the Iowa State Fair but was not taken up in a plane until she was twenty-three; in 1932, at age thirty-four, she flew solo across the Atlantic Ocean; she attempted a flight around the world 1937
- Bob Dole (1923–) Russell; U.S. Senate and House of Representatives; during the Great Depression, the family moved into the basement and rented out the rest of the house
- Walter Chrysler (1875–1940, Wamego; started Chrysler Corporation 1925; purchased the Dodge company 1928; financed the construction of the Chrysler Building in New York City
- Hattie McDaniel (1892–1952), Wichita; first black performer to win an Academy Award–Best Supporting Actress for the role of Mammy in *Gone with the Wind,* 1939; first black woman to sing on the American radio; appeared in over three hundred films but was only given credit for eighty
- Adolph Rupp (1901–1977), Halstead; became interested in basketball at age six; played basketball at the University of Kansas, 1919-1923; coached University of Kentucky basketball from 1930–1972; 80% of his players were from Kentucky; as coach, he won four NCAA championships and twenty-seven Southeast Conference titles; during his tenure at the University of Kentucky, his teams averaged losing 4.6 games per season; one season, 1953–1954, the team was undefeated
- Eddie Sutton (1936–), Bucklin; was the first coach to take four teams to the NCAA tournament and two schools to the Final Four; he coached University of Kentucky basketball teams from 1985–1989
- Vivian Vance (1909–1979), Cherryvale; born Vivian Roberta Jones; when casting for the new television show, *I Love Lucy,* in 1951, the director wanted Vance; Lucille Ball wanted Bea Benaderet, but she could not take the part because of a prior acting commitment

One of the youngest mayors elected in America was twenty-three-year-old John S. Gibson, Jr., 1924, in Geneseo, Rice County.

Interesting names include: Achilles; Adams; Admire; Agenda; Agricola; Akron; Albert; Alexander; Allen; America City; Americus; Anderson; Antelope; Arkansas City; Asherville; Ashland; Athens; Atlanta; Atlas; Augusta; Badger; Bazaar; Beagle; Beaver; Benton; Berlin; Beverly; Big Bow; Big Springs; Bird City; Birmingham; Bison; Black Jack; Black Wolf; Block; Bloom; Bloomington; Blue Hill; Blue Mound; Blue Rapids; Bluff City; Boyd; Boyle; Buck Creek; Buckeye; Buffalo; Bunker Hill; Burden; Burr Oak; Buttermilk; Caldwell; Camp Number Fortytwo; Camp Number Six; Campus; Canada; Caney; Canton; Catherine; Cave; Cave Springs; Cedar; Cedar Bluffs; Cedar Point; Centerview; Centerville; Central; Centropolis; Charleston; Chautauqua; Cherryvale

(Vivian Vance); Chevron; Cheyenne; Circleville; Clearview City; Clearwater; Cleveland; Clinton; Coalvale; Coal Valley; Coats; Coffeeville; Coldwater; Colony; Columbus; Commonwealth; Corbin; Cottage Hill; Cottonwood Falls; Council Grove; Covert; Crane; Crystal Springs; Cuba; Daily Hill; Dale; Danville; Deerfield; Deerhead; Denmark; Derby; Detroit; Diamond Springs; Dispatch; Dodge City; Douglas; Douglass; Dresden; Dry Wood; Duluth; Dundee; Durham; Dutch Hollow; Edna; Edward; Elk City; Elk Falls; Elkhart; Elmdale; Empire City; Ensign; Erie; Eureka; Everest; Fairview; Fall Leaf; Fall River; Fiat; Five Points; Fleming; Florence; Flush; Ford; Forest City; Four Corners; Fox Town; Frankfort; Franklin; Fredonia; Friend; Frisbie; Fruitland; Fulton; Garden City; Garden Plain; Gardner; Garland; Gas; Gem; Geneva; Georgia; Globe; Goldenrod; Good Intent; Goodrich; Gordon; Grainfield; Granada; Grand Summit; Grant; Great Bend; Greely; Green; Greenleaf; Greensburg; Greenwich; Gross; Grove; Grover; Groverland; Gypsum; Half Mound; Halstead (Adolph Rupp); Hamburg; Hammond; Harding; Harlan; Harper; Hartford; Hasty; Havana; Hawk; Hayden; Hill City; Hog Back; Holland; Home; Hope; Hopewell; Hopkins; Horace; Hunter; Huntsville; Huron; Independence; Indian Ridge; Iowa Point; Jamestown; Jefferson; Johnson; Kansas City; Kelly; Kendall; Kensington; La Crosse; Ladysmith; Lake City; Lancaster; Lane; Lansing; Lapland; Lawrence (Hugh Beaumont); Leavenworth; Lebanon; Lewis; Lexington; Liberal; Liberty; Lincoln; Lindsey; Litchfield; Little River; Logan; Lone Elm; Lone Star; Long Island; Lost Springs; Louisville; Lovewell; Lucerne; Madison; Manchester; Manhattan; Maple City; Maple Hill; Marion; Marquette; Marydel; Marysville; May Day; Mayfield; McAllaster; McCracken; Meade; Medicine Lodge; Mentor; Michigan Valley; Middletown; Midland; Midway; Milan; Miller; Mineral Springs; Minneapolis (George Washington Carver); Montana; Montezuma; Monticello; Monument; Moonlight; Morehead; Moscow; Mound City; Moundridge; Mound Valley; Mount Hope; Mt Vernon; Mulberry; Nashville; Neutral; Norway; Oak Hill; Oakley; Oak Mills; Oak Valley; Ogden; Oneida; Ontario; Opolis; Ottumwa; Page City; Paradise; Park; Park City; Partridge; Pearl; Peck; Peoria; Perry; Peru; Petrolia; Pierceville; Pilsbury Crossing; Piqua (Buster Keaton); Pittsburg; Pleasant Grove; Pleasant Valley; Pomona; Portland; Prairie Center; Prairie View; Prairie Village; Pratt; Pretty Prairie; Princeton; Prospect; Protection; Punkin Center; Quaker; Quartzite; Radium; Rainbow Bend; Ransom; Reading; Redwing; Reno; Republic; Reserve; Rest; Richmond; Ringer; Riverside; Rock; Rock Creek; Rockland; Rocky Ford; Rolla; Rome; Rose; Rose Hill; Roseland; Russell; Russell Springs; Saint Marys; Salter; Sand Creek; Scott; Scottsville; Scranton; Sedan (Emmett Kelly); Selma; Severance; Shady Bend; Shady Brook; Shallow Water; Shamrock; Shook; Silverdale; Silver Lake; Simpson; Skiddy; Smileyberg; Soldier; Somerset; Sparks; Spearville; Speed; Spencer; Spring; Spring Hill; Springvale; Stanton; Stark; Sterling; St Marys; Stone City; Strawberry; Strong City; Sublette; Summit; Sun City; Sunflower; Sunset Park; Sun Springs; Suppersville; Swamp Angel; Syracuse; Tampa; Tennis; Terra Cotta; Thompsonville; Toledo; Toronto; Tractor; Trading Post; Tyler; Uniontown; Upland; Utopia; Valley Center; Valley Falls; Venango; Vine Creek; Viola; Walkinghood; Walnut; Washington; Waterville; Wayside; Weaver; Webster; Wetmore; White City; White Cloud; Whitelaw; White Rock; Whiteside; Whitewater; White Woman Creek; Wichita (first fast-food chain, White Castle, 1921; hamburgers were 5 cents); Williams; Williamsburg; Williamstown; Willowdale; Wilson;

Winchester; Winifred; Winona; Wolf; Wolf Creek; Woodlawn; Woods; Xenia; Yankee Run; Zenith; Zook; Zurich

KENTUCKY – An Indian word for "meadowland." The state nickname is "Bluegrass State." From about 1650, until the arrival of the first white settlers, Shawnee tribes from north of the Ohio River, along with Cherokee and Chickasaw tribes from south of the Cumberland River, fought for control of the "Great Meadow." During this time, no Indian nation held possession of the land that would one day be known as Kentucky. The origin of Kentucky's name has yet to be positively identified, though some theories have been debunked. For example, Kentucky's name does not come from the combination of "cane" and "turkey", nor does it mean "dark and bloody ground" in any Indian language. The most likely etymology is that it comes from an Iroquois word for "meadow" or "prairie." Kentucky is the only state to have a non-contiguous part existing as an exclave surrounded by other states. Far western Kentucky includes a small piece of land, Kentucky Bend, on the Mississippi River which is accessible by land only by first going into Tennessee. This land difference was created by the New Madrid Earthquake (estimated to be 8.0 on Richter scale) occuring from December, 1811, into February, 1812.

Kentucky's ninety thousand miles of streams provides one of the most expansive and complex stream systems in the nation providing 1,100 miles of commercially navigable waterways, more than any other state, except Alaska. It is the only U.S. state to be bordered on three sides by rivers: Mississippi on the west, Ohio on the north, Big Sandy River and Tug Fork on the east. Kentucky became the fifteenth state in 1792. Of the artificial lakes east of the Mississippi River, Lake Cumberland is the largest in water volume while Kentucky Lake has the largest surface.

Kentucky and Missouri are the only two states to share a boundary with no road directly connecting them. High Bridge over the Kentucky River (Jessamine County) was the first cantilever bridge in North America and, at two hundred seventy-five feet above the water, it was the tallest railroad bridge in the world when it was completed in 1877. Louisville's Big Four Bridge is a project to reclaim unused railroad beds. When completed, the Big Four Bridge rail trail will contain the second longest pedestrian-only bridge in the world. Currently the longest pedestrian-only bridge, the Purple People Bridge, connects Newport, Kentucky to Cincinnati, Ohio. These two bridges will also be the only two pedestrian bridges in America connecting two states.

Kentucky is the nation's leading producer of burley tobacco and the second leading producer of all tobacco products. Kentucky is the leading beef cattle state east of the Mississippi River and is eighth in the nation overall. It ranks seventh is the production of broilers. Kentucky has over twelve million acres of commercial forest land comprising one-half of the state's total land area and is ranked third among hardwood producing states. The most harvested species of trees include white oak, red oak, walnut, yellow poplar, beech, sugar maple, white ash, and hickory. Kentucky is also the nation's third leading producer of coal and is an abundant producer of crushed stone, natural gas, and petroleum.

The Official State Drink is Milk (also Louisiana, Maryland, Minnesota, Mississippi, Nebraska, New York, North Carolina, North Dakota, Oklahoma, Oregon, Pennsylvania, Rhode Island, South Carolina, South Dakota, Vermont, Virginia, and Wisconsin)

> The Official State Mineral is Coal
> The Official State Fruit is Blackberry
> The Official State Tree is Tulip Poplar
> The Official State Instrument is Dulcimer
> The Official State Horse is Thoroughbred
> The Official State Rock is Kentucky Agate
> The Official State Soil is Crider Soil Series
> The Official State Fish is Kentucky Spotted Bass
> The Official State Gemstone is Freshwater Pearl
> The Official Wild Animal Game Species is Gray Squirrel
> The Official State Latin Motto is "Let Us Be Grateful to God"
> The Official State Outdoor Musical is "The Stephen Foster Story"
> The Official State Silverware pattern is Old Kentucky Bluegrass, the Georgetown pattern

Jesse Applegate (1811–1888), born in Kentucky; along with his brothers and their families, he joined what became known as the, "Great Migration of 1843" on the Oregon Trail; he led a large group of settlers along the Oregon Trail to the Oregon Country; he helped establish the Applegate Trail, as an alternate trail to the Oregon Trail.

The abbreviations for Kentucky, Ohio, and Virginia (Ken O Va) comprise the name for Kenova, West Virginia. Kentucky has more resort parks than any other state in the nation.

On May 22, 1849 Abraham Lincoln received a patent for a system of bellows and pulleys used to float boats over shallow waters. The invention never took off in Lincoln's day, though the same principle was later used to float submarines. He is the only American president to have been issued a patent.

Pueblo, Indiana, is ninety miles farther south than Newport, Kentucky. The easternmost point of Kentucky is almost due south of Cleveland, Ohio. Phelps (Pike County) is farther east than Huntington, West Virginia. The westernmost point of Virginia is farther west than Frenchburg, Kentucky.

More detailed information about Kentucky is given later in the book.

LOUISIANA – Named after King Louis XIV, king of France from 1643–1715. Statehood was April 30, 1812. The state nickname is "Pelican State." Land of Louis was named by French explorer La Salle for Louis XIV, one of France's greatest and most powerful kings. The town of Red Pole, which served as a boundary marker, was the original name of the Choctaw village. When the French arrived in the 1700s, they simply translated "red pole" into French. Baton (stick) and Rouge (red) was the result.

Famous Louisianans include:

- Louis Armstrong (1901–1971), New Orleans; for many years he often played more than three hundred engagements each year; in 1964, "Hello, Dolly!" was number one on the pop chart; at age sixty-three, he was the oldest person to accomplish that feat; "What a Wonderful World," was the biggest-selling single in the United Kingdom where at age sixty-six, he became the oldest male to top the charts; it is believed that he gave away as much money as he kept for himself
- Fats Domino (1928–), New Orleans; Born Antoine Domino; released thirty-seven singles that reached the Top 40; in 1956, "Blueberry Hill" was number two on Top 40, number one on R&B charts for eleven weeks, and was his biggest hit, selling more than five million copies in 1956 and 1957; "Blueberry Hill" was written in 1940, and recorded six times that year by such artists as the Sammy Kaye Orchestra, Gene Krupa, Glenn Miller, and Gene Autry; "Blueberry Hill" was also recorded by Elvis Presley, Little Richard, Ricky Nelson, Andy Williams, Bill Haley and His Comets, The Everly Brothers, Led Zeppelin, Freddy Fender, Jerry Lee Lewis, The Beach Boys, Elton John, The Rolling Stones; the song was premiered by Gene Autrey singing it in the 1940 western film, *The Singing Hill*
- Al Hirt (1922–1999), New Orleans; given his first trumpet at age six; by age sixteen he was playing professionally; he studied at the Cincinnati Conservatory of Music; played in bands of Tommy Dorsey, Jimmy Dorsey, Benny Goodman; recorded twenty-two albums
- Jerry Lee Lewis (1935–), Ferriday; began playing piano as a youth with cousins Mickey Gilley and Jimmy Swaggart; his parents mortgaged the farm to buy him a piano; his musical style was a mixture of rhythm and blues, boogie-woogie, gospel, and country music; became highly influential in adding piano to rockabilly recordings; appeared on *The Steve Allen Show*, 1957
- Floyd Cramer, (1933–1997), Shreveport; one of the architects of the "Nashville Sound;" taught himself to play piano and received formal classical training later; played on recordings for Elvis Presley, Brenda Lee, Patsy Cline, The Browns, Jim Reeves, The Everly Brothers, and many others; played on Presley's first national hit, "Heartbreak Hotel"
- Ray Walston (1914–2001), New Orleans; born Herman Walston; movies include *Damn yankees!, South Pacific, The Apartment, Who's Minding the Store?, Paint Your Wagon, The Sting*, and the television series, *My Favorite Martian*
- Donna Douglas (1933–), Pride; Miss Baton Rouge and Miss New Orleans; was the Letters Girl on the "Perry Como Show," 1957, and the Billboard Girl on the *Steve Allen Show*, 1959; played on *The Twilight Zone, Ozzie and Harriet*, and *Bachelor Father*; played the part of Frankie in the 1966 movie *Frankie and Johnny* with Elvis Presley; she often performs as a gospel singer and speaks at churches across America; wrote a children's book entitled, *Donna's Critters and Kids: Children's Stories with a Bible Touch*
- "Jelly Roll" Morton (1885 or 1890), New Orleans; born Ferdinand Joseph Lamothe; the first serious composer of jazz; at age fourteen, he played piano in a brothel but convinced his great-grandmother he was working in a barrel factory

42

One of the youngest mayors elected in America was twenty-two-year-old Robert Kennon, 1925, Minden, Webster Parish.

Interesting names include: Albany; Alexandria; Alfalfa; Alice; Alliance; Alpha; Anchor; Anderson; Argyle; Arizona; Ashland; Athens; Atlanta; Bagdad; Barcelona; Bat; Baton Rouge; Battle; Bayou Jack; Baywood (Donna Douglas, *Ellie May Clampett*); Bear Creek; Bear Skin; Beaver; Bedford; Bee Bayou; Beech; Beech Springs; Benton; Bermuda; Bernice; Big A Plenty Landing; Big Bayou; Big Bend; Big Cane; Big Creek; Big Woods; Bijou; Billy Goat Hill; Black Creek; Blackfoot; Black Hawk; Blanks; Bluff Creek; Bob; Bon Ami; Bond; Book; Boston; Bowie; Brake; Branch; Breezy Hill; Brian; Bridge City; Brimstone; Brownsville; Buckeye; Bull Run; Burnside; Bush; Butler; Calhoun; Campbell; Canebrake; Cane Ridge; Caney; Cargas; Carlisle; Carroll; Carterville; Cash Point; Catherine; Cedar Grove; Center Point; Centerville; Central; Charlieville; Cherry Grove; Cherry Ridge; Clay; Clearwater; Clinton; Coldwater; Columbia; Concord; Convent; Converse; Coochie; Cook; Copenhagen; Corbin; Cornerview; Cotton Plant; Cottonwood; Covington; Cow Island; Cranky Corner; Crescent; Crowville; Cuba; Cut Off; Cypress; Cypress Creek; Cypress Island; Danville; Dave; Delaware; Delhi; Delta; Diamond; Dixie; Douglas; Dry Creek; Duckroost; Dutch Town; Duty; Eden; Egg Bend; Elizabeth; Elm Grove; Elmwood; Empire; English; Enterprise; Eureka; Evergreen; Ewing; Extension; Fairlane; False River; Farmerville; Fayette; Fillmore; Fisher; Five Forks; Flat Creek; Flatwoods; Flora; Florence; Floyd; Forest; Forest Hill; Forked Island; Forksville; Fortune Fork; Four Corners; Four Forks; Franklin; Freetown; French Settlement; Friendship; Frogmore; Frost; Frost Town; Fulton; Garden City; Gardner; Garland; Garyville; Gassoway; Georgetown; Georgeville; Glade; Gold Dust; Goldridge; Goodbee; Good Hope; Goodwill; Gordon; Grand Prairie; Grand River; Grant; Gravel; Gravel Point; Grayson; Greenfield; Green Gables; Greenlaw; Greensburg; Greenville; Grim; Grimes; Grove; Grove Hill; Gum Ridge; Gypsy; Hackberry; Half Moon; Half Way; Halfway; Hamburg; Hancock; Happy Jack; Hardwood; Harmony; Henderson; Henry; Hickory; Hickory Valley; Hilltop; Hilly; Holly; Holly Beach; Hollybrook; Holly Grove; Holly Ridge; Holly Springs; Hollywood; Home Place; Hope; Hot Wells; Houston River; Hunt; Hurricane; Illinois Plant; Independence; Independent; Indian Bayou; Indian Landing; Indian Mound; Indian Village; Intercoastal City; Invincible; Iowa; Irish Bend; Island; Jackson; Jamestown; Jefferson; Jenkins; Jigger; Johnson; Junction City (shares border with Junction City, AR); Keystone; Kings Oaks; Klondyke; Laark; Lake Charles; Lake End; Latex; Laurel Hill; Laurel Ridge; Leslie; Liberty; Liberty Hill; Lindsay; Link; Lisbon; Little Creek; Little Prairie; Live Oak; Liverpool; Livingston; Loch Lomond; Loco; Locust Ridge; Logansport; Log Cabin; Lone Pine; Lone Star; Longacre; Long Bridge; Long Springs; Longstraw; Longstreet; Longview; Lower Texas; Lucky; Madisonville; Magenta; Magnolia; Major; Manchester; Manifest; Many; Maplewood; Marion; Mars Hill; Marthaville; Martin; Mason; Matthews; Maryland; Mayflower; Meeker; Metropolis; Midway; Millerton; Millerville; Mineral Springs; Mink; Missionary; Mix; Monroe; Montgomery; Monticello; Montpelier; Morgan City; Morris; Mound; Mount Lebanon; Mount Pleasant; Mt Airy; Mt Union; Mulberry; Mulberry Hill; Mystic; Natchez; New Orleans (Louis Armstrong); Nicholas; Nichols; Nickel; Nine Forks; Oak Flats; Oak Grove; Oakland; Oak Ridge; Oaks; Oil City; Old Saline; Old Shongaloo;

Omega; Oshkosh; Oxbow; Palmetto; Paragon; Peach Bloom; Pearl; Pearl River; Pecan Island; Peck; Pelican; Perry; Perryville; Philadelphia Point; Pigeon; Pikes Peak; Pine; Pine Cliff; Pine Coupee; Pine Grove; Pine Island; Pine Prairie; Pine Ridge; Pinewood; Pioneer; Plain Dealing; Plains; Pleasant Hill; Point Pleasant; Poland; Port Sulphur; Powell; Prairie Home; Prairieville; Pratt; Pride; Princeton; Prospect; Pumpkin Center; Punkin Center; Quebec; Quick; Rebecca Plantation; Red Chute; Red Fish; Red Gum; Redoak; Red Oak; Retreat; Riceville; Richmond; Ridge; River Bend; Roanoke; Robert; Rock; Rock Hill; Rocky Branch; Rocky Mount; Rosedale; Rosefield; Rose Hill; Roseland; Rosepine; Royal Pines; Ruby; Russellville; Saint Louis; Saline; Sandy Hill; Sarepta; Savoy; Scott; Scottsville; Security; Shady; Shady Grove; Shamrock; Shongaloo; Sibley (forty miles from) Sibley; Sicily Island; Simpson; Singer; Slacks; Slaughter; Smithland; Solitude; Somerset; Spencer; Spring Creek; Springfield; Springhill; Spring Hill; Spring Lake; Spring Ridge; Springville; Standard; Stanton; Staples; Star; Start; State Line; Stay; St Charles; Stephenville; Sterling; Stevensdale; Stoney Point; Stony Point; Sugar Creek; Sugartown; Sulphur; Summerfield; Summerville; Summit; Sun; Sunny Hill; Sunset; Sunshine; Superior; Supreme; Swampers; Sweet Home; Sweet Lake; Sweetville; Swindleville; Swords; Taterville; Taylor; Taylortown; Tenmile; Thirteen Points Landing; Tickfaw; Tide; Todd; Topsy; Transylvania; Trees; Trout; Tulip; Turkey Creek; Turtle Lake; Twin Oaks; Uncle Sam; Uneedus; Union; Union Hill; Union Point; Union Springs; Unionville; Upco; Upland; Utility; Valentine; Vatican; Vienna; Vixen; Walet; Wall Lake; Walnut Hill; Warden; Washington; Waterproof; Welcome; Wham; White Castle; White Hall; Whitehall; White Hills; White Kitchen; White Sulphur Springs; Whiteville; Whitley; Wickliffe; Wildcat; Wildwood; Willow Chute; Wilson; Yellow Bayou; Yellow Pine; Yucatan Landing; Zachary; Zee; Zugg; Zylks;

MAINE - Named for an old French province. Statehood was March 15, 1820, through the Missouri Compromise, in an effort to keep an equal balance between free and slave states. The state nickname is "Pine Tree State." It is the most sparsely populated state east of the Mississippi River. Ninety percent of the state is forested. For example, the Northwest Aroostook territory contains 2,668 square miles and twenty-seven residents, or one person for every one hundred square miles. The original inhabitants of this area were Algonquian-speaking peoples. English colonists settled in 1607. It was a hot bed between American and British forces during the Revolutionary War and the War of 1812. Maine is the only state to have a one-syllable name and the only state to be bordered by only one state. Lubec is the easternmost point in the United States. The morning sun shines on Maine before falling on any other part of the United States. Maine is the number one exporter of blueberries and toothpicks. A citizen of Maine is known as a Mainer.

Famous Mainers include:
- Leon Leonwood (L.L.) Bean (1872–1967), Greenwood; displayed at an early age his ability to earn and manage money; to solve the problem of wet boots when hunting, he began developing plans for waterproof boots; he had to refund the money for the first one hundred pairs of boots he sold

- Milton Bradley (1836–1911), Vienna; invented the board games *The Game of Life*, *Candy Land, Operation,* and *Battleship*
- Henry Wadsworth Longfellow (1807–1882), Portland
- Margaret Chase Smith (1897–1995), Skowhegan; first woman to be elected to both houses of congress

The easternmost point of ME is nine hundred miles east of Miami, Florida and due north of Puerto Rico. The northernmost point of ME is four hundred miles north of Windsor, Ontario.

Interesting names include: Adams; Alexander; Argyle; Ashland; Athens; Atlantic; Augusta; Bald Head; Bath; Beans Corner; Beaver Dam; Belfast; Belgrade; Benton; Bingo; Birch Harbor; Blackstone; Blackwater; Blue Hill; Blue Hill Falls; Bradley; Bradleys Corner; Bridgewater; Brooksville; Buffalo; Burlington; Burnt Mill; California; Camden; Campbell; Canton; Cape Elizabeth; Caribou; Carroll; Carson; Cash Corner; Cedar; Cedar Grove; Centerville; Charleston; Cherryfield; China; Christmas Cove; City Point; Cleveland; Clinton; Columbia; Cooks Corner; Cornville; Crows Nest; Crystal; Dallas; Danville; Dark Harbor; Deadmans Corner; Deep Cut; Deer Isle; Denmark; Derby; Detroit; Dog Corner; Dogtown; Dog Town; Douglas Hill; Drinkwater Corner; Ducktrap; Dunkertown; Eagle Lake; Edinburg; Egypt; Eight Corners; Eliot; Elizabeth Park; Fairbanks; Falmouth; Fayette; Fish Street; Five Corners; Five Mile Corners; Five Points; Forest; Fort George; Four Corners; Frankfort; Franklin; Freedom; French Settlement; Frenchville; Garland; Georgetown; Gerry; Globe; Goodrich; Goodwin; Goose Rocks; Gordon; Grand Isle; Granite Hill; Grass Corner; Great Pond; Great Works; Greely Landing; Greenbush; Greenfield; Greenlaw Crossing; Greenville; Gregorys Corner; Grindstone; Grove; Hancock Point; Happy Corner; Harding; Hardy; Harmony; Harrison; Hartford; Hay Brook; Hayden Corner; Head Tide; High Head; Hillman; Hillside; Hope; Indian Island; Indian Point; Indian River; Irish Settlement; Island Falls; Jackson; Jacksonville; Jay; Jefferson; Johnson Center; Jumbo Landing; Kendalls Corner; Kennebunk; Kennebunkport; Knox; Lagrange; Lamb Place; Lambs Corner; Lebanon; Lee; Liberty; Limestone; Lincoln; Lisbon; Litchfield; Little Canada; Little Cranberry Island; Little Falls; Little Italy; Long Beach; Long Pond; Lucerne in Maine; Lucky Landing; Lynchville; Madison; Maine; Mainstream; Manchester; Maple Grove; Mapleton; Marion; Mars Hill; Martin; Maysville; McShea; Meadowville; Mechanic Falls; Mercer; Mexico; Michigan Settlement; Miller Corner; Monroe; Monticello; Mooselookmeguntic; Morgan Beach; Morris Corner; Moscow; Mountainview; Mouse Island; Mt Desert; Mt Vernon; Naples; Nashville Plantation; Newport; Nixon; Norway; Number Four; Oakfield; Oak Hill; Oakland; Oceanville; Old City; Old Town; Olive Hill Corner; Orient; Otter Creek; Owls Head; Oxbow; Packard Landing; Parent; Paris; Pea Cove; Perry; Peru; Pigeon Hill; Pike Corner; Pine Corner; Pine Hill; Pine Knoll; Pleasant Hill; Pleasant Island; Pleasant Point; Pleasant Ridge Plantation; Poland; Prairie; Pretty Marsh; Pride; Prospect; Purgatory; Red Rock Corner; Reeds; Richmond; Ripley; Rivers End; Roberts; Robinhood; Rockwood; Rome; Round Mountain; Russell Crossing; Sandwich; Sandy Creek; Sandy Point; Sandy River Plantation; Sargentville; Scituate; Scotland; Seawall; Shady Brook; Shady Nook;

Shaker Village; Sheep Landing; Sheepscott; Shin Pond; Shy Corner; Sidney; Silver Ridge; Simpson Corners; Six Mile Falls; Smarts Corner; Snow Corner; Snow Settlement; Sodom; Soldier Pond; Somerset Junction; Split Hill; Springfield; Spring Lake; Square Lake; Stacyville; Starboard; State Road; St David (six miles from) St David; Steep Falls; Steep Landing; Stetson; Stevens Corner; Stevensville; St George; Stockholm; Strong; Stronghold; Suckerville; Sugar Hill; Summer Harbor; Sunset; Sunshine; Swans Island; Sweden; Tacoma; Ten Degree; The Forks; The Landing; The Pines; Thompson (two miles east of) Thompson Corner; Three Streams; Town Hill; Trap Corner; Troutdale; Twelve Corners; Twin Brook; Union; Unity; Upper Dam; Van Buren; Vienna; Waite; Walnut Hill; Warren; Washington; Wayne; Webster; Weld; White Oak Corner; Williamsburg; Winslow; Winter Harbor; Winterville; Woodbridge Corner

MARYLAND – Named after the wife of King Charles I. Statehood April 28, 1788. The state nickname is "Old Line State." It is the second wealthiest state in America with a median household income of $62,000. There is one point along the Pennsylvania border where the state of Maryland is about one mile wide. Streams in the western part of the state shed water into the Mississippi River. There are no natural lakes in Maryland.

The Maryland Toleration Act of 1649, (from the British Empire) was one of the first laws that explicitly dictated religious tolerance (as long as it was Christian). The Act is sometimes seen as a precursor to the First Amendment of the Constitution. The Mason-Dixon Line has nothing to do with a division of the North and South, but a division between Pennsylvania (controlled by the Penn family) and Maryland (controlled by the Calvert family). The border dispute began in 1730, and was finally settled by King George II when he established the Mason-Dixon Line in 1767. Maryland was the thirteenth state to approve the ratification of the Articles of Confederation which brought into being the United States as a united, sovereign, and national state. In 1789, it became the seventh state admitted to the Union after ratifying the new Constitution. The following year, 1790, Maryland ceded land selected by President George Washington to the federal government for the creation of Washington, D.C. During the War of 1812, the British attempted to capture the Port of Baltimore which was protected by Fort McHenry. It was after this battle that the "Star-Spangled Banner" was written.

Many federal government agencies are located in Maryland including Medicare, Medicaid, EPA, FDA, IRS, NASA, NOAA, NRC, Social Security, among others. It is also home to Aberdeen Proving Ground, Andrews Air Force Base, Camp David, and the U.S. Naval Academy, among others. There are thirty-one institutions of higher learning, not counting community colleges, nor the fifteen separate sites for the University of Maryland. In all, there are 56 campuses of higher learning in Maryland.

Signers of the Declaration of Independence include: Charles Carroll, Samuel Chase, William Paca, and Thomas Stone.

Baltimore is due north of Kingston, Jamaica.

Famous Marylanders include:
- John Wilkes Booth (1838–1865), Bel Air; fatally shot President Abraham Lincoln in Ford's Theatre in Washington, D.C., on April 14, 1865; President Lincoln died the next day and became the first president to be assassinated; Booth was killed by Union troops April 26, 1865
- Johns Hopkins (1795–1873), Anne Arundel County; Johns is a family name in his lineage; died December 24, 1873 with no heirs; his $7 million estate was left to establish institutions that bear his name, including Johns Hopkins Colored Children Orphan Asylum, Johns Hopkins University, Johns Hopkins Press, Johns Hopkins School of Nursing, Johns Hopkins University School of Medicine
- Francis Scott Key (1779–1843), Carroll County; lawyer, author, and poet who wrote the words to "The Star-Spangled Banner;" was inducted into the Songwriters Hall of Fame, 1970
- Harriet Tubman (1820–1913), Dorchester County; born into slavery, escaped to Philadelphia then returned to Maryland to rescue her family; eventually guided dozens of other slaves to freedom; known as Moses in the Underground Railroad; a Union spy during the Civil War

One of the youngest mayors elected in America and believed to be the youngest mayor in Maryland's historty was twenty-year-old Amel Morris, 2008, Westernport, Allegany County. He defeated the five-term incumbent by a vote count of 443–187.

Interesting names include: Aberdeen; Accident; Allegany Grove; Allen; Anchorage; Ancient Oak; Annapolis Rock; Apple Grove; Appletown; Asher Glade; Autumn Hill; Avenue; Back River; Bacon Hill; Bald Eagle; Ballard; Baltimore (Garry Moore); Barber; Bare Hills; Beaver Creek; Beetree; Bel Air (John Wilkes Booth); Bell; Ben Oaks; Berlin; Berry; Berrytown; Bestpitch; Big Pines; Big Pool; Big Spring; Bird Hill; Bitter Sweet; Blackhorse; Black Oak; Blackrock Mill; Blackwater; Bloom; Bloomer Spring; Bloomfield; Bloomington; Blue Hill; Blue Mount; Blue Mountain; Blue Ridge View; Boonsboro; Boot Hill; Bootjack; Boring; Bowie; Bowling Green; Bowlings Alley; Bridgeport; Bridgetown; Brink; Brownsville; Bruceville; Bucktown; Buena Vista; Bureau; Burleytown; Burnt Factory; Burnt Mills Hill; Burnt Mills Village; Burnt Woods; Bush; Cabin John; California; Callaway; Carroll; Cascade; Cash Corner; Catchpenny; Cat Creek; Cedar Beach; Cedar Cliff; Cedar Haven; Cedar Hill; Cedar Landing; Cedar Lawn; Centerville; Chaney; Charlestown; Charlesville; Cheltenham; Cherry Hill; Cherrytown; Chestnut Grove; Chestnut Hill; Chestnut Ridge; Chevy Chase; Chewsville; Choptank; Chrome Hill; Claysville; Clearfield; Clear Ridge; Clear Spring; Clevelandville; Clinton; Cloverfields; Clover Hill; Coffee Hill; College Park; Columbia; Concord; Constant Friendship; Copperville; Corbin; Cottage City; Cranberry; Crappo; Crescendo; Cumberland; Daisy; Danville; Day; Dayton; Deep Branch; Deep Run; Deer Park; Deerpark; Delight; Detour; Discovery; Dogtown; Dogwood Flats; Drybranch; Dry Run; Dublin; Dumbarton; Eagle Harbor; Eden; Elkton; Elliott; Elmwood; Evergreen; Fair Hill; Fairplay; Fair Play; Fairview; Federal Hill; Federalsburg; Ferncliff; Fishtown; Five Forks; Flint; Flintstone; Florence; Floyd; Forest Hill; Forest Park; Fork; Fort Washington; Fountain Head;

Four Locks; Four Winds; Foxcatcher at Fair Hill; Fox Chapel; Foxtown; Foxville; Franklin; Franklinville; Freeland; Frenchtown; Friendsville; Frogeye; Frogtown; Frostburg; Frostown; Fulton [Baltimore]; Furnace; Garland; Gary; Georgetown (Francis Scott Key); Germantown; Glass Hill; Good Luck; Granite; Gravel Hill; Great Falls; Green Glade; Greenmount; Green Ridge; Greensburg; Green Spring Furnace; Green Valley; Gum Swamp; Gunpowder; Hale; Halfway; Hancock; Harmony; Harpers Choice; Harpers Corner; Hayden; Henderson; Hi-Point; Hickory; Hickory Hills; Hickory Thicket; High Point; Hillside; Hill Top; Hog Island; Holler; Holly Beach; Hollywood; Hollywood Beach; Hopkins Corner; Horsehead; Horseshoe Curve; Huckleberry; Huntington Lodge; Hurry; Indianbone; Indian Head; Indian Springs; Indian Town; Iron Hill; Ivory; Ivy Hills; Ivytown; Jackson; Jasontown; Jefferson; Jenkins; Jerusalem; Jimtown; Jugtown; Jumptown; Kendall; Kensington; Kettering; Kings Creek; Knoxville; Ladiesburg; Lap; Laurel; Laurel Grove; Leslie; Level; Liberty Grove; Libertytown; Lime Kiln; Lincoln; Lisbon; Little Orleans; Locust Grove; Locust Valley; Londontown; Long Green; Long Meadow; Louisville; Lynch; Madison; Magnolia; Manchester; Maplecrest; Maple Crest; Maple Grove; Maple View; Mapleville; Marble Hill; Marshalls Corner; Marydel; Maryland Line; Maryland Point; Matthews; Mayberry; Mayfield; Mayo; Meadowview; Mechanicsville; Mechanic Valley; Mexico; Miami Beach; Middlebrook; Middleburg; Middlepoint; Middletown; Midland; Miller; Minefield; Mineral Spring; Montpelier; Monumental; Morgan; Morgantown; Morningside; Moscow; Mountain; Mount Wilson; Mousetown; Mt Airy; Mt Vernon; Murray Hill; Nichols; North East; Oakland; Oak Orchard; Oak Ridge; Oak Summit; Oakwood; Ocean City; Odessy; Oklahoma; Oldtown; Old Town; Orchard Hills; Oregon; Oriole; Ottersdale; Paradise; Parole; Pasadena; Peach Grove; Peacocks Corner; Perry Point; Perryville; Phoenix; Pilot; Pinehurst; Pine Knoll; Pine Orchard; Pine Ridge; Piney Hill; Pioneer City; Pipe Creek Mill; Pleasant View; Pleasantville; Pleasant Walk; Point of Rocks; Point Pleasant; Pomona; Poplar Hill; Poplar Knob; Port Deposit; Potomac; Pot Spring; Pratt; Prince Frederick; Princess Ann; Prospect; Providence; Pumpkin Center; Putty Hill; Quail Run; Queen Ann; Rabbit Town; Ralph; Red Hill; Redhouse; Red Point; Ripley; Rising Sun; Roberts; Rock Run; Rockville; Rocky Ridge; Rocky Springs; Roller; Royal Oak; Ruthsburg; Sand Spring; Sandy Bottom; Sandy Hook; Sandy Spring; Sassafras; Scotland (Tubby Smity); Scotland Beach; Secretary; Security; Seven Oaks; Shady Bower; Shady Oaks; Shady Side; Sharpsburg; Sharptown; Silver Rock; Silver Run; Singer; Slabtown; Snow Hill; Society Hill; Somerset; Spring Gap; Spring Valley; Standard; St Charles; St Georges; Stillmeadows; Still Pond; St Margarets; St Marys City; Street; Stringtown; St Stephen; Stumptown; Sugarland; Sunnybrook; Sunset View; Sunshine; Sunview; Surrey Ridge; Swan Creek; Sweet Air; Tall Timbers; Tannery; Taylor; Taylorsville; Texas; The Oaks; Thompson; Thompsons Corner; Thompsontown; Timber Grove; Timber Ridge; Tollgate; Tompkinsville; Topeka East; Town Creek; Treetops; Troutville; Truck; Tulip Hill; Tuxedo; Tyler; Unicorn; Union Bridge; Union Mills; Uniontown; Unionville; Unity; Urbana; Valley Stream; Vienna; Vinegar Hill; Walnut; Walnut Ridge; Warfieldsburg; Warren; Watersville; Webster; Welcome; Wenona; West Liberty; Whispering Pines; White Hall; White House; Whitehouse; White Oak; White Rock; Williamsburg; Willow Grove; Wilson; Wilson Mill; Winchester; Winston; Wolfsville

MASSACHUSETTS – An Indian word for "large hill place." Statehood was February 6, 1788. The state nickname is "Bay State" and is known as the "Cradle of Liberty." The name is derived from a local tribe of Native Americans living in the area, the Massachusett. Massachusetts is one of four commonwealths in the nation. Kentucky, Pennsylvania, and Virginia are the other three. Of the 6.5 million who live in the state, 4.4 million (two-thirds) live in the Boston area.

The first Europeans to settle in the area were Pilgrims in 1620. They were soon followed by the Puritans. The first battles of the Revolutionary War were fought in Lexington (for which Lexington, Kentucky was named) and Concord. Boston is the birthplace of the abolitionist movement that emancipated southern blacks from slavery. Crane Paper Company in Dalton produces the material used for printing U.S. Federal Reserve Notes.

Harvey Ball, a freelance graphic artist from Worcester, was paid $45 in 1963, to design an emblem that would ease tensions between workers at two insurance companies that merged. His design was the smiley face. A Belgian entreprenour copyrighted the face, which had remained uncopyrighted, and has since received millions of dollars since 1971.

Signers of the Declaration of Independence include: John Adams, Samuel Adams, Elbridge Gerry, John Hancock, Robert Treat Paine,

Massachusetts has the lowest divorce rate in America.

Famous Bay Staters include:
- Dwight L. Moody (1837–1899), Northfield; his Sunday school was so well known that newly-elected President Lincoln visited and spoke at a Sunday school meeting November 25, 1860; Moody helped promote "The Wordless Book," a teaching tool invented by Charles Haddon Spurgeon in 1866. In 1875 Moody added a fourth color—gold, to represent heaven
- Jack Lemon (1925–2001), Newton; born in an elevator at Newton-Wellesley Hospital [Boston]
- Horatio Alger (1832–1899), Chelsea; wrote over two hundred fifty dime novels, many dealing with rags to riches stories; admitted to Harvard at age sixteen; Alger never became rich from his writings
- Marshall Field (1834–1906), Conway; started Marshall Field, and Co.; famous for the slogan, "Give the lady what she wants" and, reportedly, "The customer is always right"
- Samuel Adams (1722–1803), Boston; one of the country's founding fathers and a brewer
- John Hancock (1737–1793), Braintree; only person to sign the Declaration of Independence on July 4, 1776; he is well-remembered for his large signature (he actually printed his name which is five inches long) on the Declaration of Independence, so much so that the term, "John Hancock," has become an informal synonym for "signature"

- William Prescott (1726–1795), Groton; Revolutionary War colonel who commanded the forces at Bunker Hill and said, "Do not fire (on the British) until you see the whites of their eyes." The soldiers were very low on ammunition and no rounds could be wasted
- Paul Revere (1734–1818), Boston; rode from Boston to Lexington (about ten miles) to warn John Hancock and Samuel Adams of the movements of the British Army
- John Adams, Jr. (1735–1826), Braintree; America's first vice president and second president; played a leading role in persuading congress to adopt the Declaration of Independence, 1776
- John Quincy Adams (1767–1848), Braintree (now Quincy); sixth president of the United States and son of John Adams, the second president
- George Herbert Walker Bush (1924–), Milton; forty-first president of the United States and two-term vice-president under President Ronald Reagan
- Edmund Sears (1810–1876), Sandisfield; wrote "It Came Upon the Midnight Clear," as a melancholy reflection on his times while a minister in Wayland
- Benjamin Franklin (1706–1790), Boston; the fifteenth of seventeen children (two mothers); at age seventeen ran away to Philadelphia; initiated the idea for the public library; 1733 began publishing *Poor Richard's Almanac*; there are sixteen counties and nine towns in America named for him
- Eli Whitney (1765–1825), Westborough; invented the cotton gin
- Susan B. Anthony (1820–1906), Adams; instrumental in the movement that allowed women to vote; for forty-five years she traveled the United States and Europe giving seventy-five to one hundred speeches annually
- Robert Goulet (1933–2007), Lawrence; in 1960, he appeared on Broadway as Lancelot in the musical *Camelot*

Nantucket Island extends farther south than Newport, Rhode Island and New Haven, Connecticut.

Interesting names include: Adams; Ashland; Atlantic; Avon; Barnstable; Bassets Corner; Bedford; Berlin; Beverly; Beverly Road; Big Muddy River; Black Rock; Boston (nation's 1st subway; Paul Revere); Bradford; Braintree; Briggs Corner; Briggsville; Brimstone Corner; Brookline (John F. Kennedy); Brush Hollow; Burlington; Butlerville; Buzzards Bay; Canada Mills; Carlisle; Carterville; Cedar Bushes; Cedar Grove; Cedar Hill; Central Square; Charles River Grove; Cherry Valley; Chestnut Hill; Chestnut Tree Corner; Clevelandtown; Clinton; Coldbrook Springs; Cold Spring; Concord (Along w/Lexington where American Revolutionary War began; Henry David Thoreau); Cottage Hill; Cottage Park; Cow Yard; Cranberry Bog Corner; Cummaquid; Cuttyhunk; Douglas; Douglas Corner; Duckville; Eddyville; Egypt; Factory Village; Fairview; Falmouth; Farm Hill; Fayville; Feeding Hills; Fighting Rock Corner; Fireworks; First Cliff; Five Corners; Five Pound Island; Flint Village; Florence; Florida; Four Corners; Fourth Cliff; Franklin; Freetown; Fresh Brook; Furnace; Gardner; Georgetown; Germantown; Grantville; Greenville; Halfway House; Halfway Pond; Hancock; Handy Four Corners; Happy Hills;

Harding; Hayden Row; Hemlocks; Holland; Holly Woods; Huckleberry Corner; Huntington; Indian Orchard; Ipswich; Island; Island Creek; Jefferson; Kendal Green; Killdeer Island; Lancaster; Lands End; Lawrence; Lee; Lexington (see Concord note); Liberty Plain; Lincoln; Little Bridge; Little Egypt; Little Rest; Lobsterville; Locks Village; Long Josephs Point; Long Plain; Long Pond; Lower Village; Magnolia; Manchester; Manchester-by-the-Sea; Maple Grove; Maple Park; Maple Ridge; Marblehead; Marion; Marshall Corner; Mashpee; Mayflower Grove; Mayo Beach; Meadow Brook; Mercer Square; Metcalf; Middle Pasture; Middlesborough; Mill River; Milton (George H. W. Bush); Monroe; Monroe Bridge; Montgomery; Morris Corner; Mount Washington; Mountain Park; North Orange; Oak Grove; Oakland; Ocean Spray; Ocean View; Old City; Old Furnace; Old Quaker Meetinghouse; Onset; Orange; Orleans; Otis; Oxford (Clara Barton); Packardville; Paper Mill Village; Partridgeville; Peabody (George Peabody); Perryville; Peru; Pigeon Cove; Pine Bluffs; Pinecrest; Pinefield; Pine Grove; Pinehurst; Pine Island; Pine Rest; Pine Tree Corner; Pleasant Valley; Plowed Neck; Plymouth (2nd permanent English settlement in North America in 1620); Pond Village; Pratt Junction; Pratts Corner; Prattville; Precinct; Princeton; Prospect Hill; Quincy (John Hancock; John Adams; John Quincy Adams); Red Bridge; Revere; Rice Square; Richmond; Rochester; Rock; Rockport; Rocks Village; Rock Valley; Rockville; Rocky Hill; Roosterville; Russell; Russellville; Sandwich; Scituate; Scotland; Second Cliff; Seekonk; Shakerhill; Shaker Village; Shrewsbury; Silver Hill; Silver Lake; Sixteen Acres; Skyland; Smalltown; Somerset; South Lancaster; South Lincoln; Spencer; Springfield (June Foray—voice of Chatty Kathy (1963) & many cartoon characters); Spruce Corner; Sterling; Still River; Stow; Summit; Sunnyside; Swampscott; Swan Corner; Sweet Corner; Swift River; Teaticket; Ten Hills; The Green; The Springs; The Street; The X; Third Cliff; Thompsonville; Tinkertown; Town Hall; Tree of Knowledge Corner; Trots Hills; Union Hill; Unionville; Upper Green; Uxbridge; Victory Hill; Wales; Walnut Hill; Walpole (Charles Farrell, father on *My Little Margie*); Warren; Washington; Watertown; Waterville; Wayland; Wayside; Webster; Wheelwright; Whipples; White City; White Hall; White Oaks; White Valley; Williamsburg; Williamstown; Williamsville; Willowdale; Winchester; Winter Hill; Workmans Circle Camp; Yankee Orchards

MICHIGAN – Chippewa for "great water." Statehood was January 26, 1837. The state nickname is "Great Lakes State." During the War of 1812, Michigan Territory was captured by the British and returned to Canada until the Treaty of Ghent, which implemented the policy of "Status Quo Ante Bellum," meaning "Just As Things Were Before the (Civil) War." In 1920, radio station WWJ began commercial broadcasting of regular programs, the first such radio station in the United States.

A resident of Michigan is called a Michiganian or a Michigander, but a resident of the Upper Peninsula is called a Yooper. Michigan was named after Lake Michigan whose name was a French adaptation of the Ojibwe Tribe *mishigami* meaning "large water" or "large lake." Michigan has the longest freshwater shoreline in America—3,250 miles—and more recreational boats than any state. Michigan is the only two-peninsula state. Lower and Upper Michigan are separated by the Straits of Mackinac, but joined by a five mile long bridge, the world's longest suspension bridge between its anchorages.

Windsor, Ontario is the only place where one must travel north to enter the United States from Canada. Michigan has well over one hundred lighthouses, reportedly more than any other state. Vernors Soda was invented in Michigan. Woodward Avenue in Detroit was the first paved road in America. The largest college football stadium is Michigan Stadium, with a capacity of over 100,000. It sits is on the campus of the Univesity of Michigan, Ann Arbor.

Famous Michiganders include:
- Wallace Maynard "Wally" Cox (1924–1973), Detroit; *Mr. Peepers*, 1952–1955, aired live and also starred Tony Randall and Marion Lorne (*Mrs. Gurney* and *Aunt Clara* on *Bewitched*
- Henry "Harry" Morgan (1915–), Detroit; born Harry Bratsberg; played officer Bill Gannon on *Dragnet* and Colonel Sherman T. Potter on *M*A*S*H*; the photograph on his desk of his wife was, in fact, his wife
- Joyce Randolph (1925–), Detroit; played Trixie Norton on *The Honeymooners*
- David Dunbar Buick (1854–1929), Arbroath, Scotland; founder of Buick Motor Company and was instrumental in developing the overhead valve engine
- John De Lorean (1925–2005), Detroit; at Pontiac Division of General Motors, he developed the nation's first muscle car, Pontiac *Gran Turismo Omologato* (GTO), named after the Ferrari 250 GTO
- John Dodge (1864–1920), Horace Dodge (1868–1920), Niles; co-founded Dodge Motor Company
- Henry Ford (1863–1947), Dearborn; founder of Ford Motor Company; the Model T revolutionized transportation in America; by 1918, one-half of all the cars in America were Model Ts
- William Hewlett (1913–2001), Ann Arbor; along with David Packard formed Hewlett-Packard, 1939
- Mike Ilitch (1929–), Detroit; founder of Little Caesar's Pizza, 1959
- Will Keith Kellogg (1860–1951); he and brother John pioneered the process of making flaked cereal
- Tom Monaghan (1937–), Ann Arbor; founded of Domino's Pizza, 1960
- C. W. Post (1854–1914); pioneer in the prepared-food industry; copied process to make flaked cereal from W. K. Kellogg;
- James Anthony Bailey (1847–1906), Detroit; born James Anthony McGuiness; creator of the modern circus; co-founded Barnum and Bailey Circus
- Lee Majors (1939–), Wyandott [Detroit]; born Harvey Lee Yeary; at age two was adopted by his paternal uncle and anut who moved him to Middlesboro, KY

Many cities and trownships in MI lie within two counties. Two of the youngest mayors elected in America were eighteen-year-old Michael Sessions, 2005, Hillsdale, Hillsdale County, and twenty-three-year-old Phil Tanis, 1987, Holland, on the Ottawa/Allegan County lines.

Interesting names include: Adair; Advance; Afton; Akron; Alabaster; Alamo; Alaska; Alberta; Allen; Alpha; Alpine; Amble; Anderson; Angel; Ann Arbor; Antlers; Argyle; Ashland; Athens; Atlanta; Atlas; Austin; Azalia; Bad Axe; Ballards; Ballards Corners; Baltimore; Bangor; Bark River; Basswood; Bath; Battle Creek; Beacon; Bear Town; Beaver; Beaverdam; Beaverton; Beechwood; Bell; Bell Oak; Benton; Betty B Landing; Beverly Hills; Big Bend; Big Prairie; Big Rapids; Big Rock; Billings; Birch Creek; Birch Run; Birchwood; Birmingham; Black Lake; Black River; Bliss; Bombay; Boon; Bootjack; Boston; Boyd; Bradley; Bradleyville; Breckenridge; Bridgeport; Bridgeton; Bridgeville; Bridgewater; Bristol; Brooklyn; Brownsville; Bruce Crossing; Buchanan; Buckhorn; Buck Trails; Buena Vista; Bunker Hill; Burlington; Burnside; Burnt; Burr Oak; Butler; Butterfield; Butternut; Buttersville; Cadillac; California; Camden; Canton; Carlisle; Carrollton; Carson City; Carsonville; Cash; Cedar Bank; Cedar Bluff; Cedar Creek; Cedar Haven; Cedar Lake; Cedar River; Cedar Run; Cedar Springs; Cement City; Centennial; Center Line; Centerville; Central; Charles; Charleston; Charlesworth; Charlotte; Christmas; Clinton; Coalwood; Cold Springs; Coldwater; Colon; Columbus; Commerce; Concord; Copper City; Copper Falls; Copper Harbor; Coral; Corpse Pond; Covert; Covington; Crisp; Crystal; Dailey; Dale; Dayton; Daytona; Deer Creek; Deerfield (Danny Thomas); Deerheart Valley; Deer Park; Delaware; Delhi Mills; Detroit (Wally Cox, *Mr. Peepers*; Joyce Randolph *Trixie Norton on "The Honeymooners"*); Diamond Springs; Dice; Disco; Dodge City; Dollar Bay; Dollar Settlement; Dollarville; Douglas; Dover; Dublin; Duel; Dundee; Eagle; Eagle Harbor; Eagle Nest; Eagle Point; Eagle River; Eagles Nest; Eden; Edwards; Edwardsburg; Eightmile Corner; Elk Rapids; Elkton; Elm; Elmwood; Empire; Englishville; Ensign; Erie; Eureka; Fairview; Falmouth; Fawn River; Fern; Ferndale; Fillmore; Fingerboard Corner; Firesteel; Fish Corners; Fisher; Five Corners; Fivemile Corner; Five Points; Five Points North; Flat Rock; Flint; Floodwood; Flowerfield; Forest City; Forest Grove; Forest Hill; Forest Hills; Fountain; Four Mile Corner; Four Towns; Frankfort; Franklin; Freeport; Free Soil; Frenchtown; Friendsville; Frost; Fruitport; Fruit Ridge Center; Fulton; Gardner; Garland Village; Garnet; Geneva; Gibraltar; Golden; Goodland; Goodrich; Gordon; Gordonville; Grace; Grand Rapids (Judy Garland—nee Frances Ethel Gumm; Ray Teal, *Sheriff Roy Coffee* on "Bonanza"); Grand View; Granite Bluff; Grant; Grape; Green; Green Haven; Green Lake; Greenland; Green Oak; Green River; Green Timbers; Greenville; Gregory; Hamburg; Hancock; Hand; Hard Luck; Hardwood; Harlan; Harlem; Harper Woods; Harrietta; Harrison; Hartford; Hatmaker; Hawk Head; Hawks; Helena; Hell; Helps; Hemlock; Henderson; Hickory Ridge; Highland Park (Bill Haley created the spit-curl to take attention from his blind left eye); Hillman; Hilltop; Holland; Holly; Hollywood; Holy Corners; Homestead; Honor; Hopkins; Houseman; Huron City; Indian Grove; Indian River; Indiantown; Indian Town; Interlochen; Iron River; Irons; Ironton; Ivanhoe; Jackson; Jamestown; Jefferson; Johannesburg; Juniata; Juniper; Kalamazoo; Kendall; Kenton; Kentucky; Kindle; La Grange; Lake; Lake City; Lake George; Lavender Corner; Lawrence; Lee; Leisure; Leslie; Lexington; Liberty; Lime Creek; Limestone; Lincoln; Lincoln Park; Linkville; Litchfield; Little Lake; Little Venice; London; Long Rapids; Lulu; Manchester; Maple Grove; Maple Hill; Maple Rapids; Maple Ridge; Maple Valley; Maplewood; Marine City; Marion; Marion Springs; Marshall; Martin; Mason; Mass City; Mastodon; Maybee; Mayfield;

Meade; Meadow; Memphis; Metropolitan; Miami Beach; Michigamme; Middletown; Millersburg; Moline; Monongahela; Monroe; Montgomery; Morgan; Moscow; Mount Morris; Nashville; National City; Needmore; Nelson; Nine Mile; Nirvanna; Nonesuch; North Bradley; North Star; Norway; Oak Grove; Oak Ridge; Ogden; Orangeville; Orchard Beach; Orchard Lake; Orleans; Otter Lake; Oxbow; Ozark; Palms; Pamona; Paradise; Parchment; Paris; Parisville; Pavilion; Paw Paw; Peacock; Pearl; Peatville; Peck; Penn; Perry; Petoskey (Hal Morris, *Otis Campbell*); Phoenix; Pigeon; Pine Creek; Pine Ridge; Pine River; Pine Run; Pine Stump Junction; Pioneer; Pittsburg; Planter; Pleasant Ridge; Pleasant Valley; Pleasant View; Plymouth; Podunk; Pompeii; Pontiac; Popple; Portland; Prairie; Prairieville; Prattville; Princeton; Prosper; Pulaski; Quakertown; Rabbit Bay; Rainbow Bend; Raisin Center; Ralph; Rapid City; Rapid River; Rattle Run; Ray; Redman; Red Oak; Redridge; Redstone; Reed City; Reno; Republic; Rescue; Rice Creek; Richmond; Richville; Ridge; Ripley; Riverdale; River Raisin; River Rouge [Detroit]; Riverview; Rochester; Rockland; Rockview; Roots; Roseburg; Rosebush; Rose City; Rosedale; Roseville; Rousseau; Russellville; Rust; Ruth; Saint Louis; Saline; Sand Creek; Sand Lake; Sand River; Sandstone; Sandusky; Sault Ste. Marie (200 miles north of Toronto, Canada); Seewhy; Selma; Shady Shores; Shelby; Shelbyville; Shepardsville; Shepherd; Sidney; Silver City; Silverwood; Six Lakes; Slapneck; Snowshoe; Snowville; Somerset; South Lyon; Speaker; Spencer; Spring Arbor; Springfield; Spring Lake; Spruce; Stanton; Star; Star City; Stark; St Charles; Stephenson; Sterling; Stevensville; St Louis; St Nicholas; Stony Creek; Stony Point; Strasburg; Stringtown; Sturgis; Sugar Grove; Sugar Loaf; Sugar Rapids; Summit; Summit City; Sunfield; Sunnyside; Sunshine Beach; Superior; Swan Creek; Taylor [Detroit]; Teapot Dome; Teeterville; Temperance; Texas Corners; Thayer; The Jackpines; Thompson; Thompsonville; Three Churches Corner; Three Lakes; Three Oaks; Three Rivers; Timberlost; Tioga; Topaz; Torch Lake; Tower; Traverse City; Trenton; Trimountain; Trout Lake; Turtle; Twelve Corners; Twin Lake; Twin Lakes; Union; Union City; Unionville; Vandalia; Vanderbilt; Vienna; Vulcan; Walnut Point; Warren; Washington; Waters; Watersmeet; Watertown; Wayland; Webster; Welcome Corners; Wenona Beach; Wetmore; Wheatland; White; White City; White Cloud; Whitefish Point; Whitehall; White Oak; White Pigeon; White Pine; White Rock; White Star; Wildwood; Wiley; Williamsburg; Willow; Wilson; Winona; Wise; Wolf Crossing; Wolf Lake; Wolverine; Wooden Shoe Village; Woods; Wyoming; Ypsilanti; Yuma; Zeeland; Zenith Heights;

MINNESOTA – Sioux for "cloudy water." Statehood was May 11, 1858. The state nickname is "North Star State." Five million people live in Minnesota—6.5 million people live in Maine. Of those 5 million, 3.5 million (60%) live in the Minneapolis-St. Paul area. The name Minnesota comes from the word for the Minnesota River in the Dakota language, *mnisota*. The Dakota word *nmi* can be translated "water". *Mnisota* is then translated as *sky-tinted water* or *somewhat clouded water*. The many names of locations in the state that contain the Dakota word for water (mni, pronounced minnie), such as Minnehaha Falls, is not "laughing water," as many think, but is actually "waterfall." Minnesota is the northernmost state, except for Alaska, due to the Northwest Angle area. This angle area on the northern border of the states is the only part of the forty-eight contiguous states lying north of the 49th Parallel. Two continental divides meet in the northern part of Minnesota forming a triple watershed. Precipitation can follow the Mississippi River to the Gulf of Mexico, the St. Lawrence Seaway to the Atlantic Ocean, or the Hudson Bay Watershed to the Arctic Ocean.

The state's nickname, "Land of 10,000 Lakes" is not an exaggeration. There are nearly 12,000 lakes over ten acres in size. Minnesota has 6,564 natural rivers and streams that flow for a total distance of 69,000 thousand miles.

When Laura Ingles Wilder wrote of prairie adventures, she was writing about Minnesota. Sinclair Lewis wrote about Minnesota's small-town life his novel, *Main Street*.

Famous Minnesotans include:
- The Andrews Sisters; the first female singing group to sell one million records
- Richard Warren Sears (1863–1914), Stewartville; 1893 co-founded Sears, Roebuck & Co.
- James Arness, (1923–), Minneapolis; born James Aurness; played role of Marshal Matt Dillon on *Gunsmoke*; is the older brother to Peter Graves *Fury* and *Mission Impossible*; James Arness is the tallest actor to play a lead role, standing 6' 7" tall
- Joan Davis (1907–1961), St Paul; remembered best for the 1952 to 1955 television comdey *I Married Joan*; the part of her husbnd was played by Jim Backus

Minnesota is ranked first in the percentage of residents who engage in regular exercise. They also have the nation's lowest premature death rate and the second-longest life expectancies. Ninety-one percent of Minnesotans have health insurance.

Two of the youngest mayors elected in America were twenty-one-year-old John Gibeau, 1998, in Ceylon, Martin County, and twenty-two-year-old Bjorn Skogquist, 2002, Anoka, Anoka County. He was the youngest mayor in Minnesota when he was elected.

Interesting names include: Adams; Afton; Albany; Alberta; Albert Lea (Richard Carlson played Herb Philbrick in *I Led Three ALives*); Alexandria; Allen; Alpha; Angel Inlet (the northernmost town in the Lower 48); Angora; Angus; Apple Valley; Argyle; Artichoke; Artichoke Lake; Ash Creek; Assumption; Athens; Audubon; Aurora; Austin; Avon; Badger; Bain; Ball Club; Baptism Crossing; Bath; Battle Lake; Battle River; Bear River; Bear Valley; Beaver; Beaver Creek; Beaver Crossing; Beaver Falls; Bee; Belgrade; Bengal; Benton; Big Bend City; Big Falls; Bigfork; Big Spring; Big Woods; Birch; Birch Beach; Bird Island; Blackberry; Blackduck; Black Hammer; Blackhoof; Blooming Prairie; Bloomington; Blue Earth; Blue Grass; Bombay; Border; Bowstring; Boy Corner; Boyd; Boy River; Breckenridge; Breezy Point; Briggs Lake; Bristol; Brooklyn; Brownsville; Bruce; Bucksnort; Buffalo; Buffalo Lake; Butler; Butterfield; Butterfly Lake; Butternut; Buyck; Bygland; Caledonia; Callaway; Campbell; Camp Ripley Junction; Cannon City; Cannon Falls; Canyon; Caribou; Carlisle; Carp; Carpenters Corner; Casey; Casino; Castle Danger; Castle Rock; Cedar; Cedar Beach; Cedar Lake; Cedar Mills; Celina; Center City;

Centerville; Central; Ceylon; Charlesville; Cherry; Cherry Grove; Chester; Chicago City; Choice; Circle Pines; Clappers; Claybank; Clear Lake; Clearwater; Cleveland; Clinton; Clinton Falls; Clotho; Cold Spring; Collegeville; Cologne; Concord; Conger; Coon Rapids; Cosmos; Cotton; Cottonwood; Credit River; Crow River; Crow Wing; Crystal; Crystal Spring; Cuba; Current Lake; Dads Corner; Dale; Danube; Darfur; Darling; Dayton; Debs; Deer Creek; Deer Lane; Deer River; Deerwood; Delhi; Dent; Diamond Corner; Douglas; Dugdale; Dundee; Eagle Bend; Eagle Lake; Eagles Nest; Echo; Eden; Eden Prairie; Eden Valley; Edina (first indoor shopping mall, 1956); Edwards; Elbow Lake; Elevenmile Corner; Elizabeth; Elk River; Elkton; Elmdale; Elm Park; Embarrass (EM-brah); Empire; Englund; Erie; Estes Brook; Evansville; Evergreen; Fairbanks; Faith; Farming; Fertile; Fifty Lakes; Fillmore; Finland; Fisher; Five Corners; Five Points; Flaming; Floodwood; Florence; Forest City; Forest Grove; Fork; Fort Ripley; Fountain; Four Corners; Four Town; Fox; Foxboro; Foxhome; Franklin; Freeborn; French; French Lake; French River; Frost; Garden City; Gary; Geneva; Georgetown; Georgeville; Goldenrod; Golden Valley; Good Thunder; Goodview; Gordonsville; Gracelock; Graceville; Granada; Grand Meadow; Grand Prairie; Granite Falls; Granite Ledge; Green Isle; Greenleaf; Green Valley; Greenview; Gregory; Gregoryville; Gully; Hackensack; Hamburg; Ham Lake; Hancock; Happyland; Happy Wanderer; Harding; Harmony; Hart; Havana; Hay Creek; Haydenville; Hayfield; Haypoint; Heidelberg; Helena; Henderson; Herman; Hermantown; High Forest; Hill City; Hillman; Hillview; Holland; Hollywood; Hopkins; Houston; Huntersville; Iberia; Independence; Inez; International Falls; Iron; Iron Hub; Iron Junction; Ironton; Ironwood; Island; Island View; Isle; Ivanhoe; Jack Pine; Jackson; Jay See Landing; Jenkins; Johnson; Judge; Kennedy; Kensington; Kettle River; Kevin; Key West; Kevin; Kiester; Klondyke; Knife River; Lagoona Beach; Lake Center; Lake City; Lake George; Lake Wilson; Lancaster; Largo; Leader; Leaf River; Leaf Valley; Leavenworth; Leech Lake; Lexington; Lime; Lime Creek; Lincoln; Litchfield; Little Chicago; Little Falls; Little Fork; Little Pine; Little Rock; Local; London; Long Beach; Long Prairie; Lost; Lucknow; Lude; Luxemburg; Madison; Madison Lake; Magnolia; Maine Prairie; Mallard; Manchester; Manhattan Beach; Maple; Maple Bay; Maple Hill; Maple Island; Maple Lake; Maple Plain; Maple Springs; Mapleton; Mapleview; Maplewood; Marble; March; Marine On St Croix; Marion; Marshall; Martin; Mason; Meadow Brook; Meadowlands; Medicine Lake; Mentor; Middle River; Midway; Milan; Millersburg; Minneapolis (Peter Graves, *"Fury"* & *"Mission Impossible"*; James Arness, *Gunsmoke"*; Charles Schultz); Minnehaha {Minneapolis}; Minneopa; Minneota; Minnesota Boys Town; Minnesota City; Minnesota Falls; Money Creek; Montevideo; Montgomery; Monticello; Moose Lake; Morgan; Morgan Park; Morris; Morristown; Moscow; Mountain Iron; Mountain Lake; Murray; Nashville Center; Nassau; Nichols; Norcross; North Star; Norway Lake; Norwegian Grove; Oak Center; Oak Grove; Oak Park; Oakport; Oakridge; Oaks Corner; Omega; Org; Oslo; Ottawa; Otter Creek; Otter Tail; Outing; Oxlip; Page; Palisade; Palmdale; Parent; Parkers Prairie; Park Rapids; Pelican Rapids; Pigeon River; Pine Bend; Pine Brook; Pine Center; Pine City; Pinecreek; Pine Creek; Pine Island; Pine Knoll; Pine Point; Pine River; Pine Springs; Pinetop; Pineville; Pinewood; Pipestone; Platte; Pleasant Grove; Pleasant Valley; Poplar; Post Town; Prairieville; Pratt; Princeton; Prosper; Providence; Racine; Radium; Ransom; Red Lake; Red Lake Falls; Red Rock; Red Top; Regal; Reno; Rice; Rice Lake; Richmond;

Rich Valley; Ridge; River Point; River Valley; Rochester; Rock Creek; Rockville; Rollingstone; Roosevelt; Roseau; Rose City; Rose Creek; Roseville; Round Lake; Round Prairie; Royalton; Rush City; Rushmore; Rush River; Russell; Ruthton; Saginaw; Sandstone; Sargeant; Savage; Seaforth; Sedan; Shanty Town; Shovel Lake; Side Lake; Silica; Silver Creek; Silverdale; Silver Lake; Skyline; Sleepy Eye; Spring Creek; Springfield; Spring Grove; Spring Hill; Spring Lake; Springvale; Spring Valley; Spruce; Spruce Center; Stacy; Stanton; Staples; Starbuck; Star Lake; State Line; St Charles; Stephen; Sterling Center; Stevenson; St George; Stillwater; St Nicholas; Stockholm; St Paul (William Demarest—*Uncle Charley* on "My Three Sons"); Sugarloaf; Summit; Sunburg; Sunrise; Swanburg; Swan River; Swanville; Swift; Swift Falls; Taylors Falls; Tenmile Corner; Tenstrike; Thief River Falls; Toad Lake; Tower; Tracy; Trail; Traverse; Turtle River; Twig; Twin Grove; Twin Lakes; Twin Valley; Two Harbors; Two Inlets; Tyler; Union Hill; Viking; Vineland; Viola; Virginia; Wakemup; Wall Lake; Walnut Grove; Warren; Warroad; Warsaw; Watertown; Waterville; Wayland; Webster; Welcome; Western; West Virginia; White Earth; Whiteface; White Hawk; White Rock; White Willow; Wilds; Wildwood; Willow Creek; Willow River; Wilmington; Wilson; Winnebago; Winner; Winona; Winter; Wolf; Wolf Lake; Woodland; Wyoming; Yankeetown; Young America; Yucatan; Zim; Zumbro Falls

MISSISSIPPI – Chippewa for "great river," taking its name from the Mississippi River. Statehood was December 10, 1817. The state nickname is "Magnolia State." The highest point in Mississippi is Woodall Mountain with an elevation of 806 feet. Half of the state is covered in trees. The explorer Hernando de Soto was the first European in Mississippi who passed through in 1540.

Near the beginning of the Civil War in 1861, Mississippi was the first state to secede from the Union in order to form the Confederate States of America. Mississippi's rank as one of the poorest states can be traced back to the Civil War. Before the War, Mississippi was the fifth-wealthiest state in the nation. At that time, more than one-half of the state's population was enslaved, and slaves were considered valuable property when determining one's wealth. That helped to boost their ranking as being a wealthy state. The war was expensive, costing the state 35,000 lives. Plantation owners who survived the war were bankrupted by the emancipation of slaves, plus the fact that Union troops left wide-spread destruction in their wake.

The teddy bear gets its name from a hunting trip in 1902, to Sharkey County by President Theodore Roosevelt when he refused to shoot a captured bear. Mississippi became the center for several types of American music including gospel, country, jazz, blues, and rock and roll.

Greenville is 100 miles farther west than Reel Foot Lake in west Tennessee.

Famous Mississippians include:

- Elvis Presley (1935–1977), Tupelo; born in a two-room shotgun house built by his father; received his first guitar for his eleventh birthday; recorded "Heartbreat Hotel" for RCA in 1956; in December, in 1956, *Billboard* magazine reported that Elvis had placed more songs in the Top 100 than any other artist since chart records began; he enjoyed listening to the symphony and the Metropolitan Opera
- B. B. King (1925–) Itta Bene (near Indianola); born Riley B. King; admits he cannot play chords very well, relies on improvisation; performed two hundred fifty concerts annually during most of his 52-year career; Sonny Listen was his uncle
- Conway Twitty (1933–1993), Friars Point; born Harold Lloyd Jenkins; influenced by Elvis Presley
- Tammy Wynette (1942–), near Tremont; born Virginia Wynette Pugh; an all-star high school basketball player; was titled the "First Lady of Country Music;" while meeting with Epic Record producer Billy Sherrill, he said her long, blong hair in a pony tail reminded him of Tammy in the film *Tammy and the Bachelor*, and suggested Tammy as a possible name
- LeAnn Rimes (1982–), Pearl; born Margaret LeAnn Rimes; her debut single, "Blue," was released when she was thirteen years old; by age twenty-four she had sold over thirty-seven million albums
- Charley Frank Pride (1938–), Sledge; his father named him Charl Frank Pride, but due to a typing error on his birth certificate he was legally born as Charley Frank Pride; had thirty-six number one hits; his life-long goal was to play professional baseball
- Oprah Winfrey (1954–), Kosciusko; born to teenage parents; with an annual salary of $385 million her net worth is over $2.7 billion (2008); name originally spelled Orpah after the Biblical character in the Old Testament book of Ruth
- Jim Henson (1936–1990), Greenville; while in high school, began creating puppets for a Saturday morning children's show on WTOP-TV, Maryland

Interesting names include: Aberdeen; Adair; Alice; Allen; Alligator; Altitude; Anchorage; Anderson; Arm; Armory; Ashland; Ashwood; Askew; Athens; Atlanta; Austin; Avon; Bacon Springs; Bald Hill; Ballard; Ballardsville; Banks; Basic City; Basin; Battles; Beach (125 miles from the gulf); Beacon Hill; Bear Creek; Bear Town; Beauregard; Beech Grove; Beech Springs; Beechwood; Bent Oak; Benton; Benwood; Berea; Beverly; Bewelcome; Big Creek; Big Level; Big Point; Birmingham; Black Hawk; Black Jack; Blackwater; Bloody Springs; Blueberry Hill; Blue Hill; Blue Lake; Blue Mountain; Blue Ridge; Blue Springs; Bluff; Bluff Springs; Bobo; Bond; Bonus; Boone; Bourbon; Bowling Green; Boyle; Bradley; Branch; Brazil; Bright; Bright Corner; Brooklyn; Brooksville; Brownsville; Bruce; Bruce Junction; Buckhorn; Buena Vista; Bunker Hill; Burnside; Burt; Bush; Busy Corner; Butler; Cairo; Caledonia; Calhoun; Calhoun City; Camargo; Camden; Camp Hill; Canton; Carlisle; Carpenter; Carroll; Carrollton; Carson; Carter; Carter Branch; Cedar Bluff; Cedar Cove; Cedar Hill; Cedar Lake; Cedars; Cedar View; Center; Center Hill; Center Point; Center Ridge; Centerville; Central; Central Academy; Central Grove; Centre; Charleston; Cherry Creek; Christmas; Chunky; Clack; Clark; Clay; Claytown;

Clear Branch; Clear Springs; Cleveland; Clover Hill; Coal Oil Corner; Coalville; Coats; Coffeeville; Coldwater; Cold Water; College Hill; Columbia; Columbus; Compromise; Concord; Congress; Coonwood; Coral; Cornish; Cotton Plant; Cottonville; Coy; Creek; Crockett; Crossroads; Cross Roads; Crow; Crumtown; Crystal Springs; Cumberland; Cypress Corner; Dale; Dallas Jones Crossing; Darling; Days; Deep Creek; Deerfield; Delta (30 miles from) Delta; Denmark; Deposit; Derby; Dixie; Dixie Pine; Dogtown; Double Springs; Dragon; Drew; Dry Grove; Duck Hill; Dundee; Eagles Nest; East Aberdeen; Ecru; Eden; Edinburg; Edwards; Eggville; Egypt; Egypt Hill; Eldorado; Electric Mills; Elliott; Emerald; Eminence; Empire; Endville; Energy; Enola; Enterprise; Eureka Springs; Evanston; Evansville (ten miles from) Evansville; Evergreen; Expose; Fair Oaks Springs; Fairview; Falcon; Fame; Fayette; Fernwood; Flat Rock; Flat Top; Flatwood; Flora; Florence; Flowers; Ford; Forest Hill; Forkville; Forty; Four Mile; Fox; Fox Island; Franklin; Free Run; Free Trade; French Camp; Friendship; Frog Island; Frogtown; Fulton; Furry; Gallatin; Garlandville; George; Georgetown; Gift; Gin; Glens Glen; Golden; Golden Grove; Good Hope; Goodluck; Goodwater; Gordon; Grace; Grapeland; Grass Lake; Gravel Hill; Gravestown; Gray; Green Grove; Greenland; Green River; Greenville; Gregory; Grenada; Guide; Gulf Hills; Gum Ridge; Gums; Gum Springs; Guntown; Hamburg; Handle; Handy Corner; Hard Cash; Hardscrabble; Hardscramble; Harmony; Harperville; Haw Pond; Hazlenut; Heater; Heidelberg; Helm; Hermanville; Hero; Hickory; Hickory Flat; Hickory Grove; Hickory Hills; High Hill; High Point; Hightown; Hobo Station; Holly Bluff; Holly Grove; Hollyknowe; Holly Landing; Holly Springs; Hollywood; Honey Island; Horn; Horseshoe; Hot Coffee; Hot Water; House; Houston; Hub; Huntsville; Huron; Hurricane; Hurricane Branch; Hurricane Creek (3 miles from) Hurricane Creek; Improve; Increase; Independence; India; Indian Springs; Institute; It; Jackson; Jamestown; Janice; Jeff Davis; Jefferson; Jenkins; Johnson; Jolly; Jug Fork; Jumpertown; Juniper Grove; Keel; Kiln; King; King And Anderson; Kinlock; Kitchener; Klondike; Knobtown; Knoxville; Kokomo; Lackey; Lake; Lake City; Lake View; Larue; Latonia; Laurel; Laurel Hill; Leaksville; Lebanon; Lemon; Lespedeza; Lexington; Liberty; Lilac; Limerick; Little Creek; Little Italy; Little Rock; Little Springs; Little Texas; Little Yazoo; Loakfoma; Loch Leven; Loch Lomond; Logtown; Lone Pine; Long; Long Branch; Long Lake; Longshot; Longstreet; Longtown; Longview; Louisville; Love; Lucern; Lynchburg; Lyon; Madison; Madisonville; Magenta; Magnolia; Marathon; Marion; Mars Hill; Martin; Mascot; Matthews; Mayday; McElveen; Mechanicsburg; Memphis; Metcalfe; Michigan City; Midnight; Midway; Miller; Mineral Springs; Minot; Missionary; Mississippi City; Monarch; Money; Monroe; Montgomery; Monticello; Montpelier; Moon; Moon Lake; Morgan City; Morgans Store; Morgantown; Morning Star; Morris; Morriston; Moscow; Moss; Mound City; Mountain; Mount Pleasant; Mount Vernon; Mulberry; Murry; Needmore; Nevada; Newport; New Town; Nichols; Nile; Nixon; Norfolk; Norway; Oak Grove; Oakland; Oaks; Oak Vale; Oil City; Oklahoma; Old Americus; Old Georgetown; Olive Branch; Omega; Onward; Orange; Orange Grove; Orangeville; Oxberry; Palmetto; Panther Burn; Paris; Parkersburg; Pearl; Pearl River; Pecan Grove; Peoria; Perdue; Perry; Petal; Philadelphia; Phoenix; Pikeville; Pilgrim Grove; Pilgrims Rest; Pine Bluff; Pinebur; Pine Grove; Pinehurst; Pine Ridge; Pine Springs; Pine Valley; Pineview; Pineville; Pink; Pistol Ridge; Plain; Plainview; Plantation; Pleasant Grove; Pleasant Hill; Pleasant Ridge;

Plum Grove; Plum Point; Pluto; Point; Poplar Creek; Poplar Springs; Poplarville; Possum Corner; Possumneck; Possum Trot; Post; Prairie; Prairie Hill; Prairie Mount; Prairie Point; Prince Chapel; Princeton; Prismatic; Progress; Prospect; Providence; Pulaski; Pumpkin Center; Quail Valley; Quay; Quincy; Raleigh; Ratliff; Ravine; Rawhide; Red Banks; Redhill; Red Hill; Red Lick; Red Top; Redwater; Redwood; Reform; Refuge; Remus; Revive; Riceville; Richmond; Ripley; Rising Sun; Riverview; Roberts; Robinwood; Rock Creek; Rockhill; Rock Hill; Rocky Hill; Rocky Mount; Rocky Point; Rocky Springs; Rolling Fork; Rome; Rosebloom; Rosebud; Rosedale; Rose Hill; Rough Edge; Roundaway; Round Lake; Rural Hill; Russell; Russellville; Ruth; Sable; Sanatorium; Sand Hill; Sandy Hook; Sandy Ridge; Savage; Savannah; Scotland; Scott; Self Creek; Service; Sessions; Seven Springs; Shady Grove; Shady Oak; Shake Rag; Shankstown; Sharpsburg; Shepherd; Sherwood Forest; Short; Shucktown; Shutersville; Signal; Silver City; Silver Creek; Silver Run; Six Towns; Skyline; Slate Spring; Sledge (Charley Pride); Society Hill; Soso; Speedtown; Splinter; Spring Cottage; Spring Creek; Springfield; Spring Hill; Spring Ridge; Springville; Stamper; Standard; Stanton; Starkville; State Levee; State Line; St Catherine; Steel; Stephen; Stephens; Stephenville; Sterling; Stevens; Stonewall; Stout; Stringer; Stringtown; Strong; Sturgis; Success; Sugar Hill; Summit; Sunflower; Sunkist; Sunrise; Sunset; Swan Lake; Swiftown; Swiftwater; Taylor; Taylorsville; Tchula; Temperence Hill; Ten Mile; Texas; Thompson; Thompsonville; Thorn; Thrasher; Threadville; Three Rivers; Tie Plant; Timberlane; Togo; Topeka; Touchstone; Triplets Corners; Tupelo (Elvis Presley); Turkey Creek; Turnpike; Twelve Oaks; Twin; Twin Lakes; Tyler; Union; Union Hill; Uniontown; Unity; Value; Van Buren; Vancleave; Veto; Vidalia; Villanova; Vowell; Waco; Wallhill; Walnut; Walnut Creek; Walnut Grove; Warsaw; Washington; Water Valley; Way; Wayside; Webster; West; Whistler; White Apple; White Bluff; White Cap; White House; White Oak; White Plains; Whitesand; Whynot; Wildwood; Williamsburg; Williamsville; Willows; Winona; Winstonville; Winterville; Wolf Springs; Woodland; Wood Springs; Wool Market; Wren; X-Prairie; Yazoo; Yazoo City; Zero

MISSOURI - Algonquin for "river of canoes." Statehood was August 10, 1821. The state nickname is "Show Me State." Missouri was originally acquired from France as part of the Louisiana Purchase. St Louis is known as the "Gateway to the West" because it served for a departure point for the settlers heading west as well as the starting point and return destination of the Lewis and Clark Expedition. The Missouri River flows from Kansas City, eastward to St. Louis. The Baltimore Orioles were once the St. Louis Browns. *The Adventures of Tom Sawyer* and *The Adventures of Huckleberry Finn* were set in the town of Hannibal, Mark Twain's boyhood home.

Famous Missourians include:
- Burt Bacharach (1928–), Kansas City; pianist, composer; wrote seventy Top 40 hits
- Lawrence Peter "Yogi" Berra (1925–), St Louis; because Berra waited to bat with arms and legs crossed, a friend noted he resembled a Hindu holy man (Yoga) they had seen in a movie, thus the nickname "Yogi;" the Hanna-Barbera cartoon character Yogi Bear was named after Yogi Berra; he is famous for his "Yogiisms,"

"Nobody goes there (to that restaurant) anymore, it's too crowded," and "When you come to a fork in the road, take it."

- Omar Bradley (1893–1981), Clark; was the last surviving U.S. Army five star general; first to hold the position of Chairman of the Joint Chiefs of Staff, 1949
- Calamity Jane (1852–1903), Princeton; born Martha Jane Canary; at age fifteen, after both parents died, became the head of the household, including five siblings; a frontierswoman and scout; friend of Wild Bill Hickock beside whom she is buried
- George Washington Carver (1864?–1943), Old Calibrator (now Diamond); discovered nearly 100 uses for the peanut, from cosmetics to gasoline; his slave owner, Moses Carver, had bought his parents for $700; he, a sister and his mother were kidnapped and sold in Kentucky; when Carver was finally found he was near death; when slavery was abolished, his slave owner and wife raised George and his brother as their own; as a teenager he witnessed a black man being beaten to death by a group of white men; by 1896, he had earned a master's degree in botany from the Iowa State Agricultural College; he taught forty-seven years at Tuskegee (Alabama) College
- Walter Cronkite (1916–), St Joseph; on July 7, 1952 the term "anchor" was coined to describe Cronkite's role as both the Democratic and Republican National Conventions, which were the first nationally-televised conventions; anchored the CBS Evening News from 1962–1981
- Robert Cummings (1908–), Joplin; born Charles Clarence Robert Orville Cummings; his grandfather, Orville Wright, taught him to fly; starred in *The Bob Cummings Show* from 1955 to 1959
- Jesse James (1847–1882), Kearney; an outlaw in Missouri and the most famous member of the James-Younger gang; his father was a hemp farmer and Baptist minister in Kentucky who, after moving to Missouri, helped found Liberty College (Liberty); Jesse and Frank (1843–1915) robbed the Southern Deposit Bank in Russellville (Logan County), KY; allegedly Jesse shot the weather vane atop the bank leaving a hole that is visible today
- James Cash (J.C.) Penney (1875–1971), Hamilton; in 1898 he began working in a small chain called Golden Rule stores; in 1902, the owners offered him a one-third partnership for $2,000 in a new store in Wyoming; he helped open two more stores; when the other two owners disolved their partnership, Penney purchased full interest in all three stores; in 1913 the company was renamed J.C. Penney Company; by 1924 his annual income was $1.5 million
- Marlin Perkins (1905–1986), Carthage; at the Wentworth Military Academy he kept blue racer snakes in his barracks room; dropped out of college to work at St. Louis Zoo; he was director of the Buffalo Zoological Park, Buffalo, NY, Lincoln Park Zoo, Chicago and Saint Louis Zoological Park; hosted *Wild Kingdom* from 1963–1988
- Vincent Price (1911–1993), St. Louis; made his film debut in 1938; first horror film was made with Boris Karloff in 1939; aired ninety-one episodes on the radio as *The Saint*
- T. S. Eliot (1888–1965) – Thomas Stearns Eliot was known to his family as Tom

- Porter Wagoner (1927–2007), West Plaines; started performing on a radio station in Springfield which led to a contract by RCA Records; he had eighty-one charted recordings; Porter Wagoner and Dolly Parton ("Now, there's a couple of big ones," said Lester "Roadhog" Moran) appeared together on his TV show from 1967–1976
- Harry S. Truman (1884–1972), Lamar; thirty-third president; he used executive orders to begin desegregation of the U.S. armed forces; his grandfathers could not agree on what his middle name should be, so they settled on using only the initial "S," however, no one knows whether the S stood for Anderson Shipp Truman or Solomon Young, since both grandfathers each touted it was his own
- Nellie Tayloe Ross (1876–1977), St Joseph; governor of Wyoming from 1925 to 1927, and the first female governor in the United States; she remains the only female governor of Wyoming; director of the National Mint from 1933 to 1953

Red Onion (Dunklin County) is thirty miles farther south than Styra (Clay County), Arkansas. Missouri's easternmost point is twenty-five miles farther east than Kentucky's westernmost point. Missouri's boot heel extends thirty-five miles south into Arkansas. One of the youngest mayors elected in America was twenty-two-year-old Scott Faughn, 2002, in Poplar Bluff, Butler County.

Interesting names include: Acorn Corner; Acorn Ridge; Adair; Adams; Adel; Advance; Affton [St Louis]; Agency; Aid; Airline Acres; Akron; Albany; Alberta; Alexandria; Alice; All; All Saints Village; Alpha; Americus; Amsterdam; Anaconda; Anderson; Ann; Annapolis; Antler; Apex; Apple Creek; Arab; Argyle; Ark; Arrow Rock; Ashland; Athens; Atlanta; Austin; Austria; Auxvasse; Avenue City; Avon; Bachelor; Ballard; Bannister; Barren; Bass; Beach; Bear Branch; Beaverdam; Bee Fork; Belfast; Belgrade; Bellflower; Bell Grove; Bend; Benjamin; Benton City; Bentonville; Berlin; Beverly; Big Creek; Big Ridge; Bigspring; Billings; Birch Tree; Birds Corner; Birdsong; Birds Point; Bird Springs; Birmingham; Black; Blackbird; Blackjack; Black Jack; Black Oak; Black Walnut; Blackwater; Bland; Bliss; Bloodland; Blooming Rose; Bloomington; Blue Eye (across the state line from Blue Eye, AR); Blue Lick; Blue Mound; Blue Ridge; Blue Springs; Blythedale; Boone; Boonesboro; Boonesborough; Boston; Boulder City; Bourbon; Bowling Green; Boys Town; Bracken; Brazil; Breckinridge; Brian; Briar; Bridge Creek; Bridgeport; Broadway; Brookfield; Brooklyn; Brown Shanty; Brush Arbor; Brussells; Buckeye; Buckhorn; Budapest; Buffalo; Buick; Bunker; Bunker Hill; Burksville; Burrows; Bute; Butler; Buzzards Roost; Cabool; Cadet; Cairo; Caledonia; Calhoun; California; Callaway; Calleaway; Cambridge; Camden; Cannon; Cape Girardeau; Carbon Center; Carbon Hill; Carrollton; Carsons Corner; Carter; Cash; Catherine Place; Cave; Cave City; Cave Hill; Cave Spring; Cawood; Cedar Bluff; Cedar Cliffs; Cedar Creek; Cedar Ford; Cedar Gap; Cedar Hill; Cedar Ridge; Cedar Springs; Cedar Valley; Cedar Vista; Cement City; Center; Center Post; Centertown; Centerview; Centerville; Central; Centropolis; Chain of Rocks; Chalk Level; Chamois; Champ; Champion; Champion City; Chantilly; Charity; Charleston; Cherry Box; Cherry Dell; Cherry Vale; Cherry Valley; Cherryville; Chesapeake; Chestnutridge (eight miles from) Chestnutridge; Chestnut Ridge; Chillicothe; China; Chloride; Cincinnati; Circle City; Clark; Clark City; Clay; Clear Creek;

Clear Springs; Clearwater; Cleopatra; Cleveland; Clever; Clinton; Clover Bottom; Coal; Coal Hill; Cobbler; Cold Springs; Coldwater; Colony; Columbia; Columbus; Comet; Commerce; Competition; Conception; Concord; Cook Station; Cooter; Copper Mine; Corbin; Cornertown; Cornland; Cottage; Cottleville [St Louis]; Couch; Covington; Crane; Cream Ridge; Crescent Hill; Crooks Springs; Crosstown; Crystal City; Cuba; Cul de Sac; Currentview (across the stateline from Current View, AR); Cyclone; Cypress; Daisy; Dale; Danville; Dawn; Day; Dayton; Deep Ford; Deepwater; Deer; Deerfield; Deer Park; Deer Ridge; Defiance; Delaware; Denver; Diamond; Dixie; Dixon; Dodge City; Doe Run; Dogwood; Dolittle; Douglas; Dove; Dover; Dry Valley; Duncans Bridge; Dundee; Dutchtown; Dye; Eagle Rock; Eaglette; Eagleville; Echo; Economy; Edinburg; Edmonson; Edwards; Egypt Grove; Egypt Mills; Eldorado; El Dorado Springs; Elixer; Elk City; Elk Creek; Elkhorn; Elkton; Elliott; Elm; Eminence; Empire; Empire Prairie; Energy; English Town; Enough; Enterprise; Erie; Estes; Estill; Eureka; Evansville; Eve; Evening Shade; Ewing; Excelsior; Fairdealing; Fair Grove; Fair Haven; Fair Play; Fairport; Fairview; Fairville; Faith; Falcon; Fanning; Farmer; Farmersville; Far West; Fawn; Fayette; Fidelity; Fillmore; Flag Springs; Flat Creek; Flat River; Flatwood; Fleming; Flint Hill; Florence; Florida (Samuel Clemens, *Mark Twain*); Floyd; Forest City; Forest Green; Forest Springs; Forker Boomer Post Office; Fortyville; Fourmile; Fourmile Corner; Four Points; Fox Creek; Fox Springs; Frankenstein(steen); Franklin; Fredericksburg; Freedom; French Town (fifteen miles from) French Village; Friendly Valley; Fulton; Gainesville; Gallatin; Gamma; Garden City; Gardner; Garrett; Gazette; Georgetown; Georgeville; Germantown; Gipsy; Glasgow; Globe; Gobbler; Golden City; Goodhope; Goodland; Goodville; Good Water; Gordonville; Grace; Grain Valley; Granada; Grand Center; Grand Eddy; Grand Port; Grand River City; Grandview; Grave Hill; Grayson; Greenbrier; Green Castle; Green City; Greendoor; Green Grove; Greenlawn; Green Mountain; Green Ridge; Greenstreet; Greentop; Green Town; Greenview; Greenville; Gregory Landing; Gumbo; Half Rock; Halfway; Hamburg; Hams Prairie; Hancock; Handy; Happy Hollow; Hardin; Harmony; Harper; Hartford; Harvester; Hatch; Hawkeye; Hawk Point; Hayden; Helena; Helm; Henderson; Hercules; Hickman; Hickory Creek; Hickory Hill; Hickory Ridge; High Gate; High Hill; High Point; High Prairie; High Ridge; Hilldale; Holland; Hollywood; Holstein; Homeland; Homestead; Honey Creek; Hopkins; Hopkinsville; Hornet; Hot Coffee; House Springs; Houston; Humansville (Edgar Buchanan, *Uncle Joe on "Petticoat Junction"*); Huntington; Huntsville; Huron; Hurricane; Hybrid; Iberia; Imperial; Independence [Kansas City] (Ginger Rogers); Indian Creek; Indian Grove; Indian Mound; Indian Point; Ink; Iron Center; Iron Gates; Iron Mountain; Ironton; Island City; Jacket; Jackson; Jacksonville; Jake Prairie; James Brothers; Jamestown; Japan; Johns Cross Timbers; Joplin (Robert Cummings); Judge; Kansas City (first subruban shopping center in America, 1922); Kendall; Kennet; Keystone; Kinloch [St Louis]; Klondike; Knob Lick; Knob Noster; Knox; Knox City; Knoxville; Kodiak; La Grange; Lake Creek; Lake Winnebago; Lanes Prairie; Laredo; Laura; Lawrenceburg; Lead Mine; Lebanon; Lemons; Lewis and Clark Village; Lewistown; Lexington; Liberal; Liberty; Libertyville; Licking; Lickskillet; Light; Lincoln; LinNeus; Lisbon; Lithium; Little Berger; Little Union; Lively; Livingston; Local; Loch Lloyd; Lock Springs; Locust; Locust Hill; Logan; London; Lone Corner; Lone Elm; Lone Jack; Lone Star; Lone Tree; Long Lane; Longtown; Loose Creek; Louisiana;

Louisville; Lucerne; Lulu; Lynchburg; Lyon; Macon; Madison; Madisonville; Magnolia; Maiden; Main City; Mammoth; Manchester [St Louis]; Manila; Mansfield (Laura Ingles Wilder lived here as an adult); Many Springs; Maple Grove; Maple Hill; March; Marion; Marshall; Maryville; Matthews; Mayberry; Mayfield; Mayflower; Maysville; Mechanicsville; Memphis; Mexico; Miami; Middletown; Midway; Milan; Miles Point; Miller; Millersburg; Miner; Mineral City; Mineral Point; Mineral Spring; Mines; Minimum; Minnie; Missouri City; Mock Corner; Monastery; Monkey Run; Monroe City; Montana; Montgomery City; Monticello; Montreal; Morgan; Moscow Mills; Mound City; Mountain; Mountain Grove; Mountain View; Mount Pleasant (one-half mile from Pleasant Mount); Mount Sterling; Mt Airy; Mulberry; Murry; Musselfork; Mystic; Narrows Creek; Nashville; Nausau Junction [Nevada]; Neck City; Needmore; Nelson; Nevada; Newark; New Bourbon; New Castle; Newcomer; New York; Nichols [Springfield]; Nichols Grove; Nile; Nodaway; Noel; Nogo; Not; Novelty; Number Eight; Oak; Oak Grove; Oak Hill; Oakland; Oak Ridge; Oasis; Ohio; Oil City; Old Appleton; Old Bland; Old Greenville; Oldham; Old Monroe; Old Success; Olive; Olympia; Olympian Village; Orange; Orchard Farm; Orchid; Ore; Oregon; Origana; Oriole; Owls Bend; Owsley; Ozark; Ozark Springs; Pacific; Pack; Page City; Palace; Palisades; Paradise; Paris; Paris Springs; Parkway; Passover; Paw Paw; Paydown Ford; Peace Valley; Peach Orchard; Pea Ridge; Pearl; Pearl City; Peculiar; Pendleton; Peoria; Pepsin; Perry; Perryville; Persia; Peru; Philadelphia; Pilgrim; Pine; Pine Crest; Pinhook; Pin Hook; Pink Hill; Piper; Pipertown; Pitcher; Pittsburg; Plainview; Platte City; Platte River; Pleasant Grove; Pleasant Hill; Pleasant Hope; Pleasant Mount (one-half1/2 mile from Mount Pleasant); Pleasant Retreat; Pleasant Ridge; Pleasant Valley; Plum Ford; Plum Valley; Points; Polk; Polo; Pomona; Ponce de Leon; Ponder; Poplar Bluff; Portland; Possum Trot; Possum Walk; Postal; Post Oak; Powell; Prairie City; Prairie Home; Prairie Ridge; Precinct; Princeton; Prohibition City; Prospect Grove; Prosperine; Prosperity; Protem; Providence; Pulaski; Pumpkin Center; Punkin Center; Pure Air; Quaker; Queen City; Quick City; Quincy; Quote; Racine; Racket; Radar; Rat; Raytown (fictional home of *Mama's Family*); Red Bird; Red Oak; Red Onion; Red Point; Red Top; Reeds; Reform; Regal; Renfro; Republic; Rescue; Revere; Rhineland; Rich Fountain; Rich Hill; Richmond; Ripley; Riverside; Riverview; Roach; Roads; Roanoke; Rochester; Rock; Rockbridge; Rock Creek; Rock Ford; Rock Port; Rock Springs; Rockville; Rocky Mount; Rocky Ridge; Romance; Rome; Roosevelt; Roosterville; Rosebud; Rose Hill; Rosewood; Round Grove; Round Spring; Royal Oak; Rush Hill; Russellville; Safe; Saginaw; Saline; Saline City; Salt River; Salt Springs; San Antonio; Sandals; Sand Hill; Sandy Hook; Santa Fe; Santiago; Sargent; Savannah; Scotsville; Sebree; Sedan; Selma; Senate Grove; Seventysix; Shade; Shady Grove; Shakertowne; Shamrock; Shantytown; Sharp; Sharpsburg; Shelbyville; Shoal; Shook; Short Bend; Sidney; Signal; Sikeston (90 miles east of Quincy, IL); Silver Creek; Silver Lake; Silverleaf; Silver Mine; Silver Springs; Simpson; Skinner; Slabtown; Sleeper; Smoky Hollow; Snow; Solo; South Carrollton; South West City; Sparrow; Speed; Spokane; Spring Bluff; Spring Creek; Springfield; Spring Forest; Spring Fork; Spring Garden; Spring Grove; Springhill; Springtown; Spruce; St Annie; Stanton; Stapletown; Starfield; St Catherine; St Charles; St Elizabeth; Stephens; Sterling; St George; Stillhouse Springs; St Marys; Stockbridge; Stone Hill; Stony Hill; Stringtown; Sturges; Sublette;

Success; Sue City; Sugar Creek; Sugar Lake; Sugartree; Sumach; Summerville; Summit; Summit City; Sundown; Sunlight; Sunnyside; Sunrise; Sunset; Susanna; Sutherland; Sweden; Sweet Hollow Ford; Sweet Springs; Sweetwater; Swift; Swiss; Sycamore; Syracuse; Table Rock; Taps; Tavern; Taylor; Tea; Teal; Ten Mile; Terre Haute; Texas Bend; The Diamonds; Theodosia; Thirty Four Corner; Thompson; Thousand Oaks; Thralls Prairie; Three States; Thrush; Tightwad; Tigris; Timber; Tin Town; Tipperary; Todd; Toledo; Topaz; Topsy; Torch; Toronto; Trenton; Trimble; Tulip; Turkey Ridge; Turnback; Turtle; Twelvemile; Twin Springs; Tyler; Umpire; Union; Union Star; Uniontown; Unionville; University City [St Louis]; Useful; Valley City; Valley Forge; Valley View; Van Buren; Van Cleve; Vandalia; Venice; Venus; Versailles; Vienna; Village of Four Seasons; Viola; Violet; Virginia; Vista; Voyage; Wall Steet; Walnut; Walnut Grove; Walnut Shade; Wanamaker; Warren; Warsaw; Washington; Wayland; West Glasgow; West Keystone; West Liberty; West Plains (Dick Van Dyke; Porter Wagoner); Wheatland; Wheeling; White Bear; White City; Whitecloud; Whitecorn; White House; White Oak; White Rock; Whitewater; Wilderness; Wildwood; Williamsburg; Williamstown; Willow Brook; Willow Springs; Wilson; Wilson City; Wilsons Creek; Winchester; Windy Curve; Windyville; Winner; Winona; Winslow; Winston; Wintersville; Wolfe; Wood; Wood Hill; Woodlandville; Woodlawn; Woodridge; Woodville; Worcester; Yarrow; Yukon; Zig

MONTANA - Spanish for "mountain." Butte (b-Ü-tte) is a hill; Statehood was November 8, 1889. The state nickname is "Treasure State." Other nicknames include, "Land of Shining Mountains," "Big Sky Country," and "The Last Best Place." In land mass it ranks fourth; in population it ranks forty-fourth. Even though the Rocky Mountains make up part of the state, still 60% of the land is prairie. Montana contains Glacier National Park, Little Bighorn Battle National Monument, and Yellowstone National Park. Using one's imagination, one may see the resemblence of President Nixon's silhouette looking southwesterly on the Montana-Idaho border.

Famous Montanans include:
- Gary Cooper (1901–1961), Helena; tried out unsuccessfully for the high school drama club
- Myrna Loy (1905–1993), Radersburg; most noted for her role as Nora Charles, wife of detective Nick Charles (William Powell) in *The Thin Man* series; her first name came from a train station, a name which her father liked
- Martha Raye (1916–1994), Butte; born Margie Reed; made first film appearance in 1934; during WWII, the Korean War, and Vietnam War she traveled extensively to entertain the troops; hosted *The Martha Rae Show*, from 1954–1956; she closed her TV show by saying, "Goodnight, Sisters," referring to the nuns at St. Francis Hospital, Miami, Florida who helped her through an emotional time
- Patrick Duffy (1949–), Townsend; played roles on *Dallas, Step by Step, The Bold and the Beautiful*
- Chet Huntley (1911–1974), Cardwell; when NBC executives decided to replace John Cameron Swayze, they could not decide between Huntly or David Brinkley and finally decided on both; *The Huntly-Brinkley Report* began in 1956;

the catchphrae closing of, "Good night, Chet, Good night, David…and good night for NBC News" was developed by the show's producer; both men disliked it

- Evel Kenievel (1938–2007), Butte; born Robert Craig Kenievel; at age eight he attended a George Rice "Joie" Chitwood Auto Daredevil Show which he credits for his career choice; dropped out of high school after completing his sophomore year and was given a job with Anaconda Mining Company; while operating a large earth mover he made it do a wheelie and drove it into Butte's main power line; he was dismissed; his first public daredevil act was to jump a twenty-foot long box of rattlesnakes and two mountain lions; despite having his rear wheel hit the box of rattlesnakes, he escaped unharmed; partnered with Six Flags Over St. Louis to build a wooden roller coaster and name it for him; the ride opened in 2008.

Interesting names include: Aberdeen; Adel; Agency; Aloe; Alpine; Amazon; Amsterdam; Anaconda; Andes; Antelope; Ant Flat; Apex; Archer; Arrow Creek; Ashland; Augusta; Austin; Avon; Bainville; Bald Butte; Barber; Baseline; Basin; Bay Horse; Bear Spring; Beartown; Beaver Creek; Beaver Hill; Bedford; Beehive; Belfry; Belgrade; Belt; Belt Creek; Bend; Bernice; Big Arm; Bigfork; Bighorn; Big Sag; Big Sandy; Big Sky (nickname of state); Big Timber; Birdseye; Bison; Black Eagle; Blackfoot; Blackleaf; Blacktail; Blackwood; Bluegrass; Bone Crossing; Borax; Boulder; Bowler; Box Elder; Boyd; Bradley; Brandenberg; Brown; Buckingham; Buffalo; Bull Mountain; Butte (Kirby Grant, *Sky King*); Cabin City; Cabin Creek; Caldwell; Calypso; Camp Three; Canyon Creek; Canyon Ferry; Capitol; Cardwell (Chet Huntley); Carpenter; Carter; Cartersville; Cascade; Cassidy Curve; Castle Rock; Castle Town; Cat Creek; Champion; Chance; Checkerboard; Cherry Ridge; Chestnut; Chimney Rock; Chinatown; Chinook; Circle; Clearwater; Cleveland; Cliff Lake; Clinton; Coal Banks Landing; Coalridge Reserve; Coalwood; Coffee Creek; Cold Spring; Colgate; Columbia Falls; Columbus; Comet; Contact; Content; Copper City; Copper Cliff; Corbin; Corral; Cottonwood; Crackerville; Crane; Crow Rock; Crystal Ford; Crystal Point; Cut Bank; Dayton; Deer Lodge; Diamond City; Divide; Dixon; Dover; Dovetail; Durham; DY Junction; Eagles Nest; Eden; Edwards; Eightmile Saddle; Electric; Elkhorn; Elmdale; Emigrant; Eureka; Evergreen; Fairfield; Fairview; False Summit; Fee; Finch; First Creek; Fishtail; Fishtrap; Flatwillow; Flaxville; Florence; Ford; Forest Green; Forestgrove; Forest Grove; Fort Kipp; Fort Logan; Four Buttes; Four Corners; Franklin; French Town; Fresno; Frontier Town; Gallaltin; Gallatin Gateway; Garland; Garnet; Garrison; Georgetown; Geraldine; Geyser; Glacier Colony; Glasgow; Gold Creek; Golden Ridge; Goldstone; Gordon; Grace; Granite; Grant; Grass Range; Great Falls; Gunsight; Halfmoon; Happys Inn; Happy Valley; Happy Wanderer; Hardin; Harlem; Harrison; Heart Butte; Helena, (Gary Cooper); Hellgate; Highview; Highwood; Hill; Hillside Colony; Holland; Homestead; Hopkins; Hot Springs; Hungry Hollow; Hungry Horse; Hungry Joe; Independence; Indian Arrow; Inkstar; Intake; Iris; Jackson; Jefferson City; Johnson; Kevin; Keystone; Kicking Horse; Kildeer; Knife River; Knox; Kremlin; Lakeside; Lame Deer; Laurel; Libby (farther west than Needles, CA); Lima; Limestone; Lincoln; Lindsay; Living Springs; Livingston; Locate; Lodge Grass; Lodge Pole; Lodgepole Saddle; Logan; Lonepine; Lost Creek; Macon; Maiden; Maiden Rock; Mammoth; Manchester; Manger; Manhattan; Marion; Marsh; Marshall; Marysville;

Mason; Matthews; McAllister; Medicine Lake; Medicine Springs; Mid Canon; Midway; Mill Creek; Miller; Miller Colony; Mill Iron; Miner; Mission; Missoula; Moccasin; Molt; Monarch; Montana City; Montanapolis Springs; Moose Town; Morgan; Moss Agate; Muddy; Munster; Musselshell; Navy; New Year; Nichols; Nimrod; Nine-mile; Ninemile; Noble; Number Seven; Offer; Ohio Camp; Oilmont; Old Agency; Old Town; Olive; Opportunity; Ops; Otter; Outlook; Pacific Junction; Packers Roost; Paisley; Paradise; Paragon; Peerless; Pine Creek; Pine Prairie; Pinnacle; Pioneer; Pioneer Junction; Pipestone; Plateau; Pleasant Prairie; Pleasant Valley; Pleasant View; Plentywood; Poland; Polaris; Polebridge; Pompeys Pillar; Pony; Poplar; Portal; Porters Center; Post; Post Creek; Potomac; Potomac Post Office; Power; Pray; Primrose; Prison Farm; Quartz; Quebec; Queen; Queens Point; Quietus; Racetrack; Rainbow; Rapelje; Rapids; Rattlesnake; Red Eagle; Red Lodge; Red Rock Point; Redstone; Red Top; Reed Point; Reserve; Riceville; Ridge; Rimrock; Rim Rock Colony; Ripley; Rising Sun; Riverbend; Riverside; Riverview; Roberts; Rochester; Rock Springs; Rockvale; Rocky Boy; Rosebud; Round Butte; Round Prairie; Roundup; Ruby; Saddle Butte; Sage Creek Colony; Salmon Prairie; Sand Springs; Sapphire Village; Savage; Sedan; Shelby; Shepherd; Sidney; Silver Bow; Silver City; Silver Gate; Silver Star; Singleshot; Sixteen; Skyline; Slab Crossing; Smelter Hill; Snowslip; Soda; Soda Springs; Sourdough; Spear; Sphinx; Split Rock Junction; Spotted Robe; Spring Creek Junction; Spring Gulch; Springhill; Springs; Springtime; Springtown; Square Butte; Stacey; Stanford; Stark; Sterling; Steve Forks; Stevensville; Stillwater; St Mary; Stone; Stonehill; Story; Straw; Stump Town; Summit; Summit Valley; Sunburst; Sundance; Sunlight; Sunnyside; Sun Prairie; Sun River; Superior; Sweetgrass; Swiftcurrent; Sylvanite; Talc; Thompson Falls; Three Forks; Tobacco; Top O'Deep; Trail; Triple Divide; Troy (200 miles west of Felt, ID); Truly; Tungsten; Turtle Lake; Twin Bridges; Twin Creeks; Two Dot; Ulm; Valencia; Valentine; Valleytown; Vandalia; Virginia City; Vista; Volt; Wall City; Warm Springs; Warren; Weed; Wheat Basin; White; White City; Whitefish; White Pine; White Sulphur Springs; Whitetail; Whitewater; Williamsburg; Winifred; Winston; Wisdom; Wise River; Wolf Creek; Wolf Point; Wolf Prairie; Wood Place; Woodside; Woodville; Yaak; Yakt; Ynot; Yukon Saddle; Zap; Zero; Zurich

NEBRASKA - Chiwere word for "flat river." Statehood was March 1, 1867. The state nickname is "Cornhusker State." At the time of statehood, the capital was moved from Omaha to Lancaster and renamed Lincoln, to honor the assassinated president. The Arbor Day Foundation is headquartered in Nebraska City. Nebraska claims to have more miles of rivers than any other state. Kool-Aid, created in 1927 by Edwin Perkins, makes Hastings the "Birthplace of Kool-Aid." CliffsNotes were invented in Rising City by Clifton Hillegass. The world's largest railroad yard is in North Platte. It covers 2,850 acres, is eight miles long, and has over 315 miles of track. The yard receives and sends ten thousand cars every day, as well as repairs fifteen hundred cars and seven hundred fifty locomotives each month. The yard is recognized in the *Guinness Book of World Records*. The Vice Grip wrench was invented and is still manufactured in De Witt. The swing in the Hebron city park is claimed to be the world's largest porch swing, holding 18 adults or 24 children.

Famous Nebraskans include:

- Richard "Dick" Bruce Cheney (1941–), Lincoln; vice president under George W. Bush; Secretary of Defense under President George H. W. Bush; U.S. House of Representatives; White House Chief of Staff under President Gerald Ford
- Gerald Ford (1913–2006), Omaha; born Leslie Lynch King, Jr.; thirty-eighth president and 40th vice president; he was the first person appointed to the vice-presidency under the terms of the 25th Ammendment, and became president upon Richard Nixon's resignation in 1974; the fifth president never to have been elected to that position and the only one to never have won any national election; the longest-lived president in U.S. history, dying at age 93
- Lady Charles Cavendish or Adele Astaire (1896–1981), Omaha; dancer and entertainer; elder sister to Fred Astaire
- Fred Astaire (1899–1987), Omaha; born Frederick Austerlitz; his stage and film career span seventy-six years
- Ward Bond (1903–1960), Benkelman; at UCLA played football with John Wayne; the TV series *Wagon Train* was based on a 1950 movie, *Wagon Master,* in which Bond also appeared; he appeared in *Gone with the Wind, Tobacco Road, Sergeant York, It's a Wonderful Life*, and 39 other movies
- Henry Fonda (1905–1982), Grand Island; nominated for Academy Award in *Grapes of Wrath*, 1935

Interesting names include: Able; Adams; Agate; Akron; Alexandria; Allen; Alliance; Angora; Angus; Arabia; Arbor; Arborville; Archer; Arizona; Ashland; Assumption; Atlanta; Aurora; Badger; Battle Creek; Beacon View; Beaver City; Beaver Crossing; Bee; Belfast; Belgrade; Berea; Beverly; Big Springs; Birdwood; Bloomfield; Bloomington; Blue Hill; Blue Springs; Boone; Bordeaux; Bow Valley; Boys Town; Bradley; Bridgeport; Briggs; Broadwater; Broken Bow; Brookdale; Buckeye; Bucktail; Buffalo; Burr Oak; Butte; Cairo; Callaway; Cambridge; Campbell; Carlisle; Carroll; Carter Lake; Cascade; Catalpa; Cedar Bluffs; Cedar Creek; Cedar Rapids; Center; Centerville; Central City; Champion; Chase; Clay Center; Clearwater; Clinton; Cody; Coker; Columbus; Concord; Cook; Council Bluffs; Covert; Crab Orchard; Craft; Crete; Dakota City; Dakota Junction; Davey; David City; Decatur; Dixon; Doughboy; Douglas; Duff; Duluth; Eagle; Eddyville; Eldorado; Elk City; Elk Creek; Elkhorn; Elm Creek; Elmwood; Emerald; Enola; Ewing; Fairfield; Falls City; Falter Place; Finchville; Five Points; Flats; Fort Calhoun; Franklin; Freedom; Friend; Gables; Garland; Garrison; Geneva; Glen; Goodwin; Gordon; Grand Island; Grant; Greely; Gross; Guide Rock; Harrisburg; Harrison; Hastings; Hay Springs; Hazard; Henderson; Henry; Herman; Hershey; Hickman; Hire; Holland; Holstein; Horace; Horn; Houston; Hyannis; Imperial; Inez; Inland; Ithaca; Jackson; Janise; Johnson; Juniata; Kennedy; Keystone; Knox; Knoxville; Lakeside; Laurel; La Vista; Lawrence; Lebanon; Lexington; Liberty; Lime Grove; Lincoln; Lindsay; Litchfield; Lodgepole; Logan; Long Pine; Louisville; Lynch; Macon; Madison; Madrid; Magnet; Marion; Marquette; Marsland; Martin; Mascot; Mason City; Maxwell; Mayberry; McLean; Mead; Meadow; Meadow Grove; Meek; Memphis; Menominee; Mercer; Midway; Miller; Minersville; Monroe; Monterey; Moomaw Corner; Morse Bluff; Mount Vernon; Mumper; Murray; Nashville;

Nebraska City; Nelson; Newark; Newport; Nonparell; Norfolk; North Star; Norway; Oakland; Oak Mill; Odessa; Ohiowa; Omaha (Fred Astaire); Ong; Opportunity; Orchard; Orleans; Oshkosh; Ough; Paddock; Page; Palisade; Panama; Perry; Peru; Pierce; Pine Ridge; Piper; Plainview; Pleasant Hill; Pleasant Valley; Point of Rocks; Polk; Powell; Prague; Prairie Center; Prairie Home; Precept; Primrose; Princeton; Quick; Redbird; Red Cloud; Red Willow; Republican City; Rising City; Riverside; Riverview; Roach; Rockville; Rose; Rosedale; Rounds Place; Round Valley; Royal; Sacramento; Sandridge; Sargent; Scotia; Sedan; Shelby; Sidney; Silver Creek; Sioux City; Somerset; South Bend; Sparks; Springfield; Springview; Spurior Place; Stanton; Star; St Charles; St Edward; Sterling; St Mary; Story; St Paul; St Stephens; Sumter; Superior; Surprise; Swan Lake; Swedeburg; Swedenhome; Sweetwater; Syracuse; Table Rock; Taylor; Thayer; Thompson; Timber Creek; Todd; Townhall; Trenton; Trout; Tryon; Ulysses; Union; Valentine; Valley; Valparaiso; Venango; Venice; Venus; Virginia; Waco; Wahoo; Walnut; Walton; Washington; Wausau; Wayne; Webster; Weeping Water; Wee Town; Western; Whiteclay; Willow Island; Wilsonville; Winslow; Woodcliff; Wood Lake; Wood River; Worms; Wynot; Wyoming; York

NEVADA - Spanish for "snow clad." Statehood was October 31, 1864. The state nickname is "Silver State," due to the large number of silver deposits that were discovered and mined there. "The Battle Born State" is the state's official slogan since it was admitted to the Union during the Civil War. In 1931, construction began on the Hoover Dam, near Las Vegas. When completed, it was the largest concrete structure in the world. The Nevada Test Site, sixty-five miles east of Las Vegas, was built in 1951, for the testing of nuclear weapons. The underground testing of nuclear weapons ended in 1992. Nellis Air Force Base houses Area 51. The location is known for the highest amount of concentrated nuclear deposited weapons in America. Over 87% of the state is owned by the federal government. The primary reason for this is that homesteads were not deeded out in large enough sizes to be useful in the arid conditions. Instead, early settlers would homestead land surrounding a water source, then graze livestock on the adjacent public land, which is useless for agriculture with the absence of water. This pattern of ranching is still in use today. Nevada has the highest divorce rate in America. Needles, California, is thirty miles farther east than Las Vegas.

Famous Nevadans include:
- James E. Casey (1888–1983), Pick Handle Gulch, near Candelaria; in 1907, nineteen-year-old Jim founded the American Messenger Company in Seattle, Washington with $100 borrowed from a friend; in 1913, he merged with Everet McCabe's Motorcycle Messengers; in 1919, the company expanded its territory beyond Seattle and changed the name to United Parcel Service; Casey said, "One measure of your success will be the degree to which you build up others who work with you. While building up others, you will build up yourself."
- Thelma Katherine "Pat" Nixon (1912–1993), Ely; given the nickname Pat due to the fact that her father is of Irish descent and her birthday was March 16; wife of President Richard Nixon

Interesting names include: Afton; Alamo; Alkali; Alpha; Alpine; Alum; American Flat; Anderson; Antelope Springs; Arabia; Arrowhead; Ash Springs; Atlanta; Austin; Awakening; Babylon; Barrel Spring; Basic; Battle Mountain; Beaver; Bernice; Birch; Black Forest; Black Horse; Bliss; Blue Diamond; Bolivia; Bonnie Briar; Borax; Border Town; Boulder City; Boyd; Bracken; Broadway; Broken Hills; Bronco; Buckhorn; Buckskin; Buffalo Meadows; Bull Fork; Bullion (2); Burnt Cabin; Cactus Springs; Camp Douglas; Canon City; Canyon City; Canyon Creek Station; Carp; Carroll; Carson City; Carson Hot Springs; Cavecreek; Centerville; Central; Central Rochester; Charleston; Charleston Park; Cherry Creek; Chinatown; Clark; Clinton; Clover; Coaldale; Cold Spring; Columbia; Columbus; Contact; Copper Basin; Copperfield; Copper Flat; Copper Hill; Copper Run; Coral Hill; Cornish Camp; Cornucopia; Cottonwood; Coyote; Coyote Hole; Crescent Valley; Crossroads; Crows Nest; Crystal; Crystal Springs; Currant; Danville; Dayton; Decoy; Deep Creek; Deep Hole; Deer Lodge; Diamond City; Dinner Station; Divide; Dixie; Dixie Valley; Double Springs; Douglas; Dry Creek; Dry Lake; Duckwater; Eagle Station; Eagleville; Eden; Elkhorn; Empire; Erie; Eureka; Excelsior; Fair Play; Fairview; Fay; Fiddlers Green; Fillmore; Fish Lake; Fitting; Five Mile House; Flat Nose; Flowery City; Frenchman; Frisbie; Garden Pass; Geneva; Geyser; Gold Acres; Gold Bar; Goldbud; Gold Bug; Gold Butte; Gold Center; Golden; Golden Arrow; Golden Valley; Goldfield; Gold Hill; Gold Hit; Gold Point; Gold Reef; Gold Run; Goldville; Goldyke; Good Hope; Gouge Eye; Granite; Grass Valley; Greens; Green Springs; Greenville; Gregory; Groom; Happy Creek Station; Heinz; Henderson; Highland; Hilltop; Horseshoe Bend; Hot Creek; Hot Springs; Hunter; Huntington; Incline Village; Indian Cove; Indian Springs; Iron Point; Island City; Island Mountain; Jackpot; Jackrabbit; Jackson; Jamestown; Jean; Jefferson; Jenkins; Jersey; Jumbo; Junction; Kennedy; Keystone; Klondike (one mile south of Southern Klondike); Kodak; Kyle Hot Springs (2); Lane City; Laurel; Lee; Liberty; Lima; Logan; Lost City; Lower Gold Hill; Lucky Boy; Maggie Blues; Mammoth Ledge; Manhattan; Martin; Mason; Massacre Lake; Mayberrys; Maysville; Mesquite; Metalic City; Middlegate; Middletown; Midway; Mill City; Mineral; Mineral City; Monarch; Montezuma (2); Morton; Mound House; Mountain City; Mountain House; Mountain Springs; Mountain View; Mt Airy; Mud Springs; Mustang; National; Nelson; Neptune City; Nevada City; Nevada Hills; Nevada Scheelite Camp; Newark; Nightingale (2); Ninemile Rocks; Nixon; North Battle Mountain; Number One Oasis; Number One Settlement; Oak Springs; Oasis; Old Battle Mountain; Old Bullion; Pahrump; Panama; Pancake Summit; Panther Valley; Paradise [Las Vegas]; Paradise Hill; Paradise Valley; Pick Handle Gulch; Pilot; Pine Creek; Pine Grove; Pinto; Pioneer; Pittsburgh; Pleasant Valley; Point of Rocks; Poker Brown (2); Potomic; Princeton; Pronto; Prospect; Pueblo; Pyramid; Quartz Mountain; Queen City; Ragtown; Raiser City; Rapids City; Raspberry Creek; Rawhide; Rebel Creek; Red Butte; Red House; Red Top; Reno (300 miles west of Needles, CA); Reservation; Ripley (2); Riverside; Rochester; Rock House; Rosebud; Rose Creek; Rose Valley; Round Hill; Round Mountain; Ruby Hill; Ruby Valley; Rye Patch; Sage; Salt Wells; San Antonio; Sand Pass; Sand Springs; San Juan; Scranton; Scraper Springs; Searchlight; Secret; Settlement; Seven Troughs; Shamrock; Shanty Town; Sheepshead; Shores; Sierra Way; Silverbow; Silver City; Silver Peak; Silver Springs; Silver Zone; Simpson; Southern Klondike (one mile north of Klondike);

Spanish Springs; Sparks; Spring City; Spring Creek; Spruce; Sprucemont; Stagecoach; Star City; Stateline; Steamboat; Steptoe; Stillwater; Stone Cabin; Stone House; Stonehouse; Strawberry; Strawberry Hill; Sulphur; Summit; Sundown; Sunnyside; Sunshine Camp; Sunvalley; Sweetwater; Taylor; Tempest; Thompson; Thousand Springs; Three Bar; Tippecanoe; Tunnel Camp; Twain; Twin Flat; Union; Upper Pyramid; Upper Town; Valley View; Veteran; Viola; Virginia City; Vista; Volcano; Vya; Warm Creek; Warm Farm; Warm Springs; Washington; Welcome; White; White Caps; White River; White Rock; Willow Grove; Willow Point; Willowtown; Wilson; Wilson Creek; Winchester [Las Vegas]; Winnemucca; Wood; Yankee Blade;

NEW HAMPSHIRE – Named after a county in England. Statehood was June 21, 1788. The state nickname is "Granite State." It was one of the original Thirteen Colonies that revolted against British rule in the American Revolution. It was the first state to have its own state constitution. Its license plates carry the famous state motto, "Live Free or Die." New Hampshire has the only two-lane Interstate Highway with a cobblestone median for a short section. It was the last of the New England states to observe Fast Day, a day of prayer for a bountiful harvest. It was a legal holiday until 1991, when it was replaced by Civil Rights Day, which was later renamed Martin Luther King, Jr., Civil Rights Day, becoming the last state to have a Martin Luther King Jr., Day.

Signers of the Declaration of Independence include: Josiah Bartlett, Matthew Thornton, and William Whipple.

Famous New Hampshireians include:
- Daniel Webster (1782–1852), Salisbury; U.S. House of Representatives; U.S. Senate; 14th and 19th Secretary of State
- Franklin Pierce (1804–1869), Hillsborough; fourteenth U.S. president; U.S. House of Representatives, U.S. Senate; brigadier general in the Mexican-American War; his birthplace is now submerged in Franklin Pierce Lake
- John Sargent Pillsbury (1828–1901), Sutton; served as governor of Minnesota during the Grasshopper Plague of 1877; called for a day of prayer after which a sleet storm killed all the grasshoppers; a chapel was built in Cold Spring to honor the miracle; founder of the Pillsbury Company, 1872
- Alan Shephard (1923–1988), East Derry; as a Mercury astronaut he was the second person and the first American in space on May 5, 1961; when reporters asked Shepherd what he thought about as he sat atop the Redstone rocket waiting for liftoff, he replied, "Every part of this ship was built by the low bidder;" later commanded Apollo 14
- Horace Greeley (1811–1872), Amherst; U.S. House of Representatives; places named for him include Greely, CO; Greeley, PA; Greeley, TX; Greely County, NE; in Greely County, Kansas is the town of Horace, the county seat is Tribune

New Hampshire has the highest percentage of high school graduates, ninety-two percent.

Interesting names include: Albany; Appalachia; Ashland; Bath; Bean Island; Beans; Bedford; Benton; Berlin; Blackwater; Bow Bog; Bowman; Breakfast Hill; Breezy Point; Brick School Corner; Bristol; Bucks Corner; Bungy; Campton; Cantebury; Carroll; Cascade; Cemetery Corners; Center; Center Sandwich; Charlestown; Chicks Corner; Chickville; Cold River; Columbia; Concord; Cooks Crossing; Copperville; Cornish; Cornish City; Cornish Flat; Cornish Mills; Cotton Mountain; Cowbell Corners; Cricket Corner; Crockett Corner; Crystal; Danbury; Danville; Deerfield; Dixieville Notch; Dover; Dublin; Ducks Head; Dundee; Elkins; Elmwood; Fairview; Federal Corner; Five Corners; Franklin; Freedom; Gaza; Georges Mills; Goose Hollow; Granite; Grape Corner; Great Boars Head; Greenfield; Greenland; Greenville; Hancock; Happy Corner; Happy Valley; Hardscrabble; Hell Hollow; Hemlock Center; Highbridge; Hill; Hometown; Horses Corner; Ireland; Jackson; Jefferson; Jockey Hill; Johnson Center; Kensington; Lancaster; Lawrence Corner; Lebanon; Lincoln; Lisbon; Litchfield; Little Boars Head; Livermore; Londonderry; Lost Nation; Lost River; Lower Shaker Village; Lower Village; Madison; Manchester; Maplewood; Marshall Corner; Martin; Mason; Meadows; Milan; Mill Hollow; Monroe; Mountain Base; Murray Hill; Nelson; New Castle; Newport; Noone; Orange; Ossipee; Paris; Pearls Corner; Peppermint Corner; Pierce; Pierce Bridge; Pike; Pine Cliff; Pine River; Pittsburg; Place; Plymouth; Powwow River; Quaker City; Quebec Junction; Redstone; Richmond; Rim Junction; Rochester; Russell; Rye; Sandwich; Sandwich Center; Scotland; Scott; Shaker Village; Silver Lake; Slab City; Soo Nipi; Springfield; Stark; State Line; Stillwater; Sugar Hill; Swiftwater; Thompson Corner; Tinkerville; Tripoli Mill; Troy; Twin Mountain; Tyler; Union Wharf; Unity; Upper Shaker Village; Upper Village; Warren; Washington; Water Village; Waterville Valley; Webster; Whiteface; Wildwood; Wilson; Winchester; Winona; Woodsville

NEW JERSEY – Named after an English island. Statehood was December 18, 1787. The state nickname is "Garden State." The area was first settled by Native Americans known as the Lenni-Lenape, but the Dutch and the Swedes, who were the first white settlers to enter the area in the 1600s, called them Delaware Indians. New Jersey was one of the original Thirteen Colonies that revolted against British rule in the American Revolution. The New Jersey Constitution was passed July 2, 1776, just two days before America became a nation. State Representative Richard Stockton, and a signer of the United States Constitution, sacrificed his royal judicial title and his considerable international economic interest in order to be an elected delegate for New Jersey at the General Congress. He was a renowned Presbyterian minister from Scotland. On Christmas Day, 1776, General George Washington crossed the Delaware River and engaged the unprepared Hessian troops in the Battle of Trenton. Princeton was the nation's capital for four months. In 1804, it became the last state to abolish slavery. PT-109 was built in New Jersey. The zeppelin Hindenburg went up in flames over Lakehurst.

In an April 12, 2007 automobile accident, Jon Corzine was the third straight Jew Jersey governor to break a leg while in office. New Jersey is the birthplace of the FM radio; motion picture camera; light bulb; transistors; electric trains; the drive-in movie; cultivated blueberries; cranberry sauce; the postcard; boardwalk; zipper; phonograph; saltwater taffy;

dirigible; first use of a submarine in warfare; and ice cream cones. The properties in the board game Monopoly are named after streets in Atlantic City. The four-mile long boardwalk in Atlantic City was the world's first and remains the world's longest. New Jersey is home to many manufacturers of diners. Jew Jersey has more diners in operation than anywhere in the world. New Jersey and Oregon are the only two states in America where self-service gas stations are outlawed.

Signers of the Declaration of Independence include: Abraham Clark, John Hart, Francis Hopkinson, Richard Stockton, and John Witherspoon.

Famous New Jersians include:
- Francis Albert "Frank" Sinatra (1915–1998), Hoboken; in March, 1939 he recorded his first song; in June, 1939 Harry James hired him on a one-year contract for $75 per week; joined Tommy Dorsey band in January, 1940
- William "Count" Basie (1904–1984), Red Bank; took piano lessons as a child; as a youth he did odd jobs at the Palace Theater; one day when the pianist did not show, he played for the silent movie; formed his first band in 1935
- William Alexander "Bud" Abbott (1895–1974), Asbury Park; his parents worked for the Barnum and Bailey Circus; teamed up with Lou Costello in 1936; during WWII the duo were among the most popular and highest paid stars in the world; together they made thirty-six movies
- Lou Costello (1906–1959), Paterson; born Louis Francis Cristello; he excelled in basketball; he also boxed under the name Lou King; he did not use off-color material, a trait that continued throughout his career; the Japanese military showed movies of Abbott and Costello to demonstrate how inept the American military was; in 1942, Costello had an attack of rheumatic fever and was unable to work for a year; on November 4, 1943, the day he returned to the show, his infant son accidentally drowned in the family pool; the baby was only a few days short of his first birthday; Lou had asked his wife to keep Butch up that night so the boy could hear his dad on the radio for the first time; rather than cancel the broadcast, Lou said, "wherever he is tonight, I want him to hear me," and went on with the show; the audience did not know of his son's death until after the show; Abbott and Costollo split up in 1957
- Martha Stewart (1941–), Jersey City; born Martha Helen Kostyra; she appeared in several television commercials including Tareyton's famous "I'd rather fight than switch" cigarette ads
- Stephen Grover Cleveland (1937–1908), Caldwell; was the twenty-second and twenty-fourth president of the United States; governor of New York; mayor of Buffalo, NY; sheriff of Erie County, NY; grew up in Fayetteville, NY; entered the White House a bachelor but married the next year; he was the second president to marry while in office and the only president to have a wedding in the White House

Interesting names include: Aberdeen; Adams; Afton; Alpine; Ampere; Amsterdam; Anderson; Archers Corner; Asbury Park (Bud Abbott); Atlantic City; Auburn;

Avon-by-the-Sea; Barber; Barley Sheaf; Bear Tavern; Beaver Dam; Beaver Lake; Berlin; Beverly; Big Oak; Big Springs; Black Horse; Blue Bell; Bound Brook; Brass Castle; Brick; Bridgewater; Broadway; Brownsville; Burnt Mills; Butler; California; Campgaw (Jane Wyatt, *Father Knows Best*); Cape May Court House; Capitol Hill; Cedar Bridge; Cedar Brook; Cedar Grove; Cedar Knolls; Cedar Lake; Centerville; Centre Grove; Changewater; Charleston Springs; Charlestown; Cheesequake; Cherry Hill; Cherry Ridge; Cherryville; Cherrywood; Chestnut Ridge; Chimney Rock; Clark; Clearwater; Clinton; Clover Hill; Cloverhill; Coffins Corner; Cold Spring; Cologne; Colts Neck; Columbus; Comical Corners; Commercial; Coontown; Copper Hill; Corbin City; Creamridge; Cumberland; Dayton; Deepwater; Dogs Corners; Double Trouble; Dutch Neck; Dutchtown; Eagle; Echo Lake; Edinburg; Edison; Egg Harbor City; Elizabeth; Ellis Island; Fair Lawn; Fair Play; Fairview; Fish House; Five Points; Flagtown; Floral Hill; Florence; Foot of Ten; Forest Grove; Foul Rift; Four Corners; Four Mile; Four Mile Circle; Frankfort; Franklin (10 miles from) Franklin; Franklin Grove; Franklinville; Franklin Lakes; Frenchtown; Friendship; Gary Corner; Georgetown; Georgia; Gigantic City; Gillette; Good Intent; Gravel Hill; Green Bank; Green Grove; Green Knoll; Green Pond; Greensand; Greenville; Gum Tree Corner; Guttenberg; Hackensack; Hacklebarney; Half Acre; Hamburg; Hamilton; Harding; Harmony; Harmonyvale; Harrison; Hi-Nella; High Bridge; Hilltop; Ho-Ho-Kus; Hoboken (Frank Sinatra); Holland; Hoot Owl; Hopatcong; Hope; Indian Mills; Interlaken; Iron Rock; Jackson; Jacksonville; Jefferson; Jenkins; Jersey City (Ozzie Nelson); Jerseyville; Jumbo; Junction; Kendall Park; Lauderdale; Laurel Springs; Lawrenceville; Lebanon; Liberty Corner; Liberty Island (Statue of Liberty); Libertyville; Lincoln; Lincoln Park; Little Brook; Little Egg Harbor; Little Falls; Little Ferry; Little Silver; Livingston; Logan; Long Branch; Long Hill; Long Valley; Love Ladies; Madison; Madison Park; Magnolia; Manchester; Maple Grove; Maple Shade (40 miles from) Maple Shade; Maplewood; Marble Hill; Marshalls Corner; Marshalltown; Marshallville; Maryland; Matthews; McKee City; Meadowbrook; Meadows; Mechanicsville; Merchantville; Merrygold; Miami Beach; Middletown; Middle Valley; Millstone; Milltown; Mine Brook; Mine Hill; Monroe; Monroeville; Montana; Montgomery; Morgan; Morganville; Morris; Morris Plains; Morristown; Morrisville; Mountainside; Mountain View; Mount Airy; Mount Misery; National Park; Neptune; Neptune City; Newark (Jerry Lewis; Connie Francis); Newfoundland; Newport; Nixon; Normandy Beach; Oak Grove; Oak Ridge; Oak Shade; Oak Tree; Oak Valley; Oakville; Ocean; Ocean Beach; Ocean City; Ogden; Old Tappan; Orange; Palisades Park; Paterson (Lou Costello); Peapack-Gladstone; Penns Beach (20 miles west of Philadelphia); Penny Pot; Perryville; Pheasant Run; Pill Hill; Pine Brook; Pine Crest; Pine Grove; Pine Hill; Pine Lane; Pine Valley; Piscataway; Plains; Pleasantdale; Pleasant Grove; Pleasant Plains; Pleasant Run; Pleasant Valley; Pleasant View; Pleasantville; Plumbsock; Porchtown; Possumtown; Princessville; Princeton; Prospect; Prospect Plains; Prospect Point; Prospertown; Quaker Gardens; Quakertown; Quarryville; Ramtown; Raven Rock; Red Bank; Red Hill; Red Lion; Red Mill; Red Oak Grove; Red Valley; Retreat; Ridgewood; River Edge; Riverside; Robertsville; Rockport; Rocktown; Rockwood; Roosevelt; Roosevelt City; Rosedale; Roseland; Rosemont; Roseville; Rudeville; Russia; Saddle Brook; Saddle River; Sand Hills; Sandtown; Sandy Hook; Sandy Ridge; Scotch Bonnet; Scotch Plains; Sea Breeze (on the Delaware River);

Sea Bright; Sea Girt; Sergeantsville; Seven Stars; Shaytown; Shell Pile; Ship Bottom; Sickleville; Silver Springs; Six Points; Slabtown; Smoke Rise; Somerset; South Egg Harbor; South Orange; Speedwell; Spring Mill; Spring Mills; Springtown; Spring Valley; Stanton; Star Cross; Stephensburg; Still Valley; Stillwater; Stockholm; Stone Mill; Stonetown; Summit; Sunnyside; Surf City; Swedesboro; Sweetwater; Swinesburg; Taylors Mills; Taylortown; Teaneck; Tenafly; Ten Mile Run; Texas; Thompson Beach; Thompsontown; Thorofare; Three Bridges; Timbuctoo; Tranquility; Two Bridges; Two Rivers; Undercliff Junction; Union; Union City; Union Grove; Union Hill; Union Mills; Uniontown; Unionville; Uttertown; Vail; Valley; Vienna; Wading River; Walnut Valley; Warren; Warren Glen; Washington; Washington Park; Washington Valley; Washingtonville; Waterwitch; Weekstown; Wenonah; West Egg Harbor; West New York; Whig Lane; White Horse [Trenton]; Whitehouse; White Oak Bottom; Wildwood; Williamstown; Willow Grove; Wood-Ridge [Hackensack]; Wyoming;

NEW MEXICO – Named after the country. Statehood was January 6, 1912. The state nickname is "Land of Enchantment." The first permanent European settlement there, San Juan, was established in 1598. A decade later, 1609, Santa Fe was established. The Santa Fe Trail started in central Missouri, went southwest to Santa Fe, then south into Mexico. New Mexico became a state in 1912, followed by Arizona five weeks later. The United States government built Los Alamos Research Center in 1943, while fighting World War II. The atomic bomb was developed there with testing done at White Sands Proving Grounds July 16, 1945.

When Ralph Edwards, host of the radio show "Truth or Consequences," went there to do a program, the obliging town fathers changed the name from Hot Springs to Truth or Consequences.

Famous New Mexicans include:
- John Denver (1943–1997), Roswell; born John Henry Deutschendorn, Jr.; released about three hundred songs, nearly half of which he composed; adopted the surname after the capital of his favorite state, Colorado; in the mid to late 1960s sang with the Chad Mitchell Trio
- Tom Blackburn (1913–1992), Raton; wrote the lyrics to "The Ballad of Davy Crockett"

Bennett, NM is two hundred miles farther east than El Paso, TX.

Interesting names include: Acoma (on an outcropping 365 feet tall is the home of the oldest continually inhabited settlement in North America); Aden; Afton; Air Base City; Alamo; Alaska; Alcatraz; Alta Vista; Anchor; Angel Fire; Antelope; Antelope Wells; Arena; Arkansas Junction; Aztec; Banning Place; Bard; Big Mill; Black Lake; Black Rock; Bland; Bluewater; Boyd; Bread Springs; Brilliant; Broadview; Buchanan; Buckeye; Buckhorn; Buena Vista; Buffalo Springs; Cameo; Campbell; Canyon Mill; Caprock; Captain Hill; Casa Blanca; Cedar Crest; Cedar Grove; Cedar Hill; Centerville (2 miles from) Centerville

Corner; Central; Chaparral; Chili; Chloride; Cimarron; Cleveland; Cliff; Cloudcroft; Columbus; Continental Divide; Coolidge; Copper City; Copperton; Cotton City; Cottonwood; Counselor; Coyote; Coyote Canyon; Crisp; Crossroads; Crowther Cow Camp; Crystal; Cuba; Cutter; Dahlia; Deep Tunnel; Deer; Deer Creek Landing; Deer Lake; Defiance; Des Moines; Double Crossing; Double Mills; Dunes; Dusty; Eagle Nest; Eldorado at Santa Fe; Elephant Butte; Elk; Fence Lake; Five Mile Crossing; Florida; Floyd; Flying-E; Flying H; Folsom; Four Forks; Four Points; French; Frontier Post; Fruitland; Gallup; Garrison; Gary; Golden; Grants; Greenville; Guy; Halfway; Hard Luck Crossing; Hatch; Hayden; High Lonesome Wells; Highway; Hollywood; Hooverville; Hope; Hot Springs; House; Humble City; Illinois Camp; Inez; Johnson; Kennedy; Lake Valley; Lama; Las Vegas; Lava; Lincoln; Lingo; Lisbon; Little Water; Lizard; Lobo; Loco Hills; Logan; Lone Wolf; Loving Place; Madison; Madrid; Maxwell; McAlister; McCrystal Place; McGreggor Place; Meadow Lake; Mesquite; Mexican Springs; Miami; Midnight; Midway; Milan; Mirage; Montezuma; Monticello; Monument; Mountainair; Mountainview; Mule Creek; New York; Oak Grove; Oasis; Oil Center; Old Horse Springs; Old Town; Old Moses; Olive; Page; Park Springs; Philadelphia; Pierce; Pie Town; Pinehill; Pine Lodge; Pines; Pine Springs; Pleasant Hill; Point of Sands; Ponderosa; Ponderosa Pines; Potato Patch; Pot Creek; Pounds; Prairieview; Pronto; Queen; Radium Springs; Rainsville; Rattlesnake; Red Bluff; Red Hill; Red Mill; Red River; Redrock; Red Rock; Redstone; Reserve; Ring Place; River Mill; Riverside; Rock Cabin; Rock Springs; Rodeo; Rosebud; Route 66; Sacramento; Salt Lake; San Antonio; Sands; Sand Springs; San Francisco; Sedan; Seven Lakes; Seven Rivers; Seven Springs; Shady Brook; Shakespeare; Sheep Springs; Ship Rock; Shoemaker; Silver Acres; Silver City; Six Mile Gate; Spears; Spur Lake; Standing Rock; Sublette; Sugarite; Sulphur Springs; Summit; Sunny Side; Sunrise; Sunset; Sunshine; Sunshine Valley; Sun Valley; Sweetwater; Taylor Springs; Texico; Thoreau (10 miles from) Thoreau; Three Rivers; Thunderbird; Tingle; Top of the World; Trout Springs; Truth Or Consequences; Turquoise; Two Grey Hills; Upper Fruitland; Valencia; Virginia City; Vista; Wagon Mound; Water; Waterflow; Weed; Whitehorse; White Lakes; White Oaks; Whitetail; Whitewater; White Rock; White Sands; White Signal; Williamsburg; Willow Creek; Willow Mountain; Willow Springs; Winston; Yankee

NEW YORK – Named for the Duke of York. Statehood was July 26, 1788. The state nickname is "Empire State." It is one of the original Thirteen Colonies. New York City is the most populous city in America and boasts forty percent of the state's population at nearly 3 million, followed by Buffalo with less than 300,000. New York City is made up of five counties (boroughs): The Bronx, Manhattan, Queens, Brooklyn, and Staten Island. The Bronx is the only part of the city that is part of the United States mainland; the others are islands. Brooklyn was an independent city until 1898. Manhattan's Central Park divides that part of the city into east side and west side. New York City has the most non-vehicle households in America—58%—while in the borough of Manhattan more than 75% of the households do not own a car. The national average is 8%. About one-third of the nation's mass transit users and about two-thirds of the rail users in America live in New York City. Schenectady is a joint Indian and Dutch word.

The Iroquois called the area "the place of the pines;" the Dutch took what they heard from the Indians and called it Scheaenedstede; stede in Dutch means "a town."

In 1869, exiled former Mexican president and general Santa Anna (the Alamo) was living in New Jersey. He brought a ton of Mexican chicle with him in hopes of selling it to raise funds in order to return to power in Mexico. He persuaded Thomas Adams of Staten Island to buy it. Adams, a photographer and inventor, intended to vulcanize the chicle for use as a rubber substitute. Those efforts failed, but he noticed that Santa Anna liked to chew the chicle, as the ancient Myans had done. Adams boiled a small batch of chicle in his kitchen to create a chewing gum. He gave some to a local store and people bought it. In 1871, Adams received a patent on a gum-making machine and began mass-producing chicle-based gum. His first product, Snapping and Stretching, was pure chicle with no flavoring so he began to expriment with flavorings, beginning with sarsaparilla (spelled correctly). In 1884, he began adding licorice flavoring and called his invention Adams' Black Jack, the first flavored gum in America. It was also the first gum to be offered in sticks. Black Jack Gum sold well into the 1970s, when production ceased due to slow sales. In 2002, Adams was purchased by the Cadbury Company. Cadbury Adams continues to manufacture Black Jack, Beaman's, and Chiclets.

The largest man-made structure in the world is the Fresh Kills Garbage Landfill in New York City. Before it closed in March, 2001, New York deposited two billion tons of garbage there. The landfill is twenty times the size of the Great Pyramid in Egypt and rises to a height of 155 feet, the highest point on the eastern seabord south of Maine. In 1991, it overtook the Great Wall of China as the largest man-made object on earth. It currently produces two percent of the worlds's man-made methane.

Elizabeth Blackwell was the first female to graduate from medical school and the first female physician in America. Born in England, 1821, her family moved to New York City when she was eleven. A summer program at the Philadelphia Hospital in 1848, allowed her to practice medicine for the first time.

In 1918, the first three-color traffic light was erected in New York City.

The Empire State Building is the tallest building in New York City at 102 stories (1,472 feet) and is the second tallest building in America behind Sears Tower. It has its own Zip Code, 10118. Construction on the building began in January, 1930 and was completed in May, 1931. Since 1890, eleven structers in the city have held the title of world's tallest building. The history of skyscrapers in New York City began with the completion of the World Building in 1890. At 348 feet it was the first building to surpass the 284-foot spire of Trinity Church. New York City went through a high rise construction boom from the early 1910s to the early 1930s, during which time sixteen skyscrapers were built.

Signers of the Declaration of Independence include: William Floyd, Francis Lewis, Philip Livingston, and Lewis Morris.

Famous New Yorkers include:

- Franklin Delano Roosevelt (1882–1945), Hyde Park; thirty-second president of the United States; elected to four terms in office; a distant relative of Theodore Roosevelt; created the New Deal during the Great Depression; other programs include Federal Deposit Insurance Corporation, Tennessee Valley Authority, and the United States Securities and Exchange Commission
- Gene Barry (1919–), New York City; born Eugene Klass; starred in *Our Miss Brooks, Bat Masterson, The Name of the Game,* and *Burke's Law;* trained in violin and voice; he adopted his professional name after John Barrymore
- Carroll O'Connor (1924–2001), Bronx, NY; Jackie Gleason and Mickey Rooney were asked to play the part of Archie Bunker before O'Connor; *All in the Family* aired from 1970–1979
- Billy the Kid (1859–1881), New York City; born Henry McCarty; became legendary after sheriff Pat Garrett wrote a biography titled *The Authentic Life of Billy, the Kid*
- Lucille Ball (1911–1989), Jamestown; attended John Murray Anderson School for the Dramatic Arts but was told she had no future as a performer; made movies with the Marx Brothers and the Three Stooges; married Desi Arnaz in 1940; in 1948, she starred in the radio show *My Favorite Husband*; CBS asked her to develop the show for television; it resulted in *I Love Lucy,* airing from 1951–1957
- Frances Bavier (1902–1989), New York City; played Aunt Bea on *The Andy Griffith Show* and *Mayberry, RFD,* from 1960-1970; in 1972 she bought a home, sight unseen, in Siler City, North Carolona
- William Bendix (1906–1964), Manhattan; was a bat boy for the New York Yankees where he watched Babe Ruth hit more than one hundred homeruns; in 1948, he played the part of Babe Ruth in *The Babe Ruth Story*; played the part of Chester A. Riley on the radio show *The Life of Riley,* airing from 1944–1951, and in the television series by that name from 1953–1958
- Shirley Booth (1898–1992), New York City; born born Marjory Ford; began her career on the stage as a teenager, but made her first movie at age 54; at age 63, in 1961, began starring in the television series *Hazel*
- George Samuel "Sammy" Davis Jr (1925–1990), Harlem, Manhattan; served in World War II; singer, dancer, impersonationist, comedian, drummer, vibraphoneist, and trumpeter
- Jimmy Durante (1893–1980), Brooklyn; dropped out of school in eighth grade to become a full-time ragtime pianist
- Jackie Gleason (1916–1987), Bushwick, Brooklyn; born Herbert Walton Gleason, Jr; played the role of Chester A. Riley on the original television series *The Life of Riley,* 1949; *The Jackie Gleason Show* aired from 1952-1970; *The Honeymooners* aired from October, 1955 to September, 1956; signs at the approaches to the Brooklyn Bridge read: Welcome to Brooklyn "How Sweet it Is"
- Danny Kaye (1913–1987), Brooklyn; born David Daniel Kaminsky; hosted *The Danny Kaye Show* from 1963–1967

- Mickey Rooney (1920–), Brooklyn; born Joseph Yule, Jr; entered the *Guinness Book of Records* as the actor with the longest record on both stage and screen
- Rose Marie (1923–), New York City; born Rose Marie Mazetta; at age three she started performing under the name Baby Rose Marie; at age five she became a radio star on NBC and made a series of films; she may be best remembered as Sally Rogers on *The Dick Van Dyke Show*
- The Marx Brothers:
  - Leonard "Chico" (1887–1961), New York City; originally nicknamed Chicko due to his reputation as a ladies' man or a "chicken chaser," in the popular slang of the day
  - Arthur "Harpo" (1888–1964), New York City; born Adolph; inspired to develop his "silent" routine after reading a review, "Adolph Marx performed beautiful pantomime which was ruined whenever he spoke;" taught himself to play the harp because he could not sing or dance and did not speak well
  - Julius Henry "Groucho" (1890–1977), New York City; his early career goal was to become a doctor but the family's need for income forced him out of school at age 12; he was a voracious reader which helped to make up for his lack of formal education; the quiz show *You Bet Your Life* started on radio in 1947, moved to television in 1950 and ceased airing in 1961
  - Milton "Gummo" (1893–1977), New York City; served in the Army during World War I; he was given his nickname because he had a tendancy to be sneaky backstage and would creap up on others without them knowing (like a gumshoe)
  - Herbert Manfred "Zeppo" (1901–1979), New York City; though a straight man on stage, he was reputed to be very funny in person, perhaps the funniest of all his siblings

Long Island extends under Connecticut almost to the Rhode Island line. Three of the youngest mayors elected in America were twenty-one-year-old Mike Sellers, 2005, Cobleskill, Schoharie County, thirty-two-year-old Hugh Grant, 1889, New York City, and thirty-one-year-old Seth Low, 1881, Brooklyn. After Low was mayor of Brooklyn, he became the only person to be president of Columbia University and mayor of New York City.

Interesting names include: Adams; Afton; Akron; Alabama; Alleganey; Alpine; Amsterdam; Anderson; Andes; Antwerp; Arabia; Arcade; Arctic; Argyle; Atlanta; Avon; Bains Corner; Basket; Bath; Belcher; Belfast; Berlin; Big Moose; Bird; Bronx (Dion); Brooklyn (Jackie Gleason); Buchanan; Buena Vista; Buffalo (Buffalo Bob Smith, *Howdy Doody Show*, 1947); Bullet Hole; Burnt Hills; Butternut Grove; Cairo Junction; Calcium; Cascade; Cat Elbow Corner; Catskill; Cattaraugus (the continental divide between the Mississippi River and the Great Lakes runs through Cattaraugus County); Cattown; Cherry Creek; Cherry Valley; Chestnut Ridge; Chili Center; China; Chipmunk; Cincinnatus; Cobleskill; Coffins Mills; Copenhagen; Cornwall on Hudson; Covert; Coxsackie; Crafts;

Cuba; Dayton; Deposit; Dibbletown; Dogtown; Dresden; Drunkard Creek; Dublin; Dutch Hollow; Dutch Settlement; Eagle Nest; Eden; Edwards; Elizabethtown; Fillmore; Fishkill; Five Corners; Five Points; Florida; Flushing; Forest Hills (Michael Landon *Little Joe; Charles Ingalls*); Fort Edward; Friend; Friendship; Frost Hollow; Garland; Geneva; Grant; Graphite; Gravesend; Greece; Greenville; Groverville; Gypsum; Hague; Half Acre; Halfway; Hamburg; Hampshire; Happy Valley; Hardscrabble; Harrison; Hemlock; Hicksville; Hogtown; Holland; Honk Hill; Horseheads; Horshshoe; Horseshoe Hill; Hungry Hill; Hurricane; Idle Hour; Index; Interlaken; Irelandville; Irish Settlement; Irishtown; Italy Hill; Jamestown (Lucille Ball); Johnson; Kabob; Kendall; Kennedy; Killawog; Kill Buck; Kripplebush; Lake George; Lava; Lawyersville; Lebanon; Liberty; Lincoln [NYC]; Lisbon; Liverpool; Locust Grove; Logan; Lonelyville; Lost Village; Lynbrook (Bob Keeshan, *Clarabell & Captain Kangaroo*); Madrid; Manhattan (Milton Berle); Marshall; Marshalls; Martin; Mechanicville; Melody Lake; Model City; Monroe; Morningside; Mountain House; Mountain Lodge; Mount Vernon (Dick Clark; Art Carney); Mud Hill; Mud Mills; Muitzeskill; Muttontown; Naples; Nassau; Neversink; New Scotland; New York City (Long Island is over 100 miles long); Niagara Falls; Nichols; Nile; Ninety Six Corners; North Cuba; North Pole; Norway; Number Four; Ohio; Oniontown; Orangeburg; Orchard Park; Oregon; Orient; Otter Kill; Owls Nest; Oxbow; Panama; Paradise; Paradox; Peas Eddy; Peekskill; Penelope; Penn Yan; Perfection; Persia; Peru; Philadelphia; Phoenix; Pilgrim Corners; Pleasant Valley; Pleasantville; Poland; Pumpkin Hill; Pumpkin Hollow; Pumpkin Hook; Purchase; Quackenkill; Quaker Hill; Quaker Settlement; Ripley; Rome; Rotterdam; Rough and Ready; Russia; Schenectady (1st TV station, WRGB, 1928); Scotchtown; Shady Corner Curve; Shamrock; Sheds; Shin Hollow; Sidney; Silver Creek; Silver Springs; Skunks Corner; Sleepy Hollow; Sodom; South Dayton; Sparkill; Sparrow Bush; Squirrels Corners; State Line; Staten Island; Stockholm; Sulphur Springs; Sun; Sunny Brae; Sunnyside; Swastika; Taylor; Texas; Texas Valley; Thompson; Thompson Ridge; Thompsons Corner; Thompsons Crossing; Thompsons Lake; Thompsonville; Tip Top; Toll Gate Corner; Town Line; Tripoli; Troy; Tuckahoe; Utica (Annette Funicello); Van Buren; Versailles; Vienna; Wallkill; Warsaw; Webster; Weckerly Park [NYC]; Welcome; Wellsville (Gabby Hayes); White Plains; Wynantskill; Wyoming; Yaddo; Yaphank; Yonkers

NORTH CAROLINA – Named after King Charles, I. Statehood was November 21, 1789. The state nickname is "Old North State." It is one of the original Thirteen Colonies. On May 20, 1861, it became the last of the southern states to secede from the Union; it was readmitted July 4, 1868. North Carolina provided one one hundred twenty-five thousand troops for the Confederate cause, more than any other state. About forty thousand of those troops never returned. The first Confederate soldier killed in the Civil War was Private Henry Wyatt. At the Battle of Gettysburg in July, 1863 the 26th North Carolina Regiment advanced the farthest of any Confederate regiment. At Appomattox Court House in Virginia, April, 1865 the 75th North Carolina Regiment fired the last shots of the Civil War. For many years North Carolinians proudly boasted that they had been "First at Bethel, Farthest at Gettysburg, and Last at Appomattox." New Bern is home to the drug store where Pepsi Cola was invented.

Signers of the Declaration of Independence: Joseph Hewes, William Hooper, and John Penn.

Famous North Carolinians include:
- James Knox Polk (1795–1849), Pineville; (the L is silent) eleventh president of the United States; U.S. House of Representatives (two terms); governor of Tennessee; suffering from poor health as a child, his father attempted to seek medical help in Philadelphia but, because of his severe pain, instead visited the nearer Dr. Ephraim McDowell in Danville, Kentucky who removed urinary stones
- Andrew Johnson (1808–1975), Raleigh; seventeenth president of the United States following Lincoln's assassination; 16th vice president of the United States; U.S. Senator; U.S. House of Representatives (five terms); governor of Tennessee; never attended any type of school and taught himself to read and spell; his wife later taught him arithmetic; was included in the plot that assassinated President Lincoln but the would-be assassin failed to carry out his orders to kill Johnson
- Rev. Billy Graham (1918–), Charlotte; has preached to more persons around the world than any Protestant who has ever lived; according to his staff, as of 1993, more than two and one-half million persons have responded to the invitaion to receive Jesus; as of 2002, his lifetime audience topped two billion
- David Brinkley (1920–2003), Wilmington; co-anchored NBC's nightly news program from 1956–1970
- Howard Cosell (1918–1995), Winston-Salem; served during World War II; began his career in law; clients included Willie Mayes
- Andy Griffith (1926–), Mount Airy; as a very young child he slept in chest of drawers for a few months; a minister at Grace Moravian Church taught him to sing and play the trombone; began college in hopes of becoming a Moravian minister but changed his major to music in which he earned a bachelor's degree in 1949 from the University of North Carolina at Chapel Hill; after graduation, he taught English for a few years at Goldsboro High School, Goldsboro, NC; *The Andy Griffith Show* aired from 1960 to 1968
- Earl Scruggs (1924–), Shelby; joined Bill Monroe's Blue Grass Boys in 1945; he and Lester Flat left Monroe's band to form Flatt and Scruggs in 1948, which lasted until 1969
- George "Meadowlark" Lemon (1932–), Wilmington; chosen to play with the Harlem Globetrotters in 1955, he played sixteen thousand games in twenty-two years
- Soupy Sales (1926–), Franklinton; born Milton Supman; served in World War II; earned a Master's Degree in journalism from Marshall College, Huntington, West Virginia; was a morning DJ on WKRC, Cincinnati, Ohio; his first pie in the face was on a Cleveland, Ohio television show called *Soupy's On!*; he is best known for his long-running daily television children's television show, *Lunch with Soupy Sales*; the title was later to *The Soupy Sales Show*; he claims to have been hit by over twenty-five thousand pies

The westernmost point of North Carolina is due south of greater Cincinnati, Ohio. Sutherland, North Carolina is one mile north of Goose Pimple Junction, VA.

Interesting names include: Aberdeen; Acorn Hill; Acre; Adams; Advance; Afton; Alert; Alexander; Allegheny; Allen; All Healing Springs; Alligator; Andeson; Apex; Apple Ridge; Ash; Ashland; Asylum; Atlantic; Austin; Avon; Bahama; Ballard; Baltic; Bamboo; Bandana; Barbecue; Barber; Bat Cave; Bath; Battleground; Bayleaf; Bear Creek; Bear Grass; Bear Poplar; Bearskin; Beaverdam; Beech Creek; Bee Log; Belgrade; Bent Creek; Belfast; Berea; Berry Hill; Berry Mill; Beverly; Big Hill; Bird Cage; Black Creek; Black Jack; Black Mountain; Black Water; Blackwood; Blowing Rock; Blue Ridge; Blue Ridge Forest; Blue Rock; Bob White Fork; Boiling Springs; Bolivia; Boone; Boonville; Bowman Bluff; Brake; Brasstown; Bricks; Brief; Brightwater; British Woods; Broadway; Brown Mountain Beach (300 miles from the coast); Bruce; Buffalo; Buffalo Cove; Bug Hill; Bunker Hill; Burger Town (100 miles west of Bristol, TN); Burlington; Burnt Chimney Corner; Burnt Mills; Buzzards Crossroads; Cabin; Calabash; Caldwell; California; Calypso; Camden; Campbell; Cane Brake; Cane River; Cape Fear; Carolina; Carpenter; Carroll; Carter; Casablanca; Cashiers; Catherine Lake; Cat Square; Cedar Creek; Cedar Falls; Cedar Grove; Cedar Village; Central; Central Falls; Charles; Cherry; Cherry Grove; Cherry Lane; Cherryville; Chestnut Dale; Chestnut Grove; Chestnut Hill; Chimney Rock; China Grove; Chip; Clark; Clear Creek; Cleveland; Clinton; Clover Garden; Cobblestone; Cold Springs; Cold Water; Columbia; Columbus; Comfort; Concord; Cool Springs; Cotton Grove; Council; Country Lane; Covington; Cranberry; Cranberry Gap; Creek; Crisp; Crooked Oak; Crossnore; Crumpler; Cuba; Dallas; Dark Ridge; Day Book; Deep Gap; Deep River; Deep Run; Deer Run; Democrat; Denver; Derby; Dixie; Dodgetown; Double Island (400 miles from the coast); Double Shoals; Douglas Crossroads; Dublin; Duck; Duff Creek; Eagle Springs; Eagletown; Eden; Edinburgh; Edward; Edwards Crossroads; Egypt; Eldorado; Elf; Eli Whitney; Elizabeth City; Elizabethtown; Elkin; Elk Mountain; Elk Valley; Elm City; Elm Grove; Emerald Isle; English; Enola; Ether; Eureka; Fairview; Faith; Falcon; Falling Creek; Farmer; Farmville; Fig; Finger; Five Forks; Five Points; Flat Branch; Flat Creek; Flat Rock; Flat Shoals; Flat Springs; Flat Top; Flatwood; Flint Hill; Florence; Flowers; Folly; Forest; Forest Grove; Fork; Fountain; Four Corners; Four Oaks; Franklin; Friendship; Frog Level; Frog Pond; Frogsboro; Fruitland; Frying Pan; Garland; George; Georges Mills; Georgetown; Georgeville; Globe; Goat Neck; Gold; Golden; Gold Hill; Gold Point; Gold Rock; Gold Sand; Goldston; Goodluck; Goose Hollow; Gooseneck; Goose Pond; Gordonton; Gordontown; Grabtown; Grand Oaks; Granite Falls; Granite Quarry; Grape Creek; Grapevine; Grapewood; Graphite; Grassy Creek; Grayson; Green Hill; Green Mountain; Green Needles; Greentown; Green Valley; Greenville; Gregory; Gregory Crossroads; Gregory Forks; Gulf; Gum Corner; Gum Neck; Gum Springs; Gumtree; Hairtown; Half Moon; Handy; Happy Home; Happy Valley; Hare; Harmony; Harmony Grove; Harper; Harpers Crossroads; Harrisburg; Hasty; Hawk Branch; Healing Springs; Hemlock; Henderson; Hickory; Hickory Crossroads; Hickory Point; Hickory Rock; High Shoals; Hills; Hog Island; Holland; Holly Grove; Holly Park; Holly Ridge; Holly Springs; Honey Hill; Honey Island; Honolulu; Hopkins; Horse Neck; Horse Shoe; Horseshoe; Hothouse; Hot Springs; Hunting Creek; Huntsville; Hurricane; Husk;

Index; Inez; Institute; Intelligence; Ivy Hills; Ivy Ridge; Jackson; Jackson Springs; Jacksonville; Jason; Jefferson; Jugtown; Jupiter; Justice; Kendall Acres; Kill Devil Hills; Kinston; Kitty Hawk; Knob Creek; Laboratory; La Grange; Laurel; Laurel Hill; Laurel Springs; Lawrence; Leaksville; Lemon Springs; Lewis; Lexington; Liberty; Liberty Hill; Lickskillet; Lincolnton; Listening Rock; Little Creek; Little Switzerland; Loafers Glory; Locust; Locust Hill; Logan; Lone Hickory; Lower Pig Pen; Luck; Lumber Bridge; Madison; Magnolia; Magnum; Maiden; Maine; Manchester; Maple; Maple Grove; Maple Springs; Mapleton; Marble; Margaret; Margarettsville; Marion; Marshall; Marshallberg; Mars Hill; Matthew; Matthews Crossroads; Mayfield; Maysville; Meadow; Meadow Summit; Meadow View; Meat Camp; Mechanic; Merry Hill; Merry Oaks; Middletown; Midway; Mill Neck; Mineral Springs; Minuet; Money Island Beach; Monogram; Monroe; Montezuma; Monticello; Morehead City; Morgan Ford; Morning Star; Morrisville; Mountain Island; Mountain Page; Mountain Park; Mountain Valley; Mountain View; Mount Airy (Andy Griffith); Mount Energy; Mount Pleasant; Mount Valley; Mount Vernon; Mt Holly; Mt Sterling; Mt Vernon Springs; Mud Castle; Muddy Creek; Mulberry; Nags Head; Naples; Nashville; Needmore; New Bern (birthplace of Pepsi Cola); New Castle; Nob Hill; Oak City; Oak Grove; Oak Hill; Oak Ridge; Oaks; Oakville; Ocean; Ogden; Old Ford; Old Hundred; Olive Grove; Olive Hill; Orange; Orange Factory; Orange Grove; Oregon Hill; Oriental; Orion; Orlando; Othello; Otter Creek; Owltown; Paint Gap; Paint Rock; Paint Town; Panther Creek; Paris; Peach; Peacock Crossing; Peacock Crossroads; Pea Hill; Pea Ridge; Pee Dee; Pendleton; Penelope; Penny Hill; Pensacola; Peppers; Perfection; Pet Crossroads; Philadelphia; Pigeonroost; Pikeville; Pilot Mountain (for which Mt. Pilot was named on *Tha Andy Griffith Show*); Pine Hill; Pinetown; Pineview; Pine View; Pinewood; Pink Hill; Pittsburg; Plateau; Pleasant Grove; Pleasant Hill (2); Pleasant Ridge; Pleasantville; Plumtree; Poor Town; Poplar; Poplar Branch; Poplar Springs; Pricetown; Princeton; Prospect; Prospect Hill; Prosper; Providence; Pumpkin Center; Pumpkintown; Quail Hollow; Quail Ridge; Quail Roost; Quaker Gap; Quebec; Rabbit Corner; Rainbow Springs; Ranger; Rebel City; Red Brush; Red Cross; Redcross; Red Hill; Red House; Red Oak; Red Springs; Relief; Republican; Retreat; Rich Hill; Riddle; Ridgeway; River Ridge Run; Riverside; Roaring Creek; Roaring River; Rock Creek; Rockfish; Rockyhock; Rocky River; Rocky Springs; Rosebud; Rose Hill; Roseville; Roundhill; Round Peak; Rowan; Ruby City; Russellville; Ruth; Saddletree; Sandy Bottom; Sandy Ridge; Savages Crossroads; Savannah; Sawmills; Scotch Grove; Scotland Neck; Scranton; Seaboard (miles from the ocean); Seven Bridges; Seven Hills; Seven Lakes; Seven Paths; Seven Springs; Shacktown; Shanghai; Sharp Point; Sharpsburg; Shelby; Sherwood Forest; Shine; Shoals; Shoe; Shoofly; Shooting Creek; Sign Pine; Silk Hope; Silver Springs; Silverstone; Silver Valley; Simpson; Six Forks; Small; Snow Camp; Snow Hill; Social Plains; Soda Hill; Solo; Somerset; Soul City; Speed; Speedwell; Spies; Spout Springs; Spray; Spring Creek; Spruce Pine; Stacey; Stacy; Star; Steel Creek; Sterling; Stoneville; Stony Creek; Stony Fork; Stoney Knob; Stony Point; Strawberry Ridge; St Stephens; Stumptown; Sugar Grove; Sugar Ridge; Sugar Town; Sulphur Springs; Summit; Sunburst; Sunnyvale; Sunny View; Sunset Hills; Sunshine; Sun Valley; Supply; Surf City; Sutherland; Sweetgum; Sweetwater; Swiss; Tar Corner; Tar Heel; Tar River; Taylortown; Thankful; Thermal City; Three Forks; Three Mile; Toast; Tobaccoville; Todd; Toledo;

Tomahawk; Topnot; Tree Top; Trenton; Triangle; Triple Springs; Troy; Turkey; Turkey Ford; Tuxedo; Twin Oaks; U-No; Union; Union Cross; Union Grove; Union Hill; Union Hope; Union Mills; Union Point; Upper Pig Pen; Upward; Vein Mountain; Volunteer; Wake Forest; Walnut; Walnut Cove; Walnut Creek; Warsaw; Washington; Wayside; Webster; Welcome; West Philadelphia; Whalebone; Wheat Swamp; Whipporwill Hills; White Hill; Whitehouse; White Oak; White Plains; Whiterock; Whynot; Williamsburg; Willow; Willow Ridge; Willow Springs; Wilmington (David Brinkley); Wilson; Wilsonville; Wilson's Mills; Wind Blow; Windy Gap; Winston-Salem; Wintergreen; Winterville; Wolf Mountain; Woodrow; Yellow Creek; Yellow Gap

NORTH DAKOTA - Sioux for "united allies." Statehood was November 2, 1889. The state nickname is "Peace Garden State." The first Europeans to reach the area were French-Canadian explorers and fur traders who visited about 1740. Lewis and Clark had already visited the area and made contact with the local Indian tribes.

Famous North Dakotans include:
- Angie Dickinson (1931–), Kulm; born Angeline Brown; in ;1954, she made her acting debut on *Death Valley Days*; she also appeared on *Gunsmoke, Cheyenne, Perry Mason, Wagon Train, The Fugative,* and *Dr. Kildare;* starred on *Police Woman* as Sgt. Leann "Pepper" Anderson from 1974 to 1978
- Louis L'Amour (1908–1988), Jamestown; all one hundred one of his works were in print at the time of his death
- Peggy Lee (1920–2002), Jamestown; born Norma Deloris Egstrom; her singing range was contralto (from G below middle C to two Gs above middle C); sang with Benny Goodman's band for two years; wrote the lyrics for such songs as "Fever," He's a Tramp," "The Siamese Cat Song," and numerous others
- Ann Southern (1909–2001), Valley City; was a high school classmate of Eddie Albert (then Edward Heimberger); in 1956, she was heard as the voice of Gladys Crabtree (the car) in the short-lived series *My Mother the Car*
- Lawrence Welk (1903–1992), Strasburg; born to German-speaking immigrant parents, he did not learn English until the age of twenty-one; the term "Champagne Music" was derived from an engagement at the William Penn Hotel, Pittsburgh, Pennsylvania when a dancer referred to his band's sound as "light and bubbly as champagne;" *The Lawrence Welk Show* began airing in 1955, and ending in 1971
- Bobby Vee (1943–), Fargo; born Robert Thomas Velline; when Buddy Holly, Richie Valens, and The Big Bopper were killed in an airplane accident in 1959, Velline, age fifteen, hastily assembled a band of Fargo, North Dakota schoolboys and volunteered for the job of filling in for Holly and his band at their next engagement; their performance was a success; recordings include "Devil or Angel," "Rubber Ball," "Take Good Care of My Baby," "The Night Has a Thousand Eyes"

Interesting names include: Abercrombie; Adams; Agate; Alamo; Alexander; Alice; Alpha; Antelope; Antler; Apple Valley; Arena; Auburn; Bathgate; Battleview; Beach; Berea;

Berlin; Big Bend; Blackstone Post Office; Bloom; Bluegrass; Bonetrail; Bounty; Bowbells; Briarwood; Brisbane; Buchanan; Bucyrus; Buffalo; Buffalo Springs; Burlington; Burt; Buttzville; Cannon Ball; Carson; Cavalier; Center; Christine; Cleveland; Colgate; Columbus; Concrete; Cooperstown; Crete; Crocus; Crystal; Crystal Springs; Cuba; Daily; Davenport; Dawson (seven miles from) Dawson; Dazey; Divide; Dodge; Douglas; Dresden; Eagle Nest; Edinburg; Elliott; Erie; Everest; Fairfield; Fayette; Fillmore; Fleece; Flora; Forest River; Four Bears Village; Friend; Fryburg; Gardner; Golden Valley; Goodrich; Grace City; Grand Rapids; Greene; Greenfield; Hague; Hamberg; Hamilton; Harding; Harlem; Harrisburg; Havana; Hawkeye; Hope; Hunter; Huron City; Independence; Inkster; Interlaken; Jamestown (Peggy Lee); Johnson; Joliette; Kellogg; Keystone; Killdeer; Knox; Lignite; Lincoln; Lincoln Valley; Lisbon; Logan; Logan Center; Lone Tree; Lostwood; Madison; Magnolia; Mapleton; Marion; Marseilles; Marshall; Martin; Mason; Maxbass; Mazda; McKenzie; Mercer; Michigan; Midway; Montpelier; Mound; Mountain; Munich; Munster; Murray; Napoleon; Nash; New England; Niagara; Nine Mile Corner; Nome; Northgate; North Lemmon; Norway; Oakdale; Ops; Otter Creek; Overly; Oxbow; Page; Park River; Parshall; Penn; Pick City; Pillsbury; Pittsburg; Plaza; Pleasant Valley; Poland (seven miles south of Warsaw); Porcupine; Power; Prairie Junction; Price; Prosper; Raleigh; Ralston; Ransom City; Ray; Revere; Rider; Rising; Riverdale (ten miles east of) Riverdale; Riverside; Roseglen; Roseville; Rugby; Ruso; Russell; Satratoga Springs; Scranton; Sentinel Butte; Sevenmile Corner; Sheyenne; Silverleaf; Spring Creek; Stampede; Stanton; Starkweather; Sterling; St George; Still; Strasburg; Surrey; Sweet Briar; Sweetwater; Taylor; Temple; Thompson; Three V Crossing; Tioga; Tokio; Tower City; Trenton; Trotters; Turtle Lake; Twin Buttes; Valley City; Wales; Walhalla; Warren; Warsaw (seven miles north of Poland); Weaver; Webster; Westby (6 miles from Westby, Montana); Wheatland; White Earth; White Shield; Wild Rice; Wildrose; Willow City; Wimbledon; Wing; York; Yorktown Post Office; Ypsilanti; Zap; Zeeland; Zenith;

OHIO - Iroquois for "good river." Statehood was March 1, 1803. The state nickname is "Buckeye State." Natives are known as Ohioans. Seven U.S. presidents hailed from Ohio at the time of their election. Only Virginia has more presidents with eight. Ohio's central position and its population gave it an important place during the Civil War, and the Ohio River was a vital artery for troop and supply movements, as were Ohio's railroads. In the 1800s, long before the invention of the automobile, B. F. Goodrich built the first rubber manufacturing plant in Akron. Canton was named for Canton, China.

The population of the Greater Cincinnati Area, including nearby Kentucky and Indiana towns, is estimated to be over two million. Cincinnati was founded in 1788, and named Losantiville, derived from four terms from four different languages. The name means "The city opposite the mouth of the Licking River." The "L" was used from "Licking River;" "os" is Latin for "mouth;" "anti" is Greek for "opposite;" and "ville" is French for "city." L-os-anti-ville. The name Cincinnati (changed in 1790), is from Cincinnatus, a Roman general who saved his city then retired to his farm. After the American Revolution, military officers and other patriots bonded together in the Cincinnati Society. Apparently, the fathers of Cincinnati admired these patriots—hence the tribute to Cincinnatus. George Washington was considered a latter day Cincinnatus.

On April 1, 1853, Cincinnati's fire department became the first full-time, paid fire department in America and was the first fire department in the world to use steam fire engines. The Cincinnati Red Stockings began playing ball in the 1800s, and in 1869, it became the first permanent, professional baseball team in the country. It is reported that from 1953 to 1958, the name was changed from Red Stockings to Red Legs, to avoid any idea of being a Communist sympathizer. Proctor and Gamble began making Ivory Soap in 1879. After fire destroyed the first factory, they moved to a new factory on Mill Creek and began soap production again which eventually led to the area being known as Ivorydale. The Anderson Ferry has been in continuous operation since 1817. The ferry crosses the Ohio River about eight miles downstream from Cincinnati. The Greater Cincinnati Airport is about three miles from the ferry. Prior to 1980, the Cincinnati skyline was featured on the opening and closing sequence of the daytime drama "The Edge of Night," as was "WKRP in Cincinnati." There are no natural lakes in Ohio. The abbreviations for Kentucky, Ohio, and Virginia (Ken o va) make up the name for Kenova, West Virginia.

The first electric traffic light was erected on the corner of 105th Street and Euclid in Cleveland on August 5, 1914, although Salt Lake City claims a rudimentary traffic signal was operating there in 1912. The light in Cleveland had two colors, red and green, and a buzzer to provide a warning for color changes. In 1918, it was reported that a traffic light with three colors was operational in New York City.

The first rock and roll concert, The Moondog Coronation Ball, was held in Cleveland on March 21, 1952. After seven thousand tickets were sold in a matter of days, a riot ensued when police closed the concert due to the tremendous overcrowing. In 1949, Modern Records released the R&B 78 rpm single by Wild Bill Moore, the first song to use the term "rock and roll" and sounded like it. Others consider the first true rock and roll song to have been "Rocket 88," recorded by Ike Turner in 1951. The term "rock and roll" derives from its original usage as an African American street slang expression for sex during the 1920s and 1930s. "Rock and roll" was first used in reference to music by Cleveland disc jokey Alan Freed in the 1950s, although a group called the Boswell Sisters recorded a song called "Rock and Roll" in 1934.

Newark, Ohio (locals jockingly call it Nerkahia) is due north of Havana, Cuba.

Famous Ohioans include:
- William Howard Taft (1857–1930), Cincinnati; twenty-seventh president of the United States; Chief Justice of the United States, and the only former president to serve on the Supreme Court; at three hundred pounds, he was the heaviest president and the last president to have facial hair; he graduated from Yale College and Cincinnati Law School; in 1904, President Theodore Roosevelt appointed Taft Secretary of War in order to groom Taft as his successor to the presidency

- Thomas Alva Edison (1847–1931), Milan; moved to Louisville at age ninteen; held over 1,000 patents; he did not invent the first electric light bulb but the first commercially practical incandescent light
- William "Hopalong Cassidy" Boyd (1895–1972), Hendrysburg; in 1935, he was offered the lead role in the movie, *Hopalong Cassidy*
- Roy Rogers (1911–198), Cincinnati; Born Leonard Franklin Slye; in 1934, he formed *Sons of the Pioneers*; began working in western films in 1935; in 1938, when Gene Autry temporarily walked out on his movie contract, Slye was immediately christened "Roy Rogers;" Dale Evans wrote "Happy Trails"
- Zane Grey (1872–1939), Zanesville; born Pearl Zane Gray
- George Edward "Eddie" Arcaro (1916–1997), Cincinnati; american Thoroughbred Hall of Fame jockey; wom more American Classic Races than any other jockey in history and is the only rider to win the U.S. Triple Crown twice
- Powel Crosley Jr. (1886–1961), Cincinnati; built the Crosley car, owned the Cincinnati Reds, and for whom Crosley Field was named; by 1924, Crosley Radio Corporation was the largest manufacturer of radios in the world; in 1922, Crosley went on the air with a 50-watt commercial station whose call sign was WLW; by 1934, WLW was broadcasting with five hundred thousand watts and aired such famous entertainers as Red Skelton, Doris Day, Fats Waller, and the Mills Brothers; by 1930, he had added refrigerators and other household appliances to his list of products; in 1932, he pattented the idea of putting shelves in the doors of the refrigerator; in 1934, he purchased the Cincinnati Reds baseball team; on May 24, 1935, the first nighttime baseball game in history was held between the Cincinnati Reds and the Philadelphia Phillies in the newly-named Crosley Field; in 1949, he introduced the first disc brakes on his automiblies; he also introduced the push-button radio
- Albert Sabin (1906–1993), born in Russia (now Poland); became a naturalized citizen 1930; developed the oral polio vaccine
- Doris Day (1924–), Evanston neighborhood in Cincinnati; born Doris Mary Ann von Kappelhoff; starting out as a dancer in the mid 1930s, an automobile accident curtailed her dreams as a professional dancer; during her recovery she took up singing and by age seventeen began performing locally; she released "Sentimantal Journey" with the Les Brown orchestra in 1945
- Annie Oakley (1860–1926), near Willowdell; born Phoebe Ann Mosey; it is believed she took her name from Cincinnati's Oakley neighborhood; began hunting at age nine to support the family; the game was sold to locals for money enabling her to pay off the mortgage; in 1881, a traveling show marksman bet $100 that he could beat any local fancy shooter; after missing his twenty-fifth shot, he lost the match and the bet; however, he married Oakley in 1882, and became her business manager; joined Buffalo Bill's Wild West Show in 1885
- Steven Spielberg (1946–), Cincinnati; In the 1996 video, "Elmo Saves Christmas," we learn that Snuffleupagus' grandmother lives in Cincinnati

- Ransom E. Olds (1864–1950), Geneva; namesake for Reo (R. E. Olds Motor Company) and Oldsmobile; founded Olds Motor Vehicle Company; in 1901 he designed the Curved Dash Oldsmobile which, rather than the Model-T, was the first mass-produced, low-priced American motor vehicle
- Jim Backus (1913–1989), Cleveland; played the role of the husband on the television comdey *I Married Joan* and Thurston Howell III on the television comedy *Gilligan's Island*

One of the youngest Mayors elected in America was thirty-one-year-old Dennis Kucinich, Cleveland, Cuyahoga County.

Interesting names include: Aberdeen; Adair; Advance; Africa; Afton; Albany; Alert; Alexandria; Alice; Alliance; Amsterdam; Anderson; Angel; Antwerp; Apex; Apple; Apple Creek; Ashland; Ashwood; Assumption; Athens; Atlanta; Attitude; Aurora; Bacon; Badgertown; Baltic; Baltimore; Bangs; Bath; Battlesburg; Beach City; Beagle; Bear Creek; Beartown; Beaver; Beaver Creek; Beaverdam; Beaver Park; Beaver Pond; Beavertown; Belfast; Ben; Benton; Berlin; Bernice; Beverly; Beverly Gardens; Beverly Hills; Big Prairie; Big Rock; Big Springs; Birmingham; Bismark; Blackband; Blackberry Corner; Blackhawk; Black Horse; Blacktop; Blessing; Bloody Corners; Bloomville; Blue Jay; Blue Rock; Bobo; Bogart; Boston; Bowling Green; Bridgewater; Briggs; Broadway; Brush Ridge; Buchanan; Buckeye; Buckeye City; Buckhorn; Buena Vista; Buffalo; Bunker Hill; Burlington; Burr Oak; Businessburg; Busniess Corner; Butler; Cabinet; Cable; Cadiz (Clark Gable); Calcutta; Caldwell; Calm; Camden; Canada; Candy Town; Cannelville; Carlisle; Carpenter; Carroll; Cars Run; Carter; Caywood; Cedar Grove; Cedar Run; Cedar Springs; Cedar Valley; Celeryville; Centennial; Center; Center Village; Centerville; Central City; Champion; Charleston; Charm; Chattanooga; Chautauqua; Cherry Fork; Cherry Valley; Chuckery; Cincinnati (Jimmy Dodd, original Head Mouseketeer; Doris Day); Circleville; Clark; Clearview; Cleveland (Jim Backus; Henry Mancini); Clover; Clover Hill; Cloverleaf; Coalburg; Coal Hill; Coal Run; Coats; Coldwater; Columbia; Columbus; Columbus Grove; Comet; Concept; Concord; Confederate Crossroads; Congress; Constitution; Continental; Convoy; Coolville; Coon Crossing; Cork; Covington; Crabapple; Cranberry Prairie; Crayon; Cream City; Crescent; Crooked Tree; Crystal Rock; Crystal Springs; Cuba; Cumberland; Cuyahoga Falls; Cynthiana; Dadsville; Dale; Danville; Dart; Dawn; Dayton (Dayton Engineering Laboratories Company [Delco] started by Charles Kettering and Edward Deeds. Both left NCR where Kettering had invented the motor that made the electric cash register possible); Deadman Crossing; Defiance; Delaware; Delightful; Denver; Derby; Dixie; Dodo; Douglas; Dover; Dresden; Dry Run; Dublin; Duck Creek; Dull; Dundee; Dutch Ridge; Eagle City; Eagleville; Eden; Edinburg; Edinburgh; Egypt; Eight Square; Eldorado; Elizabethtown; Elk; Elk Fork; Elk Lick; Elkton; Elliott; Emerald; Empire; England; Equity; Evanston; Evergreen; Ewing; Fairlawn; Farmer; Farmers; Farmersville; Fay; Fayette; Federal; Feed Springs; Fiat; Fillmore; Firebrick; Fireside; Fisher; Five Corners; Five Forks; Five Points; Flag; Flat Iron; Flat Iron Corner; Flat Ridge; Flat Rock; Flatwood; Fleatown; Flint; Florence; Florida; Flushing; Fountain Park; Four Corners; Fourmile House Corner; Fourmile Run; Fox; Frankfort;

Franklin Square; Freedom; Frenchtown; Fresno; Friendship; Frost; Fruit Hill; Fryburg; Fulton; Funk; Garland; Gaysport; Gem; Geneva; Geneva on-the-Lake; Georgesville; Georgetown (boyhood home of General Ulysses S. Grant); German; Germantown; Germany; Getaway; Gettysburg; Ginghamsburg; Glasgow; Goes; Goodwin; Gordon; Grand Rapids; Grandview; Grape Grove; Grayson; Greasy Ridge; Green Creek; Green Springs; Greentown; Greenville; Gregory; Grover Hill; Hamburg; Hamilton; Hancock; Hanging Rock; Happy Corners; Happy Hollow; Harbor; Hardscrabble; Harlem; Harlem Springs; Harper; Harpersfield; Harriett; Harriettsville; Harrisburg; Harrison; Hartford; Havana; Hayden; Heidelberg Beach; Hemlock; Hemlock Grove; Hendrysburg (William "Hopalong Cassidy" Boyd); Hickory Grove; Hicksville; Highwater; Hilltop; Hoboken; Holland; Honesty; Honeytown; Hope; Huber Heights; Hunter; Hunting Valley; Huntsville; Iberia; Idaho; Independence; Industry; Ink; Ireland; Iron City; Irondale; Ironville; Ivorydale; Jackson; Jacksonville; Jamestown; Jay Bird; Jefferson; Jeffersonville; Jelloway; Jerusalem; Jim Town; Joe; Johnson; Jug Run; Jugs Corners; Jumbo; Jump; Kensington; Kettering (named for Charles Kettering who, along with Edward Deeds, left NCR); Killbuck; Kingsville; Kingsville on-the-Lake; Klondike; Knockemstiff; Knox; Knoxville; La Grange; Lancaster; Lansing; La Rue; Lawrence; Lexington; Liars Corner; Liberty Center; Lickskillet; Liggett Crossing; Lima (Phyllis Diller); Lime City; Limerick; Limestone; Limestone City; Limpytown; Lindsey; Lisbon; Litchfield; Little Chicago; Lock; Lock Seventeen; Locust Grove; Logan; Logansville; London; Londonderry; Long; Louisville; Lucerne; Lynchburg; Madison; Madison on-the-Lake; Mad River; Magnetic Springs; Magnolia; Manchester; Maplecrest; Maple Grove; Maple Ridge; Maple Valley; Maplewood; Marathon; Marble Furnace; Marion; Marseilles; Marshall; Marshallville; Martin; Marysville; Mason; Maysville; Meade; Mecca; Mechanicsburg; Mechanicstown; Mechanicsville; Memphis; Mentor; Mentor-on-the-Lake; Mercer; Mesopotamia; Mexico; Miami; Miamisburg; Miamitown; Middle Point; Middletown; Midway; Milan; Miller; Miller City; Miller Grove; Millersburg; Mineral; Mineral City; Mineral Springs; Modest; Monday; Monroe; Montezuma; Monticello; Montpelier; Morgan Center; Morgan Run; Morgantown; Morning Sun; Morningview; Morristown; Morrisville; Moscow; Mount Repose; Mount Sterling; Mount Vernon (Paul Lynde); Mt Sterling; Mudsock; Mulberry; Mulberry Grove; Mule Town; Mutual; Nashville; Nebraska; Needful; Needmore; Nelson; Neptune; Nevada; Newark; Newcomerstown; New England; New Guinea; Newport; New Rumley (General George Armstrong Custer); Nicholsville; North Dayton; North Star; Novelty; Oak; Oakgrove; Oak Hill; Oakland; Oak Shade; Oakwood; Oco; Ogden; Ohio City; Oklahoma; Old Town; Omega; Ontario; Orange; Orangeburg; Oregon; Orient; Ottawa; Otter; Paintsville; Pandora; Panhandle; Paradise; Paradise Hill; Patriot; Pee Pee; Peninsula; Peoria; Pepper Pike; Perrysburg; Peru; Pigeon Run; Pigeye; Pigtown; Pikeville; Pinhook; Pink; Pioneer; Plain City; Pleasant Grove; Pleasant Hill; Pleasant Home; Pleasant Valley; Pleasant View; Point Pleasant (birthplace of Ulysses S. Grant); Point Rock; Polk; Poplar Ridge; Powers; Pratts Fork; Prattsville; Pricetown; Pride; Prospect; Providence; Pulaski; Punity; Pyro; Quaker City; Quarry; Rainbow; Rain Rock; Range; Ray; Redbird; Redbush; Red Diamond; Red Oak; Red River; Reedtown; Reform; Republic; Revenge; Rich Hill; Richmond; Rich Valley; Ripley; Risingsun; River Corners; Roanoake; Rochester; Rock; Rockbridge; Rock Creek; Rock Hill; Rock Springs; Rocky Ridge;

Rocky River; Rome; Rosedale; Roseland; Rosewood; Rosseau; Round Bottom; Roundhead; Royalton; Rush; Rushmore; Rushsylvania; Russell; Russellville; Russia; Salineville; Saltillo; Santa Fe; Sargents; Savannah; Science Hill; Scotch Ridge; Scotland; Scott; Sedan; Senior; Seven Hills; Seven Mile; Seventeen; Shade; Sharpeye; Sharpsburg; Shepherdstown; Sicily; Sidney; Silver Creek; Sinking Spring; Six Corners; Six Mile; Six Points; Skit; Slabtown; Smock; Smoketown; Snowville; Somerset; South Logan; Spencer; Spokane; Springfield; Spring Grove; Spring Mill; Spring Valley; Squirrel Town; Starbucktown; State Road; Station 15; St Charles; Steel Point; Sterling; Steubenville (Dean Martin); Stillwater; St Louisville; Stone; Stone Creek; Stoneville; Stony Ridge; Storms; Stow; St Paul; Strassburg; Stringtown; Success; Sugar Bush Knolls; Sugarcreek; Sugar Creek; Sugar Grove; Sugar Ridge; Sugar Tree Ridge; Sulphurgrove; Sulphur Springs; Summit; Summitville; Sunnyside; Sunrise; Superior; Sycamore; Tacoma; Taylorsville; Taylortown; Temperanceville; Terre Haute; Texas; The Bend; The Eastern; The Point; Thompson; Three Forks; Three Locks; Tipp City; Tippecanoe; Toledo (Teresa Brewer; Charlie Weaver); Tom Corwin; Toronto; Tranquility; Trenton; Triadelphia; Trimble; Triumph; Tucson; Tunnel; Tunnel Hill; Turkey; Turkey Foot Corner; Umbria; Union Furnace; Union Station; Uniontown; Unionville; Uniopolis; Unity; Uno; Valley; Valley City; Valley View; Van Buren; Venice; Versailles; Veto; Vienna; Walnut Creek; Walnut Grove; Warren; Warsaw; Washington; Washington Court House; Washington Hall; Washingtonville; Way; Wayne; Weavers; Weavers Corners; Webster; Welcome; West Liberty; White Fox; Whitehouse; Whiteoak; White Oak; Wickliffe; Widowville; Williamsburg; Williamstown; Willoughby (Tim Conway); Winchester; Winona; Winterset; Wolf Creek; Wolfpen; Wren; Yellow Springs; Yellowtown; Zanesville; Zuck

OKLAHOMA – The name comes from the Choctaw words "okla" meaning "red" and "homma" meaning "people." Statehood was November 16, 1907. The state nickname is "Sooner State." Oklahoma was almost named Sequoya in honor of the Cherokee who created the Cherokee alphabet (symbols). Oklahoma has what is officially considered the highest hill in the world, Cavanal Hill, at 1,999 feet. This is due to the fact that a "mountain" is two thousand feet or higher. The highest peak is 4,973 feet tall. Oklahoma has more than two hundred lakes created by dams, more than any other state, over one million surface acres of water and two thousand more miles of shoreline than the Atlantic and Gulf Coasts combined. Oklahoma thunderstorms from April through July, tend to be the most severe than anywhere in the world. Central Oklahoma, known as Tornado Alley, is the most tornado-prone area in the world. The highest wind speed ever recorded on earth was 318 mph, measured during a tornado in May, 1999.

The motto for Drumright is, "Town of Oil Repute." Enid has the most grain storage capacity in America. Frank Philips of Bartlesville established Philips Petroleum Company in 1905, when it was still Indian Territory. Shawnee is home of the first Sonic Drive-In franchise, 1953, originally known as Top Hat. Will Rogers was born in Oologah, twenty-eight years before Oklahoma became a state. Both parents had Indian blood in them. Will often said, "My ancestors didn't come over on the Mayflower, they met it."

Country stars Garth Brooks and Trisha Yearwood live on a ranch in Owasso with Brooks' three daughters. This down-to-earth Grammy winning couple is often seen around town talking with the locals. Toby Keith also comes there to visit relatives. Ardmore was named after the affluent Philadelphia suburb and historic Pennsylvania Main Line stop at Ardmore, Pennsylvania which was named after Ardmore, Ireland by the Pennsylvania Railroad in 1873.

Altus is home to Altus Air Force Base where pilots and crews are trained in the C-5, C-17, and KC-135. Each C-5 costs $167 million. The cargo compartment in a C-5 is one hundred twenty feet long—the same distance the Wright Brothers flew their first plane. The nose of the craft swings up and the tail swings down allowing drive-through loading and unloading. The plane is equipped with a "kneeling" landing gear which allows the plane to be lowered to truck bed height for ease of loading and unloading from a flatbed or semi. The landing gear consists of twenty-eight wheels. There is a separate passenger area above the cargo bay for seventy-three troops, facing backward. The overall dimensions are 250 feet long, 220 feet wide, and 65 feet high. The volume of unusable space in the tail assembly is greater than the cargo space of a C-130 Hercules. It requires sixteen hours of maintenance for each hour of flight.

In 1936, Carl Magee of Oklahoma City is generally accredited with originating the parking meter. Oklahoma has more astronauts than any other state. Watonga is home of Clarence Nash, the voice of Donald Duck until 1985. The first YIELD sign was used on a trial basis in Tulsa. Oklahoma was the last state to legalize tattooing in 2006. Venita was originally called Downingville. The name was changed to Vinita in honor of Vinnie Ream, the sculptress who created the life-size statue of Abraham Lincoln in the United States Capital. During World War II, Boise City was the only city in the continental United States to be bombed. A B-17 bomber dropped six practice bombs on the town instead of on a bombing range in Texas. Sylvan Goldman, an Oklahoman, invented the first shopping cart—his was the one without the bumpy wheel.

Famous Oklahomans include:
- Lon Chaney Jr (1906–1973), Oklahoma City; known for his roles in moster movies
- James Garner (1928–), Norman; born James Scott Baumgarner; served fourteen months in the Korean War; awarded the Purple Heart; starred in the television series *Maverick* from 1957 to 1960; in 1974, Garner starred in the television series *The Rockford Files* which was a remake of the former *Maverick* character, but this time as a modern-day private detective; many of the *Maverick* plats were re-used
- Ron Howard (1954–), Duncan; played the role of Opie Taylor on *Andy Griffith* and Richie Cunningham on *Happy Days*. His brother Clint (1959–), born in Burbank, CA was the little boy on *Andy Griffity* dressed in a cowboy outfit who offered a bite of his sandwich to passersby
- Chuck Norris (1940–), Ryan; born Carlos Ray Norris; an Air Policeman in the Air Force (1958–1962); stationed in Korea where he acquired the nickname Chuck and began studying Tang Soo Do; in 1969, made his acting debut in the Dean Martin

movie *The Wrecking Crew;* began filming *Walker, Texas Ranger* in 1993; has authored several Christian books

- Tony Randall (1920–2004), Tulsa; born Arthur Leonard Rosenberg; served during World War II, refusing an entertainment assignment with Special Services; on the television show *Mr. Peepers* he played the role of Harvey Weskit, the gymn teacher; 1970–1975, he starred in the television series *The Odd Couple*
- Dale Robertson (1923–), Harrah; born Dayle Lamoine Robertson; served during World War II; his is best remembered for the television series *Tales of Wells Fargo* in which he played the character Jim Hardie; from 1969–1972, he hosted the television series *Death Valley Days;* in 1981, he was in the original starring cast of *Dynasty* but his character disappeared after the first season; Will Rogers, Jr., gave him this advice, "Don't ever take a dramatic lesson. They will try to put your voice in a dinner jacket, and people like their hominy and grits in everyday clothes."
- Earl Grant (1931–1970), Oklahoma City; served in the U.S. Army during the Korean War; his first album, "Ebb Tide," was released in 1961; he recorded five singles and six more albums; he was killed instantly in an automobile accident in New Mexico while returning from an engagement in Juarez, Mexico; he was 39
- Patti Page (1927–), Claremore; born Clara Ann Fowler; the best-selling female artist of the 1950s; has sold over 100 million recordings; her signature song, "Tennessee Waltz," recorded in 1950, was one of the biggest-selling singles of the 20th century; she made the country charts in five separate decades; sustained her success amid the 1950s Rock and Roll era with such recordings as "Old Cape Cod," and "Allegheny Moon;" at age eighteen she was a regular on a fifteen-minute radio program at a Tulsa radio station; the show was sponsored by Page Milk Company; she was dubbed on the air as Patti Page
- Paul Harvey (1918–2009), Tulsa; born Paul Harvey Aurandt; served in the U.S. Army Air Forces during World War II; in September, 2008, he became the oldest syndicated radio personality in America; at a high school teacher's suggestion he began working at radio station KVOO in Tulsa cleaning the offices and studio and was eventually allowed to read the news and commercials; in 1951, he began broadcasting *Paul Harvey News and Comment*
- Sam Walton (1918–1992), Kingfisher; served in the U.S. Army during World War II; with a $20,000 loan and $5,000 he had saved up while in the army, he purchased a Ben Franklin variety store in Newport, Arkansas; the first Wal-Mart opened in 1962, in Rogers, Arkansas; Walmart is the world's largest retailer, the largest private employer in the world, and the largest grocery retailer in the United States
- Leroy Gordon Cooper, Jr. (1927–2004), Shawnee; grew up in Murray, KY; one of the original seven astronauts in Project Mercury; the first American to sleep in orbit; served during World War II

One of the youngest mayors elected in America was twenty-two-year-old Stephen Brinlee, 2007, in Wilburton, Latimer County, and ninteen-year-old John Tyler Hammons in Muskogee. He won over 70 per cent of the votes over a three-time incumbent mayor and was a freshman at the University of Oklahome when elected. Kenton (Cimarron County) is

92

one hundred fifty miles farther west than Magoun, (Lipscomb County) Texas.

Interesting names include: Adair; Adams; Adel; Afton; Albert; Alex; Alfalfa; Allen; Alpha (5 miles from Omega); America; Anchor; Anderson(2); Antlers; Apple; Arkoma (on the border with Arkansas); Asher; Ashland; Ballard; Barber; Battiest; Beaver; Bee; Bell; Bengal; Berlin; Bernice; Bessie; Big Cabin; Bigheart; Big Rocks; Billings; Bison; Black Bear; Blackgum; Blackjack; Bluejacket; Boggy Depot; Boise City; Boone; Boudinot; Bowlegs; Box; Boyd; Bradley; Bray; Breckinridge; Briartown; Briggs; Brink; Broken Arrow; Broken Bow; Bromide; Brooksville; Buffalo; Bug Tussle; Bull Hollow; Bunch; Burg; Burns Flat; Burt; Butler; Byng; Cache; Cairo; Calhoun; Camargo; Canadian; Canadian Fork; Caney; Caney Ridge; Carbon; Carlisle; Carpenter; Carson; Carter; Carter Nine; Carters Corner; Cartersville; Castle; Cedar; Cedars; Cedar Village; Cement; Center; Centerville; Centrahoma; Chance; Chattanooga; Cheek; Cherry Tree; Chewey; Chili; Cimarron City; Claremore (Patti Page); Clearview; Cleveland; Cloud Chief; Cloud Creek; Cloudy; Coal Creek; Cocklebur Flat; Cody; Cold Springs; Colony; Commerce; Cook; Cookietown; Copic Slab; Corn; Cornish; Corral Crossing; Cotton Valley; Cottonwood; Council Hill; Counts; Covington; Crescent; Crusher; Custer City; Dale; Dead Women Crossing; Deer Creek; Delaware; Denver; Dill City; Dirty Butter Creek; Divide; Dog Creek; Douglas; Dripping Springs; Drumright; Dry Creek; Duncan (Ron Howard *Opie Taylor*); Dundee; Eagle City; Eldorado; Elk City; Elliott; Elmwood; Empire City; England; Evening Shade; Fairview; Falls Creek; Fame; Fay; Felt; Fillmore; Fivemile Corner; Flint Creek; Flute Springs; Fogel (across the border from Fogel, AR); Foss; Four Mile Crossing; Frankfort; Freedom; Friendship; Frogville; Frost; Garland; Gas City; Gate; Gene Autry (name changed from Berwin in 1941 when Gene Autry bought a ranch and moved his rodeo livestock there); Goodlake (200 miles south of Booker, TX); Goodnight; Goodwater; Goodwin; Gotebo; Granite; Gray; Gray Horse; Grayson; Greasy; Green; Greenville; Gregory; Gypsy; Half Bank Crossing; Happy Land; Hardshorne; Hardy; Harrisburg; Harrison; Hatchetville; Haw Creek; Haydenville; Helena; Herd; Herman; Hickory; Hickory Hill; High Hill; Highway 9 Landing; Hogshooter; Hollow; Homestead; Hominy; Hoot Owl; Hoover; Hopkins; Horntown; Hunter; Hydro; Independence; Indiahoma; Indianapolis; Indian City; Indian Meadows; Indian Springs; Ironbridge; Iron Stob Corner; IXL; Jefferson; Jester; Jet; Jimtown; Johnson; Jumbo; Justice; Kansas; Kenton; Kingfisher; Kremlin; Last Chance; Lawrence; Lawrence Creek; Leader; Leedy (Darla Hood, *Our Gand Comedy*); Lexington; Liberty; Lima (Phyllis Diller); Limestone Gap; Lincoln; Lincolnville; Lindsay; Little Axe; Little Chief; Little City; Little Ponderosa; Loco; Locust Grove; Logan; Lone Chimney; Lone Grove; Lone Wolf; Long; Longtown; Lookout; Lost City; Loving; Loyal; Manchester; Maple; Marble City; Marshall; Martin; Mason; Mayfield; Maysville; McAlester; Miami; Midway; Midwest City; Mill Creek; Monroe; Moon; Morgans Corner; Morris; Morrison; Mouser; Mule Barn; Muse; Mustang; Mutual; Needmore; Nelson; Nichols Hills; Noble; Nobletown; Noel; Non; Norman (Harlow Wilcox); North Pole; Nowhere; Oak Ridge; Oaks; Oil Center; Oil City; Okay; Oklahoma City (Lon Chaney Jr.; 1935 parking meters first used); Old Retrop; Olive; Omega (5 miles from Alpah); Oneida; Ontario; Oologah (Will Rogers); Oriental; Orion; Orlando; Oscar;

Ottawa; Ozark; Page; Panama; Panther; Paoli; Paradise Hill; Paradise View; Parkersburg; Peachtree Crossing; Peavine; Pensacola; Peoria; Perry; Pharaoh; Piedmont; Pierce; Pine Knot Crossing; Pine Ridge; Pine Top; Pink; Pittsburg; Plainview; Player; Pleasant Grove; Pleasant Valley; Pond Creek; Porter; Post Oak; Prague (Jim Thorpe); Prattville; Pulaski; Pumpkin Center; Pyramid Corners; Quapaw; Ralph; Range; Rattan; Reagan; Redbird; Red Oak; Red Rock; Reed; Retrop (Porter, spelled backward); Richmond; Ripley; Rock Creek; Rock Island; Rocky; Rocky Ford; Rocky Mountain; Roll; Roosevelt; Rose; Rosedale; Russell; Russellville; Salina; Salt Fork; Sandbluff; Sand Creek; Santa Fe; Sapulpa; Savanna; Scott; Sedan; Sentinel; Sequoyah; Sevenmile Corner; Seven Oaks; Shady Grove; Shady Point; Shamrock; Shoals; Short; Silo; Silver City; Slapout; Slaughtersville; Slick; Smacker; Smith-Lee; Snake Creek; Snow; Sooner; Sparks; Spencer; Spring Creek; Springhill; Squaretop; Star; Sterling; Stillwater; Stillwell; St Louis; Stonebluff; Stonewall; Stoney Point; Stony Point; Story; Straight; Strawberry Spring; Stringtown; Strong City; Sturgis; Success; Sugar Creek; Sulphur; Sunkist; Sunrise; Sunset; Sunset Corner; Sunsweet; Sweetwater; Sycamore; Taft; Taylor; Taylor Corner Gin (cotton gin); Tenkiller; Texhoma (on the border with Texhoma, TX); The Holy City; The Village; Thompson Corner; Three-Way Corner; Ti; Tiger; Tip; Titanic; Todd; Torpedo; Trail; Trestle Ford; Tullahassee; Tupelo; Turkey Ford; Twin Oaks; Tyler; Union City; Union Valley; Unity; Victory; Walls; Warren; Washington; Wayne; Weathers; Weeks; Wheeless; Whippoorwill; White Bead; Whitebread; White Eagle; White Oak; Wildcat Point; Wildhorse; Willow; Willow View; Wilson; Winchester; Wolf; Woodford; Woods; Wynona; Yukon; Zincville;

OREGON - French for "hurricane." Statehood was February 14, 1859. The state nickname is "Beaver State." In 1778, an explorer used the name Oregon, rather than Ouragon, in journaling his trip. One living in Oregon is known as an Oregonian. James Cook explored the coast in 1778, searching for the Northwest Passage, a sea route connecting the Atlantic and Pacific Oceans through the Arctic regions of Canada. It was not successfully done until 1906. The Lewis and Clark expedition traveled through the region during their expedition to explore the Louisiana Purchase. After the United States agreed to jointly settle the Oregon Territory with the United Kingdom, it almost led to another war between the two nations, but the border dispute was settled at the 49th parallel and the Oregon Territory was officially organized in 1848. Crater Lake National Park in southern Oregon was made when the twelve thousand foot high Mount Mazama erupted. The lake receives its water supply from an average of forty-four feet of snowfall each year. At two thousand feet, it is the deepest lake in America but only the seventh deepest in the world. The "Old Man" of Crater Lake is a mountain hemlock log that has been floating upright in the lake for more than 100 years. Wind currents move the old man around the lake. Mount Hood is considered the Oregon volcano most likely to erupt.

Bly, Oregon, is the only place on American soil where death resulted from enemy action during World War II. From late 1944 to April, 1945, the Japanese released more than nine thousand balloons with attached bombs, hoping the winds would carry them across the ocean to the United States. An estimated one thousand actually reached North America, and on May 5, 1945, Elsie Mitchell and five children were killed outside the town of Bly by an explosion from one such device they found in the woods.

Famous Oreganders include:
- Dallas R. McKennon (1919–), La Grande; a voice actor whose best roles are that of Gumby, Archie, and Buzz Buzzard in the Woody Woodpecker cartoons; his best-known live action role is for that of Cincinnatus in the *Daniel Boone* television series starring Fes Parker

Interesting names include: Action; Adams; Adel; Advance; Albany; Alfalfa; Allegany; Aloha; Alpha; Alpine; Amsterdam; Anderson; Antelope; Antler; Arlington (Doc Severinsen); Artesian City; Asbestos; Ash; Ashland; Atlanta; Atomic City; Azalea; Barber; Barview (Coos County); Barview (Tillamook County); Beagle; Bear Creek; Beaver; Beaver Creek; Beaver Homes; Beaver Springs; Beech Creek; Bernice; Beverly Beach; Black Rock; Blitzen; Blue River; Boone; Boring; Bourbon; Boyd; Bradwood; Bridal Veil; Bridge; Brothers; Brown City; Brownsville; Browntown (ten miles from) Browntown; Bruce; Buchanan; Buckboard; Bucks Corners; Buena Vista; Bull Run; Bunker Hill; Burlington; Burns; Burnt Woods; Bush [Salem]; Cableville; Cake; Calloway; Camp Carson; Canary; Cannon Beach; Canyon City; Caribou City; Carroll; Carson; Cedar Flat; Cedar Mill; Central Point; Charleston; Charlestown; Chase; Cherry Grove; Cherryville; China Town; Christmas Valley; Chrome; Clear Creek; Clear Lake; Clearwater; Cleveland; Clover; Cold Springs; Columbine; Concord; Copper; Corbin; Corner; Cornucopia; Cottage Grove; Cottonwood; Courtrock; Cow Creek; Cracker City; Crane; Crescent; Crocus; Crow; Crowfoot; Crystal; Curtain; Dads Creek; Dallas; Dayton; Deadwood; Deerhorn; Deer Island; Denmark; Denver; Detour; Detroit; Diamond; Dixie; Dixon; Dollar; Douglas; Drain; Dry Creek; Dundee; Eagle Creek; Eagle Crest Corner; Eagle Point; Echo; Eddyville; Eden; Edwards; Eightmile; Eldorado; Elk City; Elkhead; Elkhorn; Elk Horn; Elkton; Elliott Prairie; Emigrant; English; Eugene; Evarts; Ewing; Fairbanks; Fair Oaks; Fall Creek; Falls City; Farewell Bend; Fern; Fern Corner; Fern Hill; Fir; Fishhawk; Five Corners; Five Points; Flora; Florence; Forest Grove; Fossil; Four Corners; Fourmile; Fox; French Lane; Friend; Frost Mill; Fulton; Gateway; Gem; George; Giveout; Gladtidings; Glasgow; Glide; Gold Beach; Gold Creek; Gold Hill; Gooseberry; Gooseberry Mountain; Government Camp; Grace; Grade; Grandview; Granite; Granite Hill; Granite Mountain; Grass Valley; Grave Creek; Gray; Greenback; Greenhorn; Greenleaf; Green Meadows; Greenville; Gregory; Grouse; Halfway; Hamilton; Hamlet; Happy Hollow; Happy Valley; Hardin; Hare; Harlan; Harmony; Harper; Harper Junction; Havana; Hayden; Hemlock; Hidaway Springs; High Rock; Hindman; Holland; Homestead; Hoover; Horseshoe Bend; Hot Lake; Hot Springs; Huntington; Huron; Idiot Creek; Igo; Independence; Indian Valley; Interlachen; Ireland Springs; Ironside; Island City; Jacksonville; Jamestown; Jean; Jefferson; Jimtown; Johnson; Juniper; Kansas City; Kettering; King Cole; Klondike; Knoxville; Laurel Grove; Leap; Lebanon; Lee; Lewis; Lexington; Liberal; Liberty; Lightning; Lime; Lincoln Beach; Lincoln City; Link; Little Alps; Little Valley; Lockit; Locust Grove; Loganville; Log Cabin; London; London Springs; Lone Pine; Lone Star; Lone Pine; Lone Star; Long Creek; Looking Glass; Lost Prairie; Lost River; Lovely; Love Station; Lower Bridge; Magic; Maple Grove; Maples; Margaret; Marion; Marion Forks;

Mason; Mayo; McKee; Meadow; Medical Springs; Medley; Meteor; Michigan; Midway; Military Crossing; Miller; Milwaukie; Mineral; Mink Creek; Mist; Mistletoe; Monitor; Monroe; Monument; Morgan; Morgan Landing; Mountain Home; Mount Vernon; Mule; Narrows; Nashville; Natal; Needy; Niagara; Nichols; Nixon; Nonpareil; Noon; Norway; Oak Grove; Oak Hills; Oak Springs; Oasis; Oceanside; Old Town; Ontario; Ordnance; Oregon City; Oregon Slope; Orient; Otter Rock; Oxbow; Pacific City; Page; Paisley; Panther Creek; Paradise; Paradise Park; Parkersburg; Paris; Park Place; Parliament; Peach; Peck; Peel; Pelican City; Pendleton; Perry; Persist; Phoenix; Pilot Rock; Pine; Pine City; Pine Hollow; Pine Ridge; Pioneer City; Pistol River; Pittsburg; Pleasant Hill; Pleasant Home; Pleasant Valley; Plum Trees; Plush; Poison Creek; Ponderosa; Poplar; Porter; Post; Prairie City; Prairie Creek; Princeton; Progress; Promise; Prospect; Quartz; Quartz Mountain; Rainbow; Range; Ranier; Redwood; Remote; Rhododendron; Rice Hill; Richmond; Riddle; Ridgeway; Ring; Ringtail Pine; Ripple; Ripplebrook; Rising River; Riverside; Roads End; Roberts; Rock Creek; Rock Point; Rockville; Rocky Ford; Rocky Point; Rogue Elk; Rogue River; Rome; Roots; Rosedale; Round Prairie; Rural; Rye Valley; Sailor; Salmon; Salmonberry; Salt Creek; Sand Hollow; Sargent Place; Seal Rock; Seaside; Selma; Service Creek; Shady; Shady Cove; Shale City; Silver Falls City; Silver Lake; Simpson; Sinks; Sisters; Sixers; Skull Spring; Smock; Snake; Snark; Snooseville Corner; Soda Springs; Sodaville; Sparks; Spray; Springfield; Spring Valley; Springwater; Stanton; Starvation Heights; Stavebolt; Steamboat; Stephens; Stone; St Paul; Strawberry; Sublimity; Sulphur Springs; Summerville; Summit; Sunnyside; Sunnyslope; Sunset; Sunset Beach; Sun Valley; Superior; Susanville; Swan; Swastika; Swedetown; Sweet Home; Swisshome; Table Rock; Talent; Tangent; Tanks; Tenmile; The Dalles; Thirtymile; Thompson; Thorn Hollow; Three Forks; Three Lynx; Three Rivers; Three Rocks; Three Springs; Timber; Timber Grove; Timbuktu; Tioga; Toledo; Tollgate; Tongue Point Village; Tophill; Trail; Tri-City; Triangle; Trout; Trout Creek; Tulsa; Twin Rocks; Twomile; Ucon; Umpqua; Union; Union Creek; Union Point; Unity; Upper Soda; Utopia; Virginia; Vistallas (10 miles from) Vistallas; Voltage; Wagontire; Warm Springs; Warren; Wayland; Webfoot; Wheatland; Whiskey Dick; Whitehill; White Pine; Whitewater; Wildwood; Williamsburg; Willowcreek; Willow Forks; Willow Springs; Winchester; Wind Rock; Winona; Winslow; Winston; Winterville; Witch Hazel; Wolf Creek; Wolverine; Wonder; Woods; Wood Village; Wren; Zigzag

PENNSYLVANIA – Meaning "Penn's Woods." Statehood was December 12, 1787. The state nickname is "Keystone State." It has been known as the Keystone State since 1802, based on its central location among the original Thirteen Colonies. It was a keystone state economically, having industry common to the north (Conestoga wagons and rifles) and agriculture common to the south, producing feed, food, and tobacco. In 1681, Charles II granted a land charter to William Penn to pay a debt of £20,000 ($30 million) owed to William's father, Admiral Penn. This was one of the largest land grants to an individual in history. The land included present-day Delaware and Pennsylvania. It was called Pennsylvania, meaning Penn's Woods, in honor of Admiral Penn. William Penn, who had wanted his province to be named Sylvania, was embarrassed at the change, feeling that people would think he had named it after himself, but King Charles would not rename the grant. Penn established a government with two innovations that were copied in the New World, namely, the county commission and freedom of religious conviction. The Pennsylvania colony made its own paper money which is generally regarded as the most successful currency experiment by any government that ever existed. Banjamin had a hand in creating this currency.

The Pennsylvania Turnpike between Somerset and Bedford is the oldest stretch of interstate in America. James Buchanan, Lancaster, was the only bachelor president of the United States. Pennsylvania ranks number one in the growing and selling of mushrooms. The term "Dutch," when referring to Pennsylvania Dutch, means "German" rather than "Netherland." State cookie: chocolate chip. The state toy is Slinky.

Pennsylvania was the second state but it was first in many other ways, including the.....
first public school in the Colonies, 1698, Philadelphia
first life insurance company, 1717, Presbyterian Minister's Fund
first public library, 1731, Philadelphia
first volunteer fire department, 1736, Philadelphia
first hospital in America, 1751, Philadelphia
   Continental Marines established, 1755, U.S. Marines
first flag of the United States sewn by Betsy Ross, 1777
first university in America,1779
first daily newspaper, 1784, Philadelphia
first stock exchange, 1790
first United States Mint, 1792
first turnpike, 1795, between Philadelphia and Lancaster
first wire cable suspension bridge, 1816
first electrically-powered street car, 1826, Scranton
first steam locomotive to run on railroad tracks in the U.S., 1829
first accordion, 1854
first pharmacy school, 1871
first commercially packaged toilet paper, 1857
first pencil with an attached eraser, 1858
first oil well, 1859
first pretzel factory, 1861
first zoo, 1874
first X-ray taken, 1874, Philadelphia
first World's Fair in America, 1876
first department store, 1877, Wannamaker's
first typewriter, 1881
first taxi service, 1884, Philadelphia
first chlorine discovery, 1887
first revolving door, 1888
Ferris wheel, 1893, George Ferris
first escalator, 1901, Philadelphia

first banana split, 1904
first Flag Day, 1912, Allentown
world's first gas station, 1913
first Mother's Day, 1914, Ann Jarvis of Philadelphia
first Thanksgiving Day Parade, 1919, Philadelphia
first commercial radio station, 1920, KDKA, Pittsburgh
First Bingo, 1924
first bubblegum, 1928, Philadelphia
first paper towels, 1931, Arthur Scott of Philadelphia
first hard surfaced runway, 1930, Allegheny County
Zippo lighter, 1932, Bradford
PSFS Building (Philadelphia Saving Fund Society) was the first totally air-conditioned
  building, 1932; it was also the first modern skyscraper
first toll road, 1940, Pennsylvania Turnpike
first Slinky, 1945
first cable television system, 1948
first polio vaccine, 1952
first diabetic "dip and read" tests, 1956
first automotive bridge to be named for a woman, 1976, the Betsy Ross Bridge,
  Philadelphia;
first license plate with a website address, 2000

The City Hotel in Sunbury, was the first building to be lit by Edison's three-wire system; the hotel's name was changed to The Hotel Edison

Philadelphia Cream Cheese was first made in Chester, New York in 1872. The product was so named because, at that time, top-quality food products often originated in, or were associated with, Philadelphia and were often referred to as being "Philadelphia quality."

The first radio station in America, KDKA. On November 2, 1920, Leo Rosenberg broadcast the returns of the Harding-Cox presidential race from the studios of the station. The station was a wooden shack on the roof of a Pittsburgh factory. KDKA also broadcast the first baseball game and football game. The first sports announcer, Harold Arlin, treated the new medium with such reverence that he often wore a tuxedo while on the air.

In August, 1928 Walter Diemer, an accountant with the Fleer gum company who had been conducting gum experiments on the side, put one of his concoctions into his mouth and blew a large bubble that easily peeled off his face, unlike other bubble gums. That discovery became Dubble Bubble Gum, first sold on December 26, 1928. Incidentally, pink is the predominant bubble gum color because that is the only food coloring Diemer had around when he first invented the chew.

Signers of the Declaration of Indepencence include: George Clymer, Benjamin Franklin,

Robert Morris, John Morton, George Ross, Benjamin Rush, James Smith, George Taylor, and James Wilson.

Famous Pennsylvanians include:
- Louisa May Alcott (1832–1888), Germantown [northwest Philadelphia]; author of <u>Little Women</u> series
- Charles Darrow (1879–1967), Germantown [northwest Philadelphia]; invented Monopoly
- Marion Lorne MacDougall (1883–1968), West Pittston; played the role of Mrs. Gurney, an absent-minded English teacher, on *Mr. Peepers*
- Lionel Barrymore (1878–1954), Philadelphia; elder brother of Ethel and John Barrymore
- Bill Cosby (1937–), Philadelphia; maintains homes in Shelburne, MA and Cheltenham [Philadelphia], PA
- Broderick Crawford (1911–1986), Philadelphia; played Chief Dan Matthews in *Highway Patrol,* 1955–1959; his parents were Lester Crawford and Helen Broderick
- W.C. Fields (1880–1946), Darby; born William Claude Dunkenfield; started out as a jugler and received world-wide acclaim; some of his famous quotes are: "I am free of all prejudice. I hate everyone equally"
- Shirley Jones (1934–), Charleroi; played Shirley Partridge on *Partridge Family* where her actual step-son (David Cassidy) played her TV son Keith
- Gene Kelly (1912–1996), Pittsburgh; appeared in the musicals *An American inParis*, 1951, and *Singin' in the Rain*, 1952
- Jack Klugman (1922–), Philadelphia; starred in the original Broadway production of *The Odd Couple* as well as on the TV series
- Mr. Rogers (1928–2003), Latrobe; born Frederick McFeely Rogers; ordained as a Presbyterian minister
- James Stewart (1908–1997), Indiana; began acting while attending Princeton University and was a head cheerleader; he rose from private to colonel in four years and finally to the rank of brigadier general, USAF Reserves
- Frankie Avalon (1939–) Philadelphia; had thirty-one singles on the Billboard charts; still tours with two sons
- Perry Como (1912–), Canonsburg; was the seventh son of a seventh son; opened a barber shop, 1933; was the first artist to have ten records sell more than one million copies; in 1950, starred on *The Perry Como Show*, a fifteen-minute show on Monday, Wednesday and Friday after the CBS evening news
- Carl Betz (1921–1978), Pittsburgh; served during World War II; best known for the role of Dr. Alex Stone on the television series *The Donna Reed Show* from 1958 to 1956
- Bobby Vinton (1935–), Cannonsburg; born Stanley Robert Vintula, Jr.; has a degree in music composition from Duquesne University; served in the U. S. Army; "Roses Are Red" was his first hit; his second hit, "Blue Velvet," was also a hit for

Tony Bennett in 1951; after Epic Records dropped him from his contract, he recorded and number three hit, "My Melody of Love," sung partially in Polish; he hosted *TheBobby Vinton Show* from 1975 to 1978

- Stephen Foster (1826–1864), Lawrenceville; "My Old Kentucky Home" was originally titled "Poor Uncle Tom, Good Night!;" the song was published in 1853, and adopted by the Kentucky General Assembly as the state song in 1928
- Daniel Boone (1734–1820), Oley Valley, Berks County; in 1775 he blazed the ilderness Trail through the Cumberland Gap into Kentucky; founded Boonesborough (Clark County, KY), one of the first English-speaking settlement west of the Appalachian Mountains; it is estimated that within the next twenty-five years two hundred thousand people enteed Kentucky by following the trail he blazed; in 1782, he fought in the Battle of Blue Licks, one of the last battles of the Revolutionary War
- Bil Keane 1922–), Philadelphia; created "The Family Circus," first published in 1960; taught himself to draw; served in the U. S. Army from 1942 to1945
- John Wanamaker (1838–1922), Philadelphia; United States postmaster general, 1889–1893; credited by his friends with introducing the first commemorative stamp, and many efficiencies to the postal pervice; the first to make plans for the free rural postal service in the United States; opened his first store at Sixth and Market Streets in 1861; considered to be the father of modern advertising; Wanamaker's is thought the first department store in Philadelphia; in 1896 he opened a store in New York City; he opened other stores in London and Paris; his country estate was the Lindenhurst Mansion in Cheltenham on York Road; from 1904 to 1914, he financed Anna Jarvis' successful campaign to have a national Mother's Day holiday officially recognized
- William Wrigley, Jr. (1861–1932), Philadelphia
- Robert Aitken (1734–1802), born in Scotland, lived in Philadelphia; first to publish a Bible in America
- Betsy Ross (1752–1836), Philadelphia; said to have sown the first American flag which incorporated stars representing the first thirteen colonies
- Fabian (1943–), Philadelphia; born Fabiano Anthony Forte; he was sitting on the front steps of his house crying because an ambulance had just taken away his sick father; the co-owners of Chancelor Records asked him if he wanted to get into the record business; being the older of three brothers he took the chance to financially help out his family; he charted eleven hit singles in the Billboard Hot 100 and appeared in over thirty films
- Eddie Fisher (1928–), Philadelphia; Served in the U.S. Army in Korea from 1952–1953; appeared on *Arthur Godfrey's Talent Scouts*; from 1950–1956, he had seventeen songs in the Top 10 and thirty-five songs in the Top 40
- Sebastian S. Kresge (1867–1966), Bald Mountain near Wilkes Barre; in 1897, he started in a five and ten cent story with James McCrory in Memphis, Tennessee; in 1899, he co-founded a store with Charles Wilson; in 1912, he incorporated the S. S. Kresge Corporation with eighty-five stores; by 1924, he was worth nearly $400 million; the first Kmart opened in 1962

- Earl "Fatha" Hines (1903–1983), Duquesne [Pittsburgh]; pianistwho helped shape the history of jazz; played jazz "before the word 'jazz' was ever invented"

Four of the youngest mayors elected in America were eighteen-year-old Jeffrey Dunkel, 2003, in Mount Carbon, Schuylkill County, nineteen-year-old Christopher Portman, 2002, Mercer, Mercer County, twenty-two-year-old Robert Prah, 2006, Smithton, Westmorland County, and eighteen-year-old Christopher Seeley, 2005, Linesville, Crawford County. Twenty-year-old G. Michael Peccon, 2002, Carmichaels, Greene County, was originally appointed by the council, ran for office and received 85% of the votes making him the youngest re-elected mayor in Pennsylvania.

Interesting names include: Abbott (near Costello); Aberdeen; Advance; Aladdin; Alaska; Albert; Alice; Allen; Allentown (Lee Iacoca); Ambler; Amsterdam; Anderson; Andreas; Angels; Anise; Arbor; Asylum; Atlantic; Bagdad; Bala Cynwyd {KIN-wid} (two separate towns that USPS combined to form one name); Bald Eagle; Bangor; Basket; Bear Creek; Bear Swamp; Beaver; Beaver Dam; Beaver Falls (Joe Namath); Beaver Meadows; Beaver Springs; Beaver Valley; Beech Grove; Beechwood; Belfast; Benjamin; Bens Creek; Bernice; Beverly; Beverly Heights; Beverly Hills; Big Beaver; Big Bend; Big Mountain; Big Pond; Big Spring; Bills Place; Birch; Bird-in-Hand; Birmingham; Black; Black Ash; Black Diamond; Black Gap; Black Mountain; Black Ridge; Black Walnut; Bloomington; Blue Ball; Blue Bell; Blue Goose; Blue Jay; Blue Knob; Bogus Corners; Boiling Springs; Bordertown; Boyd; Bradley Junction; Bradleytown; Breakneck; Briggsville; Brooklyn; Brownsville; Bruceton; Buckhorn; Buena Vista; Buffalo; Buffalo Run; Bullion; Burlington; Burning Bush; Burning Well; Burnt Cabins; Burrows; Bute; Buttermilk Falls; Butternut Grove; Buttonwood; Buzz; California; Camargo; Camp Hill [Harrisburg]; Camptown; Cannelton; Cannonsburg (Perry Como; "Catch a Falling Star" was the first ever Gold Record, 1958); Canoe Camp; Carbon; Carlisle; Carsontown; Carsonville; Carter; Carter Camp; Cashtown; Catfish; Ceasetown; Cedar Grove; Cedar Hill; Cedar Pines; Cedar Run; Cedar Springs; Centennial; Centerville; Central; Central City; Cereal; Chaintown; Challenge; Chaneysville; Charleroi (Shirley Jones); Charleston; Cheesetown; Cheltenham; Cherry City; Cherry Corner; Cherry Flats; Cherry Grove; Cherry Hill; Cherry Mills; Cherry Ridge; Cherry Run; Cherry Tree; Cherry Valley; Chestnut Grove; Chestnut Hill; Chestnut Ridge; Chickentown; Christmas; Chrome; Clay; Clinton; Clover; Coal Center; Coal City; Coal Hollow; Coal Junction; Coal Run; Coaltown; Cocolamus; Coffeetown; Cold Point; Cold Run; Cold Spring; Collegeville; Columbia; Columbus; Compass; Concord; Conestoga; Confluence; Congo; Congress Hill; Congruity; Cook Tomb; Cool Spring; Coon Corners; Coon Hunter; Corner Store; Costello (near Abbott); Cottage; Cottage Grove; Cottles Corner; Cotton Town; County Line; Coupon; Covert; Covington; Cranberry; Creamery; Crete; Crooked Creek; Crumb; Crystal Springs; Cyclone; Cypher; Dale; Dallas; Dark Water; Darlington; Day; Dayton; Defiance; Delaware Water Gap; Dice; Divide; Dividing Ridge; Dogtown; Donation; Douglas; Dresher; Drinker; Drums; Dry Tavern; Dublin; Duck Run; Duquesne [Pittsburgh] Earl "Fatha" Hines); Dutch Corner; Dutch Hill; Eagle Point; Eau Claire; Echo; Economy; Eden; Edenburg; Edinburg; Edna Number One; Edna Number Two; Effort; Egypt; Eighty Four; Elephant, Eleven Mile;

Elizabeth; Elizabethtown; Elkin; Emporium; Equinunk; Evansville; Ewingsville; Excelsior; Experiment; Factoryville; Fades; Fairbanks; Falls Creek; Farmers; Fayette; Fearnot; Federal; Fern; Filetown; Fillmore; Finch Hill; First Fork; Five Corners; Five Forks; Five Locks; Five Points; Flat Rock; Flatwoods; Flora; Foot of Ten; Forest Lake; Fort Washington; Fountain Springs; Four Corners; Four Points; Fox Hill; Franklin; Fredericksburg; French Settlement; Frenchtown; Friendsville; Frisbie; Frogtown; Frostproof; Fruittown; Furlong; Gallows Hill; Garden City; Gardner; Georgetown; Georgeville; Germans; German Settlement; Germantown [Philadelphia] (Louisa Mae Alcott); Germany; Girard; Glasgow; Glass City; Glen Campbell; Gobbler Knob; Gold; Gold Mine; Good Intent; Good Spring; Granite Hill; Grant; Gravity; Gray; Greece City; Greenback; Greenland; Greenville; Gregory; Grindstone; Grover; Gum Tree; Hamburg; Hancock; Happy Valley; Harlan; Harlem; Harper Tavern; Harrisburg (Nancy Kulp); Harrison; Harrow; Hatboro; Heidelberg; Hellertown; Hemlock; Henderson; Henry Clay; Hermit Spring; Hershey; Hickory; Hickory Grove; Hollywood; Home; Hometown; Honey Brook; Honey Creek; Honey Grove; Honey Hole; Hoover; Hop Bottom; Hungry Hollow; Hunter; Huntsville; Idaho; Imperial; Independence; Indiana (James Stewart); Indian Creek; Indian Crossing; Indian Head; Indian Orchard; Inez; Intercourse; Irishtown; Ironton; Irvine; Jackson; Jacksonville; Jamestown; Japan; Jeanville; Jefferson; Jersey Shore (120 miles west of the New Jersey state line); Jim Thorpe; Jimtown; Jobs Corners; Jo Jo; Jugtown; Juniata; Kendall; Kennedy; Keystone; King of Prussia; Kissimmee; Klondike; Knox; Knoxville; Laboratory; Larue; Laurel Grove; Laurel Hill; Laurel Lake; Laurel Mountain; Laurel Park; Laurel Run; Laurel Summit; Lawrenceburg; Lebanon; Lemon; Liberty; Library; Limerick; Lime Ridge; Lime Rock; Limestone; Lincoln; Litchfield; Little Hope; Little Jack Corners; Liverpool; Lock Haven; Logan Mills; Logansport; Logantown; Loganville; London; Lookout; Lovely; Lucerne; Lumber City; Madison; Madisonville; Manhattan; Maple Grove; Maple Hill; Maple Shade; Maple Summit; Marble; Margaret; Marion; Mars; Marshall; Marshall Hollow; Marshallton; Marsh Creek; Marsh Hill; Marysville; Mason; Matthews Run; Maysville; Mechanicsburg; Mechanicsville; Mercer; Metal; Mexico; Middletown; Milan; Mineral Point; Minister; Mixtown; Monroe; Montgomery; Monument; Moon; Morgan; Morgan Hill; Morgantown; Morningside; Morris Run; Morrisville; Moscow; Mount Misery; Mt Air; Mt Airy; Mt Morris; Muddy Creek; Mud Run; Muhlenberg; Mulberry Center; Munster; Murray; Mustard; Mutual; Napier; Nay Aug; Nectarine; Needful; Needmore; Nelson; Neversink; New Castle; Newfoundland; New Philadelphia; Newport; Niagara; Ninepoints; Nixon; Nolo; North East; Northumberland; NuMine; Nuremberg; Oak Grove; Oak Hill; Oak Shade; Oak Tree; Ohioview (near) Ohioville; Ohl; Oil City; Oklahoma; Ono; Ontario; Opp; Orange; Oriental; Oriole; Outlet; Overshot; Owl Hollow; Owls Nest; Paint; Paisley; Palm; Palo Alto; Pancake; Panic; Panther; Paoli; Paradise; Patience; Peach Bottom; Peanut; Pearl; Pecan; Peru; Philadelphia (Bill Cosby; W. C. Fields; Grace Kelly; Sherman Helmsley; Ed Winn); Picture Rocks; Pierce; Pigs Ear; Pikeville; Pillow; Pine; Pine City; Pine Flats; Pine Grove; Pine Mill; Pine Run; Pine Summit; Pine Swamp; Pine Top; Pine Valley; Pink; Pleasant Hill; Pleasant View; Plum; Polk; Porky; Possum Hollow; President; Primrose; Progress; Promised Land; Prospect; Prosperity; Pulaski; Punxsutawney; Purchase Line; Puzzletown; Quakake; Quaker City; Quakertown; Quarryville; Quecreek; Queen; Queen

City; Queens Run; Quicks Bend; Quicktown; Quiet Dell; Quiggleville; Racine; Railroad; Raven Creek; Raytown; Red Bank; Red Barn; Redbird; Red Bridge; Red Cross; Red Hill; Red Hot; Red Lion; Red Mill; Red Oak; Red Rock; Red Run; Red Schoolhouse Corner; Reduction; Reed; Reliance; Rembrant; Republic; Revere; Richmond; Rich Valley; Ricketts; Ringing Hill; Ripple; Riverside; Rochester; Rolling Stone; Rome; Roslyn; Rough and Ready; Roulette; Round Head; Roundtop; Rural Valley; Russell; Russellville; Sandy Hook; Savage; Scab Hill; Scalp Level; Schubert; Scotch Hill; Scotch Hollow; Scotland; Scott; Sergeant; Seven Points; Seven Springs; Seven Stars; Seven Valleys; Shade Valley; Shadow Shuttle; Shamrock; Sharpsburg; Shaytown; Shenandoah (Tommy & Jimmy Dorsey); Silver Creek; Silver Lake; Singersville; Sinking Spring; Sistersville; Skytop; Slabtown; Slate Run; Slate Valley; Slippery Rock; Smithland; Smoketown; Snow Hill Falls; Snow Shoe; Somerset; Speedwell; Split Rock; Spring Brook; Spring Creek; Springfield; Spring Garden; Spring Hill; Spring Mills; Spruce; Spruce Creek; Spruce Hill; Square Corner; Squirrel Hill; Standing Stone; Stanton; Starlight; State College; State Line; Station; Sterling; Stevens; St George; Still Creek; Stillwater; Stiltz; Strawberry Ridge; Stump Creek; Sudan; Sugarcreek; Sugar Grove; Sugar Hill; Sugar Run; Sulphur Springs; Summit; Sunflower; Sunnyside; Sunrise; Sunset Valley; Sunshine; Sun Valley; Swamproot; Swede Hill; Sweden; Sweet Valley; Sweetwater; Swiftwater; Sycamore; Tallyho; Taylor; Telescope; Ten Mile; Texas Corner; Thompson; Thompson No 1; Thompsons Mills; Three Mile; Time; Tingley; Tioga; Tippecanoe; Todd; Top; Torpedo; Trade City; Transfer; Triumph; Trooper; Tuna; Tunnelhill; Turkeyfoot; Tyler; Ulysses; Union City; Union Hill; Union Valley; Universal; Utahville; Valencia; Van Buren; Vanilla; Venango; Venice; Vineyard; Walnut (twelve miles from Walnut Grove); Walnut Bottom; Walnut Grove (twelve miles from Walnut); Warren; Warsaw; Washington; Washington Square; Webster; West Liberty; Whig Hill; White; White Deer; White House; White Oak; White Pine; Whitesburg; White Springs; Wigwam; Williamsburg; Willow Grove; Willow Hill; Willow Springs; Wilson; Wilsons Corner; Wilsonville; Windsor Castle; Wolfs Corner; Woodchoppertown; Wyoming; Yellow House; Yellow Spring; Yukon; Zenners; Zeno; Zerbe; Zerby

RHODE ISLAND – Named after the Greek island. Statehood was May 29, 1790. The state nickname is "Ocean State." It is the smallest state by area, the state with the longest name, and it is not an island. It was the first of the original Thirteen Colonies to declare independence from British rule, starting the American Revolution. It was also the last of the original Thirteen Colonies to ratify the Constitution. The first bloodshed of the American Revolution took place in Rhode Island. During the Civil War, Rhode Island provided over twenty-five thousand Union troops. During World War I, Rhode Island furnished 28,900 troops.

The total square mileage is 1,214. However, with a population of just over one million, the density ratio is one thousand residents per square mile. Rhode Island is mostly flat with no real mountains. The state officially adopted the nickname, "The Ocean State" because about ten percent of the inland area is covered by salt water and no resident is more than thirty minutes from the ocean.

Rhode Island features the highest number of coffee/donut shops per capita in the country, with over one hundred Dunkin' Donuts locations in the state. If you order regular coffee, it comes with cream and sugar already added. The Official State Drink is coffee milk. Instead of adding chocolate syrup to milk, coffee syrup is added. This unique syrup was invented in the state and is bottled and sold in most Rhode Island supermarkets. Wieners, sometimes called "gaggers" or "weenies," are smaller than a standard hot dog but are covered in a meat sauce, chopped onions, mustard, and celery salt. Submarine sandwiches are called "grinders." "Dynamites" are similar to a sloppy Joe. Rhode Island milkshakes are called "cabinets." Spinach pies are similar to a calzone but filled with seasoned spinach instead. New England clam chowder is white, Manhattan clam chowder is red, but Rhode Island clam chowder is clear. A clam cake is a deep fried ball of buttery dough with bits of chopped clam inside.

There are thirty-nine cities and towns in Rhode Island. Providence is home to First Baptist Church, the oldest Baptist church in America, founded by Roger Williams in 1638. The first synagogue was founded in Newport in 1763. The nation's first nine-hole golf course was completed in Newport in 1890. The Rhode Island State House was the first building in America with an all-marble dome, completed in 1901. The Newport Bridge, a suspension bridge, is the longest bridge in New England. Its overall length is 11,247 feet and the towers reach 400 feet above the surface of the water; the roadway is 215 feet above the water's surface.

Signers of the Declaration of Independence include: William Ellery and Stephen Hopkins.

Famous Rhode Islanders include:
- Norm Abram (1950–); born in Rhode Island and reared in Massachusetts; *This Old House* began airing in 1979; on the television situation comedy *Home mprovement*, Tim Allen played the part of Tim Taylor, a character inspired by Bob Vila and Richard Karn played the part of Al Borland, a character inspired by Norm Abram
- Nelson Eddy (1901–1967), Providence; he was "discovered" by Hollywood when he substituted at the last minute for the noted diva Lotte Lehmann, at a sold-out concert in Los Angeles in February, 1933; he scored a professional triumph with eighteen curtain calls; several film offers immediately followed; in 1935, he sang for the first time with Jeanette McDonald; John Kenneth Hilliard, a sound engineer backstage at MGM from 1933 to 1942, reported in 1981, that though Eddy and McDonald were a screen couple, they "hated each other with a vengence"
- George M. Cohan (1878–1942), Providence; a baptismal certificate indicated that he was born on July 3, but the Cohan family always insisted George was "born on the Fourth of July;" by his teens he was well known as one of the stage's best male dancers and he also started writing original skits and songs for the family act in both vaudeville and minstrel shows; soon he was writing professionally, selling his first songs to a national publisher in 1893; Cohan has his first Broadway hit in 1904, which introduced his tunes, "Give My Regards to Broadway" and "The Yankee Doodle Boy;" he published nearly fifteen hundred original songs

- Oliver Hazard Perry (1785–1819), South Kingston; an officer in the U.S. Navy who served in the War of 1812; on September 10, 1813, Perry's fleet defended against an attacking British fleet at the Battle of Lake Erie; during the battle Perry's flagship was destroyed and Perry rowed a half mile through heavy gunfire to transfer command to the *Niagara*, carrying his battle flag which read, "DONT GIVE UP THE SHIP [*sic*], the famous final words of Captain James Lawrence; his battle report to William Henry Harrison after victory is famous: "We have met the enemy and they are ours…"; Perry County, KY and its county seat, Hazard, were named for him

Interesting names include: Arctic; Black Plain; Charlestown; Cherry Valley; Chopmist; Cooks Corner; Cumberland; Cumberland Hill; Darlington; Diamond Hill; Fountain Spring; Frenchtown; Fruit Hill; Galilee (three-fourths mile from Jerusalem); Garden City; Green Hill; Greenville; Harmony; Harriet; Hog Island; Homestead; Hopkins Mills; Jackson; Jamestown; Jerusalem (3/4 mile from Galilee); Kettle Corner; Laurel Hill; Liberty; Lime Rock; Lincoln; Middletown; Moosehorn Corner; Moscow; Newport; Nichols Corner; Nooseneck; Oak Valley; Pawtucket; Pine Hill; Places Corner; Plum Point; Primrose; Providence; Quonochontaug; Rice City; Richmond; River View; Rocky Brook; Rocky Point; Round Top; Salyersville; Silver Spring; Spring Grove; Spring Lake; Stillwater; Summit; Tarbox Corner; Tug Hollow; Warren; Washington; Watch Hill; Whitehall; Woods Corner; Wyoming

SOUTH CAROLINA – Named after King Charles, I. Statehood was May 23, 1788. The state nickname is "Palmetto State." The Province of South Carolina, one of the original Thirteen Colonies, revolted against British rule leading into the American Revolution. The state is named after King Charles I of England, Scotland and Ireland. *Carolus* is Latin for Charles. The colony of Carolina was settled by English settlers, mostly from Barbados. The Carolina upcountry was largely settled by Scots-Irish immigrants from Pennsylvania and Virginia. The formal colony of "The Carolinas" split into two parts in 1712. South Carolina became a royal colony in 1729. The state declared its independence from Great Britain and set up its own government in March, 1776, but became the eighth state in May, 1788. South Carolina was the first state to secede from the Union to form the Confederate States of America in December, 1860. In April, 1861, Confederate batteries began shelling Fort Sumter and the Civil War had begun. African Americans make up the largest ancestry group in South Carolina, thirty percent.

Signers of the Declaration of Independence include: Thomas Heyward, Thomas Lynch, Arthur Middleton, and Edward Rutledge.

Famous South Carolinians include:
- Bill Anderson (1937–), Columbia; holds a degree in journalism from the University of Georgia; released more than forty studio albums; thirty-six singles have reached the Top Ten; in 1965, he appeared on the game show *To Tell the Truth*.

According to the affidavit read at the beginning of his segment, Bill was at the time "generally considered to be the top composer of country music in the nation." Kitty Carlisle asked, "Why are you wearing this costume?" After looking down at his brightly decorated suit, he deadpanned, "Well, its all I had."

- James Brown (1933–2006), Barnwell; known as "Godfather of Soul;" began his professional music career in 1953, and continued to score hits through the 1980s
- Chubby Checker (1941–), Spring Gulley; born Ernest Evans; grew up in south Philadelphia where one of his classmates was Fabiano Forte (Fabian); after school Evans would entertain customers at his various jobs, including Fresh Farm Poultry on 9th Street with songs and jokes, and it was his boss who gave him the name "Chubby;" the store owner and his friend arranged for Chubby to do a private recording for Dick Clark; Clark's wife asked Evans what his name was; "Well, my friends call me 'Chubby;'" since he had just finished a Fats Domino impression, she smiled and said, "As in Checker?" That little play on words ("chubby" meaning fat and "checkers" like dominos) got an instant laugh and the name stuck
- "Dizzy" Gillespie (1917–1993), Cheraw; born John Birks Gillespie; started to play the piano at age four; played with such orchestras as Cab Calloway, Ella Fitzgerald, and Earl "Fatha" Hines; his trademark trumpet had the bell bent up at a forty-five degree angle which came quite by accident at a job in 1953; the constriction at the bend altered the tone and Gillespie liked the effect
- Andrew Jackson (1767–1845), Waxhaws area on the North and South Carolina border; seventh president of the United States; at age thirteen became a courier in the Revolutionary War; he and his brothers were British prisoners of war where they nearly starved to death; he was the last American president to have been a veteran of the American Revolution and the second president to have been a prisoner of war (General Washington was captured by the French in the French and Indian War); Jackson's portrait appears on the twenty dollar bill, but it has also appeared on the $5, $10, $50, and $10,000 bills
- Eartha Kitt (December 25, 1927–2008), Columbia; recorded "Santa Baby;" played Cat Woman for the third season of the 1960s televlision series *Batman*; she spoke French fluently
- Peggy Parish (1927–1988), Manning; author of the children's story series Amelia Bedelia; after her sudden death, her nephew, Herman Parish, continued the series
- Vanna White (1957–), North Myrtle Beach; born Vanna Marie Rosich; she first appeared on *Wheel of Fortune* in 1982

Interesting names include: Allen; Anderson; Argyle; Ashland; Back Swamp; Bath; Baton Rouge; Battlecreek; Beech Island; Bell Town; Berea; Berlin; Beverly; Birdtown; Blossom; Blue Brick; Blue Heaven; Blue Ridge; Boiling Springs; Bowling Green; Boyd; Bradley; Brick House; Brooksville; Brownsville; Buffalo; Bunker Hill; Bush River; Calhoun; Calhoun Falls; Calhoun Mill; Campbell; Campton; Cane Brake; Carlisle; Carolina; Carters Crossroads; Cartersville; Cash; Cashville; Cedar Creek; Cedar Grove; Cedar Rock; Cedar Springs; Cedar Swamp; Centenary; Central; Charity; Charleston; Cheddar; Cherry Hill; Chestnut Springs; Chick Springs; Chisolm; Clear Pond; Clearwater; Cleveland; Clinton;

Clover; Cold Point; Columbia; Cook Corner; Cool Spring; Coward; Crescent; Cross Roads; Cumberland; Daisy; Dale; Denmark; Denver; Dog Bluff; Douglas; Douglass; Dover; Dry Branch; Due West; Edwards; Estill; Eureka; Evergreen; Fair Play; Fairview; Farewell Corner; Filbert; Fingerville; Finland; Five Forks; Five Points; Flat Rock; Flat Shoals; Fleet; Florence; Forest Lake; Fork; Four Holes; Four Mile; Foxtown; Friendship; Fudges; Fulton; Garden City; Gary; Georgetown; Germantown; Giant; Goose Creek; Grace; Green Bay; Green Hill; Green Pond; Green Sea; Greenville; Grover; Guess; Haddock; H and B Junction; Hamburg; Hancock; Hand; Harmony; Harmony Hill; Harper Crossroads; Healing Springs; Health Springs; Hickory Grove; Hickory Hill; Hickory Tavern; High Point; Hogeye Crossroads; Hollow Creek; Holly Hill; Holly Ridge; Holly Springs; Hollywood; Honey Hill; Hopkins; India Hook; Iron Crossroads; Isle of Palms; Italy; Jackson; Jamestown; Jefferson; Kensington; Ketchuptown; Kings Creek; Klondike; La France; Lake City; Lancaster; Laurel Hill; Lebanon; Lexington; Liberty; Liberty Hill; Lima; Limehouse Station; Limerick; Limestone; Little Africa; Little Mountain; Little River; Little Rock; Little Texas; Little Town; Live Oak; Lodge; Lone Oak; Lone Star; Long Creek; Longtown; Lookout Mountain; Lucknow; Madison; Maplewood; Marion; Martin; Marydell; Mascot; Mayo; Maysville; Mayo Mills; Mechanicsville; Meeting Street; Merchant; Mexico; Midway; Monarch; Montgomery; Monticello; Morgan; Morningside; Morrisville; Mountain Rest; Mountain View; Mulberry; Newport; Nichols; Nine Times; Ninety-Six; North; Norway; Oak Grove; Oak Ridge; Oak View; Oats; Ogden; Old House; Old Joe; Orangeburg; Palmetto; Paris; Park Place; Pee Dee; Pendleton; Phoenix; Picket Post; Pimlico; Pine Grove; Pine Ridge; Pineville; Play Cards; Pleasant Hill; Pleasant Lane; Pleasant Valley; Plum Branch; Polecat Landing; Pond Town; Ponpon; Poplar Forks; Poplar Hill; Poplar Springs; Possum Corner; Poverty Hill; Princeton; Promised Land; Prosperity; Providence; Pumpkintown; Quail Hollow; Quarantine; Quick Crossroads; Rainbow Falls; Rains; Red Bank; Red Bluff; Red Hill; Red Oak Corner; Red River; Red Star; Retreat; Return; Rice Hope; Ricetown; Richmond; Ridge Spring; River Falls; Robbins Neck; Rock Bluff; Rock Hill; Rocky Bottom; Rocky River; Rome; Round O; Russellville; Salters; Salters Depot; Scott; Scranton; Seaside; Seven Mile; Seven Oaks; Silver; Silverstreet; Six Mile; Sixty Six; Snow Town; Society Hill; South of the Border; Spiderweb; Spring Branch; Springfield; Spring Hill; State Farm; State Park; St Charles; Steamboat Landing; St George; St Matthews; Stomp Springs; Stone Lake; Stone Station; Strawberry; St Stephen; Sunny Brook; Sunny Side; Sunset; Sweden; Sweetwater; Switzerland; Sycamore; Tall Pines; Taxahaw; Temperance Hill; Ten Mile; Tenmile; Testo; Thompson Corner; Three Trees; Tigerville; Tip Top; Townville; Travelers Rest; Trenton; Trio; Turkey Pond; Twelvemile; Una; Union; Valentine; Valley Falls; Walhalla; Walnut Grove; Warsaw; Washington; Weeks; Welcome; Whetstone; White Hall; Whitehall; White Oak; White Plains; White Pond; White Rock; White Stone; Wilson Crossroads; Winona; Winterseat; Winterville; Wise; Woodford; Workman; Yarn Mill; Zemp;

SOUTH DAKOTA - Sioux for "united allies." Statehood was November 2, 1889. The state nickname is "Mount Rushmore State." It was named after the Lakota and Dakota Sioux American Indian Tribes. It became a state in 1889. The population density ratio is nine people per square mile. The word "butte" (b-Ü-tte) derives from a French word meaning "small hill." A butte is an isolated hill with steep sides and a small, flat top. Buttes are formed by erosion when a cap of hard rock, usually of volcanic origin, covers a layer of softer rock that is easily worn away. The rock on top avoids erosion while the earth around it wears away. Badlands National Park is an area of over five hundred thousand acres of such terrain. Mount Rushmore National Memorial attracts two million visitors annually. The work began in 1927, and ended in 1941, with few injuries and no deaths.

Famous South Dakotans include:
- George Lee "Sparky" Anderson (1934–), Bridgewater; played for the Philadelphia Phillies, coached the Cincinnati Reds (two World Series titles) and Detroit Tigers (one World Series title)
- Myron Floren (1919–2005), Roslyn; started playing the accordian at age six; turned down by the Army due to rheumatic fever; in 1950, he went to a dance where the Lawrence Welk Orchestra was playing, was recognized by Welk, and asked to play one piece with the orchestra; he afterward became a permanent member
- Chief Crazy Horse (1840–1877); his name literally means, "his horse is crazy;" became a respected war leader of the Oglala Lakota who fought against the federal government in an effort to preserve the traditions and values of the Lakota way of life; was born with the name In the Wilderness or Among the Trees, meaning he was one with nature; his nickname was Curly because he had the same light, curly hair as his mother
- Billy Mills (1938–), Pine Ridge; the second Native American to win an Olympic gold medal; he won the ten thousand meter run at the 1964, Tokyo Olympics and is the only American to win the ten thousand meter run and win a gold medal while setting a new Olympic record for the event

Wall Drug in Wall, SD has signs for several hundred miles away advertising free ice water. They may give away twenty thousand cups of water during peak holidays. One of the youngest mayors elected in America was eighteen-year old Shane Mack, 1988, Castlewood, Hamlin County.

Interesting names include: Aberdeen; Academy; Advance; Akaska; Alaska; Alexandria; Allen; Alto; Antelope; Argyle; Armour; Artesian; Aurora; Avon; Badger; Bad Nation; Baltic; Bath; Bear Butte; Bear Creek; Beaver Crossing; Benchmark; Big Bend; Big Springs; Big Stone City; Bijou Hills; Bison; Blackhawk; Black Hawk; Black Horse; Blackpipe; Blunt; Bonesteel; Box Elder; Bradley; Bridgewater; Bristol; Brittin; Brownsville; Bruce; Buffalo; Buffalo Gap; Buffalo Ridge; Buffalo Trading Post; Bullhead; Bunker; Butler; Cactus Flat; Camp Crook; Canning; Carbonate; Carlock; Carpenter; Carter; Carterville; Cascade Springs; Cash; Castle Rock; Cedar Canyon; Center Point; Centerville; Central City; Chance; Chancellor; Chase; Chautauqua; Cherry Creek (15 miles from) Cherry Creek; Chinatown; Clark; Clearfield; Clear Lake; Coal Springs; Columbia; Cottonwood; Council House; Crook City; Crooks; Crow Creek; Crow Lake; Custer; Dallas; Date; Deadwood; Diamond; Diamond City; Dixon; Douglas City; Dry Wood Lake; Eagle; Eden; Edna; Elizabethtown; Elk Point; Elkton; Elm Springs; Empire; Eureka;

Fairview; Farmer; Fedora; Firesteel; Five Points; Florence; Forest City; Fort Thompson; Fourmile; Fox Ridge; Frankfort; Franklin; Frenchtown; Frisby; Fulton; Garden City; Gary; Gettysburg; Glad Valley; Goodwin; Grandview; Gray Goose; Green Grass; Greenville; Gregory; Grindstone; Grover; Hammer; Harding; Harrisburg; Harrison; Hartford; Haydraw; Hayti; Henry; Hidden Timber; Hill City; Hoover; Hot Springs; Houston; Hub City; Huron; Ideal; Igloo; Interior; Ipswich; Iron Lightning; Java; Jefferson; Jolly; Jolly Dump; Kenel; Keystone; Kodaka; Lake City; Lebanon; Letcher; Lily; Littleburg; Little Eagle; Lodgepole; Lone Tree; Long Lake; Long Valley; Lucerne; Madison; Manchester; Maple Leaf; Marion; Marshalltown; Martin; Mayfield; Meadow; Midway; Miller; Moe; Monroe; Morningside; Morristown; Mound City; Mount Vernon; Mud Butte; Mystic; Naples; Norway Center; Oldham; Old Town; Oral; Orient; Ottumwa; Parade; Pelican; Piana; Pine Ridge; Pine Run; Plainview; Plum Creek; Porcupine; Potato Creek; Powell; Prairie City; Prairie Queen; Prairie Village; Promise; Provo; Pumpkin Center; Ralph; Rapid City; Red Elm; Redfern; Redfield; Red Owl; Red Scaffold; Red Shirt; Reliance; Reno; Richmond; Ridgeview; Riverside; Rocky Ford; Rosebud; Rousseau; Rumpus Ridge; Running Water; Scenic; Scotland; Sevenmile Corner; Shadehill; Shelby; Slim Butte; Snake Creek; Soldier Creek; Spain; Spencer; Spokane; Spring Creek; Spring Grove; Star Corner; St Charles; Stevens; Stockholm; Stone Bridge; Stratosphere Bowl; Sturgis; Sulphur; Summerville; Sunnyview; Swan Lake; Tea; Tennis; Thunder Butte; Thunder Hawk; Tigerville; Timber Lake; Tomahawk; Toronto; Trail City; Troy; Turkey Ridge; Twin Brooks; Two Strike; Valley; Victor; Vienna; Violin; Virginia; Volunteer; Wall; Watertown; Webster; White; White Butte; Whitehorse; White Lake; White Owl; White River; White Rock; Willow Lake; Winner; Wolf Creek; Wood; Wounded Knee; Yellowhorse Ford; Zell

TENNESSEE - Cherokee for "village." Statehood was June 1, 1796. The state nickname is "Volunteer State." The name Tennessee comes from the Cherokee town Tanasi which, along with its neighbor town Chota, were two of the most important Cherokee towns. It earned the nickname "Volunteer State" during the War of 1812, in which volunteers from Tennessee played a prominent role, especially during the Battle of New Orleans. Many Civil War battles were fought in Tennessee, but most of them were Union victories. After the War, Tennessee adopted a new constitution abolishing slavery.

In 1933, the Tennessee Valley Authority was established and quickly became the nation's largest utility. During World War II, Oak Ridge was selected as a U.S. Department of Energy national laboratory, one of the principal sites for the Manhattan Project, to develop the first nuclear weapon, jointly sponsored by the United States, Great Britain, and Canada.

The word "Chattanooga" is based on a Muskogean term for "rock" (chatta), and may refer to Lookout Mountain which, when viewed from Moccasin Bend, appears as a "rock rising to a point." Clarksville, incorporated in 1785, was named for frontier fighter and Revolutionary War hero General George Rogers Clark. The average elevation of the Blue Ridge area is five thousand feet above sea level. Clingman's Dome, the highest elevation in Tennessee, is located in the Blue Ridge area.

Knoxville was named for Secretary of War Henry Knox, as was Fort Knox, Kentucky. Memphis and western Tennessee was settled seventy years before Knoxville and eastern Tennessee. Memphis was named after the ancient capital of Egypt on the Nile River.

Nashville was founded in 1779, and originally named Fort Nashborough after the Revolutionary War hero Francis Nash. It was the advent of the Grand Ole Opry, combined with an already thriving publishing industry that positioned Nashville to become "Music City, USA." In 1963, Nashville was the first major city in America to join governments with the county government. The city of Bristol is shared by both Tennessee and Virginia. The state line runs down the center of State Street. Here were the first commercial recordings made of country music, showcasing Jimmie Rodgers and the Carter Family. Congress recognized Bristol as the "Birthplace of Country Music."

Tennessee has seven state songs. Crossville is the location of the United States Chess Federation. Knoxville houses the Women's Basketball Hall of Fame. Tennessee was home to three Presidents: Andrew Jackson, Andrew Johnson, and James K. Polk.

Famous Tennesseeans include:
- Roy Acuff (1903–1992), Maynardville; he seemed unable to get his early career off the ground until he began singing "The Great Speckled Bird" in his weekly shows; his popularity quickly spread across east Tennessee; he was asked by ARC, a record label in Chicago with national distribution, to record the song
- Chester Burton "Chet" Atkins (1924–2001), Luttrell; his style was inspired, in part, by Merle Travis and Les Paul; he started out on the ukelele, moved to the fiddle, then traded his brother for a guitar when he was nine years old; because of a near-fatal asthma condition he was sometimes forced to sleep in a straight-backed chair in order to breathe comfortably; on those nights he played the guitar until he fell asleep holding it, a habit that lasted the rest of his life; he did not have a strong style of his own until he heard Merle Travis playing on the radio in 1939; wheras Travis' right hand used his for the melody and thumb for bass notes, Atkins learned to pick with his first three fingers while the thumb played the bass; he was famous for playing "Yankee Doodle Dixie" in which he played "Yankee Doodle" and "Dixie" at the same time on the same guitar
- Polly Bergen (1930–), Knoxville; born Nellie Pauline Burgin
- Davy Crockett (1786–1836), Dotsontown; killed at the Alamo, age forty-nine; member of the U.S. House of Representatives from two different Tennessee congressional districts
- Lester Flatt (1914–1979), Sparta; came to prominence in the 1940s as a member of Bill Monroe's Blue Grass Boys; in 1948, he and a former member of the Blue Grass Boys, Earl Skruggs, started the Foggy Mountain Boy
- Ernest Jennings "Tennessee Ernie" Ford (1919–1991), Bristol; studied at the Cincinnati Conservatory of Music; served in World War II as First Lieutenant Ford as a bombardier on a B-29 Superfortress flying missions over Japan; became a

household name largely as a result of playing "Cousin Ernie" on the *I Love Lucy Show*; in 1955, recorded "Sixteen Tons" which was number one on the country charts for eight weeks and number one on the pop charts for eight weeks; it became his signature song; in 1956, he released "Hymns," his first gospel album which remained on Billboard's Top Album charts for five years and four months

- Winston Conrad "Wink" Martindale (1934–), Jackson; in 1957, he graduated from Murray State University, Murray, KY; was close friends with Elvis; he is only the second television personality to have hosted fifteen game shows (Bill Cullen hosted twenty-three), the most-remembered being *Tic Tac Dough*
- Dolly Rebecca Parton (1946–), Seviereville; she has twenty-six number-one singles, a record for a female performer, and forty-two top-ten country albums; she has the distinction of having performed on a Top-40 country hit in each of the last five decades; the fourth of twelve children, her family lived in a one-room, dilapidated cabin; Dolly and her husband have raised several of her younger siblings at their home in Nashville, leading her nieces and neephews to refer to her as Aunt Granny; by age nine she was appearing on *The Cas Walker Show* in Knoxville, and at age thirteen she was appearing on the *Grand Ole Opry;* in 1967, she was asked to join the *Porter Wagoner Show*, leaving the show in 1976
- Minnie Pearl (1912–1996), Centerville; born Sarah Ophelia Colley Cannon; the price tag on Minnie's hat read $1.98; her first performance onstage as Cousin Minnie Pearl was in 1939; Grinder's Switch is an actual railroad switch just outside her hometown; she and her husband lived next door to the Governor's Mansion in Nashville
- Dinah Shore (1916–1994), Winchester; born Frances Rose Shore; her parents were Jewish immigrants from Russia; in 1918, at the age of two, she was stricken with polio; graduated from Vanderbily University, Nashville, in 1938, with a degree in sociology; after failing several singing auditions, she struck out on her own to become the first singer of her era to achieve a hugh solo success; she recorded over eighty charted pop hits lasting from 1940 to the late 1950s; she starred on her own television series, *The Dina Shore Show*, from 1951 to 1963
- Sergeant Alvin York (1887–1964), Pall Mall; was awarded the Medal of Honor for leading an attack on a World War I German machine gun nest, taking thirty-two machine guns, killing twenty-eight German soldiers, and capturing one hundred thirty-two others; he attempted to enlist in World War II but was denied entry due to age

The easternmost point in TN is due north of Jacksonville, Florida. Clarksville is farther north than Fulton (Fulton County), KY.

Interesting names include: Adair; Adams; Afton; Alamo; Alcoa; Alexandria; Alpine; Anderson; Ashland; Backwoods; Bain; Bald Hill; Baltimore; Bath Springs; Beans; Bean Station; Bear Spring; Bear Stand; Bear Wallow; Beaver Hill; Beech Bottom; Beech Grove; Beech Springs; Beechnut City; Belfast; Bell Buckle; Bell Town; Bending Chestnut; Berea; Berlin; Beverly Hills; Big Creek; Big Rock; Big Sandy; Big Springs; Bird; Bitter End;

111

Black Jack; Black Oak; Block; Blondy; Blossom; Blue Creek; Blue Goose; Blue Ridge; Blue Sky; Blue Springs; Board Valley; Bogota; Bold Spring; Bon Aqua; Bond; Boone; Booneville; Boston; Boyd; Brazil; Bride; Bright Hope; Brimstone; Bristol (Tennessee Ernie Ford); Brooksville; Brownsville; Bruceville; Buchanan; Buckeye; Bucksnort; Buena Vista; Buffalo; Buffalo Mop; Buffalo Ridge; Buffalo Valley; Bug Scuffle; Bungalow; Burt; Busy Corner; Cairo; Calhoun; Calico; Calls; Camelot; Campaign; Campbellsville; Capital Hill; Car Branch; Carlisle; Carter; Carter Crossing; Carter Crossroads; Carters Creek; Cartertown; Cash; Cash Point; Cat Corner; Catlettsburg; Cave Spring; Cedar Bluff; Cedar Grove; Cedar Hill; Cedar Lane; Center; Central; Central Point; Chalk Level; Charleston; Cherry; Cherry Corner; Cherry Hill; Cherry Valley; Chestnut Glade; Chestnut Grove; Chestnut Hill; Chestnut Mound; Chestnut Ridge; Chestnut Valley; Christmasville; Claysville; Clear Springs; Cleveland; Clinch River; Cloud Creek; Coal Hill; Cold Spring; Cold Springs; Coldwater; Columbia; Combs; Comfort; Concord; Cooktown; Cookville; Cottontown; Couch; County Line; Covington; Crab Orchard; Crackers Neck; Creek Store; Crescent; Crockett; Crooked Creek; Crossville; Crystal; Cuba; Cumberland City; Cumberland Gap; Cumberland View; Cyprerss; Cypress Creek; Daddys Creek; Dale Hollow; Danville; Deep Gap; Deer Lodge; Defeated; Denmark; Denver; Difficult; Disco; Dismal; Dixie; Dixieland; Dog Hill; Dogtown; Dogwood; Dollar; Dotsontown (Davy Crockett); Double Bridges; Double Springs; Double Top; Douglas; Dover; Dresden; Drop; Dry Hill; Duck Creek; Duck River; Ducktown; Duff; Dumplin; Dumplin Mill; Duo; Duplex; Dutch; Dutch Valley; Eagle Creek; Eagle Furnace; Economy; Edna; Edward Grove; Egypt; Elizabeth; Elizabethtown; Elkins; Elk Valley; Elkton; English Creek; Estill Springs; Eureka; Evanston; Evansville; Evergreen; Ewing; Factory; Fairview; Falcon; Fall Creek; February; Finger; Five Forks; Flat Gap; Flat Hollow; Flemingsburg; Fly; Forest Home; Forge Ridge; Forks of Piney; Forks of the River; Forty Forks; Foundry Hill; Four Points; Fox Den; Fox Fire; Friendship; Friendsville; Frost; Frost Bottom; Fruitland; Fulton; Gabtown; Gap of the Ridge; Garland; Gause; Genesis; Georgetown; Germantown; Gismonda; Glasgow; Glass; Gnat Hill; Goat City; Golddust; Gooseneck; Gordonsburg; Grace; Grant; Grasshopper; Grassland; Gravel Hill; Gray; Gray Mule;Greenland; Greenlawn; Green River; Green Valley; Greenville; Gum; Gum Flat; Gum Springs; Hackberry; Half Acre; Halfway; Hamburg; Hanging Limb; Happy Hill; Happy Valley; Hardscrabble; Harmony; Harrison; Head of Barren; Henderson (Eddie Arnold); Herbert Domain; Hickman; Hickory Flats; Hickory Grove; Hickory Point; Hickory Tree; Hickory Valley; High Point; Hilltop; Hohenwald; Holiday (Benton Co., only place in nation where fresh water pearls are cultivated); Hollow Rock; Holly Creek; Holly Grove; Holly Leaf; Holly Springs; Hollywood; Holy Hill; Hoodoo; Hornbeak; Hornet; Horse Creek; Houston; Huckleberry; Hurricane; Hurricane Mills (Loretta Lynn's ranch); Iconium; Idol; India; Indian Mound; Irish Cut; Ivory; Jackson; Jamestown; Jaybird; Jefferson; Jimtown; Jumbo; Juno; Kansas; Kensington; Kinderhook; Klondike; Ko Ko; La Grange; Lancaster; Lantana; Laurel Bluff; Laurel Fork; Lawrenceburg; Lebanon; Lexington; Liberty; Liberty Hill; Lick Skillet; Life; Lightfoot; Lincoln; Lisbon; Little Creek; Little Hope; Littlelot; Little Texas; Little White Oak; Livingston; Locust Springs; London; Lone Mountain; Lone Star; Long Rock; Louisville; Love Lady; Lucky; Madisonville; Magnolia; Manchester; Maples; Maple Spring; Marrowbone; Marshall; Martin; Mary Chapel; Marys Grove; Maryland;

Maryville; Mascot; Mason; Mayberry; Mayday; McKenzie; Melbourne; Memphis; Middle City; Midway; Milan; Miller; Millstone; Moccasin; Model; Monroe; Montezuma; Montgomery; Monticello; Moon; Moons; Moscow; Mound Bottom; Mountain City; Mountain Home; Mount Airy; Mount Orange; Mount Vernon; Mulberry; Mulberry Hill; Mule Hollow; Nameless; Napier; Natural Bridge; Needmore; Neverfail; New Johnsonville (after Johnsonville was flooded by TVA, New Johnsonville was established); Nickletown; Ninemile; Nixon; Normandy; Oak Grove; Oak Hill; Oak Ridge; Obey City; Old Glory; Oldham; Old Hickory; Only; Opossum; Overall; Owl City; Owl Hoot; Ozone; Pacific; Paint Rock; Pall Mall (Sgt. Alvin C. York State Historic Park); Pandora; Papaw; Paris; Pawpaw Plains; Peach; Peeled Chestnut; Persia; Philadelphia; Pierce; Pigeon Forge; Pikeville; Pine Grove; Pine Ridge; Pine Spring; Pinnacle; Pioneer; Plant; Plateau; Plato; Pleasant Shade; Pleasant View; Polecat; Ponderosa; Ponders; Poplar Grove; Poplar Springs; Portland; Powder Springs; Princeton; Promise; Prospect; Prosperity; Providence; Pulaski; Pumpkin Center; Quebeck; Rabbit Bluff; Rafter; Range; Reagan; Red Hill; Red Walnut; Regret; Reliance; Rest; Rich; Ridgetop (Grandpa Jones and Stringbean lived there); Right; Ripley; Roaring Springs; Robertson; Rock Bridge; Rock City; Rock Hill; Rock House; Rock Island; Rock Springs; Rocky Fork; Rocky Springs; Roe; Rome; Rose Hill; Round Pond; Round Top; Ruby Falls; Russellville; Sailors Rest; Sale Creek; Sand Switch; Sandy Hook; Santa Fe; Savannah; Sawdust; Scott; Screamer; Sequatchie; Sequoia Grove; Seven; Shady Grove; Shady Rest; Sharp Place; Shea; Shelbyville; Sheybogan; Shining Rock; Sideview; Signal Mountain; Skullbone; Slide; Smithland; Snow Hill; Soddy Daisy; Solo; South Fulton (on the border with Fulton, KY); Speck; Speedwell; Spencer; Spot; Spout Springs; Spring Hill; Springfield; Spruce Pine; Squirrel Flat; Stacy; Stanton; State Line; Static; Stinking Creek; Stone; Strawberry Plains; Stringtown; Sugar Grove; Sugar Hill; Sugar Hollow; Sugar Tree; Sulphura; Sulphur Springs; Summer City; Summit; Sunbright; Sunny Side; Sunnyside; Sunrise; Sunset; Surprise; Swannsylvania; Sweetgum; Sweet Lips; Sweetwater; Sycamore; Sycamore Spring; Tater Peeler; Taylorsville; Tennessee City; Tennessee Ridge; Thick; Thompson Crossroads; Thompson Mill; Thompsons Station; Thompsons Store; Thorn Hill; Three Forks; Three Points; Tin Cup; Todd Town; Trade; Tranquility; Trigg; Trimble; Turnpike; Twin Oaks; Two Chestnut; Union Camp; Union City; Unity; Utah; Versailles; Victory; Virtue; Walnut Grove; Walnut Log; Walnut Shade; Wartburg; Water Valley; Webster; Well Spring; West; Wheel; White City; White Hill; White Hollow; White Horn; White House; Whitehouse; White Oak; White Oak Forest; White Pine; White Rock; Wildwood; Williamsburg; Willow Grove; Wilson Hill; Wilson Station; Winchester (Dinah Shore); Windy City; Winesap; Winslow; Wolf Creek; Wolverine; Xenophon; Yankeetown; Yell; Yellow Springs; Yukon; Zenith;

TEXAS – From the Caddo Indians meaning "friendly." Statehood was December 29, 1845. The state nickname is "Lone Star State." Texas is the only state to enter the U.S. by treaty instead of annexation, which means it can fly its flag at the same height as the U.S. flag. Texas declared its independence from Mexico in 1836, and existed as the independent Republic of Texas for nearly a decade. In 1845, Texas joined the United States as the twenty-eighth state. Six different flags have flown over Texas: the Fleur-de-lis of France, the national flags of Spain, Mexico, the Republic of Texas, the Confederate States of Americ, and the United States of America. In February, 1861, Texas seceded from the Union and joined the Confederate States of America. The last battle of the Civil War was fought in Texas at Palmito Ranch, May 12, 1865, six weeks after Lee surrendered at Appomattox Court House, Virginia, on April 9, 1865. Texas was readmitted to the Union in 1870. The poorest place in America with one thousand or more population is South Alamo with a per capita income of $3,162. Numbers two, four, five, seven, and ten are also in Texas. The motto for the town of Happy is "The Town Without a Frown." More than one-third of Texans are of Hispanic origin. Texas is the only state in America that has three cities whose population is over one million—Houston, Dallas, and San Antonio.

The largest ranch in America is in Texas. Nearly the size of the state of Rhode Island, the King Ranch was founded by a former steamboat captain in 1853, and encompases nearly one million acres on which are hundreds of oil wells. However, this is on four tracts of land. The Ford Motor Company has a King Ranch Edition for their F-Series Super Duty truck line as well as the Expedition Full Size SUV. The largest ranch within one fence in the country is Waggoner Ranch, spreading over 500,000 acres. Texas has the lowest percentage of high school graduates–seventy-seven percent.

Fort Worth is the setting for the Christmas movie *Blossoms in the Dust* in which the character Edna Gladney (Greer Garson), founder of the Texas Children's Home and Aid Society, says the line, "There are no illegitimate babies…only illegitimate parents." Gladney successfully lobbied the Texas Legislature to remove the term "illigitimate" from birth certificates and to ensure adopted children the same rights as other children.

Famous Texans include:
- Orvon Gene Autry (1907–1998), near Tioga; family moved to Oklahoma in the 1920s; began performing on local radio in 1928 as "Oklahoma's Yodeling Cowboy;" signed a recording deal with Columbia Records in 1929; made his first film in 1935, *In Old Santa Fe*; during World War II he servided as a pilot in the Army Air Forces in which he flew the C-47 Skytrain in dangerous missions over the Hump between Burma and China; he is the only star to have five stars on the Hollywood Walk of Fame, one in each of the five categories maintained by the Hollywood Chamber of Commerce
- Carol Burnette (1933–), San Antonio; before her first television appearance on the Paul Winchel show her grammdmother tolder her to say hello to her; explaining that would not be allowed, they worked out a signal—she tugged on her left ear lobe
- Scott Joplin (1868–1917), near Linden; when he was fifteen his mother purchased a piano; in 1899, he sold his most famous composition, "Maple Leaf Rag," to John Stark and Son; it sold over one million copies
- Dan Blocker (1928–1972), DeKalb; served in the Korean War; played the role of Eric "Hoss" Cartwright on the television series *Bonanza*; in high school Blocker was 6' 3" and weighed three hundred pounds; he and Pernell Roberts were the same age

114

- Gale Storm (1922–), Bloomington; born Josephine Owaissa Cottle; best remembered for her roles in the television series *My Little Margie* and *The Gale Storm Show*; recorded "I Hear You Knockin' "
- Sandra Day O'Connor (1930–), El Paso; first woman to serve on the U. S. Supreme Court

The distance of Texas, north to south, is comparable to the distance from Dallas to Chicago, Houston to Miami, Atlanta to New York City, or Washington, D.C. to Memphis. Brownsville (Cameron County) is four hundred seventy-five miles farther south than Tijuana, Mexico.

One of the youngest mayors elected in America was eleven-year-old Brian Zimmerman, 1983, Crabb, Fort Bend County. Zimmerman worked to incorporate the small unincorporated town, which had a population of less than two hundred when he was elected. This threatened his mayorship because Texas state law prohibits anyone under the age of eighteen from serving as mayor.

Interesting names include: Aberdeen; Academy; Adair; Adams; Admiral; Advance; Afton; Albany; Albert; Alcoa; Alexander; Alfalfa; Alice Acres; Allen; Alpine; Alto; Alum Creek; Anchorage; Anderson; Angel City; Angus; Antelope; Arbor; Argyle; Arizona; Arkansas City; Ash; Ashland; Asia; Athens; Atlanta; Atlas; Avenger Village; Back; Bacon; Badger; Bagdad; Bainville; Bangs; Bardwell; Bath; Beach City; Beacon; Bear Creek; Bee Cave; Bee House; Belgrade; Bell; Ben; Bend; Ben Franklin; Benjamin; Berea; Berlin; Best; Beverly Hills; Bigfoot; Birch; Birthright; Black; Blackberry; Black Hill; Blackjack; Black Oak; Bland; Blanket; Blessing; Bloomington (Gale Storm {born Josephine Cottle} "I Hear You Knockin,'" 1956); Blossom; Blowout; Blue; Blue Berry Hill; Blue Ridge; Boise; Bonus; Booker (farther north than Nashville, TN); Boone; Bootleg; Boston; Bounce; Boyd; Brad; Brand; Briggs; Bright Star; Bronco; Brownsville; Bruceville; Buckeye; Buckhorn; Buena Vista; Buenos Aires; Buffalo; Bug Tussle; Bunker Hill; Burlington; Burns; Burrow; Butler; Cactus; Cadiz; Caldwell; Calf Creek; Camden; Camelot; Campbell; Canadian; Cannon; Canyon; Cap Rock; Carbon; Carlisle; Carolina; Carrollton; Carson; Carter; Carter Settlement; Carterville; Cash; Cat Spring; Cedar Creek; Cedar Grove; Cedar Hill; Cee Vee; Center; Cereal; Chalk; Champion; Chancellor; Chaney; Charleston; Charlie; Chat; Cheapside; Check; Cheek; Chillicothe; China; China Grove [San Antonio]; Chocolate Bayou; Chocolate Springs; Choice; Christine; Chunky; Circle; Citrus City; City-by-the-Sea; Clark; Clay; Clear Creek; Clear Springs; Cleveland; Click; Close City; Coal Mine; Coffee City; Coffeeville; Coke; Cold Springs; Cold Water; Cologne; Colorado; Columbus; Combine; Comfort; Commerce; Concord; Concrete; Cone; Converse; Cook; Corner Windmill; Corn Hill; Cost; Cotton; Cotton Flat; Cotton Gin; Cotton Patch; Cottonwood; County Line; Covington; Coyote; Crane; Crisp; Crockett; Crow; Crusher; Crystal City; Crystal Falls; Cuba; Cut; Cut and Shoot; Cyclone; Cypress; Dads Corner; Dallas (George "Spanky" McFarland, *Our Gang Comedy*); Danville; Darling; Dawn; Dayton; Deal; Deer Creek; DeKalb (Dan Blocker *Hoss* or *Eric*); Democrat; Dennison (Dwight D. Eisenhower, 34th President); Dent; Desert; Dew; Dial; Dies; Dime Box; Dimple; Ding Dong; Direct;

Divide; Divot; Dixie; Dixon; Dog Ridge; Domino; Double Bayou; Double Mountain; Douglas; Douglasville; Draw; Dripping Springs; Drop; Dry Valley; Dublin; Duff; Dundee; Dye; Eagle Flat; Earth; Easter; Ebony; Echo; Eden; Edge; Edinburg; Edmonson; Edna; Edna Hill; Edwards; Egypt; Elbow; Eldorado; Electric City; Elevation; El Paso (closer to California than Dallas; US 62 originates in El Paso and terminates in Niagara, NY); Elliott; Elm Creek; Elm Flat; Elm Grove; Elm View; Emblem; Energy; English; Era; Eulogy; Eureka; Fairview; Faker; Falcon; Fall Creek; Falls City; Farmer; Fate; First Crossing; Fivemile; Fivemile Crossing (8 miles from Fourmile Crossing); Five Points; Flat; Flat Fork; Flat Prairie; Flat Rock; Flat Top; Fleming; Flint; Flora; Florence; Flower Grove; Flower Mound; Floyd; Fog Town; Forest; Fort Worth (Fes Parker); Foster; Four Corner Windmill; Fourmile Crossing (eight miles from Fivemile Crossing); Franklin; Fredericksburg; Friday; Friendship; Frog Hop; Frognot; Frost; Fruitland; Garden City; Garland; Gary; Gasoline; Gem; George; Georges Creek; George West; Georgetown; Georgia; Germany; Gilmer (Johnny Mathis); Ginger; Glass; Globe; Goldfinch; Golly; Goober Hill; Good Springs; Goodnight; Goodwin; Gordon; Gordonville; Grace; Grandview; Grapevine; Grassland; Gray Mule; Green; Green Hill; Greenville; Gregory; Groom; Grow; Gum Springs; Gun Barrel City; Gunsight; Hackberry; Hail; Hall; Hancock; Hanger; Happy; Happy Hollow; Happy Valley; Hardin; Hardy; Harmony; Harper; Harpersville; Harriet; Harrison; Hay City; Henderson; Hickory Creek; Hickory Ridge; High; Hi Ho; Hindman; Hogeye; Holland; Holly Springs; Homestead; Honey Creek; Honey Grove; Hood; Hoop and Holler; Hoot; Hoover; Horizon City; Houston (first word spoken from the moon); Huber; Humble; Hunt; Huntington; Huron; Illinois Bend; Impact; Independence; Index; India; Indian Creek; Indian Gap; Indian Hot Springs; Industry; Iowa Colony; Ireland; Italy; Jackson; Jacksonville; Jamestown; Jean; Jefferson; Joe; Johnson; Jolly; Jot 'Em Down; Jumbo; Junction; Kentucky Town; Kermit; Key; King; Kingston (Audie Murphy); Klondike; Knickerbocker; Knob Hill; Knott; La Grange; LaRue; Las Vegas; Lawn; Lawrence; Leaky; Lebanon; Lemonville; Lexington; Liberty; Lime City; Lincoln; Lindsay; Little Mexico; Little New York; Lively; Live Oak; Liverpool; Loco; Locust; Locust Grove; Logan; Log Cabin; Lollipop; London; Lone Cedar; Lone Oak; Lone Star ("Lone Star State"); Lone Willow; Looneyville; Loop; Los Angeles; Love; Loving; Lubbock (Buddy Holly); Lucky Ridge; Madisonville; Magic City; Mallard; Maple; Marathon; Marble Falls; Margaret; Margie; Marion; Marsh; Marshall; Marshall Ford; Marshall Springs; Mart; Marysville; Mason; Matador; Matthews Place; Mayfield; Mayflower; McLean; Meadow; Medicine Mound; Memphis; Merit; Mesquite; Miami; Middle Water; Midway; Mile High; Mineral; Missouri City; Monroe; Montgomery; Monticello; Morgan; Morris Grove; Morris Ranch; Moscow; Moss Hill; Mound City; Mountain Home; Mulberry; Muleshoe; Murray; Mustang; Nameless; Napier; Naples; Necessity; Needmore; Negros Liberty Settlement; Nelson; Nevada; New Deal; Newport; New York; Nicholas; Nickel; Ninteen Mile Crossing; Nix; Nixon; Nobility; Noodle; Noonday; Notrees; Novice; Nursery; Oak Flat; Oak Grove; Oak Hill; Oakland; Oak Leaf; Oak Ridge; Oatmeal; Ogden; Ogg; Oil City; Oklahoma; Oklahoma Flat; Okra; Old Glory; Oldham; Old Navy; Old R; Omaha; Omen; Onion Creek; Orange; Orange Grove; Orchard; Ore City; Orient; Owenton; Owl Creek; Paducah; Paint Creek; Paint Rock; Palmetto; Panama; Pancake; Panhandle (300 miles from the Texas panhandle); Paradise; Paris; Parkway; Peach Creek; Peach Tree Village;

Peacock; Pearl City; Pear Valley; Pecan Bay; Pecan Grove; Pecan Hill; Pegasus; Pelican; Pendleton; Penelope; Peoria; Pep; Pert; Pheasant; Pierce; Pilgrim; Pine Branch; Pine Forest; Pine Hill; Pine Prairie; Pine Ridge; Pine Springs; Pine Valley; Pin Oak; Pinto; Pioneer; Pittsburg; Placid; Plains; Plainview; Plateau; Pleasant Springs; Pleasant Valley; Pluck; Plum Creek; Poetry; Point; Pointblank; Polar; Ponder; Pone; Post; Post Oak; Prairie Grove; Prairie Hill; Prairie Point; Prairie View; Price; Pride; Primrose; Princeton; Progress; Prospect; Prosper; Providence; Puerto Rico; Pumpkin; Punkin Center; Quail; Quarry; Quebec; Queen City; Quicksand; Quitman; Raccoon Bend; Racetrack; Radar Base; Radium; Rainbow; Raisin; Ratler; Rattan; Rattlesnake Gap; Ray; Reagan; Red Bluff; Red Branch; Red Gate; Red Hill; Red Lake; Red Level; Red Mud; Red Oak; Red River City; Red Rock; Red Springs; Red Top; Redwater; Redwood; Refuge; Reliance; Retreat; Rhode Island; Rice; Richmond; Ridge; Ring Gold; Rising Star; River Hill; Riverside; Roach; Roaring Springs; Robertson; Rochester; Rock Creek; Rock Hill; Rock House; Rock Island; Rock Springs; Rocky Mound; Roosevelt; Rosebud; Rosewood; Round Mountain; Round Prairie; Round Rock; Roundup; Royalty; Rule; Rural Shade; Russellville; Rye; Sabine Pass (The Big Bopper); Saline; Salt Flat; Salty; Sam Houston; Sam Rayburn; San Antonio (Carol Burnette); Sand; San Diego; Sandusky; San Juan; Sargent; Satin; Savage; Scenic Oaks; Scissors; Scotland; Scott; Scranton; Seclusion; Second Crossing; Senate; Senior; Seven Heart Crossing; Seven Knobs; Seven L Crossing; Sevenmile Corner; Seven Oaks; Seven Pines; Seven Points; Seventeen Mile Crossing; Shadowland; Shady Grove; Shamrock; Shelbyville; Shiner; Short; Sidney; Silver; Sixmile Crossing; Six Point; Sixteen Mile Crossing; Slabtown; Slide; Small; Smithland; Snow Hill; Soda Springs; Somerset; Sour Lake; South Point (farther south than Fort Lauderdale, FL); Spade; Speaks; Spring; Spring Creek; Springfield; Spring Hill; Spring Valley; Stacy; Stag Creek; Stagecoach; Stairtown; Stamps; Stanton; Star; State Line; Stellar; Stephen Creek; Stevens; Stout; Strain; Stranger; Stringtown; Structure; Stumptown; Sublime; Sudan; Sugar Land [Houston]; Sugar Valley; Sulphur; Summer; Sundown; Sunny Side; Sunray; Sunset; Sunshine; Sweet Home; Sweetwater; Swift; Swiss Alps; Sycamore; Tarzan; Taylor; Taylorsville; Telegraph; Telephone; Tell; Tenmile Crossing; Tennessee Colony; Terrace; Texarkana (on the border with Texarkana, AR); Texas City; Texhoma (on the border with Texhoma, OK); The Grove; Thicket; Thompson Grove; Thompsons; Thompsonville; Thorn Hill; Thornberry; Three Leagues; Three Oaks; Three Rivers; Three States (Texas, Arkansas, Louisiana); Thrift; Tigertown; Tigerville; Tin Top; Tioga (Gene Autry); Todd; Toledo; Tool; Toronto; Triangle; Tribune; Trinidad; Trio; Trophy Club; Trout Creek; Truce; True; Tulip; Turkey; Tuxedo; Twin Mountains; Twin Sisters; Two F Crossing; Tyler; Uncertain; Union; Utopia; Uvalde (Dale Evans); Valentine; Valley Creek; Valley Spring; Valley View; Valley Wells; Venus; Verbena; Veribest; Vienna; View; Vineyard; Violet; Waco (Dr Pepper invented 1885); Wall; Walnut Grove; Walnut Ridge; Walnut Springs; Warren; Warsaw; Washer; Washington; Water Valley; Wealthy; Webster; Welcome; Welfare; Wheatland; White City; White Deer; Whitehouse; White Mound; White Oak; White Oak Springs; White Rock; White Shed; Wild Horse; Wildwood; William Penn; Willow City; Willow Grove; Willow Springs; Wilson; Winchester; Windy Hill; Wink; Winona; Winter Haven; Wise; Wolfe City; Zipperlandville

UTAH - Navajo for "upper." Statehood was January 4, 1896. The state nickname is "Beehive State." Sixty-two percent of Utahns claim to be Mormon. The state motto is "Industry." Utah, Colorado, New Mexico, and Arizona make up the "four corners" states. The Wasatch Mountain Range receives about forty feet of snow each year. The Bonneville Salt Flats is so large you can see the curvature of the earth on its surface. The salt is six feet deep in many places. Southwest Utah is the lowest and hottest place in Utah. It is known as Dixie because early settlers were able to grow limited amounts of cotton there. This is also the area of the Mojave Desert. Seventy percent of Utah is either owned or controlled by the federal government. Salt Lake City is the Jell-O capital of the world due to its consumption of the product. The title was briefly lost to Des Moines, IA in 1999, but has again been retaken by Salt Lake City. Lime is the favorite flavor.

Famous Utahns include:
- Butch Cassidy (1866–1908), Beaver; born Robert Leroy Parker; a notorious train robber, bank robber, and leader of the Hole in the Wall gang; Hole-in-the-Wall is a remote hideout in the Big Horn Mountains in northern Wyoming
- Philo Farnsworth (1906–1971), Beaver; invented the first completely electronic television
- John Willard Marriott (1900–1985), Marriott Settlement near Ogden; his company rose from a small root beer stand in Washington, D. C., in 1927, to a chain of family restaurants in 1932, to his first motel in 1957
- Merlin Olsen (1940–), Logan; played professional football from 1962-1976
- Olive Marie Osmond (1959–), Ogden; although she appeared on *The Andy Williams Show* with her brothers when she was three, she was never a part of the family singing group, but did make a name for herself with her country music recordings
- Donald "Donnie" Clark Osmond (1957–), Ogden; after seeing the Osmond Brothers perform at Disneyland as a barbership quartet, Andy Williams asked the boys to audition for his television show
- Loretta Young (1913–2000), Salt Lake City; born Gretchen Young; in 1930, at age seventeen, eloped with twenty-seven-year-old actor Grant Withers; the marriage was annulled the next year, just as their second movie together, *Too Young to Marry*, was released; her movie, *The Bishop's Wife*, was remade with Whitney Houston as *The Preacher's Wife*
- Parley Baer (1914–2002), Salt Lake City; in 1952, he began playing the role of Chester on the radio series *Gunsmoke*; he played the role of Mayor Stoner (the second mayor) on the television series *The Andy Griffith Show*

Interesting names include: Agate; Alpine; American Fork; Angle; Antimony; Aspen Grove; Aurora; Avon; Ballard; Bear River City; Beaver; Beaver Dam; Big Water; Birdseye; Black Rock; Bloom; Blueacre; Bluebell; Blue Creek; Bone Valley; Boulder; Bountiful; Brian Head; Bullion Falls; Bullionville; Castle Rock; Cedar; Cedar City; Cedar Springs; Cedar Valley; Central; Charleston; Christmas City; Circleville; Clear Creek; Clearfield; Clear Lake; Cleveland; Clover; Coal City; Coalville; Columbia; Consumers;

Cook Corner; Cornish; Cotton; Crystal Springs; Desert; Desert Mound; Diamond; Dividend; Dragon; Dry Fork; Dutch John; Eagle Mountain; Echo; Eden; Eggnog; Eighteenmile Point; Elk Ridge; Eureka; Fayette; Fillmore; Fountain Green; Freedom; Fruitland; Fry Canyon; Garden; Garden City; Garland; Georgetown; Gold Hill; Gooseberry; Green River; Greenville; Grouse Creek; Grover; Gunlock; Gusher; Hailstone; Harding; Hardup; Harrisburg; Hatch; Hayden; Heist; Helper; Horse Canyon; Huntington; Hurricane; Indian Village; Iron Basin; Iron Mountain; Iron Springs; Liberty; Lincoln; Logan; Low; Manila; Maple Grove; Marshall; Martin; Marysvale; Mayfield; Meadow; Mexican Hat; Midway; Monarch; Monroe; Montezuma Creek; Monticello; Morgan; Mound City; Mountain Home; Mount Sterling; Naples; Oak City; Oak Creek; Oasis; Orangeville; Paradise; Perry; P Hill; Pigeon; Pines; Pine Valley; Plain City; Pleasant View; Price; Promontory; Providence; Rainbow; Red Point; Red Wash; Richmond; Rockville; Roosevelt; Saline; Salt Lake City (Parley Baer *the neighbor on "Ozzie & Harriet" and the Mayor Stoner on Mayberry*); Shivwits; Silver City; Silver Reef; Sixmile Point; Snowville; Soldier Summit; Solitude; Spanish Valley; Spearmint; Spry; Sterling; St George; Strong; Summit; Sunnyside; Sunset; Sutherland; Taylor; Taylorsville; Thistle; Thompson; Thompson Springs; Thompsonville; Three Forks; Three Pines; Ticaboo; Trenton; Tropic; Trout Creek; Upper Sunnyside; Venice; Virgin; Washington; West Valley City; Wheatgrass; White Horse Village; White Mesa; Wildcat; Wildwood

VERMONT - French for "green mountain." Statehood was March 4, 1791. The state nickname is "Green Mountain State." Only Wyoming has a smaller population. It is the only New England state with no Atlantic Ocean coastline. The area was first claimed by the French but became a British possession after France's defeat in the French and Indian War. New Hampshire and New York disputed for possession of the land but the Green Mountain Boys prevailed in creating an independent state. During the Revolutionary War, and for fourteen years thereafter, it was the independent Republic of Vermont. The state is ninety miles wide (thirty-seven miles wide at the narrowest point), and one hundred sixty miles long; by comparison, it is one hundred sixty miles from Greenville, KY to Lexington, KY; During the Civil War, Vermont sent more than thirty-four thousand men into service.

The most expensive college in America in 2004 was Landmark College, Putney, at a cost of $35,300, excluding room and board.

Famous Vermontians include:
- John Calvin Coolidge, Jr. (1872–1933), Plymouth; thirtieth president of the United States and the only president to be born on the Fourth of July; twenty-ninth vice president of the United States; governor of Massachusetts; lieutenant governor of Massachusetts
- Chester A. Arthur (1829–1886), Fairfield; twenty-first president of the United States; twentieth vice president of the United States; Arthur spent some of his childhood years living in Perry, New York; served in the Civil War as acting quartermaster general

Interesting names include: Albany; Alpine Village; Athens; Baltimore; Beanville; Berlin Corners; Birdland; Blissville; Braintree Hill; Bread Loaf; Brimstone Corners; Bristol; Brooksville; Brownsville; Buck Hollow; Burlington; Butlers Corners; Butternut; Cedar Beach; Centertown; Centerville; Charleston; Checkerberry Corner; Chimney Corner; Cold River; Cold Spring; Concord; Concord Corner; Copper Flat; Cozy Corner; Crystal Beach; Danville; Derby; Dover; Eden; Egypt; Evansville; Fays Corner; Fayville; Florence; Franklin; French Hollow; Georgia Center; Georgia Plains; Goodrich Four Corners; Goose Green; Gordon Landing; Graniteville; Hancock; Happy Corner; Hardscrabble Corner; Hartford; Holland; Huntington; Island Pond (Rudy Vallee); Jacksonville; Jamaica; Joes Pond; Johnson; Killington; Lewis; Lincoln; Londonderry; Lost Nation; Manchester; Maple Corner; Mechanicsville; Michigan; Middletown; Mile Point; Montgomery; Montpelier; Morgan; Morrisville; Moscow; Mosquitoville; Nashville; Newport; Old City; Orange; Orleans; Peach Four Corners; Peru; Pittsburg; Pleasant Valley; Podunk; Prosper; Red Village; Richmond; Riverside; Rochester; Russellville; Rutland; Scottsville; Smugglers Notch; Somerset; Stacy Crossroads; Stevens; Summit; Texas; The Four Corners; Thompsons Point; Thompsonburg; Tinmouth; Troy; Victory; Warren; Washington; Waterville; Williamstown; Willow Point; Woodford; Worcester

VIRGINIA – Named in honor of Queen Elizabeth, I. Statehood was June 25, 1788. The state nickname is "Old Dominion." Jamestown Colony was the first permanent English settlement in North America. Virvinia is named after Queen Elizabeth I, who was known as the *Virgin Queen.* Virginia is known as the "Mother of Presidents" because it is the birthplace of eight U.S. presidents: George Washington, Thomas Jefferson, James Madison, James Monroe, William Henry Harrison, John Taylor, Zachary Taylor, and Woodrow Wilson. Virginia has also been known as the "Mother of States" because portions of the original Virginia subsequently became Kentucky, Indiana, Illinois, and West Virginia, as well as portions of Ohio. Virginia is one of the states that seceded from the Union and operated independently until it joined the Confederacy during the Civil War. In 1863, during the Civil War, forty-eight counties in the northwest part of the state that remained loyal to the Union separated from Virginia to form the state of Kanawah, later becoming West Virginia. During the Civil War, more battles were fought on Virginia soil than any other state. The city of Richmond served as the capital of the Confederacy during the Civil War. Virginia rejoined the Union in 1780, after a period of post-war military rule.

All municipalities incorporated as cities are independent of the county. Thirty-nine of America's forty-two independent cities are in Virginia. The other independent cities are Baltimore, MD, Saint Louis, MO and Carson City, NV. When Douglas Wilder became governor of Virginia in 1990, he became the first African American governor in America. The abbreviation for Kentucky, Ohio, and Virginia (Ken o va) make up the name for Kenova, WV.

The Statler Brothers (Staunton), only two of the group members were brothers; in 1955, they were originally a church trio comprised of bass Harold Reid, lead Phil Balsley, and tenor Lou DeWitt. In 1960 Reid's younger brother Don joined the group singing lead. The quartet sang gospel music under the name The Kingsmen. After arranging a meeting with the promotion department of a Johnny Cash concert, the Kingsmen were asked to open for the concert. Cash was so impressed that he invited the group to join the tour. After changing their name to the Statler Brothers, they remained with Cash from 1963–1971. The Statlers signed with Columbia Records in 1964, and one year later scored a huge country and pop hit with DeWitt's "Flowers on the Wall." In 1969, the quartet signed with Mercury Records where they remained for over twenty years. In 1973, they recorded "Alive at the Johnny Mack Brown High School" performed by Lester "Roadhog" Moran and the Cadillac Cowboys (aka The Statler Brothers). In 1982, DeWitt was forced to leave the group as a result of Crohn's Disease; he died in 1990. They performed their last concert in 2002. Although no longer touring, the group has produced at least three more albums.

Two of Virginia's counties lie twenty miles off the Atlantic Coast. Kate Smith attended a Philadelphia Flyers hockey game and was asked to sing "God Bless America" before the game. She consented. The Flyers won the game. She was asked to sing at another home game. They won again. From that time on, the Flyers wonover two-thirds of their home games at which Kate Smith sang. As a result of that record, a fan was reported to have said, "It ain't begun 'til the fat lady sings."

Cumberland Gap National Historic Park is due south of Natural Bridge State Resort Park (Powell County), KY, Toledo, OH, and Flint, MI. The northernmost point of Virginia is farther north than Chillicothe, OH, Kansas City, KS, and San Francisco, CA.

Signers of the Declaration of Independence include: Carter Braxton, Benjamin Harrison, Thomas Jefferson, Francis Lightfoot Lee, Thomas Nelson, and George Wythe.

Famous Virginians include:
- George Rogers Clark (1752–1818), Albemarle County, Virginia; served as a leader in the Kentucky militia during much of the Revolutionary War; was instrumental in convincing Governor Patrick Henry to create Kentucky County, Virginia
- Patrick Henry (1736–1799), Hanover County, Virginia; in a speech made in the House of Burgess, urging the legislature to take military action against the encroaching British military force, said, "Is life so dear, or peace so sweet, as to be purchased at the price of chains and slavery? Forbid it, Almighty God! I know not what course others may take; but as for me, give me liberty or give me death!" The crowd jumped up and shouted, "To arms! To arms!" After the Revolution he was an outspoken critic of the United States Constitution, arguing it gave the federal government too much power
- Robert E. Lee (1807–1870), Stratford Hall Plantation, Westmoreland County; served in the Mexican-American War and the Civil War; President Lincoln asked Lee to take command of the entire Union Army, but he refused because his home state of Virginia was seceding from the Union; Lee was defeated at the Battle of Gettysburg but escaped to Virginia
- Patsy Cline (1932–1963), Winchester; killed at age thirty-one; millions of her albums have been sold since her death; ten years after her death she became the first female

solo artist inducted to the Country Music Hall of Fame; she played the piano by ear and sang with perfect pitch; she won an audition and sang on *Arthur Godfrey's Talent Scouts* and reappeared on the show for several months thereafter

- Willard Scott (1934–), Alexandria; from 1959–1962 he was the local Bozo the Clown on WRC-TV, Washington, D.C., and was the original Ronald McDonald
- Ralph Stanley (1927–), Big Spraddle Creek; he received his first banjo as a teenager and learned to play clawhammer style (a style of picking) from his mother
- Booker T. Washington (1856–1915), Hale's Ford; freed from slavery as a child by the Thirthteenth Amendment following the Civil War; the first black to be an honored guest of a U.S. president
- Ella Fitzgerald (1917–1996), Newport News; her voice spanned three octaves; her recording career spanned 57 years
- Statler Brothers, Staunton; neither man's last name is Statler; they were named after a brand of facial tissue; they joked that they could have been called the Kleenex Brothers; the Statler Brothers started their career at a performance at Lynhurst Methodist Church, near Staunton; in 1963 they started an eight-year run with Johnny Cash as his warm-up act; they have released over forty albums
- Wayne Newton (1942–), Norfolk; while still a child, his family moved to a home near Newark, Ohio; achieved nationwide recognition in 1962, when he and his brother performed on *The Jackie Gleason Show*, where he made twelve appearances in two years; in 1994, he performed his 25,000th solo show in Las Vegas

Interesting names include: Acorn; Afton; Alexandria; Alleghany; Alpine; Alps; Amsterdam; Annex; Antlers; Appalachia; Apple Grove; Arbor Hill; Avon; Bachelors Hall; Backbone; Bagdad; Barracks; Bath; Bath Alum; Beaverdam; Bee; Bent Creek; Berea; Berlin; Big Meadows; Big Spring; Birdsnest; Blackberry; Bland; Bleak; Blue Grass; Blue Hole; Blue Mountain; Boone; Boston; Bowmans; Bradley Acres; Bradley Forest; Brand; Briery Branch; Briggs; Brightwood; Britain; Broken Hills; Brownsville; Buchanan; Buckeye; Buena Vista; Buffalo Bend; Buffalo Ford; Buffalo Forge; Buffalo Hill; Buffalo Ridge; Buffalo Springs; Bull Run; Burnt Chimney; Burnt Factory; Burnt Tree; Callaway; Campbell; Cape Charles; Captain; Cash; Cash Corner; Catherine Furnace; Cats Bridge; Cedar Branch; Centerville; Chalk Level; Chance; Chantilly; Charity; Charles City; Charles Corner; Check; Chericoke; Cherry Grove; Chestnut Grove; Chestnut Hill; Chestnut Knob; Christian; Clover; Clover Creek; Clover Hill; Coffee; Coke; Cold Spring; Cologne; Combat Village; Commonwealth; Concord; Contra; Convent; Convent Station; Converse; Convict Lake; Cook; Cookertown; Cooktown; Corbin; Corn Valley; Cotton Town; Crab Orchard; Crooked Oak; Crouch; Crows; Crystal Springs; Cuckoo; Cutalong; Dale City; Danville; Davids Crossroads; Dayton; Deep Hole; Disputanta; Dixie Hill; Double Tollgate; Douglass Park; Dover; Dublin; Duet; Dugwell; Dumbarton; Dutch Gap; Edinburg; Eggbornsville; Elk Run; Falls Church; Falmouth; Farmers Fork; File; First Colony; Five Forks (1 mile from Four Forks); Five Mile Fork; Flat Iron; Flat Run; Flint Hill; Flood; Ford; Four Corners; Four Forks (one mile from Five Forks); Fourway; Fox; Fredericks-burg; Free Union; Friendship; Fritters Corner; Frogtown; Frytown; Furnace; Garden City; Georges Fork; Georges Mill; Germantown; Gibson Mill (eight miles farther west than

122

Morehead, KY); Glasgow; Goblintown; Gold Hill; Goldvein; Gordonsville; Granite Springs; Grant; Grassland; Great Falls; Green Bay; Green Springs; Green Valley; Greenville (Kate Smith); Greenwich; Gregory Corner; Gum; Gum Springs; Halfway; Hamburg; Hamilton; Happy Creek; Hardscrabble; Harmony; Harper; Hawk; Hayfield; Head Waters; Healing Springs; Hickory Grove; Hightown; Holland; Hollywood; Honeyville; Hopkins Spring; Horse Head; Horse Pasture; Horsepen; Horsey; Hot Springs; Huntington; Hurricane; Hustle; Hyacinth; Igo; Independence Hill; Index; Indian Field; Indian Neck; Indian Town; Inlet; Iron Gate; Ivory; Ivy; Jackson; Jamaica; James Store; Java; Jefferson; Jersey; Kentuck; Kermit; Kidville; King and Queen Court House; King George; King William; Kremlin; Lagrange; Larrys Store; Lawyers; Leaksville; Lebanon; Legato; Lent; Lexington; Liberty; Lick Skillet; Lignum; Lincoln; Little Duck; Little Texas; Loch Lomond; Locust Grove; Logan; Lone Fountain; Long Island; Looney; Lost Corner; Louisa; Luck; Lynchburg; Madison; Madrid; Maherrin (Roy Clark); Maple Grove; Marshall; Marshalltown; Maryland; Maryton; Mayfield; McLean; Mechanicsburg; Mechanicsville; Meter; Midway; Midway Island; Mineral; Monitor; Monroe; Montezuma; Montpelier; Moon Corner; Moonlight; Morgantown; Moscow; Mountain Grove; Mountain View; Mount Airy; Mt Garland; Mulberry Hill; Natural Well; Navy; Negro Foot; Nesting; New Castle; Newport; Newport News (Ella Fitzgerald); Nicelytown; Nicholas; Noel; Nuttsville; Oak Grove; Oak Hill; Oak Ridge; Oak Shade; Office Hall; Olive; Opal; Orange; Orchid; Ordinary; Overall; Owenton; Ox Place; Panorama; Paris; Passing; Peach Grove; Pendleton; Penneys Crossroad; Petunia; Philadelphia; Pine Grove; Pine View; Pleasant Shade; Pleasant Valley; Pleasant View; Plum Tree; Pocket; Poorhouse Corner; Poplar; Possum Trot; Potomac Falls; Pound; Prices Store; Prim; Prince George; Progress; Prospect; Public Fork; Pumpkin Center; Quail; Quantico; Quebec; Radiant; Rawhide; Red Apple Orchard; Redeye; Red Oak Hollow; Refuge; Reliance; Republican Grove; Rich Patch Mines; Rip Rap; Riverside; Rock Hill; Rocky Mt; Roman; Rose Hill; Roseville; Round Hill; Running Deer; Ruth; Saint Louis; Sales Corner; Sassafras; Sawmill Corner; Scotland; Scrabble; Screamersville; Scuffletown; Seminary; Seven Corners; Seven Fountains; Shady Grove; Sheep Town; Shenandoah; Sign Post; Singerly; Singers Glen; Skinquarter; Snowflake; Snow Hill; Solitude; Somerset; Sparkling Springs; Spostylvania; Spotsylvania Courthouse; Spring Creek; Springfield; Spring Hill; Spring Valley; Star Tannery; Staunton (Statler Brothers); St Charles; St Davids Church; Stephens City; Stephens Fort; Sterling; Stevensburg; Stony Point; Storck; Strasburg; Stratford Hall (Robert E. Lee); Stringtown; Success; Summerdream; Summerduck; Sunbeam; Sunbright; Sunny Point; Sunny Side; Sunrise; Sunset Village; Supply; Surprise Hill; Sutherland; Swift Run; Switch Back; Sycamore; Syria; Taylor; Telegraph Spring; Tenth Legion; The Cross Roads; The Plains; Thompson Valley; Threemile Corner; Three Square; Threeway; Ticktown; Tightsqueeze; Timber Ridge; Tiny; Tiptop; Tobaccoville; Toms Brook; Topnot; Triangle; Trimble; Triplet; Troy; True Blue; Tryme; Tulip; Turkey Fork; Unionville; Uno; Upper Pocosin; Upright; Vesuvius; Vienna Woods; Viscose City; Walnut Grove; Walnut Point; Warm Springs; Warsaw; Washington; Waterfall; Welcome; Wheatland; White Oak; Wickliffe; Wildcat Corner; Wilderness; Wiley; Williamsburg; Willow Grove; Wilson Springs; Winchester; Windsor; Winterville; Winston; Wise; Wolf Trap; Woodford; Yankeetown; Yellow Sulphur; Youngers Store

WASHINGTON – Named for George Washington. Statehood was November 11, 1889. The state nickname is "Evergreen State." It is the only state named after a president. Residents are called Washingtonians. On May 18, 1980, following a period of heavy tremors and eruptions, the northeast face of Mount St. Helens exploded outwardly, destroying a large part of the top of the volcano. The eruption flattened the forests, killed fifty-seven people, flooded the Columbia River and its tributaries with ash and mud, and blanketed large parts of Washington in ash, making the day look like night.

Famous Washingtonians include:
- Bob Barker (1923–), Darrington; served in the U.S. Navy during World War II as a fighter pilot; hosted *Truth or Consequences* 1956–1975; do you remember Beulah the Buzzer? Barker hosted *The Price Is Right* 1972–2007; he appeared on an episode of *Bonanza* in 1960
- Elinor Donahue (1937–), Tacoma; best remembered for the role of Betty Anderson on the television series *Father Knows Best* 1954–1960 and for the role of Ellie Walker, the drugist, on the television series *The Andy Griffith Show* 1960–1961

Interesting names include: Aberdeen; Aberdeen Gardens; Agate Bay; Agate Point; Aladdin; Allen; Aloha; Alto; American River; Apricot; Artesian; Artic; Ash; Bacon; Bangor; Basin City; Battle Ground; Beacon Hill; Beaver; Berry Patch; Beverly; Beverly Beach; Birch Bay; Birdsview; Blockhouse; Bluelight; Blueside; Bluestem; Blue Town; Boise; Boston Harbor; Boundary; Bow; Bristol; Brooklyn; Brownsville; Bruce; Burrows; Bush Prairie; B Z Corner; Cabin Creek; Cactus; Calhounville; Camas (Jimmie Rodgers, "Honeycomb," 1957); Carnation; Cascade Valley; Cashmere; Cashup; Castle Rock; Cedar Falls; Cedar Mountain; Cedarville; Centerville; Centralia; Chain Hill; Charleston; Chautauqua; Cherry Grove; Cherry Point; Chew; Clay City; Clearwater; Cleveland; Clipper; Coal Canyon; Coal Creek; College Place; Columbia; Concrete; Cougar; Cozy Nook; Crabtree; Crystal Mountain; Cumberland; Danville; Davenport; Dayton; Deep Creek; Deep River; Deer Trail; Deer Valley; Des Moines; Diamond; Dixie; Dollar Corner; Dolomite; Dolphin; Dot; Douglas; Downs; Dry Creek; Duckabush; Du Pont; Dusty; Dutch Settlement; Dynamite; Echo; Eden; Edna; Edwards; Electric City; Electron; Elk; Elk Creek; Elliott; Emerald; English Boom; Estes; Eureka; Farmer; Fern Hill; Fern Prairie; Fernwood; Fish Town; Five Corners; Flint; Ford; Forks; Four Corners; Four Lakes; Fox Island; Frankfort; Freedom; Friday Harbor; Fruitland; Fruitvale; Gardena; Gate; Geneva; George; Ginger; Glacier; Globe; Gold Bar; Goldstake; Gooseneck; Goose Prairie; Grand Mound; Green River; Greenwater; Grotto; Grouse; Happy Valley; Harmony; Harper; Hay; Hazard; Headquarters; High Point; Hilltop; Home; Horse Heaven; Humorist; Humptulips; Independence; Index; Ireland; Iron Springs; Jackson; Jefferson; Johnson; Kendall; Kooskooskie; La Push; Laurel; Lavender; Lawrence; Leadpoint; Leavenworth; Lee; Lexington; Lincoln; Little Oklahoma; Lone; Long; Low Gap; Lucerne; Maiden; Manchester; Maple Beach; Maple Falls; Maple Grove; Marble; Marshall; Martin; Mason; Matthew; Matthews Corner; Mayfield; Medical Lake; Melbourne; Meteor; Michigan Hill;

Milan; Mill A; Mineral; Minnehaha; Mock City; Monitor; Monroe; Mountain Brook; Mountain View; Mount Vernon; Mud Springs; National; Neah Bah (westernmost point in the lower 48); Nelson; Nighthawk; Nile; Noble; Noon; Novelty; Oak Harbor; Ocean City; Ocean Grove; Ohop; Oil City; Old Town; Onion Creek; Opportunity; Orchard Prairie; Orient; Oysterville; Pacific; Paddock; Page; Palisades; Palm Lake; Pamona; Paradise; Perry; Pigeon Springs; Pillar Rock; Pine City; Ping; Plain; Pleasant Hill; Pleasant Valley; Pleasant View; Prairie; Prairie Ridge; Providence; Rainier; R Corner; Regal; Reliance; Relief; Republic; Revere; Rimrock; Ritzville; Rochester; Rock Island; Rocky Point; Rocky Ridge; Roosevelt; Rose Springs; Rose Valley; Royal City; Ruff; Ruth; Rye; Saginaw; Saint Helen; Salmon Creek; Scenic; Sea Acre; Seal Rock; Shadow; Sightly; Silver Beach; Silver Creek; Silver Lake; Sixprong; Skookumchuck; Sleepy Hollow; Snake River; Soap Lake; South Bend; Spangle; Spring Valley; Stampede; Standard; Starbuck; Startup; State Line (on the border with Oregon); Steptoe; Stillwater; Stringtown; Sulphur; Summit; Sunbeach; Sunny Hill; Sunny Shores; Sunnyside; Sunnyslope; Sunrise; Sunrise Beach; Sunset; Sunset Beach; Sunshine; Surprise Valley; Susie; Swantown; Swede Heaven; Swede Hill; Swift; Tacoma (Elinor Donahue, *Father Knows Best*; Bing Crosby); Tampico; Tanner; Thompson; Thompson Place; Thrift; Tiger; Toledo; Trinidad; Trout Lake; Tulips; Tumtum; Tumwater; Tweedie; Twin; Twisp; Two Rivers; Tyler; Union; Union Gap; University Place; Valley; Vancouver; Venice; Virginia; Vista; Voltage; Waits; Walla Walla; Walnut Grove; Warden; Warm Beach; Warren; Washington Harbor; Waterville; Welcome; White Pass; White Swan; Wild Goose; Wilderness; Wildwood; Wilson; Wilson Creek; Winchester; Winona; Winston; Yakima; Zenith

WASHINGTON, D.C. – Named for George Washington. The city was founded on July 16, 1790. The city is under the jurisdiction of the U.S. Congress. The nickname is "The District." It is represented by a non-voting, at-large Congressional delegate, but no senator. Duke Ellington was born there in 1899.

WEST VIRGINIA - Broke away from Virginia, June 20, 1863, to join the Union. The state nickname is "Mountain State." West Virginia broke away from Virginia during the Civil War and was admitted to the Union as a separate state in 1863. It is the only state formed as a direct result of the Civil War. It is one of only two states to form by seceding from a pre-existing state, the other being Vermont. President Abraham Lincoln approved its joining the Union on the condition the abolition of slavery be included in the Constitution. The area which became West Virginia furnished about 36,000 soldiers to the Federal armies and fewer than 10,000 to the Confederate. The top of the panhandle is on equal parallel with New York City. Because its extremities reach into different parts of America, West Virginia can be noted as the southernmost Northeastern state, the northernmost Southeastern state, the easternmost Midwestern state, and the westernmost Eastern state. It is the only state in the nation located entirely within the Appalachian Mountains. The abbreviations for Kentucky, Ohio, and Virginia (Ken o va) make up the name for Kenova, West Virginia.

Don Knotts graduated from West Virginia University with a degree in theater. At one time, he was a ventriloquist with a figure named Danny. He received his first break on *Search for Tomorrow* where he appeared from 1953–1955. He gained greater popularity on the *Steve Allen Show*, appearing in the Man on the Street interviews. In 1958, he appeared in the movie *No Time for Sergeants* with Andy Griffith. That movie started a relationship between the two that lasted for decades. Starting in 1960, and for five seasons, he played the role of Deputy Barney Fife on *The Andy Griffith Show*. When the show first aired, Andy was to be the comic and Barney the straight man, but it was found to be funnier the other way around. Macular degeneration in both eyes caused him to become virtually blind. He died in 2006 at the age of eighto-one.

Mary Lou Retton, gold medal gymnast in 1984, was the first woman to appear on the front of a box of Wheaties. However, Elinor Smith appeared on the back of a Wheaties box in 1934 for setting the woman's endurance record—twenty-six hours, twenty-three minutes—for an airplane flight.

Famous West Virginians include:
- Mary Lou Retton (1968–), Fairmont; Olympic Gold Medal gymnast
- Little Jimmy Dickens (1920–), Bolt; born James Cecil Dickens; 4' 11" tall
- Red Sovine (1918–1980), Charleston; born Woodrow Wilson Sovine; he was taught to play the guitar by his mother; in 1963, he helped Charley Pride break into country music
- Pearl S. Buck (1892–1973), Hillsboro
- Nancy Hanks (1784–1818), Hampshire County, Virgnina, now Mineral County, West Virginia; mother of Abraham Lincoln; married Thomas Lincoln in Washington County, Kentucky
- William Anderson "Devil Anse" Hatfield (1839–1921), of the Hatfield-McCoy feud
- Harry Randall Truman (1896–1980), Wise; served in the U.S. Navy during World War I; lived near Mount St. Helens and died in its 1980 eruption when he stubbornly refused to leave

The northernmost point of West Virginia's panhandle is as far north as New York City.

Interesting names include: Aberdeen; Adams; Advent; Afton; Alexander; Alexandria; Alice; Alloy; Alum Bridge; Anthem; Antler; Apple Grove; Argyle; Arkansas; Ashland; Assurance; Athens; Auto; Ballard; Barren Creek; Bass; Bean Settlement; Beauty; Beaver; Beaverdam; Beech; Beech Grove; Beechwood; Beelick Knob; Bens Run; Berea; Berlin; Beverly; Beverly Hills; Bias; Big Branch; Big Four; Big Run; Big Sandy; Big Springs; Birds Creek; Blackberry City; Black Wolf; Blennerhassett; Blue; Blue Bend; Blue Creek; Bluefield; Blue Jay; Blue Pennant; Blue Rock; Blue Spring; Blues Beach; Bluestone; Blue Sulphur Springs; Bluewell; Board; Bob White; Bolt; Bottom Creek; Bradley; Brake; Brownsville; Bruce; Bruceton Mills; Brush Camp Lower Place; Buckeye; Bud; Buffalo; Buffalo Creek; Bull Run; Burlington; Burning Springs; Burnt Factory; Burnt House;

Calcutta; Caldwell; Calhoun; Camden; Camp Ground; Canebrake; Canvas; Canyon; Carbide; Carbon; Caress; Carolina; Carter; Cascade; Cashmere; Cedar; Cedar Grove; Centennial; Center Point; Charles Town; Charleston; Cheat Lake; Cheat Neck; Cherry; Cherry Falls; Cherry Grove; Chestnut Hill; Chestnut Ridge; Chimney Corner; Christian; Cinderella; Circle View; Clear Creek; Clear Fork; Clinton; Clothier; Clover; Clover Lick; Coal City; Coal Fork; Coal Mountain; Coalridge; Coal Valley; Coalwood; Coketown; Cold Stream; Coldwater; Concord; Confidence; Congo; Cool Ridge; Core; Cornstalk; Cottle; Cotton; Cottontown; Creamery; Crimson Springs; Crooked Creek; Crow; Crown; Crystal Block; Cuba; Cucumber; Cutlips; Cyclone; Czar; Daisy; Dallas; Danville; Davy; Daybrook; Dayton; Deep Valley; Deer Creek; Deer Run; Deerwalk; Dent; Diamond; Dillie; Dingy; Divide; Dixie; Doe Gully; Dog Patch; Douglas; Dry Creek; Dublin; Duck; Duo; Dutch; Echo; Eden; Edna; Egypt; Elizabeth; Elk; Elk City; Elkhorn; Elm Grove; Elm Terrace; English; Entry; Evansville; Excelsior; Extra; Factory; Fairplay; Fairview; Faithful; Fallen Timber; Falling Rock; Falling Spring; Fame; Fayette; Filbert; Finch; Fink; Five Block; Five Forks; Flat Top; Flint; Flipping; Flower; Forks Of Cacapon; Forks of Coal; Four Mile; Four States; Franklin; Freeze Fork; Frenchburg; Friendly; Friendsville; Frost; Frozen Camp; Fry; Gary; Georgetown; Glasgow; Goldtown; Good; Goodwin; Gordon; Grace; Grave Creek; Green Hill; Greenland; Green Ridge; Green Spring; Greenville; Gregory; Grove; Gum Spring; Gypsy; Hacker Valley; Half Way; Halo; Hampshire; Hancock; Harding; Hardy; Harmony; Harper; Harper Heights; Harpers Ferry; Harpertown; Harriet; Harrison; Hatfield (two miles from Hatfield, KY, Martin County); Hemlock; Henderson; Hickory Grove; Holly; Holly Grove; Hollywood; Hoohoo; Horseneck; Horsepen; Horse Shoe Run; Hot Coal; Hundred; Hurricane; Independence; Industrial; Industry; Inez; Institute; Ireland; Irontown; Jockeycamp; Joe Branch; Johnnycake; Johnson; Joker; Jumbo; Junction; Justice; Kalamazoo; Kale; Kermit; Kettle; Keystone; Kitchen; Klondike; Knob Fork; Knoxville; Laurel Creek; Laurel Fork; Lawrenceville (sixty miles north of Sandrock, PA); Lead Mine; Left Hand; Lego; Liberty; Lightbeam; Lightburn; Lillydale (one-half mile from) Lillyhaven; Limestone; Limestone Hill; Little; Little Georgetown; Little Italy; Little Otter; Little Pittsburg; Lively; Liverpool; Locust; Logan; Logansport; London; Lone Oak; Longpole; Long Run; Loom; Looneyville; Lost City; Lost Creek; Lucerne; Madison; Magnolia; Mammoth; Man; Manheim; Manila; Maple; Maple Acre; Maple Fork; Maple Meadow; Maple View; Margaret; Marion; Market; Marshall; Martin; Marytown; Mason; Maxwelton; Maybeury; Meadow Bridge; Mechanicsburg; Miami; Midway; Mineral City; Mink Shoal; Minnehaha Springs; Minnie; Miracle Run; Monitor; Montpelier; Morgan Grove; Morgantown (Don Knotts); Morning Star; Moscow; Mountain; Mountain View; Mount Vernon; Mozart; National; Needmore; Nelson; Neptune; New England; Next; Nitro; Norway; Oak Grove; Oak Hill; Oak Ridge; Odd; Ogden; Olive; Orchard; Organ Cave; Page; Pancake; Pansy; Panther; Paradise; Parsley Bottom; Paw Paw; Peapatch; Peewee; Pepper; Perry; Peru; Petroleum; Pew Hill; Pie; Pierce; Pigeon; Pike; Pinch; Pine Creek; Pineknob; Pineville; Pink; Pipestem; Pleasant Hill; Pleasant Run; Pleasant Valley; Pleasant View; Pleasure Valley; Plum Orchard; Plum Run; Point Pleasant; Points; Poland; Polk; Porto Rico; Potomac; Power; Prairietown; Premier; Price; Princeton; Prosperity; Providence; Pumpkintown; Pursglove; Quick; Quiet Dell; Ragtown; Ralph; Ramp; Raven Rocks; Redbird; Red Creek; Red House; Red Jacket;

Red Spring; Replete; Republic; Revere; Rift; Rig; Ripley; Riverside; Roach; Roberts; Rock; Rock Castle; Rock Cliff; Rockridge; Romance; Ronceverte (Tom T. Hall was radio DJ on WRON); Rorer; Rosebud; Round Bottom; Rumble; Rum Junction; Russellville; Salt Rock; Salt Sulphur Springs; Saltwell; Sand Hill; Sandstone; Sandusky; Sassafras; Scarlet; Scary; Scotch Hill; Scrabble; Sedan; Shady Brook; Shady Grove; Shadyside; Shady Spring; Shamrock; Shanghai; Shanks; Shock; Short Gap; Silver Hill; Sincerity; Sistersville; Six; Six Hill; Skygusty; Skyline; Slab; Slabtown; Slate; Smoke Hole; Smokeless; Snow Flake; Snow Hill; Snoeshoe; Sod; Sovereign; Speed; Speedway; Spencer; Springfield; Spring Gap; Spruce; Spruce Valley; Star; Star City; St George; Stony Bottom; Strange Creek; Stringtown; Stumptown; Sue; Sugar Valley; Sulphur City; Summers; Summit; Sun; Sundial; Sunflower; Sun Hill; Sunlight; Sunrise; Sunset Beach; Sun Valley; Superior; Superior Bottom; Swan Pond; Sweet Springs; Sycamore; Table Rock; Tad; Tallyho; Tango; Teaberry; Three Churches; Three Forks; Thursday; Tioga; Tomahawk; Tornado; Toronto; Trainer; Triadelphia; Trolleys; Trout; Troy; True; Turkey; Turkey Knob; Turtle Creek; Twilight; Uneeda; Union; Union Corner; Union Ridge; Uniontown; Vandalia; Veto; Vienna; Viola; Violet; Virginville; Vulcan; Wahoo; Walnut; Walnut Bottom; Walnut Grove; War; Warfield; Washington; Wasp; Weaver; Webster; Wenonah; West; West Liberty; Wheatland; Whirlwind; White Hall; White Oak; White Oak Springs; White Sulphur Springs; Wick; Widen; Wildcat; Wild Meadow; Wiley; William; William Mountain; Williamsburg; Willow Bend; Willow Island; Wilson; Wilsonburg; Wilsondale; Wilsontown; Winona; Winter; Wolfe; Wolf Pen; Wolf Run; Wyoming; Wyoming City

WISCONSIN - Indian for "grassy place." Statehood was May 29, 1848. The state nickname is "Badger State." The modern Ojibwe name means "muskrat lodge place" or "little muskrat place." Wisconsin ranks first in the production of corn for silage, cranberries, ginseng, and snap beans for processing. It is also the leading producer of oats, potatoes, carrots, tart cherries, maple syrup, and sweet corn for processing.

Famous Wisconsonians include:
- Frank Lloyd Wright (1867–1959), Richland Center; architect, interior designer, writer, and educator
- Spencer Tracy (1900–1967), Milwaukee; served in the U. S. Navy during World War I; he died seventeen days after completing the film *Guess Who's Coming to Dinner*
- Don Ameche (1908–1993), Kenosha; his radio career included being the announcer and sketch participant on *The Edgar Bergen/Charlie McCarthy Show* and playing on *The Bickersons*; he played in the film *Harry and the Hendersons* in 1987
- Ellen Corby (1911–1999), Racine (grew up in Philadelphia); appeared on *Wagon Train, The Rifleman, I Love Lucy, The Virginian, Alfred Hitchcock Presents*, and *Andy Griffith* (sold Barney his first car), and in 1971, she was Grandma Esther Walton on *The Waltons*; she appeared in over two hundred plays, movies, and TV shows in her career; her movies include, *It's a Wonderful Life, The Ghost and Mr. Chicken*, and *The Glass Bottom Boat*

- Orson Welles (1915–1985), Kenosha; probably best remembered for his October 30, 1938 radio broadcast of *The War of the Worlds*
- Les Paul (1915–), Waukesha; born Lester William Polfuss; by the age of thirteen he was playing guitar semi-professionally; he backed up Nat King Cole, Bing Crosby, The Andrews Sisters, and more; he is a pioneer in the development of the solid-body electric guitar which helped advance the rock and roll sound; helped create the recording process known as multi-tracking
- Allen Ludden (1917–1981), Mineral Point; he was a captain in the U.S. Army during World War II; hosted the gameshow *Password* from 1961–1975
- Liberace (1919–1987), West Allis [Milwaukee]; full name is Wladziu Valentino Liberace; known as Lee to his friends and Walter to his family; he was a twin but the other child died at birth; he began playing the piano at age four; at age eight he met the famous Polish pianist Paderewski; in 1940, at age twenty-one, he played with the Chicago Symphony; in 1944, he made his first appearance in Las Vegas; in 1950, he performed for President Harry S. Truman in the East Room in the White House; in 1954, he performed in Madison Square Garden for $138,000; by the mid 1950s, he was making $1 million from public appearances and millions from television appearances; his shows ended with an invitation for the audience to meet him on stage to touch his clothes, piano, jewelry, and hands; *The Liberace Show* appeared on syndicated television in 1955
- John Bradley (1923–1994), Antigo; one of six men who raised the American flag on Iwo Jima

It is reported that Arthur Kneibler, an executive at a Kenosha underware company, came up with the idea for men's briefs after seeing a photo of a man wearing a short swimming suit on the Riviera in 1934. He redesigned the bathing suit, added an elastic waistband, and on May 29, 1935, received a patent.

The Republican Party was founded in Ripon (Fon du Lac County).

One of the youngest mayors elected in America was twenty-year-old Michael Raatz, 2007, Abbotsford, Clark and Marathon Counties.

Interesting names include: Adams; Advance; Afton; Agenda; Alaska; Albany; Allen; Almond; Alpha; Alto; Anderson; Apple Creek; Arena; Argyle; Arkansaw; Athens; Avalanche; Avon; Bangor; Bavaria; Bear Creek; Bear Valley; Beaver; Beaver Brook; Beaver Dam; Beaver Edge; Beetown; Berlin; Big Falls; Big Flats; Big Patch; Big Spring; Birch; Black Earth; Black Hawk; Black River Falls; Bloomer; Blueberry; Blue Mounds; Blue River; Bowler; Boyd; Bradley; Breed; Briggsville; British Hollow; Brownsville; Bruce; Brussels; Buck Creek; Buena Vista; Buffalo; Buffalo City; Burr Oak; Cable; Calamine; Caldwell; Calm Falls; Camp Douglas; Carter; Cascade; Castle Rock; Cataract;

Cedar Lake; Cedarville; Center Valley; Centerville; Chain o' Lakes; Chase; Cheeseville; Chicago Corners; Chili; City Point; Clam Falls; Clay Banks; Clear Lake; Cleveland; Clinton; Cloverland; Cold Spring; Cold Springs; Columbus; Comfort; Commonwealth; Concord; Coon Rock; Coon Valley; Cornucopia; Council Bay; County Line; Cozy Corner; Cranberry Marsh; Cream; Creamy; Crescent; Cuba City; Cumberland; Cutter; Dairyland; Dakota; Dale; Dallas; Danville; Deer Park; Delta; Denmark; Diamond Bluff; Diamond Grove; Dilly; Disco; Dover; Dundee; Eagle; Eagle Corners; Eagle Point; Eagle River; Eagleton; Eau Claire; Eden; Edwards; Eight Corners; Eldorado; Elk Creek; Elk Grove; Elkhorn; El Paso; Elm Tree Corners; Elmwood; Embarrass (EM-brah); Emerald; Emerald Grove; Endeavor; Eureka; Euren; Evansville; Evergreen; Exile; Fall Creek; Fall Hall Glen; Falls City; Farmersville; Fayette; Fillmore; Five Corners; Florence; Fon du Lac (Foot of the Lake); Footville; Forward; Fountain City; Four Corners; Fox Creek; Franklin; Freedom; Frenchville; Friendship; Fulton; Genoa City (from *The Young and the Restless*, perhaps?); Georgetown; Germantown; Globe; Gordon; Grand View; Green Bay; Green Lake; Green Valley; Greenville; Hamburg; Hancock; Harmony; Harrison; Hartford; Hay Creek; Hay Stack Corner; Hemlock; Hickory Corners; Hickory Grove; Hill Point; Holland; Horse Creek; Horseman; Hub City; Hunting; Huntington; Hurricane; Independence; Indian Creek; Institute; Ipswich; Iron Ridge; Iron River; Jackson; Jamestown; Jefferson; Jersey City; Jimtown; Johannesburg; Jump River; Junction; Juneau; Keenland; Kennedy; King; La Grange; Lake Ripley; Lancaster; Land O' Lakes; Lebanon; Liberty; Lima; Lime Ridge; Lincoln; Little Chicago; Little Hope; Little Norway; Little Prairie; Little Rose; Livingston; Loganville; London; Lone Rock; Loyal; Luck; Madison; Magnolia; Manchester; Maple; Maple Grove; Maple Hill; Marathon; Marblehead; March Rapids; Marion; Marshall; Marytown; Mason; Mayfield; McAllister; McNaughton; Meadow Valley; Meeme; Meteor; Milan; Mineral Point; Minnesota Junction; Monroe; Montana; Monticello; Montreal; Moon; Moon Valley; Moose Junction; Morgan; Moscow; Mountain; Mount Morris; Mount Sterling; Mount Vernon; Murry; Nashville; Nelson; Neptune; Neuern (1/2 mile from) Neureru; New York; Niagara; Nichols; North Star; Norway Grove; Norway Ridge; Oak Grove; Oil City; Onalaska; Ono; Ontario; Orange Mill; Oregon; Orion; Oshkosh; Oulu; Ourtown; Oxbo; Paoli; Paris; Peru; Phlox; Pierce; Pigeon Falls; Pine River; Pipe; Plain; Pleasant Prairie; Pleasant Ridge; Pleasant Valley; Plugtown; Plum City; Poland; Polar; Poplar; Porcupine; Pound; Prairie Corners; Prairie Farm; Pray; Price; Primrose; Princeton; Prospect; Pulaski; Red Banks; Red Cedar; Red River; Red Rock; Reserve; Retreat; Richmond; Ring; Rising Sun; River Falls; Riverside; Roberts; Rock Elm; Rock Falls; Rolling Ground; Romance; Rome; Royalton; Ruby; Rural; Russell; Salyersville; Sand Bay; Sand Creek; Sandrock; Sandy Hook; Scandinavia; School Hill; Shamrock; Shantytown; Shelby; Shell Lake; Silver Creek; Siren; Sister Bay; Slab City; Slabtown; Snows Corner; Soldiers Grove; Somerset; Speck Oaks; Spencer; Split Rock; Springfield; Spring Green; Spring Prairie; Spring Valley; Spruce; Stanton; Star Prairie; State Line; Stevens Point; Stevenstown; Stephensville; Stockholm; Strawbridge; Strum; Sugar Bush; Sugar Grove; Sugar Island; Sunnyside; Sun Prairie; Sunset; Superior; Sutherland; Sweetheart City; Taylor; Tell; Thompson; Thompsonville; Timberland; Tioga; Tomahawk; Trade River; Trenton; Tripoli; Troy; Truman; Tunnel City; Twelve Corners; Twin Grove; Twin Town; Two Creeks; Two Rivers; Une; Union Grove; Unity; Vinnie Ha Ha; Viola; Wales;

Washington; Watertown; Wayne; Wheatland; White City; White Lake; White Oak; White River; Whitewater; Wilson; Winter; Wisconsin Dells; Wisconsin Rapids; Wolf; Wolf Creek; Wolfe; Woodford; Wyoming; Yellowstone; Young America

WYOMING – Algonquin for "great plains." Statehood was July 10, 1890. The state nickname is "Equality State." Their constitution included women's suffrage. Wyoming is the least populous state with just over five hundred thousand in the 2000 Census. Old Faithful Inn, Yellowstone National Park, has a seven-story lobby. The inn opened in 1903.

Famous Wyomans include:
- Eliza Stewart Boyd, 1833–1912), Laramie; first woman in America to be selected and serve on a jury
- Anne M. Burford (1942–2004), Casper; first female administrator of the Environmental Protection Agency from 1981 to 1983

Interesting names include: Afton; Albany; Alberta; Alpine; Antelope; Arrowhead Springs; Aspen; Atlantic City; Badger Basin; Badwater; Banner; Basin; Battle; Beartown; Beaver Creek; Big Horn; Big Sandy; Bill; Bitter Creek; Blue Hill; Border; Boulder; Boulder Flats; Boxelder; Breakneck Hill; Bronx; Buckhorn; Buckskin Crossing; Buffalo; Buffalo Ford; Burlington; Burntfork; Camel Hump; Carbon; Carpenter; Carter; Carter Cedars; Centennial; Chugwater; Clay Spur; Cody (co-founded by "Buffalo Bill" Cody); Cokeville; Continental Divide; Cow Hollow; Coyote Springs; Crane; Crowheart; Cuba City; Cyclone; Dad; Days; Dayton; Deadmans Corner; Diamond; Diamondville; Dines; Dixon; Douglas; Dry Creek; Dumbell; Eden; Elk Basin; Elk Mountain; Emblem; Emigrant Hill; Encampment; Evanston; Evansville; Fairview; Farthing; Federal; Fish Cut; Fisher; Fishing Bridge; Flattop; Fossil; Four Corners; French Vee; Fry; Garland; Goose Egg; Granite; Grass Creek; Green River; Grover; Halfway; Harmony; Harper; Hat Creek; Hawkeye; Hawk Springs; Hells Half Acre; Holly; Horse Creek; Horseshoe Bend; Iron Mountain; Jackson; Jackson Hole; Jay Em; Keystone; Kleenburn; LaGrange; Lariat; Little America; Little Medicine; Lonetree; Lookout; Lost Cabin; Lost Springs; Lucerne; Marshall; Medicine Bow; Midway; Midwest; Miller; Miners Delight; Monarch; Moose; Morgan; Mountain Home; Mountain View; Muddy Gap; Node; Oil Springs; Owl Creek; Paradise; Paradise Valley; Pavilion; Peru; Pine Haven; Pitchfork; Point of Rocks; Powder River; Prairie Center; Price Place; Purple Sage; Recluse; Redbird; Red Butte; Red Desert; Red Lane; Reliance; Rendezvous; Riverside; Riverview; Robertson; Rock Creek; Rock River; Rock Springs; Rockypoint; Ryegrass Junction; Saddlestring; Sage; Sales Place; Salt Creek; Salt Wells; Sand Draw; Shell; Shiprock; Silver Crown; Skull Creek; Sleepy Hollow; Soda Well; Sodium; South Pass City; Spencer; Spotted Horse; Spring Valley; Story; St Stephens; Sundance; Sunrise; Sunrise Hill; Sunshine; Superior; Sweetwater Crossing (one mile from) Sweetwater Station; Table Rock; Tenmile; Ten Sleep; Teton Village; Themopolis; Three Forks; Tie Siding; Twin Groves; Ucross; Ulm; Valley; Verse; Veteran; Viola; Vocation; West Thumb; Wheatland; Widdowfield; Wildcat; Wiley; Willow Creek; Willow Springs; Wilson; Winchester; Wind River (twenty miles from) Wind River; Wolf; Wyoming

ALPHABETICAL LIST OF COUNTIES IN AMERICA

(Names with an asterisk are also used in Kentucky)

ALABAMA: Autauga; Baldwin; Barbour; Bibb; Blount; Bullock; *Butler; Calhoun; Chambers; Cherokee; Chilton; Choctaw; Clarke; *Clay; Cleburne; Coffee; Colbert; Conecuh; Coosa; Covington; Crenshaw; Cullman; Dale; Dallas; DeKalb; Elmore; Escambia; Etowah; *Fayette; *Franklin; Geneva; Greene; Hale; *Henry; Houston; *Jackson; *Jefferson; Lamar; Lauderdale; Lawrence; *Lee; Limestone; Lowndes; Macon; *Madison; Marengo; *Marion; *Marshall; Mobile; *Monroe; *Montgomery; *Morgan; *Perry; Pickens; *Pike; Randolph; *Russell; St Claire; *Shelby; Sumter; Talladega; Tallapoosa; Tuscaloosa; Walker; *Washington; Wilcox; Winston. Of the 67 counties, Etowah is the smallest (535 sq. mi.) and Baldwin is the largest (1,596 sq. mi.). Baldwin County is larger than the state of Rhode Island.

ALASKA: (Boroughs) Aleutians East; Anchorage; Bristol Bay; Denali; Fairbanks North Star; Haines; Juneau; Kenai Peninsula; Ketchikan Gateway; Kodiak Island; Lake and Peninsula; Matanuska-Susitna; North Slope; Northwest Arctic; Sitka; Skagway; Wrangell; Yakutat. Over half of Alaska lies in what is called the Unorganized Borough, although it is divided into census areas. Of the 18 boroughs, Wrangell is the smallest (45 sq. mi.) and North Slope is the largest (88,817 sq. mi.) which is slight larger than the state of Kansas. The Unorganized Borough measures 330,000 square miles. The entire state measures 655,000 square miles.

ARIZONA: Apache; Cochise; Coconino; Gila; Graham; Greenlee; La Paz; Maricopa; Mohave; Navajo; Pima; Pinal; Santa Cruz; Yyavapai; Yuma. Of the 15 counties, Santa Cruz is the smallest (1,238 sq. mi.) and Coconino is the largest (18,681 sq. mi.).

ARKANSAS: Arkansas; Ashley; Baxter; Benton; *Boone; Bradley; Calhoun; *Carroll; Chicot; *Clark; *Clay; Cleburne; Cleveland; Columbia; Conway; Craighead; Crawford; *Crittenden; Cross; Dallas; Desha; Drew; Faulkner; *Franklin; *Fulton; Garland; *Grant; Greene; Hempstead; Hot Spring; Howard, Independence; Izard; *Jackson; *Jefferson; *Johnson; Lafayette; *Lawrence; *Lee; *Lincoln; Little River; *Logan; Lonoke; *Madison; *Marion; Miller; Mississippi; *Monroe; *Montgomery; Nevada; Newton; Ouachita; *Perry; Phillips; *Pike; Poinsett; Polk; Pope; Prairie; *Pulaski; Randolph; St. Francis; Saline; *Scott; Searcy; Sebastian; Sevier; Sharp; Stone; *Union; Van Buren; *Washington; White; Woodruff; Yell. Of the 75 counties, Lafayette is the smallest (526 sq. mi.) and Union is the largest (1,039 Sq. mi.).

CALIFORNIA: Alameda; Alpine; Amador; Butte; Calaveras; Colusa; Contra Costa; Del Norte; El Dorado; Fresno; Glenn; Humboldt; Imperial; Inyo; Kern; Kings; Lake; Lassen; Los Angeles; Madera; Marin; Mariposa; Mendocino; Merced; Modoc; Mono; Monterey; Napa; Nevada; Orange; Placer; Plumas; Riverside; Sacramento; San Benito; San Bernadino; San Diego; San Francisco; San Joaquin; San Luis Obispo; San Mateo; Santa Barbara; Santa Clara; Santa Cruz; Shasta; Sierra; Siskiyou; Solano; Sonoma; Stanislaus;

Sutter; Tehama; Trinity; Tulare; Tuolumne; Ventura; Yolo; Yuba. Of the 58 counties, San Francisco is the smallest (46 sq. mi.) and San Bernadioo the largest (20,062 sq. mi.)

COLORADO: Adams; Alamosa; Arapahoe; Archuleta; Baca; Bent; Boulder; Broomfield; Chaffee; Cheyenne; Clear Creek; Conejos; Costilla; Crowley; Custer; Delta; Denver; Dolores; Douglas; Eagle; Elbert; El Passo; Fremont; Garfield; Gilpin; Grand; Gunnison; Hinsdale; Huerfano; *Jackson; *Jefferson; Kiowa; Kit Carson; Lake; La Plata; Larimer; Las Animas; *Lincoln; *Logan; Mesa; Mineral; Moffat; Montezuma; Montrose; *Morgan; Otero; Ouray; Park; Phillips; Pitkin; Prowers; Pueblo; Rio Blanco; Rio Grande; Routt; Saguache; San Juan; San Miguel; Sedgwick; Summit; Teller; *Washington; Weld; Yuma. Of the 64 counties, Broomfield is the smallest (33 sq. mi.) and Las Animas is the largest (4,773 Sq. mi.).

CONNECTICUT: Fairfield; Hartford; Litchfield; Middlesex; New Haven; New London; Tolland; Windham. Of the eight counties, Middlesex is the smallest (396 sq. mi.) and Litchfield is the largest (920 sq. mi.). In 1960, their county government was abolished. Local government now consists of cities and towns.

DELAWARE: Kent; New Castle; Sussex. Of the 3 counties, New Castle is the smallest (494 sq. mi.) and Sussex is the largest (1,196 sq. mi.). For the record, the third county is 800 square miles. Delaware has the fewest counties of all the states.

FLORIDA: Alachua; Baker; Bay; Bradford; Brevard; Broward; Calhoun; Charlotte; Citrus; *Clay; Collier; Columbia; DeSoto; Dixie; Duval; Escambia; Flagler; *Franklin; Gadsden; Gilchrist; Glades; Gulf; Hamilton; Hardee; Hendry; Hernando; Highlands; Hillsborough; Holmes; Indian River; *Jackson; *Jefferson; Lafayette; Lake; *Lee; Leon; Levy; Liberty; *Madison; Manatee; *Marion; *Martin; Miami-Dade; *Monroe; Nassau; Okaloosa; Okeechobee; Orange; Osceola; Palm Beach; Pasco; Pinellas; Polk; Putnam; Saint Johns; Saint Lucie; Santa Rosa; Sarasota; Seminole; Sumter; Suwannee; *Taylor; *Union; Volusia; Wakulla; Walton; *Washington. Of the 67 counties, Union is the smallest (240 sq. mi.) and Palm Beach is the largest (2,034 sq. mi.).

GEORGIA: Appling; Atkinson; Bacon; Baker; Baldwin; Banks; Barrow; Bartow; Ben Hill; Berrien; Bibb; Bleckley; Brantley; Brooks; Bryan; Bulloch; Burke; Butts; Calhoun; Camden; Candler; *Carroll; Catoosa; Charlton; Chatham; Chattahoochee; Chattooga; Cherokee; Clarke; *Clay; Clayton; Clinch; Cobb; Coffee; Colquitt; Columbia; Cook; Coweta; Crawford; Crisp; Dade; Dawson; Decatur; DeKalb; Dodge; Dooly; Dougherty; Douglas; Early; Echols; Effingham; Elbert; Emanuel; Evans; Fannin; *Fayette; *Floyd; Forsyth; *Franklin; *Fulton; Gilmer; Glascock; Glynn; Gordon; Grady; Greene; Gwinnett; Habersham; Hall; *Hancock; Haralson; Harris; *Hart; Heard; *Henry; Houston; Irwin; *Jackson; Jasper; Jeff Davis; *Jefferson; Jenkins; *Johnson; Jones; Lamar; Lanier; Laurens; *Lee; Liberty; *Lincoln; Long; Lowndes; Lumpkin; Macon; *Madison; *Marion; McDuffie; McIntosh; Meriwether; Miller; Mitchell; *Monroe; *Montgomery; *Morgan;

Murray; Muscogee; Newton; Oconee; Oglethorpe; Paulding; Peach; Pickens; Pierce; *Pike; Polk; *Pulaski; Putnam; Quitman; Rabun; Randolph; Richmond; Rockdale; Schley; Screven; Seminole; Spalding; Stephens; Stewart; Sumter; Talbot; Taliaferro; Tattnall; *Taylor; Telfair; Terrell; Thomas; Tift; Toombs; Towns; Treutlen; Troup; Turner; Twiggs; *Union; Upson; Walker; Walton; Ware; *Warren; *Washington; *Wayne; *Webster; Wheeler; White; Whitfield; Wilcox; Wilkes; Wilkinson; Worth. Of the 159 counties, Clarke is the smallest (121 sq. mi.) and Ware is the largest (903 sq. mi.). Georgia has the second highest number of counties in the United States, second to Texas which has 254. Kentucky weighs in third with 120.

HAWAII: Hawaii; Honolulu (metro); Kolawao; Kauai; Maui. Of the five counties, Kalawao is the smallest (52 sq. mi.) and Hawaii is the largest (5,000 sq. mi.). Delaware has the fewest counties (3) and Hawaii has the second fewest.

IDAHO: Ada; Adams; Bannock; Bear Lake; Benewah; Bingham; Blaine; Boise; Bonner; Bonneville; Boundary; Butte; Camas; Canyon; Caribou; Casia; *Clark; Clearwater; Custer; Elmore; *Franklin; Fremont; Gem; Gooding; Idaho; *Jefferson; Jerome; Kootenia; Latah; Lemhi; *Lewis; *Lincoln; *Madison; Minidoka; Nez Perce; Oneida; Owyhee; Payette; Power; Shoshone; Teton; Twin Falls; Valley; *Washington. Of the 44 counties, Idaho is the largest (8,500 sq. mi.) and Payette is the smallest (400 sq. mi.).

ILLINOIS: Adams; Alexander; Bond; *Boone; Brown; Bureau; Calhoun; *Carroll; Cass; Champaign; *Christian; *Clark; *Clay; *Clinton; Coles; Cook; Crawford; *Cumberland; De Witt; DeKalb; Douglas; DuPage; Edgar; Edwards; Effingham; *Fayette; Ford; *Franklin; *Fulton; *Gallatin; Greene; Grundy; Hamilton; *Hancock; *Hardin; *Henderson; *Henry; Iriquois; *Jackson; Jasper; *Jefferson; Jersey; Jo Daviess; *Johnson; Kane; Kankakee; Kendall; *Knox; Lake; LaSalle; *Lawrence; *Lee; *Livingston; *Logan; Macon; Macoupin; *Madison; *Marion; *Marshall; *Mason; Massac; McDonough; McHenry; *McLean; Menard; *Mercer; *Monroe; *Montgomery; *Morgan; Moultrie; Ogle; Peoria; *Perry; Piatt; *Pike; Pope; *Pulaski; Putnam; Randolph; Richland; Rock Island; Saline; Sangamon; Schuyler; *Scott; *Shelby; St. Clair; Stark; Stephenson; Tazwell; *Union; Vermillion; Wabash; *Warren; *Washington; *Wayne; White; Whiteside; Will; Williamson; Winnebago; *Woodford. Of the 102 counties, McLean is the largest (1,200 sq. mi.) and Pulaski is the smallest (200 sq. mi.).

INDIANA: Adams; *Allen; Bartholomew; Benton; Blackford; *Boone; Brown; *Carroll; Cass; *Clark; *Clay; *Clinton; Crawford; *Daviess; Dearborn; Decatur; DeKalb; Delaware; Dubois; Elkhart; *Fayette; *Floyd; Fountain; *Franklin; *Fulton; Gibson; *Grant; Greene; Hamilton; *Hancock; *Harrison; Hendricks; *Henry; Howard; Huntington; *Jackson; Jasper; Jay; *Jefferson; Jennings; *Johnson; *Knox; Kosciusko; LaGrange; Lake; LaPorte; *Lawrence; *Madison; *Marion (Indianapolis metro); *Marshall; *Martin; Miami; *Monroe; *Montgomery; *Morgan; Newton; Noble; *Ohio; Orange; *Owen; Parke; *Perry; *Pike; Porter; Posey; *Pulaski; Putnam; Randolph; Ripley; Rush; St. Joseph; Scott; Shelby; *Spencer; Starke; Steuben; Sullivan; Switzerland;

Tippecanoe; Tipton; *Union; Vanderburg; Vermillion; Vigo; Wabash; *Warren; Warrick; *Washington; *Wayne; Wells; White; *Whitley. Of the 92 counties, Allen is the largest (660 sq. mi.) and Ohio is the smallest (90 sq. mi.).

IOWA: *Adair; Adams; Allamakee; Appanoose; Audubon; Benton; Black Hawk; *Boone; Bremer; Buchanan; Buena Vista; *Butler; Calhoun; *Carroll; Cass; Cedar; Cerro Gordo; Cherokee; Chickasaw; Clarke; *Clay; Clayton; *Clinton; Crawford; Dallas; Davis; Decatur; Delaware; Des Moines; Dickinson; Dubuque; Emmet; *Fayette; *Floyd; *Franklin; Fremont; Greene; Grundy; Guthrie; Hamilton; *Hancock; *Hardin; *Harrison; *Henry; Howard; Humboldt; Ida; Iowa; *Jackson; Jasper; *Jefferson; *Johnson; Jones; Keokuk; Kossuth; *Lee; Linn; Louisa; Lucas; *Lyon; *Madison; *Marion; *Marshall; Mashaka; Mills; Mitchell; Monona; *Monroe; *Montgomery; Muscatine; O'Brien; Osceola; Pagae; Palo Alto; Plymouth; Pocahontas; Polk; Pottawattamie; Poweshiek; Ringgold; Sac; *Scott; *Shelby; Sioux; Story; Tama; *Taylor; *Union; Van Buren; Wapello; *Warren; *Washington; *Wayne; *Webster; Winnebago; Winneshiek; Woodbury; Worth; Wright. Of the 99 counties, Kossuth is the largest (980 sq. mi.) and Dickinson (380 sq. mi.).

KANSAS: *Allen; *Anderson; Atchison; Barber; Barton; *Bourbon; Brown; *Butler; Chase; Chautauqua; Cherokee; Cheyenne; *Clark; *Clay; Cloud; Coffey; Comanche; Cowley; Crawford; Decatur; Dicinison; Doniphan; Douglas; Edwards; Elk; Ellis; Ellsworth; Finney; Ford; *Franklin; Geary; Gove; Graham; *Grant; Gray; Greeley; Greenwood; Hamilton; Harper; Harvey; Haskell; Hodgeman; *Jackson; *Jefferson; Jewell; *Johnson; Kearny; Kingman; Kiowa; Labette; Lane; Leavenworth; *Lincoln; Linn; *Logan; *Lyon; *Marion; *Marshall; McPherson; *Meade; Miami; Mitchell; *Montgomery; Morris; Morton; Nemaha; Neosho; Ness; Norton; Osage; Osborne; Ottawa; Pawnee; Phillips; Pottawatomie; Pratt; Rawlins; Reno; Republic; Rice; Riley; Rooks; Rush; *Russell; Saline; *Scott; Sedgwick; Seward; Shawnee; Sheridan; Sherman; Smith; Stafford; Stanton; Stevens; Sumner; Thomas; Trego; Wabaunsee; Wallace; *Washington; Wichita; Wilson; Woodson; Wyandotte. Of the 105 counties, Butler is the largest (1,400 sq. mi.) and Wyandotte is the smallest (150 sq. mi.).

KENTUCKY: Adair; Allen; Anderson; Ballard; Barren; Bath (280 sq. mi.); Bell; Boone; Bourbon; Boyd; Boyle; Bracken; Breathitt (500 sq. mi.); Breckinridge; Bullitt; Butler; Caldwell; Calloway; Campbell; Carlisle; Carroll; Carter; Casey; Christian; Clark (254 sq. mi.); Clay (470 sq. mi.); Clinton; Crittenden; Cumberland; Daviess; Edmonson; Elliott; Estill; Fayette (285 sq. mi.); Fleming (350 sq. mi.); Floyd (400 sq. mi.); Franklin; Fulton; Gallatin; Garrard; Grant; Graves; Grayson; Green; Greenup; Hancock; Hardin; Harlan; Harrison; Hart; Henderson; Henry; Hickman; Hopkins; Jackson; Jefferson; Jessamine; Johnson; Kenton; Knott (350 sq. mi.); Knox; Larue; Laurel; Lawrence; Lee; Leslie; Letcher; Lewis; Lincoln; Livingston; Logan; Lyon; McCracken; McCreary; McLean; Madison (440 sq. mi.); Magoffin (310 sq. mi.); Marion; Marshall; Martin; Mason; Meade; Menifee; Mercer; Metcalfe; Monroe; Montgomery (200 sq. mi.); Morgan (380 sq. mi.);

Muhlenberg; Nelson; Nicholas; Ohio; Oldham; Owen; Owsley; Pendleton; Perry; Pike; Powell; Pulaski; Robertson; Rockcastle; Rowan; Russell; Scott; Shelby; Simpson; Spencer; Taylor; Todd; Trigg; Trimble; Union; Warren; Washington; Wayne; Webster; Whitley (440 sq. mi.); Wolfe; Woodford. Of the 120 counties, Pike is the largest (790 sq. mi.) and Robertson is the smallest (100 sq. mi.). Of Kentucky's 120 counties, 85 names are also used in other states.

LOUISIANA: (Parishes) Acadia; *Allen; Ascension; Assumption; Avoyelles; Beauregard; Bienville; Bossier; Caddo; Calcasieu; *Caldwell; Cameron; Catahoula; Clairborne; Concordia; De Soto; East Baton Rough; East Carroll; East Feliciana; Evangeline; *Franklin; *Grant; Iberia; Iberville; *Jackson; *Jefferson; Jefferson Davis; Lafayette; Lafourche; La Salle; *Lincoln; *Livingston; *Madison; Morehouse; Natchitoches; Orleans; Ouachita; Plaquemines; Pointe Coupee; Rapides; Red River; Richland; Sabine; St. Bernard; St. Charles; St. Helena; St. James; St. John the Baptist; St. Landry; St. Martin; St. Mary; St. Tammany; Tangipahoa; Tensas; Terrebonne; *Union; Vermillion; Vernon; *Washington; *Webster; West Baton Rough; West Carroll; West Feliciana; Winn. Of the 64 parishes, Terrebone is the largest (5,390 sq. mi.) and West Baton Rough is the smallest (530 sq. mi.).

MAINE: Androscoggin; Aroostook; *Cumberland; *Franklin; *Hancock; Kennebec; *Knox; *Lincoln; Oxford; Penobscot; Piscataquis; Sagadahoc; Somerset; Waldo; *Washington; York. Of the 16 counties, Aroostook is the largest (6,830 sq. mi.) and Sagadahoc is the smallest (370 sq. mi.).

MARYLAND: Allegany; Anne Arundel; Baltimore; Baltimore City; Calvert; Caroline; *Carroll; Cecil; Charles; Dorchester; Frederick; Garrett; Harford; Howard; Kent; *Montgomery; Prince George; Queen Ann; Saint Mary; Somerset; Talbot; *Washington; Wicomico; Worcester. Of the 24 counties, Dorchester is the largest (980 sq. mi.) and Baltimore City is the smallest (92 sq. mi.).

MASSACHUSETTS: Barnstable; Berkshire; Bristol; Dukes; Essex; *Franklin; Hampden; Hampshire; Middlesex; Nantucket; Norfolk; Plymouth; Suffolk; Worcester. Of the 14 counties, Worcester is the largest (1,508 sq. mi.) and Suffolk is the smallest (120 sq. mi.).

MICHIGAN: Alcona; Alger; Allegan; Alpena; Antrim; Arenac; Baraga; Barry; Bay; Benzie; Berrien; Branch; Calhoun; Cass; Charlevoix; Cheboygan; Chippewa; Clare; *Clinton; Crawford; Delta; Dickinson; Eaton; Emmet; Genesee; Gladwin; Gogebic; Grand Traverse; Gratiot; Hillsdale; Houghton; Huron; Ingham; Ionia; Iosco; Iron; Isabella; *Jackson; Kalamazoo; Kalkaska; Kent; Keweenaw; Lake; Lapeer; Leelanau; Lenawee; *Livingston; Luce; Mackinac; Macomb; Manistee; Marquette; *Mason; Mecosta; Menominee; Midland; Missaukee; *Monroe; Montcalm; *Montgomery; Muskegon; Newaygo; Oakland; Oceana; Ogemaw; Ontonagon; Osceola; Oscoda; Otsego; Ottawa; Presque Isle; Roscommon; Saginaw; St. Clair; St. Joseph; Sanilac; Schoolcraft;

Shiawassee; Tuscola; Van Buren; Washtenaw; *Wayne; Wexford. Of the 83 counties, Marquette is the largest (3,400 sq. mi.) and Benzie is the smallest (300 sq. mi.).

MINNESOTA: Aitkin; Anoka; Becker; Beltrami; Benton; Big Stone; Blue Earth; Brown; Carlton; Carver; Cass; Chippewa; Chisago; *Clay; Clearwater; Cook; Cottonwood; Crow Wing; Dakota; Dodge; Douglas; Faribault; Fillmore; Freeborn; Goodhue; *Grant; Hennepin; Houston; Hubbard; Isanti; Itasca; *Jackson; Kanabec; Kandiyohi; Kittson; Koochiching; Lac qui Parle; Lake; Lake of the Woods; Le Sueur; *Lincoln; *Lyon; McLeod; Mahnomen; *Marshall; *Martin; Meeker; Mille Lacs; Morrison; Mower; Murray; Nicollet; Nobles; Norman; Olmsted; Otter Trail; Pennington; Pine; Pipestone; Polk; Pope; Ramsey; Red Lake; Redwood; Renville; Rice; Rock; Roseau; *Scott; Sherburne; Sibley; St. Louis; Stearns; Steele; Stevens; Swift; Todd; Traverse; Wabasha; Wadena; Waseca; *Washington; Watonwan; Wilkin; Winona; Wright; Yellow Medicine. Of the 87 counties, St. Louis is the largest (6,200 sq. mi.) and Ramsey is the smallest (150 sq. mi.).

MISSISSIPPI: Adams; Alcorn; Amite; Attala; Benton; Bolivar; Calhoun; *Carroll; Chickasaw; Choctaw; Claiborne; Clarke; *Clay; Coahoma; Copiah; Covington; DeSoto; Forrest; *Franklin; George; Greene; Grenada; *Hancock; *Harrison; Hinds; Holmes; Humphreys; Issaquena; Itawamba; *Jackson; Jasper; *Jefferson; Jefferson Davis; Jones; Kemper; Lafayette; Lamar; Lauderdale; *Lawrence; Leake; *Lee; Leflore; *Lincoln; Lowndes; *Madison; *Marion; *Marshall; *Monroe; *Montgomery; Neshoba; Newton; Noxubee; Oktibbeha; Panola; Pearl River; *Perry; *Pike; Pontotoc; Prentiss; Quitman; Rankin; *Scott; Sharkey; *Simpson; Smith; Stone; Sunflower; Tallahatchie; Tate; Tippah; Tishomingo; Tunica; *Union; Walthall; *Warren; *Washington; *Wayne; *Webster; Wilkinson; Winston; Yalobusha; Yazoo. Of the 82 counties, Bolivar is the largest (875 sq. mi.) and Alcorn is the smallest (400 sq. mi.).

MISSOURI: The city of St. Louis is independent from St. Louis County and is referred to as a "city not within a county." *Adair; Andrew; Atchison; Audrain; Barry; Barton; Bates; Benton; Bolliger; *Boone; Buchanan; *Butler; *Caldwell; Callaway; Camdem; Cape Girardeau; *Carroll; *Carter; Cass; Cedar; Chariton; *Christian; *Clark; *Clay; *Clinton; Cole; Cooper; Crawford; Dade; Dallas; *Daviess; DeKalb; Dent; Douglas; Dunkin; *Franklin; Gasconade; Gentry; Greene; Grundy; *Harrison; *Henry; Hickory; Holt; Howard; Howell; Iron; *Jackson; Jasper; *Jefferson; *Johnson; *Knox; Laclede; Lafayette; *Lawrence; *Lewis; *Lincoln; Linn; *Livingston; Macon; *Madison; Maries; *Marion; McDonald; *Mercer; Miller; Mississippi; Moniteau; *Monroe; *Montgomery; *Morgan; New Madrid; Newton; Nodaway; Oregon; Osage; Ozark; Pemiscot; *Perry; Pettis; Phelps; *Pike; Platte; Polk; *Pulaski; Putnam; Ralls; Randolph; Ray; Reynolds; Ripley; Saint Charles; Saint Clair; Saint Francois; Sainte Genevieve; Saint Louis; Saint Louis City; Saline; Schuyler; Scotland; *Scott; Shannon; *Shelby; Stoddard; Stone; Sullivan; Taney; Texas; Vernon; *Warren; *Washington; *Wayne; *Webster; Worth; Wright. Of the 114 counties, Texas is the largest (1,200 sq. mi) and Worth is the smallest (270 sq. mi.).

MONTANA: Beaverhead; Big Horn; Blaine; Broadwater; Carbon; *Carter; Cascade; Chouteau; Custer; Daniels; Dawson; Deer Lodge; Fallon; Fergus; Flathead; *Gallatin; Garfield; Glacier; Golden Valley; Granite; Hill; *Jefferson; Judith Basin; Lake; Lewis and Clark; Liberty; *Lincoln; *Madison; McCone; Meagher; Mineral; Missoula; Musselshell; Park (contains a portion of Yellowstone National Park); Petroleum; Phillips; Pondera; Powder River; *Powell; Prairie; Ravalli; Richland; Roosevelt; Rosebud; Sanders; Sheridan; Silver Bow; Stillwater; Sweet Grass; Teton; Toole; Treasure; Valley; Wheatland; Wibaux; Yellowstone. Of the 56 counties, Beaverhead is the largest (5,500 sq. mi.) and Silver Bow is the smallest (700 sq. mi.).

NEBRASKA: Adams; Antelope; Arthur; Banner; Blaine; *Boone; Box Butte; *Boyd; Brown; Buffalo; Burt; *Butler; Cass; Cedar; Chase; Cherry; Cheyenne; *Clay; Coalfax; Cuming; Custer; Dakota; Dawes; Dawson; Deuel; Dixon; Dodge; Douglas; Dundy; Fillmore; *Franklin; Frontier; Furnas; Gage; Garden; Garfield; Gosper; *Grant; Greeley; Hall; *Hamilton; *Harlan; Hayes; Hitchcock; Holt; Hooker; Howard; *Jefferson; *Johnson; Kearney; Keith; Keya Paha; Kimball; *Knox; Lancaster; *Lincoln; *Logan; Loup; *Madison; McPherson; Merrick; Morrill; Nance; Nemaha; Nuckolls; Otoe; Pawnee; Perkins; Phelps; Pierce; Platt; Polk; Red Willow; Richardson; Rock; Saline; Sarpy; Saunders; Scotts Bluff; Seward; Sheridan; Sherman; Sioux; Stanton; Thayer; Thomas; Thurston; Valley; *Washington; *Wayne; *Webster; Wheeler; York. Of the 93 counties, Cherry is the largest (6,000 sq. mi.) and Sarpy is the smallest (240 sq. mi.).

NEVADA: Carson City is not part of a county. Churchill; *Clark; Douglas; Elko; Esmeralda; Eureka; Humboldt; Lander; *Lincoln; *Lyon; Mineral; Nye; Pershing; Storey; Washoe; White Pine. Of the 16 counties, Nye is the largest (18,000 sq. mi.) and Storey is the smallest (260 sq. mi.).

NEW HAMPSHIRE: Belknap; *Carroll; Cheshire; Coos; Grafton; Hillsborough; Merrimack; Rockingham; Straford; Sullivan. Of the 10 counties, Coos is the largest (1,800 sq. mi.) and Sullivan is the smallest (540 sq. mi.).

NEW JERSEY: Atlantic; Bergen; Burlington; Camden; Cape May; *Cumberland; Essex; Gloucester; Hudson; Hunterdon; *Mercer; Middlesex; Monmouth; Morris; Ocean; Passaic; Salem; Somerset; Suxxes; *Union; *Warren. Of the 21 counties, Ocean is the largest (900 sq. mi.) and Hudson is the smallest (60 sq. mi.).

NEW MEXICO: Bernalillo; Catron; Chaves; Cibola; Colfax; Curry; De Baca; Dona Ana; Eddy; *Grant; Guadalupe; Harding; Hidalgo; Lea; *Lincoln; Los Alamos; Luna; McKinley; Mora; Otero; Quay; Rio Arriba; Roosevelt; Sandoval; San Juan; San Miguel; Santa Fe; Sierra; Socorro; Taos; Torrance; *Union; Valencia. Of the 33 counties, Catron is the largest (6,900 sq. mi.) and Los Alamos is the smallest (110 sq. mi.).

NEW YORK: Albany; Allegany; Bronx; Broome; Cattaraugus; Cayuga; Chautauqua; Chemung; Chenango; Clinton; Columbia; Cortland; Delaware; Dutchess; Erie; Essex; *Franklin; *Fulton; Genesee; Greene; Hamilton; Herkimer; *Jefferson; Kings; *Lewis; *Livingston; *Madison; *Monroe; *Montgomery; Nassau; New York; Niagara; Oneida; Onondaga; Ontario; Orange; Orleans; Oswego; Ostego; Putnam; Queens; Rensselaer; Richmond; Rockland; St. Lawrence; Saratoga; Schenectady; Schorarie; Schuyler; Seneca; Steuben; Suffolk; Sullivan; Tioga; Tompkins; Ulster; *Warren; *Washington; *Wayne; Westchester; Wyoming; Yates. Of the 62 counties, St. Lawrence is the largest (2,800 sq. mi.) and New York City is the smallest (35 sq. mi.). Five of New York's counties are co-extensive with the five broughs of New York City and do not have functioning county governments. New York City is the county seat of New York County (Manhattan), Kings County (Brooklyn), Bronx County (The Bronx), Richmond County (Staten Island), and Queens County (Queens).

NORTH CAROLINA: Alamance; Alexander; Alleghany; Anson; Ashe; Avery; Beaufort; Bertie; Bladen; Brunswick; Buncombe; Burke; Cabarrus; *Caldwell; Camden; Carteret; Caswell; Catawba; Chatham; Cherokee; Chowan; *Clay; Cleveland; Columbus; Craven; *Cumberland; Currituck; Dare; Davidson; Davie; Duplin; Durham; Edgecombe; Forsyth; *Franklin; Gaston; Gates; Graham; Granville; Greene; Guilford; Halifax; Harnett; Haywood; *Henderson; Hertford; Hoke; Hyde; Iredell; *Jackson; Johnston; Jones; *Lee; Lenoir; *Lincoln; McDowell; Macon; *Madison; *Martin; Mecklenburg; Mitchell; *Montgomery; Moore; Nash; New Hanover; Northampton; Onslow; Orange; Pamlico; Pasquotank; Pender; Perquimans; Person; Pitt; Polk; Randolph; Richmond; Robeson; Rockingham; *Rowan; Rutherford; Sampson; Scotland; Stanley; Stokes; Surry; Swain; Transylvania; Tyrrell; *Union; Vance; Wake; *Warren; *Washington; Watauga; *Wayne; Wilkes; Wilson; Yadkin; Yancey. Of the 100 counties, Dare is the largest (1,560 sq. me.) and Clay is the smallest, (221 sq. mi.).

NORTH DAKOTA: Adams; Barnes; Benson; Billings; Bottineau; Bowman; Burke; Burleigh; Cass; Cavalier; Dickey; Divide; Dunn; Eddy; Emmons; Foster; Golden Valley; Grand Forks; *Grant; Griggs; Hettinger; Kidder; LaMoure; *Logan; McHenry; McIntosh; McKenzie; McLean; *Mercer; Morton; Mountrail; *Nelson; Oliver; Pembina; Pierce; Ramsey; Ransom; Renville; Richland; Rolette; Sargent; Sheridan; Sioux; Slope; Stark; Steele; Stutsman; Towner; Traill; Walsh; Ward; Wells; Williams. Of the 53 counties, McKenzie is the largest (2,750 sq. mi.) and Eddy is the smallest (630 sq. mi.).

OHIO: Adams; *Allen; Ashland; Ashtabule; Athens; Auglaize; Belmont; Brown; *Butler; *Carroll; Champaign; *Clark; Clermont; *Clinton; Columbiana; Coshocton; Crawford; Cuyahoga; Darke; Defiance; Delaware; Erie; Fairfield; *Fayette; *Franklin; *Fulton; Gallia; Geauga; Greene; Guernsey; Hamilton; *Hancock; *Hardin; *Harrison; *Henry; Highland; Hocking; Holmes; Huron; *Jackson; *Jefferson; *Knox; Lake; *Lawrence; Licking; *Logan; Lorain; Lucas; *Madison; Mahoning; *Marion; Medina; Meigs; *Mercer; Miami; *Monroe; *Montgomery; *Morgan; Morrow; Muskingum; Noble;

Ottowa; Paulding; *Perry; Pickaway; *Pike; Portage; Preble; Putnam; Richland; Ross; Sandusky; Sciota; Seneca; *Shelby; Stark; Summit; Trumblull; Tuscarawas; *Union; Van Wert; Vinton; *Warren; *Washington; *Wayne; Williams; Wood; Wyandot. Of the 88 counties, Ross is the largest (700 sq. mi.) and Lake is the smallest (230 sq. mi.).

OKLAHOMA: *Adair; Alfalfa; Atoka; Beaver; Beckham; Blaine; Bryan; Caddo; Canadian; *Carter; Cherokee; Choctaw; Cimarron; Cleveland; Coal; Comanche; Cotton; Craig; Creek; Custer; Delaware; Dewey; Ellis; Garfield; Garvin; Grady; *Grant; Greer; Harmon; Harper; Haskel; *Jackson; *Jefferson; Johnston; Kay; Kingfisher; Kiowa; Latimer; Le Flore; *Lincoln; *Logan; Love; Major; *Marshall; Mayes; McClain; McCurtain; McIntosh; Murray; Muskogee; Noble; Nowata; Okfuskee; Oklahoma; Okmulgee; Osage; Ottawa; Pawnee; Payne; Pittsburg; Pontotoc; Pottawatomie; Pushmataha; Roger Mills; Rogers; Seminole; Sequoyah; Stephens; Texas; Tillman; Tulsa; Wagoner; *Washington; Washita; Woods; Woodward. Of the 77 counties, Osage is the largest (2,250 sq. mi.) and Marshall is the smallest (370 sq. mi.).

OREGON: Baker; Benton; Clackamas; Clatsop; Columbia; Coos; Crook; Curry; Deschutes; Douglas; Gilliam; *Grant; Harney; Hood River; *Jackson; *Jefferson; Josephine; Klamath; Lake; Lane; *Lincoln; Linn; Malheur; *Marion; Morrow; Multnomah; Polk; Sherman; Tillamook; Umatilla; *Union; Wallowa; Wasco; *Washington; Wheeler; Yamhill. Of the 36 counties, Harney is the largest (10,100 sq. mi.) and Multhnomah is the smallest (430 sq. mi.).

PENNSYLVANIA: Adams; Allegheny; Armstrong; Beaver; Bedford; Berks; Blair; Bradford; Bucks; *Butler; Cambria; Cameron; Carbon; Centre; Chester; Clarion; Clearfield; *Clinton; Columbia; Crawford; *Cumberland; Dauphin; Delaware; Elk; Erie; *Fayette; Forest; *Franklin; *Fulton; Greene; Huntingdon; Indiana; *Jefferson; Juniata; Lackawana; Lancaster; *Lawrence; Lebanon; Lehigh; Luzerne; Lycoming; McKean; Mercer; Mifflin; *Monroe; *Montgomery; Montour; Northampton; Northumberland; *Perry; Philadelphia; *Pike; Potter; Schuylkill; Snyder; Somerset; Sullivan; Susquehanna; Tioga; *Union; Venango; *Warren; *Washington; *Wayne; Westmoreland; Wyoming; York. Of the 67 counties, Erie is the largest (1,550 sq. mi.) and Montour is the smallest (130 sq. mi.).

RHODE ISLAND: Bristol; Kent; Newport; Providence; *Washington. Of the 5 counties, Washington is the largest (560 sq. mi.) and Bristol is the smallest (45 sq. mi.).

SOUTH CAROLINA: Abbeville; Aiken; Allendale; *Anderson; Bamberg; Barnwell; Beaufort; Berkeley; Calhoun; Charleston; Cherokee; Chester; Chesterfield; Claredon; Colleton; Darlington; Dillon; Dorchester; Edgefield; Fairfield; Florence; Georgetown; Greenville; Greenwood; Hampton; Horry; Jasper; Kershaw; Lancaster; Laurens; *Lee; Lexington; McCormick; *Marion; Marlboro; Newberry; Oconee; Orangeburg; Pickens; Richland; Saluda; Spartanburg; Sumter; *Union; Williamsburg; York. Of the 46 counties, Charleston is the largest (1,360 sq. mi.) and Calhoun is the smallest (392 sq. mi.).

SOUTH DAKOTA: Aurora; Beadle; Bennett; Bon Homme; Brookings; Brown; Brule; Buffalo; Butte; *Campbell; Charles Mix; *Clark; *Clay; Codington; Corson; Custer; Davison; Day; Deuel; Dewey; Douglas; Edmunds; Fall River; Faulk; *Grant; Gregory; Haakoh; Hamlin; Hand; Hanson; Harding; Hughes; Hutchinson; Hyde; *Jackson; Jerauld; Jones; Kingsbury; Lake; *Lawrence; *Lincoln; Lyman; *Marshall; McCook; McPherson; *Meade; Mellette; Miner; Minnehaha; Moody; Pennington; Perkins; Potter; Roberts; Sanborn; Shannon; Spink; Stanley; Sully; *Todd; Tripp; Turner; *Union; Walworth; Yankton; Ziebach. Of the 66 counties, Meade is the largest (3,470 sq. mi.) and Clay is the smallest (400 sq. mi.).

TENNESSEE: *Anderson; Bedford; Benton; Bledsoe; Blount; Bradley; *Campbell; Cannon; *Carroll; *Carter; Cheatham; Chester; Clairborne; *Clay; Cocke; Coffee; Crockett; *Cumberland; Davidson; Decatur; DeKalb; Dickson; Dyer; *Fayette; Fentress; *Franklin; Gisbon; Giles; Grainger; Greene; Grundy; Hamblen; Hamilton; *Hancock; Hardeman; *Hardin; Hawkins; Haywood; *Henderson; *Henry; *Hickman; Houston; Humphreys; *Jackson; *Jefferson; *Johnson; *Knox; Lake; Lauderdale; *Lawrence; *Lewis; *Lincoln; Loudon; McMinn; Macon; *Madison; *Marion; *Marshall; Maury; McNairy; Meigs; *Monroe; *Montgomery; Moore; *Morgan; Obion; Overton; *Perry; Pickett; Polk; Putnam; Rhea; Roane; *Robertson; Rutherford; *Scott; Sequatchie; Sevier; *Shelby; Smith; Stewart; Sullivan; Sumner; Tipton; Trousdale; Unicoi; *Union; Van Buren; *Warren; *Washington; *Wayne; Weakley; White; Williamson; Wilson. Of the 95 counties, Shelby is the largest (750 sq. mi.) and Trousdale is the smallest (115 sq. mi.).

TEXAS: *Anderson; Andrews; Angelina; Aransas; Archer; Armstrong; Atascosa; Austin; Bailey; Bandara; Bastrop; Baylor; Bee; Bell; Bexar; Blanco; Borden; Bosque; Bowie; Brazoria; Brazos; Brewster; Briscoe; Brooks; Brown; Burleson; Burnet; *Caldwell; Calhoun; Callahan; Cameron; Camp; Carson; Cass; Castro; Chambers; Cherokee; Childress; *Clay; Cochran; Coke; Coleman; Collin; Collingsworth; Colorado; Comal; Comanche; Concho; Cooke; Coryell; Cottle; Crane; Crockett; Crosby; Culberson; Dallam; Dallas; Dawson; Deaf Smith; Delta; Denton; DeWitt; Dickens; Dimmit; Donley; Duval; Eastland; Ector; Edwards; El Passo; Ellis; Erath; Falls; Fannin; *Fayette; Fisher; *Floyd; Foard; Fort Bend; *Franklin; Freestone; Frio; Gaines; Galveston; Garza; Gillespie; Glasscock; Goliad; Gonzales; Gray; Grayson; Gregg; Grimes; Guadalupe; Hale; Hall; Hamilton; Hansford; Hardeman; *Hardin; Harris; *Harrison; Hartley; Haskel; Hays; Hemphill; *Henderson; Hidalgo; Hill; Hockley; Hood; Hopkins; Houston; Howard; Hudspeth; Hunt; Hutchison; Irion; Jack; *Jackson; Jasper; Jeff Davis; *Jefferson; Jim Hogg; Jim Wells; *Johnson; Jones; Karnes; Kaufman; Kendall; Kenedy; Kent; Kerr; Kimble; King; Kinney; Kleberg; *Knox; Lamar; Lamb; Lampasas; La Salle; Lavaca; *Lee; Leon; Liberty; Limestone; Lipscomb; Live Oak; Llano; Loving; Lubbock; Lynn; McCulloch; McLennan; McMullen; *Madison; *Marion; *Martin; *Mason; Matagorda; Maverick; Medina; Menard; Midland; Milam; Mills; Mitchell; Montague; *Montgomery; Moore; Morris; Motley; Nacogdoches; Navarro; Newton; Nolan; Nueces; Ochiltree; Oldham; Orange; Palo Pinto; Panola; Parker; Parmer; Pecos; Polk; Potter; Presidio; Rains; Randall; Reagan; Real; Red River; Reeves; Refugio; Roberts; *Robertson; Rockwall;

141

Runnels; Rusk; Sabine; San Augustine; San Jacinto; San Patricio; San Saba; Schleicher; Scurry; Shackelford; *Shelby; Sherman; Smith; Somervell; Starr; Stephens; Sterling; Stonewal; Sutton; Swisher; Tarrant; *Taylor; Terrell; Terry; Throckmorton; Titus; Tom Green; Travis; Trinity; Tyler; Upshur; Upton; Uvalde; Val Verde; Van Zandt; Victoria; Walker; Waller; Ward; *Washington; Webb; Wharton; Wheeler; Wichita; Wilbarger; Willacy; Williamson; Wilson; Winkler; Wise; Wood; Yoakum; Young; Zapata; Zavala. Of the 254 counties, Brewster is the largest (6,100 sq. mi.) and Robertson is the smallest (130 sq. mi.).

UTAH: Beaver; Box Elder; Cache; Carbon; Daggett; Davis; Duchesne; Emery; Garfield; Grand; Iron; Juab; Kane; Millard; *Morgan; Piute; Rich; Salt Lake; San Juan; Sanpete; Sevier; Summit; Tooele; Uintah; Utah; Wasatch; *Washington; *Wayne; Weber. Of the 29 counties, San Juan is the largest (7,800 sq. mi.) and Davis is the smallest (300 sq. mi.).

VERMONT: Addison; Bennington; Caledonia; Chittenden; Essex; *Franklin; Grand Isle; Lamoille; Orange; Orleans; Rutland; *Washington; Windham; Windsor. Of the 14 counties, Windsor is the largest (970 sq. mi.) and Grand Isle is the smallest (80 sq. mi.).

VIRGINIA: Accomack; Albemarle; Alleghany; Amelia; Amhurst; Appomattox; Arlington; Augusta; *Bath; Bedford; Bland; Botetourt; Brunswick; Buchanan; Buckingham; *Campbell; Caroline; *Carroll; Charles City; Charlotte; Chesterfield; Clarke; Craig; Culpeper; *Cumberland; Dickenson; Dinwiddie; Essex; Fairfax; Fauquier; *Floyd; Fluvanna; *Franklin; Frederick; Giles; Gloucester; Goochland; Grayson; Greene; Greensville; Halifax; Hanover; Henrico; *Henry; Highland; Isle of Wright; James City; King and Queen; King George; King William; Lancaster; *Lee; Loudon; Louisa; Lunenburg; *Madison; Mathews; Mecklenburg; Middlesex; *Montgomery; *Nelson; New Kent; Northampton; Northumberland; Nottoway; Orange; Page; Patrick; Pittsylvania; Powhatan; Prince Edward; Prince George; Prince William; *Pulaski; Rappahannock; Richmond; Roanoke; Rockbridge; Rockingham; *Russell; Scott; Shenandoah; Smyth; Southampton; Spotsylvania; Stafford; Surry; Sussex; Tazewell; *Warren; *Washington; Westmoreland; Wise; Wythe; York. Of the 95 counties, Pittsylvania and Augusta are the largest (971 and 972 sq. mi. respectively) and Arlington is the smallest (25 sq. mi.).

WASHINGTON: Adams; Asotin; Benton; Chelan; Clallam; *Clark; Columbia; Cowlitz; Douglas; Ferry; *Franklin; Garfield; *Grant; Grays Harbor; Island; *Jefferson; King; Kitsap; Kittitas; Klickitat; *Lewis; *Lincoln; *Mason; Okanogan; Pacific; Pend Oreille; Pierce; San Juan; Skagit; Skamania; Snohomish; Spokane; Stevens; Thurston; Wahkiakum; Walla Walla; Whatcom; Whitman; Yakima. Of the 39 counties, Okanogan is the largest (5,200 sq. mi.) and San Juan is the smallest (175 sq. mi.).

WEST VIRGINIA: Barbour; Berkeley; *Boone; Braxton; Brooke; Cabell; Calhoun; *Clay; Doddridge; *Fayette; Gilmer; *Grant; Greenbrier; Hampshire; *Hancock; Hardy; *Harrison; *Jackson; *Jefferson; Kanawah; *Lewis; *Lincoln; *Logan; McDowell; *Marion; *Marshall; *Mason; *Mercer; Mineral; Mingo; Monongalia; *Monroe; *Morgan;

Nicholas; *Ohio; *Pendleton; Pleasanta; Pocahontas; Preston; Putnam; Raleigh; Randolph; Ritchie; Roane; Summers; *Taylor; Tucker; Tyler; Upshur; *Wayne; *Webster; Wetzel; Wirt; Wood; Wyoming. Of the 55 counties, Randolph is the largest (1,000 sq. mi.) and Hancock is the smallest (80 sq. mi.).

WISCONSIN: Adams; Ashland; Barron, Bayfield; Brown; Buffalo; Burnett; Calument; Chippewa; *Clark; Columbia; Crawford; Dane; Dodge; Door; Douglas; Dunn; Eau Claire; Florence; Fon du Lac; Forest; *Grant; *Green; Green Lake; Iowa; Iron; *Jackson; *Jefferson; Juneau; Kenosha; Kewaunee; La Crosse; Lafayette; Langlade; *Lincoln; Manitowoc; Marathon; Marinette; Marquette; Menominee; Milwaukee; *Monroe; Oconto; Oneida; Outagamie; Ozaukee; Peppin; Pierce; Polk; Portage; Price; Racine; Richland; Rock; Rusk; Saint Croix; Sauk; Sawyer; Shawano; Sheboygan; *Taylor; Trempealeau; Vernon; Vilas; Walworth; Washburn; *Washington; Waukesha; Waupaca; Waushara; Winnebago; Wood. Of the 72 counties, Marathon is the largest (1,500 sq. mi.) and Ozaukee and Peppin are the smallest (230 sq. mi. each).

WYOMING: Albany; Big Horn; *Campbell; Carbon; Converse; Crook; Fremont; Goshen; Hot Springs; *Johnson; Laramie; *Lincoln; Natrona; Niobrara; Park; Platte; Sheridan; Sublette; Sweetwater; Teton; Uinta; Washakie; Weston. Of the 23 counties, Sweetwater is the largest (10,500 sq. mi.) and Hot Springs is the smallest (2,000 sq. mi.).

The U.S. Census Bureau lists 3,141 counties (or the county equivalent) in the United States. Only eight states have a population greater than Los Angeles County. The county with the least population is Loving County, Texas with a population of fewer than 100. The next smallest county is Kalawao County, Hiwaii, a leper colony with a population of fewer than two hundred. Thirty-one states have a Washington County.

States in order of greatest to least number of counties:

254 – Texas	75 - Arkansas	33 – New Mexico
195 – Georgia	72 - Wisconsin	29 - Utah
134 – Virginia	76 - Pennsylvania	27 - Alaska
120 - Kentucky	67 - Florida	24 - Maryland
115 - Missouri	67 - Alabama	23 - Wyoming
105 – Kansas	66 – South Dakota	21 – New Jersey
102 – Illinois	64 - Louisiana	17 - Nevada
100 – North Carolina	64 – Colorado	16 - Maine
99 – Iowa	62 – New York	15 - Arizona
95 – Tennessee	58 - California	14 - Vermont
93 – Nebraska	56 - Montana	14 - Massachusetts
92 – Indiana	55 – West Virginia	10 – New Hampshire
88 – Ohio	53 – North Dakota	8 - Connecticut
87 – Minnesota	46 – South Dakota	5 – Rhode Island
83 – Michigan	44 – Idaho	5 - Hawaii
82 – Mississippi	39 – Washington	3 - Delaware
77 – Oklahoma	37 - Oregon	

The city of Dallas, Texas lies within five counties while New York City contains five counties within itself.

KENTUCKY

Following are lists of interesting names across Kentucky along with some historical facts. Many names deal with nature, women's names, and family names. Some names have no particular significance, other than the fact that they are unusual, such as, Decoy, Elmrock, Fisty, Handshoe, Mousie, Pippa Passes, Sassafras, and Vest.

ADAIR COUNTY (1802) Formed from Green County. The county is named for John Adair, Kentucky House of Representatives, helped draft Kentucky's Constitution, governor of Kentucky (1820–1824), U.S. House of Representatives, and U.S. Senate. He was born in South Carolina (1757) to a Scottish immigrant and served in the Revolution and the War of 1812. He moved to Kentucky in 1788, and continued a military career rising to the rank of brigadier general. During his term as governor he helped establish the state's university system. He died and was buried in Harrodsburg in 1840, but in 1872 his remains were moved to the Frankfort Cemetery. He also has counties named for him in Iowa and Missouri as well as the town of Adair, Iowa.

Columbia is the county seat. The post office at Columbia was opened on April 1, 1806, by John Field, who also ran a local store. It is alleged that he named the community in honor of Christopher Columbus.

Lindsey Wilson College, affiliated with the United Methodist Church, began in 1903 as a training school for Vanderbilt University which, at that time, was affiliated with the Methodist Episcopal Church, South.

Interesting names include: Basil; Bliss; Breeding; Cane Valley; Chance; Christine; Craycraft; Crocus; Ella; Eunice; Fairplay; Feathersburg; Flatwood; Gadberry; Inroad; Joppa; Knifley; Low Gap; Milltown; Montpelier; Neatsville; Nell; Ozark; Pickett; Picnic; Pyrus; Settle; Sparksville; Speck; Weed

ALLEN COUNTY (1815) Formed from Barren and Warren Counties. The county is named for Colonel John Allen, an army officer killed in the War of 1812, Battle of River Raisin near Detroit, Michigan. Born 1771 in Virginia and died 1813. He left his senate seat in Frankfort, from Shelby County, to serve in the war. He also has counties named for him in Indiana and Ohio.

Scottsville is the county seat.

Notable residents include:
- Mordecai Ham (1877–1961) – born on a farm near Scottsville; he is the evangelist under whose preaching Billy Graham was converted
- Charles Napier (1936–) – Scottsville; actor; he is a blond, square-jawed man who usually plays tough guy parts; has appeared in thirty films including: "Nutty Professor, II," two Austin Powers movies, "The Cable Guy," "Ernest Goes to Jail," and "The Blues Brothers"

- Cal Turner Sr. – businessman who founder the Dollar General Corporation Scottsville; was illiterate

Interesting names include: Adolphus; Amos; Butlersville; Cedar Springs; Chapel Hill; Clare; Fleet; Forest Springs; Gainesville; Halfway; Halifax; Holland; Mount Aerial; Mount Zion; Mt Union; Oak Forest; Petroleum; Pope; Red Hill; Settle; Walnut Grove; Walnut Hill; Yesse

ANDERSON COUNTY (1827) Formed from Franklin, Washington, and Mercer Counties. The county is named for Richard Clough Anderson, Jr., Kentucky House of Representatives (Speaker of the House), U.S. House of Representatives, and the first minister to the Republic of Columbia. Born in Louisville 1788 and buried at Soldiers' Retreat near Louisville, 1826.

Lawrenceburg is the county seat.

Notable residents include:
- James Beauchamp Clark (1850–1921) – Lawrenceburg; An unsuccessful candidate for the Democratic nomination for president in 1912; U.S. House of Representatives from Missouri, 1911-1919 and Speaker of the House
- Andrew McKee (1896–1976) – Lawrenceburg; pioneer in modern submarine design and development; the submarine tender USS McKee (AS-41) is named for him

Interesting names include: Alton; Anderson City; Antioch; Ashbrook; Ballard; Birdie; Drydock; Fairview; Fox Creek; Gee; Hickory Grove; Klondyke; Ninevah; Sinai; Sparrow; Stringtown; Van Buren; Wayside

BALLARD COUNTY (1842) Formed from Hickman and McCracken Counties. The county is named for Captain Bland Ballard who fought in the Revolutionary War and the War of 1818 and was a member of the Kentucky General Assembly; born in Fredericksburg, Virginia in 1761; moved to Kentucky at age eighteen; served as a scout in George Rogers Clark's 1780 expedition in Ohio, and as a scout and in 1786 for Clark's Wabash Campaign during the Northwest Indian War; was wounded and taken prisoner at Raisin River near Detroit, Michigan; died in 1853; Blandville in Ballard County is named for him

Wickliffe, the county seat, is named for Charles Anderson Wickliffe, Kentucky House of Representatives, lieutenant governor, governor (1839–1840), U.S. Postmaster General, and U.S. Congress; born in Bardstown where he also practiced law; served in the War of 1812; a wealthy man with contempt for the poor, he earned the nickname "The Duke;" he died in Maryland. When looking at a map, Ballard County favors a monkey's head. The town of Monkeys Eyebrow is located where the monkey's eyebrow would be.

Wickliffe Mounds State Historic Site is the archaeological site of a prehistoric Native American village of the Mississippian mound builders. Located on the bluff overlooking the Mississippi River, the village was occupied from about AD 1100 to 1350. The Mississippians built a complex settlement with permanent houses and earthen mounds situated around a central plaza. They farmed the river bottoms and participated in a vast trade network. Their dead were buried with great dignity and respect.

Interesting names include: Bandana; Barlow; Blandville; East Cairo; Gage; Ingleside; Kevil; La Center; Monkeys Eyebrow; Needmore; New York; Oscar

BARREN COUNTY (1799) Formed from Green and Warren Counties, the county is named for the barrens, a region of grassland in the northern third of the county. Barren County, like most of south central Kentucky, was settled by the Scots-Irish, and still bears many cultural aspects that trace back to that heritage.

Glasgow, the county seat, was founded in 1799 by a group of Revolutionary War veterans and named for Glasgow, Virginia. Four days of Scottish family entertainment, known as Glasgow Highland Games, are held each year on the weekend following Memorial Day at Barren River Lake State Resort Park. The event draws many thousands of visitors. In 2007 *The Progressive Farmer* magazine voted Barren County the Number One best place to live in rural America. The county is reported to have the most fertile land in the state.

Notable residents include:
- James Greene Hardy (1795–1856) – born in Virginia; lieutenant governor, 1855-1856; Hardyville in Hart County is named for him
- Louis Broady Nunn (1924–2004) – Park; Kentucky governor from 1967-1971
- Billy Vaughn (1919–1991) – Glasgow; served during World War II; learned to play the mandolin at age three; had more chart successes than any other orchestra leader
- Julian Goodman (1922–) – Glasgow; former CEO and chairman of the board of NBC
- Lisa Diane Sawyer (1945–) – Glasgow; TV journalist; soon after her birth the family moved to Louisville; in 1963, she won the America's Junior Miss scholarship pageant representing Kentucky; in 1970, she was hired by the White House press secretary to serve in the administration of President Richard Nixon and assisted him with his memoirs after his resignation; co-anchored CBS Morning News, correspondent for 60 Minutes, co-anchored Primetime Live, co-hosted Good Morning America
- The first Wigwam Village Motel, in the shape of a teepee, was built by Frank A. Redford, from Cave City

Interesting names include: Apple Grove; Austin; Berry Store; Cave City; Cooktown; Coral Hill; Dry Fork; Eighty Eight; Freedom; Goodnight; Halfway; Highland Springs; Kino; Merry Oaks; Nobob; Oil City; Park; Park City; Red Cross; Rocky Hill; Roseville; Salt Lick; Slick Rock; Temple Hill

BATH COUNTY (1811) Formed from Montgomery County. The county is named for springs within the county which were thought to have medicinal value.

Land for Owingsville, the county seat, was donated by Richard Menefee, a politician, and Thomas Dye Owings, owner of a local iron foundry. The largest earthquake in Kentucky (5.1 magnitude) happened July 7, 1980 near Sharpsburg. The earthquake was felt in 15 states as well as Ontario. It caused property damage in Kentucky, Indiana, and Ohio. Property damage at Maysville was estimated at $1 million. East of the epicenter, near Owingsville, cracks in the ground were estimated to be 4 inches deep and 30 yards long. On June 6, 2003 an earthquake measuring 4.0 was felt in western Kentucky. The epicenter was near the Mississippi River. On September 17, 2004 an earthquake measuring 3.7 was felt in southeast Kentucky near Corbin. Earthquakes have been reported in all fifty states from as early as 1727 to as late as January 31, 2007 when a 2.9 hit western Kentucky. The epicenter was at Wickliffe (Ballard County). A series of earthquakes, centered in the New Madrid Fault occurred from December 16, 1811 to February 11, 1812. The following quote is from the *Kentucky Gazette*, a Lexington newspaper and the first newsaper published in Kentucky (1787):

> About half after two o'clock yesterday morning a severe shock of an earthquake was felt at this place; the earth vibrated two or three times a second, which occurred for several minutes, and so great was the shaking that the windows were agitated to what they would have been in a hard gust of wind.

At the onset of the earthquake the ground rose and fell bending the trees until their branches intertwined; deep cracks in the ground opened; landslides swept down bluffs and hillsides; large areas of land were uplifted; still larger areas sank and were covered with water emerging through fissures; huge waves on the Mississippi River overwhelmed many boats and washed others high on the shores; high banks collapsed and caved into the river; sandbars and points of islands gave way; whole islands disappeared; log cabins were destroyed as far as Cincinnati; large waves were generated on the Mississippi River by fissures opening and closing below the surface; local uplifts of the ground and water gave the illusion that the river was flowing backward; Reelfoot Lake in Tennessee was created as a result of that earthquake. Shock waves were felt in every state east of the Mississippi River with the exception of Maine.

Notable residents include:
- John Bell Hood (1831–1879) – Owingsville; Confederate general during the Civil War
- Henry S. Lane (1811–1881) – near Sharpsburg; U.S. House of Representatives; U.S. Senator; served the shortest term as governor of Indiana governor, having served two days
- Alvin Hawkins (1821–1905) – born in Kentucky; Tennessee governor

Interesting names include: Bald Eagle; Bethel; Clear Creek Furnace; Harpers; Hope; Midland; Moores Ferry; Mud Lick; Oakla; Olympia (3 miles north of) Olympia Springs;

Peasticks; Pebble; Peeled Oak; Pittsburg; Red Bush; Salt Lick; Sharpsburg; State Valley; Wyoming

BELL COUNTY (1867) Formed from Harlan and Knox Counties. The county is named for Joshua Fry Bell, born in Danville, graduated from Centre College, U.S. House of Representatives (Whig), Kentucky Secretary of State, and sent by Kentucky as a commissioner to the Peace Conference held in Washington, D.C., in 1861, in an unsuccessful attempt to divert what became the Civil War.

Pineville, the county seat, is one of the oldest communities in Kentucky dating back to 1781, when it was known as Cumberland Ford. Isaac Shelby, Kentucky's first governor, once owned part of the land that makes up the present-day city. The floodwall completed in 1952, was no match for the flood of 1977, that inundated the town. The U.S. Army Corps of Engineers extended the flood wall in 1988.

It was not Daniel Boone who discovered Cumberland Gap, but Dr. Thomas Walker in 1750, and who first named it Cave Gap. Near the river, which he named Cumberland, he built a cabin. Twenty-five years later Daniel Boone led a group of men who marked what later became known as the Wilderness Road. By 1796, the Gap had been widened enough to allow Conestoga Wagons to pass. By the time Kentucky was admitted to the Union in 1792, it is estimated that 100,000 people passed through Cumberland Gap. By 1810, that figure had grown to 300,000. During the Civil War it was known as the "Keystone to the Confederacy," and the "Gibralrar of America." Noted historian Frederick Jackson Turner said of Cumberland Gap in 1894, "Stand at the Cumberland Gap and watch the procession of civilization." Twin, mile-long tunnels were opened to automobile traffic in 1996, at a cost of $250 million.

Middlesboro, established 1886, is the only city in the United States built inside a meteor crater. The theory is that a meteor fifteen hundred feet in diameter struck the earth there some 300 million years ago creating the four-mile wide crater. In 2003, the Kentucky Society of Professional Geologists designated the area as a Distinguished Geologic Site. Pine Mountain State Resort Park became Kentucky's first state park in 1924.

Interesting names include: Arjay; Ark; Beverly; Blackmont; Black Snake; Blanche; Callaway; Calvin; Cardinal; Cary; Clear Creek Springs; Crockett; Cubage; Davisburg; East Pineville; Edgewood; Ferndale; Field; Fourmile; Frakes; Harbell; Hutch; Iverdale; Ivy Grove; Kettle Island; Meldrum; Middlesboro; Miracle; Noetown; Oaks; Paramount; Pearl; Premier; Pruden (one mile from Pruden, TN); Stoney Fork; Straight Creek; Tejay; Varilla; Wallsend; Wasioto; Yellow Creek

BOONE COUNTY (1798) Formed from Campbell County. The county is named for Daniel Boone, an American settler, pioneer, and hunter who also fought in the Revolutionary War. Boone served three terms in the Virginia general assembly the war. Burlington is the county seat.

Florence, in its earlier years, was known as Polecat, Pow Wow, Maddentown, and Connersville, but was originally called Crossroads due to the several roads that converged at that location. Originally the water tower read "Florence Mall," but before the mall was finished travelers would stop with the intent to go shipping. The state told them to remove the sigh sighting false advertising. Rather than repaint the entire sign, they simply removed the outer legs of the "M" and left the bottom stem of the "Y". They intended to change it back after the mall was completed but the residents liked the new sign and decided to leave it. In 1784, John Filson wrote about the salt lick where large bones were found: "the head appears to have been about three feet long, the ribs seven feet long, and the thigh bones about four feet long. It is said that one of the bones weighs seventy-eight pounds. The grinders (teeth) are about five inches square and eight inches long." Rabbit Hash: C. W. Craig's General Store in Rabbit Hash is said to be the best known and best preserved general store in the state. It was established in 1831.

Notable residents include:

- Abner Gaines – moved from Virginia in 1804, opened a post office in his tavern in 1815, began the first stagecoach line between Cincinnati and Lexington; built a 17-room, two and one-half story house in Walton
- James and Martha Dinsmore – purchased seven hundred acres six and one-half miles west of Burlington in 1839 where they raised sheep, grew grapes, and harvested willow trees for a basket-making business
- Steve Cauthen (1960-) – Covington; first jockey to win $6 million in one season; youngest jockey to win the U. S. Triple Crown, riding Affirmed
- John Uri (YOUR-eye) Lloyd – born in New York; scientist, pharmasist, novelist (1849-1936)

Interesting names include: Beaverlick; Belleview; Bellevue; Big Bone; Bullitsville; Commissary Corner; Constance; Florence (formerly Polecat, formerly Pow Wow); Francisville; Hebron; Hueys Corner; Kensington; Limaburg; Marydale; Oakbrook; Rabbit Hash; Richwood; Stringtown; Sugartit; Taylorsport; Union; Waterloo

BOURBON COUNTY (1786) Formed from Fayette. The county is named for House of Bourbon, a European royal house whose rule extended mostly in France and Spain dating from the 1500s. Currently Spain and Luxembourg have Bourbon monarchs. There is also a Bourbon County in Kansas.

Paris, the county seat, was settled in 1775 and originally called Hopewell, Virginia. The name was changed in 1790 to reflect appreciation for the French assistance during the American Revolution. Triple Crown winner Secretariat was retired to Clairborne Farms and is buried there.

Notable residents include:

- Garrett Morgan (1877–1963) – Paris; an African-American who invented a respiratory protective hood, similar to the modern-day gas mask (1912); invented a hair-straightening preparation; invented a type of traffic signal (1923)
- George Snyder – the fishing reel he developed in the 1820s became the basis for what were known as the Kentucky Reel
- John Fox Jr. - wrote *The Little Shepherd of Kingdom Come*

Duncan Tavern, a 3-story stone tavern on court house square, was built in 1788, four years before Kentucky became a state. It served as a gathering place for pioneers such as Daniel Boone and Simon Kenton. The Shinner Building is listed by Ripley's *Believe It Or Not* as the world's tallest three-story building. It was built in 1891. Six miles east of Paris is the Cane Ridge Meeting House built in 1791. It is said to be the largest one-room log structure in the country. This is one of the sites of the Great Revival in 1801 where an estimated twenty-five thousand worshipers gathered for a protracted meeting. From that revival, the Christian Church (Disciples of Christ) was begun.

Bourbon County is reported to be the birthplace of bourbon whiskey, although the original Bourbon County covered a large territory comprising mostly of what is now northern Kentucky which includs thirty-four modern-day counties. While the fact of the original naming of bourbon whiskey may have come from Bourbon County, it should be understood that the original Bourbon County covered an area of land much larger than the Bourbon County of today. Incidentally, Bourbon County is dry.

Interesting names include: Austerlitz; Blacks Crossroads; Bunker Hill; Centerville; Clintonville; Currentsville; Elizabeth Station; Escondida; Jacksonville; Jackstown; Jimtown; Little Rock; Millersburg; Monterey; North Middletown; North Millersburg; Plum; Ruddels Mills; Shawhan; Stony Point

BOYD COUNTY (1860) Formed from Greenup, Carter, and Lawrence Counties. The county is named for Linn Boyd of Paducah, U.S. House of Representatives and Speaker of the House (elected to seven terms), Kentucky House of Representatives (representing two different counties), and lieutenant governor of Kentucky but died during the first year.

Catlettsburg is the county seat. The post office was opened in this area in 1808, as Mouth of Sandy (Big Sandy River) and Catlettsburg was incorperated as a city in 1848. In 1973, an archaeological dig revealed a serpent-shaped mound of rocks dating to 2000 B.C., and stretching for nine hundred feet. One of the early settlers was Charles "One-Handed Charlie" Smith who served under Colonel George Washington in the French and Indian War, 1754. For that service he received roughly four hundred acres of land. After his death the land was passed to Alexander Catlett, for whom Catlettsburg was named in 1848. The original Catlett log cabin, built in1808, is still standing.

In 1999, Ashland Oil merged with Marathon. The Scotch-Irish Poage family from Staunton (home of the Statler Brothers), VA, came through Cumberland Gap and founded Poage's

Landing, which later became Ashland. The Kentucky Iron, Coal, and Manufacturing Company was incorporated in 1854, and is responsible for having laid out the town of Ashland. The town's architect was criticized for designing 100-foot wide streets. Levi Hampton, one of the founders of the Kentucky Iron, Coal, and Manufacturing Company and an admirer of Henry Clay, suggested the name be changed from Poage's Landing to Ashland. The first child born in the new town of Ashland was named Ashland Poage. The iron furnaces in Ashland were sold to American Rolling Mill Company in 1921 which later developed into Armco Steel Corporation. The new steel mill featured a continuous rolling method which produced steel sheets, the first of its kind in the nation. In 1954, Armco employed 7,500 people. In 1969, Armco built the Amanda furnace, one of the largest blast furnaces in the world. The company is now known as AK Steel. The C & O Railroad Company operated one of the largest switchyards in the world in nearby Russell and Raceland.

Notable residents include:
- Billy C. Clark – nationally recognized author of numerous novels including *Goodbye Kate*, which had its right sold to the Walt Disney Company
- Naomi Judd (1946–) – Ashland; born Diana Ellen Judd
- Wynonna Judd (1964–) – Christina Claire Ciminella; born in Ashland
- Billy Ray Cyrus (1961–) – Flatwoods
- Chuck Woolery (1941–) Ashland; attended Morehead State University; his third wife was Teri Nelson, granddaughter of Ozzie and Harriet Nelson; he is a Christian and spends a great deal of his time involved in volunteer ministries; starting as an enterprising folk/pop singer, he was soon recognized as having master of ceremonies qualities; at the urging of Merv Griffin, he accepted the position as host for the still young TV show Wheel of Fortune (1975–1981) {succeeded by Pat Sajak}; other shows include Scrabble, the Dating Game, and Lingo; an avid bass fisherman, he often speaks about bass fishing and sells his own line of fishing products, including "MotoLure," a motorized lure that emulates a small fish; he is the official outdoor spokesman for QVC.
- Venus Ramey (1924–) – the first Miss America with red hair, 1944

Interesting names include: Ashland; Big Sandy; Cliffside; Cloverdale; Coalton; Fairview; Flatwoods; Grassland; Horse Creek; Ironville; Millseat; Normal; Princess; Rush; Sandy Furnace; Savage Branch; Summit; Unity; West Fairview; Winslow

BOYLE COUNTY (1842) Formed from Lincoln and Mercer Counties. The county is named for John Boyle, U.S. House of Representatives (three terms), Kentucky House of Representatives, U.S. District Judge, and served as Chief Justice of the Kentucky Court of Appeals until his death in 1834 or 1835. He is buried in Bellevue Cemetery in Danville. During the Civil War, the Battle of Perryville was fought here October 8, 1862, between the Confederate Army of the Mississippi and the Union Army of the Ohio. More than seven thousand men fell in that battle making it the most destructive battle in Kentucky. It was the South's last serious attempt to gain possession of Kentucky. A reenactment of that battle is held on the same battleground annually.

Danville, the county seat, was established in 1887, by the Virginia Legislature. The city is named in memory of Walker Daniel who purchased the original site of the settlement from John Crow, another early settler. Danville was the capital of Kentucky while it was still a district of Virginia. The city is called the "Birthplace of the Bluegrass" since the state's Constitutional Convention was held at what is now known as Constitution Square in 1792, when Kentucky's first Constitution was signed. Danville is called the "City of Firsts:"

- first courthouse in Kentucky
- first U.S. post office west of the Alleghenies
- first state-supported school for the deaf
- first physician in the world to successfully remove an ovarian tumor (Dr. Ephraim McDowell)

The oldest log meetinghouse in Kentucky was built in 1804, during a period of religious revival. Many Revolutionary War soldiers and pioneers, including Daniel Boone's sister, Hannah, are buried there. The structure has twelve corners in the shape of a cross and three doors, symbolic of the Holy Trinity. Penn's Store, near Danville, has been a store since 1845, and has been owned by the Penn family since 1850. It is reported to be America's oldest country store. Danville was the original home of Transylvania University. Centre College was founded in 1819. The Kentucky School for the Deaf was founded on April 10, 1823, becoming the first state supported school of its kind in the nation and in the western hemisphere. In 2007, they won the National Boys Soccre Championship and became a contender in twelfth region boys basketball. There are thirty-two Historic markers placed throughout the county.

Notable residents include:
- Ephraim McDowell (1771–1830) - born in Virginia; family moved to Danville; performed first successful surgery by removing an ovarian tumor, 1809; his most famous patient was James K. Polk, eleventh president of the United States; he was a founding member of Centre College, Danville (1819)
- John Marshall Harlan (1833–1911) - Boyle County; Supreme Court Associate Justice; fought in the Civil War; during his tenure as justice, he taught Sunday school at a Presbyterian church in Washington, D.C.; his grandson, John Marshall Harlan II, was also a Supreme Court Associate Justice
- Major General John C. Breckinridge (1821–1875) - Cabell's Dale (near Lexington); vice president under James Buchanan (the nations youngest vice president), U.S. Senate, Kentucky House of Representatives, Confederate general in the Civil War, the last Confederate secretary of war, and served as a major of the Third Kentucky Volunteers during the Mexican-American War
- Eddie Montgomery - country music singer; brother of John Michael Montgomery, country singer; forms the duet of Montgomery Gentry
- John Michael Montgomery (1965–) – Danville; country music singer-songwriter; #1 singles are, "I Swear," and "Sold (The Grundy County Auction Incident)

- John Baptiste Ford (1811–1903), Danville; faught in the War of 1812; founded Pittsburg Plate Glass Company
- Larnelle Harris (1948–), Danville; won five Grammy Awards and eighteen Dove Awards

Interesting names include: Aliceton; Alum Springs; Atoka; Beverly Hills; Craintown; Davis Hill; Forkland; Green Acres; Junction City; Little Needmore; Needmore; Shelby City

BRACKEN COUNTY (1796) Formed from Mason and Campbell Counties. The county is named for William Bracken, an early pioneer and surveyor who was killed by Indians. Bracken County played a major role in the Underground Railroad. There are several "stations" in the Augusta area, including the Bradford/Payne House in Augusta on the Ohio River. White burley tobacco, a light, adaptable leaf that revolutionized the industry, was first produced here in 1867.

Brooksville is the county seat and the birthplace of John Gregg Fee, founder of Berea College. Before 1800, the town was known as Woodwards Crossroads. County government moved from Augusta to Woodwards Crossroads in 1833, due to its more central location, although it did not become the official county seat for six years in 1839.

Augusta is the site of Augusta Methodist College (1820) the first Methodist college in the world. Augusta is named after Augusta County, VA and was the original county seat. Augusta Male College and Augusta Female College, an Underground Railroad station, both opened in 1845 and closed in 1847. In 1847 Augusta Male and Female College was opened.

Notable residents include:
- Rosemary Clooney (1928–) – Maysville; pop and jazz vocalist from the 1940s and 1950s; married Jose' Ferrer; aunt to George Clooney
- George Clooney (1961–) – born in Lexington, KY; Debbie Boone married Clooney's cousin, Gabriel Ferrer
- Don Galloway (1937–) – Brooksville; actor best known for playing Detective Sergeant Ed Brown on *Ironside*
- Heather French (1974–) - former Miss America
- Stephen Collins Foster (1826-1864) – born in Lawrenceville, PA; frequently visited his uncle in Augusta who was president of Augusta Male College

Interesting names include: Berlin; Bridgeville; Germantown; Gertrude; Lenoxburg; Neave; Petra; Rock Springs; Santa Fe; Stonewall; Stoney Point; Willow; Willow Grove

BREATHITT COUNTY (1839) Formed from Clay, Perry, and Estill. The county is named for John Breathitt, Kentucky Senator, lieutenant governor, and governor of

Kentucky from 1832-1834. Born in Henry County, Virginia the family moved to Logan County, KY. Breathitt died of tuberculosis in the governor's mansion in 1834, making him the second governor to die in office. He is buried at Maple Grove Cemetery, Russellville (Logan County).

Jackson, the county seat, is home to "The Kentucky Explorer," a monthly magazine that features Kentucky history and genealogy.

Notable residents include:
- Jeffrey Reddick – reared in Jackson; screenwriter, probably best known for creating the *Final Destination* series
- Chad Warrix - singer in the duo "Halfway to Hazard"

Two movies were filmed in Jackson, *Next of Kin* and *Fire Down Below*

Interesting names include: Altro; Beech; Canoe; Crockettsville; Dalesburg; Evanston; Fivemile; Flintville; Frozen Creek; Guage (a narrow gauge railroad went through the area during World War I; the misspelling was never corrected); Hardshell; Houston; Little; Lost Creek; Macedonia; Moct; Morris Fork; Mountain Valley; Ned; Noble; Noctor; Oakdale; Panhandle; Press; Quicksand; Rock Lick; Roosevelt; Rousseau; Shoulderblade; Taulbee; Turkey; Vancleve; War Creek; Whick; Widecreek; Wolf Coal; Wolverine

BRECKINRIDGE COUNTY (1800) Formed from Hardin County. The county is named for John Breckinridge, Kentucky Attorney General, Legislator, U.S. Senator, and U.S. Attorney General.

In the 1800s Victoria Coal Mines were the first to produce coal oil. The oil was exported to Great Britain where it was used to light Buckingham Palace. The Breckinridge County Archives, formed in 1984, was the first state-funded archival repository in the history of the United States and is known across the nation as an excellent resource for genaelogical and historical research.

Hardinsburg is the county seat. The city's namesake, Captain William Hardin, established the city as a fort in 1780.

In 1816 ferryman Jacob Weatherholt piloted the family of Abraham Lincoln, then age seven, across the Ohio River to Indiana.

Rough River Dam State Resort Park was built in the 1950s.

Notable residents include:
- Joseph Holt (1807–1894) - United States Postmaster General Secretary of the Interior, Attorney General, Secretary of War, Commissioner of Patents, and Judge Advocate General

- Wiley Blount Rutledge (1894–1949) – born in Tar Springs near Cloverport; former United States supreme court justice
- Alfred "Butch" Beard (1947–) – Hardinsburg; former NBA player/coach for the New Jersey Nets 1994–1996; also played for Atlanta Hawks, Cleveland Cavaliers, Seatle SuperSonics, Golden State Warriors, and New York Knicks
- Percy Beard (1908–1990) – Hardinsburg; In 1931 he set a world record of 14' 2" in thd 120-yard high hurdle then tied his recoed in 1934; he was a silver medalist for hurdle jump in the 1932 Summer Olympics; later became an outstanding coach at University of Florida from 1937–1964; he used his civil engineering degree to help develop all-weather tracks
- Ralph Beard (1927–2007) – Hardinsburg; one of the University of Kentucky's Fabulous Five, 1945-1948; drafted by Chicago Stage in 1949; gold medal winner in basketball at the 1948 Olympics
- Perry T. Ryan (1962–) – Kentucky lawyer and author who writes books on American history

Interesting names include: Basin Spring; Big Spring; Bullitt; Cannons Point; Cave Spring; Cloverport; Cobblers Knob; Constantine; Corners; Custer; Falls of Rough; Fisher; Garfield; High Plains (3 miles from) High Plains Corner; Horn Back Mill; Kathryn; Locust Hill; Madrid; Mook; Mystic; Rosetta; Sample; Scuffletown; Se Ree; Simpson; Solitude; Stephensport; Tar Fork; Union Star; Webster

BULLITT COUNTY (1797) Formed from Jefferson and Nelson Counties. The county is named for Alexander Scott Bullitt, one of the architects of Kentucky's government. In the late 1700s to the mid 1800s, Bullitt County was the site of a thriving salt and iron works industry.

Shepherdsville, the county seat, was founded and named for Adam Shepherd in 1793. In 1836, a mineral water spa called Paroquet Springs opened. The mineral water supposedly had medicinal properties which drew suffers with a variety of ailments to Shepherdsville to drink and bathe in the healing waters. In 1879 the Paroquet Hotel burned down but water from the spring continued to be bottled and sold until 1915.

Mount Washington was founded in the early 1800s, and was known as The Cross Roads. It was officially chartered in 1822, as Mount Vernon, but when a post office was applied for, it was discovered that Rockcastle County was already using that name. In 1822, the population was seven hundred with three churches, two schools, several stores, five doctors, two taverns, and twelve mechanical trades. During the Civil War the bridge over the Salt River at Shepherdsville was guarded by Union troops.

The previous mayor of Mount Washington was a contestant on The Price Is Right, playing The Money Game and winning $185, but losing a PT Cruiser.

Bernheim Arboretum and Research Forest is a fourteen thousand acre arboretum, forest, and nature preserve near Clermont. In 1928, the land was purchased for $1 per acre because the land had been stripped for mining iron ore. The grounds in the arboretum were designed by Frederick Law Olmstead who also designed Central Park in New York City and the gardens around Biltmore Estate, Asheville, NC, as well as the forest. Opening in 1950, it is the largest privately owned area in the state.

Jim Beam and Knob Creek bourbon whiskey is made at Clermont.

Notable residents include:
- Charles Kurtsinger (1906–1946) – Shepherdsville; U.S. Racing Hall of Fame jockey; won U. S. Triple Crown in 1937
- Wayne Edwards (1967–) – Shepherdsville; NASCAR driver

Interesting names include: Beech Grove; Cedar Grove; Cupio; Fox Chase; Gap in Knob; Hunters Hollow; Katharyn; Kosmosdale; Lebanon Junction; Lee; Limestone Springs; Lotus; Mount Washington; Pitts Point; Poplar Level; Ridgetop; Salt River; Scuffletown; Shepherdsville; Solitude; Zoneton

BUTLER COUNTY (1810) Formed from Logan and Ohio Counties. The county is named for General Richard Butler, a major in the Continental Army who fought in the Revolutionary War. Following the war he served in the Pennsylvania House of Representatives. The city of Butler, Pennsylvania, Butler County, Pennsylvania and Butler County, Ohio are also named for him.

Morgantown is the county seat. The first industry in the area was making salt. Butler County has one of only two Civil War monuments dedicated to the soldiers who served and died on both sides. The zinc Civil War monument was dedicated in 1907 on the Butler County courthouse lawn in Morgantown.

It is reported that Morgantown may have initially been called Funkhouser Hill, named after Christopher Funkhouser who donated the Land for the town. It is further reported that Funkhouser may have given the town its present name to honor Daniel Morgan Smith, the first child born there. Morgantown is home to the annual Green River Catfish Festival each Fourth of July.

Prior to 1917, the primary means of transportation was the Green River. However, in 1917, the river froze, leaving the town without supplies for two months. A subsequent period of road-building began, and by 1930, a road connecting Morgantown to Bowling Green provided an alternate route for commerce. Rochester, at the confluence of the Mud and Green Rivers, was named for Rochester, New York. With a current population of less than two hundred, it is the smallest municipality by that name in the United States.

Notable residents include:

- Admiral Claude C. Bloch (1878–1967); - Woodbury; commanded the Naval district when Pearl Harbor when was attacked
- William S. Taylor (1853–1928); - Kentucky governor from 1899-1900, was born near Morgantown

Interesting names include: Aberdeen; Boston; Brooklyn; Casey; Dimple; Eden; Elfie; Flat Rock; Harper Crossroads; Horsemail; Huntsville; Jetson; Logansport; Love; Mining City; Needmore; Pleasant Hill; Provo; Quality; Region; Rochester; Silver City; Sugar Grove; Vineyard; Welcome

CALDWELL COUNTY (1809) Formed from Livingston County. The county is named for John Caldwell (1757-184), who participated in the George Rogers Clark Indian campaign of 1786, was a Kentucky state senator, and was Kentucky's second lieutenant governor. He died while presiding over the senate in his first year as lieutenant governor. He was also a member of the Danville Conventions of 1787 and 1788 which adopted a petition "demanding admission into the Union."

Princeton is the county seat. In the early nineteenth century Caldwell County witnessed the forced migration of the Cherokee Indians on the Trail of Tears. The Cherokee spent several weeks in Caldwell County during the winter of 1838, notably at Big Springs at downtown Princeton and at Centerville near Fredonia. At the turn of the century an agricultural boon in dark leaf tobacco had made Caldwell County a major tobacco growing center. However, the monopolization of the tobacco market by James B. Duke left many farmers financially strapped. Under the organization of Dr. David Amoss, a vigilante group formed known as the Night Raiders. The Night Raiders terrorized those who cooperated with the tobacco conglomerate by destroying crops, burning warehouses, and physical intimidation. The "Black Patch Wars" came to an end around 1908.

Interesting names include: Black Hawk; Cedar Bluff; Crowtown; Fairview; Farmersville; Flat Rock; Friendship; Fryer; Harper Ford; Midway; Needmore; Otter Pond; Pumpkin Center; Ruth; Shady Grove; The Bluff; White Sulphur

CALLOWAY COUNTY (1822) Formed from Hickman County. The county is named for Colonel Richard Callaway (note the spelling) (1724–1780), one of the founders of Fort Boonesborough having helped mark the trail with Daniel Boone. Two of Callaway's daughters and one of Boone's daughters were captured by the Indians. Callaway led one of the parties in the now famous rescue of the girls. On March 8, 1780 Callaway was caught outside Boonesborough by Shawnees and was killed, scalped, and mutilated.

Murray is the county seat. It began as a post office and trading center in the 1820s when it was called Williston in honor of James Willis, an early settler. The name was changed to Pleasant Springs then in 1884 to Murray in honor of U.S. Congressman John L. Murray. Murray is host to the annual Freedom Fest held the last week of June. Murray is home to Murray State University, Ohio Valley Conference, established 1922.

Notable residents include:

- Jackie DeShannon (1944–) – Hazel; Born Sharon Lee Byers; one of the first female singer/songwriters of the rock and roll period; her parents in show business, she was introduced to performing at the age of six; by age eleven she was hosting her own radio program; her first hit song was, "Dum Dum" recorded by Brenda Lee in 1960; DeShannon dated Elvis Presley and formed friendships with Ricky Nelson and the Everly Brothers; in 1968, she recorded, "Put a Little Love in Your Heart"
- Nathan Stubblefield (1860–1928) – Murray; American inventor and melon farmer. It is reported that he successfully demonstrated wireless voice transmission (radio), 1892; he said, "I have solved the problem of telephoning without wires;" some say it was the first radio—others deny that statement; he was issued four U.S. patents which include the electric battery, a wireless telephone, a lightning device, and the mechanical telephone; from 1907–1911 he operated a home school called The Nathan Stubblefield Industrial School, built on his eighty-five-acre melon farm; it is not the campus of Murray State University
- W. Earl Brown ((1963–) – Murray; character actor who has appeared on TV shows including *CSI, Six Feet Under,* as well as several movies
- Theodore Roosevelt Mason Howard (1908–1976) – Murray; a black physician, surgeon, and civil rights activist
- Frank Albert Stubblefield (1907–1977) – served in the U. S. Navy during WW II; U.S. House of Representatives serving eight terms; lost his ninth re-election bid to Carroll Hubbard; a distant cousin to Nathan Stubblefield; is buried in the Murray City Cemetery
- Molly Simms (1973–) – actress and model; appeared in ads for Old Navy and is a "Cover Girl" model; appeared in two moveis and in the NBC television series "Las Vegas"
- Stan Key – Former UK basketball player and current alumni director

Interesting names include: Almo; Cherry; Coldwater; Crossland; Five Points; Hamlin; Hazel; Hico; Midway; New Concord; New Providence; Normal; Penny; Pleasant Hill; Protemus; Shiloh; Stella; Taylors Store; Van Cleave; Wiswell

CAMPBELL COUNTY (1793) Formed from Harrison, Mason, and Scott Counties. The county is named for John Campbell, the founder of Louisville. Alexandria, one of two county seats (along with Newport), was settled in 1793 by a family named Spillman and named for Alexandria, Virginia. A post office was established in 1819. The second oldest road in Kentucky was the Old State Road which ran from Newport to Winchester, a distance of nearly one hundred miles. The road is now US Highway 27.

Newport was established in 1795 by James Taylor and named in honor of Admiral Christopher Newport. He led the first English setlement of Jamestown, Virginia. Newport's development took a major boost in 1803 when the Army agreed to build a military post there. The Army purchased five acres of land from James Taylor for $1. The land was located at the mouth of the Licking River and named Newport Barracks. Gangsters became a part of Newport's history in the 1920s after the invention of the Thompson submachine gun. Campbell County has two county seats—Alexandria and Newport. The World Peace Bell in Newport is the world's largest free-swinging bell weighing over seventy-eight thousand pounds (thirty-nine tons). The Newport Aquarium is billed as the "number one aquarium in the Midwest" with one million gallons of water.

Notable residents include:
- John Thompson (1860–1940) – Newport; Inventor of the Thompson submachine gun (Tommy gun); in 1883, graduated from West Point and became the youngest colonel in Army history, eventually reaching the rank of brigadier general
- Dave Cowens (1948–) – Newport; fourth-round draft pick to Boston Celtics; NBA player and coach; voted one of the "50 Greatest Players in NBA History"
- Lonnie Burr (1943–) – Dayton; one of the original Mouseketeers

Interesting names include: Alexandria; Aspen Grove; Beagle; California; Camp Springs; Cold Spring; Cote Brilliant; Dayton (a merger between the towns of Brooklyn and Jamestown, 1867); Flag Spring; Melbourne; Mentor; Persimmon Grove; Silver Grove; Wilder

CARLISLE COUNTY (1886) Formed from Hickman County. The county is named for John Griffin Carlisle (1834–1910), Speaker of the U.S. House of Representatives, Kentucky State Senate, lieutenant governor (1871–1875), appointed as U.S. Senator to fill an unexpired term, and U.S. Secretary of the Treasury. Carlisle was born in what is now Kenton County and practiced law in Covington. He died in New York City. Bardwell is the county seat.

A portion of the county, approximately two miles wide and four miles long, extends across the Mississippi River into Missouri. It was the result of the earthquake of 1811–1812.

Interesting names include: Arlington; Berkley; Fillmore; Kirbyton; Magee Springs; Winford

CARROLL COUNTY (1838) Formed from Gallatin, Trimble, and Henry Counties. The county is named for Charles Carroll (1737–1832) of Carrollton, Maryland who became the last surviving signer of the Declaration of Independence and the only Roman Catholic to sign it. He was one of the wealthiest men in America. He came out of retirement to help create the Baltimore and Ohio Railroad in 1827. He was a member of the first U.S. Senate representing Maryland. He is buried in the chapel attached to the north end of the Doughregan Manor near Elliott City, Maryland. Also, counties in Arkansas, Georgia, Illinois, Indiana, Iowa, Lousiana, Maryland, Mississippi, Missouri, New Hampshire, Ohio, and Virginia are named for him as well as the Carroll Gardens neighborhood in Brooklyn, New York. Carroll County, Kentucky is home to General Butler State Resort Park.

Carrollton is the county seat. The city is at the confluence of the Kentucky and Ohio Rivers. When it was founded in 1794 it was known as Port Williamson. On Saturday, May 14, 1988 Larry Mahoney, a drunk driver traveling in the wrong direction on Interstate 71, collided with a gasoline-powred former school bus being used as a church bus. The impact ruptured the forward gasoline tank making it impossible to exit the bus via the front doors and sending fire and black smoke throughout the cabin which further impaired the bus evacuation. Out of 67 passengers, 27 were killed and 34 were injured. Only six escaped without significant injury. As of March, 2009 it remains the worst bus crash in U.S. history tied for fatalities with the Prestonsburg (Floyd County) school bus disaster in 1958 when a loaded school bus careened into the swollen Levisa Fork of the Big Sandy River after striking the rear of a wrecker. Twenty-six children and the bus driver lost their lives. As a result of the Carrollton County bus accident, Kentucky now requires more exit doors from its school busses than any other state and Canada.

Interesting names include: Carson; Eagle Station; Easterday; English; Langstaff; Locust; Prestonville; Worthville

CARTER COUNTY (1838) Formed from Greenup and Lawrence Counties. The county is named for Colonel William Grayson Carter who served in the Revolutionary War as aide-de-camp to General George Washington, rising to the rank of lieutenant colonel. He was a member of the first U.S. Senate.

Grayson, the county seat, lies on the Little Sandy River. In 1919 the Christian Normal Institute was founded. As a "normal school" it included a high school, a junior college, and a training program for public school teachers. Today the Kentucky Christian University and is recognized by "U.S. News and World Report" as one of the top 50 comprehensive baccalaureate level universities in the south. The school is fully accredited to confer both bachelor and master degrees. In 2007 the cost per credit hour was $390.

Grayson Lake State Park, about five miles south of Grayson, was once a favorite camping site for Shawnee and Cherokee Indians.

Notable residents include:
- Tom T. Hall (1936–) – Olive Hill; country singer and songwriter; has eleven Number one hits and twenty-six more hits in the top ten; has been nicknamed "The Storyteller," and has written songs for dozens of country stars, including, Johnny Cash, George Jones, Loretta Lynn, and Waylon Jennings; one of his most successful songwriting ventures was "Harper Valley P.T.A." which alone sold over six million copies

Interesting names include: Access; Aden; Beech Grove; Beetle; Boone Furnace; Carter; Cold Springs; Fairview Hill; Globe; Gregoryville; Iron Hill; Johns Run; Limestone; Mountain Top; Mt Savage; Music; Olive Hill; Pactolus; Poplar; Rush (town is shared by both Carter and Boyd counties); Silica; Soldier; Sophi; Wolf

CASEY COUNTY (1807) Formed from Lincoln County. The county is named for Colonel William Casey, a Revolutionary War veteran from Virginia who explored the area in 1779. It is the only Kentucky county situated entirely in the Knobs Region of the state.

Liberty is the county seat. The city was established in 1806 by several Revolutionary War veterans and named for one of the values of their new country. Liberty is proud to be "Home of the world's largest apple pie." The recipe includes: forty-five bushels of apples, three hundred pounds of pastry, one hundred fifty pounds of granulated sugar, fifteen pounds of butter, two and one-half pounds of cinnamon, one and one-half pounds of salt, and seventy-five pounds of cornstarch. Such festivities abound each September at the Annual Casey County Apple Festival. Liberty is also home to Tarter Gate Company, makers of tubular gates used for the farm, for which it also bears the title of Gate Capitol of the World. Middleburg is a small community on the Green River first settled by Abraham Lincoln, I, grandfather of the president.

Notable residents include:
- Silas Adams (1839–1896) – born in Pulaski County, moved to Casey County at age two; served in the Union Army during the Civil War; member of the United States House of Representatives
- The Costello Twins – actresses and models; appeared on Levi's commercials, *Buffy the Vampire Slayer, The Drew Carey Show,* and *The Man Show*

Interesting names include: Argyle; Bass; Beech Bottom; Bethelridge; Butchertown; Cantown; Chilton; Evona; Gilpin; Honey Acre; Kidds Store; Labascus; Middleburg; Moore; Mount Olive; Peytons Store; Pine Grove; Pricetown; Teddy; Walltown; Windsor; Yosemite (YO-se-mite)

CHRISTIAN COUNTY (1797) Formed from Logan County. The county is named for Colonel William Christian (1743–1786), a soldier and politician from Augusta County, Virginia who served in the Continenal Army during the Revolutionaty War. He worked in the law office of Patrick Henry and married Henry's sister Annie. He settled in Louisville in 1785 and was killed in Indiana by Indians in 1786. Counties in Illinois and Missouri are named for him as well as Christiansburg, Virginia. Christian County is the second largest county in Kentucky with 724 square miles (Pike is the largest with 789 square miles). Joshua Grant was an early settler in Christian County who married into the McNeil Family. Almost all of Joshua's sons had McNeil as their middle name.

Hopkinsville, the county seat, was settled in 1796, by Bartholomew and Martha Ann Wood and was then known as Old Rock Spring. Wood donated five acres of land and a half interest in the spring for the county seat. The new town, Christian Court House, was renamed Elizabeth in 1799, in honor of Wood's eldest daughter. However, since Hardin County already had Elizabeth Town, and when the city incorporated in 1804, the General Assembly renamed the settlement Hopkinsville in honor of General Samuel Hopkins of Henderson County. Hopkinsville is the primary manufacturing facility for Ebonite bowling balls and one of the oldest and largest bowling ball manufacturers in existence. Ebonite owns other well-known brand names including Hammer Bowling, Dyno-Thane, Columbia 300, Track International, and Robby's. Hopkinsville was a stop along the Trail of Tears and a Pow Wow is celebrated there each September commemmorating the event.

During the total eclipse on August 17, 2021, Hopkinsville will be the closest metropolitan area to the expected point of the greatest eclipse, which will occur about twelve miles northwest of the city center.

In the early 1900s, tobacco planters formed a protectionist Dark Tobacco District Planters' Protective Asociation of Kentucky and Tennessee. This was in opposition of a corporate monopoly of the American Tobacco Company (ATC) owned by James B. Duke. Many farmers could not sell their tobacco at a profit and the ATC was the region's only buyer. Some farmers formed the Silent Brigade in an effort to boycott the sale of any tobacco to the ATC. The Silent Brigade, later known as Night Riders, were heros to some tobacco farmers but vigilantes to those who sold their tobacco at a cheap rate to the ATC. On December 7, 1907, two hundred fifty masked Night Riders captured police and sheriffs posts and cut off the town from outside contact. They then pursued city officials and tobacco executives who were buying cheap tobacco from farmers who were not members of the Association. Three tobacco warehouses were burned during that night of lawlessness. Peace Park in Hopkinsville was created on the site of one of those warehouses. It is now one of the town's major visitor attractions.

Fort Campbell North is a community on the Army base so designated in order to count the soldiers and their families in the U.S. census. Generally speaking, northern Christian County supported the North while southern Christian County supported the South during the Civil War.

Pennyrile Forest State Resort Park, in the northwest section of the county, is named for the tiny pennyroyal plant found in the woodlands surrounding this resort. The fragrant pennyroyal plant, a member of the mint family, is useful as a mosquito repellant.

Notable residents include:
- Jefferson Davis (1808–1889) – Fairview in Christian County, now Todd County; president of the Confederate States of America, 1860–1865; U.S. House of Representatives (Mississippi); U.S. Senate (Mississippi); U.S. Secretary of War from 1853–1857; his father was from Philadelphia, PA; fell in love with Zachary Taylor's daughter who did not approve of the romance; Davis resigned his commission and married Sarah Knox Taylor fourteen years before her father was elected President; Sarah died three month after from malaria
- Adlai Ewing Stevenson Sr., (1835–1914) – U.S. vice president under Grover Cleveland, 1893–1897; his parents were Presbyterians of Scotch-Irish descent; his wife Letitia helped found the Daughters of the American Revolution as a way to help heal the division between North and South after the Civil War; he served as

Postmaster General for Grover Cleveland in 1885; during that time he fired over 40,000 Republican workers and replaced them with Democrats from the South; he attended school at Blue Water, Kentucky

- Thomas Rust Underwood (1898–1956) – Hopkinsville; Kentucky House of Representatives, U.S. House of Representatives; appointed to the U.S. Senate to fill a vacated seat
- Edward Thompson "Ned" Breathitt (1924–2003) – Hopkinsville; Kentucky governor from 1963–1967; Kentucky House of Representatives; while governor, he established Kentucky Educational Television (KET); successfully sought anti-descrimination and civil rights legislation from the General Assembly, making Kentucky the first southern state to enact such laws
- Wayne Edward "Ed" Whitfield (1943–) – Hopkinsville; U.S. House of Representatives since 1995 and a member of the Kentucky House of Representatives 1974–1979
- Jerry Claiborne (1928–2000) – Hopkinsville; former UK football coach 1982–1989; played halfback under coach Paul "Bear" Bryant at the University of Kentucky and became Bryant's assistant at Texas A & M and Alabama before becoming head football coach for the University of Kentucky
- Mac King (1959–) – Hopkinsville; comedy magician; you may have seen him on television do a magic trick before a commercial then tell how the trick is performed after the commercial; while performing the cut and restore rope routine, he accidentally cut off the tip of a finger; he tried to tape the finger and continue the show, but the bleeding became so severe that he had to stop and ask if a nurse were in the audience; a nurse stopped the bleeding enough to allow him to finish the show and do a second show before going to the hospital; he has also performed with magician Lance Burton from Louisville
- Brice Long (1972–) – Hopkinsville; Country music singer and songwriter; recordings include "Its Only Monday," "Anywhere But Here," and "Meat and Potato Man;" graduated from Middle Tennessee State University
- Christopher Antoine Whitney (1971–) – Former NBA point guard. During his eleven-year career he played for San Antonio Spurs, Washington Bullets/Wizards, Denver Nugets, and Orlando Magic

Interesting names include: Apex; Askew; Beverly; Bluff Spring; Carl; Church Hill; Dogwood; Empire; Era; Fairview; Fidelio; Fort Campbell North; Fruit Hill; Gracey; Honey Grove; Kelly; Kennedy; Macedonia; Oak Grove; Outwood; Peedee; Pleasant Green Hill; Pleasant Hill; Saint Elmo; Sinking Fork

CLARK COUNTY (1793) Formed from Bourbon and Fayette Counties. The county is named for Revolutionary War hero George Rogers Clark. Although his military achievements came before his thirtieth birthday, he spent the final years of his life in increasing poverty and obscurity because he had to finance his own campaigns since he was never reimbursed by Virginia government. At least ninteen pioneer stations or settlements are believed to have been established in the area. They include Strode's Station (1799), McGee's Station (c 1780), Holder's Station (1781), and Boyle's Station (1785). Clark County Illinois and Ohio are named for him as are Clarksville in Clark County, Indiana, Clarksburg, West Virginia, Clarksville, Tennesee, and Clark Street in Chicago.

Winchester, the county seat, is named for Winchester, Virginia. Daniel Boone and his men reached the Kentucky River on the southern border of the county and established Boonesborough as Kentucky's second settlement. Most pioneers had already passed through Fort Boonesborough before it was established as a permanent settlement in Clark County. Among the early settlers was a group of forty Baptist families led by Captain William Bush who settled on Lower Howard's Creek in 1775. In 1793, the group erected the Old Stone Meeting House. Clark County actually began as Bourbon County, Virginia in 1785, when it was created from the very large Fayette County. Among the residents of Clark County were Governor Charles Scott (1808–1812) and Governor James Clark (1836–1839). James Clark was born in Bedford County, Virginia, but while very young his family moved to Clark County. He died in Frankfort and is buried in a private cemetery in Winchester. In addition to serving as governor of Kentucky, he also served two separate terms as U.S. House of Representatives, the Kentucky House of Representatives, and the Kentucky State Senate. His administration oversaw the establishing of the State Board of Education.

During the Civil War about one thousand men joined either the Confederate or the Union Armies. The entrance of the railroad made Winchester a transportation, commercial, and educational center, and gave rise to small service communities such as Hedges Station, six miles east of town, and Ford, a once-prosperous mill town on the Kentucky River. Hemp, which was grown to make rope, suffered from foreign competition and vanished as a cash crop around World War I. The crop was brought back during World War II, and a processing plant was built. When the war ended, so did the need for hemp.

In the 1950s and 1960s, industry began moving into the county, mostly around Winchester due, in large part, to the completion of I-64 and the Mountain Parkway. Today farmland makes up ninety-five percent of the county.

Ale-8-One, Kentucky's soft drink, is bottled here.

The George Rogers Clark High School Marching Band performed in the Orange Bowl Parade, 1980 and in the Macy's Thanksgiving Day Parade, 1987.

There are ninteen historic markers placed throughout the county.

Notable residents include:
- Charles Scott (1739–1813) – born in Cumberland County, Virginia; Kentucky's fourth governor 1808–1812, served in the French and Indian War and spent the

winter at Valley Forge under George Washington in the Revolutionary War; after his term as Governor he retired to Clark County where he died the following year; he was buried in a family plot but the body was moved to Frankfort in 1854; Scott County, Kentucky, Scott County, Indiana, and Scottsville, Virginia are named for him

- James Clark (1779–1839) – born in Bedford County, Virginia; thirteenth governor of Kentucky 1836-1839, Kentucky House of Representatives, Kentucky Court of Appeals, U.S. House of Representatives (two separate terms), and Kentucky Senate where he was elected Speaker; while governor, he oversaw the creation of the State Board of Education and established a public school system in every county; he is buried in a private cemetery in Winchester
- Jane Lampton - mother of author Samuel Clemens (Mark Twain)
- Helen Thomas (1920–) – Winchester; born to Lebanese immigrants; since 1961 she has been the UPI White House correspondent; raised in Michigan; she has covered every president from John F. Kennedy to Barack Obama.
- Robert Trimble (1776–1828), Berkeley County, VA; family moved to Clark County; Kentucky House of Representatives from Bourbon County; Kentucky Court of Appeals; U.S. District Judge for Kentucky; appointed to U.S. Supreme Court by John Quincy Adams, sixth president; he is said to have appointed Trimble on the advice of Henry Clay, Secretary of State; Trimble County is named for him

Interesting names include: Agawam; Bel Air; Elkin; Hootentown; Indian Fields; Kiddville; L and E Junction; Locust Grove; Old Pine Grove; Pilot View; Pine Grove; Rabbit Town; Rightangle; Thompson

CLAY COUNTY (1807) Formed from Madison, Floyd, and Knox Counties. The county is named for General Green Clay (1757–1826), a Madison County legialator and early Kentucky surveyor. He was also a member of the Virginia and Kentucky State Legislaltures, U.S. Senator, and Secretary of State. He was the father of Cassius Marcellus Clay of White Hall and a cousin of Henry Clay.

Manchester is the county seat.

Near the town of Oneida, the Red Bird River and Goose Creek confluence to form the South Fork of the Kentucky River. The Red Bird River is named for Chief Red Bird, a Cherokee who was murdered on its banks in the late 1700s by two men from Tennessee. There are ten historic markers placed throughout the county.

Notable residents include:
- Bert T. Combs (1911–1991) – Manchester; governor of Kentucky 1959–1963, born in Manchester, died in Powell County, attended Oneida Baptist Institute; began his law career as city attorney in Prestonsburg and later became Commonwealth Attorney for Floyd County; was elected to fill a vacancy on the Kentucky Court of Appeals until he resigned in 1955 to run for governor which he lost to Happy

Chandler; four years later he was elected governor; during his administration he established the merit system for state workers, formed the state's first Human Rights Commission, and ordered the desegragation of all public accommodations in Kentucky; he improved the Education Department and expanded the state's highway system; the Bert T. Combs Mountain Parkway is named in his honor; after his term as governor, he was appointed by President Lyndon B. Johnson to the U.S. Court of Appeals for the Sixth Circuit; in 1971, he unsuccessfully ran for governor being defeated by Wendell Ford; on the evening of December 4, 1991 he was driving home from Frankfort when his car was swept from a roadway near Rosslyn, Powell County, into the flooded Red River; the eighty-year-old former governor drowned in that accident; he was buried in Manchester; his widow, Sarah Walter Combs, sits as Chief Judge on the Kentucky Court of Appeals

- Richie Farmer (1969–) – Manchester; Named Mr. Basketball in the state of Kentucky in 1988; a former University of Kentucky basketball shooting guard 1988–1992 where he was known as one of "The Unforgetables;" his #32 jersey was retired; since 2003 he has been the Kentucky Commissioner of Agriculture; in November, 2007 he and Trey Grayson, Secretary of State, became the first Republicans since 1915, to win a statewide office in an election won by a Democratic guberneratorial candidate

Interesting names include: Ammie; Ashers Fork; Bernice; Big Creek; Bluehole; Botto; Brightshade; Brutus; Burning Springs (so named for its ignitable release of natural gas); Chestnutburg; Creekville; Deer Lick; Fall Rock; Felty; Flat Woods; Fogertown; Gardner; Garrard; Goose Creek; Goose Rock; Grace; Hooker; Horse Creek; Katies Creek; Larue; Laurel Creek; Levi; Lincoln; Littleton; Newfound; Ogle; Oneida; Pigeonroost; Plank; Queendale; Shepherdtown; Spring Creek; Trixie; Urban; Vine; Wild Cat

CLINTON COUNTY (1836) Formed from Cumberland and Wayne Counties. The county is named in honor of lieutenant governor of New York, New York State Senator, U.S. Senator, and seventh governor of New York, DeWitt Clinton. As governor, he was largely responsible for the construction of the Erie Canal. DeWitt County Illinois and Clinton County Illinois are named for him. The county seat of DeWitt County, IL is Clinton. It is the only instance in the United States where one person has two counties name for him in the same state.

Among the early settlers to Clinton County, Kentucky were Simon Barber and his family from Albany, NY, where the county seat of Albany is now located. Albany has a high population of single people and an unusually rate of single women. In the 2000 Census, for every one hundred females age eighteen and over, there were ninety-one and one-half males. The community grew around a tavern established by Benjamin Dowell in the early 1800s. In 1837, the residents voted to make the location the seat of county government, and named the newly-formed town after Albany, New York.

Notable residents include:

- Thomas Bramlette (1817–1875) – born in Cumberland County, now Clinton; Kentucky's twenty-third governor
- Preston Leslie (1819–1907) – born in Wayne County, now Clinton; twenty-sixth governor of Kentucky, 1871-1875; territorial governor of Montana, 1887-1889; U.S. District Attorney, Montana, 1894-1898

Interesting names include: Aaron; Alpha; Browns Crossroads; Bug; Cedar Knob; Cumberland City; Decide; Desda; Fairland; Highway; Ida; Narvel; Nora; Savage; Seminary; Seventy Six; Shipley; Snow; Static; Upchurch; Wago

CRITTENDEN COUNTY (1842) Formed from Livingston County. The county is named for John Jordan Crittenden, Kentucky's seventeenth governor from 1848–1850, Kentucky House of Representatives (Speaker of the House), the sixteenth and twenty-third U.S. Attorney General, U.S. Senate (three separate terms), and Associate Justice of the Supreme Court of the United States. Author of the Crittenden Compromise, he fought desperately for conciliation on the eve of the Civil War. He had two sons, one fought for the Union Army and one for the Confederate Army. He died in Frankfort and is interred in the Frankfort Cemetery.

Marion, the county seat, is twenty-three miles from Princeton in Caldwell County, twenty-three miles from Providence in Webster County, and twenty-three miles from Sturgis in Union County. It is named for Francis Marion, a brigadier general from South Carolina in the Revolutionary War. He became known as the "Swamp Fox" for his ability to use decoys and ambushes to disrupt enemy communications, capture supplies, and free prisoners. Marion is considered one of the fathers of modern guerrilla warfare, and is credited in the lineage of the U.S. Army Rangers.

Interesting names include: Frances; Irma; Levias; Mattoon; Mexico; Midway; New Salem; Nunn; Repton; Shady Grove; Susan Creek; The Bluff; Tolu; Tribune; View

CUMBERLAND COUNTY (1799) Formed from Green County. The county is named for the Cumberland River which flows through it.

Burkesville, the county seat, began as a small riverside settlement even before the Iroquois Indians officially sold the land in 1768 to establish Cumberland County. In 1846 it was incorporated and named Burkesville after Sam Burk, a prominent citizen leader at that time. Just as Kentucky was a border state in the Civil War, Burkesville was a border town. The Cumberland River became a natural barrier between opposing army forces, which meant that there were soldiers and encampments from both sides throughout the county. After the Civil War, and on to the turn of the century, when people and goods were mainly transported by water, Burkesville became a busy and important town.

Today Burkesville's downtown boasts a courthouse square around which all traffic flows, and one traffic light. Thomas Lincoln, father of Abraham, lived in the Meshack Creek area of the county and served two terms as constable. Two Kentucky governors, Thomas E. Bramlette and Preston H. Leslie were born in the county. General John Edwards, King of Burkesville, commanded the Third Brigade in the Battle of the Thames during the War of 1812. King's home later became the home of Joel Cheek and his family, the originators of Maxwell House Coffee. The first American oil well was struck three miles north of Burkesville in 1829, but it is not generally recognized as such because the drillers were not searching for oil. It was the first county in America to have a female sheriff. Burkesville is home to Smith Pharmacy, the oldest, continuously operating pharmacy in Kentucky beginning in 1814.

Notable residents include:
- Thomas E. Bramlette (1817–1875) – born in Cumberland County, now Clinton County; twenty-third governor of Kentucky 1863–1867; in 1862 President Abraham Lincoln appointed him as U.S. District Attorney for Kentucky; died in Louisville and is buried in Cave Hill Cemetery
- Thomas Lincoln (1778–1851) – born in Rockingham County, Virginia; father of Abraham Lincoln
- Joel Cheek - founder of Maxwell House Coffee

Interesting names include: Amandaville; Arat; Bow; Cloyds Landing; Douglas Town; Dubre; Frogue; Green Grove; Judio; Kettle; Leslie; Long Ridge; Marrowbone; Modoc; Mud Camp; Tanbark; Waterview; Whetstone

DAVIESS (pronounced Davis) **COUNTY** (1815) Formed from Ohio County. The county is named for Colonel Joseph Hamilton Daveiss (1774–1811), the U.S. District Attorney for Kentucky who prosecuted Aaron Burr. He was killed at the Battle of Tippecanoe, Indiana. Although the correct spelling of his last name seems to be Daveiss, it is uniformly spelled Daviess in other places named for him, which include Jo Daviess County, Illinois, Daviess County, Indiana, and Daviess County, Missouri.

Josiah Henson (1789–1883), a slave in Daviess County, escaped to Canada in 1830. That event is thought to be the basis for Harriet Beecher Stowe's book, *Uncle Tom's Cabin*.

It has been reported that Owensboro, the county seat, has more restaurants per capita than any city in America. The city was named after Abraham Owen (also after whom Owen County was named) who was born in Prince Edward County, VA and moved to Kentucky in 1785. He was a member of the Kentucky Legislature and a member of the State Constitutional Convention. Owensboro was originally called Yellow Banks, an allusion to the color of the banks of the Ohio River. The city of Henderson, in the next county down the Ohio River, was called Red Banks.

In 1910, the Carriage Woodstock Company began to manufacture the Ames automobile. Production ceased in 1915. The company instead began making replacement bodies for the

Model T Ford. In 1922, the company began making furniture under the name of Ames Corporation. The company sold out to Whitehall Furniture in 1970.

On August 14, 1936, Owensboro became the sight of the last public hanging in the United States (in 2005, this writer talked with a lady who, as a young girl, witnessed that hanging. She and a friend skipped school that day and happened upon the event). Owensboro is home to Brescia University and Kentucky Wesleyan College. In 2006, plans were announced for a research center operated by the University of Louisville to study how to make the first ever human papillomavirus (HPV) vaccine from tobacco plants. If successful, the vaccine will be made in Owensboro.

Owensboro is home to the International Bluegrass Music Museum. The museum hosts a bluegrass jam session the first and third Saturdays of each month from 6 to 10 PM. Finally, Owensboro is home to the Western Kentucky Botanical Garden. The nine-acre garden is open to the public year round from sunrise to sunset. They boast a butterfly garden, rose, iris, daylily gardens, an herb garden, and fruit and berry gardens. The William Natcher Bridge, completed in 2002, was at the time of completion, the longest cable-supported bridge over an inland waterway in America. The bridge spans the Ohio River connecting Owensboro and Rockport, Indiana.

Notable residents include:
- Wendell Hampton Ford (1924–) – Owensboro; governor of Kentucky 1971–1974, Kentucky senator, lieutenant governor of Kentucky, and the longest-serving U.S. Senator from Kentucky (1974–1999). The Western Kentucky Parkway bears his name
- W. Ralph Basham – Owensboro; former director of the United States Secret Service
- Steve Henry (1953–) - lieutenant governor of Kentucky, 1995–2003
- Rex Chapman (1967–) – born in Bowling Green and reared in Owensboro; former UK basketball starter and 14 years with the NBA; he was the first player signed by the Charlotte Hornets, 1988
- Cliff Hagan (1931–) – Owensboro; former University of Kentucky basketball player, NBA basketball player, and former UK athletic director
- NASCAR drivers Darrell Waltrip, Michael Waltrip, Jeremy Mayfield, Jeff Green, David Green, Mark Green, and Stuart Kirby
- Nick Varner (1948–) Owensboro; Professional Pool Players Association World Open Pocket Billiard Champion, 1980; Billiard Congress of America National Eight-ball Championship, 1980, 1981; Professional Pool Players Association World Nine-ball Championship 1982
- Johnny Depp (1963–) – Owensboro; actor
- Tom Ewell (1909–1994) – Owensboro; Tony Award-winning actor; his most successful role came in the Broadway production of "The Seven Year Itch" which co-starred a lovely actress; when the movie version was made, the girl in the Broadway play was not asked to audition for the part but Marilyn Monroe was; the

scene of Ewell slyly admiring Monroe as she stood over a subway grate with her skirt blowing has become one of the most iconic moments in films; his final acting role was in a 1986 episode of "Murder, She Wrote"
- Moneta Sleet Jr. (1926–1996) – Owensboro; First black American to win Pulitzer Prize in photography, 1969; it was a photograph of Coretta Scott King at her father's funeral; he attended Kentucky State University, Frankfort

Interesting names include: Boston; Curdsville; Delaware; Grandview; Habit; Handyville; Livia; Maceo; Maple Mount; Maxwell; Oak Ridge; Oklahoma; Panther; Philpot; Red Hill; Rome; Ruin; Scythia; Spice Knob; Sutherland; Tuck; West Louisville

EDMONSON COUNTY (1826) Formed from Hart, Grayson, and Warren Counties. The county is named for Captain John Edmonson, hero in the War of 1812 and killed at the Battle of River Raisin, near Detroit, Michigan. A monument was erected in Monroe, Michigan to honor the Kentuckians who died as a result of that battle. Brownsville is the county seat. It is commonly held that in 1798, Mammoth Cave was discovered when John Houchins chased a bear into a large opening. Mammoth Cave is the largest cave system in the world with more than three hundred sixty miles of charted passageways. In 1981, the United Nations designated Mammoth Cave as a World Heritage Site, along with the Grand Canyon and the Great Pyramids of Egypt. It is the second oldest tourist attraction in the United States having begun in 1816. Niagara Falls is the nation's oldest tourist attraction. Nearly two million people visit the cave each year.

Brownsville is the county seat.

Residents of note include:
- Joe Blanton (1980–) – born in Nashville, grew up in Edmonson County, graduated from Franklin-Simpson High School, Simpson County; starting pitcher for Oakland Athletics; played baseball at the University of Kentucky where he finished eighth among all NCAA Division I pitchers; in the minor leagues he ranked second overall among all minor league pitchers (2003); in game 4 of the 2008 World Series, Blanton hit his first major league home run to become the thirteenth pitcher overall, and the first since 1974, to hit a home run in a World Series game; he was credited with the Philadelphia Phillies' 10-2 win over the Tampa Bay Rays

Interesting names include: Asphalt; Bee Spring; Black Gold; Broadway; Cedar Spring; Chalybeate; Dripping Spring; Elko; Fairview; Faye; Grassland; Hillview; Huff; Kyrock; Nash; Newfoundland; Oak Ridge; Ollie; Pig; Prosperity; Rhoda; Rocky Hill; Roundhill; Stockholm; Straw; Sunfish; Sweeden; Union City; Windyville; Woodside

ELLIOTT COUNTY (1869) Formed from Morgan, Lawrence, and Carter Counties. Elliott County is named for John Milton Elliott whose family moved from Virginia to what is now Elliott County when Elliott was an infant. He later became a lawyer and polititian in Prestonsburg, a member of the U.S. House of Representatives, and a Confederate Justice of the Kentucky Court of Appeals during the Civil War, Kentucky House of Representatives for two terms. He was assassinated in Frankfort on March 26, 1879.

Sandy Hook, the county seat, had population of 678 in the 2000 census.

Residents of note include:
- Jackie "Keith" Whitney (1954–1989) – country music singer; Whitney, along with Ricky Skaggs, were discovered by Ralph Stanley when the two teenagers sang Stanley Brothers songs at an opening act for the Clinch Mountain Boys and soon joined Ralph's band; Whitney also played with J. D. Crowe and the New South in the mid 1970s; during this period he established himself as one of the most versatile and talented lead singers in bluegrass; he released twenty singles and eighteen albums; his brother-in-law found him one day lying face down on his bed; the coroner ruled that he died of alcohol poisoning since his alcohol blood level was .447, five times over the legal limit to drive

Interesting names include: Ault; Bascorn; Beartown; Bell City; Bigstone; Bruin; Brushy Fork; Clay Fork; Dewdrop; Edsel; Faye; Gimlet; Gomez; Green; Ibex; Little Sandy; Lucile; Newfoundland; Ordinary; Roscoe; Ruin; Sarah; Shady Grove; Sideway; Spanglin; Stark; Stephens; The Ridge

ESTILL COUNTY (1808) Formed from Clark and Madison Counties. The county is named for Captain James Estill, a Kentucky militia officer killed during the Revolutionary War, killed at the Battle of Little Mountain. Seventy-five percent of the county is forest. Prior to pioneer settlement, Estill County was the site of a Shawnee village where they mined lead from the area. A large hotel with landscaped grounds at Estill Springs attracted many famous Kentuckians for summer retreats prior to the Civil War. Henry Clay, John Crittenden, and John C. Breckinridge were among the notables who summered there. The resort survived the Civil War and operated beyond 1900.

Irvine, the county seat, hosts the annual Mushroom Festival each April and is home to the manufacturing headquarters of Carhartt, Inc. Ravenna and Irvine together are known as the "Twin Cities."

Ravenna is named for Ravenna, Italy. It was reported by early railroad officials (L & N) that an Italian foreman and interpreter with the construction crew of about sixty Italian men building the railroad yards, requested that the railroad officials name the station in honor of his birthplace, Ravenna, Italy. A design on a glazed tile was sent to Ravenna from its sister city in Italy as a token of sympathy for the tornado disaster of June 9, 1961. The tile is a copy of one of the famous mosaic panels in the Church of Vitale, Ravenna. Christ is shown as a young beardless man clothed in a purple robe and tunic embroidered with gold, flanked by two archangles, clothed in white. Christ holds the seven seals in His left hand and with His right hand offers the crown of martyrdom. The tile is on display in the Ravenna (KY) City Hall.

(The following information is taken from the May, 2007 issue of *Kentucky Monthly* magazine, POB 559, Frankfort, KY 40602, Steven M. Vest, Editor and Publisher. Used by permission) The movie and TV series, "M*A*S*H," was based on the 8055th, which was the Army's pioneer mobile surgical hospital, a new concept designed to treat soldiers' wounds as quickly as possible and send the wounded to more specialized care in Tokyo or the United States. Army nurse Captain Lelia Jeanette Jones of Irvine was assigned to the Double-Nickle (8055th) unit at Uijongbu, Korea. In writing *Memoirs of an Army MASH Nurse in Korea*, fellow nurse Frances Barnes wrote, "Lelia had a hush-hush affair with a married Army doctor, a romance that did not survive the war." It was also noted that Capt. Jones would not hesitate to express her opinion and was the first one in line to defend her patients against everyone, including visiting generals. She had a great figure and never wore a bra, according to Barnes. Was she the inspiration for "Hot Lips" Houlihan? "She was feisty, outspoken, strong- willed, known for her romance with a married doctor, and she served in the 8055th with Captain Richard Hornberger. Incidentally, it was Hornberger who wrote the 1968 novel that became the basis for the movie *M*A*S*H*, which became the basis for the TV series *M*A*S*H.*

Notable residents include:
- Harry Dean Stanton (1926–) – West Irvine; served during World War II; a character actor who has played in 51 movies; film critic Roger Ebert said, "No movie featuring Harry Dean Stanton…in a supporting role can be altogether bad"

Interesting names include: Bogie; Calloway Crossing; Cobhill; Cow Creek; Cressy; Crystal; Doe Creek; Drip Rock; Evelyn; Fox; Furnace; Happy Top; Iron Mound; Jinks; Locust Branch; Lynch Town; North Irvine; Patsey; Pea Ridge; Pilot; Powell; Ravenna; Sand Hill; Shade; South Irvine; Sprout Springs; Station Camp; Stump; Sweet Lick; Texola; Union Hall; Wagersville; Walnut Gap; West Irvine; Wilder; Willow Tree; Winston; Wisemantown

FAYETTE COUNTY (1780) One of three original counties formed out of Kentucky County, Virginia. The county is named for Marquis de Lafayette who participated in both the Revolutionary War (without pay) and the French Revolution. Although he spent a total of less than five years in America he was more admired than perhaps any other foreign visitor. There are six counties, fifteen towns, four townships, one college, six high schools, one Naval carrier, and one Naval submarine named in his honor. There must also be added to the list thirteen towns named Fayette, and eleven towns named Fayetteville.

Lexington, the county seat and "The Horse Capital of the World," was founded in June, 1775 and named for the Battle of Lexington, Massachusetts, the first battle of the American Revolution, "the shot heard around the world". It was founded seventeen years before Kentucky became a state. A party of frontiersmen camped on the Middle Fork of Elkhorn Creek, today called Town Branch and rerouted under Vine Street, at the location today known as McConnell Springs. The first building, a blockhouse, was built in 1779. A blockhouse is a small, isolated fort comprised of one building designed to serve as a defense against an enemy that does not possess siege equipment. The town of Lexington was established on May 6, 1782, by an act of the Virginia General Assembly. By 1820, it was one of the largest and wealthiest towns west of the Allegheny Mountains. So cultured was its lifestyle that Lexington became known as the "Athens of the West." One prominent citizen, John Wesley Hunt, became the first millionaire west of the Alleghenies. In 1850, twenty percent of the state's population was slaves, and Lexington had the highest concentration of slaves in the state. Jefferson Davis attended Transylvania University (1923–1924). Mary Todd Lincoln was born and raised in Lexington. John Wesley Morgan built a home in 1814. Thomas Hunt Morgan also resided there.

Ashland, the 18-room mansion of Henry Clay from 1806–1852, contains a rare collection of many artifacts belonging to the Clay family. In 1935 Lexington opened the Addiction Research Center, one of the first drug rehabilitation clinics. Lexington also opened the first alcohol and drug rehabilitation hospital in the United States. It was known as "Narco" of Lexington. It is now a federal prison.

Poa pratensis, bluegrass, is native to Europe, Asia, and northern Africa. Bluegrass thrives on the limestone beneath the soil's surface. Lexington has the dubious distinction of being recognized as a high allergy area by the Asthma and Allergy Foundation of America.

There are three public universities, five private colleges, and two theological seminaries in the Lexington area. Lexmark is a Fortune 500 company employing nearly 3,500 people. The Jiff Peanut Butter plant in Lexington is the world's largest peanut butter making facility. The University of Kentucky has an annual budget of $1.5 billion. Lexington was ranked number ten in a list of America's most educated cities with a population of two hundred fifty thousand. The University of Kentucky Wildcats basketball team has won more games than any other team in college basketball history.

On the Fourth of July, annual festivities include a reading of the Declaration of Independence on the steps of the old courthouse.

Lexington has been chosen to be the site of the 2010 World Equestrian Games. As early as 1800, the quality of Kentucky horses was known through the country and by 1840, Kentucky had reached the zenith in horse breeding, a position it still holds today. The Junior League Horse Show is the largest outdoor saddlebred show in the country. There are more than five hundred thoroughbred farms in the Bluegrass vicinity.

There are eighty-four historic markers placed throughout the county. Only Jefferson County has more (one hundred sixteen).

In 1974, Fayette County merged its government with the city of Lexington creating a consolidated city-government.

Notable residents include:
- Gideon Shyrock – Architect; introduced Greek Revival style to the "West"; his younger brother was Cincinnatus Shyrock who in 1872, built the First Presbyterian Church on North Mill Street with a one hundred fifty-foot spire; one of eleven children, Gideon went to Philadelphia to study architecture (to date it was not a recognized profession); he designed the Old State Capital, Frankfort; he was the state's most prominent architect from 1827–1837, designing public and residential buildings in Louisville, Frankfort, and Lexington
- Mary Todd Lincoln (1818–1882) – Lexington; wife of Abraham Lincoln; to escape a difficult relationship with her step-mother, Mary moved to Springfield, Illinois where she met Lincoln; it is reported that, on learning that her surname was spelled with two "d"s, Lincoln asked, "Why? One was enough for God?" She married Abraham Lincoln on November 4, 1842; the Mary Todd Lincoln House is located at 578 West Main Street, Lexington, KY
- John Breckenridge (1872–1920) – Cabell's Dale, near Lexington; U.S. vice president under James Buchanan, 1857-1861, the youngest vice president in history, thirty-six, the minimum age required by the Constitution
- William Wells Brown (1814–1884) – Lexington; America's first black novelist; born into slavery; on New Year's Day,1834, he slipped away from a steamboat docked in Cincinnati; after nine years as a conductor for the Underground Railroad, and as a steam boatman on Lake Erie (a position he used to ferry slaves to freedom in Canada), he began lecturing for the abolition movement in New York City; in 1853, Brown published The President's Daughter, a novel based on what was at the time considered to be a rumor about Thomas Jefferson fathering a daughter with his slave Sally Hemings; historians consider this the first novel written by an African American; however, the book was published in England
- Kevin Richardson (1971–) – former member of The Backstreet Boys
- Jim Varney (1949–2000) – Lexington; best known as Ernest P. Worrell ("Know what I mean, Vern?")
- George Timothy Clooney (1961–) – Lexington; actor

Interesting names include: Athens (Ā-thens); Avon; Baralto; Blueberry Hill; Centerville; Chevy Chase; Columbus; Dixie Plantation; Elmendorf; Fort Spring; Frogtown; Gardenside; Greendale; Hi-Acres; Hollywood; Jimtown; Little Georgetown; Little Texas; Loradale; Monticello; Nihizertown; Spears; Walnut Hill; Yamallton

FLEMING COUNTY (1798) Formed from Mason County. The county is named for Colonel John Fleming, a Virginia judge and early settler in Kentucky. In 1998 the Kentucky general assembly designated Fleming County as the Covered Bridge Capital of Kentucky. There are twelve historic markers placed throughout the county.

Flemingsburg is the county seat.

Notable residents include:

- Landaff Watson Andrews (1803–1887) – 1803-1887) – Flemingsburg; U.S. House of Representatives, Kentucky House of Representatives, and Kentucky Senate; he is buried in the Fleming County Cemetery
- Leander Cox (1812–1865) – born in Cumberland County, Virginia; U.S. House of Representatives and Kentucky House of Representatives; moved to Flemingsburg where he practiced law; Captain in the 3rd Kentucky Volunteers in the Mexican War; he is buried in Fleming County Cemetery
- Lawrence Trimble (1825–1904) – U.S. House of Representatives and Kentucky House of Representativews; born in Flemingsburg and practiced law in Paducah; after his political career, he moved to Albuquerque, New Mexico where he continued to practice law; he is buried there.
- Herman Chittison (1908–1967) – Jazz pianist in the 1920s and 1930s; early in his career he worked with Ethel Waters
- Woodrow "Woodie" Thompson Fryman (1940–) – born in Ewing, known as the Fleming Flame; pitching career spanned from 1967–1983; threw four one-hitters; as a rookie with the Pirates he threw three consecutive shutouts; pitched for the Cincinnati Reds, Chicago Cubs, Detroit Tigers, Montreal Expos, Pittsburgh Pirates, and Philadelphia Phillies; he makes his home in Ewing
- Franklin Sousley, PFC (1925–1945) - Hilltop, three miles south of Elizaville; on February 25, 1945, he helped raise the U.S. flag on Mount Suribachi; said to be the most famous war photograph in history taken by Joe Rosenthal of the Associated Press; the importance of the photograph as a propaganda tool was recognized immediately, and word was sent that Sousley was to be brought back to America for a publicity tour but word did not reach him in time; on March 21, 1945, Marine PFC Sousley, age ninteen, was shot in the back by a Japanese sniper; originally buried on Iwo Jima, as were all casualties, his body was reinterred on May 8, 1947, in Elizaville Cemetery. Note: The family of Rev. Charles G. Thompson, Jr., has photographs of Rev. Thompson assisting in a tribute ceremony to PFC Sousley at the Elizaville Cemetery; Rev. Thompson was pastor of nearby Ewing Baptist Church at the time

Interesting names include: Bald Hill; Battle Run; Beechburg; Bluebank; Concord; Dalesburg; Elizaville; Ewing; Fairview; Farmville; Flemingsburg Junction; Foxport; Goddard; Hill Top; Locust; Marthas Mills; Mount Carmel; Olive Branch; Pea Ridge; Pleasureville; Plummers Landing (two miles from) Plummers Mill; Poplar Grove; Poplar Plains; Ringos Mills; Stringtown; Sunset

FLOYD COUNTY (1800) Formed from Fleming, Montgomery, and Mason Counties. The county is named for Colonel John Floyd, a pioneer and surveyor. The final boundary was not set for another eighty-five years, 1884, by which time the county included parts of Lawrence, Pike, Morgan, Breathitt, Letcher, Johnson, Rowan, Magoffin, Wolfe, Elliott, Menifee, Martin, Knott, and Perry. Elevation ranges from 580 to 2,320 feet.

Prestonsburg, the county seat, and the only American town with that name, was founded in 1797. It was originally known as Preston's Station, named for John Preston. It was renamed Prestonsburg in 1799, when it became the seat of the newly-formed Floyd County. The first post office opened in 1816 as Floyd Court House. In Prestonsburg is the May House which, built in 1817, is the oldest brick house in the Big Sandy Valley. About three miles west of Prestonsburg is the Middle Creek national Battlefield, site of the largest and most significant Civil War battle in eastern Kentucky.

Dewey Lake, in Floyd County, was achieved by damming Johns Creek in 1949. John's Creek flows northwest out of Pike County, through Floyd, and into Johnson County where it empties into the Levisa Fork River. The largest tiger muskie ever taken in the state of Kentucky (13 lb., 12, oz.) was caught in Dewey Lake. The lake is approximately ten miles long. Jenny Wiley State Resort Park was originally known as at Dewey Lake State Park. It is named for Virginia "Jenny" Wiley, a pioneer woman who, in 1789, was captured by a group of Indians from four different tribes. She endured the slaying of her brother and four children, one three-months-old, and escaped after eleven months of captivity.

Lackey - (1880) named for the family of a prominent Floyd County businessman and public official Alexander Lackey, a Virginia-born pioneer who settled at the forks of the Beaver (now Martin) around 1808.
Amba - named for Amba Walters, daughter of a local physician.
Banner - named for David Banner, settler.
Betsy Layne - (1875) named for a local resident.
Blue Moon - named for a type of perfume.
Bypro - named for the Byproduct Coal Company.
David - named for David L. Francis, president of Patsy Stoker Coal.
Galveston - named for Galveston, TX.
Harold - named for Harold Hatcher, merchant.
Ligon - named for Charles Yancy Ligon, railroad engineer.
Martin - named for Martin Van Allen, postmaster.
Price - named for Emory R. Price, steel company manager.
Stanville - named for Robert E. Stanley, sheriff and judge.
Wayland - named for U.S. Senator Clarence Wayland Watson.
Wheelwright - named for Jere H. Wheelwright, president of the Consolidation Coal Company.

There are nine historic markers placed throughout the county.

Interesting names include: Allen; Alphoretta; Alvin; Amba; Arkansas; Auxier; Banner; Beaver; Beaver Junction; Betsy Layne; Blue Moon; Blue River; Bonanza; Buckingham; Bull Creek; Bypro; Cliff; Dada; Dana; David; Dema; Dock; Drift; Dwale; Eastern; East Point (the northernmost community in the county); Emma; Estill; Galveston; Glo; Halo; Harold; Hi Hat; Hippo; Hot Spot; Hunter; Lackey; Lancer; Ligon; Mare Creek; Martin; Melvin; Midas; Minnie; Northern; Orkney; Price; Prince; Printer; Pyramid;

Rough and Tough; Stanville; Teaberry; Tram; Watergap; Wayland; Weeksbury; West Prestonsburg; Wheelwright; Wonder; Woods;

FRANKLIN COUNTY (1795) Formed from Mercer, Shelby, and Woodford Counties. The county is named for the American inventor and statesman Benjamin Franklin. It was the state capital for three years before it was the county seat.

Frankfort, the county seat, probably received its name from an event that took place in 1780 when Indians attacked a group of pioneers from Bryan's Station who were making salt in a ford on the Kentucky River. One of the pioneers, Stephen Frank, was killed and the crossing became known as Franks Ford. The name soon evolved into Frankford.

Frankfort became state capital in 1792, after pledging more manpower toward the construction of a statehouse than any other city. The Kentucky General Assembly appropriated funds to provide a house to accommodate the governor in 1796. The construction was completed in 1798. The old governor's mansion is thought to be the oldest official executive residence still in use in the United States. In 1829, the old capital, the third capital building, introduced Greek Revival west of the Appalachian Mountains. The building, designed by Gideon Shryock when he was twenty-five years old, served the Commonwealth as its capital from 1830 to 1910. The building is widely recognized as a beautiful masterpiece of nineteenth-century American architecture. During the Civil War, this was the only pro-Union capital occupied by the Confederate Army. Plans to swear in a Confederate governor and establish a Confederate state government were thwarted by the approaching Union Army only days before the Battle of Perryville in 1862. On February 3, 1900, Governor-elect William Goebel, while walking to the capital to be inaugurated, was assassinated by a gunman who was hiding in an office in the old capital annex next door. He is the only governor in the history of the United States to die in office as a result of assassination. Only three states have capitals with smaller populations than Kentucky: Augusta, Maine, Pierre, South Dakota, and Montpelier, Vermont.

Bibb lettuce was first cultivated by Jack Bibb in Frankfort in the late nineteenth century. There are fifty-two historic markers placed throughout the county.

Interesting names include: Big Eddy; Camp Pleasant; Elmville; Evergreen; Farmdale; Flag Fork; Forks of Elkhorn; Indian Hills; Kennebec; Ottusville; Slickway; Swallowfield; Switzer; Woodlake

FULTON COUNTY (1845) Formed from Hickman County. The westernmost county in Kentucky, was named for Robert Fulton, the engineer and inventor of the first successful steamboat. Across America, at least five counties, six towns, and many streets are named in his honor.

Hickman is the county seat. In order to see all of Fulton County, one must travel south into Tennessee about four miles, west three miles, then north four miles in order to get back into Kentucky. There is a piece of land, approximately four miles long and three miles wide, which is completely cut off from the rest of the state. There are two roads, Kentucky Bend Road and Stepp Road, but no houses. It is used for farming. The Mississippi River borders this piece of land on three sides as it makes a loop north, west, then south again on its way to the Gulf of Mexico. This separation of land was caused by the New Madrid Earthquake in 1860-1861. Another piece of Fulton County is completely cut off from the county with no road access due to the Mississippi River making a natural course change. As far as can be determined from aerial photographs, the area is neither cultivated nor inhabited.

The city of Fulton was once known as the "Banana Capital of the World" because seventy percent of imported bananas to the U.S. were shipped there. Fulton is one of only two cities in Kentucky that provides passenger rail service by Amtrak. The station is a small, unmonitored building on the edge of town. The southbound City of New Orleans stops at 3:00 AM, and the northbound City of New Orleans stops at 1:00 AM.

Interesting names include: Anna Lynne; Fulton (on the border with South Fulton, TN; the street named State Line Road divides the two states and the two cities); Jordan; Miller; Moscow; Sassafras Ridge; State Line

GALLATIN COUNTY (1799) Formed from Franklin and Shelby Counties. The county is named for Albert Gallatin, a Swiss native who became a financier, U.S. House of Representatives, U.S. Senate, Secretary of State under Thomas Jefferson, and is the longest-serving Secretary of the Treasury. He helped found the House Ways and Means Committee and founded New York University. He is honored with a statue in front of the U.S. Treasury Building, Washington, D.C. His portrait was on the face of the $500 bill, 1862-1863. His portrait was also on the 1¼ cent stamp from 1967-1973. Three counties in other states are named after him. The United States Department of the Treasury's highest career service award bears his name, as does Gallatin Street in Washington, D.C. Gallatin was the first cabinet secretary to ever be photographed, though not while in office.

At the close of the Civil War, the Ohio River near Warsaw was the scene of one of the worst steamboat accidents in history. Two passenger steamers, the "America" and the "United States" collided. The "United States" carried barrels of kerosene which caught fire, and soon both boats were in flames. The death toll reached one hundred sixty-two.

Warsaw is the county seat. Warsaw began as a landing on the Ohio River in 1789. In 1805, founder Colonel Robert Johnson surveyed and built a road from from this landing to his former home in Scott County. The landing soon became a busy shipping port. In 1814, Colonel Johnson and Henry Yates purchased two hundred acres of land to establish a rivertown to be named Fredricksburg, after Johnson's hometown in Virginia. In 1831, the town was renamed Warsaw. The oldest home in Warsaw is the Henry Yates house, built of logs circa 1809.

Interesting names include: Munk; Napoleon; Poplar Grove

GARRARD (GAIR-ad) **COUNTY** (1797) Formed from Madison, Lincoln, and Mercer Counties. The county is named James Garrard (1796–1804), Kentucky's second governor. Garrard was born in Virginia and moved to to an area near Paris at age thirty-three where he became a member of the committee that helped frame Kentucky's Constitution. He was the first Kentucky governor to serve two full successive terms and the first one to live in the governor's mansion (today the lieutenant governor's mansion). In addition to his political duties he was an ordained Baptist minister, a miller, a farmer, and a whiskey maker. During his terms in office he added twenty-six counties (including Garrard) to the state. He died in Bourbon County and is buried in the Garrard Famial Burial Grounds at Rudells Mills in Bourbon County.

Lancaster is the county seat. It is home of the Kennedy Plantation which became the inspiration for Harriet Beecher's Stowe's novel, *Uncle Tom's Cabin*. Paint Lick, an unincorporated community, is said to have received its name from settlers' descriptions of the peeled tree trunks that served as a means of marking the salt licks along the creek by Native Americans.

Notable residents include:
- William Owsley (1782–1862) – born in Virginia, family moved to Lincoln County, near Crab Orchard; sixteenth governor of Kentucky 1844–1848, Kentucky House of Representatives (two separate terms), Kentucky Senate, Kentucky Court of Appeals, and appointed to a vacated term of Kentucky Secretary of State; he worked as a teacher, surveyor, and deputy sheriff, after which he stueied law and opened a practice in Garrard County
- Robert Perkins Letcher (1788–1861) – born in Goochland County, Virginia after which the family moved to Garrard County; fifteenth governor of Kentucky 1840–1844; he practiced law near Danville; he is buried in the Frankfort Cemetery
- Simeon H. Anderson (1802–1840) – born in Lancaster; U.S. House of representatives
- William O'Connell Bradley (1847–1914) – born in Lancaster; nicknamed Billy O. B; Kentucky's thirty-second governor, 1895-1899, and Kentucky's first Republican governor; known as the father of the Republican Party; after his term as governor he served in the U.S. Senate; his family moved to Somerset when Bradley was young; on two different occasions he dropped out of school and ran off to join the Union Army during the Civil War; despite having no college education, Bradley was allowed to take the Kentucky bar exam at age eighteen by special permission of the Kentucky Legislature which he passed; he died in Washington D.C., just after announcing his retirement and is buried in the Frankfort Cemetery
- Carrie Nation (1846–1911) – Temperance crusader known as "the lady with the hatchet;" her last name is from her second husband; she was nearly 6' tall and weighed 175 lbs; she described herself as "a bulldog running along at the feet of Jesus, barking

at what He does not like;" she claimed a divine ordination to promote temperance by smashing up bars; she is buried in Belton, Missouri

Interesting names include: Buckeye; Buena Vista; Cartersville; Manse; Marcellus; McCreary; Nina; Paint Lick; Stone; Three Forks; White Oak

GRANT COUNTY (1820) Formed from Pendleton County. The county is named for Samuel Grant, Colonel John Grant, or Squire Grant, early settlers of Kentucky.

Williamstown, the county seat, is about three miles from the Grant/Pendleton County line.

Interesting names include: Cherry Grove; Cordova; Corinth; Crittenden; Delia; Dry Ridge; Four Corners; Hilltop; Holbrook; Jericho; Lawrenceville; Mason; Mount Zion (500 yards from) Mt Zion; Stringtown; Zion Station

GRAVES COUNTY (1824) Formed from Hickman County. It is named for Benjamin F. Graves, a soldier killed during the War of 1812 at the Battle of River Raisin in Michigan. As one of Kentucky's largest counties, Graves' history of legends and leaders includes a U.S. vice president, four U.S. Congressmen, famous and infamous heroes, singers and songwriters, noted authors, and a legacy of historic sites.

The fertile land attracted early settlers from Virginia, North Carolina, South Carolina, and Tennessee, who brought with them a degree of fierce determination to succeed on the land. Tobacco was a large part of the local economy and over the years Graves County has a rich history of the dark-fired and dark-air cured leaf tobacco used in smokeless tobacco farming. A woolen mill began operation prior to the American Civil War and continued to grow with the men's clothing market. Several other clothing companys were added to the county's commerce. Mayfield's minor league baseball team was called the Mayfield Clothiers.

Mayfield is the county seat.

Dukedom is connected with Confederate General Nathan Bedford Forrest. Regiments camping near here were given permission to seek food, horses, get recruits, and visit families. No one deserted; all returned to their units.

Graves County is home to Fancy Farm. They celebrated their 128th annual picnic in 2009.

Notable residents include:
- Lucien Anderson (1824–1898) – born near Mayfield; correct spelling is Lucian; U.S. House of Representatives and Kentucky House of Representatives
- Andrew Rechmond Boone (1831–1886) – born in Davidson County, Tennessee, moved to Mayfield; U.S. House of Representatives

- Alben Barkley (1877–1956) – born near Lowes; U.S. vice president under Harry S. Truman, 1949-1953; born Willie Alben Barkley, he changed his name after law school to Alben William Barkley. He practiced law in McCracken County (Paducah). He was elected to both the House of Representatives and the U.S. Senate. At the time of his inauguration, at age seventy-one, he was the oldest vice president to date, and he is the only vice president to marry while in office (to a lady half his age). After his term as vice president, he was reelected to the U.S. Senate and served until his death. Just before his death, he said, "I would rather be a servant in the House of the Lord than to sit in the seats of the mighty." He is buried in Mount Kenton Cemetery near Paducah. Barkley Lodge and Lake Barkley are named for him
- William Voris Gregory (1877–1936) – U. S. House of Representatives 1927–1936 and the brother of Representative Noble Jones Gregory
- Noble Jones Gregory (1897–1971) – Mayfield; U.S. House of Representatives serving eleven terms and the brother of William Voris Gregory
- Carroll Hubbard (1937–) – Murray; Kentucky senator 1968–1975, U.S. House of Representatives for nine terms

Interesting names include: Baltimore; Bell City; Boaz; Clear Springs; Cooksville; Cuba; Dogwood; Dublin; Dukedom; Fairbanks; Fancy Farm; Feliciana; Golo; Hickory; Hicksville; Kansas; Lynnville; Pilot Oak; Roper; South Highland; Tri City; Viola; Water Valley; Westplains; West Viola; Wheel

GRAYSON COUNTY (1810) Formed from Hardin and Ohio Counties. The county is named for William Grayson (of Scotish descent) who served as an aide-de-camp to General George Washington during the Revolutionary War and later served Virginia as its U.S. Senator. George Washington once owned five thousand acres in Grayson County. He purchased the land from Henry "Light Horse Harry" Lee, father of Robert E. Lee by trading his favorite horse for it.

Each July Grayson County hosts the Official Kentucky State Old Time Fiddlers Contest which brings fiddlers from several states to the Rough River Dam State Resort Park area. In September the city of Clarkson hosts the annyal Honeyfest. This festival celebrates the city and contributions of of Clarkson's Walter T. Kelley Beehive Factory.

Leitchfield is the county seat. It was incorporated in 1866, and named for Major David Leitch. It is believed that the settlement dates back to the 1700s, and was once known as Shaw's Station

Interesting names include: Anneta; Black Rock; Church; Concord; Do Stop; Duff; Eveleigh; Fairbanks; Falling Branch; Falls of Rough; Fragrant; Grayson Springs; Hanging Rock; Hickory Corner; Indian Valley; Jugville; Lilac; Lone Oak; Meredith; Neafus; Pine Knob; Ponderosa; Post; Ready; Rock Creek; Royal; Short Creek; Snap; South;

Spring Lick; Spurrier (10 miles from Spurrier in Hardin County); Tar Hill; Tri City; Wax; West City

GREEN COUNTY (1793) Formed from Lincoln and Nelson Counties. The county is named for Nathaniel Greene, a major general in the Continental Army during the Revolutionary War. By the end of the war he was known as General George Washington's most gifted and talented officer.

Greensburg is the county seat.

Notable residents include:
- William Herndon, Abraham Lincoln's law partner. The house of his birth still stands

Interesting names include: Black Gnat; Blowing Springs; Bloyd; Bluff Boom; Eve (the only one I found in America); Exie; Fry; Grab; Little Barren; Mount Gilead; Pierce; Roachville; Summersville; Whitewood

GREENUP COUNTY (1804) Formed from Mason County. The county and the county seat, also named Greenup, are named for Christopher Greenup, the third governor of Kentucky, 1804–1808. He was born in Virginia and served in the Revolutionary War. He was one of Kentucky's first two members of the U.S. House of Representatives which he served from 1792–1797. He died in Frankfort and is buried in the Frankfort Cemetery.

Flatwoods was originally named Advance. The name was later changed to Cheap, after John Cheap, a blind Methodist preacher. The city returned to the name of Advance in 1918. In 1938 the post office was renamed Flatwoods. The name of Flatwoods comes from the area's original topography, a strip of flat, wooded land which runs parallel to the Ohio River.

Notable residents include:
- Jesse Hilton Stuart (1906–1984) - Writer and Kentucky poet laureate; wrote his first short story when he was a sophomore in high school; in addition to seven novels and five autobiographical works, he had 460 short stories printed, as well as several poems; the lodge at Greenbo Lake State Resort park is named for him
- Don Gullet (1951–) – Lynn; Major league pitcher for Cincinnati Reds from 1970-1976; signed on with the New York Yankees in 1977, but shoulder trouble ended his career in 1980; he then joined the Cincinnati Reds as a pitching coach; he had a career 3.1 ERA and a career batting average of 194; although he only played for nine seasons, he was a member of five World Series teams
- Billy Ray Cyrus (1961–) – Flatwoods; Country singer, songwriter, actor; his father is a former member of the Kentucky house of representatives (Ron Cyrus, 1975–1996); the song "I Miss You," by Miley Cyrus, was written for Ron Cyrus after his death and is featured on her 2007 album *Hannah Montana 2: Meet Miley Cyrus*);

Billy was raised in a Pentecostal family; his parents divorced during his youth; he attended Georgetown College on a baseball scholarship, but dropped out to form a band called, "Sly Dog," with his brother Kevin Cyrus; since 2006, he is known as Robby, the father of *Hannah Montana,* a Disney Channel television series in which *Hanna Montana* is played by his biological daughter, Miley Cyrus

Interesting names include: Argentum; Argillite; Beechy; Bellefonte (Kentucky's youngest town, incorporated 1951); Flatwoods; Frost; Hunnewell; Letitia; Limeville; Lloyd; Load; Lynn; Naples; Oldtown; Poplar Highlands; Raceland; Riverview; Russell; Samaria; Siloam; South Shore; Sunshine

HANCOCK COUNTY (1829) Formed from Ohio, Breckinridge, and Daviess Counties. The county is named for John Hancock, the first and only signer of the Declaration of Independence on July 4, 1776. The other 55 delegates signed on August 2.

Hawesville, the county seat, has the second oldest courthouse in Kentucky. The Greek Revival building was completed in 1867. Main Street in front of the courthouse was the scene of one of the most widely published gunfights in Kentucky before the Civil War. In March, 1859 a shootout between factions led by merchant Thomas Lowe and district prosecutor Cicero Maxwell, left one man dead and two wounded, and was publicized nationally in the well-known newspaper *Harper's Weekly.*

Lewisport's claim to fame is that Abraham Lincoln won his first law case in the "Pell Home," which at the time was the site of the circuit court. Descendents of Judge Pell live in Lewisport today. The Pate House, built in 1822, was the scene of Abraham Lincoln's first trial in which he defended himself against charges of operating a ferry across the Ohio River without a license.

The paddlewheel steamer Robert E. Lee was built by Captain John Cannon, a Hawesville native. The boat defeated the Natchez in the 1870 steamboat race from New Orleans to St. Louis in 1870.

Interesting names include: Adair; Cabot; Dukes; Floral; Indian Lake; Little Tar Springs; Petri; Roseville; Skillman; Sunny Corner; Utility

HARDIN COUNTY (1793) Formed from Nelson County. The county is named for John Hardin, an officer in the Continental Army during the Revolutionary War. After the war he settled in Washington County. He was also a Kentucky militia commander in the Northwest Indian War. He was killed by Shawnee Indians while serving as an emissary in that war.

Thomas Lincoln, a resident of Hardin County, married Nancy Hanks in 1806, and they lived in a log cabin in Elizabethtown. Their daughter Sarah was born there in 1808. Afterward, they moved to the Sinking Spring Farm (La Rue County) where Abraham was born. After moving to Indiana in 1816, Thomas Lincoln moved back to Elizabethtown after Nancy died. Here he married Sarah Johnston who had the privilege of rearing Abraham from the age of ten. The log home of pioneer Hardin Thomas was bult in part by Abraham Lincoln's father, Thomas Lincoln. That home still stands.

Elizabethtown, the county seat, was founded on July 4, 1797, and named in honor of the wife of Andrew Hynes.

In 1862, Elizabethtown was attacked by General John Hunt Morgan with a cavalry of three thousand. During the battle more than one hundred cannon balls were fired into the town. After the battle, one cannon ball was lodged in the side of a building in the Public Square. The building burned in 1887. When it was rebuilt, the cannon ball was replaced in the side of the new building, as close as possible to its original point of impact, where it remains. From 1871-1873 General George Custer was stationed in Elizabethtown. The movie, "Elizabethtown" (2005), was largely filmed in Versailles and Louisville because Elizabethtown had lost most of its historic buildings due to development and sprawl.

A few miles north of Elizabethtown on US 31 is Ft. Knox which, since 1936, has been home of the U.S. Bullion Depository with over $6 billion worth of gold, the largest amount stored anywhere in the world. In 1951, Abbott and Costello starred in a movie titled, "Comin' Round the Mountain," in which they use a treasure map to find a stash of gold. At the end of the film they find themselves in the middle of Ft. Knox and are immediately arrested. The 1964 James Bond film, "Goldfinger," was partly filmed there.

West Point was established in 1796, and so named because it was the westernmost outpost of the English civilization coming down the Ohio River.

Notable residents include:
- Kelly Rutherford (1968–) – Elizabethtown; actress, perhaps best known for her roles on "Generations" and "Melrose Place"

Interesting names include: Arch; Booth; Cecilia; Cranks; Crest; Crummies; Eastview; Flint Hill; Four Corners; Hardin Springs; Kraft; Limp; Long View; Nolin; Old Stephensburg; Perryville; Red Hill; Rose Terrace; Seven Corners; Sonora; Spurrier (10 miles from Spurrier in Grayson County); Stephensburg; Summit; Tiptop Station; Tunnel Hills; Vine Grove; West Point

HARLAN COUNTY (1819) Formed from Knox County. Both the county and county seat, Harlan, are named for Silas Harlan, a soldier in the Battle of Blue Licks, the last battle of the Revolutionary War. Journeying to Kentucky with James Harrod in 1774 Harlan served as scout, hunter, and military leader, achieving the rank of major. Harlan assisted James Harrod's party in Harrodsburg to pick up gun powder to be delivered to the Kentucky settlers to assist them against the British in the Revolutionary War.

Harlan County is the site of a rare criminal case in which Condy Dabney was convicted in 1924 of murdering a person who was later found alive.

Harlan County is home to Kingdom Come State Park.

In 1913 Harlan countians formed the state's first forest fire protective association. In 1919, the county was the site of the first state forest, Kentenia, on Pine Mountain.

Lynch, a coal town, was named for the head of the company, Thomas Lynch. It had a population of ten thousand in the 1940s. The town boasted a movie theater and a hospital. The 2000 census reported a population of nine hundred. Lynch, near Black Mountain (elevation 1,600 feet), is Kentucky's highest incorporated city. Black Mountain is Kentucky's highest peat at 4,145 feet above sea level.

Harlan is the longest county in Kentucky, about fifty miles long and only twenty miles wide.

Blanton Forest is the largest old-growth forest in Kentucky and one of the oldest in America. The trees that tower one hundred feet over the forest floor are the same ones the early settlers saw.

Notable residents include:
- Wallace "Wah Wah" Clayton Jones (1926–) – Harlan; holds the unique distinction of being an All-American under the legendary Adolph Rupp (basketball) and Bear Bryant (football) when both men coached at the University of Kentucky; the Wildcats were NCAA basketball champions 1948 and 1949; he played in the NBA from 1949-1952 with the Indianapolis Olympians
- Cawood Ledford (1926–2001) – Cawood; long-time play-by-play announcer for the University of Kentucky basketball and football teams, the men's NCAA Final Four, and the Kentucky Derby; he was employed by WHAS; the basketball court in Rupp Arena is named Cawood's Court
- Bernard "Bernie" Bickerstaff (1944–) – Benham; Current executive vice-president for the Charlotte Bobcats; formerly coached Seattle SuperSonics, Denver Nuggets, and Washington Bullets/Wizards; played with the Harlem Globetrotters several seasons and coached them for three years before coaching in the NBA
- Paul "Showtime" Gaffney – in his twelfth season with the Harlem Globetrotters; replaced George "Meadowlark" Lemon
- Willis Thomas - Harlem Globetrotters
- George Ella Lyon (1949–) – Harlan; poet and author; lives in Lexington
- Joanna Carter – claims to have seen Bigfoot in Harlan County crossing Highway 1137

Interesting names include: Ages; Bailey Creek; Benham; Benito; Big Laurel; Black Bottom; Black Mountain; Bobs Creek; Cawood (for which Cawood Ledford was named);

Chad; Chevrolet; Closplint; Clover; Clovertown; Clutts; Coldiron; Colts; Cranks; Crummies; Cumberland; Cutshin; Divide; Dizney; Farmers Mill; Fresh Meadows; Georgetown; Golden Ash; Harlan Gas; Highsplint; Hilo; Laden; Liggett; Louellen; Low; Lynch; Mary Alice; Mary Helen; Pansy; Pathfork; Pine Mountain; Redbud; Ridgeway; Rio Vista; River Ridge; Sampson; Sand Hill; Short Town; Sunshine; Tacky Town; Ten Spot; Three Point; Totz; Tway; Twila; Wallins Creek; Woods

HARRISON COUNTY (1794) Formed from Bourbon and Scott Counties. The county is named for Colonel Benjamin Harrison V, a signer of the Declaration of Independence, an advocate for Kentucky statehood, one of the framers of Kentucky's Constitution, and a Kentucky legislator. His son William Henry Harrison and his great-grandson Benjamin Harrison would both become president of the United States.

Cynthiana, the county seat, is named after Cynthia and Anna Harrison, daughters of Robert Harrison who donated land known as the Public Square. In 1969 the 3M Company built a factory there where Post-It Notes were developed in the 1970s and later produced. Until patents expired in the 1990s this was the only place where Post-It Notes were produced. Today it still accounts for nearly all the world's Post-It Notes production.

Notable residents include:
- Joe Beasman Hall (1928–) Cynthiana; head basketball coach for the University of Kentucky (1972–1985), succeeding Adolph Rupp under whom he was an assistant coach from 1965; his record at UK is 297–100 and 373–156 career; Coach Hall is only one of three men to have played on a NCAA championship team (1949– Kentucky) and coach a NCAA championship team (1978–Kentucky); the others to achieve this feat are Bob Knight and Dean Smith; Hall was named National Coach of the Year in 1978, the same year they won the NCAA Tournamant

Interesting names include: Alberta; Antioch; Berry; Boyd; Breckinridge; Buena Vista; Claysville; Lair; Oddville; Poindexter; Shady Nook; Sunrise; Sylvandell; Venus

HART COUNTY (1819) Formed from Hardin and Barren Counties. The county is named for Captain Nathaniel G. T. Hart, Kentucky militia officer in the War of 1812 who was captured at the Battle of River Raisin in Michigan. The Battle of Munfordville, a Confederate victory, was fought in the county in 1862, during the Civil War.

Munfordville, the county seat, was once known as Big Buffalo Crossing. The current name came from Richard Jones Munford who donated the land in 1816.

The visitor center for Mammoth Cave National Park is in Hart County. Horse Cave is a town best known for the large natural cave opening on the south side of Main Street. Around the time of World War I, the world's only air conditioned tennis courts were located in the entrance of the cave. Likewise, many of the early buildings along Main Street received air conditioning from the cave. There is a fast-flowing river in the cave which allowed them to be the only city, other than Louisville, to have electric lights in the late 1880s.

Uno, pronounced "You Know," came from the days of selling moonshine during the days of prohibition. Another name for this community is Clearpoint, derived from Clear Pint, again referring to a place to buy moonshine. Cub Run Cave, fifteen miles west of Munfordville, features a "boxwood" pattern that, according to some speleologists, is found in only four caves in the United States. The cave tour includes a small pool where a constant, single drip falls from the ceiling every few seconds creating perpetual concentric circles on the water's surface.

Interesting names include: Bear Wallow; Bee; Big Windy; Blowing Springs; Cash; Cub Run; Defries; Dogcreek; Eudora; Forestville; High Hickory; Horse Cave; Lone Star; Monroe; Mt Beulah; Northtown; Pascal; Pike View; Powder Mill; Rex; Rio; Rosebud; Three Springs; Uno; Wax; Winesap

HENDERSON COUNTY (1799) Formed from Christian County. The county is named for Colonel Richard Henderson who originally purchased seventeen million acres of land (an area half the size of Kentucky) from the Cherokee Indians, only to have it voided by the Virginia Legislature. However, in 1778, the Richard Henderson Company was granted two hundred thousand acres in recognition of the $50,000 paid to the Indians in the Treaty of Wauagua. Henderson's roots lie in a scheme by North Carolina judge, Colonel Richard Henderson, and a group of investors who sought to buy much of modern-day Kentucky and Tennessee from the Cherokee Indians and resell it to settlers. Henderson's group, the Transylvania Land Company, hired Daniel Boone to help settle the region.

Henderson is the county seat. General Samuel Hopkins and surveyor Thomas Allin visited Red Banks in 1797, and laid out plans for a town. One of the characteristics of their planning included wide streets to help prevent the spread of fire. The streets in downtown Henderson are so wide that even with diagonal parking delivery trucks are able to park in the middle of the street without disrupting the flow of traffic.

In the last half of the 1800s, Henderson was famous for exporting tobacco, mostly to Great Britain. Just prior to World War I it was home to more millionaires per capita than any city in the world for its size. The city of Henderson was called Red Banks (Owensboro was called Yellow Banks) by the Indians who lived there because of the reddish clay soil on the banks of the river.

The city was called home by ornithologist, painter, and naturalist John James Audubon who lived there in the early 1800s. Audubon State Park bears his name. It is also home to blues legend W. C. Handy. In his autobiography, Handy said, "I did not write any songs in Henderson, but it was there I realized that the experiences I had, along with the things I had seen and heard, could be put on paper in a kind of music characteristic of my race. There I learned to appreciate the music of my people......then the blues were born, because from that day on I started to think about putting my own experience down in that particular kind of music."

For more than 100 years Henderson has also been home to the Southern Cherokee Nation.

Notable residents include:
- A. B. "Happy" Chandler (1898–1991) – Corydon; Kentucky governor 1935–1939 and 1955–1959; U.S. senator; Major League Baseball Commissioner 1945–1951; entered Transylvania University in 1917, starred in football, baseball, basketball, and track, sang in the glee club, and worked part-time jobs to pay for his education; in 1921 he emerged with a bachelor's degree and the nickname, "Happy;" started practicing law in Versailles in 1925; was inducted into the Major League Baseball Hall of Fame as the second commissioner; was known as a "player's commissioner"
- Grandpa (Louis Marshall) Jones (1913–1998) – Niagara; spent his teenage years in Akron, Ohio, where he began singing country music tunes on a local radio station; in 1935, his career took him to Boston, Massachusetts, where he met musician/songwriter Bradley Kincaid who gave him the name "Grandpa" due to his off-stage grumpiness at early-morning radio shows; Jones liked the name and decided to create a stage persona based around it; moved to Nashville and became a part of the Grand Ole Opry and was a regular on the television series *Hee-Haw;* a resident of Ridgetop, TN (two counties north of Nashville) he was a neighbor of David "Stringbean" Akeman; on the morning of November 11, 1973, Jones discovered the bodies of Akeman and his wife who were murdered in the night; it was a well-known fact that Akeman did not keep his money in a bank but carried large amounts of money on his person; the would-be robbers found none of Akeman's money; it was discovered several years later in the chimney of their very modest, very small, frame home

Traveling north of Henderson on US 41 one crosses the Ohio River but stays in Kentucky for another mile. Ellis Park Racetrack is in Kentucky but north of the Ohio River.

Mother's Day was first observed in Henderson by teacher Mary S. Wilson. It became a national holiday in 1916.

Interesting names include: Anthoston; Baskett; Bluff City; Cairo; Coraville; Corydon; Dixie; Euterpe; Geneva; Niagara; Reed; Rock Springs; Scuffletown; Tunnel Hill; White City; Zion

HENRY COUNTY (1799) Formed from Shelby County. The county is named for Patrick Henry. There is no documented proof that he spoke the words: "Give me liberty or give me death." There is also a Henry County in Alabama, Georgia, Illinois, Missouri, Ohio, Tennessee, Virginia, and one Patrick County in Virginia. Henry and eleven other counties became part of Kentucky in an eleven-day span. The second session of the 1798 legislature voted to create these twelve new counties from December 10 through December 21. Henry County was approved on December 14, followed later that same day by Green, Gallatin, and Muhlenberg Counties. Other counties formed during that period were Pendleton, Livingston, Boone, Ohio, Jessamine, Barren, Henderson, and Pulaski.

New Castle is the county seat.

Interesting names include: Bellview; Bethlehem; Black Jack; Eminence (highest point between Louisville and Cincinnati); Gest; Harpers Ferry; Jericho; Lacie; Lockport; North Pleasureville (one mile north of Pleasureville in Shelby County); Pendleton; Port Royal; Slabtown; Sligo; Sulphur; Tarascon

HICKMAN COUNTY (1822) Formed from Christian County. The county is named for Captain Paschal Hickman who was killed in the massacre at the River Raisin, Michigan, 1818.

A portion of Hickman County (approximately four miles wide and five miles long) lays across the Mississippi River and appears to be in Missouri. It is called Kentucky Bend (also Madrid Bend, New Madrid Bend, and in Tennessee it is called Bessie Bend).

Clinton is the county seat.

During the Civil War the Confederates established Fort de Russey on the strategically-located, 120-foot-high bluffs on the east side of the Mississippi River, opposite Belmont, Missouri. General Ulysses S. Grant attacked Belmont in his first battle but was repelled by the Confederate forces from Columbus. The site of the Battle of Columbus-Belmont is now a state park. During the presidency of Thomas Jefferson, a fire in Washington, D.C., prompted Jefferson to propose that the U.S. capital be moved to the more centrally-located Columbus, Kentucky. The proposal failed in the Senate by one vote. From 1880–1925, the population of Columbus was over ten thousand; today it is just over two hundred.

- Harry Lee Waterfield (1911–1988) – Served two terms as Kentucky's lieutenant governor (1955–1959 and 1963–1967) under Happy Chandler and Edward Breathitt; was the first person to serve in that position twice; ran for governor but lost to Bert Combs

Interesting names include: Beulah; Columbus; Fulgham; Hailwell; Moscow; New Cypress; Nichols; Old Cypress; South Columbus; Spring Hill

HOPKINS COUNTY (1807) Formed from Henderson County. The county is named for General Samuel Hopkins who participated in the Revolutionary War and the War of 1812, Kentucky House of Representatives, Kentucky Senate, as well as U.S. House of Representatives. He was born in Virginia and moved to Kentucky at the age of forty-three to the community of Red Banks, later called Henderson.

Madisonville, the county seat, was founded in 1807 and named for James Madison, then secretary of state who later became the fourth president of the United States (1809-1817).

Lee Trover Todd (Earlington), known by his close high school friends as, "Tro," is president of the University of Kentucky. Frank Ramsey (1931–), a native of Corydon (Henderson County) is a long-time resident of Madisonville. He played basketball for UK (1949–1954) and helped them win the NCAA title in 1951 against Kansas State. After being drafted in the first round by the Boston Celtics in 1953, Ramsey stayed one more season and led the Wildcats to a 25-0 record in 1954. At that time, NCAA rules would not allow graduate students to play in post-season games. Rather than risk their perfect record, UK declined to play in the NCAA tournament. Ramsey played for the Boston Celtics from 1954-1964. During his professional career he averaged 13.4 points a game. He was inducted into the Basketball Hall of Fame in 1981. His jersey, #23, is retired by the Celtics. He coached the ABA Kentucky Colonels (led by Dan Issel and Louis Dampier) for one season, 1970-1971. On November 15, 2005, Ramsey's house was destroyed by a tornado. Papers from his house were found as far away as Indiana. He survived the storm by getting into a closet. The chimney is all that remained of the house.

Dawson Springs, in extreme southwest Hopkins County, was once the spring training ground for the Pittsburgh Pirates from 1914–1917. Dawson Springs is home to Kentucky's 61st Governor, Steven Lynn "Steve" Beshear.

Notable residents include:
- Ruby Laffoon, Kentucky governor 1931–1936 – Madisonville; the two-room cabin in which he was born still stands and contains some original furniture
- Jimmy Roberts (1924–1999) – Madisonville; sang on the Lawrence Welk Show
- Lee Trover Todd (1946–) – Earlington; president of the University of Kentucky; he owns six U.S. patents in the area of high-resolution display technology
- Dottie Rambo (1934–2008) – Madisonville; born Joyce Reba Lutteell; after becoming a Christian at age twelve, her father gave her the ultimatum to either give up Christian music or leave home; she left home
- Howard and Vestal Goodman – Madisonville; southern gospel singers, *The Singing Goodmans*
- Travis Ford (1969–) – Madisonville; former University of Kentucky basketball player and currently head basketball coach at the University of Massachusetts
- Steve Beshear (1944–) – Dawson Springs; sixty-first governor of Kentucky governor, lieutenant governor under Governor Martha Layne Collins, Attorney General under Governor John Y. Brown Jr.

Interesting names include: Anton; Beulah; Carbondale; Charleston; Coiltown; Daniel Boone; Dawson Springs; East Diamond; Fiddle Bow; Fies; Grapevine; Jewel City; Little Valley; Manitou; Mortons Gap; Mount Carmel; Nebo; Nortonville; Oak Hill; Oriole; Pee Vee; Rabbit Ridge; Richland; Sixth Vein; St Charles; Vandetta; Victoria; White Plains; Wicks Well

JACKSON COUNTY (1858) Formed from Madison, Estill, Owsley, Clark, Laurel, and Rockcastle Counties. The county is named for Andrew Jackson, seventh president of the Unite States, U.S. Senate and U.S. House of Representatives. He joined the Revolutionary War as a courier – at age thirteen. He was the last president to have served in the Revolutionary War and the second president to be a prisoner of war. He and his brother were captured by the British and George Washington was captured by the French in the French and Indian War.

McKee is the county seat.

Interesting names include: Annville; Bond; Brazil; Clover Bottom; Cornelius; Datha; Drip Rock; Egypt; Foxtown; Gray Hawk; Green Hill; Herd; High Knob; Loam; Macedonia; Mildred; Mummie; Olin; Parrot; Peoples; Privett; Sand Springs; Sandgap; Sourwood; Threelinks; Turkey Foot; Tyner; Waneta; Wind Cave; Zekes Point

JEFFERSON COUNTY (1780) One of three original counties formed out of Kentucky County, Virginia. The county is named for Thomas Jefferson, principal author of the Declaration of Independence, third president of the United States, second vice president of the United States, first Secretary of State, and second governor of Virginia. In addition to statesman, he also achieved distinction as a horticulturist, architect, archaeologist, paleontologist, author, inventor, and founder of the University of Virginia.

The settlement that became the city of Louisville was founded in 1778 by George Rogers Clark and is named after King Louis, XVI, of France, whose soldiers at that time were aiding Americans in the American Revolutionary War.

In 1803 explorers Meriwether Lewis and William Clark organized their expedition across America at the Falls of the Ohio in Louisville. Louisville is often referred to as the southernmost northern city and the northernmost southern city in the United States.

In 1820, slaves made up about 25% of Louisville's population. Louisville had one of the nation's largest slave trades in the United States before the Civil War, but by 1860, that figure dropped to about 8%. During the Civil War, Louisville was a major stronghold of Union forces which kept Kentucky firmly in the Union. It was the center of planning, supplies, transportation, and recruiting for numerous campaigns. By the end of the war, Louisville had not been attacked even once, even though several battles were fought in that vicinity.

In the 1860, presidential election, Abraham Lincoln received fewer than 1% of Kentucky's votes. Kentuckians owned two hundred fifty thousand slaves, but also loved the Union. Kentucky wanted to keep slavery and stay in the Union. In 1861, eleven southern states seceded from the Union except Kentucky. Senator Henry Clay had worked for compromise and the state followed his lead.

After firing upon Fort Sumter, South Carolina which started the Civil War, President Lincoln asked for seventy-five thousand volunteers, but Kentucky Governor Beriah Magoffin refused to send any men to act against another southern state. President Lincoln secretly sent rifles to Louisville for defense. The weapons were kept hidden in the court house basement. On May 20, 1861, Kentucky declared its neutrality. President Lincoln and Confederate President Jefferson Davis kept a hands-off policy when dealing with Kentucky, hoping not to push the state into one camp or the other.

On September 4, 1861, Confederate General Polk, outraged by Union intrusions in the state, attacked Columbus (Hickman County), forever shattering Kentucky's neutrality policy. As a result of that invasion, Union General Ulysses S. Grant entered Paducah (McCracken County). President Jefferson Davis allowed Confederate troops to stay in Kentucky. Confederate forces were sent to invade Bowling Green (Warren County). Three days later on September 7, the Kentucky State Legislature, angered by the Confederate invasion, ordered the Union flag to be raised over the state capital in Frankfort, declaring its allegiance with the Union.

By early 1862, Louisville had eighty thousand Union troops throughout the city. With the Confederate Army under General Braxton Bragg prepared to take Louisville, and with Frankfort in Confederate hands for about a month, Governor Magoffin maintained his office in Louisville, and the state legislature held their sessions in the Jefferson County Courthouse.

The Thomas Edison House, in Louisville's Butchertown community, is where Edison boarded while working as a telegraph operator in 1866 and 1867. The museum features many of Edison's inventions.

Louisville Steam Engine Company 7, formed in 1871, was the oldest continuously operated firehouse in the United States. Due to budget constraints, the doors were closed January, 2009. Responding to about two thousand calls per year, the engine company served the largest neighborhood of Victorian homes, outside of New York's Soho area.

In 1926 the Brown Hotel became the home of the Hot Brown "sandwich." A few blocks away, the Seelbach Hotel, which F. Scott Fitzgerald references in *The Great Gatsby*, is also famous for a secret back room where Al Capone would regularly meet with associates during the Prohibition era. The Belle of Louisville is the oldest Mississippi-style steamboat in operation in the United States. Louisville is the only city in the United States that contains two-consecutively numbered, three-digit interstate highways (I-264 and I-265). Colorado, Georgia, and Tennessee also have a city named Louisville, but theirs is pronounced with the "s." There are one hundred sixteen historic markers placed throughout the county, more than any other county (Fayette is number two with eighty-four).

The United States Marine Hospital in the Portland neighborhood of Louisville was built in 1845 and is considered to be the best remaining antebellum hospital in America. Of the seven hospitals built in the mid-ninteenth century by the Marine Hospital Service, it is the only one standing. The hospital closed in 1933. Many of the wrought iron railings lining the building's galleries were either restored or replaced by the same Covington-based iron works company that created the original ones. The building was designed by Robert Mills, who designed the Washington Monument, the Department of Treasury, and the U.S. Patent Office buildings in Washington, D.C. The hospital was a cutting edge facility with indoor plumbing and an air circulation system that helped prevent infections. Mills was an early advocate of buildings designed to include fireproof materials.

Louisville is situated at the only obstacle on the Ohio River, the Falls of the Ohio (there are actually more shoals than water falls). Goods brought by barge or boat down the river had to be off loaded, carried across land about one-half mile downstream, and reloaded back onto the boat. The procedure was reversed for traffic going up river. Empty boats were usually able to cross the falls. Because cargo had to be transported across land, that portion of Louisville became known as Portland.

Notable residents include:
- Fontaine Fox (1884–1964) - near Louisville; best known for writing and illustrating the *Toonerville Folks* comic panel that appeared from 1913 to 1955, in which he displayed a total of fifty-three different characters
- Zachary Taylor (1784–1850) – born in Virginia, family moved to Jefferson County; 12th U. S. president; died in office 16 months into his term and is buried in the Zachary Taylor National Cemetery, Louisville; second cousin to James Madison and a third cousin to Robert E. Lee; after a forty-year military career he was known as "Old Rough and Ready;" first American president to never have been elected to previous public office; daughter Sarah married Jefferson Davis three months before her death
- Madame Sul-Te-Wan (1873–1959) – Louisville; born Nellie Crawford; her acting career spanned over five decades; she was the first black actor to sign a film contract and be a featured performer; she often played the part of a domestic servant, as in *King Kong*
- Victor Mature (1915–1999) – Louisville; also buried in Louisville
- Richard Mentor Johnson (1780–1850) – Beargrass; lived in Scott County; U.S. vice president under Martin Van Buren (1837–1841); he never married but had a long-term relationship with Julia Chinn, a family slave; they had two daughters; Johnson was completely open about their relationship, treating Chinn as his wife, which greatly offended many race-minded slaveholders
- Ned Beatty (1937–) – Louisville; played in 149 movies and television shows
- Foster Brooks (1912–2001) – Louisville; his career started in broadcasting with WHAS; Perry Como discovered Brooks in 1969, giving the comedian his major break; Como chose Brooks to open for him, but when the manager balked at the newcomer, Como threatened to walk; the manager gave in and Brooks was an instant success; he regularly appeared on the Dean Martin Celebrity Roast, sit-coms, and talk shows; Brooks drew on his own battles with alcohol for his acts;

during the period of his greatest fame he was able to avoid alcohol the most effectively; Brooks said, "A fellow bet me $10 that I could not quit drinking, and I haven't had a drink since. I needed the $10." He asked Dean Martin to join "Alcoholics Unanimous" with him; he said that he and Martin were charter members of the DUI Hall of Fame; the first Las Vegas show Brooks did was a smashing success because the audience thought he really was drunk; at the end of his act he responded to the applause by soberly saying, "Thank you very much, ladies and gentlemen." The audience booed him, thinking they had been scammed.

- Thomas Alva Edison (1847–1931) – Milan, Ohio; grew up in Michigan; at age nineteen he moved to Louisville where he worked for Western Union; holds 1,093 U. S. patents in his name
- William Conrad (1920–1994) – Louisville; was a fighter pilot in World War II; the voice for Dudley Dooright (late 1950s) on the *Rocky and Bullwinkle Show*; performed 120 episodes of *Cannon* (1971–1976); *Jake and the Fat Man* (1987–1992); acted in over 130 TV shows and movies; started work in radio in the late 1930s playing the part of U. S. Marshall Matt Dillon in the radio version of *Gunsmoke* from 1952–1961; was considered for the TV role of Matt Dillon but his increasing obesity led the studio to James Arness; John Wayne was also offered that role but declined; died of congestive heart failure at the age of 73
- Irene Dunn (1898–1990) – Louisville; at age eleven her father died causing her, her mother, and brother to move to Madison, Indiana, her mother's hometown; after retiring in 1952, she said, "Acting is not everything; living is;" was married to Dr. Francis Dennis Griffin from 1928 until his death in 1965; they had one adopted daughter
- Lionel Hampton (1908–2002) – Louisville; reared in Chicago where as a child began his career as a drummer; he relocated to Los Angeles and joined the house band for the New Cotton Club; Benny Goodman heard him and asked Hampton to join the Benny Goodman Trio (Goodman, Teddy Wilson, and Gene Krupa) and changed the name to the Benny Goodman Quartet; this was among the first racially mixed groups to be widely accepted; in the 1940s, Hampton left Goodman and started out on his own; His wife Gladys was his manager throughout most of his years of performing; during a 1930 recording date in Los Angeles, Louis Armstrong saw a vibraphone and asked Hampton if he could play it; already able to play the xylophone, he tried it, they decided to include it on a few recordings—the rest is history
- Thelma Hopkins (1948–) – Louisville; actress; singer (Tony Orlando and Dawn)
- Sue Grafton (1940–) – Louisville; author of famous alphabet mystery series
- Cheeseburgers were first tasted at Kaelin's Restaurant in Louisville, 1934
- Mary Travers (1936–) – Louisville; folksinger with *Peter, Paul, and Mary* from 1961–1970
- Paul Hornung (1935–) – Louisville; professional football player
- Muhammad Ali (1942–) – Louisville; born Cassius Marcellus Clay Jr.; his father was named for the 19th century abolitionist and politician Cassius Marcellus Clay

from Madison County; Ali is a three-time World Heavyweight Champion boxer and winner of an Olympic gold medal
- Tom Kennedy (1927–) – Louisville; game show host
- Mildred and Patty Hill - kindergarten teachers who wrote "Good Morning To You," published in 1893; the lyrics were changed and in 1912, "Happy Birthday To You," was published

In 1856, the first enamel bathtub was made in Louisville. The world's largest baseball bat, a full one hundred twenty feet tall and weighing thirty-four tons, is leaning against the outside of the Louisville Slugger Museum in Louisville.

Interesting names include: Anchorage; Ashville; Bancroft; Beckley; Beechwood; Berrytown; Bethany; Boston; Coldstream; Douglas Hill; Fern Creek; Fisherville; German Town; Goose Creek; Hickory Hill; Jeffersontown (originally named Town of Jefferson); Keenland; Kosmosdale; Long Run; Middletown; Northfield; Okolona; Penile; Pleasure Ridge Park (known to the locals as PRP); Portland; Prospect; Seminary Village; Shawneeland; Smyrna; Sycamore; Valley Station; Wildwood

JESSAMINE COUNTY (1799) Formed from Fayette County. The county is named for the jasmine flower that grew in the area or Jessamine Creek near Wilmore.

Camp Nelson Civil War Site is located about five miles south of Nicholasville. The Union Army turned the rolling pasture land into an enormous base of operations. Camp Nelson was built in 1863, and dismantled in 1866, after the Civil War ended. The camp helped defend central and eastern Kentucky from guerilla attacks. It was also a commissary depot that supplied Federal troops in Ohio, Kentucky, and east Tennessee. There was a pump house on the river, a five hundred thousand gallon reservoir, thousands of feet of piping that supplied water all over the camp, indoor water faucets, and water closets in the soldiers' homes and the hospital. It was the largest depot and permanent encampment in Kentucky, outside Louisville, and served a critical function to the Union war effort by providing supplies, livestock, and troops for the Army of the Ohio in Kentucky.

It was the largest recruiting, training, and mustering center for African American troops (called U.S. Colored Troops) in the United States. The Camp provided the Union Army with over ten thousand African-American soldiers. Since the Black soldiers were emancipated upon enlistment, many of them brought their families with them to Camp Nelson and eventually the Army established a refugee camp for the families.

The Camp Nelson Cemetery was begun in 1863, and contains the remains of 1,600 Camp Nelson soldiers, including approximately six hundred African American soldiers. In 1868, the cemetery was designated a National Cemetery and over 2,200 Civil War dead from several Kentucky Civil War sites were reburied there. Interment is still taking place there.

Nicholasville is the county seat.

High Bridge was the first cantilever bridge built in America. The construction of this bridge marked the beginning of scientific bridge building in America. It was designed by Charles Shaler Smith who also designed the Brooklyn Bridge. The bridge was replaced in 1911, using the same foundations. It is the highest railroad bridge in the United States over a navigable stream (308 feet). It was originally designed as a suspension bridge but the Civil War brought early construction to a halt.

Interesting names include: Bethel; Brooklyn; Catnip; Dixon Town; Hall; High Bridge; Jessamine; Keene; Little Hickman; Logana; Lucky Stop; Mount Lebanon; Nina; Pink; Providence; Sulphur Wells; Union Mills; Vineyard

JOHNSON COUNTY (1843) Formed from Floyd, Lawrence, and Morgan Counties. The county is named for General Richard Mentor Johnson, War of 1812, vice president of the United States under Martin Van Buren, 1837-1841, U.S. House of Representatives (five terms), U.S. Senate, and Kentucky House of Representatives (elected to three terms but died just after his third election to that position). He is the only vice president elected by the United States Senate under the provisions of the Twelth Ammendment rather than electoral votes. He was born on the Virginia frontier at Beargrass, now a suburb of Louisville. He was a pallbearer when Daniel Boone was interred in the Frankfort Cemetery. There are Johnson Counties in Illinois, Iowa, Missouri, and Nebraska.

Paint Creek and Paintsville, the county seat, were named in reference to drawings found on trees, believed to have been drawn by Native Americans. The founder of Paintsville is acknowledged to be William Henry Dixon. Van Lear in general, and Butcher Hollow ("Holler") in particular, is the home of Loretta Lynn and Crystal Gayle. The former coal company office building is now the Coal Miners' Museum. Mayo Mansion, in Paintsville, is a forty-three-room mansion built in 1910 by C. C. Mayo, the first coal baron in eastern Kentucky. He also built the nearby Methodist church. In the church is a Pilcher pipe organ donated by Andrew Carnegie. The stained glass windows are works of art.

Notable residents include:
- Loretta (Webb) Lynn (1934–) – Van Lear; named in honor of Loretta Young; her mother, Clara Marie Ramey Webb, is distantly related to Patty Loveless (Particia Lee Ramey) from Pike County
- Crystal Gayle (1951–) - Paintsville; born Brenda Gail Webb; her older sister, Loretta, born seventeen years earlier, had already married and moved away from home when Crystal was born; her family moved to Wabash, Indiana when Crystal was four years old; when Crystal signed with Decca Records after high school graduation, older sister Loretta suggested the name Crystal, inspired by Krystal Hamburgers; Crystal changed the spelling of her middle name to Gayle
- John Pelphrey (1968–) – Paintsville; Kentucky's "Mr. Basketball" in 1987; men's head basketball coach at the University of Arkansas; served under Eddie Sutton at Oklahoma State University and Billy Donovan at Marshall College and the

University of Florida; in 2003, his infant son, John Patrick, died of a rare blood disorder

Interesting names include: Asa; Barnrock; Boons Camp; Chestnut; Denver; East Point; Elna; Flatgap; Henrietta; Manila; Nero; Nippa; Odds; Offutt; Oil Springs; Redbush; Relief; Riceville; River; Sip; Swamp Branch; Thealka; Thelma; Tutor Key; Van Lear; Volga; West Van Lear; Whitehouse; Winifred

KENTON COUNTY (1840) Formed from Campbell County. The county is named for Simon Kenton, a frontiersman and friend of Daniel Boone. He saved Boone's life at Fort Boonesborough. Born in Virginia, at age sixteen, thinking he had killed a man in a jealous rage he fled into the wilderness of Kentucky and Ohio with the assumed name of Simon Butler. In 1782, after learning that the victim was still alive, he returned to Virginia and took up his original name. Kenton was a scout against the Shawnee Indians and served on the famous George Rogers Clark expedition to capture Fort Sackville at what is now Vincennes, Indiana. Kenton County, Ohio is also named in his honor.

Covington, the county seat, is situated at the confluence of the Ohio and Licking Rivers. Prominent in the city are the nineteenth century Roman Catholic Cathedral Basilica of the Assumption, loosely styled on Notre Dame, and Holmes High School, originally built as a castle in 1866 by New Orleans businessman Daniel Henry Holmes. The church is home to the world's largest hand-blown stained glass window known to exist today. It measures twenty-four feet by sixty-seven feet and contains 117 different figures.

Covington's first radio station, WCKY (**C**ovington,**KY**), was built in 1929. It is a clear channel station sharing the frequency with a station in Sacramento, California. The studio is in Kenwood {Cincinnati}, and the transmitter is in Villa Hills (Kenton County), KY.

Notable residents include:
- James Lamont "Haven" Gillespie (1888–1975) – Covington; who wrote "Santa Claus Is Coming to Town;" wrote songs for Dean Martin, Frank Sinatra, Louis Armstrong, George Straight, and others
- Durward Kirby (1911–2000) – Covington; was host, comic, and sketch artist for the Gary Moore Show; later he co-hosted Candid Camera with Alan Funt from 1961-1966; a common misspelling of his first name, Durwood, was spoofed in the *Rocky and Bulwinkle Show* about a man's derby hat that gave the wearer unusual wisdom, known as the Kerwood Derby
- Ron Ziegler (1939–2003) – Covington; White House Press Secretary for President Richard Nixon, 1969–1974 making him the youngest press secretary to serve that office. He died of a heart attack at age sixty-three
- John White Stevenson (1812–1886) – born in Richmond Virginia; Kentucky Governor (1867–1871) and the only governor from northern Kentucky; he was also U.S. senator
- Trey Grayson (1972–) - Kentucky Secretary of State

- Daniel Carter "Uncle Dan" Beard (1850–1941), Cincinnati; reared in Covington; founded Sons of Daniel Boone in 1905, and merged with Boy Scouts of America when it was founded in 1910; helped found Camp Fire Girls

The city of Elsmere was named after Elsmere Avenue, Norwood {Cincinnati}, Ohio.

Interesting names include: Alexandria (one of the largest land mass cities in KY); Bank Lick; Bellevue; Bracht; Edgewood; Fairview; Fiskburg; Forest Hills; Fort Mitchell; Fort Wright; Grant; Independence; Kenton; Lamb; Melbourne; Morning View; Oak Ridge; Piner; Silver Grove; Sunny Acres; Visalia; West Covington; White Tower; White Villa; Winston Park

KNOTT COUNTY (1884) Formed from Perry, Letcher, Floyd, and Breathitt Counties. The county is named for James Proctor Knott (born in Marion County), U.S. House of Representatives (two separate terms) and Kentucky governor from 1883–1887. After his term of governor he became co-founder and dean of the law school at Centre College, Danville. He died in Lebanon (Marion County) and is buried there. He is the last Kentucky Governor after whom a county is named.

When Knott County was formed there were only a few log houses and a McPherson post office. McPherson, founded in 1847, was the original name of Hindman. Hindman was founded in 1884 as the county seat and named for James P. Hindman, then lieutenant governor serving under Governor Knott. Postmaster Peyton Duke donated the land for the county seat. Wagon roads were the only ways out to Whitesburg, Hazard, Jackson, and Prestonsburg. Political strife began in Hindman soon after its formation when Clabe Jones lost a race for jailer to his old Civil War opponent Anderson Hays. The two men and their factions warred for several years. After the feud ended, other men perpetuated violence in the city.

The town of Proctor (originally named Proctorknott), Minnesota, is named for Governor Knott.

Hindman Settlement School: Professor George Clarke (1862–1940) came from Greenup County to practice law in Hindman. Citizens learning of his six years teaching experience asked him to teach their children soon after his arrival. He selected the site and started a school. After lawless elements burned his school, he tracked them down and had them sent to prison. He visited the governor at one time to get guns to stop the feuding in the county which threatened the decent citizenry. He taught into the 1920s, built a school in Floyd County, and was superintendent of schools in Letcher County. "No other man ever started with less and did more in the education field......he was truly one of eastern Kentucky's greats," wrote historian Henry Scalf. Clarke's school was the predecessor of Hindman Settlement School.

Knott, and surrounding counties, is home to a herd of over five thousand elk.

Hindman Settlement School was founded in 1902 by May Stone and Katherine Petit. Hindman was the first and the most successful rural social settlement school in America. The purposes and goals for which the settlement was founded were to provide educational opportunities for the boys and girls of this region, to keep them mindful of their heritage, and to provide community services. The Settlement is a nonprofit, nondenominational institution. In the early years the Settlement provided most of the educational programs in the vicinity. Many of the early instructors came from Smith, Vassar, Mt Holyoke, Wellesley, and several other prestigious colleges to teach the children of the mountains. The Hindman Settlement School became known for its outstanding academic programs throughout the regions. The Settlement encouraged the growth of the public school system but continued to supplement educational services not available from other agencies or groups. The school soon became a model center for education, health care, and social services. Earning praises as "the best school in the mountains," it not only transformed the community of Hindman, but also contributed significantly to regional progress. Students no longer live on campus. With the advent of public school consolidation and the building of better roads in the region, every student is able to travel to school by bus or private transportation.

Today the Settlement operates the East Kentucky Tutorial Program which gives remedial education to dyslexic children through after-school programs in several counties and a six-week summer school. The Settlement also provides to the community an adult basic education/GED program, a Montessori preschool, scholarship assistance for needy students, facilities for the Knott County Public Library, meeting space for community activities, workshops on Appalachian life and culture, artists-in-residence in the public schools, community education classes, used clothing for the needy, and many other services.

Carr Creek State Park, near Sassafras, features the longest lakefront sand beach in the Kentucky State park system. There are nine historic markers placed throughout the county.

Notable residents include:
- Carl Dewey Perkins (1912–1984) – Hindman; Kentucky House of Representatives, U.S. House of Representatives for eighteen terms (1949–1984); is buried at Mountain Memory Gardens, a public cemetery in Hindman; he was succeeded in Congress by his son Carl C. Perkins

KNOTT COUNTY COMMUNITIES –

Anco: This recently closed post office is six miles south SSW of Hindman. The post office was established in 1922 and named for its first postmaster, Anderson Combs.

Bearville: The post office is four miles NW of Hindman on KY 80 and was established in the early 1950s. Over the years it was necessary to distinguish between the several Combs families in that section by giving them nicknames. One family was called the "Bear

Combses," perhaps for some incident in the life of an ancestor. The post office was named for them.

Betty: This extinct post office on KY 80, ten miles NW of Hindman (close to Garrett in Floyd County), was in operation from 1950 to 1956. It was named for the granddaughter of Hattie Cox, the first postmaster.

Caney Creek, aka Pippa Passes: When Alice Geddes Lloyd of Boston established Caney Creek Junior College in 1923, among the groups from which she solicited funds was the Robert Browning Societies of New England. They agreed to build the local post office and are said to have suggested its name for the poet's heroin, the devout and simple mill girl Pippa who, as she passes through her town on New Year's Day, innocently touches the lives of those who hear her songs of joy and fulfillment. The Post Office Department's preference for one-word names led to the post offices establishment on December 31, 1917, as Pippapass, a meaningless name retained until July 1, 1955, when pressure brought about a return to the intended spelling. Local people still call their community Caney or Caney Creek as they always have.

Carr Creek: This hamlet, with recently discontinued post office, is on the new Carr Fork Lake, six miles south of Hindman, close to the junction of KY 160 and KY 15. For many years, the community centered on a boarding school founded in 1920 by two Massachusetts women, Olive Marsh and Ruth Watson. The post office of Dirk, established 1905 to serve this area, was renamed Carr Creek in 1928 to honor the school which had just sent its basketball team to compete in the national high school tournament in Chicago.

Cody: One of several communities completely inundated by the recent flooding of Carr Fork Lake. Cody was six miles S of Hindman. Its post office established in 1897, was named for a local family.

Decoy: This hamlet, twelve miles NNW of Hindman and fifteen miles E of Jackson, sits on the county line. Though the area was first settled around 1810, the post office was not established until 1904. Henry Shepherd, postmaster, was the hero of a most unusual place-naming account. Henry's goal of intellectual self-improvement included systematic study of a mail order dictionary. One day therein he came across the word "decoy - to entrap," and was shortly able to apply this concept when he successfully set a trap for his unfaithful wife and her man. He was later to say to his neighbors that he had decoyed them. When it came time to establish a post office in the community, Henry was asked to be the postmaster. He requested it be named Decoy, for his word has such significance to him.

Elmrock: This hamlet with post office on Laurel Fork of Quicksand Creek, is seven miles NNW of Hindman. The post office, established 1884, was named for Emma Thurman, the wife of the local school teacher who had petitioned for it, and Orlena Combs Morgan, the storekeeper and first postmaster.

Fisty (f-Ī-stee): This hamlet is about five miles W of Hindman. With so many Combses in this area that they had to be distinguished by nicknames. One was called "Fisty Sam," and, according to local tradition, he suggested that the new post office be named for him. Margaret Ritchie became the first postmaster in 1906.

Handshoe (Soft Shell): This post office on KY 1087 and Balls Fork of Troublesome Creek, four miles NNE of Hindman, were established in 1926, with Sarah Slone, postmaster, and given the name popularly applied to the Regular Baptists to distinguish them from the Hard Shell or Primitive Baptists.

Hindman: The McPherson post office established here on February, 1874, with Peyton Duke, postmaster, was renamed in October, 1884, for then Lieutenant Governor James P. Hindman. Duke gave the land for the town of Hindman, which was incorporated in 1886.

Larkslane (Handshoe): This hamlet is on KY 80 and Jones Fork of Right Beaver Creek, five miles NE of Hindman. Its post office was established and named by its first postmaster, Elizabeth Slone, for her husband, Lark Slone, and the lane that went past his home. That section of KY 80 has also been locally called Stringtown for the arrangement of houses along the highway.

Littcarr: This hamlet with post office is centered five miles S of Hindman. The post office was established in 1922, by Burnard Smith whose request to name it Little Carr for its location was accepted by the postal authorities on the condition that it be shortened to its present form.

Mousie: Named for the pet name of the younger daughter of the landowner Clay Martin.

Pippa Passes: This village with post office, home of Alice Lloyd College, lies along Caney Creek about five miles E of Hindman. It was named from the poetic drama by Robert Browning. The lead character Pipa utters those now famous lines, *"God's in His heaven- All's right with the world."* Caney Creek, above, has full details.

Puncheon (Kite): This post office, up Puncheon Branch of the Right Fork of Beaver Creek, ten miles ESE of Hindman, was established in 1900, with John Franklin as postmaster. It is said to have been named for the puncheon flooring of the building in which it was located. However, if the stream bore this name before 1900, it may well have been named for a local industry, the splitting of logs for the floors of early cabins.

Ritchie: This hamlet, with recently discontinued post office on the Clear Creek of Troublesome Creek and KY 721, is about five miles WSW of Hindman. The post office was established in 1900 with Abbie Ritchie as postmaster and named for the large number of local Ritchies, the descendants of pioneer Crockett Ritchie.

Sassafras: This coal town with post office is on Carr fork of the North Fork of the Kentucky River about seven miles SSW of Hindman. In 1879, Manton Cornett is said to have established the post office under a large sassafras tree at the mouth of Sassafras Creek, a branch of Carr Fork. Around the turn of the century it was moved two miles down the fork to its present site at the mouth of Yellow Creek and the community bearing its name grew up around it.

Smithboro (Blackey): The site of this extinct community on KY 15 at the mouth of Smith Branch of Carr fork of the North Fork of the Kentucky River is about six miles S of Hindman. It is now under Carr Fork Lake. Its recently discontinued post office, established in 1902, with George Francis as postmaster, was named for the brothers Jeremiah and Thomas Smith, local landowning sons of William and Millie (Combs) Smith, early Perry County residents.

Vest: This hamlet with post office is on KY 1087 and Balls Fork of Troublesome Creek about three miles N of Hindman. The post office was established in 1886, with William Grigsby, postmaster, and named for the postal inspector who had been sent to validate the need for a post office and who stayed to assist in its establishment. Nothing else is known about him.

Other interesting names include: Amelia; Bath; Brinkley; Carrie; Dema; Drew; Dry Creek; Emmalena; Hall; Hollybush; Ivan; Ivis; Kite; Mallie; May; Omaha; Pine Top; Raven; Redfox; Spider; Talcum; Tina; Topmost; Wiscoal; Yellow Mountain

KNOX COUNTY (1810) Formed from Lincoln County. The county is named for General Henry Knox, born in Boston to Scots-Irish immigrants. The Continental Congress made him Secretary of War under the Articles of Confederation until he became the first Secretary of War of the United States in President George Washington's Cabinet. Knox was in charge of General Washington's crossing of the Delaware which included horses and artillery. One day later, following the battle, he returned the soldiers along with hundreds of prisoners, captured supplies, and all the boats. He was promoted to brigadier general as a result of that feat.

Many incidents in his career attest to his character. One example is when he and his wife were forced to leave Boston in 1775, his home was used to house British officers who looted his bookstore. Despite personal financial hardships, he managed to make the last payment of £1,000 to Longman Printers in London to cover the price of a shipment of books he never received. Fort Knox, Kentucky and Fort Knox, Maine are named for him. There is a Knox County in Illinois, Indiana, Maine, Missouri, Nebraska, Ohio, Tennessee, and Texas. Knoxville, Tennessee is also named for him.

Barbourville is the county seat. Governor James Dixon Black (May, 1919–December, 1919) was co-founder and president of Union College, Barbourville.

Dr. Thomas Walker was the first frontiersman in Kentucky, preceding Daniel Boone by seventeen years. Dr. Walker led the first expedition through Cumberland Gap in 1750. Near the river Dr. Walker built the first cabin in Kentucky.

Notable residents include:
- Green Adams (1812–1884) – Barbourville; Kentucky House of Representatives, U.S. House of Representatives, practiced law in Philadelphia and died there; is buried in West Laurel Hill Cemetery, Bala Cynwyd, Pennsylvania
- Silas Woodson (1819–1896) – Barbourville; governor of Missouri
- Kerri Mitchell – Barbourville; Miss Kentucky, 2005
- Arthur Lake (1905–1987) – Corbin; best known for playing Dagwood Bumstead on the television series *Blondie* (1957), in the series of films (1938–1950) by the same title, and on the *Blondie* radio series during most of the same years

Interesting names include: Arkle; Baileys Switch; Barnyard; Bertha Station; Bimble; Bryants Store; Callaway; Cannon; Cardinal; Crane Nest; Dishman Springs; Emanuel; Erose; Flat Lick (one-half mile from Old Flat Lick); Fount; Girdler; Gray; Green Road; Hammond; Himyar; Jarvis Store; Kayjay; King; Knoxfork; Old Flat Lick; Permon; Providence; Rain; Salt Gum; Siler; Sprule; Stinking Creek; Swan Lake; Swanpond; Trosper; Walker; Warren; Woodbine; Woollum

LaRUE COUNTY (1843) Formed from Hardin County. The county is named for John LaRue, an early settler of Kentucky.

Hodgenville is the county seat.

During the Civil War, Kentucky was one of only two states to have a star on both the North and the South flags.

Notable residents include:
- Abraham Lincoln (1809–1865) - Sinking Spring Farm (now in LaRue County); sixteenth president of the United States; the first president born outside the original Thirteen Colonies; mother died when he was nine; ending slavery was a primary goal of his administration; wife Mary Todd Lincoln was born in Lexington to a family that owned slaves; shot April 14, pronounced dead 7:22 AM, April 15, 1865; in 1916 the Lincoln Farm Association donated the land and buildings to the federal government which established the Abraham Lincoln National Park; just a few miles from his birthplace is Knob Creek, his boyhood home

Interesting names include: Atlanta; Attilla; Boundary Oak; Buffalo; Ginseng; Gleanings; Jericho; Leafdale; Lyons; Magnolia; Maxine; Roanoke; South Buffalo; Talley; Tanner; Tonieville; Upton (partly in Hardin County); White City

LAUREL COUNTY (1826) Formed from Rockcastle, Clay, Knox, and Whitley Counties. It is believed that the county is named for the mountain laurel shrub that is prominent in the area.

The evergreen, flowering plant blooms between May and June. All parts of the plant are poisonous including honey made from the flower. The mountain laurel is poisonous to several animals including horses, goats, cattle, sheep, and deer. It is also known as Ivybush, Calico Bush, Spoonwood (because the Indians made their spoons from it), Sheep Laurel, Lambkill, and Clamoun. It is in the division of the magnolia.

London is the county seat. It was reported by a postal employee who sorted mail on a train that London is the highest point between Cincinnati and Knoxville.

Notable residents include:
- Colonel Harland Sanders (1890–1980) - born in Henryville, Indiana; at the age of forty Sanders cooked chicken dishes for people in his living quarters who stopped at his service station in North Corbin; his popularity grew so he moved into a motel with a restaurant that seated 142 people; he was given a chance to turn around a failing Kentucky Fried Chicken restaurant to a young Dave Thomas; working with Colonel Sanders, Dave turned four ailing stores into million-dollar successes; later, Dave Thomas sold his KFC franchises and opened his first Wendy's restaurant in Columbus, Ohio in 1969; Lee's Famous Recipe Chicken was started by Sanders' nephew Lee Cummings; after Sanders's death, his body lay in the Kentucky State Capital rotunda

Interesting names include: Atlanta; Baldrock; Billows; Blackwater; Boreing; Brock; Bush; Camp Grounds; Cane Creek; Cruise; Darthoe; Greenmount; Hare; Hazel Patch; Hightop; Hopewell; Horse Creek; Keavy; Lake; Langnau; Lida; Lily; Lynn Camp; Maplesville; Marydell; Mershons; North Corbin; Oakley; Pine Grove; Pittsburg; Sasser; Sublimity City; Symbol; Victory; Vox

LAWRENCE COUNTY (1822) Formed from Greenup and Floyd Counties. The county is named for James Lawrence, an American naval hero during the War of 1812. On being attacked by British vessels and himself being mortally wounded, he told his officers, "Fight her 'til she sinks and don't give up the ship." His death was reported to fellow officer and friend Oliver Hazard Perry (for whom the city of Hazard and Perry County are named) who ordered a large battle ensign stitched with the phrase "DONT GIVE UP THE SHIP" [sic] in bold white letters. That flag was hoisted on Perry's flagship. Counties in Alabama, Illinois, Indiana, Missouri, Ohio, and Tennessee are named for him as well as the cities of Lawrenceville in Georgia and Illinois.

Louisa, the county seat, was established in 1822, and named for the Levisa (Louisa) Fork of the Big Sandy River which had been named by Dr. Thomas Walker in honor of the wife of the Duke of Cumberland. George Washington surveyed the land that is now Louisa.

Notable residents include:
- Governor Paul Patton (1937–) – fifty-ninth Governor of Kentucky; first governor to succeed himself under a new law; fiftieth lieutenant governor of Kentucky
- Fred Moore Vinson (1890–1953) - Louisa; served in all three branches of the U.S. government: Chief Justice of the Supreme Court, House of Representatives, and Secretary of the Treasury; born in the front part of the Lawrence County jail where his father was jailer
- Ricky Skaggs (1954–) – Cordell; at age six, he played mandolin on stage with Bill Monroe; at age seven, he appeared on television with Lester Flatt and Earl Scruggs; at age sixteen, he and two other musicians began opening for Ralph Stanley; soon they joined Stanley's band, the Clinch Mountain Boys

Interesting names include: Adams; Adeline; Ben Bow; Buchanan; Catalpa; Charley; Cherokee; Deephole; Ellen; Evergreen; Five Forks; Gallup; Georges Creek; Hannah; Irad; Joe Fork; Laurel; Ledocio; Martha; Mazie; Morgans Creek; Needmore; Overda; Peach Orchard; Ray; Stringtown; Summit; Torchlight; Trinity; Ulysses; Wilbur; Zelda

LEE COUNTY (1870) Formed from Breathitt, Owsley, Estill, and Wolfe Counties. The county may have been named for Robert E. Lee, but Lee County was pro Union. It may have also been named for Lee County, Virginia, or for Henry "Light Horse Harry" Lee III, a cavalry officer in the Continental Army during the Revolutionary War. Henry Lee was the governor of Virginia, a U.S. Congressman, and the father of Robert E. Lee.

Beatyville is the county seat of Lee County. Since 1987, during the third weekend in October, the Main Street of Beatyville is closed to traffic as the annual Wooly Worm Festival swings into action. Activities include flea market, parade, car show, non-stop musicians, helicopter rides over Lee County, and the main event, coaxing wooly worms, untouched, up a string. The correct name for the wooly worm is wooly bear caterpillar.

Natural Bridge is a sandstone arch that is seventy-eight feet long and sixty-five feet high. When the Kentucky State Park System was established with four parks in 1925, Natural Bridge was one of them.

Interesting names include: Airedale; Arvel; Belle Point; Canyon Falls; Crystal; Delvinta; Enoch; Evelyn; Fillmore; Fincastle; Fixer; Greeley; Heidelberg; Idamay; Leeco; Lone; Lower Buffalo; Mount Olive; Old Landing; Old Orchard; Pinnacle; Primrose; St Helens; Vada; White Ash; Williba; Willow; Yellow Rock; Zachariah; Zoe

LESLIE COUNTY (1878) Formed from Clay, Harlan, and Perry Counties. The county is named for Preston Hopkins Leslie, Kentucky governor from 1871–1875. He was born in Wayne County and was a resident of Glasgow in Barren County. He sponsored the establishment of a school system for African American children and the admission of African American testimony in state courts. He died in 1907 in Montana, where President Grover Cleveland had appointed him Territorial Governor (1887–1889).

Hyden is the county seat. In the town of Wendover, about two miles south of Hyden, is the oldest school of nurse-midwifery in America.

The town of Hell for Certain was named for Hell for Certain Creek. There is a Hell for Certain Creek in Lee County, also. Hell for Certain is a carboniferous volcanic ash in the eastern United States. The Hell for Certain flint clay bed is a new name for the flint clay parting of the fire clay coal and the coal's lateral equivalents in certain Appalachian basins. The bed has been mapped in Tennessee, Kentucky, Virginia, and West Virginia where it was known as "the flint clay parting" or the "jackrock parting" of the coal. "Jackrock" is a mining term that refers to the suitability of the hard flint clay as a floor for mining jacks and other roof support systems. Numerous researchers in the last twenty years have agreed that the widespread bed is an altered volcanic ash. The Fire Clay (Hazard No. 4) coal was extensively mined in this area. The name Hell for Certain is appropriate because conditions must have been very difficult during the heavy ash fall.

Notable residents include:
- Tim Couch (1977–) – Hyden; quarterback for the University of Kentucky and Cleveland Browns; became quarterback for the Browns in the second game of his rookie year and played five years
- The Osborne Brothers, Sonny (1937–) and Bobby (1931–) - were an influential and popular Bluegrass act which came to prominence in the 1950s; two of their hits are "Ruby (Honey Are You Mad At Your Man)" and "Rocky Top;" Sonny retired in 2005 but Bobby continues to make personal appearances

Interesting names include: Asher; Bear Branch; Big Fork; Big Rock; Cinda; Confluence; Creekville; Cutshin; Divide; Dryhill; Essie; Frew; Grassy; Hare; Hell for Certain; Jason; Kaliopi; Mozelle; Napier; Shoal; Sizerock; Smilax; Spruce Pine; Thousandsticks; Upper Laurel Fork; Warbranch; Yeaddiss

LETCHER COUNTY (1842) Formed from Perry and Harlan Counties. The county is named for Robert P. Letcher, Kentucky House of Representatives (two terms), U.S. House of Representatives, and Kentucky governor from 1840–1844. Born in Virginia, the family moved to Garrard County around 1800. Letcher was educated at a private school near Danville where he also practiced law. His term as governor was dominated by the panic of 1837. He drastically cut spending, eliminating the state's deficit.

The Panic of 1837 was built on a speculative fever. The bubble burst on May 10, 1837 in New York City when every bank stopped payment in specie (gold and silver coinage). The Panic was followed by a five-year depression with the total failure of banks and record high unemployment levels. Out of 850 banks in the United States, 343 were completely closed.

Whitesburg, the county seat, was named for state representative Daugherty White of Clay County, who championed the creation of the new county. Whitesburg was originally called

Summit City. Whitesburg is known for its ubiquitous cut stone. The city was home to a community of Italian stone masons who moved with the coming of the Louisville and Nashville Railroad in 1911–1912. The city includes numerous ashlar stone retaining walls, foundations and bridge abutments, as well as several buildings covered entirely of sandstone pulled from the Kentucky River. Ashlar is stone work of any type stone. Ashlar blocks are large rectangular blocks, sculpted to have square edges and even faces.

Whitesburg streets were paved for the first time in 1924, and some of the original concrete streets are still in use. Broadway, one of those streets, is marked with the hoof prints of a cow, the footprints of chickens, and the footprints of a barefoot child who ran across the street while the concrete was still wet.

The Cumberland River originates in Letcher County, goes through Nashville, and empties into the Ohio River at Smithland, about five miles upstream from Paducah. Cumberland River forms Lake Cumberland and Lake Barkley in Kentucky, Dale Hollow Lake, shared by Kentucky and Tennessee, and Old Hickory Lake in Tennessee. The river is 687 miles long.

Democrat (Razorblade): This hamlet with post office is now located on KY 7 at the mouth of Lower Appletree on Rockhouse Creek about eight miles north of Whitesburg. According to Arthur Dixon, a former County Judge, it was first called Razorblade Branch of Rockhouse Creek, close to the present site. A post office called Stick was established in this vicinity in 1889 with Elhanan King as postmaster, though the exact location is uncertain. The post office was renamed Democrat on October 31, 1902. In 1915, it was located at the mouth of Big Branch of Rockhouse, but was later moved to its present site. Though no one seems to know why the Razorblade and Stick names were applied, everyone agrees that Democrat was named for the one lone Democrat in a staunchly Republican precinct, the postmaster himself.

Notabale residents include:
- Harry M. Caudill (1922–1990) – Whitesburg; historian, professor of law at the University of Kentucky (1976–1984), lawyer, legislator in the Kentucky House of Representatives, environmentalist (opposes strip mining), and author of six books, including *Night Comes to the Cumberlands*; faced with an advancing case of Parkinson's Disease, Caudill took his life with a gunshot to the head in 1990
- Perhaps you have seen a roadside sign depicting a mother duck with several ducklings following and the words "Duck X-ing;" the signs were commissioned by local radio host Jim Webb, who at the time hosted a show under the alias, "The Ducktor;" Webb appeared in newspaper photos publicizing the placement of the signs while wearing a rubber duck mask

Interesting names include: Banks; Beefhide; Bellcraft; Big Branch; Blackey; Bottom Fork; Carbon Glow; Carcassonne; Crafts Colly; Cromona; Crown; Day; Deane; Defeated Creek; Democrat; East Jenkins; Eolia; Ermine; Fleming; Fleming-Neon; Flint; Gordon; Hallie;

Head of Linefork; Hot Spot; Ice; Jenkins; Jeremiah; Kingdom Come; Kings Creek; Letcher; Linefork; Little Colly; Mayking; Millstone; Neon; Oscaloosa; Oven Fork; Partridge; Polly; Potters Fork; Premium; Roxana; Sergent; Skyline; Southdown; Tillie; Ulvah

LEWIS COUNTY (1807) Formed from Mason County. The county is named for Meriwether Lewis who explored the territory of the Louisiana Purchase (along with William Clark). The alpine plant *Lewisis*, popular in rock gardens, and Lewis' Woodpecker were named for him. Also named for him are Lewis County, Tennessee, Lewisburg, Tennessee, Lewiston, Idaho, Lewis County, Washington, and the U.S. Army installation Fort Lewis, Washington. Vanceburg is the county seat.

Concord is the smallest city in Kentucky with a population of twenty-eight in the 2000 census.

Notable residents include:
- Faith Esham - opera singer

Interesting names include: Awe; Brandy Lick; Buena Vista; Charters; Concord; Cottageville; Crum; Firebrick; Garrison; Harris; Head of Grassy; Kinniconick; Oak Ridge; Poplar Flat; Queens; Quincy; Ribolt; Rugless; Sand Hill; Tannery; Trinity; Upper Bruce

LINCOLN COUNTY (1780) One of three original counties formed out of Kentucky County, Virginia. The county is named for Major General Benjamin Lincoln of the Continental Army who served during the Revolutionary War. Also named for him are counties in Georgia, North Carolina, Tennessee and the town of Lincoln, Vermont. Some mistakingly report that the county was named for President Abraham Lincoln, but it was named twenty-nine years before the future president was born.

Stanford, the county seat, is the second oldest settlement in Kentucky (Harrodsburg being first). Stanford was originally founded in 1775 by Benjamin Logan as Logan's Fort. The term Fort Logan is still used today, such as Fort Logan Hospital. The name Stanford is believed to have come from Standing Fort, which Fort Logan became known as in the late 1770s, because it survived multiple attacks by Indians. Main Street is part of an old buffalo trail. Stanford is the site of the first automobile garage in Kentucky, 1905.

In nearby Crab Orchard stands the first brick home built in Kentucky. It was built by pioneer William Whitley who came from Virginia, explored the area, returned to Virginia, and brought back more settlers with him. The house, still standing, has a secret passage in the event of an Indian attack. The home boasted a horse race track which was the first of its kind in the United States to be made of clay rather than turf. It was also the first time horses ran counterclockwise rather than clockwise, as in Great Britain. These differences are attributed to Whitley's hatred for anything British, probably stemming from the Revolutionary War. Whitley was elected to the Kentucky General Assembly and the

Kentucky House of Representatives. In 1813, at the age of 61, he volunteered in the Kentucky Mounted Infantry as part of the War of 1812. In the Battle of the Thames, October 5, 1813, he led the charge against Tecumseh, the Shawnee Indian leader. Both Tecumseh and Whitley were killed in the battle. He left behind three sons and eight daughters. In 1818, Whitley County was named for him. In 1883, Whitley County, Indiana was also named for him.

The Wilderness Trail did not go far enough west to reach Fort Logan, so Benjamin Logan was instrumental in creating a spur from where the Wilderness Trail went north and extended it in a northwesterly direction to Crab Orchard and on to the Falls of the Ohio. Logan County (Russellville) is also named for Benjamin Logan.

Interesting names include: Blue Lick; Boneyville; Chicken Bristle; Crab Orchard; Dog Walk; Geneva; Hubble; Jumbo; Kings Mountain; Logantown; Maywood; Miracle; Preachersville; South Fork; Sugar Grove; Turkeytown; Walnut Flat

LIVINGSTON COUNTY (1799) Formed from Christian County. The county is named for Robert R. Livingston who helped draft the Declaration of Independence and was one of five who presented the document to the Continental Congress. In a famous painting by John Trumbull, Livingston is standing in the middle of John Adams, Roger Sherman, Thomas Jefferson, and Benjamin Franklin. He also administered the oath of office to George Washington, the only presidential ceremony held in New York City, which was the capital of the United States at that time. He teamed up with Robert Fulton and developed the first steamboat. Livingston parish, Louisiana and Livingston County, New York are also named for him.

Smithland is the county seat. The Cumberland River dissects the county and empties into the Ohio River at Smithland.

Interesting names include: Bayou; Birdsville; Burna; Grand Rivers; Heater; Iuka; Joy; Lake City; Lola; Newbern; Pinckneyville; Salem; Tiline; Vicksburg

LOGAN COUNTY (1792) Formed from Lincoln County. The county is named for Benjamin Logan who was second in command of the Kentucky County, Virginia militia during the Revolutionary War, was a delegate in the writing of Kentucky's Constitution, and was a member of the Kentucky House of Representatives. Logan died of stoke at his home in 1802 and is buried in a family cemetery in his native Shelby County.

Russellville is the county seat. Before it was incorporated in 1798, Russellville was also known as Cook's Station, Logan Court House, Rogues' Harbour, and Big Boiling Spring. The name Russellville was chosen in honor of Revolutionary War general William Russell. Russell County is named for his son, William Russell III. During the Civil War the Russellville Convention met in Russellville to establish Kentucky's Confederate government. The convention ratified an ordinance of secession, adopted a new state seal, designated Bowling Green as the Confederate State Capital, and elected George W. Johnson as governor. The Confederate States of America recognized the convention and admitted Kentucky into the Confederacy, but the fledgling government faced enormous challenges from the beginning. The government formed by the Russellville Convention lacked any real power after 1863, and was dissolved in 1865. Eleven southern states formed the Confederate States of America between the years of 1861 and 1865. Seven states had declared their independence from the United States before Abraham Lincoln was elected president. Four more states followed suit after the Civil War began. The Union held secession illegal and failed to recognize the Confederacy. The town of Auburn was originally Federal Cove. In the 1860s, the name was changed to honor Auburn, New York.

The Red River Meeting House was the site of the first religious camp meeting in the United States and the start of the Second Great Awakening from June 13–17, 1800, which lasted into the 1830s. Logan County is also home to a Shaker community known as South Union. The community opened in 1807 and closed in 1922. Although the Shakers chose not to fight on either side of the Civil War, they were still drawn in by conscription. At any given time soldiers from either side could ride through demanding food.

Jesse James robbed the Southern Deposit Bank in Russellville on March 20, 1868. Jesse is said to have shot a hole in the weathervane atop the bank. A hole in the weathervane is visible today.

Ten other states have a Logan County.

Notable residents include:
- Jim Bowie (1796–1836) - died in the Battle of the Alamo; made the famous Bowie knife
- Terry Wilcutt - astronaut and veteran of four space shuttle missions, two of which he commanded
- Otis Key - Harlem Globetrotter

Interesting names include: Agnes; Anderson; Beechland; Buffalo Fork; Cave Springs; Chandlers Chapel; Cooperstown; Corinth; Costelow; Crossroad; Deer Lick; Dennis; Diamond Springs; Dot; Edwards; Gasper; Gordonsville (is 1 mile from) Gordonville; Halls Store; Hilltop; Hollow Bill; Jerico; Justice; Keysburg; Lickskillet; Lost City; Oakville; Schochoh; South Union (Shaker settlement); Spa; Whippoorwill; Williams Store; Wolf Lick

LYON COUNTY (1845) Formed from Caldwell County. The county is named for Chittenden Lyon, a U.S. Representative from Kentucky and a member of the Kentucky House of Representatives (1822–1824) and the Kentucky Senate (1827–1835). He died in Eddyville in 1842 and is buried in the Eddyville Cemetery.

Eddyville, the county seat, was so named for the eddies in the nearby Cumberland River prior to the formation of Lake Barkley. About one-half of the county is taken up by Lake Barkley, Kentucky Lake, and the Land Between the Lakes.

Eddyville is the home of the Kentucky State Penitentiary. Governor Luke Pryor Blackburn (1879–1883), greatly improved conditions in the prison system and was instrumental in establishing the penitentiary at Eddyville. It took six years to build this massive stone structure (1884–1890). Viewed from Lake Barkley it is often called "The Castle of the Lake." The electric chair was first used in 1936, but has not been used since 1999, in favor of lethal injection.

Governor Blackburn also reorganized the agricultural and mechanical college into what is today the University of Kentucky. Governor Blackburn and Governor Fletcher are the only physicians to have served as governor of Kentucky.

Following the completion of the Kentucky Dam on the Tennessee River in the 1940s, rumors began to surface that another dam would be built, this time on the Cumberland River. By the mid 1950s, the rumors were confirmed and plans were underway to relocate the city of Eddyville and Kuttawa (cut-TAH-wa). Enter Lee S. Jones, a native of Lyon County who had gained considerable wealth as a tax lawyer in Louisville. Jones had already purchased farms in the Fairview community (where Eddyville now sits) and presented the following plan to the Eddyville City Council: "each person owning land in the towns of Eddyville and Kuttawa to be flooded would receive a free lot in the new Eddyville site, including acreage for a school and public buildings. This also applied to businesses." The residents accepted his offer and declared August 28, 1959, as "Dedication and Free Deed Day."

Eddyville was home to the former AM radio station WEAK.

Interesting names include: Carmack; Confederate; Cross Road; Fairview; Greenacres; Koon; Kuttawa (ku-TAW-wa); Lamasco; Palisades; Saratoga; Suwanee;

MADISON COUNTY (1786) Formed from Lincoln County. This sixth county in Kentucky is named for Virginia statesman James Madison, Secretary of State, and the fourth president of the United States. Being the principle author of the Constitution, he is considered to be the "Father of the Constitution." As a leader in the First Congress, he drafted many basic laws and was responsible for the first ten amendments to the Constitution and is thus known as the "Father of the Bill of Rights." As president, he led the nation into war against Great Britain in the War of 1812 in order to protect the economic rights of the United States. He graduated from Princeton University in two years.

Richmond, the county seat, was founded in 1798 by Colonel John Miller, Revolutionary War soldier, and named in honor of Miller's birthplace, Richmond, VA. Madison County was formed in 1785 from Lincoln County, Virginia.

Another report tells that Madison County was named for Kentucky's sixth governor, George Madison (1816–1816), second cousin to President James Madison. He was born in Rockingham County, Virginia and fought in the American Revolution. He was living in Bourbon County when he won his gubernatorial election. However, being too ill to travel to Frankfort for the inauguration, he was sworn in by a justice of the peace in Bourbon County. He died six weeks later, making him the first Kentucky governor to die in office. Madison is buried in Frankfort Cemetery.

In the northern part of the county, near Fort Boonesborough, is White Hall State Historic Site. It was the home of Cassius Marcellus Clay, emancipationist, newspaper publisher, Minister to Russia, and friend to Abraham Lincoln. Clay's daughter, Laura Clay, was politically active for women's suffrage and states' rights. In 1920, Laura became the first woman to be nominated for U.S. president by a major political party. The innovative home had indoor running water and central heating. There are twenty-seven historic markers placed throughout the county.

Bybee Pottery, Bybee, is the oldest existing pottery west of the Alleghenies and the oldest industry in Madison County. It is believed to have been established in 1809. The location of the operation was selected because of the large clay deposits in the area.

Notable residents include:
- Samuel Freeman Miller (1816–1890) – Richmond; United States Supreme Court Justice
- Christopher Houston "Kit" Carson (1809–1868) – born near Richmond; Indian agent, trapper, scout; his father was of Scotch-Irish descent; the family moved to Missouri where they bought a piece of land owned by the sons of Daniel Boone; Kit was number eleven of fifteen children; at age sixteen, Kit went to Santa Fe, New Mexico, where he became fluent in Spanish, Navajo, Apache, Cheyenne, Arapaho, Paiute, Shoshone, and Ute; he and his third wife raised fifteen children (there were at least two children by his first wife)
- Cassius Marcellus Clay (1810–1903) – The Lion of White Hall; Ambassador to Russia; abolitionist; a founder of the Republican Party; in 1844 he delivered campaign speeches for his relative Henry Clay

Berea: In 1850 the area known as Glade was a community of scattered farms with a racetrack and citizens sympathetic to emancipation. In 1853, the wealthy and politically ambitious Cassius Marcellus Clay gave Rev. John Gregg Fee a tract of land in the Glade where, with local supporters and other abolitionists, Fee established a church, a college, and a tiny village. Fee named Berea after a biblical town of whom it was said, "received the Word with readiness of mind" (Acts 17:10–11).

Berea College, founded in 1855, became the only integrated college in the south for nearly forty years. In the 1880s there was a growing national interest in the culture and traditions of Appalachia by writers, academics, missionaries, and teachers. Fascinated by the rich culture and dismayed by the isolation and poverty, college donors were excited by the coverlets brought by students in exchange for tuition. College President William Frost took many of these coverlets with him on his fund raising trips to the north. Frost, perceiving a national market for traditional crafts, established the first Berea College Fireside Industries. The college built a loom house and hired a supervisor to train and maintain the quality of student work.

Interesting names include: Arlington; Berea; Bighill; Blue Grass; Bobtown; Boonesboro; Buggytown; Bybee; College Hill; Cottonburg; Crow Valley; Cuzick; Duluth; Happy Landing; Middletown; Million; Paint Lick; Panola; Redhouse; Robinsville; Round Hill; Ruthton; Silver Creek; Slate Lick; Speedwell; Stringtown; Union City; Valley View; Waco; White Hall; Whites

MAGOFFIN COUNTY (1860) Formed from Floyd, Johnson, and Morgan Counties. The county is named for Beriah Magoffin, Governor of Kentucky at the outbreak of the American Civil War (1859-1862) and Kentucky House of Representatives. As governor at the start of the Civil War, Magoffin refused President Lincoln's call for troops by writing, "I will send not a man nor a dollar for the wicked purpose of subduing my sister Southern States." Though Magoffin also rejected a similar Confederate request, he was forced to resign because of his sympathies but was permitted to name his successor, James F. Robinson (1862–1863). Magoffin was born, died, and buried in Harrodsburg. He married Anna Nelson Shelby, daughter of Kentucky's first and fifth governor, Isaac Shelby.

Salyersville, the county seat, was established in 1794, but the settlers were driven off by the Indians and did not return until 1800. The post office opened as Burning Springs in 1829, was moved and renamed Licking Station in 1839, moved and renamed Adamsville in 1849, and was finally renamed Salyersville in 1860 for Samuel Salyer.

During the Civil War, Salyersville fell on hard times. Because of its location, families were often divided on the issues between the North and the South. In 1871, "Uncle Billy" Adams gave land on which to build a court house and other public buildings. In 1890, the first court house was completed. That building stood until it caught fire (twice) in 1957. In 2002, the court house (only the second one) was razed to make room for a new Justice Center which opened in 2006. The architecture of the new Justice Center pays tribute to the original court house.

Magoffin County Institute, Salyersville's first high school, was founded in 1908 by Rev. A. C. Harlowe. In 1963, the Mountain Parkway was completed, stretching seventy-six miles from Salyersville to Winchester. The first annual Magoffin County Founder's Day was held in 1978.

In the winter of 1997, as part of Kentucky's elk restoration project, Salyersville became one of the locations selected to release elk into the wilderness. It was hoped that by the year 2000, Kentucky would have the largest free-ranging, wild elk herd east of Montana.

As of 2006, Magoffin was one of the poorest counties in the United States.

Pioneer Village is a complex of fifteen original log cabins restored and rebuilt on the grounds of the former Salyersville Graded School. The cabins serve as a living historical center with displays and demonstrations of early crafts. Some of the cabins date back to the early 1800s. There are six Historic Markers placed throughout the county.

Notable residents include:
- Rebecca Lynn Howard (1979–) – Salyersville; country music singer-songwriter

Interesting names include: Arthurmabel; Bethanna; Bradley (named for Governor William O. Bradley); Burning Fork (named for the Burning Fork Creek which was named for natural gas ignited by the Indians); Cisco; Cutuno; Cyrus; Dale; Dixie; Duco (derives its name from the Latin phrase, "I read"); Edna; Elsie; Ever; Falcon; Flat Fork; Foraker; Fredville; Fritz; Galdia; Gapville; Gifford; Grayfox; Gunlock; Gypsy; Harper (named for Nanie Harper Arnett, postmaster); Ivyton; Kerney; Lacey; Lakeville; Leatha; Lickburg; Logville; Lower Burning Fork; Lykins; Maggard; Marshallville; Mashfork; Mid; Minefork; Netty; Ova; Plutarch; Puncheon; Right Middle Fork; Royalton; Stringtown; Sublett (named for David D. Sublett, settler); Tiptop; Waldo; Wheelersburg (named for the family of Greenville P. Wheeler, postmaster); Wonnie

MARION COUNTY (1834) Formed from Washington County. The county is named for Lieutenant Colonel Francis Marion in the Continental Army, who later became a brigadier general in the Revolutionary War. He became known as the Swamp Fox for his ability to use decoy and ambush tactics to disrupt enemy communications, capture supplies, and free prisoners. The residents of some of Marion County's first communities were a result of one of Maryland's first migration movements beginning in 1785.

Lebanon was established in 1814, and named for the Lebanon in the Bible because of the abundance of cedar trees. It became the county seat in 1835. Several structures were burned to the ground, including the depot, when John Hunt Morgan's troops raided the town during the Civil War. Because a branch of the Louisville and Nashville Railroad extended to Lebanon, it was important to both sides of the war and thus changed hands several times.

The Lebanon National Cemetery is located just outside the city limits. The fourteen acre cemetery contains about five thousand graves. In 1862, it was first established as a cemetery for nearby Camp Crittenden, the Union supply depot in Lebanon, and the military hospitals in the area. It was designated a national Cemetery in 1867. Holy Cross Church is the first Catholic church west of the Allegheny Mountains. Major General George Thomas led Union forces from Lebanon to Mill Springs (on the Cumberland River near Burnside, a distance of about fifty air miles) to engage in the first major Civil War battle in Kentucky.

The geographic center of Kentucky is about three miles NNW of Lebanon.

Notable residents include:
- Phil Simms (1955–) – Lebanon; quarterback for New York Giants; MVP of Super Bowl XXI; now a football analyst for CBS

Interesting names include: Belltown; Calvary; Frogtown; Gandertown; Gravel Switch; Green Acres; Greenbriar; Holy Cross; Mount Pisgah; Nerinx; New Market; Poplar Corner; Raywick; St Joseph; St Mary

MARSHALL COUNTY (1842) Formed from Calloway County. The county is named for John Marshall, an American statesman and jurist who shaped American constitutional law and made the Supreme Court a center of power. Marshall was the fourth Chief Justice of the United States serving from 1801, until his death in 1835, U.S. House of Representatives, and Secretary of State. He is the longest serving judge in Supreme Court History.

Benton is the county seat. The county was formed in 1842, from part of Calloway County. The first settlement was established about 1818, when the area was bought from the Chickasaw Indians as part of the Jackson Purchase. The creation of Kentucky Lake by the Tennessee Valley Authority in the 1940s, led to the destruction of two towns, Birmingham and Gilbertsville. Gilbertsville, at the site of the dam, was relocated about one and one-half mile to the north. Marshall County is home to Kentucky Dam Village State Resort Park and the Kentucky Lake Motor Speedway.

Shape-note singers gather annually at the court house in Benton on the fourth Sunday in May to sing from a tunebook called the *Southern Harmony*. Organized in 1884, and called the Big Singing or the Big Singing Day, it is considered by many to be the oldest indigenous musical tradition in the United States. It is the only singing in the world to use the William Walker Southern Harmony system of shape-note singing. Benton is also known for an annual festival day called Tater Day at which Marshall Countians gather on the court house square to eat, listen to music, and hear political speeches. Tater Day began in 1842, as a day for farmers to gather at the county seat to trade agricultural goods, mainly sweet potato slips. Tater Day is the world's only celebration of the sweet potato.

Calvert City was named for Potilla Calvert. He built his home, Oak Hill, in 1860, and gave a portion of his land to a new railroad, specifying that a station be built near his home. The town grew up around the train station.

Notable residents include:
- Tom Rickman – screenwriter of *Coal Miner's Daughter*

Interesting names include: Aurora; Birmingham; Brien; Briensburg; Buena Vista; Cloud Crossing; Dogtown; Elva; Fairdealing; Glade; Grand Rivers (the only city to front both Lake Barkley and Kentucky Lake); Hardin; Ida; Iola; Little Cypress; Marshall; Oak Level; Olive; Possum Trot; Scale; Shady Grove; South Marshall; Walnut Grove

MARTIN COUNTY (1870) Formed from Floyd, Johnson, Pike, and Lawrence Counties. Martin County is named for Congressman John Preston Martin, U.S. House of Representatives and Kentucky House of Representatives. He was born in Virginia and moved to Prestonsburg (Floyd County). Inez is the county seat. The Martin County Airport is seven air miles from Prestonsburg, eight air miles from Inez, and 400 yards from the Johnson County line.

Interesting names include: Add; Beauty; Calf Creek; Castle; Davella; Joe Branch; Job; Laura (is nine miles from) Laura; Lovely; Milo; Oppy; Pilgrim; Preece; Threeforks; Tomahawk; Warfield; West Lovely

MASON COUNTY (1789) Formed from Bourbon County. The county is named for George Mason (1725–1792), the Virginian who wrote the Virginia Constitution and who authored the Bill of Rights for the United States. Along with James Madison, he is called the "Father of the Bill of Rights." The Bill of Rights is based on Mason's earlier Virginia Declaration of Rights. He was a Virginia delegate to the U.S. Continental Convention. West Virginia and Illinois also have counties named for him.

Maysville is the county seat. Mason County was formed by an act of the Kentucky Legislature from Bourbon County in May, 1788. When seen at night from above, the streetlights of downtown Maysville form an outline of the Liberty Bell, including the crack. President Andrew Jackson vetoed a bill that would have allowed a road built from Lexington to Maysville. While Harriet Beecher visited the home of Marshall Key in Maysville, she witnessed a slave auction on the lawn of the Washington Courthouse which may have inspired her writing of Uncle Tom's Cabin. The national Underground Railroad Museum is located in the Bierbower House.

Notable residents include:
- Stanley Forman Reed (1884–1980) - Minerva; served on U.S. Supreme Court 1938–1957; received his B.A. degree from Kentucky Wesleyan College, Owensboro
- Heather French (1974–), Augusta; Miss America 2000; in October, 2003, she struck and subsequently killed a German bicyclist in Louisville
- Judge Phantly Roy Bean (1825–1903) - Infamous "hangin' judge" of Langtry, Texas; he was a saloon keeper and self-appointed judge who called himself, "The law west of the Pecos;" he killed a man in Mexico then fled to California to live with a brother who later became the first mayor of San Diego; during the Civil War he smuggled guns from Mexico, through a Union blockade, to the Confederate Army
- Rosemary Clooney (1928–2002) – Maysville; popular singer/actress in the 1940s and 1950s; her father was an alcoholic, so the children kept moving back and forth between their parents; in 1951, Columbia Records chose a song for her to sing which she hated, but recorded rather than be in breech of contract; "Come On-a My House" became her first single hit; in 1954 she starred in "White Christmas" and

sang with Bing Crosby and Danny Kaye; in 1956, she had her own thirty-minute *Rosemary Clooney Show*; the next year it went to NBC as *The Lux Show Starring Rosemary Clooney*; even into the 1980s, Clooney was still singing, "Extra value is what you get when you buy Coronet;" in 1994, she guest starred on the medical drama *ER* for which she was nominated for an Emmy; she was married twice to Jose' Ferrer, a Puerto Rican-born actor; they have five children, one of whom is married to Debbie Boone; Rosemary is buried at St. Patrick's Cemetery, Maysville

- Joseph Desha (1768–1842) – born in Monroe County, Pennsylvania; served in the War of 1812; Kentucky's ninth governor (1824–1828), Kentucky House of Representatives and Senate, as well as U.S. Senate; he is buried in Georgetown Cemetery

Interesting names include: Brandywine Creek; Dover; Fernleaf; Helena; Lewisburg; Marshall; Mill Creek; Mount Gilead; Old Washington; Orangeburg; Plumville; Sardis; Somo; Springdale; Washington; Weedonia

McCRACKEN COUNTY (1825) Formed from Hickman County. The county is named for Captain Virgil McCracken of Woodford County. McCracken was killed in the Battle of the River Basin near Detroit, Michigan during the War of 1812.

Paducah is the county seat. According to legend, Paducah, originally called Pekin, which began around 1815, was a mixed community of Indians and white settlers who were attracted by its location at the confluence of several waterways. Chief Paduke, most likely a Chickasaw, welcomed the people traveling down the Ohio and Tennessee Rivers on flatbeds. His wigwam, located on a low bluff at the mouth of Island Creek, served as the council lodge for his village. The settlers, appreciative of his hospitality and respectful of his ways, settled across the creek. The two communities lived in harmony, trading goods and services and enjoying the novelty of each other's culture.

Things went smoothly until 1827 when William Clark, of the Lewis and Clark expedition, arrived with a title deed to the land on which Pekin sat. Clark asked the Indians and settlers to move along, which they did offering little resistance, most likely because deed was issued from the United States Supreme Court. Clark surveyed his new property and laid out the grid for a new town which remains evident to this day. The Chief and his villagers moved to Mississippi allowing Clark to continue with the building of the new city which he named Paducah in honor of the Chief.

On September 6, 1861, General Ulysses S. Grant captured Paducah, giving Union troops control of the mouth of the Tennessee River. It remained that way for most of the war. On December 17, 1862, thirty Jewish families, longtime residents, were forced from their homes. A prominent Jewish businessman, Cesar Kaskel, sent a telegram to President Abraham Lincoln and met with him, eventually succeeding in getting the order revoked.

In 1950, the U.S. Atomic Energy Commission selected Paducah as the site for a new uranium enrichment plant. Paducah is home to the Museum of the American Quilter's Society, the world's largest quilt museum.

On December 1, 1997, a fourteen-year-old boy named Michael Carneal carried five loaded guns to Heath High School. He shot a group of fellow students in the school's foyer as they were leaving a prayer group before school. Three girls were killed and five others were wounded.

Dippin' Dots was invented in Paducah in 1988, by Curt Jones, a microbiologist who pioneered the process of cryogenic encapsulation. The company is headquartered in Paducah. Very small pieces of ice cream are dropped into a vat of liquid nitrogen. After being frozen instantly the droplets are scooped off the liquid oxygen.

The Whitehaven Welcome Center, Paducah, houses some of former Vice-President Alben W. Barkley's personal memorabilia.

Notable residents include:
- Julian Morton Carroll (1931–) – West Paducah; Kentucky House of Representatives, lieutenant governor of Kentucky, governor of Kentucky (1974–1979), and a State Senator since 2004
- Steven Curtis Chapman (1962–) – Paducah; contemporary Christian singer who sang at the funerals of those students killed at Heath High School
- John Scopes (1900–1970) – Paducah; Defendant in Scopes "Monkey" Trial for violating a Tennessee state law against teaching evolution; buried in Paducah
- Marcy Walker (1961–) – Paducah; played the part of Liza Colby on *All My Children*, Eden Capwell on *Santa Barbara*, Tangie Hall on *Guiding Light*, then back to *All My Children*; currently serves as a Childrens' Ministry Director in North Carolina
- Hoyt Hawkins (1927–) - sang with the Jordanaires
- Vernon Carver Rudolph - founded Krispy Kreme donuts after moving to Winston-Salem, North Carolina; Paducah has never had a local Krispy Kerme donut shop
- Charles "Speedy" Atkins (1875–1928) – born in Tennessee; his mummified body was on display at a local funeral home from 1928 to 1994
- Homer Louis "Boots" Randolph (1927–) – Paducah, but grew up in Cadiz (Trigg County); he played for the U.S. Army Band; moved to Nashville in 1961, after recording "Yackety Sax;" was the first to play saxophone on a recording with Elvis Presley and the only one to ever play a solo with him and played on the soundtrack for eight Elvis movies; recorded with Roy Orbison, Al Hirt, REO Speedwagon, Brenda Lee, Chet Atkins, Buddy Holly, Floyd Cramer, Alabama, Johnny Cash, Pete Fountain, Tommy Newsom, Doc Severinsen, among others; he is a member of the Kentucky Music Hall of Fame, Renfro Valley
- Bigfoot sightings in 2002, 2003, two in 2005, and one on April 17, 2007
- The first known set of all male quintuplets was born in Paducah, 1896

- Jean Byron (1925–2006), Paducah; best known for the role of Natalie Lane, Patty Lane's mother on *The Patty Duke Show*

Paducah is home to the Paducah International Raceway owned by Dale Earnheardt Jr., Tony Stewart, Kenny Schrader, and Bob Sargent.

Interesting names include: Camelia; Cecil; Cimota City; Concord; Elva; Forest Hill; Fremont (one mile from) Freemont; Future City; Hardmoney; Heath; High Point; Krebs; Littleville; Massac; Oakdale; Oaks; Ragland; Riverview; Shady Grove; West Future City; West Paducah; Woodville

At the November, 2008 election, the 175 residents of Lone Oak voted to dissolve the thirty-year-old charter that made them a city. The town is one-half mile square.

McCREARY COUNTY (1912) Formed from Pulaski, Wayne, and Whitley Counties. The county is named for James Bennett McCreary, the twenty-seventh and thirty-seventh governor of Kentucky (1875–1879 and 1912–1916), Kentucky House of Representatives (Speaker of the House), U.S. Representative (1885–1897), and U.S. Senator (1903–1909). He was born in Richmond, graduated from Centre College, and practiced law in Richmond. Having been a member of the Confederate States Army he participated in raids on the nerby towns of Monticello and Burkesville. As governor, much of his time was spent quelling feuds in eastern Kentucky. His wife remains the youngest First Lady of the Commonwealth. He died in Richmond and is buried in Richmond Cemetery.

Whitley City is the county seat and is named for Colonel William Whitley. It is the only county in Kentucky not to have an incorporated city. Sixty-three percent of the county is owned and managed by Daniel Boone National Forest. McCreary was the last county to be named in Kentucky in 1912.

Cumberland Falls State Resort Park is in McCreary County, although the Cumberland River is the dividing line between it and Whitley County. Cumberland Falls is the only falls in the Western Hemisphere to consistently display a moonbow or lunar rainbow. The Falls have been seen in three movies: *The Kentuckian*, 1955, staring John Wayne; "Raintree County," 1997, during Civil War days, starring Montgomery Clift, Elizabeth Taylor, Eva Marie Saint, Agnes Morehead, and Lee Marvin; "Fire Down Below," 1997 with Steven Seagal (Cumberland Falls can be seen in a flyover).

Yahoo Falls drops 113 feet from the top of a cliff making it the tallest waterfall in Kentucky. It was here that over one hundred children, women, and older Chickamauga Indians had gathered waiting to be taken to Lookout Mountain and safety from Indian fighters. Before morning most of them lay dead, killed by several Indian fighters who heard of their trip. Only a few managed to escape because the falls had them trapped. By the same token, as the massacre was ending, two Indians came upon the scene and were able to kill all the murderers one by one because they, like their victims, could not escape.

Interesting names include: Bell Farm; Beulah Heights; Blue Heron; Co-Operative; Comargo; Creekmore; Fidelity; Flat Rock; Funston; Greenwood; Hickory Grove; Hill Top; Hollyhill; Honeybee; Monticello; Oz; Pine Knot; Sawyer; Smith Town; Strunk; White Oak Junction; Whitley City; Wiborg; Yamacraw

McLEAN COUNTY (1854) Formed from Daviess, Muhlenberg, and Ohio Counties. The county is named for Judge Alney McLean, Kentucky House of Representatives, U.S. House of Representative (two separate terms), and a captain in the War of 1812. After leving Congress he served as judge of the fourteenth districe for ten years until his death in 1841. He was born in North Carolina, moved to Kentucky and was appointed surveyor of Muhlenberg County in 1799. He began practicing law in Greenville in 1805. He is buried in the Old Caney Station Cemetery near Greenville.

Calhoun is the county seat. The county was formed by an act of the Kentucky Legislature in 1854 from portions of surrounding Daviess, Ohio, and Muhlenberg Counties.

Dividing the county in half is the Green River, Kentucky's longest river that flows totally within state boundaries.

In McLean County, it is possible to cross two rivers, leave one county, drive through another county, and reenter the first county, all within the span of less than one-fourth mile. This is how it is done. Traveling north on U.S. Highway 431, one enters the Livermore Bridge that crosses the GreenRiver, then passes over a small sliver of Ohio County that extends under the bridge. Next, the bridge crosses the Rough River (a narrow river), and lastly it reenters McLean County.

Sacramento was originally named Cross Roads, but after returning from the California Gold Rush, John Vickers suggested changing the name to Sacramento. This town of five hundred holds the county's largest tourist attraction each year, a reenactment of the Battle of Sacramento from the Civil War. The city of Island, population four hundred, was so named because when the Green River flooded it totally surrounded the town, which sits on a slight elevation.

Interesting names include: Beech Grove; Buttonsberry; Cleopatra (cleo-PAY-tra); Comer; Elba; Guffie; Lemon; Nuckols; Poplar Grove; Poverty; Semiway

MEADE COUNTY (1824) Formed from Breckinridge and Hardin Counties. The county is named for James Meade, honored after he was killed in the Battle of Raisin River near Detroit, Michigan, War of 1812.

Brandenburg is the county seat. Muldraugh, about half way between Elizabethtown and Louisville on U.S. Highways 31 and 60, was so named because it is located at the bottom of a very steep hill. The only way to get to the top of the hill before automobiles was with a "mule drawn" wagon.

Notable residents include:
- Rick Stansbury (1959–) – Louisville; played basketball for Meade County High School; Mississippi State University's men's head basketball coach

Interesting names include: Battletown; Beechland; Buck Grove; Cedar Flat; Cold Springs; Ekron; Fair Acres; Garrett; Hillgrove; Liberty; Lickskillet; Maples Corner; Midway; Oolite; Rhodelia; Roberta; Rock Haven; Sirocco; Wolf Creek

MENIFEE COUNTY (1869) Formed from Bath, Montgomery, Morgan, Powell, and Wolfe Counties. The county is named for Richard Hickman Menefee (note the spelling). He was born in Owingsville (Bath County), graduated from Transylvania University, and practiced law in Mount Sterling where he was appointed Commonwealth Attorney. He was a member of the Kentucky House of Representatives and the U.S. House of Representatives. After leaving Washington, D.C., he practiced law in Lexington. He died in Frankfort, was interred in a private cemetery in Fayette County, and later reinterred in Cave Hill Cemetery, Louisville.

Frenchburg is the county seat.

Interesting names include: Artville; Back; Ballard; Big Woods; Blackwater; Dan; Dog Trot; Flat Rock; Hill Top; Korea; Laurel Grove; Mariba; Means; Pine Grove; Pomeroyton; Rebelsville; Scranton; Stonequarry; Stroll; Sudith; Trimble Bend

MERCER COUNTY (1786) Formed from Lincoln County. The county is named for General Hugh Mercer, physician and brigadier general in the Continental Army and close friend to George Washington. Mercer was born near Aberdeenshire, Scotland. He moved to Mercersberg, Pennsylvania where he practiced medicine for eight years. He was commissioned a captain in a Pennsylvania regiment and was wounded and separated from his unit while attacking Indians in 1756. He trekked several miles through the woods for fourteen days, injured and with no supplies, until he found his way back to Fort Shirley where he was recognized for such a feat and, as a result, promoted.

After befriending several Virginia men, Mercer moved to Fredericksburg, a thriving Scottish community, where he opened an apothecary and medical practice. George Washington's mother, Mary Washington, was one of Dr. Mercer's patients. That establishment is now a museum. In 1774, George Washington sold Ferry Farm, his childhood home, to Mercer which he intended to use for his family estate. Two of his direct descendants include Army General George S. Patton and songwriter Johnny Mercer.

Counties in Illinois, New Jersey, Ohio, Pennsylvania, and West Virginia and the town of Mercerville, New Jersey are named for him.

Harrodsburg is the county seat where James Harrod established the first permanent settlement west of the Alleghenies in 1774.

Shaker Village of Pleasant Hill was active from 1805–1910. Many of the early residents of Shakertown were influenced by the Cane Ridge Revival near Paris (Bourbon County). In the early 1830s they constructed a water tower on a high plot of ground. A horse-drawn pump lifted the water into the tower, and from there a system of pipes carried the water to kitchens, cellars, and wash houses. In the wash houses, washing machines (also powered by horse) were built to reduce the enormous chore of laundering the community's clothing and linens. When a group of Lexington-area residents decided to restore the grounds and buildings in 1961, they asked a former Woodford County resident and the first curator of Colonial Williamsburg, James Lowry Cogar, to supervise the project. Today, with thirty-four original buildings and 2,800 acres of farmland, Shaker Village claims to be the largest historic community of its kind in America. The oldest continuous horse show in America, dating back to 1827, is at the Mercer County Fair in Harrodsburg.

Notable residents include:
- John Adair (1757–1840) – born in South Carolina; in 1788, he moved to Mercer County; U.S. House of Representatives, U.S. Senate, and eighth Kentucky governor

Interesting names include: Bohon; Bondville; Burgin; Bushtown; Cornishville; Deep Creek; Ebenezer; Jackson; Mavo; Mayo; Nevada; Oregon; Pleasant Hill; Rose Hill; Salvisa; Seaville; Stringtown; Tablow; Terrapin; Vanarsdell

METCALFE COUNTY (1860) Formed from Adair, Butler, Cumberland, Green, Hart, and Monroe Counties. The county is named for Thomas Metcalfe, U.S. House of Representatives (five terms), U.S. Senate, Kentucky governor from 1828 to 1832, Kentucky House of Representatives (four terms), Kentucky Senate and served in the War of 1812. As governor, President Andrew Jackson vetoed money to build a turnpike connecting Maysville and Lexington, Governor Metcalfe built it anyway and paid for it entirely with state funds. Born in Fauquier County, Virginia, he moved with his family to Fayette County where he learned the trade of stone mason and helped construct the Old State Capitol. He died near Carlisle and was interred in the family burial ground at Forest Retreat, his estate in Nicholas County.

Edmonton is the county seat. The area was first surveyed by Revolutionary War veteran Edmund P. Rogers in 1800. The town was established by the Kentucky Legislature as a trading post in 1836, and was named the county seat in 1860. The post office first opened on February 18, 1830, and was named, though incorrectly spelled, for Edmund Rogers. The population was 1,586 at the 2000 census.

The population is thirty-four persons per square mile with sixteen housing units per square mile.

Notable residents include:
- the rock band Black Stone Cherry
- the country music band Kentucky Headhunters

Summer Shade is home to Kingsford Charcoal factory

Interesting names include: Beechville; Cave Ridge; Cedar Flats; Center; Clarks Corner; Cofer; Cork; Curtis; East Fork; Echo; Gascon; Goodluck; Knob Lick; New Liberty; Node; Red Lick; Savoyard; Shady Grove; Sulphur Well; Willow Shade; Wisdom

MONROE COUNTY (1820) Formed from Barren and Cumberland Counties. Monroe County is named for President James Monroe (1817–1825). He was the fifth president of the United States and the fourth Virginian to hold that office. He was also Secretary of State and Secretary of War under President James Madison, a member of the U.S. Senate, and governor of Virginia twice. His daughter Maria Monroe was the first to be married in the White House. In the famous painting, *Washington Crossing the Delaware* (also depicted on the New Jersey state quarter), Monroe is standing behing Washington holding the American flag. Monroe is considered to be the president who is in the most paintings; through the 1800s, he was in over 350 paintings.

Tompkinsville is the county seat and was named for vice president (1817–1825) Daniel D. Tompkins who served under President James Monroe, for whom the county was named. Freetown, six miles west of Tompkinsville, was so named when, about 1845, slave owner William Howard freed his slaves and gave them four hundred acres on which to build homes.

Interesting names include: Blythe; Bugtussle; Bushong; Center Point; Coe; Cyclone; Ebenezer; Emberton; Flippin; Forkton; Fountain Run; Gamaliel; Grandview; Gum Tree; Harlan Crossorads; Jeffrey; Lamb; Meshack; Mount Hermon; Mud Lick; Otia; Persimmon; Raydure; Rockbridge; Sulphur Lick

MONTGOMERY COUNTY (1797) Formed from Clark County. The county is named in honor of Richard Montgomery, Revolutionary War brigadier general killed December 31, 1775, while trying to capture Quebec City, Canada. Six cities are named for him, including Montgomery, Alabama, as well as eight counties.

Mount Sterling, the county seat, was settled in 1792 by Hugh Forbes, a Scotsman who held a land grant near an ancient tribal burial site known as "Little Mountain." In choosing a name for the growing settlement, Forbes chose Sterling, a town in his native Scotland. Each year, hundreds of thousands of visitors flock to Mount Sterling for Court Day. The event is held on the third Monday of October.

Notable residents include:
- Ernie Fletcher (1952–) – Mount Sterling; Kentucky Governor from 2003–2007

Interesting names include: Camargo; Ewington; Grassy Lick; Hope; Jeffersonville; Judy; Klondike; Levee; Lower Spencer; Lucky Stop; Sideview; Stepstone; Stoops; Upper Spencer

MORGAN COUNTY (1823) Formed from Bath and Floyd Counties. The county is named for General Daniel Morgan, an American pioneer and gifted soldier who was one of the most gifted battlefield tacticians of the Revolutionary War. The Virginia House of Burgess chose Daniel Morgan to form a rifle company and give assistance to the fighting at Boston. He recruited ninety-six men in ten days and assembled them at Winchester on July 14, 1775. He then marched them to Boston in twenty-one days. He led a group of snipers named "Morgan's Sharpshooters."

West Liberty is the county seat. One of Abraham Lincoln's uncles, Fielding Hanks, is reportedly one of several who helped establish the town and county in 1822. Cannel coal is derived from the word "candle" because pencil-shaped pieces were once used as candles.

West Liberty celebrates the annual Sorghum Festival on the last weekend of September. The festival is locally known for the horse-drawn sorghum mill which is operated during the festival. There are four historic markers placed throughout the county.

Interesting names include: Adele (named for the daughter of the Ohio and Kentucky Railroad president); Bearwallow; Blairs Mills; Blaze; Bonny; Burg; Caney (named for Elcaney Lykins, local resident); Cannel City (named for the cannel coal mined there); Cottle; Crockett (named for David Crockett Fannin, son of postmaster Peter Fannin); Dingus; Ebon; Elkfork; Ezel; Florress; Gordon Ford; Grassy Creek; Hickory Grove; Holliday; Index; Jeptha; Jericho; Kellacy; Leisure; Lick Branch; Licking River; Lost Creek; Malone (named for Malone Lykins, settler); Matthew; Maytown; Mima; Mize; Moon; Murphyfork; Oak Hill; Ophir; Panama; Pomp; Redwine; Relief; Right Fork; Rockhouse; Salem; Silverhill; Stacy Fork; Straight Creek; Tarkiln; Twentysix; Wheel Rim; White Oak; Woodsbend; Wrigley; Yocum (named for Billy Yocum, resident); Zag

MUHLENBERG COUNTY (1798) Formed from Christian and Logan Counties. The county is named for John Peter Gabriel Muhlenberg, Revolutionary War general, U.S. Senator (for six months), U.S. House of Representatives (three separate terms) (his brother was Speaker of the House during the first term), as well as an ordained Lutheran minister, and an ordained Anglican priest. He was born in Trappe (Montgomery County), Pennsylvania, educated at the Academy of Philadelphia. He died in Montgomery County and is interred at the Augustus Lutheran Church, Trappe. Only Muhlenberg County, KY bears his name.

Greenville, the county seat, is named for Revolutionary War General Nathaniel Greene. In 1795, a small group of soldier-settlers under the leadership of Colonel William Campbell and General William Russell, having served in the Revolutionary War under Nathaniel Greene, came to this area to claim their land grants given to them in payment for their service in the war. This group came from Virginia, North Carolina, and a few from Pennsylvania. They first settled one and one-half miles from downtown Greenville in a community they called Caney Station, however, the area proved to be too low and too far from their fresh water supply. In 1799, they moved to a "site on seven hills" where there were two good springs and where several old trails met. The new location was named Greenville in honor of General Nathan Greene.

The easternmost boundary of the county is the Green River which starts in Lincoln County (Stanford), flows through Mammoth Cave, and empties into the Ohio River near Evansville, Indiana, 300 miles from its beginning. Muhlenberg County, once the largest coal-producing county in America, depended heavily on the Green River to export the coal.

Following the Revolutionary War many veterans staked claims along the Green River as payment for their military service. Unfortunately, the valley also attracted a number of ne'er-do-wells, earning it the dubious nickname Rogue's Harbor. In 1842 the river was canalized with a series of locks and dams which created a navigable channel as far inland as Bowling Green.

The Green River produces some of the largest freshwater fish in the world. The following catches are on record as being the biggest in the state: Flathead Catfish, 97 lbs; Freshwater Drum, 38 lbs; Bowfin, 15 lbs; Blue Sucker, 4 lbs, 15, oz; Bighead Carp, 52 lbs., Blue Sucker, 4 lbs, 15 oz.

(Personal note: it has been reported by those who do underwater rescue in Kentucky's rivers that some have encountered fish as big as any man. A fish that size has not actually been seen due to the dim light or muddy water, but the divers conclude that nothing else could move the water so strongly around the diver.)

Muhlenberg County and the Green River will forever be linked in the minds of many by the John Prine song, "Paradise," about a small town in Muhlenberg by that name which was situated on the Green River. On the site of the old town of Paradise is the present-day Paradise Fossil Fuel Steam Plant, part of the Tennessee Valley Authority.

Lake Malone State Park, in the southern end of the county (also shared by Logan and Todd Counties), displays up to fifty-feet tall sandstone cliffs rising above the water's edges.

Bremen was named by German immigrants who settled the area and named it after Bremen, Germany. Central City was named for the Central Railroad Company that maintained a large yard and a roundhouse.

Until 2007, Central City was also home to Brewco Motorsports, a NASCAR Busch Series racing team. The team included drivers Casey Atwood, Scott Wimmer, Greg Biffle, Ken Schrader, and Brad Coleman. The company and the name Brewco Motorsports was sold and moved to another location.

Powderly was named for Terence Powderly who opened a coal mine there in 1887.

Greenville is home to the House of Onyx, the world's largest gemstone dealer.

There are 11 historic markers placed throughout the county.

Notable residents include:
- Warren Oates (1928–1982) – Depoy; died of a sudden heart attack at age 53; memoribalia displayed at Duncal Cultural Center, Greenville
- Tom Christerson – Central City; the second-ever recipient of an artificial heart transplant
- The city of Drakesboro erected the Four Legends Fountain, honoring four pioneers of the "thumb-picking" style of guitar playing; those names are Kennedy Jones, Isaac "Ike" Everly, Mose Rager, and Merle Travis; the last three have close ties to Muhlenberg County
- James Best (1926–) Powderly; best known for his role as Sheriff Roscoe P. Coltrane in the television series *Dukes of Hazzard*
- Don and Phil Everly (1937–) (1939–) – Don was born in Brownie, a now-defunct coal mining town in Muhlenberg County while Phil was born in Chicago; in addition to both being competent guitarists, the brothers used a style of close harmony in which each one sang a tune that could often stand alone as a plausible melody line; this is in contrast to typical harmony lines which would sound strange if sung by themselves; sometimes they were mistaken for women, particularly Phil who actually imitated a woman on several Buddy Holly recordings; the Beatles and the Beach Boys were influenced by the Everly Brothers; the Beatles based the vocal arrangement of their song, "Please, Please Me," directly on that of "Cathy's Clown;" Chet Atkins produced their first recording, but it flopped; their second recording, "Bye Bye, Love," had been rejected by thirty other acts, including Elvis Presley (thank you very much); it reached number two on the Pop charts and number one on both County and R & B charts selling one million copies; their enlistment into the Marine Corps took them out of the spotlight just before the Beatles (whose harmonies were influenced by the Everly Brothers) took the United States by storm and changed forever the face of rock and roll music; in 1983, the duo came together again to perform a song written especially for them my Paul McCartney; "On the Wings of a Nightingale" was a hit both in the United States and United Kingdom; the Everly Brothers were among the first to be inducted into the Rock and Roll Hall of Fame
- Merle Travis (1917–1983) – Rosewood; singer, guitarist, and songwriter; his lyrics often discussed the exploitation of coal miners, i.e. "Sixteen Tons," "Dark As A Dungeon;" others include, "So Round, So Firm, So Fully Packed," and "Smoke, Smoke, Smoke that Cigarette;" he is responsible for introducing thumb picking, known as "Travis Picking;" he was inducted into the Nashville Song-writers Hall of Fame, 1970, and the Country Music Hall of Fame, 1977; his original guitar was made by his brother; several local guitar players caught his attention, including

Mose Rager who played a thumb and index finger picking style method which essentially created a solo style that blended lead lines and a rhythmic bass plucked by the thumb (with pick), similar to the style Travis developed; Travis also learned guitar from Kennedy Jones and Ike Everly, the Everly Brothers' father; hits like "Divorce Me C.O.D," "Steel Guitar Rag," and "Fat Girl" gave him national prominence, although they rarely showed off his playing abilities; in his personal life he was a heavy drinker and suffered from serious stage freight; his other talents include prose writing, taxidermy, cartooning, and watch repair; his greatest claims to fame are when he appeared in the 1953 film, *From Here to Eternity*, and when his good friend Tennessee Ernie Ford recorded "Sixteen Tons;" Glen Campbell's middle name is Travis, in honor of Merle Travis; after his death he was cremated and his ashes scattered around a monument erected to him at the Ebenezer Baptist Church Cemetery just outside Drakesboro; today his son Thom Bresh continues playing in Travis' style

Interesting names include: Bancroft; Bards Hill; Beech Creek; Beechmont; Belton; Bevier; Browder; Brown Town; Cleaton; Depoy; Drakesboro; Dunmore; Earls; Ebenezer; Ennis; Graham; Gus; Harps Hill (where Jesse James allegedly hid a cache of money); Hillside; Knightsburg; Luzerne; Lynn City; Martwick (named after Mr. Martin and Mr. Wickliffe who co-owned the coal mine); Mercer; Midland; Millport; Mog; Moorman; Morehead; Nebo; Nelson; New Cypress; Nonnell; Paradise; Penrod; Rosewood; Sandy; Skilesville; South Carrollton; Stringtown; Union Ridge; Weir

NELSON COUNTY (1785) Formed from Jefferson County. The county is named for Thomas Nelson Jr., a Virginia Governor who signed the Declaration of Independence. He was born in Virginia and was a delegate of Virginia in the Continental Congress and, as such, signed the Declaration of Independence. He was also a Governor of Virginia, succeeding Thomas Jefferson. His grandfather Thomas "Scotch Tom" Nelson was an immigrant from Scotland. Nelson County, Virginia is also named for him.

Bardstown, the county seat, is named for David Bard, the man who obtained the land for the city from the Governor of Virginia. His brother William Bard was the surveyor who laid out the city. Bardstown is the second oldest city in Kentucky, having been settled in the 1770s, and receiving its charter in 1790. It was the first center of Catholicism west of the Appalachian Mountains. The world's largest crucifix, sixty feet tall, is in Bardstown.

The Old Talbot Tavern on court house square, built around 1797, can boast of several notable American icons who passed through the tavern's doors, including Abraham Lincoln and Daniel Boone. It is the oldest western stagecoach stop in America.

- The Kentucky Railway Museum is in nearby New Haven; the museum owns four steam locomotives and six diesel locomotives as well as over one hundred pieces of rolling stock

- The Tobacco Festival in Bloomfield used to have a tobacco spitting contest. It was a major event for many years

Interesting names include: Balltown; Bellwood; Bloomfield; Blue Gap; Boston; Bourbon Springs; Chaplin; Coxs Creek; East Bardstown; Fairfield; Fort Knox (not the Army base); Gethsemane; Greenbrier; Highgrove; Hunters; Hurricane Hills; Lenore; Nazareth; Nelsonville; New Haven; New Hope; Pine Mountain; Samuels; Woodlawn

NICHOLAS COUNTY (1800) Formed from Mason and Bourbon Counties. The county is named for George Nicholas, Revolutionary War colonel and father of the Kentucky Constitution.

Carlisle is the county seat.

Samuel Kimbrough Barlow (1792–1867); a pioneer in the area that later became the state of Oregon; he was a key figure in establishing the Barlow Road over the Cascade Ridge, the most widely chosen final segment of the Oregon Trail; the road opened in 1846

Interesting names include: Barefoot; Barterville; Carlisle; East Union; Headquarters; Hooktown; Milltown; Morning Glory; Pleasant Valley; Sprout; Upper Blue Licks

OHIO COUNTY (1799) Formed from Hardin County. The county is named for the Ohio River which is in the next county, about fifteen miles north of the Ohio County's north border.

Hartford, the county seat, is believed to have derived its name from a deer crossing (hart, meaning deer, and ford, meaning crossing) on the nearby Rough River.

Notable residents include:
- Wyatt Earp had three step-brothers: James, Virgil, and Morgan. Wyatt was born in Illinois but his mother was a native of Ohio County. Virgil, Morgan, and Wyatt were with Doc Holliday at the OK Coral
- Ray Chapman (1891–1920) – Beaver Dam; an American baseball player who spent his entire career with the Cleveland Indians; he is notable as the only Major League baseball player to have been killed in a game when he was hit on the head by a pitch thrown by Carl Mays of the New York Yankees; it appears that Chapman did not see the ball coming; pitchers did everything they could to dirty up the ball for their own benefit; often by the latter innings the ball was difficult to see; chapman was hit in the fifth inning; his death led Major League Baseball to establish a rule to require umpires to replace the ball when it became dirty; his death was also one of the examples used to emphasize the need for wearing batting helmets, although that rule would not be adopted for thirty more years
- Bill Monroe (1911–1996) – Rosine (he was actually born at Jerusalem Ridge, near the small community of Rosine); developed the style of music known as

Bluegrass which takes its name from his band, the Blue Grass Boys; as a mandolin player Monroe brought a virtuosity previously unknown to his instrument in country music; in 1945, he hired Earl Scruggs who similarly elevated the role of the banjo; this version of the Blue Grass Boys, which also included Lester Flatt, Chubby Wise, and Howard Watts, aka Cedric Rainwater, made the first recordings that featured all the elements that later came to be known as bluegrass music; this particular group broke up when Flatt and Scruggs left to form their own group, the Foggy Mountain Boys; more than one150 musicians played in the Blue Grass Boys; Bill Monroe was inducted into the Country Music Hall of Fame, the International Blue Grass Music Hall of Honor, and the Rock and Roll of Fame; he is the only performer honored in all three; his well-known song "Blue Moon of Kentucky" has been sung by many artists including Elvis Presley, Paul McCartney, and Patsy Cline and is Kentucky's official state bluegrass song

Interesting names include: Adaburg; Aetnaville; Alta; Beaver Dam; Beda; Bells Run; Centertown; Ceralvo; Cool Springs; Dan; Dogwalk; Dundee; Equality; Flint Springs; Highview; Horse Branch; Jerusalem Ridge (Bill Monroe); Jingo; Matanzas; Mt Pleasant; Narrows; Ninteen; No Creek; Oak Grove; Oaks; Pleasant Ridge; Point Pleasant; Ralph; Render; Rob Roy; Rockport; Rosine; Scottown; Select; Sulphur Springs; Sunnydale; Taffy; Trisler; White Run; Windy Hill

OLDHAM COUNTY (1824) Formed from Henry, Jefferson, and Shelby Counties. The county is named for Colonel William Oldham of Jefferson County, a Revolutionary War officer.

La Grange is the county seat. Oldham is the wealthiest county in Kentucky and the forty-eighth wealthiest county in the U.S. and ranks second highest in Kentucky for the percent of college educated residents.

Crestwood's first name was Beard's Station, in honor of Joe Beard. From that, people would jokingly call it Whiskers. Some of the residents did not take kindly to that nickname. In 1909, the name was changed to Crestwood. One product that has figured prominently in Crestwood's history is orchard grass seed. Oldham County was considered to be the top producer in the country—and possibly the world—until the late 1960s.

The only state burial ground for southern veterans of the Civil War is in Peewee Valley.

Notable residents include:
- Admiral William J. Crowe Jr. (1925–) – La Grange; Ambassador to the United Kingdom under President Bill Clinton and Chairman of the Joint Chiefs of Staff under Presidents Ronald Reagan and George H.W. Bush; he was succeeded by General Colon Powell; in 1989, he made one appearance on the sitcom Cheers

- D. W. Griffith (1875–1948) – La Grange; American film director; his father was a Confederate Army colonel and a Civil War hero; between 1908–1913, he produced 450 short films, an enormous feat for this time; this work enabled him to experiment with cross-cutting (a way of editing disjunct scenes to make it seem as though they happened sequentially), camera movement, close-ups, and other methods of manipulation; some hold that he invented the close-up shot; Griffith found a quaint little town in California in which to film his first film making him the first to shoot a film in Hollywood; he was the first to produce a film that lasted more than an hour; other producers believed that watching a movie very long would hurt the eyes; Charlie Chaplin called Griffith, "The teacher of us all."

Interesting names include: Ballardsville; Cedar Point; Centerfield; Crestwood; Demplytown; Floydsburg; Glenarm; Goshen; Greenhaven; Harmony Village; Lake Louisvilla; Liro; Oldham; Orchard Grass Hills; Park Lake; River Bluff; Russell Corner; Skylight; Westport

OWEN COUNTY (1819) Formed from Franklin, Gallatin, and Scott Counties. The county is named for Colonel Abraham Owen, killed in 1811, at the Battle of Tippecanoe (Indiana) while serving as an aide-de-camp to William Henry Harrison (who later became president of the United States). He surveyed Shelby County in 1796, was in the Kentucky legislature in 1798, and a member of the state Constitutional Convention in 1799. Owen County, Indiana and Owensboro, KY are named for him.

Owenton is the county seat. Gratz was founded in 1847, and was named for B. Gratz Brown who later became governor of Missouri.

Interesting names include: Beechwood; Canby; Cull; Eagle Hill; Fairbanks; Harmony; Holiday Ford; Long Ridge; Monterey; Moxley; Natlee; Needmore; New; New Columbus; New Liberty; Pleasant Home; Poplar Grove; Rockdale; Squiresville; Sweet Owen; Teresita; Wheatley

OWSLEY COUNTY (1843) Formed from Breathitt, Clay, and Estill Counties. The county is named for William Owsley, Kentucky Senate (1832–1834), sixteenth Governor of Kentucky (1844–1848), Kentucky House of Representatives (two terms), and appointed to the Kentucky Court of Appeals two different times.

Born in Virginia, the family moved to Lincoln County, near Crab Orchard, while he was an infant. He later practiced law in Garrard County. As Governor, he worked for improvements in public schools and higer teacher salaries. He retired to his farm in Boyle County until his wife died, after which he lived with his children until he died. He is interred in the Bellview Cemetery, Danville.

Booneville is the county seat.

- Earl Combs (1899–1976) – Pebworth; a former New York Yankee and Hall of Fame inductee (1970), was born in Pebworth; his entire baseball career (1924–1935) was spent with the Yankees; played nearly his entire career batting leadoff in front of Babe Ruth; batted no lower than .299 and scored no fewer than 113 RBIs from his rookie year, 1925 until 1933; played in three World Series championships; set the Yankees team record for the most triples in a season (23 in 1927);

Interesting names include: Chestnut Gap; Cowcreek; Endee; Eversole; Island City; Lerose; Levi; Major; Mistletoe; Pebworth; Ricetown; Southfork; Stay; Sturgeon; Taft; Travellers Rest; Turin; Whoopflarea

PENDLETON COUNTY (1799) Formed from Campbell and Bracken Counties. The county is named for Edmund Pendleton, U.S. Senator, longtime member of the Virginia House of Burgesses, a delegate to the Continental Congress, and Chief Justice of Virginia's Supreme Court. Pendleton County, West Virginia is also named for him.

During the Civil War, the county sent men to both armies. A Union Army recruiting camp was established in Falmouth in September, 1861. Two Confederate recruiters were captured and executed by the Union Army in Peach Grove. In July, 1862, a number of citizens were rounded up by Union troops during a crackdown against suspected Confederate sympathizers. One year later, June, 1863, a number of women were arrested in Demossville, believed to be potential spies against the Union Army.

Falmouth, the county seat, has been the site of three natural disasters in recent history. In 1964, the Licking River reached nineteen feet above flood state, leaving much of the town under water. A 1968 tornado leveled many homes in the town. In 1997, another major flood on the Licking River reached twenty-four feet above flood stage and put 80% of the town under water. Falmouth is where the South and the Main Forks of the Licking River meet.

Notable residents include:
- Phillip Sharp (1944–) – Falmouth; Nobel Prize winner for the discovery of split genes and for advancing research on cancer with hereditary diseases, 1993; born in Falmouth

Interesting names include: Bachelors Rest; Boston; Butler; Caldwell; Concord; Four Oaks; Gardnersville; Goforth; Greenwood; Ivor; Knoxville; Locust Grove; Morgan; Mt Auburn; Peach Grove; Pleasant Hill; Portland

PERRY COUNTY (1821) Formed from Floyd and Clay Counties. Perry County is named for Commodore Oliver Hazard Perry, a naval hero in the War of 1812. Not only did he fly under the flag "DONT GIVE UP THE SHIP," [*sic*], spoken by his friend Captain James Lawrence (for whom Lawrence County is named), his words after the Battle of Lake Erie were, "We have met the enemy and they are ours…." A total of ten Perry Counties are named for him as well as several cities, including Perryville, Kentucky, Perry, New York, Perry and Perrysburg, Ohio, Perry, Iows, and Perry Hilltop, a neighborhood in Pittsburgh, Pennsylvania.

Hazard is the county seat. Both the county and the county seat are named for the same man. Before the railroad came in 1912, the only ways out of the valley were forty-five miles down the North Fork of the Kentucky River or a two-week trip over the surrounding mountains. In July, 1999, the city of Hazard had the dubious honor of being the first stop on President Bill Clinton's tour of poverty-stricken communities that had failed to share in the boom of the late 1990s.

Vicco - This city is on KY 15 and Carr Fork of the North fork of the Kentucky River about five miles ESE of Hazard. Though there may have been a settlement here prior to the establishment of the Montgomery Creek Coal Company mines in the vicinity, it was at this time that the town and its post office were established at Montago, named for the company and the creek which join Carr Fork at this point. The Montago post office, which opened in 1921, was renamed Vicco in 1923, for the Virginia Iron Coal and Coke Company which dominated coal production in the area.

Notable residents include:
- Jean Ritchie (1922–) – Viper; folksinger and Appalachian dulcimer player

Interesting names include: Airport Gardens; Allais; Ary; Avawam; Blue Diamond; Blue Grass No 3; Boat; Bonnyman; Bowlingtown; Buckhorn; Bulan; Busy; Butterfly; Combs; Daisy; Defiance; Delphia; Diablock; Dice; Doorway; Dwarf; Fourseam; Fusonia; Happy; Hardburly; Jeff; Jimhill; Kingdom Come; Kodak; Krypton; Lamont; Leatherwood; Lothair; Manuel; Montago; Pioneer; Rowdy; Scuddy; Slemp; Stacy; Typo; Vicco; Viper; Yerkes

PIKE COUNTY (1821) Formed from Floyd County. The county is named for General Zebulon Montgomery Pike Jr., an officer in the Continental Army and an explorer for whom Pike's Peak in Colorado is named. During that expedition he mapped much of the southern portion of the Louisiana Purchase. He was also sent by the governor of the Louisiana Territory to find the headwaters of the Mississippi, Arkansas, and Red Rivers. Eight states have a Pike County including Pike County, Georgia with Zebulon as its county seat. In addition, there is Pikes Peak, Iowa; Piketon, Ohio; and Zebulon, Kentucky (Pike County).

Pikeville is the county seat. Pike, the state's largest county with 789 square miles, is the world's largest producer of coal. Pikeville College has a medical school. Pikeville has an exposition center that seats 7,000 people. The cut-through contains a four-lane, divided highway, a railroad line, and the Big Sandy River. It is one of the largest land removal projects ever completed in the western hemisphere by the U.S. Army Corps of Engineers and is the second largest earth moving project in the world. The project took fourteen years to complete at a cost of $77.6 million.

Between 1878 and 1891, the Hatfield-McCoy feud raged in Pike and bordering Mingo County, West Virginia.

Mouthcard is a small community on the Virginia border and on the banks of the Levisa Fork of the Big Sandy River. It is at the mouth of two creeks: Big Card Creek and Little Card Creek. U.S. Highway 460 runs through the city. Looming over the town and both creeks is Card Mountain. Breaks Interstate Park, shared by both Kentucky and Virginia, displays a canyon five miles long and 1,600 feet deep. Many regard it as the Grand Canyon of the South.

Fishtrap Lake, seven miles southeast of Pikeville, boasts the highest dam in Kentucky at 195 feet. The lake takes its name from the pioneers who noticed the fish traps used by the Native Americans. This is the geographical area of the Hatfield-McCoy feud.

Notable residents include:
- Patty Loveless (1957–) aka Patricia Lee Ramey – Pikeville; reared in Elkhorn City; family moved to Louisville when she was twelve years old; country singer
- Dwight Yoakam (1956–) – Pikeville; actor/country singer; reared in Columbus, Ohio
- Robert Damron (1972–) – Pikeville; professional golfer on the PGA Tour

Pikeville annually leads the nation, per capita, in consumption of Pepsi-Cola. The city of Pikeville is four air miles from Floyd County to the west and thirty air miles from West Virginia to the east. The Pikeville airport is two air miles from the Floyd County line.

Interesting names include: Aflex; Allegheny Mine; Argo; Arrow; Ashcamp; Bear Fork; Beaver Bottom; Beaver Creek; Beefhide; Belcher; Belfry; Big Branch; Big Card; Blue John; Board Tree; Bobtown; Bourbon; Broad Bottom; Burnetta; Burnwell; Camp Creek; Canada; Cedarville; Coal Run Village; Coin; Columbiatown; Crooked Creek; Dorema; Dorton; Douglas; Draffin; Drum; Dry Fork; Edgewater; Elihu; Elkhorn City; Etty; Fallsburg; Federal; Fedscreek; Ferrell; Flatwoods; Forest Hills; Freeburn; Garden Village; Goodman; Goody; Greasy Creek; Gulnare; Hardy; Hatfield (2 miles from Hatfield, WV) Hellier; Henry Clay; Honey Fork; Hurricane; Hylton; Indian Creek; Jamboree; Jonancy; Justiceville; Kettlecamp; Kewanee; Kingbee; Lick Creek; Little Dixie; Little Floyd County; Long Fork; Lookout; Majestic; Mark; Marrowbone; Mayflower; Meathouse; Mikegrady; Mossy Bottom; Myra; Nampa; New Camp; Nigh; Orinoco; Owsley; Paw Paw; Penny; Phyllis; Pigeon; Pigeon Roost; Pinson; Pinsonfork; Piso; Pleasant Valley; Raccoon; Ransom; Republic; Road Fork; Rockhouse; Rural; Senterville; Sharondale; Shelbiana; Sidney; Speight; Stone; Stopover; Stringtown; Sycamore; Tom Ray; Toonerville; Turkey Creek; Upper Elk; Varney; Virgie; Wales; Wolfpit; Woodman; Woodside; Yorktown

POWELL COUNTY (1852) Formed from Clark, Estill, and Montgomery Counties. The county is named for Lazarus Whitehead Powell the nineteenth Kentucky Governor (1851–1855), Kentucky House of Representatives, and U.S. Senator. His election as governor marked the end of the Whig dominance in Kentucky. He was born and died in Henderson County.

Stanton is the county seat. Powell County was named for Lazarus W. Powell, Kentucky House of Representatives, U.S. Senate, and governor from 1851–1855. He was born in Henderson and graduated from St. Joseph College, Bardstown. He began practicing law in Henderson in 1835. He died in Henderson.

The natural sandstone arch, from which Natural Bridge State Resort Park takes its name, spans seventy-eight feet and is sixty-five feet high. Near Natural Bridge is Red River Gorge national Geological Area. More than eighty natural arches and the Red River (Kentucky's only National Wild and Scenic River) makes this area unique.

Notable residents include:
- Woody Stephens (1913–1998) – Stanton; Hall of Fame thoroughbred horse trainer

Interesting names include: Black Creek; Cat Creek; Clay City; Crow; Happy Top; Judy; Lombard; Lone Oak; Morris Creek; Nada; Old Lombard; Paint Creek; Pecks Creek; Powell Valley; Slade; South Fork; Spout Springs; Stanton; Virden; Waltersville; Westbend

PULASKI COUNTY (1799) Formed from Green and Lincoln Counties. The county is named for Count Kazimierz Pulaski, a former Polish soldier who became a General and named the father of American cavalry. He fought in the Revolutionary War and died from wounds received at the Battle of Savannah and was buried at sea. His full name is Kazimierz Michal Waclaw Pulaski herbu Slepowron. The state of Kentucky has by law, since before 1942, recognized General Pulaski's Day. By presidential proclamation, each October 11 is General Pulaski Memorial Day. Each October Grand Rapids, Michigan, celebrates Pulaski Days. The state of Illinois has celebrated a Pulaski Day on the first Monday in March since 1977. Wisconsin and Indiana extend similar regognition and Milwaukee, Wisconsin, holds an annual parade and school holiday. On his day there is a Pulaski Day parade in New York City. There is a statue of General Pulaski on his horse (right fore leg raised) in Freedom Plaza, Washington, D.C. Counties in Arkansas, Georgia, Illinois, Indiana, Iowa, Missouri, and Virginia have counties named for him as well as towns in Georgia, Illinois, Iowa, Mississippi, New York, Tennessee, Virginia, and Wisconsin.

Somerset is the county seat. Burnside was originally named Isabel Point but the name was changed after the Civil War to honor General Ambrose Burnside who established a camp there during the war. In the 1950s, the entire town was relocated for the impounding of Lake Cumberland. Burnside is believed to the home of the first Boy Scout troop in America. Ferguson was first named Luethra for postmaster George Wynn's daughter. It was renamed in 1950 for Cincinnati attorney Edward Ferguson who helped get railroad tracks laid through the community in 1869. Science Hill was given its name by William

Gragg, its first postmaster, because local scientist William Bobbitt spent time there analyzing rocks. Somerset is home of the POW/MIA Memorial Garden, believed to be the only such memorial in Kentucky and only one of a few in the nation. It is dedicated to the American servicemen and women listed as Prisoners of War/Missing in Action since World War I.

Notable residents include:
- John Sherman Cooper (1901–1991) – Somerset; U.S. Senator for 20 years, U.S. Ambassador to India and Germany, member of the Warren Commission (investigating President John Kennedy's assassination)
- Edwin P. Morrow (1877–1935) – Somerset; Kentucky governor from 1919–1923

Interesting names include: Acorn; Albia; Alpine; Ano; Bee Lick; Bent; Blue John; Bobtown; Bourbon; Burnside; Cains Store; Cedar Grove; Clarence; Coin; Concord; Conrad; Dorena; Drum; Elihu; Estesburg; Etna; Ferguson; Floyd; Goodwater; Grade; Hail; Keno; Kingbee; Mount Victory; Mt Zion; Nancy; Naomi; Oak Hill; Oil Center; Omega; Piney Grove; Plato; Pointer; Poplarville; Public; Pulaski; Ringgold; Ruth; Sandy Gap; Sardis; Science Hill; Shopville; Squib; Stab; Sugar Hill; Trimble; Valley Oak; Walnut Grove; Whetstone; Woodstock

ROBERTSON COUNTY (1867) Formed from Bracken, Harrison, Mason, and Nicholas Counties. The county is named for Kentucky Congressman George Robertson, from 1817-1821. It is Kentucky's smallest county with one hundred square miles of land (compared to Pike County's 790 square miles) and a population of 2,226 in the 2000 Census. The density population is twenty-five people per square mile (compared to Jefferson County's 1,800 people per square mile).

Mount Olivet (county seat) was formed around 1820, and named for the biblical Mount of Olives.

Interesting names include: Abigail; Alhambra; Hittville; Mount Olivet; Piqua

ROCKCASTLE COUNTY (1810) Formed from Knox, Lincoln, Madison, and Pulaski Counties. The county is named for the Rockcastle River that runs through it. In 1750, Dr. Thomas Walker noticed a rock on a mountain above Livingston that resembled a castle and in 1767, Isaac Lindsey named this rock Castle Rock. The river below was named Rockcastle River and when the county was formed, it took the name of Rockcastle County.

Mt. Vernon became the county seat in 1818, and was named for George Washington's home Mount Vernon. Renfro Valley is famous for the historic Renfro Valley Barn Dance which was aired on WHAS, Louisville, beginning in 1939. The show actually began two years earlier, but it did not originate from Renfro Valley. Red Foley ("Peace in the Valley") hosted the barn dance for a time. Renfro Valley is also home to the Kentucky Music Hall of Fame Museum which opened in 2002.

Interesting names include: Billows; Bloss; Boone; Broadhead; Bromo; Bummer; Burr; Climax; Disputant; Flat Rock; Gum Sulphur; Hiatt; Hummel; Johnetta; Level Green; Livingston; Orlando; Ottawa; Pine Hill; Pongo; Quail; Renfro Valley; Roundstone; Sand Springs; Sinks; Spiro; Threelinks; Wabd; Wellhope; Wildie; Willailla

ROWAN COUNTY (1856) Formed from Fleming and Morgan Counties. The county is named for John Rowan, U.S. House of Representatives, U.S. Senator, two separate terms in Kentucky House of Representatives, Kentucky Secretary of State, and Kentucky Court of Appeals. Born near York, Pennsylvania, Rowan's family moved to Kentucky when he was ten years old. He studied law in Lexington and practiced law in Louisville. He was interred in the family burial ground at Federal Hill, near Bardstown (Nelson County).

Morehead, the county seat, is named for James T. Morehead, Kentucky House of Representatives, U.S. Senate, lieutenant governor of Kentucky (two terms), and twelfth governor (1834–1836) when Governor John Breathitt died. He was the first Kentucky-born governor (Bullitt County). He attended Transylvania University and practiced law in Bowling Green. He is buried in the Frankfort Cemetery. Morehead was probably the third community to be settled in the area and became the county seat when the county was formed in 1856. Rowan was formed out of Fleming and Morgan Counties in 1856. Only 32% of the county is farmland; the government owns 35% of the county.

It is believed that a party of surveyors from Pennsylvania, led by George William Thompson, first explored the area in the summer of 1773. The first settlers came mostly from Virginia to claim land granted to them from serving in the Revolutionary War. Farmers remained the largest community until around 1900, when the logging industry was depleted.

Cave Run Lake dam is 148 feet tall and one-half mile long. The largest muskie ever caught in Kentucky (44.38 lbs) was caught in Cave Run Lake. Morehead State University was originally founded as Morehead Normal School, a church-supported teachers training school, in 1887, by Phobee Button. It is said to have been comprised of thirteen buildings with a layout in the shape of a crescent moon. The university has satellite campuses in Ashland, Jackson, Prestonsburg, and West Liberty. In 1911, Moonlight Schools were first established in Rowan County to give night instructions to pupils of all ages.

Notable alumni of Morehead State University include:
- Chuck Woolery (1941–) – Ashland; game show host
- Lori Menshouse – former Miss Kentucky
- Jon Rauch (1978–) – Louisville; National League pitcher for Washington Nationals; at 6 feet 11 inches tall, he is the tallest player in the history of the major leagues
- Walt Terrell (1958–) – Jeffersonville, Indiana; Major League pitcher, 1982-1992, with Mets, Tigers, Padres, Yankess, Pirates

- Denny Doyle (1943–) – Glasgow; second baseman for Phillies, Angels, Red Sox; career batting average is .250
- Steve Inskeep – a co-host on "Morning Edition," National Public Radio
- Marsha Griffith – former Miss Kentucky
- Mike Gottfried (1945–) – former NCAA football coach for Pittsburgh, Kansas, Cincinnati, and Murray State University; currently an ESPN college football analyst and color commentator, and uncle of Alabama's head football coach Mark Gottfried
- Henry Akin (1944–) – Detroit, Michigan; delayed graduation from Morehead to be drafted by the NY Knicks; later became one of the "Original Sonics" in Seattle; also played with KY Colonels of the ABA

Interesting names include: Bangor; Bluestone; Brady; Christy; Cogswell; Elliottville; Farmers (first developed community in Rowan County); Gates; Hamin; Hays Crossing; Hilda; Lick Fork; Minor; Paragon; Rockville; Rodburn; Smile; Triplett; Waltz

RUSSELL COUNTY (1826) Formed from Adain, Wayne, and Cumberland Counties. The county is named for William Russell, soldier, pioneer, and politician from Fayette County who fought in Revolutionary War and the War of 1812. In 1773, his family left Virginia in an attempt to establish a permanent settlement in Kentucky for the British government. The party was led by Daniel Boone. However, the attempt was thwarted when Indian attacked the travelers. The Indians captured Russell's brother Henry Russell and James Boone, son of Daniel Boone. Both boys were tortured to death. Russellville in Logan County is also named for him.

Jamestown, the county seat, was first named Jacksonville in 1826, in honor of General Andrew Jackson. By the next year the settlement was incorporated and renamed Jamestown in honor of James Wooldridge who had donated the land for the town. Russell Springs is the largest city in Russell County. The area had survived since the 1850s, as a health resort because of its location near a chalybeate spring. Chalybeate is a word meaning "containing iron." Chalybeate waters are also known as ferruginous waters. Ferruginous comes from the Latin word "ferreous" meaning "made of iron." The town itself was founded in 1850 by Samuel Patterson and was referred to as Big Boiling Springs. The first post office was established in 1855, and named Kimble in honor of leading businessman George Kimble. In 1901, the town was renamed Russell Springs. Creelsboro was at one time the busiest river port on the Cumberland River between Burnside and Nashville, although its population stayed about fifty.

Notable residents include:
- Tara Conner (1985–) – Dallas, Texas; Miss USA 2006

Lake Cumberland has more miles of shoreline than the state of Florida.

Interesting names include: Bryan; Catherine; Creelsboro; Denmark; Dent; Eli; Esto; Fonthill; Freedom; Happy Acre; Helm; Horntown; Humble; Jabez; Jericho; Long Bottom; Middletown; Old Olga; Olga; Ono; Ribbon; Rose Crossroads; Rowena; Salem; Sycamore Flat; Whittle

SCOTT COUNTY (1792) Formed from Woodford County. The county is named for Kentucky's fourth governor (1808-1812) General Charles Scott who served in the French and Indian War, the Revolutionary War, weathering the winter at Valley Forge, and served as General Washington's intelligence officer in later campaigns. While governor, he was most instrumental in preparing the state to participate in the War of 1812.

Georgetown is the county seat. Scott County was explored as early as 1774. The area became subject to hostile Indian attacks and was abandoned in 1777. In 1783, Robert Johnson established the first permanent settlement at Johnsons Station. Georgetown was established in 1786 by Rev. Elijah Craig and his Baptist church members, and originally known as Lebanon Station, Virginia. In 1790, the city was incorporated and renamed Georgetown in honor of President George Washington.

Scott County was one of the first counties created after statehood. It was named for Revolutionary War hero Brigadier General Charles Scott who served in the French and Indian War and the Revolutionary War in which he served under General George Washington. He was captured by the British in 1779, and held for two years. Born in Cumberland County, Virginia he moved to Woodford County after the American Revolution. He served as governor 1808-1812. He is buried in Frankfort. Scott County, Indiana is also named for him. During the Civil War, Scott County furnished the Union Army with 118 troops and the Confederate Army with one thousand troops.

Georgetown College traces its origins to the Royal Springs (later Rittenhouse) Academy, founded in 1787 by Baptist minister Elijah Craig; Ward Hall is said to be the largest Greek Revival house in Kentucky and is often referred to as the finest example of Greek Revival Architecture in the south; Georgetown College is the site of summer training camp for the Cincinnati Bengals; it is the only NFL training camp in Kentucky.

- James Fisher Robinson (1800–1882) – twenty-second governor of Kentucky (1862–1863) serving the unfinished term of Governor Beriah Magoffin who resigned during the Civil War

Interesting names include: Biddle; Clabber Bottom; Cranetown; Double Culvert; Georgetown; Josephine; Locust; Minorsville; Muddy Ford; New Zion; Newtown; Oxford; Peak; Sadieville; Sand Lick; Shiff; Skinnersburg; Skullbuster; Stamping Ground; Stonewall; Turkey Foot; White Sulphur; Zion Hill

SHELBY COUNTY (1792) Formed from Jefferson County. Shelby County is named for Isaac Shelby, Kentucky's first (1792–1796) and fifth (1812–1816) governor. At the time, Kentucky's Constitution prevented a governor from serving consecutive terms. During the War of 1812, General William Henry Harrison called upon Kentucky to provide volunteers for his Army of the Northwest. General Harrison also personally asked Governor Shelby to lead the Kentucky units. Shelby, known as "Old Kings Mountain" among his troops, led the Kentuckians into action at the Battle of the Thames (War of 1812). Upon leaving office in 1816, President James Monroe offered Shelby the post of Secretary of War, but Shelby declined. He died at his home of Traveler's Rest in Lincoln County, 1826. He is buried in Frankfort Cemetery. Places named for Shelby include: Shelby County, Alabama, Illinois, Indiana, Iowa, Ohio, Missouri, Tennessee, Texas, and Shelby, North Carolina.

Shelbyville, the county seat, was founded on land donated by William Shannon in 1792. It is known as the Saddlebred Capital of the world, the only breed of horse that originated in Kentucky.

Notable residents include:
- Colonel Harland Sanders (1890–1980) – Henryville, Indiana; lived in Shelby County from 1960 until his death in 1980
- Martha Layne Collins (1936–) – Bagdad; first female governor of Kentucky (1983–1987)

Interesting names include: Bagdad; Chestnut Grove; Christianburg; Clay Village; Consolation; Cropper; Elmburg; Finchville; Harrisonville; Hemp Ridge; Jacksonville; Junte; Lincoln Ridge; Mt Eden; Mulberry; Old Christianburg; Olive Branch; Pleasureville; Shelbyville; Snow Hill; Southville; Waddy

SIMPSON COUNTY (1819) Formed from Allen, Logan, and Warren Counties. The county is named for Captain John Simpson who fought during Northwest Indian War and died in the Battle of River Raisin, near Detroit, Michigan, in the War of 1812.

Franklin, the county seat, was named in honor of Benjamin Franklin.

Simpson County's border with Tennessee is not a straight line, as is the case with most other border counties. Instead, the county/state line dips slightly into Tennessee. Sanford Duncan, owner of extensive holdings west of the L and N Railroad, wanted no part of his land to be in Tennessee, since he was extremely loyal to Kentucky. He requested that the surveyors include all his land in Kentucky, but the request was denied. When the surveyors reached his property at nightfall, they were invited to spend the night. During the evening the surveyors were taken to his well-stocked cellar where he saw to it that they liberally sampled his supply of wines and cider. As a result, his original request was granted. Today the Kentucky-Tennessee state line follows what were the boundaries of Duncan's holdings, making a dip of about two miles into Tennessee and stretching about four miles east and west.

Notable residents include:
- Annie Potts (1952–), Nashville, Tennessee; grew up in Franklin, Kentucky; *Designing Women* (1986-1993), *Ghostbusters* (I and II), *Little Bo Peep in Toy Story* (I and II), *Ghostbusters* (III, 2008, not yet confirmed), and *Joan of Arcadia*
- Johnny Cash (1932–2003) – Kingsland, Arkansas and June Carter Cash (1929–2003) – Maces Spring, Virginia – were married in a private ceremony March 1, 1968, at Franklin United Methodist Church
- Kentucky Downs, owned by Churchill Downs, on the Kentucky-Tennessee border near Franklin

Interesting names include: Black Jack; Flat Rock; Franklin; Geddes; Gold City; Hickory Flat; Highland; Hillsdale; Neosheo; Petroleum; Prices Mill; Providence; Rapids; Salmons; Schweizer; Temperance

SPENCER COUNTY (1824) Formed from Nelson, Shelby, and Bullitt Counties. Spencer County is named for Spier Spencer who led a company of mounted riflemen and died at the Battle of Tippecanoe, Indiana, on November 7, 1811.

Taylorsville, the county seat, was founded in1799 on the land of Richard Taylor. William Quantrill, famous Confederate guerrilla raider, was killed by Union troops near Taylorsville in 1865, just before the end of the Civil War. Confederate guerrillas burned the courthouse in January, 1865, but the county's records were saved.

Interesting names include: Elk Creek; Little Mount; Mount Eden (beside Mt Eden in Shelby County); Ninevah; Normandy; Rivals; Waterford; Wilsonville; Yoder

TAYLOR COUNTY (1848) Formed from Green County. The county is named for Zachary Taylor (1849–1850), the nation's twelfth president. He was the first president to never have held a previous political office and the only president from Louisiana. President James Madison, the nantion's fourth President, was a second cousin, and Robert E. Lee was a third cousin. Although born in Virginia, he lived in Kentucky from infancy. His daughter, Sarah Knox Taylor, married Jefferson Davis who became the president of the CSA. She died from malaria three month after the wedding. President Taylor is buried in the Zachary Taylor (twelfth president) National Cemetery, Louisville. A twelve cent postage stamp, issued in 1938, bears his likeness.

Campbellsville, the county seat, was formed in 1817, and named for Andrew Campbell and Adam Campbell who migrated from Augusta County, Virginia. From the 1830s to the 1870's, Campbellsville served as a stage coach stop on the National Mail Route between Zanesville, Ohio and Florence, Alabama.

During the Civil War, Campbellsville was on the invasion routes of both the southern and the northern armies. The Battle of Tebbs Bend on the Green River in 1863, proved to be a stunning victory for the Union Army. After the battle, private homes and churches were used as hospitals.

Chandler Novelty opened its doors in 1892, and today is the oldest business in continuous operation in Campbellsville. It is the only incorporated city in Taylor County.

Campbellsville is home to Campbellsville University.

In addition to being shaped like a heart, Taylor County is close to the geographic center of the state. Formed in 1848, Taylor County became the one hundredth county in order of establishment.

Green River Lake State Park is in Taylor County.

Notable residents include:
- Clem Haskins (1943–), Campbellsville; former basketball coach for Western Kentucky Hilltoppers and Minnesota Golden Gophers

Interesting names include: Acton; Arista; Atchison; Badger; Bengal; Black Gnat; Elk Horn; Hibernia; Maple; Merrimac; Romine; Saloma; South Campbellsville; Speck; White Rose; Willowtown; Yuma

TODD COUNTY (1820) Formed from Christian and Logan Counties. The county is named for John Todd, an early frontier military figure during the Revolutionary War. He was born in Montgomery County, Pennsylvania and was the grandfather of Mary Todd Lincoln, President Abraham Lincoln's wife. In 1774, he fought in the Battle of Point Pleasant (West Virginia), which is considered to be the first battle of the Revolutionary War. When the Virginia Legislature divided Kentucky County into the three counties of Lincoln, Jefferson, and Fayette, John Todd was placed in charge of the Fayette County militia with Daniel Boone as lieutenant colonel. Todd died in 1782 during the Battle of Blue Licks in Robertson County, the last battle of the Revolutionary War in Kentucky. The following story was told by his wife to illustrate Todd's character:

> During the winter following their marriage the provisions of the fort at Lexington became exhausted to such an extent that on her husband's return home one night with his colored man George, the two being famished with hunger, that she presented him with a small piece of bread and a gill of milk. He asked if there was food for George. When told there was none, Todd gave the bread and milk to George and went to bed hungry.

Elkton, the county seat, was founded by Major John Gray, but named for a nearby pre-pioneer watering hole used by a large elk herd. Milliken Memorial Community House, built 1928, is the first privately donated community house in America. The 13,000 square foot mansion pioneered a new architecture for public use. In 1926, the house was

242

commissioned by Mary Louise Milliken and her husband Samuel Canning Childs, two wealthy philanthropists who were also responsible for the financing of two churches and over twenty hospitals throughout the United States. The cost for the house was $75,000, which translates to a worth of at least $1,300,000 in today's market. The Milliken family lineage can be traced to Colonel John Todd, for whom the county was named and who was an uncle to Mary Todd Lincoln.

In 1865, Union troops confiscated the Confederate courthouse and used it as headquarters. After the court-house was abandoned, the Union troops left the building in shambles.

Notable residents include:
- Robert Penn Warren (1905–1989) – Guthrie; first poet laureate of the United States
- Benjamin Bristow (1832–1896) – Elkton; U.S. Treasury Secretary (1874–1876); assisted in the capture of John Hunt Morgan, July, 1863
- Paul Marvin Rudolph (1918–1997) – Elkton; an American architect and dean of the Yale School of Architecture for six years
- Jefferson Davis (1808–1889) – Christian County, now Todd County; the only president of the Confederate States of America, 1860-1865; the Jefferson Davis Monument, erected on the spot where he was born, is the tallest (371 feet) concrete obelisk in the world; the concrete walls are eight and one-half feet thick at the bottom and two and one-half feet thick at the top; eight months after Davis was born, and one hundred miles away, another great Kentucky statesman was born - Abraham Lincoln

Interesting names include: Allegre; Anderson; Britmart; Cedar Grove; Clifty; Darnell; Daysville; Elkton; Guthrie; Hadensville; Hammacksville; Horse Creek; Jason; Liberty; Pea Ridge; Pinchem; Sharon Grove; Tabernacle; Tiny Town; Trenton; Tress Shop; Tyewhoppety; Wilhelmina; Zion

TRIGG COUNTY (1820) Formed from Caldwell and Christian Counties. The county is named for Stephen Trigg, an officer in the Revolutionary War who died in the Battle of Blue Licks, Robertson County, which was the greatest defeat for Kentuckians during the war.

Cadiz is the county seat (pronounced CA-diz). The lodge at Lake Barkley State Resort Park gives one a panoramic view through three and one-half acres of glass.

Interesting names include: Black Hawk; Blue Spring; Buffalo; Cadiz; Caledonia; Canton; Cedar Point; Cerulean; Golden Pond; Horse Creek; Maggie; Maple Grove; Montgomery; Roaring Spring; Rockcastle; Trigg Furnace; Wallonia

TRIMBLE COUNTY (1837) Formed from Gallatin, Henry, and Oldham Counties. The county is named for Robert Trimble, attorney, Kentucky House of Representatives, Kentucky Court of Appeals, U.S. District Judge for Kentucky appointed by James

Madison, and Associate Justice of the U.S. Supreme Court appointed by John Quincy Adams. He is buried in the Paris Cemetery, Bourbon County.

Bedford is the county seat.

Interesting names include: Bedford; Corn Creek; Monitor; Mount Pleasant; Providence; Sligo; Trout; Wises Landing

UNION COUNTY (1811) Formed from Henderson County. Union County was formed from the united desire of the residents to form a new county.

Morganfield, the county seat, is named for Revolutionary War General Daniel Morgan who received the land on which the city now sits as pay for his military service. The courthouse, built in 1811, is still in use today and is the site of the only political speech Abraham Lincoln made in his native Kentucky, 1840. Abraham Lincoln, age 31, was campaigning for William Henry Harrison, presidential candidate for the Whig party.

The town of Sturgis is also known as Little Sturgis because they have a bikers' rally each year, modeled after the one in Sturgis, South Dakota.

Notable residents include:
- Earl Chester Clements (1896–1985) – Morganfield; Kentucky Senator, U.S. Representative, U.S. Senator (serving alongside John Sherman Cooper and Alben W. Barkley), and Kentucky governor (1948–1950); as governor, he made state parks and state roads a high priority; Kentucky's unusually wide-spread system of four-lane, divided highways is a legacy of Clements' governorship; established the Kentucky State Police to replace the semi-corrupt highway patrol; he failed to convince the Kentucky General Assembly to end segregation in Kentucky's graduate and professional schools, regulate strip mining, or establish a statewide pension for civil service programs; was succeeded by Lawrence Wetherby
- Kassie DePaiva (1961–); Morganfield; born Katherine Virginia Wesley; a soap opera actress; played the part of Chelsa Reardon on "Guiding Light" (1986–1991) and has played the part of Blair Daimler Cramer on "One Life to Live" since 1993; is one of the few characters in soap operas who changed ethnicity—from Asian to Caucasion; at the age of eighteen she made her singing debut on stage at the Grand Ole Opry

Interesting names include: Boxville; Caney Mound; Curlew; Dekoven; Grove Center; Gum Grove; Hamner; Harding; Hazel; Herman Valley; Morganfield; Pride; Raleigh; St Vincent; Salem; Seven Gums; Spring Grove; Sturgis (aka Little Sturgis); Sulphur Springs; The Rocks; Uniontown; Walnut Grove; Yuba

WARREN COUNTY (1797) Formed from Logan County. The county is named for General Joseph Warren, a doctor and soldier in the Revolutionary War and the hero of Bunker Hill. His commission had not yet taken effect when when three days later the Battle of Bunker Hill was fought. He served as a volunteer private against the wishes of General Israel Putnam and Colonel William Prescott who requested that he serve as their commander. He fought in the front lines, rallying his troops to the third and final assault of the battle when he was killed instantly by a musket ball fired into his head by a British officer who recognized him. At the time of his death, his children were staying with Abigail Adams at the John Quincy Adams birthplace in Quincy, Massachusetts. Following Warren's death, Benedict Arnold supported them until they were of age. Fourteen states have a Warren County in addition to the cities of Warren, Michigan, Warren, New Jersey, Warrenton, Virginia, and Warren, Massachusetts. John Warren, Joseph Warren's younger brother, served as a surgeon during the Battle of Bunker Hill and the remainder of the war, after which he founded Harvard Medical School.

Bowling Green, the county seat, founded in 1798, was named after Robert Moore and George Moore who donated thirty-five acres to the Warren County Trustees. Bowling Green declared itself neutral during the Civil War but because of its prime location and abundant resources, both Union and Confederate Armies sought to control the city.

The General Motors Corvette assembly plant opened in 1981, and the Cadillac XLR assembly plant opened in 2003. The National Corvette Museum opened in 1994. Western Kentucky University began in 1906. Lost River Cave has the only underground boat tour in Kentucky. Ripley's Believe It or Not reports that it is the shortest and deepest river in the world. In the 1930s, the cave was a night club complete with big bands and ballroom dancing.

Notable residents include:
- Deborah Renshaw (1975–) – Bowling Green; NASCAR driver; ran fourteen out of fifteen races of the 2004 NASCAR Craftsman Truck Series season
- Brian Rose (1979–) – driver in NASCAR Craftsman Truck Series
- Sam Bush (1952–) – Bowling Green; mandolin player and bluegrass vocalist; called a modern day Bill Monroe
- Larry Jones - founder of Feed the Children based in Oklahoma City, Oklahoma
- Jody Richards (1938–) - served with the U.S. Army Reserve; formerly Speaker of the House of the Kentucky House of Representatives
- Duncan Hines (1880–1959) – Bowling Green; restaurant-guide publisher; during his years as a traveling salesman through many states he learned where the good and bad restaurants and hotels were; his recommendations became so popular that in 1935, he published a list of his top 167 restaurants and sent them along with his Christmas cards; the response was so overwhelming that in 1936, he published *Adventures in Good Eating*, and expanded his list of excellent restaurants; by 1938, Hines had found a new career and published a guide to the best hotels and motels in America; after being featured in the "Saturday Evening Post," Hines' influence on

the American public exploded; he used this trust to help reform American restaurants; in 1949, he joined forces with another businessman and formed Hines-Park Foods, Inc., which began producing over 250 boxed, canned, and bottled products; in 1956, Hines-Park merged with Proctor and Gamble; it was after this time that the boxed cake mix was introduced to the American housewives; in August, 2007, the Kentucky Museum, on the campus of Western Kentucky University, opened its doors to a permanent exhibit showcasing the life of Duncan Hines

- Roger Davis (1939–) – Bowling Green; television actor best known for roles in *Dark Shadows* and *Alias Smith and Jones*

Interesting names include: Anna; Barren River; Blue Level; Boiling Spring; Bowling Green; Cave Hill; Girkin; Greencastle; Greenhill; Greenwood; Guy; Hardcastle; Hays; Hydro; Lost River; Loving; Motley; Oakland; Petros; Plano; Plum Springs; Rich Pond; Riverside; Sand Hill; Springhill; Sunnyside; Three Forks; Three Springs; Woodburn

WASHINGTON COUNTY (1792) Formed from Jefferson County. The county is named for George Washington, the first president of the United States. General Washington successfully led the Continental Army to victory over the British during the Revolutionary War. He is the only president to receive 100% of the electoral votes—twice. His salary as president was $25,000. During his funeral, Henry Lee said that of all Americans, he was "first in war, first in peace, and first in the hearts of his countrymen."

Springfield is the county seat. The Washington County courthouse is Kentucky's oldest courthouse still in continuous use. Mordecai Lincoln House, built in 1797 by Mordecai Lincoln, the oldest son of Captain Abraham Lincoln and uncle of President Abraham Lincoln. The only extant structure owned and occupied by a member of the Lincoln family in Kentucky still standing on its original site and in largely unaltered condition.

Interesting names include: Battle; Bearwallow; Briartown; Brush Grove; Cardwell; Croakers; Jimtown; Maud; Pleasant Grove; Seaville; Sharpsville; Tablow; Tatham Springs; Texas; Thompsonville; Valley Hill

WAYNE COUNTY (1800) Formed from Cumberland and Pulaski Counties. The county is named for Anthony "Mad Anthony" Wayne, a general in the Revolutionary War and a member of the U.S. House of Representatives. A total of thirteen counties and seventeen cities are named for him including Wayne Township, now the city of Huber Heights, Ohio. Wayne was the first to attempt to provide basic training for Army recruits. He received the nickname "Mad Anthony" because he was struck in the skull by a musket ball during the Battle of Stony Point in 1799. Military surgeon Absalom Baird removed the broken fragments of his skull and replaced them with a steel plate in an operation called cranioplasty which was pioneered in the 1600s. A side effect of the operation was

246

occasional epileptic-like seizures which would cause Wayne to fall to the ground spastically and foam at the mouth, hence, the nickname.

Monticello, the county seat, advertises itself as "The Houseboat Capital of the World" due to the many houseboat manufacturers in the city. The city sits next to Lake Cumberland.

Notable residents include:
- Hal Rogers (1937–) – Monticello; U.S. House of Representatives since 1981; in 2003, the Daniel Boone Parkway was renamed the Hal Rogers Parkway (over the objection of some historians) in honor of Rogers' efforts to have the parkway's construction bonds paid by the federal government

Interesting names include: Barrier; Bertram Mountain; Bertrum Mountain; Bethesda; Betsey; Cedar Knob; Cedarcrest; Delta; Flossie; Frisby; Gapcreek; Gregory; Jimtown; Kidder; Low Gap; Mill Springs; Monticello; Mount Pisgah; Murl; Number One; Oil Valley; Powersburg; Pueblo; Rockybranch; Short Mountain; Slat; Static; Sumpter; Sunnybrook; Susie; Touristville; Wait; Windy; Zula

WEBSTER COUNTY (1860) Formed from Henderson, Hopkins, and Union Counties. The county is named for Daniel Webster, U.S. House of Representatives, U.S. Senate, and Secretary of State. In the movie "Mr. Smith Goes to Washington," James Stewart's character is amazed to find out that he will be sitting in the same Senate seat as Daniel Webster.

Dixon, the county seat, is named for Archibald Dixon, lieutenant governor of Kentucky and U.S. Senator. The town of Providence was named after Providence, Rhode Island. Pioneer Gustavis Slaughter won the right to name the town of Slaughters during a card game in 1855. The town of Sebree is named for Colonel E. G. Sebree who founded it in 1868. The town of Wheatcroft is named for Irving Wheatcroft who laid out the town in 1899. Webster County, one of the leading coal producing counties in the Western Coal Field region, has produced more than 325 million tons of coal since 1869.

Interesting names include: Bellville; Clay, Derby; Diamond; Elmwood; Free Union; Jolly; Liberty; Little Zion; Pratt; Providence; Sebree; Slaughters; Steamport Landing; Virginia; Wanamaker; Wheatcroft

WHITLEY COUNTY (1818) Formed from Knox County. The county is named for Colonel William Whitley. He was a member of the Kentucky House of Representatives and an American pioneer who fought many times with the Indians in an effort to secure the Wilderness Road and who fought in War of 1812. In the 1790s, Whitley built the first brick house in Kentucky near the present-day town of Crab Orchard in Lincoln County. The house includes a secret passage for escape and survival during raids by Indians. Whitley City in McCreary County is also named for him. Williamsburg, the county seat, was formed in 1818, and named for Colonel William Whitley. The Cumberland River runs through the city. Williamsburg is home to the University of the Cumberlands (formerly Cumberland College).

Notable residents include:
- Patricia Neal (1926–) – Packard; actress; *The Miracle Worker, Breakfast at Tiffany's* and thirty other films

Interesting names include: Bark Camp; Carpenter; Clio; Corbin (city limits in Whitley, Laurel, and Knox counties); Dal; Dixie; Duckrun; Fairview; Goldbug; Grove; Jellico; Joe Branch; Julip; Liberty; Lot; Lucky; Meadow Creek; Mountain Ash; Packard; Pearl; Pleasant View; Rain; Red Ash; Redbird; Rockholds; Savoy; Tidal Wave; Woodbine

WOLFE COUNTY (1860) Formed from Breathitt, Owsley, and Powell Counties. The county is named for Nathaniel Wolfe, member of the Kentucky General Assembly. Wolfe County's density saturation is thirty-two persons per square mile.

Campton is the county seat. The Torrent Falls Family Climbing Adventure is the first climbing adventure park in the United States.

Interesting names include: Antioch; Baptist; Bethany; Booth; Calaboose; Daysboro; Flat; Gilmore; Grannie; Hazel Green; Helechawa; High Falls; Landsaw; Lee City; Lexie; Lower Gilmore; Malaga; Mary; Nelson; Pine Ridge; Rosefork; Rye; Standing Rock; Stillwater; Torrent; Upper Gilmore; Valerie; Vortex; Wolf Pen; Zachariah

WOODFORD COUNTY (1789) Formed from Fayette County. Woodford County is named for General William Woodford, who was with General George Washington at Valley Forge. He was captured at the Battle of Monmluth in 1789, and sent to new York where he died aboard a British prison ship.

Versailles, the county seat, was founded in 1792 on eighty acres of ground owned by Hezekiah Briscoe, who was only a child at the time. His guardian, Marquis Calmes, named the town after Versailles, France in honor of General Lafayette. The city was occupied briefly during the Civil War by both Confederate and Union forces. The town of Midway is midway between Lexington and Frankfort. Pisgah Presbyterian Church, established 1784, was the first Presbyterian church west of the Allegheny Mountains.

Notable residents include:
- Ben Chandler (1959–) – Versailles; former U.S. House of Representatives; Kentucky Attorney General
- Although "Happy" Chandler lived here, he was born in Corydon, Henderson County

Interesting names include: Bonita; Duckers; Faywood; Hunter Town; Midway; Nonesuch; Pisgah; Shetland; Shoreacres; Spring Station; Troy; Versailles; Zion Hill

INTERESTING FACTS ABOUT KENTUCKY

- 1654 – Colonel Abram Wood of Virginia arrived to survey the area
- 1720s – the French claimed most all of Kentucky and established trading posts with help from the Indians
- 1750 – Thomas Walker, a British representative, explored the area
- 1751 – Christopher Gist explored the land fronting the Ohio River
- 1763 – the British defeated the French, ending the French and Indian War
- 1767 – frontiersman Daniel Boone and others built Fort Boonesborough
- Between 1775 and 1802 the British, along with local Indians, attacked local Kentucky settlements during and after the Revolutionary War
- Originally, Kentucky was a county of Virginia. In 1780 Kentucky County was divided into three counties: Jefferson, Fayette, and Lincoln
- When Kentucky became a state in 1792 with nine counties, it was the first state on the western frontier to join the Union.
- 1811 – the first steamboat sailed up the Ohio River
- 1818 – the westernmost area of the state was purchased from the Chickasaw Indians and referred to as the Jackson Purchase in honor of Andrew Jackson
- 1833 – Kentucky banned the importation of slaves into the state. It later reversed that decision causing an increase in slave trade
- 1860 – the state tried to remain neutral in the Civil War but losses on both sides and great property damage from attacks on both sides proved to be very costly to the state
- December 10, 1861 Kentucky was admitted to the Confederate States of America by Act of the Confederate Congress
- 1875 – the first Kentucky Derby was run
- 1937 – the U.S. Treasury opened the gold depository at Fort Knox
- 1969 – Tennessee Valley Authority built its largest steam generating plant near Paradise in Muhlenberg County

The story is told that Ohio, Muhlenberg, and Butler County officials attempted to merge their county governments. All details were agreed upon except the name......OhMuhlBut.

SELECTED KENTUCKY HIGHWAYS

State highways in Kentucky are numbered 1 to the 3500s, although numbers are available through 6999. Kentucky leads the US in number of primary highways. While four-digit primary highway numbers are rare in the rest of America, the Bluegrass State has routes in the 3000s, and this does not count the "secret" numbers in the 6000s for frontage roads and the like. The first numbered route system in America was in Wisconsin in 1917; Kentucky began numbering its roads in the 1920s. In Kentucky, Highways 1 through 100 were originally numbered so that the odd numbers ran north to south and increased toward the west, while the even numbers ran east to west and increased to the south, but this does not hold true for today's route numbering. There are over 70,000 miles of state and federal roads in Kentucky. Routes with higher numbers generally have less state maintenance than lower numbers.

- Kentucky Route 1 originates at a junction with KY 3, one mile east of Cadmus, Lawrence County, in the middle of nowhere. The route continues through Grayson and Carter Counties to terminate at US 23 in Greenup, Greenup County, at the Ohio River about two miles upstream from where KY 2 terminates. The route extends fourty-eight miles through three counties.
- Kentucky Route 2 originates in Olive Hill, Carter County, travels in a northeasterly direction into Greenup County terminating in Greenup, on the Ohio River, where it intersects with US 23. The route extends approximately thirty miles through two counties.
- Kentucky Route 3 begins south of Lancer, Floyd County, where the new US 23/460 intersects with the road to Jenny Wile State Resort Park. The road follows the western shore of Dewey Lake for about six miles, turns west to Auxier, then northeast into Johnson, Martin, and Lawrence Counties, turning northwest as it follows the Tug Fork to Louisa, and terminates at US 23 south of Catlettsburg, Boyd County, near where I-64 crosses into West Virginia. The route extends seventy-nine miles through five counties.
- Kentucky Route 4 forms a loop around Lexington, Fayette County. It is locally known as New Circle Road. The official beginning and ending of the road is at the Nicholasville Road interchange. Exit numbers increase as one travels clockwise. Between Georgetown Road and Richmond Road the road is an urban principal arterial highway with a heavy mix of driveway entrances and intersections. The only exception is the interchange of US 60, Winchester Road. The western two-thirds, from Georgetown Road to Richmond Road, is all limited access. The road was under construction from 1950 to 1967. Originally constructed as a two lane road, it was widened to four lanes in 1958. Plans were made to widen the highway to sixs lanes by the year 2000 but the $31 million project never came to fruition. The route encircles the city of Lexington, a distance of twenty miles.
- Kentucky Route 5 begins at a junction with US 60 at Princess, Boyd County. The route continues through Bellefonte, Greenup County, and terminates at US 23 back

in Boyd County between Ashland and Russell. The route extends eleven miles through two counties.

- Kentucky Route 7 begins at Jeff, Perry County, continues through Letcher, Knott, and Floyd Counties, into Magoffin County where it joins US 460 at Salyersville, then through Morgan, Elliott, and Carter Counties, and finally into Greenup County where it intersects in South Shore, Greenup County, with US 23. The route extends 202 miles through nine counties.

- Kentucky Route 8 is an east-west highway divided into three distinct segments across northern Kentucky. The western terminus of the route is near the Ohio River in Boone County. The eastern terminus is at US 23 at South Shore, Greenup County. <u>The three distinct segments of this route were not meant to be connected together.</u> The western segment of the route is one mile and two tenths long and terminates at I-275, exit 11. The middle segment of Route 8 extends seventy-nine miles between rural Boone County and Maysville in Mason County. The eastern segment of Kentucky Route 8 extends forty miles from Concord to US 23 in South Portsmouth, west of South Shore in Greenup County. The route extends a total of 200 miles through Boone, Kenton, Campbell, Pendleton, Bracken, Mason, Lewis, and Greenup Counties.

- Kentucky Route 9 runs from Newport, Campbell County, and terminates at Stinson, near Grayson, Carter County, roughly paralleling the Ohio River. From the I-275 loop to Grayson the road is also known as AA. The official name is the John Y. Brown, Jr., AA Highway. The route extends 116 miles through Campbell, Pendleton, Bracken, Mason, Lewis, and Carter Counties.

- Kentucky Route 11 originates at the intersection with KY 92 in extreme southeastern Whitley County close to the Knox County (Barbourville) border and eight air miles from the Tennessee state line and extends to Maysville, Mason County, on the Ohio River. The section from Maysville to Mount Sterling is being upgraded on a new alignment as part of a "macro-corridor" within the state. The route goes through Burning Springs in Clay County, Natural Bridge in Powell County, Mount Sterling in Montgomery County, Sharpsburg and Bethel in Bath County, Flemingsburg in Fleming County, terminating in Maysville in Mason County. The route extends 182 miles through Whitley, Knox, Clay, Owsley, Lee, Wolf, Powell, Montgomery, Bath, Fleming and Mason Counties.

- Kentucky Route 15 begins at Whitesburg, Letcher County, and terminates in Winchester, Clark County, at US 60 where Winn Avenue intersects with North Main Street. The route extends 138 miles through Letcher, Knott, Perry, Breathitt, Wolfe, Powell, and Clark Counties.

- Kentucky Route 30 originates at an intersection with US 25 in Laurel County near the community of East Bernstadt (about two miles north of the Daniel Boone Parkway), travels through the communities of Jackson, Noctor, Rousseau, and Guage in Breathitt County, intersects with the Mountain Parkway, exit 72, and terminates in Magoffin County at the intersection of US 460, two miles west of Salyersville. The route extends approximately ninety miles through Laural, Jackson, Owsley, Breathitt, and Magoffin Counties.

- Kentucky Route 40 begins in Salyersville, Magoffin County, where it intersects with US 460 and proceeds through Paintsville, Johnson County. It terminates in Martin County where it junctions with KY 645 in Inez. The route extends forty-two miles through three counties.
- Kentucky Route 52 is an east-west highway beginning near Boston, Nelson County, and terminating in Jackson, Breathitt County, where it intersects with KY 30. The route extends 167 miles through Nelson, LaRue, Marion, Boyle, Garrard, Madison, Estill, Lee, and Breathitt Counties.
- Kentucky Route 70 originates at a junction with US Highway 60 in Smithland, Livingston County, on the Ohio River and terminates at a junction with US Highway 150 near Broadhead, Rockcastle County. The route extends 233 miles through Livingston, Crittenden, Caldwell, Hopkins, Muhlenberg, Butler, Edmonson, Barren, Metcalfe, Green, Taylor, Casey, Pulaski, Lincoln, and Rockcastle Counties. However, there is no bridge connecting Livingston County to Crittenden County on Highway 70. After leaving Smithland and traveling east on Highway 70 for about twelve miles, a sign reads "End of State Maintenance." This is one mile from the Cumberland River. On the other side of the river is Dycusburg in Crittenden County where once again Highway 70 resumes. It is approximately fifteen miles from Rochester to Morgantown in Butler County. The distance the GreenRiver travels between those two towns is over thirty miles.
- Kentucky Route 80 originates on the Mississippi River in Columbus, Hickman County, and terminates in Elkhorn City, Pike County, about three miles from the Virginia border. Originally, KY 80 continued via ferry across the Mississippi River into Belmont, Missouri where it intersected with Missouri Route 80 but that ferry service no longer exists. The longest state route in Kentucky, it extends 465 miles through Hickman, Carlisle, Graves, Calloway, Marshall, Trigg, Christian, Todd, Logan, Warren, Barren, Metcalfe, Adair, Russell, Casey, Pulaski, Laurel, Clay, Leslie, Perry, Knott, Floyd, and Pike Counties.
- Kentucky Route 118, southeastern Kentucky, originates at Exit 44 of the Hal Rogers Parkway near the unincorporated community of Thousandsticks, Leslie County, and terminates in Hyden, Leslie County, at the intersection of US 421. Shortly after exiting the parkway, the road climbs a hill for approximately one mile. The last mile into Hyden is a 7% downhill grade with a runaway truck ramp near the bottom of the hill. The road is locally known as Tim Couch Pass, named after the UK and NFL quarterback who is a native of Hyden. The route extends three and one-half miles within Leslie County.
- Kentucky Route 159 originates in Falmouth, Pendleton County, extends north for approximately eight miles, and terminates at Pleasant Hill.
- Kentucky Route 160 originates at the Virginia state line in Harlan County and terminates at the intersection with KY 1087 in Vest, Knott County, after passing through Hindman. The route extends sixty-one miles through Harlan, Letcher, and Knott Counties.

- Kentucky Route 165 originates at the intersection with US 68 in Fleming County, extends southeast to Ewing, and terminates one mile father at the intersection of KY 32 near Elizaville. The route extends five miles within Fleming County.
- According to the official website of the Transportation Cabinet of Kentucky, Highway 176 originates in Greenville at the intersection with US Highway 62 and terminates at Paradise on the Green River, a distance of about twelve miles.
- Kentucky Route 189 is a north-south road that originates at an intersection with Kentucky Route 507 in northwestern Todd County and terminates at South Carrollton in northwestern Muhlenberg County. The route extends approximately forty miles through Todd, Christian, and Muhlenberg Counties.
- Kentucky Route 191 originates at the intersection of KY 15 in Campton, Wolfe County, and terminates at the intersection of US 460 at Index, two miles west of West Liberty, Morgan County. The route extends approximately thirty miles through two counties, including the communities of Cannel City and Caney. At the bend in Cannel City is Railroad Fork. Immediately intersecting with Railroad Fork is Bill Lacy Road which crosses Railroad Fork Creek the by Dr. Whitaker home then extends behind the house to the property formerly owned by Emil Adams. Bill and Donna Lacy currently live in the Whitaker home.
- Kentucky Route 321 originates at an intersection with US 23/460 in Prestonsburg, Floyd County, in front of Prestonsburg High School. It is locally known as Auxier Road. It terminates at the intersection of US Business 23 at Hager Hill, Johnson County, about two miles from Paintsville. The route extends approximately fourteen miles through two counties.
- Kentucky Route 369 originates at Rochester in Butler County, estends northward for one-half mile and stops at the eastern bank of the Green River. The road resumes on the western bank of the Green River in Ohio County and terminates at Beaver Dam, a distance of about twelve miles.
- Kentucky Route 404 originates at an intersection with KY 7 in Arthurmable, Magoffin County, goes through David, and terminates at the intersection of KY 114, which is the Mountain Parkway Extension between Salyersville and Prestonsburg, Floyd County. The route extends approximately twelve miles.
- Kentucky Route 499 originates at the intersection with US 25 between Berea and Richmond, Madison County, goes through Speedwell, and terminates at the intersection of KY 52 at Irvine, Estill County. The route extends approximately twenty-five miles through two counties.
- Kentucky Route 646 originates at an intersection with KY 213 in southern Montgomery County, travels west to Kiddville just inside Clark County, then back into Montgomery Counto to terminate at the intersection with KY 713 two miles south of Mount Sterling. The route extends approximately twenty miles.
- Kentucky Route 686 is locally known in Mount Sterling as the bypass. The road begins at KY 11 and US 460 north of the city and goes counter-clockwise terminating at US 60 east of the city. The route extends six miles within Montgomery County.

- Kentucky Route 844 originates at the intersection of KY 205 at Salem in southwest Morgan County, and terminates at intersection KY 191 just south of Malone. The road is locally called Stacy Fork. Also, KY 844 intersects with the Mack Peyton-Cannel City Road.
- Kentucky Route 1958, a bypass for the city of Winchester, Clark County, originates at KY 627 which is near I-64, exit 96 and terminates at KY 2888, Rockwell Road, northwest of the city. The route is defined by the Kentucky Transportation Cabinet as a north-south route despite the east-west alignment of the road the bypass follows for most of its length. The route extends eight miles within Clark County.
- Kentucky Route 2259 originates at a junction with Tanglewood Drive in Frankfort, Franklin County, and terminates at a junction with US 60 in Frankfort. The route extends seven tenths of a mile (.7).
- Kentucky Route 2297 originates at a junction with US 27 in Somerset, Pulaski County, and terminates at KY 2292 in Somerset. The route extends two tenths of a mile (.2).
- Kentucky Route 1000 originates at the intersection of US 460 at White Oak, Morgan County, and terminates at the intersection of KY 191 in Caney. The route extends a distance of eight miles within Morgan County.
- Kentucky Route 1081 extends from the intersection of US 460 in the southeast corner of Morgan County, through Harper to Teed Amix's Store where it joins US 460 in the northwest corner of Magoffin County. It travels north with US 460 to Bethanna (Mountain Drive In) where it begins a mostly easterly trek through northern Magoffin County, terminating at the intersection of KY 40 near Falcon (two miles from Johnson County), north of Salyersville.
- Kentucky Route1098 originates at the intersection of KY 15 near Quicksand, three miles south of Jackson, Breathitt County, and traverses ESE, terminating in Decoy, Knott County. It is the most direct route to Jackson. The route extends nearly twenty-two miles through two counties.
- Kentucky Route 1116 is the shortest Highway weighing in at eight thousandth of a mile (.008) in Louisville. Also, Highway 3503 in Boone County, just west of Devan, between I-75 and US 25, appears to be about one-half mile long.
- Kentucky Route 1516 originates at Decoy (Elmrock Road) in Knott County, travels northward, and terminates with the intersection of KY 1111 (Laurel Fork Road) in Breathitt County approximately two miles north of Decoy. The road is about two miles long.
- The Elmrock-Decoy Road (non-numbered) is the most direct route to Hindman. From Decoy the road heads in a southeasterly direction until it intersects with KY 80. The Elmrock-Decoy Road is approximately twenty miles long. It is another six miles to Hindman from that intersection.

SELECTED U.S. HIGHWAYS IN KENTUCKY
(A route ending in "0" indicates transcontinental)

- US 23 originates in Jacksonville, Florida and terminates in Mackinaw City, Michigan for a total of 1,535 miles. Mackinaw City is the northernmost point in Lower Michigan before crossing the bridge into the Upper Pensinula. The road travels through Georgia, North Carolina, Tennessee, and Virginia where it crosses into Kentucky at Jenkins in Letcher County. It then travels through Pike, Floyd, Johnson, Lawrence (where it follows the Big Sandy River), Boyd (following the Ohio River), Greenup Counties where at South Portsmouth it crosses the Ohio River into West Portsmouth, Ohio. US 23 and US 460 run together from Pikeville to Paintsville. In the mid to late twentieth century when the coal industry declined in eastern Kentucky it was said the three "Rs" were reading, writing, and Route 23 to Columbus, Ohio. Law enforcement officials from Kentucky and Ohio set up the "US Route 23 Drug Taskforce" in 1996, to patrol the highway for drug trafficking, in an attempt to stop a major artery of drug networks bringing high quality cannabis (outdoor sativa) grown in Kentucky for distribution in Ohio and points north. Signs are posted along that part of US 23 warning traffickers that efforts have been taken to prevent their actions.
- US 25 originates in Savannah, Georgia at the Atlantic Ocean and terminates at the Ohio River in Covington, opposite Cincinnati, in Campbell County. It enters Kentucky from Tennessee into Whitley County and seven miles later passes through Pleasant View then Williamsburg. From Newport, Tennessee to North Corbin, Kentucky (Laurel County), the road is split three ways forming US 25W and US 25E. Route US 25E enters Kentucky from Virginia through the Cumberland Gap Tunnel. The route is locally known as Richmond Road on the south side of Lexington and as Georgetown Road on the north side. The route extends approximately 190 miles through Whitley, Laurel, Rockcastle, Madison, Fayette, Scott, Grant, Kenton, Boone, and Kenton (again) Counties.
- US 27 originates in Miami, Florida and terminates in Fort Wayne, Indiana for a total length of 1,373 miles. It enters Kentcuky from Tennessee in McCreary County and travels through Pulaski, Lincoln, Garrard, Jessamine, Fayette, Bourbon, Harrison, Pendleton, and Campbell Counties.
- US 60 (a US route ending in 0 indicates a transcontinental route) originates in Virginia Beach, Virginia and terminates in Arizona for a total of 2,670 miles. It originally terminated in Los Angeles, California but the Arizona to California section was reassigned to Interstate 10. US 60 enters Kentucky from West Virginia at Kenova and immediately turns north to follow the Ohio River through Boyd County before turning easterly at Ashland. It then travels through Carter, Rowan, Bath, Montgomery, Clark, Fayette, Woodford, Franklin, Shelby, Jefferson, Bullitt, Hardin, Meade, Breckinridge, Hancock, Daviess, Henderson, Union, Crittenden, Livingston, McCracken, and Ballard Counties where it crosses the Ohio River at East Cairo near Wickliffe. This is where the Ohio and Mississippi Rivers converge.

- US 62 originates at the US-Mexican border in El Paso, Texas and terminates at the US-Canadian border in Niagara Falls, New York for a total distance of 2,248 miles and passing through ten states. US 62 enters Kentucky from the southern tip of Illinois at East Cairo (Ballard County), Kentucky at the confluence of the Ohio and Mississippi Rivers. It then passes through Carlisle, back into Ballard for one and one-half miles, McCracken, Marshall, Lyon, Caldwell, Hopkins, Muhlenberg, Ohio, Grayson, Hardin, Nelson, Anderson, Woodford, Scott, Bourbon (for four hundred yards in the westernmost tip), Harrison, Robertson, Mason Counties where it crosses the Ohio River at Maysville into Aberdeen, Ohio. Although the even number indicates an east-west direction, the route runs mostly north and south from Georgetown, Kentucky to Niagara Falls, New York. After leaving El Paso, the route bisects the southeast corner of New Mexico, skirting Carlsbad Caverns before entering Texas again.
- US 127 originates in Chattanooga, Tennessee and terminates in Grayling, Michigan for distance of 758 miles. The road enters Kentucky from Tennessee in Clinton County then proceeds through Russell, Casey, Lincoln, Boyle, Mercer, Anderson, Franklin, Owen, Gallatin, Boone, and Kenton Counties where it crosses the Ohio River into Cincinnati, Ohio.
- US 460 originates in Norfolk, Virginia and terminates in Frankfort, KY. The route extends 655 miles through the Kentucky counties of Pike, Floyd, Johnson, Magoffin, Morgan, Menifee, Montgomery, Bourbon, Scott, and Franklin.

CITIES, COUNTIES AND TOWNS

Anderson City is in	Anderson County	Letcher is in	Letcher County
Carrollton is in	Carroll County	Marshall is in	Marshall County
Carter is in	Carter County	Nelsonville is in	Nelson County
Flemingsburg is in	Fleming County	Oldham is in	Oldham County
Fulton is in	Fulton County	Owenton is in	Owen County
Greensburg is in	Green County	Pikeville is in	Pike County
Greenup is in	Greenup County	Powell Valley is in	Powell County
Harlan is in	Harlan County	Pulaski is in	Pulaski County
Henderson is in	Henderson County	Russell Springs is in	Russell County
Jeffersontown is in	Jefferson County	Shelbyville is in	Shelby County
Jessamine is in	Jessamine County	Sweet Owen is in	Owen County
Kenton is in	Kenton County	Uniontown is in	Union County

However,

Adairville is not in	Adair County but in	Logan County
Allen is not in	Allen County but in	Floyd County
Anderson is not in	Anderson County but in	Logan and Todd Counties
Ballard is not in	Ballard County but in	Anderson County
Bath is not in	Bath County but in	Knott County
Bell City is not in	Bell County but in	Elliott and Graves Counties
Boone is not in	Boone County but in	Rockcastle County
Bourbon is not in	Bourbon County but in	Pike County
Breckinridge is not in	Breckinridge County but in	Harrison County
Bullittsville is not in	Bullitt County but in	Boone County
Butler is not in	Butler County but in	Pendleton County
Calloway Crossing is not in	Calloway County but in	Estille County
Campbellsville is not in	Campbell County but in	Taylor County
Carlisle is not in	Carlisle County but in	Nicholas County
Casey is not in	Casey County but in	Butler County
Clay is not in	Clay County but in	Webster County
Crittenden is not in	Crittenden County but in	Grant County
Cumberland is not in	Cumberland County but in	Harlan County
Edmonton is not in	Edmonson County but in	Metcalfe County
Elliottville is not in	Elliott County but in	Rowan County
Floyd is not in	Floyd County but in	Pulaski County
Franklin is not in	Franklin County but in	Simpson County
Garrard is not in	Garrard County but in	Clay County
Grant is not in	Grant County but in	Kenton County
Grayson is not in	Grayson County but in	Carter County
Green is not in	Green County but in	Elliott County
Hardin is not in	Hardin County but in	Marshall County
Harlan Crossroads is not in	Harlan County but in	Monroe County

Hickman is not in	Hickman County but in	Fulton County
Hopkinsville is not in	Hopkins County but in	Christian County
Jackson is not in	Jackson County but in	Breathitt County
Johnsonville is not in	Johnson County but in	Anderson County
Knottsville is not in	Knott County but in	Daviess County
Knoxville is not in	Knox County but in	Pendleton County
Laurel Creek is not in	Laurel County but in	Clay County
Lawrenceburg is not in	Lawrence County but in	Anderson County
Lee is not in	Lee County but in	Butler County
Leslie is not in	Leslie County but in	Metcalfe County
Lewisburg is not in	Lewis County but in	Logan County
Lincoln is not in	Lincoln County but in	Clay County
Livingston is not in	Livingston County but in	Rockcastle County
Logantown is not in	Logan County but in	Lincoln County
Madisonville is not in	Madison County but in	Hopkins County
Marion is not in	Marion County but in	Crittenden County
Mason is not in	Mason County but in	Grant and Magoffin Counties
McCreary is not in	McCreary County but in	Garrard County
Mercer is not in	Mercer County but in	Muhlenberg County
Monroe is not in	Monroe County but in	Hart County
Montgomery is not in	Montgomery County but in	Trigg County
Morgan is not in	Morgan County but in	Pendleton County
Morgantown is not in	Morgan County but in	Butler County
Nicholasville is not in	Nicholas County but in	Jessamine County
Owensboro is not in	Owen County but in	Daviess County
Owsley is not in	Owsley County but in	Pike County
Pendleton is not in	Pendleton County but in	Henry County
Russell is not in	Russell County but in	Greenup County
Scottsville is not in	Scott County but in	Allen County
Simpson is not in	Simpson County but in	Breathitt County
Taylorsville is not in	Taylor County but in	Spencer County
Union is not in	Union County but in	Boone County
Warren is not in	Warren County but in	Knox County
Washington is not in	Washington County but in	Mason County
Webster is not in	Webster County but in	Breckinridge County
Whitley City is not in	Whitley County but in	McCreary County
Wolfe is not in	Wolfe County but in	Carter County

THE COMMUNITY OF...	IS FOUND IN THE COUNTIES OF...
Anderson	Logan and Todd
Arnold	Union and Ohio
Ballardsville	Jefferson and Oldham (about 12 miles apart)
Bear Wallow	Washington and Hart
Beech Grove	Bullitt and McLean
Beechland	Meade and Logan
Beechmont	Jefferson and Muhlenberg
Bell City	Elliott and Graves
Beulah	Hopkins and Hickman
Beverly	Bell and Christian
Black Rock	Grayson (twice)
Bobtown	Madison and Pulaski
Booth	Hardin and Wolfe
Boston	Butler, Daviess, Jefferson, Nelson, and Pendleton
Bradshaw	Jackson and Todd
Bromley	Kenton and Owen
Brooks	Bullitt and LaRue
Brownsville	Edmonson and Fulton
Buena Vista	Garrard, Harrison, Marshall
Buffalo	LaRue and Trigg
Bushtown	Mercer (twice)
Cedar Grove	Bullitt, Pulaski, and Todd
Cedar Point	Oldham and Trigg
Chapman	Lawrence and Union
Clifton	Woodford and Boyle
Columbus	Fayette and Hickman
Concord	Pendleton, Lewis, Fleming, and Grayson
Congleton	McLean and Lee
Corinth	Grant and Logan
Craintown	Fleming and Boyle
Cub Run	Edmonson and Hart
Dalesburg	Fleming and Breathitt
Dan	Menifee and Ohio
Deer Lick	Logan and Clay
Dogwood	Christian and Graves
Dry Fork	Pike and Barren
Duncan	Mercer and Casey
Edgewood	Kenton and Bell
Evergreen	Franklin and Lawrence
Fairview	Caldwell, Christian, Fleming, Kenton, Lyon
Georgetown	Harlan, Scott
Halfway	Allen, Barren
Marshall	Marshall, Mason

Midway	Caldwell, Calloway, Crittenden, Woodford (Semiway is in McLean)
Morehead	Muhlenberg, Rowan
Needmore	Boyle, Butler, Caldwell, Owen
Van Cleve	Calloway (Vancleve in Breathitt)
White Oak	Garrard, Morgan

The largest county is Pike (Pikeville) measuring 789 square miles.

The second largest is Christian (Hopkinsville) measuring 724 square miles.

The smallest county is Robertson (Mt. Olivet) measuring 100 square miles.

The second smallest is Gallatin (Warsaw) measuring 105 square miles.

Jefferson is the most densely populated county with 1,800 people per square mile.

Hickman is the least densely populated county with twenty-one people per square mile.

Robertson is next densly populated with twenty-two people per square mile.

Kenton County is more densely populated than Fayette:

Kenton—935/sq.mi.; Fayette—915/sq.mi.

The population of Jefferson is 694,000; Fayette is 260,500; Robertson is 2,270.

KENTUCKY'S MAJOR RIVERS

(There are a total of thirty-three rivers in Kentucky)

CUMBERLAND RIVER 678 miles long; originates in Letcher County (Whitesburg), flows through Nashville, TN, and feeds into the Ohio River at the small western Kentucky town of Smithland (Livingston County); it forms Lake Barkley, which is the eastern boundary of the Tennessee Valley Authority's Land Between the Lakes; it is one of a few rivers in America that leaves a state, then reenters it. The Tennessee River is also such a river. The Cumberland River is the only river in Kentucky to flow southward then northward.

GREEN RIVER 300 miles long; originates in Lincoln County (Stanford); flows through Mammoth Cave; is so named because the depth of the river makes it appear green. A young man who worked his way through college by working summers for the U.S. Army Corps of Engineers related that it is one of the deepest rivers in the United States, sometimes reaching depths of 100 feet.

KENTUCKY RIVER 259 miles long; originates in Lee County (Beatyville) where the North, South, and Middle Forks of the Kentucky River converge; passes near Lexington and Frankfort before emptying into the Ohio River at Carrollton (Carroll County); Kentucky River Palisades is about 100 miles of the Kentucky River from Clays Ferry (Madison County) to Frankfort (Franklin County) where deep gorges are found. This action occurs because limestone erodes downward while other riverbeds erode outward.

LEVISA FORK RIVER 140 miles long; also called Levisa Fork or Levisa Fork of the Big Sandy; a tributary of the Big Sandy River; originates in southwestern Virginia near Grundy, flows west into Pike County, forms the Fishtrap Lake, flows past the cities of Pikeville and Prestonsburg; near Paintsville it turns to the NNE flowing through Johnson and Lawrence Counties; joins the Tug fork at Louisa on the West Virginia state line to form the Big Sandy River; in the early 1900s the river was navagible to Pikeville, but today barge traffic is greatly curtailed. The name Levisa Fork (the official name of USGS) was given by Dr. Thomas Walker as Louisa after Princess Louisa, wife of Prince William Augustus, Duke of Cumberland; Walker had also named the Cumberland River near this same time; according to some reports the frontiersmen forgot for whom the river was named and, in time, began calling it Levisa.

LICKING RIVER 320 miles long; originates in southeastern Magoffin County less than one mile from the Knott County line (ten air miles ENE of Decoy); empties in the Ohio River at Covington/Newport, across from Cincinnati; is the boundary line between Kenton and Campbell Counties; is the main river between the Kentucky River to the west and the Big Sandy River to the east; after flowing through Salyersville and West Liberty the river then forms Cave Run Lake which was home to the largest muskie ever caught in Kentucky

(44.38 lb); the dam, reaching between Rowan and Bath counties, provides a lake in Bath, Rowan, and Menifee Counties with headwaters in Morgan County; Native Americans called the river Nepternine, but when Dr. Thomas Walker discovered the river in 1750 he called it Frederick's River; one earlier name, Great Salt Lick Creek, makes reference to the many saline springs near the river that attracted animals to its salt licks; the origin of the present name is unclear, though it possibly was derived from Great Salt Lick Creek; is believed that aboriginal peoples inhabited the river basis for at least part of the year for several thousand years; river served as an important transportation route for Native Americans and early European settlers; 1782 the river was the site of the Battle of Blue Licks; the Newport Barracks, an Army installation at Newport, guarded the mouth of the river from 1803 to 1894; during the 1800s it served as a means of getting crops and products to other markets; lower river is considered to be a rare example of a native muskie stream; there are more than 50 species of mussels, eleven of which are endangered; largest common carp ever taken in the state of Kentucky (54 lb, 14 oz.) was caught in the South Fork of Licking River; there is also a Licking River in Ohio

OHIO RIVER Ohio River played a major role in Kentucky's history because it borders all of the northern counties in Kentucky. The Monongahela River originates at Fairmont, West Virginia (northeast of Charleston) and travels 180 miles to Pittsburgh, Pennsylvania. The Allegheny River originates in north central Pennsylvania, flows north into New York, passing through Salamanca, then back into Pennsylvania and ending 280 miles later at Pittsburgh. It is the joining of these two rivers at Pittsburgh that creates the Ohio River. Since most rivers in America flow south, and a few (in Kentucky) flow north, the Ohio is the only large, navigable river that flows west. This allowed settlers to have their goods exported and fresh supplies imported.

TENNESSEE RIVER The Tennessee River is the largest tributary of the Ohio River. It is 650 miles long. It was once popularly known as the Cherokee River. It originates at Knoxville, Tennessee and terminates at Paducah, Kentucky. On its journey it flows toward Chattanooga, Tennessee before crossing into northern Alabama, borders with Mississippi, and flows back into Tennessee and finally Kentucky. It is one of a few rivers that leaves a state then re-enters it. The Cumberland River is also such a river. The Tennessee Valley Authority damed the Cumberland River in Kentuckky which created Kentucky Lake. Other than Tennessee, streams from Virginia, North Carolina, Georgia, Mississippi, and Alabama feed into the Tennessee River. The river hosts a total of nine dams.

YOU LIVE WHERE?

FOREWARD

The information in this work, except where noted, is taken from Wikipedia.
Alphebetizing courtesy of Alphabetize.org

While surfing the internet for a particular subject, a website caught my attention that listed some unusual or interesting names of communities and towns across America. It was by no means a complete list since names were not included from every state. The author listed more names from Kentucky than any other state while adding a comment, something to the effect of, "You can't make up this stuff."

The author's remark stirred up the curiosity within me so much so that I needed to find out for myself if indeed Kentucky had more unusual names than the other state in America. That study has turned into a wonderful experience of learning and fun.

I first began studying a Global Positioning System map of Kentucky, which seemed to indicate that, indeed, there is a plethora of interesting, if not unusual, names for the cities, towns, communities and neighborhoods in Kentucky. In fact, so enthralled was I by the names I found in the state of Kentucky, that I conducted a county-by-county survey to insure every possible name was revealed.

But I was not satisfied searching only for names. Having a personal bent for trivial information, I then branched out into listing some historical facts found on Wikipedia. That search led further to the inclusion of historical persons, which then led to other types of persons, such as, actors, scientists, sports personalities, etc.

After two years of research, I have now reached my own conclusion concerning whether the names of Kentucky's communities and towns are more unusual or common. With the material found in these pages, you now have a similar opportunity.

There are tens of thousands of different names of cities, towns, townships and communities in the United States with more than 4,000 of those names repeated in other states and some even duplicated within the same state. Kentucky alone uses well over 2,000 names across the state, with many of them repeated from county to county.

Pennsylvania has more official names of cities and towns than any state with 1,769. New York has the second largest number of official names with 1,616. Texas has only 1,478 and Kentucky is number six on the list with 1,097 cities and towns.

Kentucky ranks third in the number of counties (120) behind Georgia (159) and Texas (254), despite the fact that Kentucky ranks 34th nationally in land mass area. The reason for so many counties in Kentucky was to ensure that residents, in the days of poor roads and horseback travel, could make a round trip from their home to the courthouse in one day.

This work does not intend to name every community and town in America, just those with curious, uncommon, or interesting names, and those with special interest to this writer.

Following are the criteria used in selecting names:

Interesting names –	Zzyck, CA
Name of a US city –	Omaha, AR
Name of a state –	Florida, IN
A community in which I lived –	Harper, KY
Names of family and close friends –	Gary, IN
Elements in nature –	Goose Egg, WY
Names of a foreign city –	Paris, KY
Names of a foreign country –	Brazil, IA

When searching for names of your own particular interest, remember to consider prefixes such as Camp Ripley Junction; Cape Elizabeth, East Thompson, Fort Gordon, Lake Bruce, Little Penny, Mount Morris, New Douglas, North Bradley, Saint Nicholas, South Logan, West Carson, etc.

Included in this work you will find names dealing with farming, colors, other states and cities, foreign countries and cities, nuts and fruits, gemstones, agruculture and farming, chemestry, electricity, sports, foods, and the list continues.

Throughout the work, parenthetical notes have been included to indicate geographical or historical facts or to indicate that a famous person was born there.

Whether you are in pursuit of trivial information or you are tracing a family name across America, you may find yourself being captivated, as I was, by the creativity and origanility of these names.

Like the town in Bulloch County, Georgia, Hopeulikeit.

George E. Thompson
Greenville, KY

In memory of my parents,
Reverend Charles Grover Thompson Jr.,
October 30, 1911–October 18, 2005, and
Margaret McAllister Kinloch Thompson,
March 5, 1917–October 22, 2005
Missionaries to eastern Kentucky from 1946–1999

INDEX OF INTERESTING NAMES IN AMERICA

Indexes of Kentucky names and all persons listed in this work are listed separately.

The numeral indicates the page on which the name is found; the numeral in parentheses (2) indicates that the name appears more than once on that page.

-A-

- Abbotsford, 128
- Abbott, 100
- Abeline, 36
- Abercrombie, 83
- Aberdeen, 7, 10, 18, 21, 25, 31, 46, 57, 65, 72, 81, 87, 100, 107, 114, 123, 125
- Aberdeen Gardens, 123
- Able, 13, 67
- Academy, 10, 107, 114
- Accident, 46
- Achilles, 37
- Acoma, 74
- Acorn, 7, 121
- Acorn Corner, 61
- Acorn Hill, 81
- Acorn Pond, 21
- Acorn Ridge, 61
- Acre, 81
- Acres of Diamonds, 18
- Action, 94
- Active, 1
- Adair, 25, 28, 34, 52, 57, 61, 78, 87, 92, 110, 114
- Adams, 1, 18, 31, 34, 37, 44, 49(2), 54, 61, 67, 72, 81, 83, 92, 94, 110, 114, 125, 128
- Addison, 1
- Adel, 21, 61, 65, 92, 94
- Aden, 74
- Admire, 37
- Advance, 7, 10, 28, 31, 52, 61, 81, 87, 94, 100, 107, 114, 128
- Advent, 125
- Aerial, 21

- Affton, 61
- Africa, 31,87
- Afton, 10, 16, 21, 34, 52, 54, 69, 72, 74, 78, 81, 87, 92, 110, 114, 121, 125, 128, 130
- Agate, 13, 67, 83, 117
- Agate Bay, 123
- Agate Point, 123
- Agency, 34, 61, 65
- Agenda, 37, 128
- Agricola, 21, 37
- Aid, 61
- Air Base City, 74
- Airline, 21
- Airline Acres, 61
- Airport Village, 24
- Akaska, 107
- Akron, 13, 28, 31, 34, 37, 52, 61, 67, 78, 84
- Alabam, 7
- Alabama, 1, 18, 60, 78
- Alabama Hill, 10
- Alabama Village, 24
- Alabaster, 52
- Aladdin, 100, 123
- Alaktak, 4
- Alamo, 7, 10, 13, 21, 52, 69, 74, 83, 110
- Alaska, 3, 39, 52, 54, 74, 100, 107, 128
- Albany, 10, 21(2), 28, 31, 34, 42, 54, 61, 71, 87, 94, 114, 119, 128, 130
- Albert, 7, 37, 92, 100, 114
- Alberta, 52, 54, 61, 130
- Albert Lea, 54
- Alcatraz, 74
- Alcoa, 110, 114

- Alert, 81, 87
- Alex, 92
- Alexander, 31, 37, 44, 81, 83, 114, 125
- Alexandria, 1, 31, 42, 54, 61, 67, 87, 107, 110, 121(2), 125
- Alfalfa, 42, 92, 94, 114
- Algiers, 31
- Alice, 13, 34, 42, 57, 61, 83, 87, 100, 125
- Alice Acres, 114
- Aliceville, 1, 28
- Alkali, 69
- All, 61
- Alleganey, 78
- Allegany, 94
- Allegany Grove, 46
- Alleghany, 10, 121
- Allegheny, 81
- Allen, 1, 10, 13, 28, 34, 37, 52, 54, 57, 67, 81, 92, 100, 105, 107, 114, 123, 128
- Allentown, 96, 100
- Alley, 21
- All Healing Springs, 81
- Alliance, 10, 42, 67, 87
- Alligator, 57, 81
- Alloy, 125
- All Saints Village, 61
- Almond, 1, 7, 128
- Aloe, 65
- Aloha, 94, 123
- Alpha, 25, 28, 34, 42, 52, 54, 61, 69, 83, 92, 94, 128
- Alpine, 1, 4, 7, 10, 13, 18, 21, 25, 31, 52, 65, 69, 72, 78, 94, 110, 114, 117, 121, 130
- Alpine Village, 119
- Alps, 21, 121
- Alta Vista, 74
- Altitude, 57
- Alto, 107, 114, 123, 128
- Altus, 90
- Alum, 69

- Alum Bridge, 125
- Alum Creek, 114
- Amateur, 7
- Amazon, 65
- Amble, 52
- Ambler, 4, 100
- America, 1, 28, 92
- American City, 13, 37
- American Falls, 25
- American Flat, 69
- American Fork, 117
- American River, 123
- Americus, 13, 21, 31, 37, 61
- Ames, 34
- Amherst, 70
- Amish, 34
- Ampere, 10, 72
- Amsterdam, 10, 25, 61, 65, 72, 78, 87, 94, 100, 121
- Anaconda, 13, 61, 65
- Anchor, 28, 42, 74, 92
- Anchorage, 3, 46, 57, 114
- Anchor Bay, 10
- Ancient Oak, 46
- Anderson, 1, 4(2), 10, 25, 28, 31, 34, 37, 42, 52, 57, 61, 69, 72, 78, 81, 87, 92(2), 94, 100, 105, 110, 114, 128
- Andes, 65, 78
- Andreas, 100
- Angel, 52, 87
- Angel City, 114
- Angel Fire, 74
- Angel Inlet, 54
- Angels, 100
- Angels Camp, 10
- Angle, 117
- Angora, 13, 54, 67
- Angus, 34, 54, 67, 114
- Anise, 100
- Ann, 61
- Annapolis, 10, 28, 61
- Annapolis Rock, 46
- Ann Arbor, 51(2), 52
- Annex, 121

- Anoka, 54
- Antelope, 10, 37, 65, 74, 83, 94, 107, 114, 130
- Antelope Springs, 13, 69
- Antelope Wells, 74
- Ant Flat, 65
- Anthem, 125
- Antigo, 128
- Antimony, 7, 117
- Antler, 61, 83, 94, 125
- Antlers, 9, 13, 52, 92, 121
- Antwerp, 78, 87
- Anvil Points, 13
- Apex, 4, 10, 13, 61, 65, 81, 87
- Appalachia, 71, 121
- Apple, 87, 92
- Apple Creek, 61, 87, 128
- Apple Grove, 1, 46, 121, 125
- Apple Ridge, 81
- Apple River, 28
- Appletown, 46
- Apple Valley, 10, 21, 25, 54, 83
- Applewood, 13
- Apricot, 123
- Apron Crossing, 4
- Apt, 7
- Arab, 1, 61
- Arabia, 67, 69, 78
- Arbor, 67, 100, 114
- Arbor Grove, 7
- Arbor Hill, 121
- Arborville, 21, 67
- Arcade, 10, 78
- Archer, 65, 67
- Archers Corner, 72
- Archery, 21
- Arctic, 78, 104
- Arctic Village, 4
- Ardmore, 90
- Arena, 74, 83, 128
- Argyle, 21, 28, 34, 42, 44, 52, 54, 61, 78, 105, 107, 114, 125, 128
- Arizona, 4(2), 42, 67, 74, 114
- Arizona City, 4
- Arizona Village, 4
- Ark, 61
- Arkadelphia, 1,7
- Arkansas, 6, 61, 91, 125
- Arkansas City, 7, 37, 114
- Arkansas Junction, 74
- Arkansaw, 128
- Arkoma, 92
- Arlington, 94
- Arm, 57
- Armory, 57
- Armour, 107
- Aroma, 31
- Aromas, 10
- Arrow, 25
- Arrow Creek, 65
- Arrowhead, 13, 69
- Arrowhead Springs, 10, 130
- Arrow Rock, 61
- Artesian, 34, 107, 123
- Artesian City, 25, 94
- Artic, 123
- Artichoke, 54
- Artichoke Lake, 54
- Asbestos, 94
- Asbestos Point, 25
- Asbury Park, 72(2)
- Ash, 81, 94, 114, 123
- Ash Creek, 54
- Asher, 4, 92
- Asher Glade, 46
- Asherville, 37
- Ash Fork, 4
- Ash Hill, 10
- Ash Iron Springs, 31
- Ashland, 1, 16, 28, 31, 37, 42, 44, 49, 52, 57, 61, 65, 67, 71, 81, 87, 92, 94, 105, 110, 114, 125
- Ash Springs, 69
- Ashwood, 57,87
- Asia, 114
- Askew, 57
- Aspen, 13,130
- Aspen Grove, 117

- Aspen Park, 13
- Aspen Valley, 10
- Aspetuck, 15
- Assumption, 7, 54, 67, 87
- Assurance, 125
- Asylum, 10, 81, 100
- Atchison, 37
- Athens, 1, 10, 21, 28, 31, 37, 42, 44, 52, 54, 57, 61, 87, 114, 119, 125, 128
- Atlanta, 7, 10, 13, 16, 20, 21, 25, 28, 31, 37, 42, 52, 57, 61, 67, 69, 78, 81, 87, 94, 114(2)
- Atlantic, 34, 44, 49, 100
- Atlantic Beach, 18
- Atlantic City, 72(2), 130
- Atlantis, 18
- Atlas, 10, 25, 28, 37, 52, 114
- Atomic City, 25, 94
- Attitude, 87
- Audubon, 54, 83
- Augusta, 28, 37, 44, 65
- Augustine, 16
- Aurora, 13, 28, 54, 67, 87, 107, 117
- Austin, 13, 52, 54, 57, 61, 65, 69, 81
- Austria, 61
- Auto, 125
- Autumn Hill, 46
- Auxvasse, 61
- Avalanche, 128
- Avenger Village, 114
- Avenue, 46
- Avenue City, 61
- Avocado, 10
- Avon, 7, 10, 13, 15, 25, 28, 31, 49, 54, 57, 61, 65, 78, 81, 107, 117, 121, 128
- Avon-by-the-Sea, 73
- Avon Park, 18
- Awakening, 69
- Axle, 1
- Azalea, 10, 94
- Azalea Park, 18
- Azalia, 31, 52
- Aztec, 4, 74

- Azure, 13

-B-

- Babylon, 69
- Baby Rock, 4
- Bachelor, 13, 61
- Bachelors Hall, 121
- Back, 114
- Backbone, 121
- Back Gate, 7
- Back River, 46
- Back Swamp, 105
- Backwoods, 110
- Bacon, 16, 31, 87, 114, 123
- Bacon Hill, 46
- Bacon Springs, 57
- Bad Axe, 52
- Badger, 10, 34, 37, 54, 67, 107, 114
- Badger Basin, 130
- Badger Grove, 31
- Badgertown, 87
- Bad Nation, 107
- Badwater, 10, 130
- Bagdad, 4, 10, 18, 42, 100, 114, 121
- Bahama, 81
- Bahama Beach, 18
- Bain, 54, 110
- Bains Corner, 78
- Bainville, 65, 114
- Bala Cynwyd, 100
- Balance Rock, 10
- Bald Butte, 65
- Bald Eagle, 46, 100
- Bald Head, 44
- Bald Hill, 57, 110
- Bald Knob, 7
- Bald Knobs, 31
- Bald Mountain, 99
- Ballard, 7, 10, 46, 52, 57, 61, 81, 92, 117, 125
- Ballards, 52
- Ballards Corners, 52

- Ballardsville, 57
- Ball Club, 54
- Ball Ground, 21
- Ballplay, 1
- Baltic, 81, 87, 107
- Baltimore, 34, 45, 46, 52, 87, 110, 119(2)
- Bamboo, 81
- Bandana, 81
- Bangor, 1, 10, 34, 52, 100, 123, 128
- Bangs, 87, 114
- Banks, 25, 57
- Banner, 7, 130
- Banning Place, 74
- Bannister, 61
- Baptism Crossing, 54
- Barbecue, 81
- Barber, 25, 46, 65, 73, 81, 92, 94
- Barber City, 10
- Barbers, 21
- Barbersville, 31
- Barberville, 18
- Barcelona, 7,42
- Bard, 74
- Bardstown, 7
- Bardwell, 114
- Bare Hills, 46
- Bark River, 52
- Barley Sheaf, 73
- Barnstable, 49
- Barnwell, 105
- Barracks, 121
- Barrel Spring, 69
- Barren, 61
- Barren Creek, 125
- Barrow, 3, 4
- Bartlesville, 89
- Barview, 94(2)
- Basalt, 13
- Baseline, 65
- Basic, 69
- Basic City, 57
- Basin, 10, 13, 25, 57, 65, 130
- Basin City, 123

- Basket, 78, 100
- Bass, 7, 61, 125
- Bassets Corner, 49
- Basswood, 52
- Bat, 42
- Bat Cave, 81
- Batesville, 6
- Bath, 10, 21, 28, 31, 44, 52, 54, 71, 78, 81, 87, 105, 107, 114, 121
- Bath Alum, 121
- Bathgate, 83
- Bath Springs, 1, 110
- Baton Rouge, 40, 42, 105
- Battery Hill, 1
- Battiest, 92
- Battle, 130
- Battle Creek, 34, 52, 67, 105
- Battle Ground, 31, 123
- Battleground, 1, 81
- Battle Ground Forks, 18
- Battle Lake, 54
- Battle Mountain, 69
- BattleRiver, 54
- Battles, 57
- Battlesburg, 87
- Battleview, 83
- Bauxite, 7
- Bavaria, 128
- Bay Horse, 65
- Bayhorse, 25
- Bayleaf, 81
- Bayonet Point, 18
- Bayou George, 18
- Bayou Jack, 42
- Bayview, 25
- Baywood, 42
- Bazaar, 37
- Beach, 57, 61, 83
- Beach City, 87, 114
- Beaches Corner, 25
- Beachville, 18
- Beacon, 1, 52, 114
- Beacon Falls, 15
- Beacon Hill, 57, 123

- Beacon View, 67
- Beagle, 37, 87, 94
- Bean Blossom, 31
- Bean City, 18
- Bean Island, 71
- Bean Rock, 1
- Beans, 71, 110
- Beans Corner, 44
- Bean Settlement, 125
- Beans Mill, 1
- Bean Station, 110
- Beanville, 119
- Bear, 4, 7, 16, 25
- Bear Branch, 31, 61
- Bear Butte, 107
- Bear Creek, 1, 7, 10, 42, 57, 81, 87, 94, 100, 107, 114, 128
- Bear Creek Springs, 7
- Bear Grass, 81
- Bear Hollow, 18
- Bear Lake, 31
- Bear Lake Hot Springs, 25
- Bear Poplar, 81
- Bear River, 4, 54
- Bear River City, 117
- Bearskin, 81
- Bear Skin, 42
- Bear Spring, 65, 110
- Bear Stand, 110
- Bear Swamp, 100
- Bear Tavern, 73
- Bear Town, 52, 57
- Beartown, 13, 65, 87, 130
- Bear Valley, 10, 16, 54, 128
- Bear Wallow, 31, 110
- Beauregard, 57
- Beauty, 125
- Beaver, 4, 7, 34, 37, 42, 52, 54, 69, 87, 92, 94, 100, 117(2), 117, 123, 125, 128
- Beaver Brook, 128
- Beaverbrook, 15
- Beaver City, 31, 67
- Beaver Creek, 13, 18, 28, 46, 54, 65, 87, 94, 130
- Beaver Crossing, 54, 67, 107
- Beaverdam, 52, 61, 81, 87, 121, 125
- Beaver Dam, 4, 44, 73, 100, 117, 128
- Beaver Edge, 128
- Beaver Falls, 54, 100
- Beaver Head, 25
- Beaver Hill, 65, 110
- Beaver Homes, 94
- Beaver Lake, 73
- Beaver Meadows, 100
- Beaver Park, 87
- Beaver Point, 13
- Beaver Pond, 87
- Beaver Springs, 94, 100
- Beaverton, 52
- Beavertown, 87
- Beaver Town, 1
- Beaver Valley, 100
- Bedford, 28, 31, 34, 42, 49, 65, 71, 96
- Bedlam, 15
- Bedlam Corner, 15
- Bedrock, 13
- Bedstead Corner, 25
- Bee, 54, 67, 92, 121
- Bee Bayou, 42
- Bee Branch, 7
- Bee Cave, 114
- Beech, 34, 42, 125
- Beech Bottom, 110
- Beech Creek, 7, 18, 28, 81, 94
- Beech Creek Crossing, 7
- Beech Grove, 31, 57, 100, 110, 125
- Beech Haven, 16
- Beech Hill, 21
- Beech Island, 105
- Beechnut City, 110
- Beech Springs, 42, 57, 110
- Beechwood, 1, 7, 18, 21, 19, 52, 57, 100, 125
- Bee Fork, 61
- Beegum, 10
- Beehive, 1, 65

- Bee House, 114
- Beehunter, 31
- Beelick Knob, 125
- Bee Log, 81
- Bee Ridge, 18, 31
- Bee Rock, 10
- Beetland, 13
- Beetown, 128
- Beetree, 46
- Beetree Ford, 18
- Beetville, 25
- Bel Air, 46, 46
- Belcher, 78
- Belfast, 7, 21, 34, 44, 61, 67, 78, 87, 100, 110
- Belfry, 65
- Belgium, 18, 28
- Belgrade, 44, 54, 61, 65, 67, 81, 114
- Bell, 1, 4, 9, 16, 18, 21, 28, 46, 52, 92, 114
- Bell Buckle, 110
- Bell City, 7
- Belleville, 18, 28
- Bell Factory, 1
- Bellflower, 61
- Bell Grove, 61
- Bell Island Hot Springs, 4
- Bell Oak, 52
- Bell Springs, 10
- Bell Town, 105, 110
- Belltown, 16
- Bellville, 27
- Belt, 65
- Belt Creek, 65
- Belvedere, 9
- Ben, 87, 114
- Bench, 25
- Benchmark, 107
- Bend, 19, 61, 65, 114
- Bending Chestnut, 110
- Benefit, 21
- Benevolence, 21
- Ben Franklin, 114
- Bengal, 31, 54, 92

- Ben Gay, 7
- Ben Hur, 10
- Benjamin, 61, 100
- Benkelman, 67
- Bennett, 74
- Ben Oaks, 46
- Bens Creek, 100
- Bens Run, 125
- Bent Creek, 81, 121
- Bent Oak, 57
- Benton, 18, 21, 28, 37, 42, 44, 52, 54, 57, 71, 87
- Benton City, 61
- Bentonville, 31,61
- Ben Town, 28
- Benville, 28
- Benwood, 57
- Berea, 7, 34, 57, 67, 81, 83, 105 ,110, 114, 121, 125
- Berlin, 1, 7, 15, 21, 28, 37, 46, 49, 61, 71, 73, 78, 84, 87, 92, 105, 110, 114, 121, 125, 128
- Berlin Corners, 119
- Bermuda, 21,42
- Bernice, 25, 42, 65, 69, 87, 92, 94, 100
- Berry, 1, 28, 46
- Berry Creek, 10
- Berrydale, 18
- Berry Hill, 81
- Berry Mill, 81
- Berry Patch, 123
- Berrytown, 16, 46
- Berryville, 7, 21
- Bessie, 92
- Best, 114
- Best Corner, 25
- Bestpitch, 46
- Beta, 13
- Bethel, 15
- Betty B Landing, 52
- Between, 21
- Beverage Town, 7

- Beverly, 21, 28, 37, 49, 57, 61, 67, 73, 81, 87, 100, 105, 123, 125
- Beverly Beach, 18, 94, 123
- Beverly Depot, 34
- Beverly Gardens, 87
- Beverly Glen, 10
- Beverly Grove, 13
- Beverly Heights, 100
- Beverly Hill, 31
- Beverly Hills, 10, 13, 18, 21, 28, 52, 87, 100, 110, 114, 125
- Beverly Road, 49
- Beverly Shores,31
- Bewelcome, 57
- Bexar, 7
- Bias, 125
- Big A Plenty Landing, 42
- Big Arm, 65
- Big Bay, 28
- Big Bayou, 42
- Big Bear City, 10
- Big Beaver, 100
- Big Bend, 10, 42, 52, 84, 100, 107
- Big Bend City, 54
- Big Bow, 37
- Big Branch, 125
- Big Bunch, 10
- Big Cabin, 92
- Big Cane, 42
- Big Cedar, 25
- Big Chief, 10
- Big Creek, 10, 21, 25, 42, 57, 61, 110
- Big Creek Corner, 7
- Big Delta, 4
- Big Eddy, 25
- Big Elk Meadows, 13
- Big Falls, 54, 128
- Big Fields, 4
- Big Flat, 7
- Big Flats, 128
- Bigfoot, 114
- Big Foot, 28
- Bigfork, 54, 65
- Big Fork, 7

- Big Four, 125
- Big George, 25
- Biggers, 7
- Bigheart, 92
- Big Hill, 7, 81
- Big Horn, 4, 130
- Bighorn, 13, 65
- Big Lake, 7
- Big Level, 57
- Big Meadows, 121
- Big Mill, 74
- Big Moose, 78
- Big Mountain, 100
- Big Muddy River, 49
- Big Oak, 21,73
- Big Oak Corners, 16
- Big Oak Flat, 10
- Big Park, 4
- Big Patch, 128
- Big Pine, 10, 18
- Big Pines, 46
- Big Point, 57
- Big Pond, 100
- Big Pool, 46
- Big Prairie, 52, 87
- Big Rapids, 52
- Big Ridge, 1, 61
- Big River, 10
- Big Rock, 7, 28, 52, 87, 110
- Big Rocks, 92
- Big Run, 125
- Big Sag, 65
- Big Sandy, 65, 110, 125, 130
- Big Scrub, 18
- Big Sky, 65
- Big Spraddle Creek, 121
- Big Spring, 35, 46, 54, 100, 121, 128
- Bigspring, 61
- Big Spring Mill, 7
- Big Springs, 4, 7, 21, 25, 31, 37, 67, 73, 87, 107, 110, 125
- Big Stone Beach, 16
- Big Stone City, 107
- Big Sur, 10

- Big Timber, 65
- Big Trees, 10
- Big Water, 117
- Big Woods, 42, 54
- Bijou, 13, 42
- Bijou Hills, 107
- Bill, 130
- Billings, 52, 61, 92
- Bills Place, 100
- Billville, 31
- Billy Goat Hill, 1, 42
- Bimini, 18
- Bingo, 44
- Birch, 54, 69, 100, 114, 128
- Birch Bay, 123
- Birch Beach, 54
- Birch Creek, 52
- Birch Groves, 15
- Birch Harbor, 44
- Birch Island, 28
- Birch Run, 52
- Birch Tree, 61
- Birchwood, 15, 52
- Bird, 78, 110
- Bird-in-Hand, 100
- Bird Cage, 81
- Bird City, 37
- Birdeye, 1, 7
- Bird Hill, 46
- Bird Island, 54
- Birdland, 15, 119
- Bird Rock, 10
- Birds, 21, 28
- Birds Corner, 16, 61
- Birds Creek, 125
- Birds Eye, 31
- Birdseye, 13, 31, 65, 117
- Birds Landing, 10
- Birdsnest, 121
- Birdsong, 1, 7, 61
- Birdsong Crossroads, 21
- Birds Point, 61
- Bird Springs, 61
- Birdsview, 123

- Birdsville, 21
- Birdtown, 7, 105
- Birdwood, 67
- Birmingham, 1, 21, 28, 31, 35, 37, 52, 57, 61, 87, 100
- Birthright, 114
- Bismarck, 7
- Bismark, 87
- Bison, 37, 65, 92, 107
- Bitter Creek, 130
- Bitter End, 110
- Bitter Springs, 4
- Bitter Sweet, 46
- Bitterwater, 10
- Bivalve, 10
- Black, 1, 61, 100, 114
- Black Ash, 100
- Blackband, 87
- Black Bear, 92
- Black Bear Spring, 4
- Blackberry, 54, 114, 121
- Blackberry City, 125
- Blackberry Corner, 87
- Blackberry Woods, 28
- Blackbird, 61
- Black Canyon, 25
- Black Canyon City, 4
- Black Cat, 2
- Black Cloud, 25
- Black Creek, 2, 18, 42, 81
- Black Diamond, 4, 7, 18, 100
- Blackduck, 54
- Black Eagle, 65
- Black Eagle Mill, 13
- Black Earth, 128
- Blackfish, 7
- Blackfoot, 7, 42, 65
- Black Forest, 13, 69
- Black Fork, 7
- Black Gap, 4, 100
- Blackgum, 92
- Black Hammer, 54
- Blackhawk, 10, 28, 35, 87, 107
- Black Hawk, 13, 42, 57, 107, 128

- Blackhawk Island, 28
- Black Hill, 114
- Blackhoof, 54
- Blackhorse, 46
- Black Horse, 73, 87, 107
- Blackjack, 21, 61, 92, 114
- Black Jack, 7, 37, 57, 61, 81, 111
- Blackjack Corner, 6
- Black Lake, 52, 74
- Blackleaf, 65
- Blackman, 18
- Black Mountain, 81, 100
- Black Oak, 7, 31, 46, 61, 111, 114
- Black Pine, 25
- Blackpipe, 107
- Black Plain, 104
- Black Point, 18, 31
- Black Ridge, 100
- Black River, 52
- Black River Falls, 128
- Blackrock, 25
- Black Rock, 2, 7, 15, 49, 74, 94, 117
- Blackrock Mill, 46
- Blacks Ford, 18
- Black Springs, 7
- Blackstone, 28, 44
- Blackstone Post Office, 84
- Blacktail, 25, 65
- Blacktop, 87
- Black Walnut, 61, 100
- Black Water, 81
- Blackwater, 4, 16, 44, 46, 57, 61, 71
- Black Wolf, 37, 125
- Blackwood, 21, 65, 81
- Blades, 16
- Bland, 18, 61, 74, 114, 121
- Blanket, 114
- Blanks, 42
- Bleak, 121
- Blennerhassett, 125
- Blessing, 35, 87, 114
- Bliss, 25, 52, 61, 69
- Blissville, 119
- Blitzen, 94

- Block, 37, 111
- Blockhouse, 123
- Blondy, 111
- Bloodland, 61
- Bloodtown, 21
- Bloody Corners, ,87
- Bloody Springs, 57
- Bloom, 13, 37, 46, 84
- Bloomer, 7, 128
- Bloomer Spring, 46
- Bloomfield, 35, 46, 67
- Blooming Grove, 2, 31
- Blooming Prairie, 54
- Blooming Rose, 61
- Bloomington, 28, 30, 31, 37, 46, 54, 61, 67, 100, 114(2)
- Bloomville, 87
- Blossom, 105, 111, 114
- Blowing Rock, 81
- Blowing Rocks, 18
- Blowing Spring, 21
- Blowout, 114
- Blue, 4, 114, 125
- Blueacre, 117
- Blue Ball, 16, 100
- Blue Bayou, 7
- Bluebell, 117
- Blue Bell, 73, 100
- Blue Bend, 125
- Blueberry, 128
- Blue Berry Hill, 114
- Blueberry Hill, 2, 57
- Blue Brick, 105
- Blue Creek, 111, 117, 125
- Blue Diamond, 69
- Blue Dome, 25
- Blue Earth, 54
- Blue Eye, 7, 61
- Bluefield, 18, 125
- Blue Ford Landing, 2
- Blue Gap, 4
- Blue Goose, 100, 111
- Bluegrass, 31, 65, 84
- Blue Grass, 35, 54, 121

- Blue Gulf Beach, 18
- Blue Heaven, 105
- Blue Hill, 37, 44, 46, 57, 67, 130
- Blue Hill Falls, 44
- Blue Hills, 15
- Blue Hole, 121
- Blue Island, 28
- Bluejacket, 92
- Blue Jay, 10, 87, 100, 125
- Blue Knob, 10
- Blue Lake, 18
- Blue Lick, 31, 61
- Bluelight, 123
- Blue Mound, 28, 37, 61
- Blue Mounds, 128
- Blue Mount, 46
- Blue Mountain, 2, 13, 46, 57, 121
- Blue Mountain Beach, 18
- Blue Pennant, 125
- Blue Point, 28
- Blue Pond, 2
- Blue Rapids, 37
- Blue Ridge, 2, 21, 28, 31, 57, 61, 105, 111, 114
- Blue Ridge Forest, 81
- Blue Ridge View, 46
- Blue River, 13, 94, 128
- Blue Rock, 81, 87, 125
- Blues Beach, 125
- Blueside, 123
- Blue Sky, 111
- Blue Spring, 125
- Blue Springs, 2, 7, 18, 21, 57, 61, 67, 111
- Blue Springs Park, 2
- Bluestem, 123
- Bluestone, 125
- Blue Sulphur Springs, 125
- Blue Town, 123
- Blue Valley, 13
- Blue Vista, 4
- Bluewater, 5, 74
- Bluewell, 125
- Bluff, 57

- Bluff City, 28, 37
- Bluff Creek, 35, 42
- Bluff Hail, 28
- Bluffs, 28
- Bluff Springs, 18, 57
- Blunt, 10,107
- Bly, 93, 94
- Blythedale, 61
- Blytheville, 7
- Board, 125
- Board Valley, 111
- Boar Tush, 2
- Bob, 42
- Bobo, 2, 31, 57, 87
- Bobtown, 31
- Bob White, 125
- Bob White Fork, 81
- Bogart, 21, 87
- Boggy Depot, 92
- Bogota, 28, 111
- Bogus Corners, 100
- Boiling Springs, 2, 7, 81, 100, 105
- Boise, 114, 123
- Boise City, 90, 92
- Bold Spring, 111
- Bold Springs,
- Bolivia, 28, 69, 81
- Bolt, 125, 125
- Bombay, 52, 54
- Bon Agua, 111
- Bon Ami, 18, 42
- Bond, 42, 57, 111
- Bone, 25
- Bone Crossing, 65
- Bonesteel, 107
- Bonetrail, 84
- Bone Valley, 117
- Boneyard, 5
- Bonnie Bell, 10
- Bonnie Briar, 69
- Bonus, 57, 114
- Book, 42
- Booker, 114
- Boon, 52

- Boone, 5, 7, 13, 33, 35, 57, 61, 67, 81, 92, 94, 111, 114, 121
- Boonesboro, 61
- Boonesborough, 61, 99
- Booneville, 10, 35, 111
- Boonsboro, 46
- Boonville, 81
- Booster, 7
- Boot Hill, 2, 46
- Bootjack, 10, 46, 52
- Bootleg, 114
- Bootlegger Crossing, 5
- Borax, 65, 69
- Bordeaux, 67
- Border, 54, 130
- Bordertown, 100
- Border Town, 69
- Boring, 46, 94
- Boston, 2, 7, 21, 31, 42, 48(2), 49(2), 52, 61, 87, 111, 114, 121
- Boston Harbor, 123
- Boston Ravine, 10
- Bothersome, 7
- Bottom Creek, 125
- Boudinot, 92
- Boulder, 13, 25, 28, 65, 117, 130
- Boulder City, 61, 69
- Boulder Creek, 10
- Boulder Flats, 130
- Boulder Oaks, 10
- Bounce, 114
- Boundary, 123
- Boundary City, 31
- Bound Brook, 73
- Bountiful, 13, 117
- Bounty, 84
- Bourbon, 28, 31, 57, 61, 94
- Bovine, 7
- Bow, 123
- Bowbells, 84
- Bow Bog, 71
- Bowie, 5, 42, 46
- Bowlegs, 92
- Bowler, 65, 128

- Bowling Green, 18, 31, 46, 57, 61, 87, 105
- Bowlings Alley, 46
- Bowman, 71
- Bowman Bluff, 81
- Bowmans, 121
- Bowstring, 54
- Bow Valley, 67
- Box, 92
- Box Ankle, 21
- Box Canyon, 25
- Boxelder, 130
- Box Elder, 65, 107
- Box Springs, 7, 21
- Boy Corner, 54
- Boyd, 2, 7, 18, 28, 31, 35, 37, 52, 54, 65, 69, 74, 92, 94, 100, 105, 111, 114, 128
- Boyle, 28, 37, 57
- Boy River, 54
- Boys Republic, 10
- Boys Town, 61, 67
- Bracken, 31, 61, 69
- Brad, 114
- Bradford, 49, 97
- Bradley, 2, 7, 10, 25, 28, 44, 52, 57, 65, 67, 92, 105, 107, 125, 128
- Bradley Acres, 121
- Bradley Forest, 121
- Bradley Junction, 100
- Bradleys Corner, 44
- Bradleytown, 100
- Bradleyville, 15, 52
- Bradwood, 94
- Braintree, 48, 49(2)
- Braintree Hill, 119
- Brake, 42, 81, 125
- Bramble, 31
- Branch, 42, 57
- Branchville, 15
- Brand, 114, 121
- Brandenberg, 65
- Brass Castle, 73
- Brasstown, 81

- Bravo, 2
- Bray, 92
- Brazil, 30, 31, 35, 57, 61, 111
- Bread Loaf, 119
- Bread Springs, 74
- Breakfast Hill, 71
- Breakneck, 15, 100
- Breakneck Hill, 130
- Breckinridge, 28, 31, 52, 54, 61, 92
- Breed, 128
- Breezewood, 16
- Breezy Hill, 42
- Breezy Point, 54, 71
- Brenda, 5
- Brian, 42, 61
- Brian Head, 117
- Briar, 61
- Briar Bluff, 28
- Briarcliff, 21
- Briar Park, 16
- Briartown, 92
- Briarwood, 84
- Brick, 73
- Brick House, 105
- Bricks, 81
- Brick School Corner, 71
- Brick Store, 16, 21
- Bridal Veil, 94
- Bride, 111
- Bridge, 25, 94
- Bridge City, 42
- Bridge Creek, 61
- Bridge House, 10
- Bridgeport, 10, 13, 15, 18, 28, 46, 52, 61, 67
- Bridges, 18
- Bridges Crossroad, 21
- Bridgeton, 52
- Bridgetown, 21, 46
- Bridgeville, 10, 17, 52
- Bridgewater, 15, 44, 52, 73, 87, 107, 107
- Brief, 81
- Briery Branch, 121
- Briggs, 5, 31, 67, 87, 92, 114, 121
- Briggs Corner, 49
- Briggsdale, 13
- Briggs Lake, 54
- Briggs Terrace, 10
- Briggsville, 7, 49, 100, 128
- Bright, 7, 31, 57
- Bright Corner, 57
- Bright Hope, 111
- Bright Star, 2, 7, 114
- Brightwater, 7, 81
- Brightwood, 121
- Brilliant, 2, 74
- Brimstone, 42, 111
- Brimstone Corner, 13, 49
- Brimstone Corners, 119
- Brink, 46, 92
- Briny Breezes, 18
- Brisbane, 84
- Bristol, 13, 15, 28, 31, 52, 54, 71, 107, 109(2), 111, 119, 123
- Britain, 121
- British Hollow, 128
- British Woods, 81
- Brittin, 107
- Broad, 21
- Broad Brook, 15
- Broad Creek, 17
- Broad Pass, 4
- Broadview, 74
- Broadwater, 67
- Broadway, 61, 69, 73, 81, 87
- Broken Arrow, 92
- Broken Bow, 67, 92
- Broken Hills, 69, 121
- Bromide, 92
- Bronco, 21, 69, 114
- Bronx, 25, 75, 77, 78, 130
- Brook, 31
- Brookdale, 67
- Brookfield, 61
- Brook Forest, 13
- Brookline, 49

- Brooklyn, 2, 15, 21, 28, 31, 35, 52, 54, 57, 61, 75, 77(2), 78(2), 100, 123
- Brookside, 17
- Brook Springs, 21
- Brooksville, 2, 18, 21, 44, 57, 92, 105, 111, 119
- Broom Hill, 31
- Brothers, 94
- Brown, 65
- Brown City, 94
- Brown Jug Corner, 31
- Brown Mountain Beach, 81
- Brownsand, 21
- Brown Shanty, 61
- Browns Still, 18
- Brownsville, 2, 7, 10, 18, 21, 28, 31, 38, 42, 46, 52, 54, 57, 73, 94, 100, 105, 107, 111, 114(2), 119, 121, 123, 125, 128
- Browntown, 94(2)
- Brownwood, 21
- Bruce, 18, 28, 54, 57, 81, 94, 107, 123, 125, 128
- Bruce Crossing, 52
- Bruce Eddy, 25
- Bruce Junction, 57
- Bruce Lake Station, 31
- Bruceton, 100
- Bruceton Mills, 125
- Bruceville, 10, 18, 31, 46, 111, 114
- Brucewell, 35
- Brush, 13
- Brush Arbor, 61
- Brush Camp Lower Place, 125
- Brush Hollow, 49
- Brush Ridge, 87
- Brussels, 28, 61, 128
- Buchanan, 10, 13, 18, 21, 31, 52, 74, 78, 84, 87, 94, 111, 121
- Buckboard, 94
- Buck Creek, 31, 35, 37, 128
- Buckeye, 5, 7, 10, 13, 31, 35, 37, 42, 61, 67, 74, 87, 111, 114, 121, 125
- Buckeye City, 87

- Buckeye Crossroads, 13
- Buckeye Mill, 5
- Buck Grove, 35
- Buckhead, 21
- Buckhead Ridge, 18
- Buck Hollow, 119
- Buckhorn, 10, 18, 28, 35, 52, 57, 61, 69, 74, 87, 100, 114, 130
- Buckingham, 65
- Buck Knob, 7
- Buckland, 15
- Bucklin, 37
- Bucks, 28
- Bucks Corner, 71
- Bucks Corners, 94
- Buckskin, 31, 69
- Buckskin Crossing, 130
- Buckskin Joe, 13
- Bucksnort, 2, 54, 111
- Buck Snort, 7
- Bucktail, 67
- Bucktown, 10, 31, 46
- Buck Trails, 52
- Buckville, 18
- Bucyrus, 84
- Bud, 31, 125
- Budapest, 61
- Budge, 25
- Buena Vista, 2, 7, 10, 13, 18, 21, 28, 31, 35, 46, 52, 57, 74, 78, 87, 94, 100, 111, 114, 121, 128
- Buenos Aires, 114
- Buffalo, 7, 28, 31, 35, 37, 44, 54, 60, 61, 65, 67, 72, 75, 78, 81, 84, 87, 92, 100, 104, 105, 107, 111, 114, 125, 128, 130
- Buffalo Bend, 121
- Buffalo Bluff, 18
- Buffalo City, 7, 128
- Buffalo Cove, 81
- Buffalo Creek, 13, 125
- Buffalo Ford, 121, 130
- Buffalo Forge, 121
- Buffalo Gap, 107

- Buffalo Grove, 28
- Buffalo Hill, 10, 121
- Buffalo Lake, 54
- Buffalo Meadows, 69
- Buffalo Mop, 111
- Buffalo Prairie, 28
- Buffalo Ridge, 107, 111, 121
- Buffalo Run, 100
- Buffalo Springs, 74, 84, 121
- Buffalo Trading Post, 107
- Buffalo Valley, 111
- Buffaloville, 31
- Buffo, 7
- Bug Hill, 81
- Bug Scuffle, 111
- Bug Tussle, 92, 114
- Buick, 12, 61
- Bull City, 2
- Bull Creek, 10
- Bullet Hole, 78
- Bull Fork, 69
- Bullhead, 107
- Bullhead Bluff, 21
- Bullhead City, 5
- Bull Hollow, 92
- Bullion, 69, 100
- Bullion Falls, 117
- Bullionville, 117
- Bull Mountain, 65
- Bull Run, 42, 94, 121, 125
- Bull Run Corner, 15
- Bulls Bridge, 15
- Bulltown, 7
- Bull Valley, 28
- Bully Hill, 10
- Bumble Bee, 5
- Bumblebee, 10
- Bummerville, 10
- Bunch, 92
- Bungalow, 111
- Bungay, 28
- Bungy, 71
- Bunker, 61, 107
- Bunker Donation, 18
- Bunker Hill, 10, 15, 18, 28, 31, 37, 49, 52, 57, 61, 81, 87, 94, 105, 114
- Burbank, 18,90
- Burden, 37
- Bureau, 28, 46
- Burg, 7, 92
- Burger Town, 81
- Burksville, 28, 61
- Burley, 25
- Burleytown, 46
- Burlington, 13, 28, 31, 35, 44, 49, 52, 81, 84, 87, 94, 100, 114, 119, 125, 130
- Burning Bush, 21,100
- Burning Springs, 125
- Burning Well, 100
- Burns, 94, 114
- Burns Flat, 92
- Burnside, 21, 28, 35, 42, 52, 57
- Burnt, 52
- Burnt Cabin, 69
- Burnt Cabins, 100
- Burnt Cane, 7
- Burnt Chimney, 121
- Burnt Chimney Corner, 81
- Burnt Corn, 2
- Burnt Creek, 21
- Burnt Factory, 46, 121, 125
- Burntfork, 130
- Burnt Fort, 21
- Burnt Hill, 7, 15, 78
- Burnt Hills, 78
- Burnt House, 125
- Burnt Mill, 13, 44
- Burnt Mills, 73, 81
- Burnt Mills Hill, 46
- Burnt Mills Village, 46
- Burnt Prairie, 28
- Burnt Ranch, 10
- Burnt Tree, 121
- Burnt Water, 5
- Burnt Woods, 46, 94
- Burnville, 7
- Burr Oak, 31, 35, 37, 52, 67, 87, 128

- Burrow, 114
- Burrows, 61, 100, 123
- Burt, 28, 35, 57, 84, 92, 111
- Bush, 2, 10, 28, 42, 46, 57, 94
- Bush Prairie, 123
- Bush River, 105
- Bushwick, 77
- Businessburg, 87
- Business Corner, 57, 87
- Business Corners, 35
- Busy Corner, 111
- Bute, 61, 100
- Butler, 2, 7, 10, 21, 28, 31, 42, 52, 54, 57, 61, 73, 87, 92, 107, 114
- Butlers Corners, 119
- Butlerville, 49
- Butte, 64, 65, 65, 67
- Butter Creek, 7
- Butterfield, 52, 54
- Butterfly Lake, 54
- Buttermilk, 7, 37
- Buttermilk Falls, 100
- Buttermilk Point, 31
- Butternut, 52, 54, 119
- Butternut Grove, 78, 100
- Buttersville, 52
- Buttonwillow, 10
- Buttonwood, 100
- Buttzville, 84
- Buyck, 54
- Buzaards Roost, 61
- Buzards Crossroads, 81
- Buzz, 100
- Buzzards Bay, 49
- Bygland, 55
- Byng, 92
- B Z Corner, 123

-C-

- Cabbage Grove, 18
- Cabbage Patch, 10
- Cabin, 81

- Cabin City, 65
- Cabin Cove, 10
- Cabin Creek, 13, 65, 123
- Cabinet, 87
- Cabin John, 46
- Cable, 87, 128
- Cable Car Crossing, 25
- Cableville, 94
- Cabool, 61
- Cache, 25, 28, 92
- Cache Lake, 7
- Cactus, 10, 114, 123
- Cactus City, 10
- Cactus Flat, 5, 107
- Cactus Springs, 69
- Cadet, 61
- Cadillac, 18, 52
- Cadiz, 10, 28, 31, 87, 114
- Cain Rock, 10
- Cairo, 21, 28, 39, 57, 61, 67, 92, 111
- Cairo Junction, 78
- Cake, 94
- Calabash, 81
- Calamine, 7, 128
- Calcium, 78
- Calcutta, 87, 126
- Caldwell, 2, 7, 25, 28, 37, 65, 72, 81, 87, 114, 126, 128
- Caledonia, 55, 57, 61
- Calendar, 25
- Calexico, 10
- Calf Creek, 114
- Calhoun, 2, 13, 21, 28, 35, 42, 57, 61, 92, 105, 111, 126
- Calhoun City, 57
- Calhoun Corners, 15
- Calhoun Falls, 105
- Calhoun Mill, 105
- Calhounville, 123
- Calico, 111
- Calico Rock, 7
- California, 9, 14, 27, 77, 46, 52, 61, 68, 73, 81, 90, 100, 120
- California City, 10

- California Hot Springs, 10
- Callaway, 18, 21, 46, 55, 61, 67, 121
- Calleaway, 61
- Calloway, 28, 94
- Calls, 111
- Calm, 87
- Calmer, 7
- Calm Falls, 128
- Calypso, 65, 81
- Camargo, 28, 57, 92, 100
- Camas, 123
- Cambridge, 61, 67
- Camden, 10, 17, 28, 31, 44, 52, 57, 61, 71, 81, 87, 114, 126
- Camden-Wyoming, 17
- Camel Hump, 130
- Camelot, 111, 114
- Cameo, 13, 74
- Campaign, 111
- Campbell, 2, 4, 7, 10, 18, 28, 35, 42, 44, 55, 67, 74, 81, 105, 114, 121
- Campbellsburg, 31
- Campbellsville, 111
- Camp Bird, 13
- Camp Carson, 94
- Camp Crook, 107
- Camp Douglas, 69, 128
- Camp Eighteen, 10
- Campgaw, 73
- Camp Ground, 126
- Camp Hill, 2, 57, 100
- Camp Logan, 28
- Camp Number Fortytwo, 37
- Camp Number Six, 37
- Camp Ripley Junction, 55
- Camp Spring, 2
- Camp Three, 65
- Campton, 18, 21, 100, 105
- Campus, 28, 37
- Campville, 15
- Canada, 37, 87
- Canada Mills, 49
- Canadian, 92, 114
- Canadian Fork, 92
- Canary, 94
- Candelaria, 68
- Candle, 4
- Candlewood Orchards, 15
- Candlewood Pines, 15
- Candlewood Point, 15
- Candlewood Springs, 15
- Candy Town, 87
- Cane, 5
- Cane Beds, 5
- Cane Brake, 81, 105
- Canebrake, 10, 42, 126
- Cane Creek, 7, 21, 111
- Canehill, 7
- Cane Island, 7
- Cane Ridge, 42
- Cane River, 81
- Caney, 7, 37, 42, 92
- Caney Creek, 18
- Caney Ridge, 92
- Caney Valley, 7
- Cannelburg, 31
- Cannelton, 100
- Cannelville, 87
- Cannery Row, 10
- Canning, 107
- Cannon, 61, 114
- Cannon Ball, 84
- Cannon Beach, 94
- Cannon City, 55
- Cannon Creek, 7
- Cannon Falls, 55
- Cannonsburg, 98, 100
- Cannon Town, 18
- Canoe, 2, 35
- Canoe Camp, 100
- Canon City, 69
- Cantaloupe, 31
- Canterbury, 15, 17, 71
- Canton, 15, 28, 37, 44, 52, 57, 84
- Canton Center, 15
- Canton Valley, 15
- Canvas, 126
- Canyon, 25, 55, 126

- Canyon City, 10, 69, 94
- Canyon Creek, 65
- Canyon Creek Station, 69
- Canyon Dam, 10
- Canyon Ferry, 65
- Canyon Mill, 74
- Cape Charles, 121
- Cape Cod, 49
- Cape Elizabeth, 44
- Cape Fear, 81
- Cape Girardeau, 61
- Cape Horn, 10
- Cape May Court House, 73
- Capetown, 10
- Capital Hill, 10, 111
- Capitol, 65
- Capitol City, 13
- Capitol Hill, 73
- Cap Rock, 114
- Caprock, 74
- Captain, 121
- Captain Cook, 24
- Captain Hill, 74
- Carbide, 126
- Carbon, 31, 35, 92, 100, 114, 126, 130
- Carbonate, 25, 107
- Carbon Center, 25, 61
- Carbon City, 7
- Carbondale, 10, 31
- Carbon Hill, 28, 61
- Car Branch, 111
- Cardinal, 13
- Cardwell, 64, 65
- Carefree, 5, 31
- Caress, 126
- Cargas, 42
- Caribou, 10, 44, 55
- Caribou City, 25, 94
- Carlisle, 2, 7, 31, 35, 42, 49, 52, 55, 57, 67, 87, 92, 100, 105, 111, 114
- Carlock, 28, 107
- Carmel, 10
- Carmel-by-the-Sea, 10

- Carmichaels, 100
- Carnation, 123
- Carol City, 18
- Carolina, 81, 105, 114, 126
- Carol Stream, 28
- Carp, 55, 69
- Carpenter, 2, 17, 57, 65, 81, 87, 92, 107, 130
- Carpenters Corner, 17,55
- Carracas, 13
- Carroll, 35, 42, 44, 46, 57, 67, 69, 71, 81, 87, 94
- Carrollton, 7, 21, 28, 31, 35, 52, 57, 61, 114
- Carson, 2, 13, 35, 44, 57, 84, 92, 94, 114
- Carson City, 52, 69, 119
- Carson Hot Springs, 69
- Carson Lake, 7
- Carsons Corner, 61
- Carsontown, 100
- Carsonville, 52, 100
- Cars Run, 87
- Carter, 57, 61, 65, 81, 87, 92, 100, 107, 111, 114, 126, 128, 130
- Carter Branch, 57
- Carter Camp, 100
- Carter Cedars, 130
- Carter Crossing, 111
- Carter Crossroads, 111
- Carter Lake, 67
- Carter Nine, 92
- Carters Corner, 92
- Carters Creek, 111
- Carters Crossroads, 105
- Carter Settlement, 114
- Cartersville, 13, 35, 65, 92, 105, 107
- Cartertown, 111
- Carterville, 28, 42, 49, 114
- Carthage, 60
- Casablanca, 81
- Casa Blanca, 5, 74
- Cascade, 13, 25, 28, 35, 46, 65, 67, 71, 78,1 26,1 28

- Cascade Springs, 107
- Cascade Valley, 123
- Casey, 2, 7, 28, 35, 55
- Cash, 7, 52, 61, 105, 107, 111, 114, 121
- Cash Corner, 44, 46, 121
- Cashiers, 81
- Cashmere, 123, 126
- Cash Point, 42, 111
- Cashtown, 100
- Cashup, 123
- Cashville, 105
- Casino, 55
- Casper, 130
- Cassidy Curve, 65
- Castle, 92
- Castle Danger, 55
- Castleford, 25
- Castle Grove, 35
- Castle Hot Springs, 5
- Castle Pines, 13
- Castle Rock, 13, 55, 65, 107, 117, 123, 128
- Castle Rocks, 25
- Castle Rock Springs, 10
- Castle Town, 65
- Castlewood, 107
- Catalpa, 7, 67
- Cataract, 128
- Catchpenny, 46
- Cat Corner, 111
- Cat Creek, 46, 65
- Cat Elbow Corner, 78
- Catfish, 100
- Catfish Paradise, 5
- Cathedral, 13
- Cathedral Pines, 25
- Catherine, 2, 13, 37, 42
- Catherine Furnace, 121
- Catherine Lake, 81
- Catherine Place, 61
- Catlettsburg, 111
- Cats Bridge, 121
- Catskill, 78
- Cat Spring, 114
- Cat Square, 81
- Cattaraugus, 78
- Cattle Creek, 13
- Cattown, 78
- Cavalier, 84
- Cavalry Hill, 21
- Cave, 3, 7, 37, 61
- Cave-in-Rock, 28
- Cave City, 7, 10, 61
- Cave Colony, 17
- Cave Creek, 5, 7, 69
- Cave Hill, 61
- Cave Spring, 7, 21, 111
- Cave Springs, 7, 37, 61
- Cawood, 61
- Caywood, 87
- Ceasetown, 100
- Cedar, 5, 25, 31, 35, 37, 44, 55, 92, 117, 126
- Cedar Bank, 52
- Cedar Beach, 55, 19
- Cedar Bluff, 35, 52, 57, 61,1 11
- Cedar Bluffs, 37, 67
- Cedar Branch, 121
- Cedar Bridge, 73
- Cedar Brook, 28, 73
- Cedar Bushes, 49
- Cedar Canyon, 107
- Cedar City, 35, 117
- Cedar Cliff, 21, 46
- Cedar Cliffs, 61
- Cedar Cove, 57
- Cedar Creek, 5, 7, 13, 18, 25, 52, 61, 67, 81, 105, 114
- Cedar Crest, 12, 74
- Cedar Crossing, 10, 21
- Cedaredge, 13
- Cedar Falls, 35, 81, 123
- Cedar Flat, 10, 94
- Cedar Ford, 61
- Cedar Gap, 61
- Cedar Glade, 7
- Cedar Glen, 10

- Cedar Grove, 2, 7, 10, 13, 18, 21, 31, 35, 42, 44, 49, 73, 74, 81, 87, 100,1 05,1 11,114, 126
- Cedar Haven, 46, 52
- Cedar Hill, 46, 49, 57, 61, 74, 100, 111, 114
- Cedar Key, 18
- Cedar Knolls, 73
- Cedar Lake, 31, 52, 55, 57, 73,1 29
- Cedar Land, 15
- Cedar Landing, 46
- Cedar Lane, 111
- Cedar Lawn, 46
- Cedar Mill, 5, 55, 94
- Cedar Mills, 54
- Cedar Mountain, 123
- Cedar Pines, 100
- Cedar Plains, 2
- Cedar Point, 13, 31, 37
- Cedar Rapids, 35, 67
- Cedar Ridge, 5, 10,6 1
- Cedar River, 52
- Cedar Rock, 21, 105
- Cedar Run, 52, 87, 100
- Cedars, 57, 92
- Cedar Slope, 10
- Cedar Springs, 2, 10, 21, 52, 61, 87, 100, 105, 117
- Cedar Swamp, 105
- Cedartown, 21
- Cedar Valley, 2, 21, 35, 61, 87, 117
- Cedar View, 57
- Cedar Village, 81, 92
- Cedarville, 123, 129
- Cedar Vista, 61
- Cee Vee, 114
- Celebration, 18
- Celeryville, 87
- Celina, 55
- Cement, 92
- Cement City, 52, 61
- Cemetery Corners, 71
- Centenary, 31, 105

- Centennial, 5, 13, 21, 31, 52, 87, 100, 126, 130
- Center, 7, 13, 21, 57, 61, 67, 71, 84, 87, 92, 111, 114
- Center City, 55
- Center Grove, 7, 35
- Center Hill, 2, 7, 21, 57
- Center Line, 52
- Center Point, 7, 21, 35, 42, 57, 107, 126
- Center Post, 61
- Center Ridge, 57
- Center Sandwich, 71
- Centertown, 61, 119
- Center Valley, 31, 129
- Centerview, 37, 61
- Center Village, 87
- Centerville, 12, 17, 10, 17, 18, 21, 25, 28, 31, 35, 37, 42, 44, 46, 52, 55, 57, 61, 67, 69, 73, 74, 87, 92, 100, 107, 110, 119, 123, 129
- Centerville Corner, 74
- Centrahoma, 92
- Central, 4, 7, 10, 25, 28, 37, 42, 52, 55, 57, 61, 69, 75, 81, 100, 105, 117
- Central Academy, 57
- Central City, 2, 7, 13, 18, 28, 35, 67, 87, 100, 107
- Central Cove, 25
- Central Falls, 81
- Central Grove, 57
- Centralia, 28, 123
- Central Park, 28
- Central Point, 94, 111
- Central Rochester, 69
- Central Square, 49
- Central Valley, 10
- Central Village, 15
- Centre, 57
- Centre Grove, 73
- Centropolis, 38, 61
- Century, 18(2)
- Cereal, 28, 100, 114
- Ceylon, 54, 55

- Chain Hill, 123
- Chain of Rocks, 61
- Chain o' Lakes, 129
- Chaintown, 100
- Chalk, 114
- Chalk Cut, 25
- Chalk Level, 61, 111, 121
- Challenge, 10,100
- Chamois, 61
- Champ, 61
- Champaign, 28
- Champion, 61, 65, 67, 87, 114
- Champion City, 61
- Chance, 2, 13, 65, 92, 107, 121
- Chancellor, 107, 114
- Chaney, 46, 114
- Chaneysville, 100
- Changewater, 73
- Chant, 3, 7
- Chantilly, 61, 121
- Chaparral, 75
- Charity, 61, 105
- Charleroi, 98, 100
- Charles, 21, 52, 81
- Charles City, 35, 121
- Charles Corner, 121
- Charles River Grove, 49
- Charleston, 5, 7, 28, 38, 44, 52, 57, 61, 69, 87, 94, 100, 105, 111, 114, 117, 119, 123, 125, 126
- Charleston Park, 69
- Charleston Springs, 73
- Charlestown, 31, 46, 71, 73, 94, 104
- Charles Town, 126
- Charlesville, 46, 55
- Charlesworth, 52
- Charlie, 114
- Charlieville, 42
- Charlotte, 7, 52, 80
- Charm, 87
- Charter Oak, 35
- Chase, 67, 94, 107, 129
- Chat, 114
- Chattanooga, 13, 87, 92, 108

- Chautauqua, 28, 35, 38, 87, 107, 123
- Cheapside, 114
- Cheat Lake, 126
- Cheat Neck, 126
- Check, 114, 121
- Checkerberry Corner, 119
- Checkerboard, 65
- Checks Corner, 7
- Cheddar, 21, 105
- Cheek, 92, 114
- Cheesequake, 73
- Cheesetown, 100
- Cheeseville, 10, 129
- Chelsea, 48
- Cheltenham, 46, 99, 100
- Chena Hot Springs, 4
- Cheraw, 105
- Chericoke, 121
- Cherry, 5, 28, 55, 81, 111
- Cherry Box, 61
- Cherry City, 100
- Cherry Corner, 100, 111
- Cherry Creek, 25, 58, 69, 78, 107(2), 126
- Cherry Dell, 61
- Cherry Falls, 126
- Cherryfield, 44
- Cherry Flats, 100
- Cherry Fork, 87
- Cherry Grove, 31, 42, 55, 81, 94, 100, 121, 123, 126
- Cherry Hill, 7, 46, 73, 100, 105, 111
- Cherry Lake, 18
- Cherrylane, 25
- Cherry Lane, 81
- Cherry Log, 21
- Cherry Mills, 100
- Cherry Park, 15, 28
- Cherry Point, 123
- Cherry Ridge, 13, 42, 65, 73, 100
- Cherry Run, 100
- Cherrytown, 46
- Cherry Tree, 92, 100
- Cherrytree, 2

- Cherryvale, 37, 38
- Cherry Vale, 61
- Cherry Valley, 10, 28, 49, 61, 78, 87, 100, 104, 111
- Cherryville, 25, 61, 73, 81, 94
- Cherrywood, 73
- Chesapeake, 61
- Cheshire, 15
- Chester, 15, 55, 97
- Chestnut, 2, 28, 65
- Chestnut Dale, 81
- Chestnutflat, 21
- Chestnut Glade, 111
- Chestnut Grove, 2, 46, 81, 100, 111, 121
- Chestnut Hill, 46, 49, 81, 100, 111, 121, 126
- Chestnut Knob, 121
- Chestnut Mound, 111
- Chestnut Mountain, 21
- Chestnutridge 61(2)
- Chestnut Ridge, 31, 46, 61, 73, 78, 100, 111, 126
- Chestnut Springs, 106
- Chestnut Tree Corner, 49
- Chestnut Valley, 111
- Chevron, 38
- Chevy Chase, 46
- Chew, 123
- Chewey, 92
- Chewsville, 46
- Cheyenne, 38
- Cheyenne Wells, 13
- Chicago, 3, 26, 27, 28, 60, 114
- Chicago City, 55
- Chicago Corners, 129
- Chicago Creek, 4
- Chicago Park, 10
- Chicken, 4, 7
- Chickentown, 100
- Chicks Corner, 71
- Chick Springs, 106
- Chickville, 71
- Chigger Hill, 2
- Childs Meadows, 10
- Chili, 28, 31, 75, 92, 129
- Chili Center, 78
- Chillicothe, 28, 35, 61, 114, 120
- Chilly, 25
- Chimes, 7
- Chimney Corner, 119, 126
- Chimney Rock, 13, 65, 73, 81
- China, 2, 31, 44, 61, 78, 114
- China Grove, 2, 81, 114
- China Hill, 21, 25
- Chinatown, 28, 31, 65, 69, 107
- China Town, 94
- Chinese Camp, 10
- Chinook, 65
- Chip, 81
- Chipmunk, 78
- Chiquita, 10
- Chisolm, 106
- Chloride, 5, 61, 75
- Chloride City, 10
- Chocolate Bayou, 114
- Chocolate Springs, 114
- Choctaw, 1
- Choice, 55, 114
- Chopmist, 104
- Choptank, 46
- Chosen, 18
- Christian, 4, 28, 121, 126
- Christine, 84, 114
- Christmas, 5, 18, 52, 58, 100
- Christmas City, 117
- Christmas Cove, 44
- Christmas Valley, 94
- Christmasville, 111
- Chrome, 10, 94, 100
- Chrome Hill, 46
- Chrysler, 2
- Chuckery, 87
- Chugwater, 130
- Chunky, 58, 114
- Churchill Downs, 2
- Cimarron, 13, 75
- Cimarron City, 92

- Cincinnati, 7, 31, 35, 39, 61, 80, 81, 84, 85(2), 86(2), 87(2)
- Cincinnati Landing, 28
- Cincinnatus, 78
- Cinderella, 126
- Circle, 4, 65, 114
- Circle City, 61
- Circle Hot Springs, 4
- Circle Pines, 55
- Circle View, 126
- Circleville, 31, 38, 87, 117
- Citrus, 10
- Citrus Center, 18
- Citrus City, 114
- Citrus Park, 18
- Citrus Springs, 18
- City-by-the-Sea, 114
- City Point, 18, 44, 129
- Clack, 58
- Clam Falls, 129
- Clam Gulch, 4
- Clappers, 55
- Claremore, 91, 92
- Clarinda, 33, 35
- Clark, 2, 13, 18, 28, 35, 58, 60, 61, 69, 73, 81, 87, 107, 114
- Clark City, 61
- Clarksville, 30, 31, 108, 110
- Clark Tree, 25
- Clay, 2, 13, 42, 58, 61, 100, 114
- Claybank, 55
- Clay Banks, 129
- Clay Center, 67
- Clay City, 28, 31, 123
- Clay Sink, 18
- Clay Spur, 130
- Claysville, 46
- Claytown, 58
- Clayville, 15, 111
- Clear Branch, 58
- Clear Creek, 10, 31, 61, 81, 94, 114, 117, 126
- Clearfield, 46, 107, 117
- Clear Fork, 126

- Clearing House, 10
- Clear Lake, 7, 28, 31, 35, 55, 94, 107, 117, 129
- Clear Pond, 106
- Clear Ridge, 46
- Clear Spring, 7, 46
- Clear Springs, 18, 58, 62, 111, 114
- Clearview, 21, 87, 92
- Clearview City, 38
- Clearwater, 7, 18, 25, 38, 42, 55, 62, 65, 67, 73, 94, 106, 123
- Clearwater Springs, 21
- Cleaton, 21
- Cleft, 25
- Cleopatria, 62
- Cleveland, 2, 18, 21, 25, 28, 31, 38, 40, 44, 55, 58, 62, 65, 75, 80, 81, 84, 85(2), 87(2), 87, 92, 94, 106, 111, 114, 117, 123, 129
- Clevelandtown, 49
- Clevelandville, 46
- Clever, 62
- Click, 114
- Clicks, 25
- Cliff, 75
- Cliff Lake, 65
- Cliffs, 25
- Climbing Hill, 35
- Clinch, 28
- Clinch River, 111
- Clinton, 2, 7, 10, 15, 22, 28, 31, 35, 38, 42, 44, 46, 49, 52, 55, 62, 65, 67, 69, 73, 81, 90, 100, 106, 126, 129
- Clinton Falls, 55
- Clipper, 123
- Close City, 114
- Clothier, 126
- Clotho, 55
- Cloud, 35
- Cloud Chief, 92
- Cloud Creek, 92, 111
- Cloudcroft, 75
- Cloud Lake, 18
- Cloudland, 22

- Cloudy, 92
- Clover, 22, 25, 69, 87, 94, 100, 106, 117, 121, 126
- Clover Bend, 7
- Clover Bottom, 62
- Clover Creek, 121
- Cloverfields, 46
- Clover Flat, 10
- Clover Garden, 81
- Clover Hill, 46, 58, 73, 87, 121
- Cloverhill, 73
- Cloverland, 129
- Cloverleaf, 87
- Clover Lick, 126
- Clovis, 10
- Coal, 62
- Coal Banks Landing, 65
- Coalburg, 87
- Coal Canyon, 123
- Coal Center, 100
- Coal City, 2, 28, 31, 100, 117, 126
- Coal Creek, 13, 31, 35, 92, 123
- Coaldale, 69
- Coal Fire, 2
- Coal Fork, 126
- Coal Hill, 7, 62, 87, 111
- Coal Hollow, 28, 100
- Coaling, 2
- Coal Junction, 100
- Coal Mine, 114
- Coal Mine Mesa, 5
- Coalmont, 13
- Coal Mountain, 22, 126
- Coal Oil Corner, 58
- Coalridge, 126
- Coalridge Reserve, 65
- Coal Run, 87, 100
- Coal Springs, 107
- Coaltown, 100
- Coalvale, 38
- Coal Valley, 28, 35, 38, 126
- Coalville, 35, 58, 117
- Coalwood, 52, 65, 126
- Coarsegold, 10

- Coats, 38, 58, 87
- Cobalt, 15, 25
- Cobalt Landing, 15
- Cobbler, 62
- Cobbleskill, 78, 78
- Cobblestone, 81
- Cockatoo Grove, 10
- Cocked Hat, 17
- Cocklebur Flat, 92
- Cocoa, 18
- Cocoa Beach, 18
- Cocolamus, 100
- Coconut, 18
- Coconut Creek, 18
- Cody, 67, 92, 130
- Coffee, 22, 121
- Coffee Bluff, 22
- Coffee City, 114
- Coffee Creek, 10, 65
- Coffee Hill, 46
- Coffee Point, 25
- Coffee Springs, 2
- Coffeetown, 100
- Coffeeville, 2, 7, 38, 58, 114
- Coffins Corner, 73
- Coffins Mills, 78
- Coin, 7, 35
- Coke, 114, 121
- Coke Oven Hollow, 31
- Coker, 67
- Coketown, 126
- Cokeville, 130
- Cold Bay, 4
- Coldbrook, 22, 28
- Coldbrook Springs, 49
- Cold Feet, 4
- Coldfoot, 4
- Cold Fork, 10
- Cold Point, 100, 106
- Cold River, 71, 119
- Cold Run, 100
- Cold Spring, 13, 49, 55, 65, 69, 73, 100, 111, 119, 121, 129

- Cold Springs, 2, 7, 10, 31, 52, 62, 81, 92, 94, 111, 114, 129
- Cold Stream, 126
- Coldwater, 2, 38, 42, 52, 58, 62, 87, 111, 126
- Cold Water, 58, 81, 114
- Colgate, 65, 84
- College City, 7, 10, 31
- College Corner, 31
- College Hill, 7, 58
- College Park, 17, 18, 22, 46
- College Place, 123
- College Springs, 35
- College Station, 18
- Collegeville, 7, 10, 55, 100
- Cologne, 55, 73, 114, 121
- Colon, 52
- Colony, 38, 62, 92
- Colony Hills, 17
- Colorado, 4, 12, 13, 70, 74, 114
- Colorado City, 5, 13
- Colorado Springs, 13
- Colt, 6
- Colts Neck, 73
- Columbia, 5, 15, 17, 31, 35, 42, 44, 46, 58, 62, 69, 71, 81, 87, 100, 104(2), 106, 107, 111, 117, 123
- Columbia City, 31
- Columbia Falls, 65
- Columbine, 12, 94
- Columbine Hills, 13
- Columbine Valley, 13
- Columbus, 13, 22, 28, 31, 38, 52, 58, 62, 65, 67, 69, 73, 75, 81, 84, 87, 100, 114, 129
- Columbus City, 35
- Columbus Grove, 87
- Combat Village, 121
- Combine, 114
- Combs, 7, 111
- Comet, 4, 7, 62, 65, 87
- Comfort, 81, 111, 114, 129
- Comical Corners, 73

- Commerce, 2, 10, 22, 35, 52, 62, 92, 114
- Commerce City, 13
- Commercial, 73
- Commissary Hill, 22
- Commonwealth, 38, 121, 129
- Compass, 100
- Competition, 62
- Compromise, 58
- Concept, 87
- Conception, 62
- Concord, 2, 7, 10, 18, 22, 28, 31, 42, 46, 48, 49, 52, 55, 58, 62, 67, 71, 81, 87, 94, 100, 111, 114, 119, 121, 126, 129
- ConcordCorner, 119
- Concrete, 13, 25, 84, 114, 123
- Cone, 114
- Conestoga, 100
- Confederate Corners, 10
- Confederate Crossroads, 87
- Confidence, 10, 28, 35, 126
- Confluence, 100
- Conger, 55
- Congo, 2, 100, 126
- Congress, 5, 58, 87
- Congress Hill, 100
- Congruity, 100
- Conifer, 13
- Connecticut, 14, 15, 49, 78
- Constant Friendship, 46
- Constellation, 5
- Constitution, 87
- Consume, 10
- Consumers, 117
- Consumme, 10
- Contact, 65, 69
- Content, 65
- Continental, 5, 13, 87
- Continental Divide, 75, 130
- Contra, 121
- Convent, 42, 121
- Convent Station, 121
- Converse, 42, 114, 121

- Convict Lake, 10, 121
- Convoy, 87
- Conway, 48
- Coochie, 42
- Cook, 18, 42, 67, 92, 114, 121
- Cook Corner, 106, 118
- Cookertown, 121
- Cookietown, 92
- Cooks Corner, 44, 104
- Cooks Crossing, 71
- Cook Station, 62
- Cooks Valley, 10
- Cook Tomb, 100
- Cooktown, 111, 121
- Cookville, 111
- Cool, 10
- Coolidge, 75
- Cool Ridge, 126
- Cool Spring, 17, 100
- Cool Springs, 2, 22, 81, 106
- Coolville, 87
- Coon Corners, 100
- Coon Crossing, 87
- Coon Hunter, 100
- Coon Rapids, 35, 55
- Coon Rock, 129
- Coontown, 73
- Coon Valley, 129
- Coonwood, 58
- Cooter, 62
- Cope, 13
- Copenhagen, 42, 78
- Copic Slab, 92
- Copper, 94
- Copper Basin, 69
- Copper City, 10, 52, 65, 75
- Copper Cliff, 65
- Copper Creek, 5
- Copper Falls, 52
- Copperfield, 69
- Copper Flat, 69, 119
- Copper Harbor, 52
- Copper Hill, 69, 73
- Copper Mine, 5, 62
- Copper Mines, 5
- Copper Mountain, 13
- Copperopolis, 10
- Copper Run, 69
- Copper Springs, 2
- Cooperstown, 84
- Copperton, 75
- Copperville, 25, 46, 71
- Coral, 28, 52, 58
- Coral Hill, 69
- Corbin, 22, 38, 42, 46, 62, 65, 94, 121
- Corbin City, 73
- Core, 126
- Cork, 5, 22,8 7
- Corkscrew, 18
- Corn, 92
- Corner, 94
- Cornerstone, 2
- Corner Store, 100
- Cornertown, 62
- Cornerview, 42
- Corner Windmill, 114
- Cornfields, 5
- Corn Hill, 114
- Cornhill, 7
- Cornhouse, 2
- Corning, 33
- Cornish, 58, 71, 92, 118
- Cornish Camp, 69
- Cornish City, 71
- Cornish Flat, 71
- Cornish Mills, 71
- Cornland, 28, 62
- Cornstalk, 31, 126
- Cornucopia, 69, 94, 129
- Corn Valley, 121
- Cornville, 5, 44
- Cornwall, 15
- Cornwall Bridge, 15
- Cornwall Center, 15
- Cornwall Furnace, 2
- Cornwall Hollow, 15
- Cornwall on Hudson, 78
- Corporal, 10

- Corpse Pond, 52
- Corral, 25, 65
- Corral Crossing, 92
- Correct, 31
- Correctionville, 35
- Cos Cob, 15
- Cosmos, 55
- Cost, 114
- Costello, 100
- Cottage, 62, 100
- Cottage City, 46
- Cottage Corners, 10
- Cottage Grove, 2, 10, 15, 94, 100
- Cottage Hill, 18, 31, 38, 49
- Cottage Mill, 17
- Cottage Park, 49
- Cottage Springs, 10
- Cottle, 22, 126
- Cottles Corner, 100
- Cottleville, 62
- Cotton, 2, 55, 114, 118, 126
- Cotton Belt, 7
- Cotton Center, 5, 10
- Cotton City, 75
- Cotton Flat, 114
- Cotton Gin, 114
- Cotton Grove, 81
- Cotton Hill, 2, 22
- Cotton Mountain, 71
- Cotton Patch, 114
- Cotton Plant, 42, 58
- Cottonton, 2
- Cottontown, 2, 111, 126
- Cotton Town, 7, 100, 121
- Cotton Valley, 2, 92
- Cottonville, 35, 58
- Cottonwood, 4, 5, 10, 25, 28, 42, 55, 65, 69, 75, 92, 94, 107, 114
- Cottonwood Corner, 7
- Cottonwood Falls, 38
- Couch, 62, 111
- Cougar, 123
- Council, 4, 25, 81
- Council Bay, 129
- Council Bluff, 2
- Council Bluffs, 35, 67
- Council Grove, 38
- Council Hill, 28, 92
- Council House, 108
- Counselor, 75
- Country Lane, 81
- Country Walk, 18
- Counts, 92
- County Line, 2, 22, 100, 114, 129
- County Line, 7, 111
- Coupon, 100
- Courtrock, 94
- Cove, 7
- Coventry, 15
- Covered Bridge, 17
- Covert, 38, 52, 67, 78, 100
- Covington, 18, 22, 28, 31, 42, 52, 62, 81, 87, 92, 100, 111, 114
- Coward, 106
- Cowbell Corners, 71
- Cow Creek, 10, 18, 25, 94
- Cow Hollow, 130
- Cow Island, 42
- Cow Mound, 7
- Cow Springs, 5
- Cow Yard, 49
- Coxsackie, 78
- Coy, 7, 58
- Coyote, 69, 75, 114
- Coyote Canyon, 75
- Coyote Field, 5
- Coyote Hole, 69
- Coyote Springs, 5, 130
- Coyote Wells, 10
- Cozahome, 7
- Cozy Corner, 13, 119, 129
- Cozy Nook, 123
- Crabapple, 22, 87
- Crabb, 114
- Crab Orchard, 28, 67, 111, 121
- Crab Town, 35
- Crabtree, 25, 123
- Cracker City, 94

- Crackers Neck, 111
- Crackertown, 18
- Crackerville, 65
- Craft, 67
- Crafts, 78
- Cranberry, 1, 46, 81, 100
- Cranberry Bog Corner, 49
- Cranberry Gap, 81
- Cranberry Marsh, 129
- Cranberry Prairie, 87
- Crane, 31, 38, 62, 65, 94, 114, 130
- Crane Eater, 22
- Cranky Corner, 42
- Crappo, 46
- Crash-Up Mountain, 5
- Crater, 10
- Crater Village, 24
- Crayon, 87
- Cream, 129
- Cream Can Junction, 25
- Cream City, 87
- Creamery, 35, 100, 126
- Cream Ridge, 62, 73
- Creamridge, 73
- Creamy, 129
- Credit, 7
- Credit Hill, 22
- Credit River, 55
- Creek, 58, 81
- Creek Store, 111
- Crescendo, 46
- Crescent, 13, 22, 25, 28, 35, 42, 87, 92, 94, 106,1 11,1 29
- Crescent City, 10, 18
- Crescent Hill, 62
- Crescent Valley, 69
- Crest, 7, 10
- Crestview, 10, 18
- Crete, 31, 67, 84, 100
- Cricket Corner, 71
- Crimson Springs, 126
- Cripple Creek, 13, 17
- Crisp, 28, 35, 52, 75, 81,1 44
- Crittenden, 7, 10
- Crocket Corner, 71
- Crockett, 7, 10, 58, 111, 144
- Crocketts Bluff, 7
- Crocus, 84, 94
- Crook, 13
- Crook City, 108
- Crooked Creek, 100, 111, 126
- Crooked Oak, 2, 81, 121
- Crooked Tree, 87
- Crooks, 108
- Crooks Springs, 62
- Crossnore, 81
- Crossroad, 7
- Crossroads, 7, 22, 28, 58, 69, 75
- Cross Roads, 7, 22, 58, 106
- Crosstown, 62
- Crossville, ,109, 111
- Crouch, 25, 121
- Crow, 58, 94, 144, 126
- Crow Creek, 7, 108
- Crowfoot, 94
- Crowheart, ,130
- Crow Lake, 108
- Crown, 7, 126
- Crown King, 5
- Crow River, 55
- Crow Rock, 65
- Crows, 121
- Crows Nest, 44, 69
- Crowther Cow Camp, 75
- Crowville, 42
- Crow Wing, 55
- Crumb, 100
- Crumb Corner, 31
- Crumpler, 81
- Crumtown, 58
- Crusher, 92, 144
- Crystal, 25, 31, 44, 52, 55, 69, 71, 75, 84, 94, 111
- Crystal Beach, 119
- Crystal Block, 126
- Crystal City, 62, 144
- Crystal Fall, 4
- Crystal Falls, 4, 114

- Crystal Ford, 65
- Crystal Lake, ,35
- Crystal Mountain, 123
- Crystal Point, 65
- Crystal River, 18
- Crystal Rock, 87
- Crystal Run, 15
- Crystal Spring, 55, 118
- Crystal Springs, 2, 7, 18, 22, 38, 58, 69, 84, 87, 100, 121
- Cuba, 2, 22, 28, 31, 38, 42, 55, 62, 75, 79, 81, 84, 87, 111, 114, 126
- Cuba City, 129, 130
- Cuckoo, 121
- Cucumber, 126
- Cul de Sac, 62
- Culdesac, 25
- Cumberland, 7, 31, 35, 46, 58, 73, 87, 104, 106, 123, 129
- Cumberland City, 111
- Cumberland Gap, 111
- Cumberland Hill, 104
- Cumberland View, 111
- Cummaquid, 49
- Currant, 69
- Current Lake, 55
- Currentview, 62
- Current View, 7
- Curtain, 94
- Cusseta, 1
- Custer, 108
- Custer City, 92
- Cut, 114
- Cutalong, 121
- Cut and Shoot, 114
- Cut Bank, 65
- Cutcane, 22
- Cutlips, 126
- Cut Off, 42
- Cutter, 75,129
- Cuttyhunk, 49
- Cuyahoga Falls, 87
- Cyclone, 31, 62, 100, 114, 126, 130
- Cyclopic, 5

- Cylinder, 35
- Cynthiana, 31, 87
- Cypher, 100
- Cypress, 2, 7, 10, 18, 28, 31, 42, 62, 111, 114
- Cypress Corner, 7, 58
- Cypress Creek, 18, 42, 111
- Cypress Gardens, 18
- Cypress Grove, 10
- Cypress Harbor, 18
- Cypress Island, 42
- Cypress Lake, 18
- Cypress Point, 18
- Czar, 126

-D-

- Dad, 130
- Daddys Creek, 111
- Dads Corner, 55, 114
- Dads Creek, 94
- Dadsville, 87
- Dagger, 5
- Dahlia, 75
- Dailey, 52
- Daily, 84
- Daily Hill, 38
- Dairy, 4
- Dairy Creek, 25
- Dairyland, 10, 129
- Daisey City, 2
- Daisy, 7, 22, 46, 62, 106, 126
- Daisy Hill, 31
- Dakota, 28, 129
- Dakota City, 35, 67
- Dakota Junction, 67
- Dale, 28, 31, 35, 38, 52, 55, 58, 62, 87, 92, 100, 106, 129
- Dale City, 121
- Dale Hollow, 111
- Dallas, 2, 13, 18, 22, 44, 81, 94, 100, 108, 113(2), 114(2), 126, 129
- Dallas City, 28

- Dallas Jones Crossing, 58
- Dalton, 48
- Dana, 30
- Danbury, 71
- Daniel Boone, 2
- Danube, 55
- Danville, 7, 10, 18, 22, 28, 31, 35, 38, 42, 44, 46, 62, 69, 71, 80, 87, 111, 114, 119, 121, 123, 126, 129
- Darby, 98
- Darfur, 55
- Dark Harbor, 44
- Dark Ridge, 81
- Dark Water, 100
- Darling, 55, 58, 114
- Darlington, 100, 104
- Darrington, 123
- Dart, 2, 87
- Dasher, 22
- Date, 5, 108
- Date City, 10
- Date Creek, 5
- Dates, 10
- Dave, 42
- Davenport, 7, 10, 18, 35, 84, 123
- Davey, 67
- David, 22
- David City, 67
- Davids Crossroads, 121
- Davy, 126
- Dawn, 62, 87, 114
- Dawson, 84(2)
- Day, 10, 18, 46, 62, 100
- Day Brook, 81
- Daybrook, 126
- Days, 58, 130
- Dayton, 2, 25, 28, 30, 31, 35, 46, 52, 55, 62, 65, 69, 73, 79, 87, 94, 100, 114, 121, 123, 126, 130
- Daytona, 52
- Daytonville, 35
- Dazey, 84
- Dead Dog Creek, 25
- Dead Horse, 4

- Deadman Crossing, 87
- Deadmans Corner, 44, 130
- Dead Mans Crossing, 31
- Dead Women Crossing, ,92
- Deadwood, 10, 94, 108
- Deal, 114
- Dearborn, 51
- Death Valley, 10
- De Beque, 13
- Debruce, 22
- Debs, 55
- Decatur, 67
- Decoy, 69
- Deep Branch, 46
- Deep Creek, 25, 58, 69, 123
- Deep Cut, 44
- Deep Elm, 7
- Deep Ford, 62
- Deep Gap, 81, 111
- Deep Hole, 69, 121
- Deep Lake, 18
- Deep Park, 10
- Deep River, 15, 31, 35, 81, 123
- Deep Run, 46, 81
- Deep Springs, 10
- Deepstep, 22
- Deep Tunnel, 75
- Deep Valley, 126
- Deepwater, 62, 73
- Deer, 7, 62
- Deer Creek, 10, 17, 28, 31, 35, 52, 55, 92, 114,1 26
- Deer Creek Crossing, 10
- Deer Creek Landing, 75
- Deer Crossing, 10
- Deerfield, 28, 31, 35, 38, 52, 58, 62, 71
- Deer Grove, 28
- Deerhead, 38
- Deerheart Valley, 52
- Deerhorn, 94
- Deer Island, 94
- Deer Isle, 44
- Deer Lake, 75

- Deerland, 18
- Deer Lane, 55
- Deer Lodge, 65, 69, 111
- Deer Park, 18, 28, 31, 46, 52, 62, 129
- Deerpark, 46
- Deer Ridge, 62
- Deer River, 55
- Deer Run, 126
- Deers, 28
- Deer Mill, 31
- Deer Trail, 13, 123
- Deer Valley, 123
- Deer View, 10
- Deerwalk, 126
- Deerwood, 17, 55
- Defeated, 111
- Defiance, 7, 35, 62, 75, 87, 100
- DeKalb, 113, 114
- Delaware, 7, 16, 31, 35, 52, 62, 87, 92, 95
- Delaware City, 17, 42
- Delaware Water Gap, 100
- Delhi, 28, 35, 42, 55
- Delhi Mills, 52
- Delight, 6, 7, 46
- Delightful, 87
- Delta, 13, 25, 35, 42, 58(2), 129
- Democrat, 7, 25, 81, 114
- Democrat Spring, 28
- Denison, 34, 35
- Denmark, 7, 22, 28, 35, 38, 44, 58, 94, 106, 111, 129
- Dennison, 114
- Dent, 25, 55, 114, 126
- Denver, 12, 22, 25, 28, 31, 35, 62, 81, 87, 92, 94, 106, 111
- Deposit, 2, 22, 58, 79
- Deputy, 31
- Derby, 13, 15, 28, 31, 35, 38, 44, 58, 81, 87, 119
- Derby Acres, 10
- Derby Junction, 13
- Derby Shores, 17
- Desert, 10, 114, 118

- Desert Camp, 10
- Desert Center, 10
- Desert Hills, 10
- Desert Hot Springs, 10
- Desert Lake, 10
- Desert Mound, 118
- Desert View, 10
- Desert Wells, 5
- Des Moines, 35, 75, 117, 123
- De Soto City, 18
- Detour, 46, 94
- Detroit, 2, 28, 38, 44, 51(2), 52, 94
- Dew, 114
- Dewberry, 31
- Dew Drop, 10
- De Witt, 66
- Dewy Rose, 22
- Diagonal, 35
- Dial, 114
- Diamond, 4, 22, 25, 28, 31, 35, 42, 60, 62, 94, 108, 118, 123, 126, 130
- Diamond Bar, 10
- Diamond Bluff, 129
- Diamond Cave, 7
- Diamond City, 7, 28, 65, 69, 108
- Diamond Corner, 55
- Diamond Fields, 5
- Diamond Grove, 7, 129
- Diamond Hill, 22, 104
- Diamond Springs, 10, 38, 52
- Diamond Valley, 10
- Diamondville, 130
- Dibbletown, 79
- Dice, 52, 100
- Dies, 114
- Difficult, 111
- Dill City, 92
- Dillie, 126
- Dilly, 129
- Dime, 2
- Dime Box, 114
- Dimple, 7, 114
- Dines, 130
- Ding Dong, 114

- Dingy, 126
- Dinner Station, 69
- Dinosaur, 13
- Dinwiddie, 31
- Direct, 114
- Dirty Butter Creek, 92
- Disco, 52, 111, 129
- Discovery, 46
- Dismal, 111
- Dispatch, 38
- Disputanta, 121
- District Path, 22
- Ditch Camp Five, 10
- Divide, 4, 13, 22, 28, 65, 69, 84, 92, 100, 115, 126
- Dividend, 118
- Dividing Ridge, 100
- Divine, 28
- Divot, 115
- Dixie, 2, 5, 7, 10, 18, 22, 25, 31, 35, 42, 58, 62, 69, 81, 87, 94, 111, 115, 123, 126
- Dixie Hill, 121
- Dixieland, 2, 10, 111
- Dixie Pine, 58
- Dixietown, 18
- Dixie Valley, 69
- Dixieville Notch, 71
- Dixon, 62, 65, 67, 94, 108, 115, 130
- Doctortown, 22
- Dodge, 84
- Dodge City, 2, 7, 36, 38, 52, 62
- Dodgetown, 81
- Dodo, 87
- Doe Gully, 126
- Doe Run, 62
- Dog Bluff, 106
- Dog Corner, 44
- Dog Creek, 92
- Dog Crossing, 22
- Dog Hill, 111
- Dog Patch, 126
- Dogpatch, 7
- Dog Ridge, 115
- Dogs Corner, 73
- Dogtown, 18, 44, 46, 58, 79, 100, 111
- Dog Town, 2, 44
- Dog Walk, 28
- Dogwood, 2, 7, 10, 62, 111
- Dogwood Flats, 46
- Dolittle, 62
- D'Olive, 2
- Dollar, 2, 94, 111
- Dollar Bay, 52
- Dollar Corner, 123
- Dollar Point, 10
- Dollar Settlement, 52
- Dollarville, 52
- Dolomite, 123
- Dolphin, 123
- Dome Rock, 13
- Domestic, 31
- Dominion, 13
- Domino, 115
- Donation, 100
- Dot, 123
- Dothan, 18
- Dotsontown, 111
- Double Bayou, 115
- Double Bridges, 2, 111
- Double Crossing, 75
- Doublehead, 2
- Double Island, 81
- Double Mills, 75
- Double Mountain, 115
- Double Run, 22
- Double Shoals, 81
- Double Springs, 58, 69, 111
- Double Tollgate, 121
- Double Top, 111
- Double Trouble, 73
- Double Wells, 7
- Doughboy, 67
- Douglas, 2, 4, 5, 7, 22, 28, 31, 38, 42, 49, 52, 55, 62, 67, 69, 84, 87, 92, 94, 100, 106, 111, 115, 123, 126, 130
- Douglas City, 10, 18, 108
- Douglas Corner, 49

- Douglas Crossroads, 18, 81
- Douglas Flat, 10
- Douglas Hill, 44
- Douglass, 35, 38
- Douglass Park, 121
- Douglasville, 2, 22, 115
- Dove, 2, 62
- Dove Canyon, 10
- Dove Creek, 13, 22
- Dover, 13, 17, 25, 28, 35, 52, 62, 65, 71, 87, 106, 111, 119, 121, 129
- Dovetail, 65
- Downs, 123
- Dragon, 58, 118
- Drain, 94
- Draw, 115
- Drawbridge, 17
- Dresden, 22, 35, 38, 79, 84, 87, 111
- Dresher, 100
- Drew, 58
- Driftwood, 7
- Drinker, 100
- Drinkwater Corner, 44
- Dripping Springs, 2, 92, 115
- Driver, 7
- Drop, 111, 115
- Drumright, 92
- Drums, 100
- Drunkard Creek, 79
- Dry Beaver Creek, 5
- Drybranch, 46
- Dry Branch, 22, 106
- Dry Creek, 42, 69, 92, 94, 123, 126, 130
- Dry Fork, 118
- Dryfork, 7
- Dry Forks, 2
- Dry Grove, 58
- Dry Hill, 28, 111
- Dry Lake, 69
- Dry Pond, 22
- Dry Run, 46, 87
- Dry Tavern, 100
- Drytown, 10

- Dry Valley, 2, 10, 62, 115
- Dry Wood, 38
- Dry Wood Lake, 108
- Dub, 7
- Dublin, 2, 7, 10, 22, 31, 46, 52, 71, 79, 81, 87, 100, 115, 121,126
- Dublin Hill, 17
- Duck, 81, 126
- Duckabush, 123
- Duck Creek, 87, 111
- Ducker, 22
- Duck Hill, 58
- Duck Key, 18
- Duck River, 111
- Duckroost, 42
- Duck Run, 100
- Ducks Head, 71
- Duck Springs, 2
- Ducktown, 22, 111
- Ducktrap, 44
- Duckville, 49
- Duckwater, 69
- Duel, 52
- Duet, 121
- Due West, 106
- Duff, 7, 31, 67, 111, 115
- Duff Creek, 81
- Dugdale, 55
- Dugdown, 22
- Dug Hill, 7, 22
- Dugwell, 121
- Dull, 87
- Duluth, 22, 38, 67
- Dumbarton, 46, 121
- Dumbell, 130
- Dumplin, 111
- Dumplin Mill, 111
- Duncan, 92
- Duncans Bridge, 62
- Dundee, 2, 28, 35, 38, 52, 55, 58, 62, 71, 87, 92, 94, 115, 129
- Dunes, 10, 75
- Dunkertown, 44
- Dunmovin, 10

- Duo, 111, 126
- Duplex, 111
- Du Pont, 123
- Duquesne, 100(2)
- Durham, 15, 38, 65
- Dusty, 75, 123
- Dutch, 111, 126
- Dutch Corner, 101
- Dutch Flat, 10
- Dutch Gap, 121
- Dutch Hill, 101
- Dutch Hollow, 38, 79
- Dutch John, 118
- Dutch Mills, 7
- Dutch Neck, 73
- Dutch Ridge, 87
- Dutch Settlement, 79, 123
- Dutchtown, 35, 62, 73
- Dutch Town, 42
- Dutch Valley, 111
- Duty, 42
- Dye, 62, 115
- DY Junction, 65
- Dynamite, 123

-E-

- Eagle, 2, 4, 13, 25, 52, 67, 73, 108, 129
- Eagle Bend, 55
- Eagle Center, 35
- Eagle City, 35, 87, 92
- Eagle Corner, 7
- Eagle Corners, 129
- Eagle Creek, 2, 94, 111
- Eagle Crest Corner, 94
- Eagle Flat, 115
- Eagle Furnace, 111
- Eagle Grove, 22, 35
- Eagle Harbor, 46, 52
- Eagle Island, 18
- Eagle Lake, 18, 28, 44, 55
- Eagle Mountain, 10, 118

- Eagle Nest, 25, 52, 75, 79, 84
- Eagle Point, 28, 31, 35, 94, 101, 129
- Eagle River, 4, 52, 62, 129
- Eagles Nest, 13, 52, 55, 58, 65
- Eagles Nest Landing, 17
- Eagle Springs, 81
- Eagle Station, 69
- Eagleton, 31, 129
- Eagletown, 81
- Eagle Tree, 10
- Eaglette, 62
- Eagle Village, 4, 31
- Eagleville, 10, 15, 62, 69, 87
- Early, 18, 22, 35
- Early Station, 31
- Earp, 5, 10
- Earth, 115
- East Aberdeen, 58
- East Chicago, 31
- East Derry, 70
- Easter, 115
- East Morris, 15
- East Thompson, 16
- Eau Claire, 101, 129
- Ebbs Corner, 16
- Ebony, 115
- Echo, 2 ,7, 13, 35, 55, 62, 94, 101, 115, 118, 123, 126
- Echo House, 13
- Echo Lake, 13, 73
- Eclectic, 2
- Economy, 7, 31, 62, 101, 111
- Ecru, 58
- Eddyville, 25, 28, 35, 49, 67, 94
- Eden, 5, 13, 18, 22, 25, 42, 46, 52, 55, 58, 65, 69, 79, 81, 87, 94, 101, 108, 115, 118, 119, 123, 126, 129, 130
- Edenburg, 100
- Eden Prairie, 55
- Eden Valley, 55
- Edenville, 35
- Edge, 115
- Edgewater, 18
- Edina, 55

- Edinburg, 28, 35, 44, 58, 62, 73, 84, 87, 100, 115, 121
- Edinburgh, 31, 81, 87
- Edison, 73
- Edler, 13
- Edmonson, 7, 62, 115
- Edna, 2, 7, 22, 35, 38, 108, 111, 115, 123, 126
- Edna Bay, 4
- Edna Hill, 115
- Edna Mills, 31
- Edna Number One, 101
- Edna Number Two, 101
- Edward, 38, 81
- Edward Grove, 111
- Edwards, 7, 10, 13, 28, 52, 55, 58, 62, 65, 79, 94, 106, 115, 123, 129
- Edwardsburg, 25, 52
- Edwards Crossroads, 81
- Edwardsville, 28
- Eek, 4
- Eel Rock, 10
- Effort, 101
- Egg Bend, 42
- Eggbornsville, 121
- Egg Harbor, 31
- Egg Harbor City, 73
- Eggnog, 118
- Eggville, 58
- Egypt, 2, 7, 22, 25, 31, 44, 49, 58, 81, 87, 101, 111, 115, 119, 126
- Egypt Grove, 62
- Egypt Hill, 58
- Egypt Mills, 62
- Eight Corners, 44, 129
- Eighteenmile, 25
- Eighteenmile Point, 118
- Eightmile, 94
- Eight Mile, 2
- Eightmile Corner, ,52
- Eightmile Saddle, 65
- Eightmile Still, 22
- Eight Square, 87
- Eighty Four, 101

- Elbow, 115
- Elbow Lake, 55
- Elder, 13
- Eldorado, 58, 62, 67, 81, 87, 92, 94, 115, 129
- El Dorado, 7
- Eldorado at Santa Fe, 75
- El Dorado Springs, 62
- Electric, 65
- Electric City, 115, 123
- Electric Mills, 58
- Electron, 123
- Elephant, 101
- Elephant Butte, 75
- Elephant Park, 13
- Elevation, 115
- Eleven Mile, 101
- Elevenmile Corner, 55
- Eleven Mile Corner, 5
- Elevenpoint, 7
- Elf, 81
- Elfers, 18
- Elgin, 27
- Eliot, 44
- Eli Whitney, 81
- Elixer, 62
- Elizabeth, 7, 13, 42, 55, 73, 101, 111, 126
- Elizabeth City, 81
- Elizabeth Park, 44
- Elizabethtown, 28, 31, 79, 81, 87, 101, 108, 111
- Elizaville, 31
- Elk, 75, 87, 123, 126
- Elk Basin, 130
- Elk City, 25, 38, 62, 67, 92, 94, 126
- Elk Creek, 10, 62, 67, 123, 129
- Elk Falls, 38
- Elk Fork, 87
- Elk Grove, 10, 129
- Elkhart, 28, 31, 35, 38
- Elkhead, 13, 94
- Elkhorn, 62, 65, 67, 69, 94, 126, 129
- Elk Horn, 35, 94

- Elkhorn Grove, 28
- Elkhorn Village, 25
- Elkin, 81, 101
- Elkins, 71, 111
- Elk Lick, 87
- Elk Mountain, 81, 130
- Elk Park, 13
- Elk Point, 108
- Elkport, 35
- Elk Ranch, 7
- Elk Rapids, 52
- Elk Ridge, 118
- Elk River, 13, 25, 55
- Elk Run, 121
- Elk Springs, 13
- Elk Summit, 25
- Elkton, 13, 18, 28, 35, 46, 52, 55, 62, 87, 94, 108, 111
- Elk Valley, 81, 111
- Elkville, 28
- Elliott, 7, 28, 31, 35, 46, 58, 62, 84, 87, 92, 115, 123
- Elliott Prairie, 94
- Ellis Island, 73
- Elm, 7, 52, 62
- Elm City, 81
- Elm Creek, 67, 115
- Elmdale, 16, 31, 38, 55, 65
- Elm Flat, 115
- Elm Grove 7, 42, 81, 115, 126
- Elm Hill, 16
- Elm Park, 7, 55
- Elm Springs, 7, 108
- Elm Store, 7
- Elm Terrace, 126
- Elm Tree Corners, 129
- Elm Tree Crossroads, 31
- Elmview, 22
- Elm View, 22, 115
- Elmwood, 7, 42, 46, 52, 67, 71, 92, 129
- El Paso, 7, 28, 74, 114, 115, 129
- Ely, 68
- Embarrass, 28, 55, 129

- Emblem, 115, 130
- Emerald, 58, 67, 87, 123, 129
- Emerald Creek, 25
- Emerald Grove, 129
- Emerald Isle, 81
- Emigrant, 65, 94
- Emigrant Gap, 10
- Emigrant Hill, 130
- Eminence, 58, 62
- Empire, 7, 13, 22, 28, 42, 52, 55, 58, 62, 58, 87, 108
- Empire City, 38, 92
- Empire Prairie, 62
- Emporium, 101
- Encampment, 130
- Endeavor, 129
- Endville, 58
- Energy, 28, 58, 62, 115
- Engineer Springs, 10
- England, 7, 87, 92
- English, 31, 42, 81, 94, 115, 126
- English Boom, 123
- English Creek, 111
- English Eddy, 22
- English Town, 10, 62
- Englishville, 52
- Englund, 55
- Enid, 89
- Enigma, 22
- Enola, 58, 67, 81
- Enough, 62
- Ensign, 38, 52
- Enterprise, 7,1 0, 22, 35, 42, 58, 62
- Entry, 126
- Equality, 2, 28
- Equinunk, 101
- Equity, 87
- Era, 25, 115
- Erie, 10, 13, 28, 38, 52, 55, 62, 69, 84, 100
- Estes, 7, 25, 62, 123
- Estes Brook, 55
- Estes Park, 13
- Estill, 62, 106

- Estill Springs, 111
- Ether, 81
- Eucalyptus Hills, 10
- Eugene, 94
- Eulogy, 115
- Eureka, 2, 4, 10, 18, 28, 31, 35, 38, 42, 52, 62, 65, 69, 81, 106, 108, 111, 115, 118, 123, 129
- Eureka Springs, 7, 58
- Euren, 129
- Evanston, 13, 28, 31, 35, 58, 87, 111, 130
- Evansville, 7, 30, 55, 58(2), 62, 101, 111, 119, 126, 129, 130
- Evarts, 94
- Eve, 62
- Evening Shade, 7, 62, 92
- Evening Star, 7
- Everest, 38, 84
- Everglade, 10
- Everglades City, 18
- Evergreen, 2, 13, 18, 25, 42, 46, 55, 58, 65, 87, 106, 111, 129
- Evergreen Park, 28
- Ewing, 10, 28, 31, 42, 62, 67, 87, 94, 111
- Ewingsville, 101
- Excelsior, 22, 62, 69, 101, 126
- Exchange, 31
- Excursion Inlet, 4
- Exile, 129
- Experiment, 7, 22, 101
- Expose, 58
- Extension, 42
- Extra, 126

-F-

- Faceville, 22
- Factory, 111, 126
- Factory Village, 49
- Factoryville, 101
- Fades, 101

- Fairbanks, 7, 10, 28, 44, 55, 94, 101
- Fairdealing, 62, 84
- Fairfield, 2, 25, 65, 67,1 18
- Fair Grove, 62
- Fair Haven, 62
- Fair Hill, 46
- Fairlane, 2, 42
- Fair Lawn, 73
- Fairlawn, 87
- Fairmont, 125
- Fairmount, 30
- Fair Oaks, 2, 5, 10, 22, 31, 94
- Fair Oak Springs, 58
- Fairplay, 7, 13, 22, 46, 126
- Fair Play, 10, 46, 62, 69, 73, 106
- Fairport, 10, 62
- Fairview, 2, 7, 13, 18, 22, 28, 31, 35, 38, 46, 49, 52, 58, 62, 65, 69, 71, 73, 81, 92, 106, 108, 111, 115, 126, 130
- Fairview Shores, 18
- Fairville, 35, 62
- Fairwell, 7
- Fairwinds, 17
- Fairylawn, 25
- Faith, 55, 62, 81
- Faithful, 126
- Faker, 115
- Falcon, 7, 13, 25, 58, 62, 81, 111, 115
- Fall Creek, 25, 94, 111, 115, 129
- Fallen Leaf, 10
- Fallen Timber, 126
- Fall Hall Glen, 129
- Falling Creek, 28, 81
- Falling Rock, 126
- Falling Rocks, 22
- Falling Spring, 126
- Falling Springs, 28
- Fall Leaf, 38
- Fallow, 35
- Fall River, 38
- Fall River Mills, 10
- Falls, 16
- Falls Church, 121
- Falls City, 2, 25, 67, 94, 115, 129

- Falls Creek, 92, 101
- Falls Village, 16
- Falmouth, 18, 28, 31, 44, 49, 52, 121
- False Pass, 4
- False River, 42
- False Summit, 65
- Falter Place, 67
- Fame, 58, 92, 126
- Fancher, 28
- Fancy Prairie, 28
- Fanning, 62
- Fantasy Hills, 22
- Farewell Bend, 94
- Farewell Corner, 106
- Fargo, 22, 83
- Farmdale, 22
- Farmer, 62, 81, 87, 108, 115, 123
- Farmer City, 28
- Farmers, 13, 31, 87, 101
- Farmersburg, 35
- Farmers Fork, 121
- Farmers Mills, 16
- Farmers Retreat, 31
- Farmersville, 2, 22, 28, 62, 87, 129
- Farmerville, 22, 42
- Farm Hill, 18, 49
- Farming, 55
- Farmland, 31
- Farm Ridge, 28
- Farmville, 81
- Farthing, 130
- Far West, 62
- Fashion, 22
- Fate, 115
- Fawn, 62
- Fawn Food, 18
- Fawn River, 52
- Fawnskin, 10
- Fay, 69, 87, 92
- Fayette, 2, 10, 13, 28, 31, 35, 42, 44, 58, 62, 84, 87, 101, 118, 126, 129
- Fayetteville, 2, 7, 22, 28, 72
- Fays Corner, 119
- Fayville, 28, 49, 119

- Fearnot, 101
- Feather Falls, 10
- Feather Sound, 18
- Featherville, 25
- February, 111
- Federal, 87, 101, 130
- Federal Corner, 71
- Federal Hill, 46
- Federal Point, 18
- Federalsburg, 17, 46
- Fedora, 108
- Fee, 65
- Feeding Hills, 49
- Feed Springs, 87
- Felt, 25, 92
- Fence Lake, 75
- Fender, 7
- Fern, 7, 10, 35, 52, 94, 101
- Ferncliff, 13, 46
- Fern Corner, 94
- Ferndale, 28, 52
- Fern Hill, 123
- Fern Hook, 17
- Fern Prairie, 123
- Fernwood, 10, 25, 58, 123
- Ferriday, 41
- Fertile, 35, 55
- Fiat, 38, 87
- Fickle, 31
- Fiddlers Green, 69
- Fiddlesticks, 18
- Fiddletown, 10, 101
- Fidelis, 18
- Fidelity, 7, 28, 62
- Field, 10
- Field Corners, 16
- Fields, 22
- Fifty-Six, 7
- Fifty Lakes, 55
- Fig, 81
- Fighting Pine, 22
- Fighting Rock Corner, 49
- Fig Orchard, 10
- Fig Tree, 2

- Figure Five, 7
- Filbert, 106, 126
- File, 121
- Fillmore, 10, 28, 31, 35, 42, 52, 55, 62, 69, 79, 84, 87, 92, 101 181, 129
- Finch, 7, 65, 126
- Finch Hill, 101
- Finchville, 67
- Findlay, 28
- Fine Gold, 10
- Finger, 81, 111
- Fingerboard Corner, 52
- Fingerville, 106
- Fink, 13, 126
- Finland, 55, 106
- Fir, 13, 94
- Firebrick, 10, 87
- Fire Clay, 13
- Fire Mountain, 10
- Fireside, 87
- Firesteel, 52, 108
- Firestone, 13
- Firetown, 16
- Fireworks, 49
- First Cliff, 49
- First Colony, 121
- First Creek, 65
- First Crossing, 115
- First Fork, 101
- First View, 13
- Fish, 22
- Fish Camp, 10
- Fish Corners, 52
- Fish Creek, 5, 22
- Fish Cut, 130
- Fisher, 7, 10, 28, 42, 52, 55, 87, 130
- Fisher Corner, 18
- Fish Haven, 25
- Fish Hawk, 18
- Fishhawk, 94
- Fish Hook,
- Fishhook, 28
- Fish House, 73
- Fishing Bridge, 130

- Fishkill, 79
- Fish Lake, 31,69
- Fishpond, 2
- Fish Rock, 10
- Fish Springs, 10
- Fish Street, 44
- Fishtail, 65
- Fishtown, 46
- Fish Town, 123
- Fishtrap, 2, 65
- Fitting, 69
- Five Block, 126
- Five Corners, 25, 44, 49, 52, 55, 71, 94, 101, 123, 129
- Five Forks, 2, 22, 42, 46, 81, 87, 101, 106, 111, 121, 126
- Five Locks, 101
- Fivemile, 7
- Fivemile Corner, 52, 92
- Five Mile Corners, 44, 79, 87
- Fivemile Crossing, 115
- Five Mile Crossing, 75
- Five Mile Fork, 121
- Five Mile House, 69
- Fivemile Still, 22
- Five Mile Terrace, 10
- Five Points, 2, 10, 16, 17, 18, 22, 25, 28, 31, 35, 38, 44, 52, 55, 67, 73, 79, 81, 87, 94, 101, 106, 108, 115
- Five Points Corner, 31
- Five Points North, 52
- Five Pound Island, 49
- Five Springs, 22
- Flag, 7, 87
- Flager, 13
- Flag Springs, 62
- Flagstaff, 5
- Flagtown, 73
- Flaming, 55
- Flamingo Bay, 18
- Flat, 4, 7, 13, 115
- Flat Branch, 81
- Flat Creek, 25, 42, 62, 81
- Flat Ford, 22

- Flat Fork, 115
- Flat Gap, 111
- Flat Hollow, 111
- Flat Iron, 87, 121
- Flat Iron Corner, 87
- Flat Nose, 69
- Flat Prairie, 115
- Flat Ridge, 87
- Flat River, 62
- Flat Rock, 2, 5, 22, 28, 52, 58, 81, 87, 101, 106, 115
- Flat Run, 121
- Flats, 67
- Flat Shoals, 22, 81, 106
- Flat Springs, 81
- Flattop, 130
- Flat Top, 2, 58, 81, 115, 126
- Flatwillow, 65
- Flatwood, 58, 62, 81, 87
- Flatwoods, 7, 28, 42, 101
- Flaxville, 65
- Fleatown, 87
- Flea Valley, 10
- Fleece, 84
- Fleet, 106
- Fleming, 7, 13, 22, 31, 38, 62, 115
- Fleming Corners, 17
- Flemingsburg, 111
- Flint, 7, 22, 25, 46, 52, 87, 115 ,120, 123, 126
- Flint Creek, 92
- Flint Hill, 22, 62, 81, 121
- Flint Springs, 7
- Flintstone, 22, 46
- Flint Village, 49
- Flipping, 126
- Flood, 121
- Floodway, 7
- Floodwood, 52, 55
- Flora, 42, 58, 84, 94, 101, 115
- Floral, 7
- Floral Chest, 2
- Floral City, 18
- Floral Hill, 22, 73

- Florence, 1, 2, 13, 18, 25, 28, 31, 35, 38, 42, 46, 49, 55, 58, 62, 65, 73, 81, 87, 94, 106, 108, 115, 119, 129
- Florenceville, 35
- Florida, 13, 17, 31, 44, 49, 62, 64, 75, 79, 87, 110
- Florida Beach, 18
- Florida City, 18
- Florida Garden, 18
- Floridale, 18
- Florida Ridge, 18
- Floridatown, 18
- Floss, 5, 7
- Flower, 126
- Flowerfield, 52
- Flower Grove, 115
- Flower Mound, 115
- Flower Pot, 10
- Flowers, 58, 81
- Flowersville, 18
- Flowery Branch, 22
- Flowery City, 69
- Floyd, 2, 7, 10, 22, 35, 42, 46, 62, 75, 115
- Floyd Crossing, 35
- Floyd School, 35
- Floydville, 16
- Fluffy Landing, 18
- Flush, 38
- Flushing, 79, 87
- Flute Springs, 92
- Fly, 111
- Fly Gap, 7
- Flying-E, 75
- Flying H, 75
- Fogel, 92
- Fog Town, 115
- Folger, 4
- Follett, 114
- Folly, 81
- Folsom, 75
- Fon du Lac, 129
- Foot of Ten, 73, 101
- Footville, 129

- Ford, 13, 31, 35, 38, 58, 65, 121, 123
- Forest, 10, 17, 25, 31, 42, 44, 81, 115
- Forest City, 18, 28, 35, 38, 52, 55, 62, 108
- Forest Falls, 10
- Forest Glen, 22
- Forest Green, 62, 65
- Forestgrove, 65
- Forest Grove, 7, 52, 55, 65, 73, 81, 94
- Forest Hill, 31, 42, 46, 52, 58
- Foresthill, 10
- Forest Hills, 52, 79
- Forest Home, 10, 111
- Forest Lake, 101, 106
- Forest Lakes, 5
- Forest Meadows, 10
- Forest Park, 17, 46
- Forest Ranch, 10
- Forest River, 28, 84
- Forest Springs, 10, 62
- Forestville, 16
- Forge Ridge, 111
- Fork, 46, 55, 81, 106
- Forked Island, 42
- Forker Boomer Post Office, 62
- Forks, 123
- Forks of Cacapon, 126
- Forks of Coal, 126
- Forks of Piney, 111
- Forks of Salmon, 10
- Forks of the River, 111
- Forksville, 42
- Forkville, 58
- Formosa, 7
- Formosa Junction, 28, 31
- Fort Calhoun, 67
- Fort Carson, 13
- Fort Douglas, 7
- Fort Edward, 79
- Fort Garland, 13
- Fort George, 44
- Fort Gordon, 22
- Fort Kipp, 65
- Fort Knox, 109

- Fort Leavenworth, 36
- Fort Logan, 65
- Fort Lonesome,
- Fort McAllister, 22
- Fort Morgan, 13
- Fort Riley, 36
- Fort Ripley, 55
- Fort Thompson, 108
- Fortune, 7
- Fortune Fork, 42
- Fort Washington, 46, 101
- Fort Wilson, 25
- Fort Worth, 113, 115
- Forty, 58
- Forty Forks, 111
- Forty Four, 7
- Fortymile Bend, 18
- Fortyville, 62
- Forum, 7
- Forward, 129
- Foss, 92
- Fossil, 94, 130
- Foster, 115
- Foul Rift, 73
- Foundry Hill, 111
- Fountain, 13, 18, 28, 31, 52, 55, 81
- Fountain City, 31, 129
- Fountain Creek, 28
- Fountain Gap, 28
- Fountain Green, 28, 118
- Fountain Head, 46
- Fountain Lake, 7
- Fountain Park, 31, 87
- Fountain Spring, 104
- Fountain Springs, 10, 101
- Fountaintown, 31
- Fountain Valley, 10
- Four Bears Village, 84
- Four Buttes, 65
- Four Corners, 10, 16, 25, 28, 31, 35, 38, 42, 44, 49, 55, 65, 73, 81, 87, 94, 101, 121, 123, 129, 130
- Four Corners Crossing, 13
- Four Corner Windmill, 115

- Four Forks, 42, 75, 121
- Four Groves, 7
- Four Gums, 7
- Four Holes, 106
- Four Lakes, 123
- Four Locks, 47
- Fourmile, 2, 62, 94, 108
- Four Mile, 2, 58, 73, 126
- Four Mile Circle, 73
- Fourmile Corner, 62
- Four Mile Corner, 52
- Four Mile Crossing, 92
- Fourmile Crossing, 115
- Fourmile House Corner, 87
- Fourmile Run, 87
- Four Miles, 106
- Four Oaks, 81
- Four Pines, 10
- Four Points, 22, 62, 75, 101, 111
- Four Presidents Corners, 31
- Four Seasons, 17
- Four States, 126
- Fourth Cliff, 49
- Fourth Crossing, 10
- Four Town, 55
- Four Towns, 52
- Fourway, 121
- Fourway Junction, 25
- Four Winds, 47
- Fox, 5, 7, 28, 31, 55, 58, 87, 94, 121
- Foxboro, 55
- Fox Catcher at Fair Hill, 47
- Fox Chapel, 47
- Fox Creek, 13, 25, 62, 129
- Fox Den, 16, 111
- Foxfield, 13
- Fox Fire, 111
- Fox Hall, 17
- Fox Hill, 31, 101
- Fox Hollow, 17
- Foxhome, 55
- Fox Island, 58, 123
- Fox Lake, 28, 31
- Fox Ridge, 108

- Fox Springs, 62
- Foxtown, 47, 106
- Fox Town, 38
- Foxville, 47
- France, 25
- Frankenstein, 62
- Frankfort, 28, 31, 35, 38, 44, 52, 73, 87, 92, 108, 123
- Franklin, 2, 5, 7, 10, 16, 18, 22, 25, 28, 31, 35, 38, 42, 44, 47, 49, 52, 55, 58, 62, 65, 67, 71, 73(2), 81, 101, 108, 115, 119, 126, 129
- Franklin Grove, 73
- Franklin Lakes, 73
- Franklin Square, 88
- Franklinton, 80
- Franklinville, 47, 73
- Fredericksburg, 10, 62, 101, 115, 121
- Fredonia, 35, 38
- Free, 31
- Freeborn,
- Freedom, 25, 44, 55, 62, 67, 71, 88, 92, 118, 123, 129
- Free Home, 22
- Free Hope, 7
- Freeland, 13, 47
- Freeport, 18, 52
- Free Run, 58
- Free Soil, 52
- Freetown, 2, 42, 49
- Free Trade, 58
- Free Union, 121
- Freeze Fork, 126
- French, 7, 31, 55, 75
- Frenchburg, 40, 126
- French Camp, 10, 58
- French Corner, 25
- French Creek, 25, 35
- French Gulch, 10
- French Hill, 2
- French Hollow, 119
- French Lake, 55
- French Lane, 94
- French Lick, 30, 31

- Frenchman, 69
- Frenchmans Bayou, 7
- French Mill, 2
- French River, 55
- French Settlement, 42, 44, 101
- Frenchtown, 31, 47, 52, 73, 88, 101, 104, 108
- French Town, 62, 65
- French Vee, 130
- French Village, 62
- Frenchville, 44, 129
- Fresh Brook, 49
- Fresh Pond, 10
- Freshwater Corners, 10
- Fresno, 7, 65, 88
- Friars Point, 57
- Frick, 13
- Friday, 115
- Friday Harbor, 123
- Fridays Crossing, 2
- Friend, 38, 67, 79, 84, 94
- Friendly, 126
- Friendly Corner, 31
- Friendly Village, 62
- Friendship, 2, 7, 22, 31, 42, 58, 73, 79, 81, 88, 92, 106, 111, 115, 121, 129
- Friendsville, 28, 47, 52, 101, 111, 126
- Frisbie, 38, 69, 101
- Frisby, 108
- Fritters Corner, 121
- Frog City, 18, 28
- Frogeye, 47
- Frog Eye, 2
- Frog Hop, 115
- Frog Island, 58
- Frog Level, 81
- Frogmore, 42
- Frognot, 115
- Frog Pond, 81
- Frogsboro, 81
- Frogtown, 28, 47, 58, 101, 121
- Frogville, 92
- Frontier Post, 75

- Frontier Town, 65
- Frost, 13, 42, 52, 55, 88, 92, 111, 115, 126
- Frost Bottom, 111
- Frostburg, 47
- Frost Hollow, 79
- Frost Mill, 94
- Frostown, 47
- Frostproof, 18, 101
- Frost Town, 42
- Frozen Camp, 126
- Fruit, 28
- Fruit Cove, 18
- Fruit Hill, 88, 104
- Fruitland, 18, 22, 25, 35, 38, 75, 81, 111, 115, 118, 123
- Fruitport, 52
- Fruit Ridge Center, ,52
- Fruittown, 101
- Fruitvale, 13, 25, 123
- Fruitville, 18
- Fry, 126, 130
- Fryburg, 84, 88
- Fry Canyon, 118
- Frying Pan, 10, 81
- Frytown, 121
- Fudges, 106
- Fulton, 2, 7, 10, 18, 22, 28, 31, 35, 38, 42, 47, 52, 58, 62, 88, 94, 106, 108, 110, 111, 129
- Funk, 88
- Furlong, 101
- Furlow, 7
- Furnace, 31, 47, 49, 121
- Furry, 58
- Future City, 28
- Futurity, 13

-G-

- Gables, 67
- Gabtown, 111
- Gainesville, 62

- Galilee, 104
- Gallatin, 7, 58, 62, 65
- Gallatin Gateway, 65
- Gallows Hill, 101
- Gallup, 75
- Gallups, 5
- Galveston, 31
- Gamble, 2
- Gamma, 22, 62
- Gap of the Ridge, 111
- Garden, 118
- Gardena, 123
- Garden City, 13, 18, 22, 25, 35, 38, 42, 55, 62, 101, 104, 106, 108, 115, 118, 121
- Garden Grove, 10, 18, 35
- Gardenland, 10
- Garden of Eden, 28
- Garden Pass, 69
- Garden Plain, 38
- Garden Prairie, 28
- Garden Valley, 10, 22, 25
- Garden Village, 31
- Gardenville, 18
- Gardner, 18, 35, 38, 42, 49, 52, 62, 84, 101
- Garland, 2, 7, 28, 35, 38, 42, 44, 47, 65, 67, 79, 81, 88, 92, 111, 115, 118, 130
- Garland City, 7, 13
- Garland Village, 52
- Garlandville, 7, 58
- Garnet, 52, 65
- Garrett, 28, 31, 62
- Garrison, 65, 67, 75
- Gary, 13, 22, 31, 47, 55, 64, 75, 106, 108, 115, 126
- Gary Corner, 73
- Gary Springs, 2
- Garyville, 42
- Gas, 38
- Gas City, 31, 92
- Gasoline, 115
- Gasoline Alley, 10

- Gas Point, 10
- Gassoway, 42
- Gate, 7, 92, 123
- Gateview, 13
- Gateway, 13, 94
- Gateway, 13
- Gause, 111
- Gayspot, 88
- Gaza, 71
- Gazelle, 10
- Gazette, 62
- Gem, 25, 31, 38, 88, 94, 115
- Gem Village, 13
- Gene Autry, 92
- Geneseo, 37
- Genesis, 111
- Geneva, 2, 7, 10, 67, 18, 22, 25, 28, 31, 35, 38, 52, 55, 69, 79, 87, 88, 123
- Geneva on-the-Lake, 88
- Genoa City, 129
- George, 7, 35, 58, 81, 94, 115, 123
- Georges Creek, 7, 115
- Georges Fork, 121
- Georges Mill, 121
- Georges Mills, 71, 81
- Georgesville, 88
- George Town, 31
- Georgetown, 2, 7, 10, 13, 16, 17, 18, 22, 25, 28, 31, 42, 44, 47, 49, 55, 58, 62, 65, 73, 81, 88, 98(2), 101, 106, 111, 115, 118, 126, 129
- Georgeville, 42, 55, 62, 81, 101
- George West, 115
- Georgia, 2, 18, 20, 31, 38, 73, 115
- Georgia Center, 119
- Georgia Plains, 119
- Gepp, 7
- Geraldine, 65
- German, 88
- German Crossing, 2
- Germans, 101
- German Settlement, 25, 101
- Germantown, 6, 35, 47, 49, 62, 88, 101, 106, 111, 121, 129

- German Valley, 28, 35
- Germany, 22, 88, 101, 115
- Gerry, 44
- Getaway, 88
- Gettysburg, 88, 108
- Geyser, 65, 69
- Giant, 10, 106
- Giants Neck, 16
- Gibson Mill, 121
- Gid, 7
- Gift, 58
- Gigantic City, 73
- Gilbraltar, 52
- Gildersleve, 16
- Gillette, 73
- Gilmer, 115
- Gin, 58
- Gin City, 7
- Ginger, 115, 123
- Ginger Hill, 28
- Ginghamsburg, 88
- Gipsy, 2, 62
- Girard, 101
- Gismonda, 111
- Giveout, 25, 94
- Glacier, 4, 123
- Glacier Colony, 65
- Glade, 35, 42
- Gladstone, 13
- Gladtidings, 94
- Glad Valley, 108
- Glasgo, 16
- Glasgow, 2, 10, 17, 22, 28, 35, 62, 65, 88, 94, 101, 111, 122, 126
- Glasgow Corner, 2
- Glasgow Pines, 17
- Glass, 2, 18, 111, 115
- Glass City, 101
- Glass Hill, 47
- Glen, 67
- Glen Campbell, 101
- Glendale, 5
- Glens Glen, 58
- Glide, 94

- Globe, 5, 10, 31, 38, 44, 62, 81, 115, 123, 129
- Gnat Hill, 111
- Gnaw Bone, 31
- Goat City, 111
- Goat Neck, 81
- Goat Rock, 10
- Goat Town, 22
- Gobbler, 7, 62
- Gobbler Knob, 101
- Gobblers Crossing, 2
- Gobblers Hill, 22
- Goblintown, 122
- Goes, 88
- Gold, 81, 101
- Gold Acres, 69
- Gold Bar, 69, 123
- Gold Beach, 94
- Goldbranch, 2
- Goldbud, 69
- Gold Bug, 69
- Goldburg, 25
- Gold Butte, 69
- Gold Camp, 5
- Gold Canyon, 5
- Gold Center, 69
- Gold Creek, 25, 65, 94
- Gold Dust, 42
- Golddust, 2, 111
- Golden, 13, 25, 28, 35, 52, 58, 69, 75, 81
- Golden Arrow, 69
- Golden Beach, 18
- Golden City, 62
- Golden Eagle, 28
- Golden Gate, 18, 28
- Golden Glades, 18
- Golden Grove, 58
- Gold Hill, 94, 118, 122
- Golden Hills, 10
- Golden Ridge, 65
- Goldenrod, 18, 38, 55
- Golden Valley, 5, 55, 69, 84
- Goldfield, 35, 69

- Goldfinch, 115
- Gold Flat, 10
- Gold Hill, 10, 69, 81
- Gold Hit, 69
- Goldmine, 22
- Gold Mine, 2, 101
- Gold Point, 25, 69, 81
- Gold Reef, 69
- Gold Ridge, 2
- Goldridge, 42
- Gold River, 10
- Gold Rock, 81
- Gold Run, 10, 69
- Gold Sand, 81
- Goldsboro, 80
- Goldsmith, 31
- Goldstake, 123
- Goldston, 81
- Goldstone, 10, 65
- Goldtown, 126
- Goldvein, 122
- Goldville, 2, 69
- Goldyke, 69
- Golf, 28
- Golly, 115
- Gonce, 2
- Goober Hill, 115
- Goobertown, 5, 7
- Good, 126
- Goodbee, 42
- Goodbys, 18
- Good Grief, 25
- Goodhope, 62
- Good Hope, 7, 18, 22, 28, 42, 58, 69
- Good Intent, 38, 73, 101
- Goodlake, 92
- Goodland, 31, 52, 62
- Goodluck, 58, 81
- Good Luck, 47
- Goodnews Bay, 4
- Goodnight, 13, 92, 115
- Goodpasture, 13
- Goodrich, 13, 25, 28, 38, 44, 52, 84
- Goodrich Four Corners, 119
- Goodrichville, 16
- Good Spring, 101
- Good Springs, 2, 115
- Goodsprings, 2
- Good Thunder, 55
- Goodview, 55
- Goodville, 62
- Goodwater, 2, 58, 92
- Good Water, 62
- Goodwill, 42, 44
- Goodwin, 5, 7, 67, 88, 92, 108, 115, 126
- Goodwins Mill, 2
- Goodyear, 5
- Goofy Ridge, 28
- Gooseberry, 94, 118
- Gooseberry Mountain, 94
- Goose Creek, 106
- Goose Egg, 130
- Goose Garden,
- Goose Green, 119
- Goose Hollow, 71, 81
- Goose Lake, 35
- Gooseneck, 81, 111, 123
- Goose Pimple Junction, 81
- Goose Point, 17
- Goose Pond, 81
- Goose Prairie, 123
- Goose Rocks, 44
- Gopher Ridge, 18
- Gordon, 18, 22, 38, 42, 44, 52, 58, 65, 67, 88, 115, 126, 129
- Gordon Heights, 17
- Gordon Landing, 119
- Gordons, 28
- Gordonsburg, 111
- Gordon Springs, 22
- Gordonsville, 2, 55, 122
- Gordonton, 81
- Gordontown, 81
- Gordonville, 18, 52, 62, 115
- Gotebo, 92
- Gouge Eye, 69
- Government Camp, 94

- Government Hill, 5
- Grabtown, 10, 81
- Grace, 2, 25, 52, 58, 62, 65, 94, 106, 111, 115, 126
- Grace City, 84
- Grace Hill, 35
- Gracelock, 55
- Graceville, 19, 55
- Grade, 94
- Graft, 13
- Grainfield, 38
- Grain Valley, 62
- Grainville, 25
- Granada, 38, 55, 62
- Grand, 10
- Grand Canyon Village, 5
- Grand Center, 62
- Grand Detour, 28
- Grand Eddy, 62
- Grand Island, 19, 67, 67
- Grand Isle, 44
- Grandjean, 25
- Grand Junction, 25
- Grand Meadow; 55
- Grand Mound, 35, 123
- Grand Oaks, 81
- Grand Point,
- Grand Port, 62
- Grand Prairie, 42, 55
- Grand Rapids, 52, 84, 88
- Grand Ridge, 19
- Grand River, 35, 42
- Grand River City, 62
- Grand Summit, 38
- Grand View, 5, 19, 25, 52, 129
- Grandview, 10, 22, 25, 28, 31, 35, 62, 88, 94, 108, 115
- Granite, 5, 13, 25, 35, 47, 65, 69, 71, 92, 94, 130
- Granite Bay, 10
- Granite Bluff, 52
- Granite City, 28
- Granite Dells, 5
- Granite Falls, 55, 81

- Granite Hill, 22, 44, 94, 101
- Granite Ledge, 55
- Granite Mountain, 94
- Granite Quarry, 81
- Granite Springs, 11, 122
- Graniteville, 11, 16, 119
- Grant, 2, 11, 13, 19, 25, 35, 38, 42, 52, 65, 67, 79, 101, 111, 122
- Grants, 75
- Grantville, 49
- Grape, 52
- Grape Corner, 71
- Grape Creek, 81
- Grape Grove, 88
- Grapeland, 11, 58
- Grapevine, 5, 7, 11, 81, 115
- Grapewood, 81
- Graphic, 7
- Graphite, 79, 81
- Grass Corner, 44
- Grass Creek, 31, 130
- Grass Flat, 11
- Grasshopper, 5, 111
- Grass Lake, 11, 28, 58
- Grassland, 111, 115, 122
- Grass Range, 65
- Grass Valley, 11, 69, 94
- Grassy Creek, 81
- Grate, 13
- Grave Creek, 94, 126
- Grave Hill, 17, 31, 62
- Gravel, 42
- Gravel Hill, 2, 47, 58, 73, 111
- Gravel Junction, 7
- Gravel Pit, 35
- Gravel Point, 42
- Graves, 22
- Gravesend, 79
- Gravestown, 58
- Gravity, 35, 101
- Gray, 58, 92, 94, 101, 111
- Gray Goose, 108
- Gray Horse, 92
- Gray Mountain, 5

- Gray Mule, 111, 115
- Grays Flat, 11
- Grayson, 2, 7, 11, 22, 42, 62, 81, 88, 92
- Greasy, 92
- Greasy Corner, 7
- Greasy Ridge, 88
- Great Bend, 38
- Great Boars Head, 71
- Great Falls, 47, 65, 122
- Great Oaks, 35
- Great Pond, 44
- Great Works, 44
- Greece, 79
- Greece City, 101
- Greekstore, 11
- Greely, 13, 38, 67, 70
- Greely Landing, 44
- Green, 25, 38, 52, 92, 115
- Greenback, 94, 101
- Green Bank, 73
- Green Bay, 19, 35, 106, 122, 129
- Green Briar, 17, 28, 35
- Greenbrier, 31, 62
- Greenbush, 44
- Greencastle, 31
- Green Castle, 35, 62
- Green Center, 31, 35
- Green City, 62
- Greencreek, 25
- Green Creek, 28, 88
- Greendale, 11, 28
- Greendoor, 62
- Greene, 84
- Greene High, 7
- Greenfield, 11, 28, 31, 42, 44, 71, 84
- Greenfield Hill, 16, 115
- Green Forest, 7
- Green Gables, 42
- Green Glade, 47
- Green Grass, 108
- Green Grove, 58, 62, 73
- Green Haven, 52
- Greenhead, 19
- Green High, 7
- Green Hill, 2, 16, 17, 31, 81, 104, 106, 126
- Green Horn,
- Greenhorn, 11, 14, 94
- Green Island, 35
- Green Isle, 55
- Green Knoll, 73
- Green Lake, 52, 129
- Greenland, 7, 14, 52, 58, 71, 101, 111, 126
- Greenlaw, 42, 62
- Greenlaw Crossing, 44
- Greenlawn, 111
- Greenleaf, 25, 38, 55, 94
- Green Meadow, 94
- Green Meadows, 31, 94,
- Greenmount, 47
- Green Mountain, 35, 62, 81
- Green Mountain Falls, 14
- Green Mountain Village, 14
- Green Needles, 81
- Greenoak, 28, 31
- Green Oak, 52
- Green Oaks, 28
- Greenpond, 28
- Green Pond, 19, 73, 106
- Green Ridge, 47, 62, 126
- Green River, 28, 52, 58, 111, 118, 123, 130
- Green Rock, 28
- Greens, 69
- Greensand, 73
- Greensboro, 19, 22, 31
- Greensburg, 38, 42, 47
- Greens Cut, 22
- Green Sea, 106
- Green Spring, 126
- Green Spring Furnace, 47
- Green Springs, 69, 88, 122
- Greenstreet, 62
- Green Street, 2
- Green Timbers, 52
- Greentop, 62

- Greentown, 31, 81, 88
- Green Town, 62
- Greenup, 28
- Green Valley, 5, 11, 28, 47, 55, 81, 111, 122, 129
- Greenview, 28, 55, 62
- Greenville, 2, 7, 11, 16, 17, 19, 22, 28, 31, 35, 42, 44, 49, 52, 56, 57, 58, 62, 69, 71, 73, 75, 79, 81, 88, 92, 94, 101, 104, 106, 108, 111, 115, 118(2), 122, 126, 129
- Greenwater, 11, 123
- Greenway, 7,
- Greenwich, 14, 38, 122
- Greenwood, 43
- Greetingville, 31
- Gregory, 7, 22, 52, 55, 58, 69, 81, 88, 92, 94, 101, 108, 115, 126
- Gregory Corner, 122
- Gregory Crossroads, 81
- Gregory Forks, 81
- Gregory Landing, 62
- Gregorys Corner, 44
- Gregoryville, 55
- Grenada, 58
- Grim, 42
- Grimes, 42
- Grinders Switch, 110
- Grindstone, 44, 101, 108
- Grizzly, 14
- Grizzly Flats, 11
- Grocery Place, 19
- Groom, 69, 115
- Gross, 19, 25, 28, 38, 67
- Grosvenor Dale, 16
- Groton, 48
- Grotto, 123
- Grouse, 94, 123
- Grouse Creek, 118
- Grove, 11, 38, 42, 44, 126
- Grove Hill, 42
- Grove Level, 22
- Grover, 14, 38, 101, 106, 108, 118, 130

- Grover Beach, 11
- Grover Hill, 88
- Groverland, 11, 19, 38
- Grovertown, 31
- Groverville, 79
- Grow, 115
- Gu-Win, 2
- Guess, 106
- Guest, 2
- Guide, 58
- Guide Rock, 67
- Gulf, 81
- Gulf City, 19
- Gulf Crest, 2
- Gulf Hammock, 19
- Gulf Hills, 58
- Gulfport, 19
- Gulf Shores, 2
- Gulf Stream, 19
- Gulls Nest, 17
- Gully, 55
- Gulscrest, 2
- Guls Stream,
- Gum, 11, 111, 122
- Gumbo, 62
- Gumboro, 17
- Gumbranch, 22
- Gum Branch, 22
- Gum Corner, 81
- Gum Flat, 111
- Gum Grove, 7
- Gumlog, 22
- Gum Neck, 81
- Gum Ridge, 42, 58
- Gums, 58
- Gum Spring, 2, 126
- Gum Springs, 7, 58, 81, 1141, 115, 122
- Gum Swamp, 47
- Gumtown, 58
- Gumtree, 81
- Gum Tree, 7, 101
- Gum Tree Corner, 73
- Gum Valley,

- Gumwood, 17
- Gunbarrel, 14
- Gun Barrel City, 115
- Gunlock, 118
- Gunpowder, 47
- Gunsight, 5, 65, 115
- Guntown, 58
- Gusher, 118
- Guttenberg, 73
- Guy, 31, 75
- Gypsum, 14, 38, 79
- Gypsy, 42, 92, 126

-H-

- Hackberry, 5, 42, 111, 115
- Hackensack, 55, 73
- Hacker Valley, 126
- Hacklebarney, 73
- Haddock, 106
- Hague, 79, 84
- Hail, 115
- Hailstone, 118
- Hairtown, 81
- Hale, 47
- Hales Ford, 121
- Half Acre, 2, 73, 79, 111
- Half Bank Crossing, 92
- Half Chance, 2
- Half Day, 28
- Halfmoon, 65
- Half Moon, 7, 19, 42, 81
- Half Moon Bay, 11
- Halfmoon Landing, 22
- Half Mound, 38
- Half Rock, 62
- Half Way, 42, 126
- Halfway, 7, 42, 47, 62, 75, 79, 94, 111, 122, 130
- Halfway House, 11, 49
- Halfway Pond, 49
- Hall, 115
- Hallelujah Junction, 11

- Halo, 126
- Halstead, 37, 38
- Hamberg, 84
- Hambone, 11
- Hamburg, 2, 6 ,7, 11, 16, 19, 28, 31, 35, 38, 42, 52, 55, 58, 62, 73, 79, 88, 101, 106, 111, 122, 129
- Hamilton, 28, 31, 60, 73, 84, 88, 94, 122
- Ham Lake, 55
- Hamlet, 7, 94
- Hammer, 108
- Hammertown, 16
- Hammond, 28, 38
- Hampshire, 28, 79, 126
- Hams Prairie, 62
- Hancock, 7, 19, 35, 42, 47, 52, 55, 62, 71, 88, 101, 106, 115, 119, 126, 129
- Hancock Point, 44
- Hand, 7, 52, 106
- H and B Junction, 106
- Handle, 58
- Hand Valley, 7
- Handy, 22, 31, 62, 81
- Handy Corner, 58
- Handy Four Corners, 50
- Hanger, 115
- Hanging Grove, 31
- Hanging Limb, 111
- Hanging Rock, 88
- Happy, 115
- Happy Camp, 11
- Happy Canyon, 14
- Happy Corner, 44, 71, 119
- Happy Corners, 7, 88
- Happy Creek, 122
- Happy Creek Station, 69
- Happy Hill, 2, 111
- Happy Hills, 50
- Happy Hollow, 62, 88, 94, 115
- Happy Home, 81
- Happy Jack, 5, 42
- Happy Land, 92
- Happyland, 16, 55

- Happy Landing, 22
- Happys Inn, 65
- Happy Valley, 4, 11, 19, 24, 65, 71, 79, 81, 94, 101, 111, 115, 123
- Happy Wanderer, 55, 65
- Harbor, 88
- Harbor Oaks, 19
- Harbor View, 19
- Hard Cash, 22,58
- Hardin, 7, 14, 28, 35, 62, 65, 94, 115
- Harding, 22, 28, 38, 44, 50, 55, 73, 84, 108, 118, 126
- Hardinsburg, 31, 108
- Hard Luck, 52
- Hard Luck Crossing, 75
- Hardscrabble, 31, 58, 71, 79, 88, 111, 122
- Hardscrabble Corner, 119
- Hardscramble, 58
- Hard Scratch, 35
- Hardshorne, 92
- Hardup, 118
- Hardwood, 42, 52
- Hardy, 7, 11, 35, 44, 92, 115, 126
- Hare, 81, 94
- Hares Corner, 17
- Harlan, 31, 35, 38, 52, 94, 101
- Harlansburg, 31
- Harlem, 11, 19, 22, 25, 28, 52, 65, 77, 84, 88, 101
- Harlem Springs, 88
- Harlemtown, 17
- Harmony, 2, 7, 11, 22, 28, 31, 42, 44, 47, 55, 58, 62, 73, 81, 94, 104, 106, 111, 115, 122, 123, 126, 129, 130
- Harmony Grove, 81
- Harmony Hill, 106
- Harmonyvale, 73
- Harp, 7, 11, 19, 22
- Harper, 11, 19, 22, 28, 31, 35, 38, 62, 81, 88, 94, 115, 122, 123, 126, 130
- Harper Crossroads, 106
- Harper Heights, 126
- Harper Hill, 2

- Harper Junction, 94
- Harpers Choice, 47
- Harpers Corner, 47
- Harpers Crossroads, 81
- Harpers Ferry, 35, 126
- Harpersfield, 88
- Harpersville, 2, 115
- Harper Tavern, 101
- Harpertown, 11, 126
- Harperville, 58
- Harper Woods, 52
- Harrah, 91
- Harriet, 7, 11, 28, 104, 115, 126
- Harriett, 88
- Harrietta, 52
- Harriettsville, 88
- Harrisburg, 11, 19, 22, 25, 31, 67, 81, 84, 88, 92, 101, 108, 118
- Harrison, 7, 19, 22, 25, 28, 44, 52, 65, 67, 73, 79, 88, 92, 101, 111, 115, 126, 129
- Harrodsburg, 31
- Harrow, 101
- Hart, 7, 11, 22, 25, 35, 55
- Hartford, 7, 16, 22, 31, 35, 38, 44, 52, 62, 88, 108 ,119, 129
- Hartford City, 31
- Harvest, 2, 22
- Harvester, 62
- Hastings, 66, 67
- Hasty, 7, 14, 38, 81
- Hatboro, 101
- Hatch, 62, 75, 118
- Hatchet, 2
- Hatchetville, 92
- Hat Creek, 11, 130
- Hatfield, 125, 126
- Hatmaker, 52
- Havana, 2, 7, 19, 28, 38, 55, 84, 85, 88, 94
- Hawaii, 23, 24
- Hawaiian-Spanish Village, 24
- Haw Creek, 92
- Hawk, 2, 38, 122

- Hawk Branch, 81
- Hawkeye, 35, 62, 84, 130
- Hawk Head, 52
- Hawk Inlet, 4
- Hawk Point, 62
- Hawk Pride, 2
- Hawks, 52
- Hawk Springs, 130
- Haw Pond, 58
- Hawthorn, 2
- Hawthorne, 2, 34
- Hay, 123
- Hay Brook, 44
- Hay City, 115
- Hay Creek, 55, 129
- Haycrop, 25
- Hayden, 5, 11, 16, 25, 31, 38, 47, 62, 75, 88, 94, 118
- Hayden Corner, 44
- Hayden Hill, 11
- Hayden Row, 50
- Haydenville, 55, 92
- Haydraw, 108
- Hayfield, 11, 35, 55, 122
- Hayfork, 11
- Haypoint, 55
- Haypress, 28
- Hays, 36
- Hay Springs, 67
- Haystack, 11
- Hay Stack Corner, 129
- Hayti, 108
- Hazard, 22, 67, 104, 123
- Hazardville, 16
- Hazlenut, 58
- Headland, 2
- Head of Barren, 111
- Headquarters, 5, 16, 25, 123
- Head River, 22
- Head Tide, 44
- Head Waters, 122
- Healing Springs, 2, 7, 81, 106, 122
- Health, 7
- Health Springs, 106
- Heart, 7
- Heart Butte, 65
- Heartstrong, 14
- Heater, 58
- Hebron, 66
- Hedgerow Hollow, 17
- Heelstring, 7
- Heidelberg, 55
- Heidelberg Beach, 88
- Heifer Landing, 7
- Heilderberg, 55, 58, 101
- Heinz, 69
- Heist, 118
- Helena, 22, 25, 52, 55, 62, 64, 65, 92
- Hell, 52
- Hellertown, 11, 101
- Hellgate, 65
- Hellhole, 25
- Hell Hollow, 71
- Hells Half Acre, 130
- Helm, 58, 62
- Helper, 118
- Helps, 52
- Hemlock, 31, 52, 79, 81, 88, 94, 101, 126, 129
- Hemlock Center, 71
- Hemlock Grove, 88
- Hemlocks, 50
- Hemp, 22
- Henderson, 1, 7, 11, 14, 22, 28, 31, 35, 42, 47, 52, 55, 62, 67, 69, 81, 101, 111, 115, 126
- Henderson Still, 22
- Hendrysburg, 86, 88
- Henpeck, 28
- Henry, 7, 11, 14, 25, 28, 31, 42, 67, 108
- Henry Clay, 17, 101
- Henryville, 30
- Hen Scratch, 19
- Hentown, 22
- Hephzibah, 22
- Herbert Domain, 111
- Hercules, 11, 62

- Herd, 92
- Herman, 55, 67, 92
- Hermantown, 55
- Hermanville, 58
- Hermit Spring, 101
- Hero, 19, 58
- Hershey, 11, 67, 101
- Hetch Hetchy Junction, 11
- Hi-Nella, 73
- Hi-Point, 47
- Hickman, 7, 11, 17, 28, 62, 67, 111
- Hickory, 42, 47, 58, 81, 92, 101
- Hickory Bluff, 22
- Hickory Corner, 31
- Hickory Corners, 28, 129
- Hickory Creek, 62, 115
- Hickory Crossroads, 81
- Hickory Flat, 2, 7, 22, 58
- Hickory Flats, 111
- Hickory Group, 35
- Hickory Grove, 2, 7, 28, 35, 58, 88, 101, 106, 111, 122, 126, 129
- Hickory Haven, 16
- Hickory Hill, 17, 62, 92, 106
- Hickory Hills, 47, 58
- Hickory Level, 22
- Hickory Point, 81, 111
- Hickory Ridge, 17, 31, 52, 62, 115
- Hickory Rock, 81
- Hickory Tavern, 106
- Hickory Thicket, 47
- Hickory Tree, 111
- Hickory Valley, 7, 42, 111
- Hicksville, 7, 79, 88
- Hidaway Springs, 94
- Hidden Timber, 108
- High, 7, 115
- High Bridge, 73
- Highbridge, 71
- High Creek, 35
- High Falls, 22
- High Fill, 7
- High Forest, 55
- High Gate, 62

- High Head, 44
- High Hill, 58, 62, 92
- Highjinks, 5
- Highland, 69
- Highland Home, 2
- Highland Park, 5, 52
- Highland Pines, 5
- High Level, 2
- High Lonesome Wells, 75
- Highnote, 2
- High Pine, 2
- High Point, 22, 35, 47, 58, 62, 106, 111, 123
- High Prairie, 62
- High Ridge, 62
- High Rock, 94
- High Shoals, 22, 81
- High Springs, 19
- Hightown, 58, 122
- Highview, 65
- Highwater, 88
- Highway, 3, 75
- Highway 9 Landing, 92
- Highway City, 11
- Highway Highlands, 11
- Highwood, 65
- Hi Ho, 115
- Hill, 65, 71
- Hill and Dale, 19
- Hill City, 22, 25, 38, 55, 108
- Hillcrest, 31
- Hilldale, 17, 62
- Hillendale, 17
- Hillman, 22, 44, 52, 55
- Hill Number 1, 2
- Hill Point, 129
- Hills, 22, 35, 81
- Hillsboro, 125
- Hillsborough, 70
- Hillside, 5, 7, 14, 42, 44, 47, 52
- Hillside Colony, 65
- Hill Top, 2, 7, 28, 47
- Hilltop, 5, 22, 42, 52, 69, 73, 88, 111, 123

- Hillview, 55
- Hilly, 42
- Hi Lo,
- Hindman, 94, 115
- Hire, 67
- Hiwaiian-Spanish Village,
- Ho-Ho-Kus, 73
- Hobby, 22
- Hoboken, 2, 22, 72, 73, 88
- Hobo Station, 58
- Hog Back, 38
- Hogeye, 8, 115
- Hogeye Crossroads, 106
- Hog Hammock, 22
- Hog Island, 47, 81, 104
- Hog Jaw, 2, 8
- Hog Landing, 4
- Hog Mountain, 22
- Hogshooter, 92
- Hogtown, 31, 79
- Hog Valley, 19
- Hohenwald, 111
- Holiday, 19, 111
- Holiday Hills, 28
- Holiday Pines, 17
- Holland, 8, 19, 22, 28, 31, 35, 38, 50, 52, 52, 55, 62, 65, 67, 73, 79, 81, 88, 94, 115, 119, 122, 129
- Holland Gin, 1
- Hollandsburg, 31
- Hollandsville, 17
- Holler, 47
- Hollis, 114
- Hollow, 92
- Hollow Creek, 106
- Hollow Rock, 111
- Holly, 14, 42, 52, 126, 130
- Holly Beach, 42, 47
- Holly Bluff, 58
- Hollybrook, 42
- Holly Creek, 111
- Hollydale, 11
- Holly Grove, 8, 42, 58, 81, 111, 126
- Holly Hill, 19, 106
- Holly Hills, 2
- Holly Island, 8
- Holly Knoll, 17
- Hollyknowe, 58
- Holly Landing, 58
- Holly Leaf, 111
- Hollymount, 17
- Holly Oak, 17
- Holly Park, 81
- Holly Point, 19
- Holly Ridge, 42, 81, 106
- Holly Spring, 22
- Holly Springs, 2, 22, 42, 58, 81, 106, 111, 115
- Hollytree, 2
- Hollyville, 17
- Hollywile Park, 16
- Hollywood, 2, 8, 11, 14, 19, 25, 42, 47, 52, 55, 58, 62, 75, 101, 106, 111, 122, 126
- Hollywood Beach, 47
- Holly Woods, 50
- Holstein, 35, 62, 67
- Holy Corners, 52
- Holy Hill, 111
- Home, 38, 101, 123
- Homedale, 25
- Home Gardens, 11
- Homeland, 11, 62
- Home Place, 42
- Homer, 27
- Homerville, 22
- Homestead, 19, 22, 35, 52, 62, 65, 92, 94, 104, 115
- Homestead Ridge, 19
- Hometown, 28, 71, 101
- Home Valley, 11
- Homewood, 2
- Hominy, 92
- Honduras, 32
- Honesty, 88
- Honey-in-the-Hills, 19
- Honey Brook, 101
- Honey Creek, 28, 32, 35, 62, 101, 115

- Honeydew, 11
- Honey Grove, 101, 115
- Honey Hill, 81, 106
- Honey Hole, 101
- Honey Island, 58, 81
- Honeypot Glen, 16
- Honeytown, 88
- Honeyville, 32, 122
- Honk Hill, 79
- Honolulu, 24(2), 81
- Honor, 52
- Hood, 11, 22, 115
- Hoodoo, 111
- Hoohoo, 126
- Hooks, 2
- Hoop and Holler, 115
- Hoosier, 28
- Hoosierville, 32
- Hoot, 115
- Hoot Owl, 73, 92
- Hoover, 92, 94, 101, 108, 115
- Hooverville, 75
- Hopatcong, 73
- Hop Bottom, 101
- Hope, 5, 6, 8, 25, 28, 32, 35, 38, 42, 44, 73, 75, 84, 88
- Hopeful, 2, 22
- Hopeulikeit, 22
- Hope Valley, 11, 16
- Hopeville, 16, 35
- Hopewell, 8, 16, 19, 22, 28, 38
- Hop Hollow, 28
- Hopkins, 22, 38, 52, 55, 62, 65, 81, 92, 106
- Hopkins Corner, 17, 47
- Hopkins Mills, 104
- Hopkins Spring, 122
- Hopkinsville, 62
- Hop Yard, 11
- Horace, 38, 67, 70
- Horizon City, 115
- Horn, 58, 67
- Hornbeak, 111
- Hornet, 62, 111

- Hornsville, 19
- Horntown, 92
- Horsecamp, 25
- Horse Canyon, 118
- Horse Creek, 11, 111, 129, 130
- Horse Head, 122
- Horsehead, 8, 47
- Horseheads, 79
- Horse Heaven, 16, 123
- Horse Lake, 11
- Horseman, 129
- Horse Mesa, 5
- Horseneck, 126
- Horse Neck, 81
- Horse Pasture, 122
- Horsepen, 122, 126
- Horses Corner, 71
- Horse Shoe, 81
- Horseshoe, 8, 19, 58, 79, 81
- Horseshoe Beach, 19
- Horseshoe Bend, 25, 69, 94, 130
- Horseshoe Curve, 47
- Horseshoe Hill, 79
- Horse Shoe Run, 126
- Horsey, 122
- Hotchkissville, 16
- Hot Coal, 126
- Hot Coffee, 58, 62
- Hot Creek, 69
- Hothouse, 22, 81
- Hot Lake, 94
- Hot Springs, 6, 8, 11, 25, 65, 69, 75, 81, 94, 108, 122
- Hot Sulphur Springs, 14
- Hot Water, 58
- Hot Wells, 42
- Hourglass, 17
- House, 58, 75
- Houseman, 52
- House Rock, 5
- House Springs, 62
- Houston, 2, 4, 8, 17, 19, 22, 25, 28, 32, 55, 58, 62, 67, 108, 111, 113, 114, 115

- Houston River, 42
- Howey-in-the-Hills, 19
- Hub, 11, 58
- Hub City, 108, 129
- Huber, 32, 115
- Huber Heights, 88
- Huckleberry, 47, 111
- Huckleberry Corner, 50
- Hull, 35
- Humansville, 62
- Humble, 115
- Humble City, 75
- Humorist, 123
- Humptulips, 123
- Humpy Creek, 4
- Hundred, 126
- Hungary, 16
- Hungry Hill, 79
- Hungry Hollow, 65, 101
- Hungry Horse, 65
- Hungry Joe, 65
- Hunt, 8, 25, 42, 115
- Hunter, 8, 28, 38, 69, 84, 88, 92, 101
- Hunter-Liggett, 11
- Hunters Point, 5
- Huntersville, 55
- Hunting, 129
- Hunting Creek, 81
- Huntington, 19, 32, 35, 40, 50, 62, 69, 80, 94, 115, 118, 119, 122, 129
- Huntington Lodge, 47
- Hunting Valley, 88
- Huntsville, 28, 32, 38, 58, 62, 81, 88, 101
- Huron, 11, 38, 58, 62, 94, 108, 115
- Huron City, 52, 84
- Hurricane, 2, 4, 28, 42, 58, 62, 79, 81, 111, 118, 122, 126, 129
- Hurricane Branch, 58
- Hurricane Creek, 58(2)
- Hurricane Grove, 8
- Hurricane Mills, 111
- Hurry, 47
- Husk, 81

- Hustle, 122
- Hyacinth, 122
- Hyannis, 67
- Hybrid, 62
- Hyde Park, 77
- Hydro, 92
- Hygiene, 14
- Hypoluxo, 19

-I-

- Iberia, 55, 62, 88
- Iceland, 11
- Iconium, 111
- Idaho, 2, 25, 88, 101
- Idaho City, 25
- Idaho Creek, 14
- Idaho Falls, 25
- Idahome, 25
- Idaho Springs, 14
- Ideal, 22, 28, 108
- Idiot Creek, 94
- Iditarod, 4
- Idle Hour, 79
- Idol, 111
- Igloo, 4, 108
- Igo, 11, 94, 122
- Illinoi, 32
- Illinois, 26, 39, 119
- Illinois Bend, 115
- Illinois Camp, 75
- Illinois City, 28
- Illinois Grove, 35
- Illinois Plant, 42
- Imboden, 6
- Impact, 115
- Imperial, 22, 62, 67, 101
- Improve, 58
- Incline, 2, 11
- Incline Village, 69
- Increase, 58

- Independence, 11, 14, 28, 32, 35, 38, 42, 55, 58, 62, 65, 84, 88, 92, 94, 101, 115, 123, 126, 129
- Independence Hill, 122
- Independent, 42
- Index, 8, 79, 82, 115, 122, 123
- India, 58, 111, 115
- Indiahoma, 92
- India Hook, 106
- Indian, 4,8
- Indiana, 30, 35, 40, 64, 84, 98, 101, 119
- Indianapolis, 30, 35, 92
- Indian Arrow, 65
- Indian Bay, 8
- Indian Bayou, 42
- Indianbone, 47
- Indian City, 92
- Indian Cove, 25, 69
- Indian Creek, 28, 62, 101, 115, 129
- Indian Crossing, 101
- Indian Falls, 11
- Indian Field, 122
- Indian Ford, 19
- Indian Gap, 115
- Indian Grove, 25, 52, 62
- Indian Gulch, 11
- Indian Head, 47, 101
- Indian Head Rock, 25
- Indian Hill, 11
- Indian Hills, 14
- Indian Hot Springs, 5, 115
- Indian Island, 44
- Indian Landing, 42
- Indian Meadows, 14, 92
- Indian Mills, 73
- Indian Mound, 42, 62, 111
- Indian Neck, 122
- Indianola, 57
- Indian Orchard, 50, 101
- Indian Pine, 5
- Indian Point, 44, 62
- Indian Ridge, 38
- Indian River, 44, 52
- Indian River City, 19
- Indian Rocks Beach, 19
- Indian Shores, 19
- Indian Springs, 2, 11, 22, 32, 47, 58, 69, 92
- Indiantown, 19, 35, 52
- Indian Town, 47, 52, 122
- Indian Valley, 25, 94
- Indian Village, 32, 42, 118
- Indian Wells, 5, 11
- Industrial, 126
- Industrial City, 22
- Industry, 2, 28, 88, 115, 126
- Inez, 55, 67, 75, 82, 101, 126
- Ingot, 11
- Ink, 8, 62, 88
- Inkstar, 65
- Inkster, 84
- Inland, 67
- Inlet, 122
- Ino, 2
- Inspiration, 5
- Institute, 2, 58, 82, 126, 129
- Intake, 65
- Intelligence, 82
- Intercession City, 19
- Intercoastal City, 42
- Intercourse, 2, 101
- Interior, 108
- Interlachen, 94
- Interlaken, 11, 73, 79, 84
- Interlochen, 19, 52
- International Falls, 55
- Invincible, 42
- Ion, 35
- Iowa, 33, 42, 117
- Iowa City, 19, 35
- Iowa Colony, 115
- Iowa Falls, 35
- Iowa Hill, 11
- Iowa Point, 38
- Ipswich, 50, 108, 129
- Ireland, 32, 71, 88, 115, 123, 126
- Ireland Springs, 25, 94

- Irelandville, 79
- Iris, 11, 14, 65
- Irish Bend, 42
- Irish Cut, 111
- Irish Settlement, 44, 79
- Irishtown, 79, 101
- Irish Town, 11
- Iron, 55
- Iron Basin, 118
- Ironbridge, 92
- Iron Center, 62
- Iron City, 14, 22, 88
- Iron Creek, 4
- Iron Crossroads, 106
- Irondale, 14, 22, 88
- Iron Gate, 122
- Iron Gates, 62
- Iron Hill, 17, 47
- Iron Hills, 35
- Iron Horse, 11
- Iron Hub, 55
- Iron Junction, 55
- Iron Lightning, 108
- Iron Mountain, 62, 118, 130
- Iron Point, 69
- Iron Ridge, 129
- Iron River, 52, 129
- Iron Rock, 73
- Irons, 52
- Ironside, 94
- Iron Springs, 8, 118, 123
- Iron Stab, 22
- Iron Stob Corner, 8, 92
- Ironton, 14, 32, 52, 55, 62, 101, 126
- Irontown, 126
- Ironville, 2, 88
- Ironwood, 55
- Iroquois Point, 24
- Irvine, 11, 19, 101
- Island, 8, 42, 50, 55
- Island City, 32, 62, 69, 94
- Island Creek, 50
- Island Falls, 44
- Island Grove, 28

- Island Mountain, 11, 69
- Island Pond, 119
- Island Town, 8
- Island View, 55
- Isle, 55
- Isle of Palms, 106
- It, 58
- Italia, 19
- Italy, 106, 115
- Italy Hill, 79
- Ithaca, 67
- Itta Bene, 57
- Ivanhoe, 11, 52, 55
- Ivory, 47, 111, 122
- Ivorydale, 88
- Ivoryton, 16
- Ivy, 35, 122
- Ivy Creek, 2
- Ivy Hills, 32, 47, 82
- Ivylog, 22
- Ivy Ridge, 17, 82
- Ivytown, 47
- IXL, 92

-J-

- Jacket, 62
- Jack Pine, 55
- Jackpot, 69
- Jackrabbit, 5, 69
- Jackson, 2, 11, 22, 25, 28, 32, 35, 42, 44, 47, 52, 55, 58, 62, 65, 67, 69, 71, 73, 82, 88, 101, 104, 106, 110, 111, 115, 122, 123, 129, 130
- Jackson Hole, 130
- Jacksonville, 19, 22, 28, 32, 35, 44, 62, 73, 82, 88, 94, 101, 110, 115, 119
- Jack Springs, 14, 82
- Jacques, 25
- Jake Prairie, 62
- Jamaica, 22, 28, 35, 119,122
- James Brothers, 62

- James Store, 122
- Jamestown, 11, 22, 28, 32, 35, 38, 42, 52, 58, 62, 69, 77, 79, 83(2), 84, 88, 94, 100, 101, 104, 106, 111, 115, 129
- Janice, 58, 67
- Janise,
- Japan, 62, 101
- Japanese Village One, 24
- Jasmine, 8
- Jason, 82
- Jasontown, 47
- Jasonville, 32
- Jasper, 1,
- Java, 11, 108, 122
- Jay, 19, 44
- Jay Bird, 88
- Jaybird, 8, 111
- Jay Bird Springs, 22
- Jay Em, 130
- Jay Jay, 19
- Jay See Landing, 55
- Jean, 69, 94, 115
- Jeanville, 101
- Jeff Davis, 58
- Jefferson, 2, 8, 11, 14, 22, 32, 35, 38, 42, 44, 47, 50, 52, 58, 69, 71, 73, 82, 88, 92, 94, 101, 106, 108, 111, 115, 122, 123, 129
- Jefferson City, 65
- Jeffersonville, 35, 88
- Jelloway, 88
- Jenkins, 28, 42, 47, 55, 58, 69, 73
- Jersey, 22, 69, 122
- Jersey City, 72, 73, 129
- Jersey Shore, 101
- Jerseyville, 73
- Jerusalem, 47, 88, 104
- Jessamine, 19
- Jester, 92
- Jet, 2, 92
- Jewelville, 22
- Jigger, 42
- Jim Thorpe, 101

- Jimtown, 11, 28, 32, 47, 92, 94, 101, 111, 129
- Jim Town, 88
- Jinks, 22
- Jobs Corners, 101
- Jockey, 32
- Jockeycamp, 126
- Jockey Hill, 71
- Joe, 88, 115
- Joe Branch, 126
- Joes, 14
- Joes Pond, 119
- Johannesburg, 11, 52, 129
- Johnnycake, 126
- Johns Cross Timbers, 62
- Johnson, 2, 4, 5, 8, 14, 17, 19, 32, 38, 42, 55, 58, 65, 67, 75, 79, 84, 88, 92, 94, 115, 119, 123, 126
- Johnson Center, 44, 71
- Johnson Crossroads, 2
- Jo Jo, 101
- Joker, 126
- Joliette, 84
- Jolly, 58, 108, 115
- Jolly Dump, 108
- Jonesboro, 6
- Jones Crossroads, 2
- Jonquil, 8
- Joplin, 60, 62
- Joshua Tree, 11
- Jot Em Down, 22
- Jot 'Em Down, 115
- Judge, 25, 55, 62
- Judge Town, 25
- Jug Fork, 58
- Jug Run, 88
- Jugs Corners, 88
- Jugtown, 47, 82, 101
- Julia, 22
- Jumbo, 2, 8, 69, 73, 88, 92, 111, 115, 126
- Jumbo Landing, 44
- Jump, 88
- Jumpertown, 47, 58

- Jump River, 129
- Jumptown,
- Junction, 69, 73, 115, 126, 129
- Junction City, 22, 42
- Juneau, 3, 4, 129
- June Lake, 11
- Juniata, 35, 52, 67, 101
- Juniper, 19, 22, 25, 52, 82, 94
- Juniper Grove, 58
- Juniper Hot Springs, 14
- Juniper Springs, 11
- Juno, 111
- Jupiter, 11, 19
- Jupiter Island, 19
- Justice, 28, 82, 92, 126

-K-

- Kaaawa, 24
- Kabob, 79
- Kalamazoo, 8, 52, 126
- Kale, 126
- Kankakee, 28, 32
- Kansas, 2, 5, 8, 13, 22, 28, 36, 70, 92, 111, 120
- Kansas City, 38, 59(2), 61, 62, 94, 120
- Kansas Settlement, 5
- Kathleen, 19
- Kay, 8
- Kearney, 60(2)
- Keddie, 11
- Keel, 58
- Keenland, 129
- Keg, 11
- Kellogg, 84
- Kelly, 38
- Kendal Green, 50
- Kendall, 38, 47, 52, 62, 79, 101, 123
- Kendall Acres, 82
- Kendall Crossroads, 2
- Kendall Hills, 28

- Kendall Park, 73
- Kendalls Corner, 44
- Kendallville, 32, 35
- Kenel, 108
- Kennebunk, 44
- Kennebunkport, 44
- Kennedy, 2, 11, 28, 35, 55, 67, 69, 75, 79, 101, 129
- Kennedy Still, 19
- Kennet, 63
- Kenosha, 127, 128(2)
- Kenova, 40, 85, 119, 124
- Kensington, 11, 16, 19, 22, 28, 38, 47, 55, 71, 88, 106, 111
- Kent Furnace, 16
- Kenton, 17, 52, 92
- Kentuck, 2, 122
- Kentucky, 8, 9, 26, 28, 30, 39, 40(2), 48, 52, 60(2), 61, 80, 84, 85, 91, 99, 109, 110(2),
115, 118, 119(2), 120(2), 122, 124, 125
- Kentucky House, 11
- Kentucky Town, 115
- Kermit, 115, 122, 126
- Ketchikan, 4
- Ketchum, 25
- Ketchuptown, 106
- Kettering, 47, 88, 94
- Kettle, 126
- Kettle Corner, 104
- Kettle River, 55
- Kevin, 55, 65
- Key, 115
- Keyhole, 14
- Keystone, 11, 14, 19, 32, 35, 42, 62, 65, 67, 69, 84, 101, 108, 126, 130
- Key West, 19, 35, 55
- Kicking Horse, 65
- Kid, 11
- Kidville, 122
- Kiester, 55
- Kilarney Shores, 19
- Kildeer, 28, 65
- Kildeer Island, 50

- Killawog, 79
- Killbuck, 88
- Kill Buck, 79
- Killdeer, 84
- Kill Devil Hills, 82
- Killington, 119
- Kiln, 58
- Kilowatt, 11
- Kinderhook, 111
- Kindle, 52
- King, 8, 58, 115, 129
- King And Anderson, 58
- King and Queen Court House, 122
- King City, 11
- King Cole, 94
- Kingfisher, 91, 92
- King George, 122
- King of Prussia, 101
- King Salmon, 4, 11
- Kings Creek, 47, 106
- Kingsland, 6
- Kings Oaks, 42
- Kingston, 115
- Kingsville, 88
- Kingsville on-the-Lake, 88
- King William, 122
- Kinloch, 58, 62
- Kinston, 82
- Kirkman, 35
- Kissimmee, 101
- Kit Carson, 11, 14
- Kitchen, 126
- Kitchener, 58
- Kite, 22
- Kitty Hawk, 15, 82
- Kleenburn, 130
- Klondike, 5, 11, 22, 28, 35, 42, 58, 62, 69, 88, 94, 101, 106, 111, 115, 126
- Klondyke, 32, 55
- Knickerbocker, 115
- Knife River, 55, 65
- Knob, 8
- Knob Creek, 8, 82

- Knob Fork, 126
- Knob Hill, 14, 115
- Knob Lick, 62
- Knob Noster, 62
- Knobtown, 58
- Knockemstiff, 88
- Knott, 22, 88, 115
- Knox, 28, 32, 44, 62, 65, 67, 84, 101
- Knox City, 62
- Knoxville, 2, 8, 11, 22, 28, 35, 47, 58, 62, 67, 88, 94, 101, 108, 109(2), 126
- Kodak, 69
- Kodaka, 108
- Kodiak, 4, 62
- Ko Ko, 111
- Kokomo, 8, 14, 24, 32, 58
- Kooskooskie, 123
- Kosciusko, 57
- Kremlin, 65, 92, 122
- Krik, 4
- Kripplebush, 79
- Kulm, 83
- K'Ville, 22
- Kyle Hot Springs, 69

-L-

- Laark, 42
- Laboratory, 82, 101
- Lackey, 58
- La Crosse, 19, 28, 32, 38
- Ladiesburg, 47
- Ladysmith, 38
- La France, 106
- Lagoona Beach, 55
- La Grande, 94
- Lagrange, 32, 44, 122
- LaGrange, 8, 22, 130
- La Grange, 11, 28, 52, 62, 82, 88, 111, 115, 129
- Lake, 58
- Lake Alpine, 11

- Lake Bird, 19
- Lake Bruce, 32
- Lake Bungee, 16
- Lake Center, 55
- Lake Charles, 42
- Lake City, 8, 11, 14, 19, 22, 28, 38, 52, 55, 58, 106, 108
- Lake Creek, 22, 62
- Lake End, 42
- Lake Fork, 25
- Lake George, 14, 52, 55, 79
- Lakehurst, 71
- Lake Lanier, 108
- Lake of the Woods, 11
- Lake Placid, 19
- Lake Ripley, 129
- Lakeside, 65, 67
- Lake Valley, 75
- Lake View, 58
- Lakeview, 25
- Lake Wilson, 55
- Lake Winnebago, 62
- Lakewood Corner, 35
- Lama, 75
- Lamar, 61
- Lamb, 28, 32
- Lamb Creek, 25
- Lamb Place, 44
- Lambs Corner, 44
- Lambs Grove, 35
- Lame Deer, 65
- Lanai City, 24
- Lancaster, 8, 32, 35, 38, 50, 55, 71, 88, 96(2), 106, 111, 129
- Land O' Lakes, 19, 129
- Lands End, 50
- Lane, 25, 38
- Lane City, 69
- Lanes Prairie, 62
- Lansing, 28, 35, 38, 88
- Lantana, 111
- Lap, 47
- Lapel, 32
- Lapland, 32, 38

- La Push, 123
- Laramie, 130
- Lardeo, 62
- Largo, 32, 55
- Lariat, 130
- Larkspur, 14
- Larrys Store, 122
- La Rue, 88
- LaRue, 115
- Larue, 8, 58, 101
- Las Animas, 14
- Last Chance, 11, 14, 25, 92
- Las Vegas, 68, 75, 115
- Latex, 42
- Latonia, 58
- Latrobe, 98
- Lauderdale, 73
- Laura, 32, 62
- Lauratown, 8
- Laurel, 11, 17, 19, 32, 35, 47, 58, 65, 67, 69, 82, 123
- LaurelBluff, 111
- Laurel Creek, 126
- Laurel Fork, 111, 126
- Laurel Glen, 16
- Laurel Grove, 19, 47, 94, 101
- Laurel Hill, 19, 42, 58, 82, 101, 104, 106
- Laurel Lake, 101
- Laurel Mountain, 101
- Laurel Park, 101
- Laurel Ridge, 42
- Laurel Run, 101
- Laurel Springs, 73, 82
- Laurel Summit, 101
- Lava, 75, 79
- Lava Hot Springs, 25
- Lavender, 123
- Lavender Corner, 52
- La Vista, 67
- Lawn, 115
- Lawrence, 2, 11, 28, 32, 38, 49, 50, 52, 67, 82, 92, 115, 123
- Lawrenceburg, 32, 35, 62, 101, 111

- Lawrence Corner, 71
- Lawrence Creek, 92
- Lawrenceville, 28, 73, 99, 126
- Laws, 11
- Lawyers, 122
- Lawyersville, 79
- Lay, 14
- Leader,
- Leader, 14, 55, 92
- Lead Hill, 8
- Lead Mine, 62, 126
- Leadore, 25
- Leadpoint, 123
- Leadville, 25
- Leaf River, 55
- Leaf Valley,
- Leaksville, 58, 82, 122
- Leaky, 115
- Leap, 94
- Leatherwood, 2, 32
- Leavenworth, 32, 38, 55,1 23
- Lebanon, 2, 5, 8, 14, 16, 17, 19, 22, 28, 32, 35, 38, 44, 58, 62, 67, 71, 73, 79, 94, 101, 106, 108, 111, 115, 122, 129
- Le Claire, 33, 35
- Lee, 2, 8, 19, 28, 32, 35, 44, 50, 52, 69, 94, 123
- Leech Lake, 55
- Leedy, 92
- Left Hand, 126
- Lefthand Bay, 4
- Legato, 122
- Lego, 126
- Lehigh, 28
- Leisure, 52
- Leisure City, 19
- Lemon, 58,101
- Lemon Bluff, 19
- Lemon Cove, 11
- Lemon Grove, 19
- Lemons, 62
- Lemon Springs, 82
- Lemonville, 115

- Lent, 122
- Leslie, 8, 22, 25, 35, 42, 47, 52
- Lespedeza, 58
- Letcher, 2, 108
- Levee, 11
- Level, 47
- Level Land, 22
- Level Plains, 2
- Levelroad, 2
- Lewis, 2, 8, 14, 19, 22, 32, 35, 38, 82, 94, 119
- Lewis and Clark Village, 62
- Lewisburg, 32
- Lewistown, 62
- Lexington, 2, 22, 28, 32, 35, 38, 48, 49, 50, 52, 55, 58, 62, 67, 82, 88, 92, 94, 106, 111, 115, 118, 122, 123
- Liars Corner, 88
- Libby, 65
- Liberal, 32, 38, 62, 94
- Liberty, 2, 5, 8, 11, 14, 17, 19, 22, 25, 28, 32, 35, 38, 42, 44, 52, 58, 60, 62, 67, 69, 79, 82, 92, 94, 101, 104, 111, 115, 118, 122, 126, 129
- Liberty Bell, 14
- Liberty Center, 32, 88
- Liberty City, 2
- Liberty Corner, 73
- Liberty Grove, 47
- Liberty Hall,
- Liberty Hill, 2, 16, 42, 82, 106, 111
- Liberty Island, 73
- Liberty Plain, 50
- Liberty Springs, 8
- Libertytown, 47
- Libertyville, 2, 29, 62, 73
- Library, 101
- Lick Branch, 8
- Lick Creek, 29
- Licking, 62
- Lickskillet, 62, 82, 88, 111
- Lick Skillet, 122
- Life, 111
- Liggett, 14, 32

- Liggett Crossing, 88
- Light, 2, 62
- Lightbeam, 126
- Lightburn, 126
- Lightfoot, 25, 111
- Lightning, 25, 94
- Lightsville, 29
- Lignite, 4, 8, 84
- Lignum, 122
- Likely, 11
- Lilac, 58
- Lillydale, 126
- Lillyhaven, 126
- Lily, 108
- Lily Lake, 29
- Lily Pond, 22
- Lima, 29, 35, 65, 69, 88, 92, 106, 129
- Lime, 2, 14, 55, 94
- Lime City, 35, 88, 115
- Lime Creek, 52, 55
- Limedale, 8, 32
- Lime Grove, 67
- Limehouse Station, 106
- Lime Kiln, 2, 47
- Limerick, 22, 29, 58, 88, 101, 106
- Lime Ridge, 101, 129
- Lime Rock, 2, 16, 101,104
- Lime Springs, 35
- Limestone, 8, 19, 44, 52, 65, 88, 101, 106, 126
- Limestone City, 88
- Limestone Creek, 19
- Limestone Gap, 92
- Limestone Hill, 126
- Lime Villagae, 4
- Limpytown, 88
- Lincoln, 2, 5, 8, 11, 14, 17, 25, 29, 32, 35, 38, 44, 47, 50, 52, 55, 62, 65, 66, 67, 67, 71, 73, 75, 79, 84, 92, 101, 104, 111, 115, 118(2), 122, 123, 129
- Lincoln Beach, 94
- Lincoln City, 19, 32, 94
- Lincoln Hills, 14
- Lincoln Landing, 22

- Lincoln Park, 14, 52, 73
- Lincolnton, 22, 82
- Lincoln Valley, 84
- Lincoln Village, 11
- Lincolnville, 32, 92
- Linden, 113
- Lindsay, 42, 65, 67, 92, 115
- Lindsey, 2, 8, 38, 88
- Linesville, 100
- Lingo, 75
- Link, 42, 94
- Linkville, 53
- LinNeus, 62
- Lisbon, 29, 32, 35, 42, 44, 47, 62, 71, 75, 79, 84, 88, 111
- Listening Rock, 82
- Litchfield, 15, 16, 29, 38, 44, 53, 55, 67, 71, 88, 101
- Lithium, 62
- Little, 126
- Little Africa, 106
- Little Alps, 94
- Little America, 130
- Little Arkansaw, 8
- Little Axe, 92
- Little Berger, 62
- Little Boars Head, 71
- Little Bridge, 50
- Little Brook, 73
- Little Buffalo, 8
- Littleburg, 108
- Little Canada, 44
- Little Cedar, 35
- Little Charley, 32
- Little Chicago, 55, 88, 129
- Little Chief, 92
- Little City, 16, 92
- Little Cranberry Island, 44
- Little Creek, 17, 42, 58, 111
- Little Creek, 82
- Little Dam, 14
- Little Duck, 122
- Little Eagle, 108
- Little Egg Harbor, 73

- Little Egypt, 26, 29, 50
- Little Falls, 44, 55, 73
- Little Ferry, 73
- Little Flock, 8
- Little Fork, 55
- Little Georgetown, 126
- Little Groves, 35
- Little Heaven, 17
- Little Hope, 22, 101, 111, 129
- Little Indian, 29
- Little Italy, 8, 44, 58, 126
- Little Jack Corners, 101
- Little Lake, 11, 53
- Little Lake City, 19
- Littlelot, 111
- Little Medicine, 130
- Little Mexico, 115
- Little Mountain, 106
- Little New York, 2, 115
- Little Norway, 11, 129
- Little Oak, 2
- Little Oklahoma, 29, 123
- Little Orleans, 47
- Little Otter, 126
- Little Paradise, 11
- Little Penny, 11
- Little Pine, 55
- Little Pittsburg, 126
- Little Ponderosa, 92
- Littleport, 35
- Little Prairie, 42, 129
- Little Red, 8
- Little Rest, 50
- Little River, 8, 11, 22, 38, 106
- Little Rock, 2, 6, 8, 25, 29, 32, 35, 55, 58, 106
- Littlerock, 11
- Little Rose, 129
- Little Silver, 73
- Little Spring, 5
- Little Springs, 58
- Little St Louis, 32
- Little Sugarloaf, 25
- Little Switzerland, 82
- Little Texas, 2, 8, 58, 106, 111, 122
- Little Torch Key, 19
- Little Town, 106
- Little Tucson, 5
- Little Turkey, 35
- Little Union, 62
- Little Valley, 11, 94
- Little Venice, 53
- Little Warrior, 2
- Little Water, 75
- Little White Oak, 111
- Little Yazoo, 58
- Little York, 29,32
- Lively, 62, 115, 126
- Live Oak, 2, 11, 19, 42, 106, 115
- Livermore, 71
- Liverpool, 29, 32, 42, 79, 101, 115, 126
- Living Springs, 14, 65
- Livingston, 2, 11, 22, 29, 35, 42, 62, 65, 73, 111, 129
- Lizard, 35, 75
- Lizzieville, 2
- Loafer, 8
- Loafers Glory, 82
- Loakfoma, 58
- Lobo, 75
- Lobsterville, 50
- Local, 55, 62
- Locate, 65
- Loch Leven, 58
- Loch Lloyd, 62
- Loch Lomond, 19, 42, 58, 122
- Lock, 88
- Lock Haven, 101
- Lockit, 94
- Lock Seventeen, ,88
- Lock Springs, 62
- Locks Village, 50
- Loco, 22, 42, 92, 115
- Loco Hills, 75
- Locust, 35, 62, 82, 115
- Locust Fork, 2

- Locust Grove, 22, 32, 47, 79, 88, 92, 94, 115, 122, 126
- Locust Hill, 62, 82
- Locust Ridge, 42
- Locust Springs, 111
- Locust Valley, 47
- Locustville, 17
- Lodge, 106
- Lodge Grass, 65
- Lodgepole, 67, 108
- Lodge Pole, 65
- Lodgepole Saddle, 65
- Lofty, 2
- Logan, 2, 8, 11, 14, 22, 29, 32, 35, 38, 62, 65, 67, 69, 73, 75, 79, 82, 84, 88, 92, 115, 118, 122, 126
- Logan Center, 84
- Logandale, 11
- Logan Mills, 101
- Logansport, 32, 35, 42, 101, 126
- Logan Square, 29
- Logansville, 11, 22, 88
- Logantown, 101
- Loganville, 94, 101, 129
- Log Cabin, 42, 94, 115
- Log Cabin Crossroads, 32
- Log Landing, 22
- Log Lane Village, 14
- Logtown, 14, 22, 58
- Lollipop, 115
- London, 2, 8, 11, 32, 53, 55, 62, 88, 94, 101, 111, 115, 126, 129
- Londonderry, 71, 88, 199
- London Springs, 94
- Londontown, 47
- London Village, 17
- Lone, 14, 123
- Lone Cedar, 115
- Lone Chimney, 92
- Lone Corner, 62
- Lone Elm, 8, 38, 62
- Lone Fountain, 122
- Lone Grove, 92
- Lone Hickory, 82

- Lone Jack, 62
- Lonelyville, 79
- Lone Mountain, 111
- Lone Oak, 14, 22, 106, 115, 126
- Lonepine, 65
- Lone Pine, 8, 11, 25, 42, 58, 94
- Lone Rock, 8, 25, 35, 129
- Lone Star, 8, 11, 14, 38, 42, 62, 94, 106, 111, 115
- Lonetree, 14, 130
- Lone Tree, 14, 32, 35, 62, 84, 108
- Lone Valley, 8
- Lone Willow, 115
- Lone Wolf, 75, 92
- Lone Wolf Colony, 11
- Long, 4, 8, 58, 88, 92, 123
- Longacre, 42
- Long Beach, 11, 19, 32, 44, 55
- Long Branch, 29, 58, 73
- Long Bridge, 42
- Long Cane, 22
- Long Creek, 29, 95, 106
- Long Green, 47
- Long Hammock, 19
- Long Hill, 16, 73
- Long Island, 38, 78, 122
- Long Josephs Point, 50
- Long Key, 19
- Long Lake, 32, 58, 108
- Long Lane, 62
- Long Meadow, 47
- Long Neck, 17
- Long Pine, 67
- Long Plain, 50
- Longpole, 126
- Long Pond, 44, 50
- Long Prararie, 55
- Long Rapids, 53
- Long Rock, 111
- Long Run, 126
- Longshot, 58
- Long Springs, 42
- Longstraw, 42
- Longstreet, 42, 58

- Longtown, 63, 92, 106
- Long Valley, 11, 73, 108
- Longview, 29, 42, 58
- Longwill, 8
- Loogootee, 29, 32
- Looking Glass, 95
- Lookout, 11, 32, 92, 101, 130
- Lookout Mountain, 22, 106
- Loom, 126
- Looney, 122
- Looneyville, 115, 126
- Loon Lake, 32
- Loop, 115
- Loose Creek, 63
- Lords Corner, 17
- Lordship, 16
- Lorida, 19
- Los Angeles, 11, 115
- Lost, 55
- Lost Cabin,
- Lost Cane, 8, 130
- Lost City, 11, 69, 92, 126
- Lost Corner, 122
- Lost Corner, 8
- Lost Creek, 65, 126
- Lost Eden, 5
- Lost Hills, 11
- Lost Nation, 29, 35, 71, 119
- Lost Prairie, 95
- Lost River, 25, 32, 71, 95
- Lost Springs, 38, 130
- Lost Village, 79
- Lostwood, 84
- Lotus, 11, 25, 32
- Louisa, 122
- Louisiana, 40, 63
- Louisville, 2, 14, 22, 29, 30, 38, 39, 47, 58, 63, 67, 86, 88, 111
- Love, 5, 8, 29, 58, 115
- Love Hill, 2, 22
- Love Ladies, 73
- Love Lady, 111
- Lovelock, 11
- Lovely, 95, 101
- Love Place, 8
- Loves Corner, 29
- Loves Park, 29
- Love Station, 95
- Loveville, 17
- Lovewell, 38
- Loving, 22, 92, 115
- Loving Place, 75
- Low, 118
- Lower Bridge, 95
- Lower Gold Hill, 69
- Lower Miami, 5
- Lower Peach Tree, 2
- Lower Pig Pen, 82
- Lower Shaker Village, 71
- Lower Texas, 42
- Lower Village, 50, 71
- Lower Village Three, 24
- Lower Wheatfields, 5
- Low Gap, 8, 123
- Low Mountain, 5
- Low Point, 29
- Loyal, 92, 129
- Lubbock, 115
- Lubec, 43
- Lucas, 6
- Lucern, 58
- Lucerne, 7, 11, 14, 32, 38, 63, 88, 101, 108, 123, 126, 130
- Lucerne In Maine, 44
- Luck, 82, 122, 129
- Lucknow, 55, 106
- Lucky, 42, 111
- Lucky Boy, 69
- Lucky Landing, 44
- Lucky Ridge, 115
- Lude, 55
- Lulu, 53, 63
- Lumber, 8
- Lumber Bridge, 82
- Lumber City, 22, 101
- Luttrell, 109
- Luxemburg, 35, 55
- Luzerne, 35

- Lynbrook, 79
- Lynch, 47, 67
- Lynchburg, 58, 63, 88, 122
- Lynchville, 44
- Lyon, 58, 63

-M-

- Mackinaw, 29
- Macon, 21, 29, 63, 65, 67
- Mad Creek, 14
- Madison, 2, 8, 11, 16, 19, 22, 25, 29, 32, 35, 38, 44, 47, 55, 58, 63, 67, 71, 73, 75, 82, 84, 88, 101, 106, 108, 122, 126, 129
- Madison Lake, 55
- Madison on-the-Lake, 88
- Madison Park, 73
- Madisonville, 42, 58, 63, 101, 111, 115
- Madrid, 2, 14, 35, 67, 75, 79, 122
- Mad River, 11, 88
- Magazine, 8
- Magenta, 42, 58
- Maggie Blues, 69
- Magic, 25, 95
- Magic City, 25, 115
- Magma, 5
- Magnet, 8, 22, 29, 32, 67
- Magnet Cove, 8
- Magnetic Springs, 88
- Magnolia, 2, 8, 11, 14, 17, 22, 29, 32, 35, 42, 47, 50, 55, 58, 63, 73, 82, 84, 88, 111, 126, 129
- Magnolia Beach, 19
- Magnolia Springs, 19
- Magnum, 82
- Magoun, 92
- Maherrin, 122
- Maiden, 63, 65, 82, 123
- Maiden Rock, 65
- Main City, 63

- Maine, 35, 43, 44, 76, 82
- Maine Prairie, 55
- Mainstream, 44
- Major, 22, 42
- Mallard, 35, 55, 115
- Mammoth, 11, 63, 65, 126
- Mammoth Lakes, 11
- Mammoth Ledge, 69
- Mammoth Spring, 8
- Man, 126
- Manassa, 13
- Manassas, 22
- Manchester, 2, 16, 22, 29, 32, 35, 38, 42, 44, 47, 50, 53, 55, 63, 65, 71, 73, 82, 88, 92, 108, 111, 119, 123, 129
- Manchester-by-the-Sea, 50
- Manger, 65
- Mango, 19
- Manhattan, 14, 19, 29, 32, 38, 65, 69, 75, 77(2), 79, 101, 103
- Manhattan Beach, 11, 55
- Manheim, 126
- Manifest, 42
- Manila, 8, 14, 63, 118, 126
- Manilla, 11, 32, 35
- Manly, 35
- Manning, 105
- Mansfield, 29, 63
- Mansfield Four Corners, 16
- Many, 42
- Many Farms, 5
- Many Island, 8
- Many Springs, 63
- Maple, 29, 55, 82, 92, 115, 126, 129
- Maple Acre, 126
- Maple Bay, 55
- Maple Beach, 123
- Maple City, 38
- Maple Corner, 119
- Maplecrest, 47, 88
- Maple Crest, 47
- Maple Falls, 123
- Maple Fork, 126
- Maple Forks, 2

- Maple Grove, 2, 8, 11, 29, 44, 47, 50, 53, 63, 73, 82, 88, 95, 101, 118, 122, 123, 129
- Maple Hill, 2, 53, 55, 63, 101, 129
- Maple Island, 55
- Maple Lake, 55
- Maple Leaf, 108
- Maple Meadow, 126
- Maple Park, 50
- Maple Plain, 55
- Maple Rapids, 53
- Maple Ridge, 32, 50, 53, 88
- Maple River, 35
- Maples, 32, 95, 111
- Maple Shade, 73(2), 101
- Mapleside, 35
- Maple Spring, 111
- Maple Springs, 8, 55, 82
- Maple Summit, 101
- Maplesville, 2
- Mapleton, 44, 55, 82, 84
- Maple Valley, 32, 53, 88
- Mapleview, 55
- Maple View, 47, 126
- Mapleville, 47
- Maplewood, 32, 42, 53, 55, 71, 73, 88, 106
- Marathon, 58, 88, 115, 129
- Marble, 8, 14, 55, 82, 101, 123
- Marble City, 92
- Marble Creek, 25
- Marble Dale, 16
- Marble Falls, 115
- Marble Furnace, 88
- Marblehead, 29, 50, 129
- Marble Hill, 22, 47, 73
- Marble Rock, 35
- March, 55, 63
- March Rapids, 129
- Margaret, 2, 82, 95, 101, 115, 126
- Margaretsville, 82
- Margie, 115
- Marianna, 18
- Marigold, 2, 14, 29

- Marine, 29
- Marine City, 53
- Marine on St Croix, 55
- Marion, 2, 8, 16, 19, 22, 25, 29, 32, 35, 38, 42, 44, 50, 53, 55, 58, 63, 65, 67, 82, 84, 88, 95, 101, 106, 108, 115, 126, 129
- Marion Forks, 95
- Marion Springs, 53
- Marked Tree, 5, 8
- Market, 126
- Marmaduke, 8
- Marquette, 29, 35, 38, 67
- Marriott Settlement, 117
- Marrowbone, 111
- Mars, 101
- Marseilles, 84, 88
- Marsh, 65, 115
- Marshall, 2, 4, 8, 11, 14, 22, 29, 32, 35, 53, 55, 63, 65, 79, 82, 84, 88, 92, 101, 111, 115, 118, 122, 123, 126, 129, 130
- Marshallberg, 82
- Marshall Corner, 50, 71
- Marshall Ford, 115
- Marshall Hollow, 101
- Marshalls, 79
- Marshalls Corner, 47, 73
- Marshall Springs, 115
- Marshallton, 17, 101
- Marshalltown, 17, 35, 73, 108, 122
- Marshallville, 22, 73, 88
- Marsh Creek, 101
- Mars Hill, 2, 8, 22, 42, 44, 58, 82, 101
- Marsh Mill, 11
- Marsh Valley, 25
- Marsland, 67
- Mart, 115
- Martha, 8
- Marthaville, 42
- Martin, 2, 4, 22, 42, 44, 53, 55, 58, 67, 69, 71, 79, 84, 88, 92, 106, 108, 111, 118, 123, 126

- Martin Box, 8
- Martinsville, 30
- Marvel, 14
- Mary, 2
- Mary Chapel, ,111
- Marydale, 29
- Marydel, 17, 38, 47
- Marydell, 47, 106
- Mary Hill, 35
- Maryland, 29, 40, 42, 45, 46, 57, 73, 111, 119, 122
- Maryland Line, 47
- Maryland Point, 47
- Marys Grove, 111
- Marysvale, 118
- Marysville, 11, 25, 35, 38, 65, 101, 115
- Maryton, 122
- Marytown, 126, 129
- Maryville, 29, 32, 35, 63, 112
- Mascot, 58, 67, 106, 112
- Mashpee, 50
- Mason, 19, 22, 29, 42, 53, 55, 66, 69, 71, 84, 92, 95, 101, 112, 115, 123, 126, 129
- Mason City, 67
- Massachusetts, 48, 118
- Massacre Lake, 69
- Mass City, 53
- Mastodon, 53
- Matador, 115
- Match, 22
- Matthew, 82, 123
- Matthews, 2, 29, 42, 47, 58, 63, 66, 73
- Matthews Corner, 123
- Matthews Crossroads, 82
- Matthews Mill, 11
- Matthews Place, 115
- Matthews Run, 101
- Maverick, 5
- Maxbass, 84
- Maxwell, 67, 75
- Maxwelton, 126

- Maybee, 53
- Mayberry, 29, 47, 63, 67, 112
- Mayberrys, 69
- Mayberry Village, 16
- Maybeury, 126
- May Day, 38
- Mayday, 14, 22, 58, 112
- Mayfield, 22, 25, 38, 47, 53, 63, 82, 92, 108, 115, 118, 122, 123, 129
- Mayflower, 42, 63, 115
- Mayflower Grove, 50
- Maynardville, 109
- Mayo, 19, 47, 95, 106
- Mayo Beach, 50
- Mayo Mills, 106
- Maysville, 8, 14, 22, 35, 44, 63, 69, 82, 88, 92, 101, 106
- Maysville Crossing, 32
- Mazda, 84
- McAlester, 92
- McAlister, 75
- McAllaster, 38
- McAllister, 66, 129
- McAllister Landing, 19
- McCoy, 14
- McCracken, 38
- McCrystal Place, 75
- McDavid, 19
- McElveen, 58
- McGreggor Place, 75
- McKee, 22, 95
- McKee City, 73
- McKenzie, 2, 84, 112
- McLean, 29, 67, 115, 122
- McNaughton, 129
- McShea, 44
- Mead, 67
- Meade, 38, 53, 88
- Meadow, 22, 53, 67, 82, 95, 108, 115, 118
- Meadow Bridge, 126
- Meadowbrook, 17, 32, 73
- Meadow Brook, 11, 50, 55
- Meadow Creek, 25

- Meadow Grove, 67
- Meadow Lake, 75
- Meadowlands, 55
- Meadowood, 17
- Meadows, 25, 29, 71, 73
- Meadow Summit, 82
- Meadow Valley, 129
- Meadow View, 82
- Meadowview, 47
- Meadowville, 44
- Meadow Woods, 19
- Meat Camp, 82
- Mecca, 32, 88
- Mechanic, 82
- Mechanic Falls, 44
- Mechanic Hill, 22
- Mechanicsburg, 29, 32, 58, 88, 101, 122, 126
- Mechanicstown, 88
- Mechanicsville, 2, 16, 17, 22, 35, 47, 63, 73, 88, 101, 106, 119, 122
- Mechanic Valley, 47
- Mechanicville, 79
- Medical Lake, 123
- Medical Springs, 95
- Medicine Bow, 130
- Medicine Lake, 55, 66
- Medicine Lodge, 38
- Medicine Mound, 115
- Medicine Springs, 66
- Medley, 95
- Meek, 67
- Meeker, 14, 42
- Meeme, 129
- Meeting House Hill, 17
- Meeting Street, 106
- Melbourne, 8, 11, 19, 35, 112, 123
- Melody, 29
- Melody Hill, 32
- Melody Lake, 79
- Melody Meadows, 17
- Memphis, 2, 19, 32, 53, 58, 63, 67, 88, 99, 109, 112, 114, 115
- Menifee, 8, 11

- Menominee, 67
- Mentor, 38, 55, 88
- Mentor on-the-Lake, 88
- Mercer, 19, 29, 35, 44, 67, 88, 100, 101
- Mercer Square, 50
- Merchant, 106
- Merchantville, 73
- Mercury, 2
- Mercuryville, 11
- Meridian, 11, 14, 19, 22, 25
- Merino, 13
- Merit, 115
- Mermaid, 17
- Merrygold, 73
- Merry Hill, 82
- Merryman, 11
- Merry Oaks, 82
- Mesopotamia, 88
- Mesquite, 69, 75, 115
- Mesquite Oasis, 11
- Metal, 101
- Metalic City, 69
- Metcalf, 29, 50
- Metcalfe, 58
- Meteor, 25, 95, 123, 129
- Meter, 122
- Metropolis, 29, 42
- Metropolitan, 53
- Mexican Hat, 118
- Mexican Springs, 75
- Mexican Town, 5
- Mexican Water, 5
- Mexico, 32, 44, 47, 63, 88, 101, 106
- Mexico Crossing, 22
- Meyers Chuck, 4
- Miami, 5, 32, 44, 63, 64, 75, 88, 92, 114, 115, 126
- Miami Beach, 17, 47, 53, 73
- Miami Bend, 32
- Miamisburg, 88
- Miamitown, 88
- Miami Valley, 22
- Michigamme, 53

- Michigan, 50, 51, 84, 95, 119, 120
- Michigan Beach,29
- Michigan Bluff, 11
- Michigan City, 32, 58
- Michigan Hill, 123
- Michigan Settlement, 44
- Michigantown, 32
- Michigan Valley, 38
- Midas, 11, 25
- Mid Canon, 66
- Mid City, 29
- Middlebrook, 47
- Middleburg, 35, 47
- Middlebury, 32
- Middle City, 112
- Middle Creek, 29
- Middlefield, 16
- Middlefork, 32
- Middlegate, 69
- Middle Pasture, 50
- Middle Point, 88
- Middlepoint, 47
- Middle River, 35, 55
- Middlesboro, 32
- Middlesborough, 50
- Middletown, 16, 17, 29, 32, 35, 38, 47, 53, 63, 69, 73, 82, 88, 101, 104, 119
- Middle Valley, 73
- Middle Village Three, 24
- Middle Water, 115
- Midland, 14, 35, 38, 47
- Midland City, 29
- Midnight, 25, 58, 75
- Midway, 2, 5, 8, 11, 14, 16, 19, 22, 29, 32, 35, 38, 42, 55, 58, 63, 66, 67, 69, 75, 82, 84, 88, 92, 95, 106, 108, 112, 115, 118, 122, 126, 130
- Midway City, 11
- Midway Corner, 8
- Midway Island, 122
- Midwest, 130
- Midwest City, 92

- Milan, 29, 38, 55, 63, 71, 75, 86, 88, 101, 112, 124, 129
- Mild Springs,
- Mile High, 11, 115
- Mile Point, 119
- Miles, 11
- Miles Point, 63
- Milestone Corner, 16
- Military Crossing, 95
- Milk Springs, 2
- Milkwater, 5
- Mill A, 124
- Mill City, 11, 69
- Mill Creek, 17, 66, 92
- Milledgeville, 21
- Miller, 2, 8, 11, 19, 29, 32, 35, 38, 47, 58, 63, 66, 67, 88, 95, 108, 112, 130
- Miller City, 29, 88
- Miller Colony, 66
- Miller Corner, 44
- Miller Grove, 88
- Millersburg, 29, 32, 35, 53, 55, 63, 88
- Millerton, 42
- Millerville, 42
- Mill Hollow, 71
- Mill Iron, 66
- Mill Neck, 82
- Mill River, 50
- Millstone, 16, 73, 112
- Milltown, 73
- Milton, 49, 50
- Milwaukee, 127
- Milwaukie, 95
- Minden, 42
- Mine Brook, 73
- Minefield, 47
- Mine Hill, 73
- Miner, 35, 63, 66
- Mineral, 8, 11, 25, 29, 69, 88, 95, 115, 122, 124
- Mineral Bluff, 22
- Mineral City, 32, 63, 69, 88, 126
- Mineral Hot Springs, 14, 88
- Mineral King, 11

- Mineral Point, 63, 101, 128, 129
- Mineral Spring, 47
- Mineral Springs, 8, 19, 38, 42, 58, 63, 82
- Miners Delight, 130
- Minersville, 67
- Mines, 63
- Minimum, 63
- Minister, 101
- Mink, 42
- Mink Creek, 25, 95
- Mink Shoal, 126
- Minneapolis, 38, 53, 54, 55
- Minnehaha, 5, 14, 55, 124
- Minnehaha Springs, 126
- Minneopa, 55
- Minneota, 55
- Minnesota, 11, 40, 53, 54
- Minnesota Boys Town, 55
- Minnesota City, 55
- Minnesota Falls, 55
- Minnesota Flat, 11
- Minnesota Junction, 129
- Minnie, 63, 126
- Minortown, 16
- Minot, 58
- Mint, 5
- Minto, 4(2)
- Mint Spring, 2
- Minuet, 82
- Miracle Hot Springs, 11
- Miracle Run, 126
- Mirage, 14, 75
- Miry Brook, 16
- Mission, 66
- Missionary, 42, 58
- Mississippi, 40, 56
- Mississippi City, 58
- Missoula, 66
- Missouri, 36, 39(2), 59, 61, 63, 74, 119
- Missouri City, 115
- Missouri Triangle, 11
- Missouri Valley, 35

- Mist, 95
- Mistletoe, 8, 95
- Mix, 42
- Mixtown, 101
- Mixville, 16
- Mize, 22
- Mobile, 1
- Moccasin, 5, 11, 29, 66, 112
- Mock, 8
- Mock City, 124
- Mock Corner, 63
- Mockingbird Hills, 17
- Model, 14, 112
- Model City, 79
- Modest, 88
- Moe, 108
- Molasses Junction, 19
- Moline, 53
- Molt, 66
- Monarch, 8, 14, 19, 58, 69, 106, 118, 130
- Monastery, 63
- Monday, 88
- Money, 58
- Money Creek, 55
- Money Island Beach, 82
- Monitor, 32, 95, 122, 124, 126
- Monkey Run, 5, 8, 63
- Monkeys Eyebrow, 5
- Monogram, 82
- Monongahela, 53
- Monroe, 8, 11, 16, 22, 32, 35, 42, 44, 50, 53, 58, 67, 71, 73, 79, 82, 88, 92, 95, 101, 108, 112, 115, 118, 122, 124, 129
- Monroe Bridge, 50
- Monroe City, 63
- Monroeville, 32, 73
- Montana, 4, 38, 63, 64, 73, 129
- Montana City, 66
- Montanapolis Springs, 66
- Monterey, 67
- Montevideo, 55

- Montezuma, 5, 11, 14, 22, 29, 32, 35, 38, 69, 75, 82, 88, 112, 122
- Montezuma Creek, 118
- Montgomery, 1, 2, 11, 22, 29, 32, 35, 42, 50, 53, 55, 58, 73, 101, 106, 112, 115, 119
- Montgomery City, 63
- Monticello, 8, 19, 22, 29, 32, 35, 38, 42, 44, 55, 58, 63, 75, 82, 88, 106, 112, 115, 118, 129
- Montpelier, 25, 32, 35, 42, 47, 58, 84, 88, 119, 122, 126
- Montreal, 63, 129
- Monument, 14, 38, 75, 95, 101
- Monumental, 47
- Moomaw Corner, 67
- Moon, 58, 92, 101, 112, 129
- Moon Corner, 122
- Moon Lake, 58
- Moonlight, 38, 122
- Moonridge, 14
- Moons, 22, 112
- Moonshine, 29
- Moonstone, 11
- Moontown, 2
- Moon Valley, 129
- Moose, 130
- Moose City, 25
- Moosehorn Corner, 104
- Moose Junction, 129
- Moose Lake, 55
- Mooselookmeguntic, 44
- Moose Town, 66
- Moosup, 16
- Morehead, 38, 122
- Morehead City, 82
- Morgan, 2, 8, 14, 22, 25, 35, 47, 53, 55, 63, 66, 73, 95, 101, 106, 115, 118, 119, 129, 130
- Morgan Beach, 44
- Morgan Center, 88
- Morgan City, 42, 58
- Morganfield, 21
- Morgan Ford, 82

- Morgan Grove, 126
- Morgan Hill, 11, 101
- Morgan Landing, 95
- Morgan Park, 55
- Morgan Run, 88
- Morgans Corner, 92
- Morgan Springs, 11
- Morgans Store, 58
- Morgantown, 19, 32, 47, 58, 88, 101, 122, 126
- Morganville, 73
- Morning Glory, 14
- Morningside, 16, 22, 32, 47, 79, 101, 106, 108
- Morning Star, 5, 8, 58, 82, 126
- Morning Sun, 35, 88
- Morningview, 88
- Moro Bottom, 6
- Morocco, 32
- Morris, 2, 8, 16, 22, 29, 32, 42, 55, 58, 73, 92
- Morris Corner, 44, 50
- Morris Grove, 115
- Morris Mill, 2
- Morrison, 92
- Morris Place
- Morris Plains, 73
- Morris Ranch, 115
- Morris Run, 101
- Morriston, 58
- Morristown, 29, 55, 73, 88, 108
- Morrisville, 73, 82, 88, 101, 106, 119
- Morse Bluff, 67
- Morton, 69
- Moscow, 2, 8, 25, 29, 32, 35, 38, 44, 47, 53, 55, 58, 88, 101, 104, 112, 115, 119, 122, 126, 129
- Moscow Mills, 63
- Mosquito Crossing, 22
- Mosquito Landing, 19
- Mosquitoville, 119
- Moss, 58
- Moss Agate, 66
- Moss Bluff, 19

- Moss Hill, 115
- Moss Oak, 22
- Mossy Creek, 22
- Mossy Head, 19
- Motion, 11
- Motor, 35
- Motor City, 11
- Mound, 42, 84
- Mound Bottom, 112
- Mound City, 29, 38, 58, 63, 108, 115
- Mound House, 69
- Moundridge, 38
- Mounds, 8
- Mound Valley, 26, 38
- Mount Adams, 8
- Mountain, 47, 58, 63, 84, 126, 129
- Mountainair, 75
- Mountain Base, 71
- Mountain Brook, 124
- Mountainbrook, 22
- Mountainburg, 8
- Mountain Center, 11
- Mountain City, 22, 69, 112, 118
- Mountain Fork, 5, 8
- Mountain Grove, 8, 63, 122
- Mountain Hill, 22
- Mountain Home, 2, 8, 26, 95, 112, 115, 118,1 30
- Mountain House, 69, 79
- Mountain Iron, 55
- Mountain Island, 82
- Mountain Lake, 55
- Mountain Lodge, 79
- Mountain Meadow, 5
- Mountain Page, 82
- Mountain Park, 22, 82
- Mountain Pass, 11
- Mountain Pine, 8
- Mountain Ranch, 11
- Mountain Rest, 106
- Mountain Scene, 22
- Mountainside, 73
- Mountain Springs, 8, 22, 69
- Mountain Top, 8
- Mountain Top Junction, 11
- Mountain Valley, 8, 82
- Mountainview, 75
- Mountain View, 2, 5, 6, 8, 11, 14, 22, 24, 44, 63, 69, 73, 82, 106, 122, 124, 126, 130
- Mountain Village, 4
- Mount Airy, 22, 73, 80, 82, 112, 122
- Mount Baldy, 11
- Mount Carmel, 100
- Mount Cuba, 17
- Mount Energy, 82
- Mount Hope, 38
- Mount Lebanon, ,42
- Mount Misery, 73, 101
- Mount Morris, 53, 129
- Mount Olive, 1
- Mount Orange, 112
- Mount Pleasant, 8, 17, 19, 42, 58, 63, 82
- Mount Repose, 88
- Mount Sterling, 63, 88, 118, 129
- Mount Valley, 82
- Mount Vernon, 8, 58, 67, 79, 82, 88, 95, 108, 112, 124, 126, 129
- Mount Washington, 50
- Mount Wilson, 47
- Mouse Island, 44
- Mouser, 92
- Mousetown, 47
- Mozart, 8, 26, 126
- Mt Air, 101
- Mt Airy, 42, 47, 63, 69, 101
- Mt Berry, 22
- Mt Desert, 44
- Mt Garland, 122
- Mt Healthy, 32
- Mt Holly, 8, 82
- Mt Idaho, 26
- Mt Lincoln, 14
- Mt Morris, 29, 101
- Mt Olympus, 32
- Mt Pleasant, 8, 29, 32, 35
- Mt Pulaski, 29

- Mt Sterling, 2, 29, 32, 35, 82, 88
- Mt Union, 42
- Mt Vernon, 22, 32, 35, 38, 44, 47
- Mt Vernon Springs, 82
- Mt Washington, 11
- Mt Wilson, 11
- Muck City, 2
- Mud Bay, 4
- Mud Butte, 108
- Mud Castle, 82
- Mud Creek, 2
- Muddy, 29, 66
- Muddy Creek, 82, 101
- Muddy Ford, 19
- Muddy Gap, 130
- Mud Hill, 79
- Mud Hole, 19
- Mud Mills, 79
- Mudrock Crossing, 11
- Mud Run, 101
- Mudsock, 88
- Mud Springs, 26, 69, 124
- Muhlenberg, 101
- Muitzeskill, 79
- Mulberry, 8, 22, 32, 38, 42, 58, 63, 82, 88, 106, 112, 115
- Mulberry Center, 101
- Mulberry Grove, 22, 29, 88
- Mulberry Hill, 42, 112, 122
- Mule, 95
- Mule Barn, 92
- Mule Creek, 75
- Mule Crossing, 5
- Mule Hollow, 112
- Muleshoe, 14, 115
- Mule Town, 88
- Mumper, 67
- Muncie, 29
- Munich, 84
- Munster, 66, 84, 101
- Murray, 8, 11, 16, 26, 32, 35, 55, 63, 67, 84, 91, 101, 110, 115
- Murray Hill, 47, 71
- Murry, 58, 63, 129

- Muscleshell, 26
- Muscle Shoals, 2
- Muse, 92
- Muskogee, 91
- Musselfork, 63
- Musselshell, 66
- Mustang, 69, 92, 115
- Mustard, 101
- Muttontown, 79
- Mutual, 88, 92, 101
- Myrtle Beach, 104
- Mystic, 11, 16, 35, 42, 63, 108

-N-

- Nags Head, 82
- Nail, 8
- Nameless, 112, 115
- Nantucket Island, 49
- Napier, 101, 112, 115
- Naples, 11, 19, 26, 29, 44, 79, 82, 108, 115, 118
- Napoleon, 84
- Narrows, 14, 95
- Narrows Creek, 63
- Nash, 84
- Nashville, 11, 22, 29, 32, 35, 38, 53, 63, 67, 82, 88, 95, 109, 110(2), 119, 129
- Nashville Center, 55
- Nashville Plantation, 44
- Nassau, 17, 19, 55, 79
- Nassauville, 19
- Natal, 95
- Natchez, 32, 42
- National, 35, 69, 124, 126
- National City, 29, 53
- National Park, 73
- Natural Bridge, 2, 112
- Natural Dam, 8
- Natural Steps, 8
- Natural Well, 122

- Nausau Junction,
- Navy, 66, 122
- Nay Aug, 101
- Neah Bah, 124
- Nebraska, 8, 40, 66, 88
- Nebraska City, 66, 68
- Necessity, 115
- Neck City, 63
- Nectar, 2
- Nectarine, 101
- Need, 11
- Needful, 88, 101
- Needles, 11, 68
- Needmore, 2, 8, 19, 22, 29, 32, 53, 58, 63, 82, 88, 92, 101, 112, 115, 126
- Needy, 95
- Negro Foot, 122
- Negros Liberty Settlement, 115
- Nelson, 2, 5, 11,14, 22, 29, 53, 63, 68, 69, 71, 88, 92, 101, 115, 124, 126, 129
- Neptune, 35, 73, 88, 126, 129
- Neptune Beach, 19
- Neptune City, 69, 73
- Nesting, 122
- Neuern, 129
- Neureru, 129
- Neutral, 38
- Nevada, 29, 32, 35, 58, 63, 68, 70, 88, 115, 119
- Nevada City, 11, 69
- Nevada Hills, 69
- Nevada Mills, 32
- Nevada Scheelite Camp, 69
- Nevadaville, 14
- Neverfail, 112
- Neverskink, 79, 101
- New Albany, 31
- Newark, 8, 11, 29, 63, 68, 69, 73, 85, 88
- New Bern, 79, 82
- Newborn, 22
- New Bourbon, 63
- Newburgh, 32
- New Castle, 2, 14, 17, 32, 63, 71, 82, 101, 122
- New City, 29
- Newcomer, 63
- Newcomerstown, 88
- New Deal, 115
- New Delhi, 29
- New Design, 29
- New Douglas, 29
- New England, 22, 84, 88, 126
- Newfoundland, 73, 101
- New Guinea, 88
- New Hampshire, 70, 118
- New Haven, 15, 49
- New Igloo, 4
- New Jersey, 71, 72, 76
- New Johnsonville, 112
- New Mexico, 74, 91
- New Moon, 2, 8
- New Orleans, 41(2), 42
- New Philadelphia, 29, 32, 101
- Newport, 22, 32, 40, 44, 49, 68, 71, 73, 88, 91, 101, 103, 104, 106, 115, 119, 122
- Newport News, 121, 122
- New Rumley, 88
- New Scotland, 79
- New Thompson, 8
- Newton, 48
- New Town, 58
- New Year, 66
- New York, 1, 19, 35, 37, 40, 63, 75(2), 97, 100, 104, 115, 118(2), 129
- New York City, 72, 75, 76(2), 77(2), 78(2), 79, 85, 99, 114, 124, 125
- Next, 126
- Niagara, 84, 95, 101, 129
- Niagara Falls, 79
- Nice, 11
- Nicelytown, 122
- Niceville, 19
- Nicholas, 19, 42, 79, 95, 122
- Nicholasville, 3, 22, 88

- Nichols, 35, 42, 47, 55, 58, 63, 66, 106, 115, 129
- Nichols Corner, 104
- Nichols Grove, 63
- Nichols Hills, 92
- Nickel, 42, 115
- Nickletown, 112
- Nighthawk, 14, 124
- Nightingale, 69
- Nightmute, 4
- Nile, 58, 63, 79, 124
- Niles, 51
- Nimrod, 66
- Nine-mile, 66
- Nine Forks, 42
- Nine Mile, 53
- Ninemile, 32, 66, 112
- Ninemile Bend, 19
- Nine Mile Corner, 84
- Ninemile Rocks, 69
- Ninepoints, 101
- Nine Times, 106
- Ninety-Six, 106
- Ninetynine Oaks, 11
- Ninety Six Corners, 79
- Ninteen Mile Crossing, 115
- Nirvanna, 53
- Nitrate City, 3
- Nitro, 126
- Nix, 3,115
- Nixon, 19, 22, 44, 58, 69, 73, 95, 101, 112, 115
- Nob Hill, 82
- Nobility, 115
- Noble, 22, 66, 92, 124
- Nobletown, 92
- Nodaway, 63
- Node, 130
- Noel, 14, 35, 63, 92, 122
- Nogales, 4
- Nogo, 8, 63
- Nolo, 101
- Nome, 4, 84
- Non, 92

- No Name, 14
- Nonesuch, 53
- Nonpareil, 95
- Nonparell, 68
- Noodle, 115
- Noon, 95, 124
- Noonday, 22, 115
- Noone, 71
- Nooseneck, 17, 104
- Norcross, 55
- Norfolk, 14, 16, 58, 61, 68
- Normal, 3, 29
- Norman, 90, 92
- Normandy, 29, 112
- Normandy Beach, 73
- North, 106
- North Battle Mountain, 69
- North Bend, 31
- North Bradley, 53
- North Carolina, 40, 77, 79, 81
- North Cuba, 79
- North Dakota, 40, 83
- North Dayton, 88
- North East, 47, 101
- Northern Ohio, 8
- Northfield, 48
- Northgate, 84
- North Lemmon, 84
- North Myrtle Beach, 105
- North Orange, 49
- North Platte, 66
- North Pole, 4, 26, 79, 92
- North Rim, 5
- North Star, 11, 17, 53, 55, 68, 88, 129
- North Thompsonville, 16
- Northumberland, 101
- Norway, 29, 32, 35, 38, 44, 53, 58, 68, 79, 84, 95, 106, 126
- Norway Center, 108
- Norway Grove, 129
- Norway Lake, 55
- Norway Ridge, 129
- Norwegian Grove, 55
- Norwich, 15

- Not, 63
- Note, 22
- Nothing, 3, 5
- Notrees, 115
- Novelty, 63, 88, 124
- Novice, 115
- Nowhere, 92
- Nowthen,
- Nuckles, 8
- Number Eight, 63
- Number Four, 44, 79
- Number Nine, 8
- Number One Oasis, 69
- Number One Settlement, 69
- Number Seven, 66
- NuMine, 101
- Nuremberg, 101
- Nursery, 115
- Nut Plains, 16
- Nut Tree, 11
- Nuttsville, 122

-O-

- Oak, 63, 88
- Oak Bottom, 11
- Oak Center, 55
- Oak City, 82, 118
- Oak Creek, 5, 14, 118
- Oakdale, 84
- Oakfield, 22, 44
- Oak Flat, 115
- Oak Flats, 42
- Oakford, 29
- Oak Forest, 8, 17
- Oak Glen, 11
- Oak Grove, 3, 5, 8, 11, 17, 19, 22, 29, 42, 50, 53, 55, 58, 63, 73, 75, 82, 95, 101, 106, 112, 115, 122, 126, 129
- Oakgrove, 88
- Oak Harbor, 124
- Oak Hill, 8, 19, 22, 38, 44, 63, 82, 88, 101, 112, 115, 122, 126
- Oak Hills, 11, 95
- Oakhurst, 11
- Oak Knoll, 11
- Oakland, 11, 16, 19, 22, 29, 35, 42, 44, 47, 50, 58, 63, 68, 88, 115
- Oakland Gardens, 16
- Oak Leaf, 115
- Oak Level, 3
- Oakley, 26, 38
- Oak Mill, 68
- Oak Mills, 38
- Oak Mountain, 22
- Oak Orchard, 47
- Oak Park, 11, 22, 29, 55
- Oakport, 55
- Oakridge, 55
- Oak Ridge, 3, 8, 19, 29, 42, 47, 53, 63, 73, 82, 92, 106, 108, 112, 115, 122, 126
- Oak Run, 11
- Oaks, 42, 58, 82, 92
- Oaks Corner, 55
- Oak Shade, 73, 88, 101, 122
- Oak Springs, 5, 69, 95
- Oak Summit, 47
- Oaktown, 32
- Oak Tree, 73, 101
- Oak Tree Crossroads, 32
- Oak Vale, 58
- Oak Valley, 11, 38, 73, 104
- Oak View, 11, 106
- Oak Village, 3
- Oakville, 11, 16, 32, 73, 82
- Oak Wells, 5
- Oakwood, 8, 22, 29, 32, 35, 47, 88
- Oaky Grove, 3
- Oasis, 11, 63, 69, 75, 95, 118
- Oatman, 5
- Oatmeal, 115
- Oats, 106
- Obed, 29
- Obey City, 112

- Oblong, 29
- Obsidian, 26
- Obtuse Hill, 16
- Ocean, 73, 82
- Ocean Beach, 73
- Ocean City, 47, 73, 124
- Ocean Grove, 124
- Ocean Roar, 11
- Oceanside, 95
- Ocean Spray, 50
- Ocean View, 17, 50
- Oceanville, 44
- Oco, 88
- O' Conee, 8
- Octagon, 3, 32
- Octave, 5
- Odd, 126
- Odessa, 68
- Odessy, 47
- Offer, 66
- Office Hall, 122
- Ogden, 29, 35, 38, 53, 73, 82, 88, 106, 115, 117(2), 126
- Ogg, 115
- Ogle, 29
- Ohio, 14, 29, 30, 40(2), 63, 79, 80, 81, 84, 85(2), 119(2), 120, 124
- Ohio Camp, 66
- Ohio City, 14, 88
- Ohioview, 101
- Ohioville, 101
- Ohiowa, 68
- Ohl, 101
- Ohop, 124
- Oil Center, 29, 75, 92
- Oil City, 42, 58, 63, 92, 101, 115, 124, 129
- Oilfield, 29
- Oil Grove, 29
- Oilmont, 66
- Oil Springs, 130
- Oil Trough, 8
- Okay, 8, 22, 92
- O'Kean, 8

- Okean, 8
- Oklahoma, 40, 47, 58, 88, 89, 90, 101, 114, 115
- Oklahoma City, 90(2), 91, 92
- Oklahoma Flat, 115
- Okra, 115
- Old Agency, 66
- Old Alabam, 8
- Old Americus, 58
- Old Appleton, 63
- Old Battle Mountain, 69
- Old Bay View, 19
- Old Beaver, 26
- Old Bland, 63
- Old Buffalo, 8
- Old Bullion, 69
- Old Calibrator, 60
- Old Camp, 4
- Old City, 44, 50, 119
- Old Cove, 8
- Old Ford, 82
- Old Furnace, 50
- Old Georgetown, 58
- Old Glory, 5, 112, 115
- Old Golden, 26
- Old Greenville, 63
- Old Halfway, 32
- Oldham, 63, 108, 112, 115
- Old Harmony, 3
- Old Hickory, 112
- Old Horse Springs, 75
- Old House, 106
- Old Hundred, 82
- Old Joe, 8, 106
- Old Lexington, 8
- Old Liberty, 8
- Old Mill Creek, 29
- Old Monroe, 63
- Old Moses, 75
- Old Mystic, 16
- Old Navy, 115
- Old Pearl, 29
- Old Peru, 35
- Old Quaker Meetinghouse, 50

- Old R, 115
- Old Rampart, 4
- Old Retrop, 92
- Old Ripley, 29
- Old River, 11
- Old Roach, 14
- Old Saline, 42
- Old Shongaloo, 42
- Old Station, 11
- Old St Louis, 32
- Old Success, 63
- Old Tappan, 73
- Old Texas, 3
- Old Thompson, 8
- Oldtown, 29, 47
- Old Town, 3, 19, 22, 32, 35, 44, 47, 66, 75, 88, 95, 108, 124
- Old Tripoli, 35
- Old Wells, 14
- Olive, 32, 63, 66, 75, 92, 122, 126
- Olive Branch, 29, 58
- Olive Grove, 82
- Olive Hill, 82
- Olive Hill Corner, 44
- Ollie, 3
- Olympia, 63
- Olympian Village, 63
- Olympic Valley, 11
- Omaha, 8, 22, 29, 66, 67(2), 68, 115
- Omega, 8, 11, 26, 32, 43, 55, 58, 88, 92
- Omen, 115
- Onalaska, 129
- One Horse Store, 8
- One Hundred Palms,
- Onehundred Palms, 11
- Oneida, 8, 29, 35, 38, 92
- One Mile, 5
- Ong, 68
- Onion Creek, 115, 124
- Oniontown, 79
- Only, 112
- Ono, 11, 101, 129
- Onset, 50

- Ontario, 11, 29, 38, 88, 92, 95, 101, 129
- Onward, 32
- Onyx, 8, 11
- Oologah, 89, 92
- Opal, 8, 122
- Opa-Locka, 18
- Opine, 3
- Opolis, 38
- Opossum, 112
- Opp, 3, 101
- Opportunity, 66, 68, 124
- Ops, 66, 84
- Optimus, 8
- Oral, 108
- Orange, 3, 11, 16, 19, 22, 29, 32, 35, 50, 58, 71, 73, 82, 88, 101, 115, 119, 122
- Orange Blossom, 19
- Orange Blossom Hills, 19
- Orangeburg, 79, 88, 106
- Orange City, 19, 35
- Orange Cove, 11
- Orangedale, 19
- Orange Factory, 82
- Orange Grove, 58, 82, 115
- Orange Hill, 19, 82
- Orange Home, 19
- Orange Lake, 19
- Orangemans Hall, 29
- Orange Mill, 129
- Orange Mills, 19
- Orange Mountain, 19
- Orange Park, 19
- Orange Prairie, 29
- Orange Springs, 19
- Orangetree, 19
- Orangevale, 11
- Orangeville, 11, 29, 32, 53, 58, 118
- Orca, 4
- Orchard, 8, 14, 26, 35, 68, 115, 126
- Orchard Beach, 53
- Orchard City, 14
- Orchard Corner, 14

- Orchard Farm, 63
- Orchard Grove, 32
- Orchard Hill, 22
- Orchard Hills, 22, 47
- Orchard Lake, 53
- Orchard Park, 14, 79
- Orchard Prairie, 124
- Orchardville, 29
- Orchid, 19, 63, 122
- Orcutts, 16
- Orcuttsville, 16
- Ordinary, 122
- Ordnance, 95
- Ore, 63
- Ore City, 115
- Oregon, 29, 40(2), 47, 63, 72, 79, 88, 93, 129
- Oregon City, 11, 95
- Oregon House, 11
- Oregon Slope, 95
- Ore Hill, 16
- Org, 55
- Organ Cave, 126
- Organ Springs, 32
- Orient, 29, 35, 44, 79, 88, 95, 108, 115, 124
- Oriental, 82, 92, 101
- Orient Park, 19
- Origana, 63
- Oriole, 47, 63, 101
- Orion, 82, 92, 129
- Orlando, 82, 92
- Orleans, 32, 35, 50, 53, 68, 119
- Oscar, 92
- Oshkosh, 43, 68, 129
- Oslo, 55
- Osprey, 19
- Ossipee, 71
- Othello, 82
- Otis, 50
- Ottawa, 29, 55, 88, 93
- Otter, 66, 88
- Otter Creek, 19, 35, 44, 55, 82, 84
- Otter Kill, 79

- Otter Lake, 32, 53
- Otter Rock, 95
- Ottersdale, 47
- Otter Trail, 55
- Otterville, 35
- Ottumwa, 35, 38, 108
- Ough, 68
- Oulu, 129
- Ourtown, 129
- Our Town, 3
- Outing, 55
- Outlet, 101
- Outlook, 66
- Overall, 112, 122
- Overbrook, 17
- Overlook, 3, 11, 16
- Overly, 84
- Overshot, 101
- Owasso, 90
- Owen, 22, 29, 32, 35
- Owensboro, 22
- Owenton, 3, 115, 122
- Owl, 5
- Owl Canyon, 14
- Owl City, 112
- Owl Creek, 115, 130
- Owl Hollow, 101
- Owl Hoot, 112
- Owls Bend, 63
- Owls Head, 44
- Owls Nest, 17, 79, 101
- Owltown, 22, 82
- Owsley, 63
- Oxberry, 58
- Oxbo, 129
- Oxbow, 26, 43, 44, 53, 79, 84, 95
- Oxford, 50
- Ox Hill, 16
- Oxlip, 55
- Ox Place, 122
- Oxville, 29
- Oxyoke, 14
- Oyster Rocks, 17
- Oysterville, 124

- Ozark, 3, 8, 29, 53, 63, 93
- Ozark Springs, 63
- Ozone, 8, 112

-P-

- Pace, 19
- Pacific, 11, 63, 112, 124
- Pacific City, 35, 95
- Pacific House, 11
- Pacific Junction, 66
- Pack, 63
- Packard Landing, 44
- Packardville, 50
- Packers Roost, 66
- Packing House Corner, 17
- Paddock, 68, 124
- Padlock, 19, 68
- Paducah, 115
- Paepcke, 8
- Page, 5, 32, 55, 68, 75, 84, 93, 95, 124, 126
- Page City, 38, 63
- Pagoda, 14
- Pahrump, 69
- Paint, 101
- Paint Creek, 115
- Painted Rock, 35, 112
- Painters Hill, 19
- Paint Gap, 82
- Paint Rock, 3, 82, 115
- Paintsville, 88
- Paint Town, 82
- Paisley, 66, 95, 101
- Palace, 63
- Palisade, 14, 55, 68
- Palisades, 26, 29, 63, 124
- Palisades Corner, 26
- Palisades Park, 73
- Pall Mall, 110, 112
- Palm, 101
- Palm Bay, 19

- Palm Beach, 19, 29
- Palm Beach Gardens, 19
- Palm City, 19
- Palm Coast, 19
- Palmdale, 11, 19, 55
- Palm Desert, 11
- Palmeto, 19
- Palmetto, 11, 43, 58, 106, 115
- Palm Grove, 11
- Palm Harbor, 19
- Palm Lake, 124
- Palms, 53
- Palm Shadows, 19
- Palm Shores, 19
- Palm Springs, 11, 19
- Palm Wells, 11
- Palo Alto, 101
- Pamona, 53, 124
- Panacea, 19
- Panama, 11, 29, 32, 35, 68, 69, 79, 93, 115
- Panama City, 19
- Panama City Beach, 19
- Pancake, 101, 115, 126
- Pancake Summit, 69
- Pandora, 88, 112
- Panhandle, 22, 88, 115
- Panic, 101
- Panorama, 122
- Pansy, 8, 126
- Panther, 36, 93, 101, 126
- Panther Burn, 58
- Panther Creek, 82, 95
- Panther Valley, 69
- Paoli, 93, 101, 129
- Papaw, 112
- Paper Mill Village, 50
- Parachute, 14
- Parade, 108
- Paradise, 5, 11, 19, 29, 32, 38, 47, 53, 63, 66, 69, 79, 88, 95, 101, 115, 118, 124, 126, 130
- Paradise City, 11
- Paradise Hill, 69, 88, 93

- Paradise Hills, 14
- Paradise Hot Springs, 11, 26
- Paradise Park, 95
- Paradise Springs,
- Paradise Valley, 5, 69, 130
- Paradise View, 8, 93
- Paradox, 14, 79
- Paragon, 3, 32, 43, 66
- Parchment, 53
- Parent, 44, 55
- Paris, 8, 11, 26, 29, 36, 44, 53, 58, 63, 71, 82, 95, 106, 112, 115, 122, 129
- Paris Crossing, 32
- Paris Springs, 63
- Parisville, 53
- Park, 26
- Park City, 22, 38
- Parker Dam,
- Parkersburg, 29, 32, 58, 93, 95, 125
- Parkers Prairie, 55
- Park Place, 8, 95, 106
- Park Rapids, 55
- Park River, 84
- Parks, 8
- Park Springs, 75
- Parkway, 63, 115
- Parliament, 95
- Parole, 47
- Parshall, 84
- Parsley Bottom, 126
- Parsons Grove, 5
- Parthenon, 8
- Partridge, 5
- Partridge Crossroads, 3
- Partridgeville, 50
- Pasadena, 47
- Passing, 122
- Passover, 63
- Passport, 29
- Pass Station, 19
- Patch, 11
- Patience, 101
- Patriot, 32, 88
- Paterson, 72, 73

- Pavilion, 53, 130
- Paw Paw, 29, 53, 63, 126
- Pawpaw Plains, 112
- Pawtucket, 104
- Paydown Ford, 63
- Peabody, 50
- Peaceburg, 3
- Peaceful Pines, 11
- Peace Valley, 63
- Peach, 8, 82, 95, 112
- Peach Bloom, 43
- Peach Bottom, 101
- Peach Creek, 115
- Peach Four Corners, 119
- Peach Grove, 47, 122
- Peach Orchard, 8, 19, 63
- Peachton, 11
- Peachtree City, 22
- Peachtree Crossing, 11, 93
- Peach Tree Hills, 3
- Peach Tree Village, 115
- Peacock, 3, 53, 116
- Peacock Corners, 17
- Peacock Crossing, 82
- Peacock Crossroads, 82
- Peacocks Corner, 47
- Peacocks Crossing, 22
- Pea Cove, 44
- Pea Green Corner, 14
- Pea Hill, 82
- Peak, 8
- Peanut, 8, 11, 101
- Peapack-Gladstone, 73
- Peapatch, 126
- Pea Ridge, 3, 8, 63, 82
- Pea Ridge Crossroads, 3
- Pearl, 14, 26, 29, 38, 43, 53, 56, 58, 63, 101
- Pearl City, 24, 29, 63, 116
- Pearl Harbor, 24
- Pearl River, 43
- Pearls Corner, 58, 71
- Pear Park, 14
- Pear Valley, 116

- Peas Eddy, 79
- Peatville, 53
- Peavine, 11, 93
- Pebble, 26
- Pecan, 19, 22, 101
- Pecan Bay, 116
- Pecan City, 22
- Pecan Grove, 8, 58, 116
- Pecan Hill, 116
- Pecan Island, 43
- Pecan Point, 8
- Peck, 19, 26, 38, 43, 53, 95
- Peculiar, 63
- Pedee, 26
- Pee Dee, 8, 82, 106
- Peekskill, 79
- Peel, 8, 95
- Peeled Chestnut, 112
- Pee Pee, 88
- Peerless, 66
- Peewee, 126
- Pegasus, 116
- Pelican, 4, 43, 108, 116
- Pelican City, 95
- Pelican Rapids, 55
- Pencil Bluff, 8
- Pendelton, 8, 32, 63, 82, 95, 106, 116, 122
- Penelope, 79, 82, 116
- Peninsula, 88
- Penn, 53, 84
- Penney Farms, 19
- Penns Beach, 73
- Pennsylvania, 3, 40, 45, 78, 100, 104
- Penn Yan, 79
- Penny Hill, 17, 82
- Penny Pot, 73
- Pennys Corner, 11
- Pennys Crossroad, 122
- Pennsylvania, 48, 70, 90, 95, 96
- Pennyville, 32
- Pensacola, 18, 82, 93
- Penzance, 5
- Peoria, 14, 38, 58, 63, 88, 93, 116

- Pep, 116
- Pepper, 17, 126
- Pepperbox, 17
- Pepper Corner, 11
- Peppermint Corner, 71
- Pepper Pike, 88
- Peppers, 82
- Peppertown, 32
- Pepperwood, 11
- Pepsin, 63
- Percale, 22
- Perdue, 58
- Perennial, 22
- Perfection, 79, 82
- Peridot, 5
- Perkins Center, 16
- Perkins Corner, 16
- Perks, 29
- Perry, 8, 11, 19, 22, 36, 38, 43, 44, 53, 58, 63, 68, 93, 95, 118, 118, 124, 126
- Perry Point, 47
- Perrysburg, 32, 88
- Perry Store, 3
- Perryville, 4, 8, 29, 43, 47, 50, 63, 73
- Persia, 36, 63, 79, 112
- Persimmon, 22
- Persimmon Grove, 3
- Persist, 95
- Pert, 116
- Peru, 29, 30, 32, 38, 44, 50, 63, 68, 79, 88, 101, 119, 126, 129, 130
- Petal, 58
- Pet Crossroads, 82
- Petoskey, 53
- Petroleum, 32, 126
- Petrolia, 38
- Petunia, 122
- Pew Hill, 126
- Pharaoh, 93
- Pheasant, 116
- Pheasant Run, 73
- Phelps, 40

- Philadelphia, 3, 8, 17, 29, 32, 46, 49, 58, 63, 73, 75, 79, 80, 82, 90, 96(2), 97(2), 98(2), 99(2), 101, 105, 112, 122
- Philadelphia Point, 43
- P Hill, 118
- Phlox, 32, 129
- Phoenix, 4, 14, 22, 29, 32, 47, 53, 58, 79, 95, 106
- Phoenixville, 16
- Piana, 108
- Piano, 26
- Pick City, 84
- Picket Post, 106
- Pick Handle Gulch, 69
- Pickles Gap, 8
- Picnic, 19
- Picture Rocks, 5, 101
- Piddleville, 22
- Pie, 126
- Piedmont, 93
- Pieplant Mill, 14
- Pierce, 11, 14, 26, 68, 71, 75, 93, 101, 112, 116, 126, 129
- Pierce Bridge, 71
- Pierceville, 38
- Pie Town, 75
- Piety Hill, 29
- Pigeon, 32, 36, 43, 53, 118, 126
- Pigeon Cove, 50
- Pigeon Falls, 129
- Pigeon Forge, 112
- Pigeon Hill, 44
- Pigeon River, 55
- Pigeonroost, 82
- Pigeon Run, 88
- Pigeon Springs, 124
- Pigeye, 3, 88
- Piggott, 8
- Pigs Ear, 101
- Pigtown, 88
- Pike, 11, 29, 32, 71, 126
- Pike Corner, 44
- Pike Creek, 17

- Pikes Peak, 43
- Pikeville, 3, 32, 58, 82, 88, 101, 112
- Pilgrim, 63, 116
- Pilgrim Corners, 16, 79
- Pilgrim Grove, 58
- Pilgrims Rest, 3, 8, 58
- Pillar Rock, 124
- Pill Hill, 73
- Pillow, 101
- Pillsbury, 84
- Pillsbury Crossing, 38
- Pilot, 47, 69
- Pilot Mountain, 82
- Pilot Rock, 95
- Pilottown, 17
- Pimento, 32
- Pimlico, 106
- Pinch, 32, 126
- Pine, 5, 14, 26, 32, 43, 63, 95, 101
- Pine Apple, 3
- Pine Barren, 19
- Pine Bend, 55
- Pine Bluff, 8, 19, 58
- Pine Bluffs, 50
- Pineboro, 22
- Pine Branch, 116
- Pine Bridge, 16
- Pine Brook, 55, 73
- Pinebur, 58
- Pine Castle,
- Pine Center, 19, 55
- Pine City, 8, 55, 95, 101, 124
- Pine Cliff, 43, 71
- Pine Corner, 44
- Pine Coupee, 43
- Pinecreek, 55
- Pine Creek, 26, 53, 55, 66, 69, 126
- Pine Crest, 63, 73
- Pinecrest, 11, 19, 50
- Pinefield, 50
- Pinefield Crossroads, 22
- Pine Flat, 3, 11
- Pine Flats, 101
- Pine Forest, 19, 116

- Pine Grove, 3, 11, 16, 19, 22, 29, 43, 50, 58, 69, 73, 101, 106, 112, 122
- Pine Haven, 3, 130
- Pinehill, 75
- Pine Hill, 3, 16, 22, 44, 73, 82, 104, 116
- Pine Hills, 11, 19
- Pine Hollow, 95
- Pinehurst, 23, 26, 47, 50, 58
- Pine Island, 19, 43, 50, 55
- Pine Island Ridge, 19
- Pineknob, 126
- Pine Knoll, 44, 47, 55
- Pine Knot Crossing, 93
- Pine Lake, 23
- Pineland, 19, 23
- Pine Lane, 73
- Pine Level, 3, 19
- Pine Lodge, 75
- Pine Log, 19, 23
- Pine Meadow, 16
- Pine Mill, 101
- Pine Mount, 19
- Pine Mountain, 3, 23
- Pine Mountain Valley, 23
- Pine Needles, 3
- Pine Nook, 14
- Pine Orchard, 3, 47
- Pine Park, 23
- Pine Point, 55
- Pine Prairie, 43, 66, 116
- Pine Rest, 50
- Pine Ridge, 8, 19, 23, 26, 43, 47, 53, 58, 68, 93, 95, 106, 107, 108, 112, 116
- Pineridge, 11
- Pine River, 53, 55, 71, 129
- Pine Run, 53, 101, 108
- Pines, 75, 118
- Pine Spring, 3, 112
- Pine Springs, 5, 55, 58, 75, 116
- Pine Stump Junction, 53
- Pine Summit, 101
- Pine Swamp, 101

- Pinetop, 5, 55
- Pine Top, 8, 93, 101
- Pinetown, 17, 82
- Pinetree, 8
- Pine Tree Corner, 50
- Pine Tree Corners, 17
- Pine Valley, 11, 23, 32, 58, 73, 101, 116, 118
- Pineview, 23, 26, 58, 82
- Pine View, 82, 122
- Pine Village, 32
- Pineville, 3, 8, 15, 55, 58, 80, 106, 126
- Pinewood, 11, 43, 55, 82
- Pinewood Springs, 14
- Piney Grove, 19, 23
- Piney Hill, 47
- Ping, 124
- Pinhook, 32, 63, 88
- Pin Hook, 63
- Pink, 23, 58, 88, 93, 101, 126
- Pink Arrow, 5
- Pink Hill, 63, 82
- Pinkstaff, 29
- Pinnacle, 66, 112
- Pinnacles, 11
- Pin Oak, 116
- Pin Point, 23
- Pinto, 69, 116
- Pioneer, 3, 5, 11, 36, 43, 53, 66, 69, 88, 112, 116
- Pioneer City, 47, 95
- Pioneer Junction, 66
- Pioneer Point, 11
- Pioneertown, 11
- Pioneerville, 26
- Pipe, 129
- Pipe Creek Mill, 47
- Piper, 63, 68
- Pipertown, 63
- Pipestem, 126
- Pipestone, 55, 66
- Piqua, 37, 38
- Pirates Cove, 19

- Piscataway, 73
- Pismo Beach, 11
- Pistol Ridge, 59
- Pistol River, 95
- Pitcher, 63
- Pitchfork, 130
- Pitchin, 29
- Pittsburg, 11, 14, 19, 23, 29, 32, 36, 38, 53, 63, 71, 82, 84, 93, 95, 116, 119
- Pittsburgh, 69, 96, 97, 98, 100
- Place, 71
- Placerville, 14
- Places Corner, 104
- Placid, 116
- Plain, 59, 124, 129
- Plain City, 88, 118
- Plain Dealing, 43
- Plainfield, 15, 23, 36
- Plains, 21, 23, 43, 73, 116
- Plainview, 8, 14, 23, 36, 59, 63, 68, 93, 108, 116
- Planet, 5
- Plant, 8, 112
- Plantation, 11, 59
- Plantation Key, 19
- Plant City, 19
- Planter, 14, 53
- Plaster City, 11
- Plastic, 14
- Plateau, 66, 82, 112, 116
- Plateau City, 14
- Platinum, 4
- Plato, 112
- Platte, 55
- Platte City, 63
- Platte River, 63
- Play Cards, 106
- Player, 93
- Plaza, 84
- Pleasant Creek, 36
- Pleasantdale, 73
- Pleasant Grove, 3, 8, 11, 19, 23, 36, 38, 56, 59, 63, 73, 82, 88, 93

- Pleasant Groves, 3
- Pleasant Hill, 3, 8, 11, 17, 23, 36, 43, 44, 59, 63, 68, 75, 82(2), 88, 95, 101, 106, 124, 126
- Pleasant Hills, 17
- Pleasant Home, 3, 8, 88, 95
- Pleasant Hope, 63
- Pleasant Island, 44
- Pleasant Lake, 32
- Pleasant Lane, 106
- Pleasant Mills, 32
- Pleasant Mount, 63
- Pleasant Plain, 32, 36
- Pleasant Plains, 3, 8, 29, 73
- Pleasant Point, 44
- Pleasant Prairie, 66, 129
- Pleasant Retreat, 63
- Pleasant Ridge, 3, 8, 32, 53, 59, 63, 82, 129
- Pleasant Ridge Plantation, 44
- Pleasant Run, 73, 126
- Pleasant Shade, 112, 122
- Pleasant Site, 3
- Pleasant Springs, 116
- Pleasant Valley, 8, 11, 23, 26, 29, 36, 38, 50, 53, 56, 63, 66, 68, 69, 73, 79, 84, 88, 93, 95, 106, 116, 119, 122, 124, 126, 129
- Pleasant Valley Place, 26
- Pleasantview, 26, 29
- Pleasant View, 3, 8, 11, 14, 26, 32, 36, 47, 53, 66, 73, 88, 101, 112, 118, 122, 124, 126
- Pleasantville, 17, 32, 36, 47, 73, 79, 82
- Pleasant Walk, 47
- Pleasure Valley, 32, 126
- Plentywood, 66
- Plowed Neck, 50
- Pluck, 116
- Plugtown, 129
- Plum, 101
- Plum Bayou, 8
- Plum Branch, 106

- Plumbs, 14
- Plum City, 129
- Plum Creek, 108, 116
- Plum Ford, 63
- Plum Grove, 59
- Plum Hill, 29
- Plum Orchard, 19, 126
- Plum Point, 59, 104
- Plum Run, 126
- Plumsock, 73
- Plum Springs, 3
- Plumtree, 82
- Plum Tree, 32, 122
- Plum Trees, 95
- Plum Valley,
- Plush, 95
- Pluto, 59
- Plymouth, 50, 53, 71, 118
- Pocatello, 26
- Pocket, 122
- Pocono, 26
- Podunk, 15, 53, 119
- Poetry, 116
- Poetry Tulip, 23
- Pogo, 3
- Poindexter, 8
- Point, 59, 116
- Point Arena, 11
- Pointblank, 116
- Point Cedar, 8
- Point Hope, 4
- Point of Pines, 5
- Point of Rocks, 47, 68, 69, 130
- Point of Sands, 75
- Point Pleasant, 11, 19, 43, 47, 88, 126
- Point Rock, 88
- Points, 63, 126
- Poison Creek, 95
- Poker Brown, 69
- Poker Flat, 11
- Poland, 32, 36, 43, 44, 66, 79, 84, 126, 129
- Polar, 116, 129
- Polaris, 66
- Polebridge, 66
- Polecat, 112
- Polecat Landing, ,106
- Pole Garden, 11
- Polk, 3, 29, 63, 68, 88, 101, 126
- Polk Springs, 11
- Polo, 8, 63
- Pomona, 23, 29, 38, 47, 63
- Pompeii, 53
- Pompeys Pillar, 66
- Ponce de Leon, 19, 63
- Pond, 11, 29
- Pond Creek, 19
- Ponder, 63, 116
- Ponderosa, 3, 11, 23, 75, 95, 112
- Ponderosa Pines, 75
- Ponders, 8, 112
- Pond Creek, 93
- Pond Meadow, 15
- Pond Spring, 23
- Pond Town, 106
- Pond Village, 50
- Pone, 116
- Ponpon, 3, 106
- Pontiac, 53
- Pony, 1, 32, 66
- Poorhouse Corner, 122
- Poorman, 4
- Poor Town, 82
- Popcorn, 32
- Pope, 3
- Poplar, 26, 56, 66, 82, 95, 122, 129
- Poplar Bluff, 61, 63
- Poplar Branch, 82
- Poplar Creek, 3, 59
- Poplar Forks, 106
- Poplar Grove, 23, 29, 112
- Poplar Head, 19
- Poplar Hill, 47, 106
- Poplar Knob, 47
- Poplar Ridge, 3, 8, 29, 88
- Poplar Springs, 3, 23, 59, 82, 106, 112
- Poplar Springs Branch, 3

- Poplarville, 59
- Popple, 53
- Porchtown, 73
- Porcupine, 4, 84, 108, 129
- Porky, 101
- Portal, 23, 66
- Port Deposit, 47
- Porter, 93, 95
- Porters Center, 66
- Portland, 14, 16, 23, 29, 36, 38, 44, 53, 63,1 12
- Port Lonesome, 19
- Port Orange, 19
- Porto Rico, 126
- Port Protection, 4
- Portsmouth, 36
- Port Sulphur, 43
- Posey, 29
- Poseyville, 32
- Possom Trot, 3
- Possum Corner, 59, 106
- Possum Grape, 8
- Possum Hollow, 101
- Possumneck, 59
- Possumtown, 73
- Possum Trot, 59, 63, 122
- Possum Walk, 63
- Post, 59, 66, 95, 116
- Postal, 63
- Post Creek, 66
- Post Falls, 26
- Post Oak, 8, 29, 63, 93, 116
- Posts, 11
- Post Town, 56
- Potash Sulphur Springs, 8
- Potato Creek, 108
- Potato Patch, 5, 75
- Pot Creek, 75
- Potlatch, 26
- Potomac, 29, 47, 66, 126
- Potomic, 69
- Potomac Falls, 122
- Potomac Post Office, 66
- Pot Spring, 47

- Poughkeepsie, 8
- Pound, 122, 129
- Pounds, 75
- Poundstone Corner, 32
- Poverty Hill, 11, 106
- Powderhorn, 14
- Powder River, 130
- Powder Springs, 23, 112
- Powder Wash, 14
- Powell, 3, 5, 8, 14, 19, 43, 63, 68, 108
- Power, 66, 84, 126
- Powers, 88
- Powwow River, 71
- Prague, 8, 68, 93
- Prairie, 3, 26, 44, 53, 59, 124
- Prairiebell, 36
- Prairie Center, 38, 68, 130
- Prairie City, 29, 32, 36, 63, 95, 108
- Prairie Corners, 129
- Prairie Creek, 8, 32, 95
- Prairie Farm, 129
- Prairie Grove, 8, 29, 36, 116
- Prairie Hall, 29
- Prairie Hill, 59, 116
- Prairie Home, 29, 43, 63, 68
- Prairie Junction, 84
- Prairie Mount, 59
- Prairie Point, 59, 116
- Prairie Queen, 108
- Prairie Ridge, 63, 124
- Prairietown, 29, 126
- Prairie Union, 8
- Prairieview, 75
- Prairie View, 8, 23, 29, 38, 116
- Prairie Village, 38, 108
- Prairieville, 43, 53, 56
- Pratt, 8, 43, 47, 56
- Pratt Junction, 50
- Pratts, 3, 38
- Pratts Corner, 50
- Pratts Fork, 88
- Prattsville, 8, 11, 50, 88
- Prattville, 53, 93
- Pray, 66, 129

- Precept, 68
- Precinct, 50, 63
- Premier, 126
- President, 101
- Presidential, 16, 23
- Pretoria, 23
- Pretty Bayou,19
- Pretty Marsh, 44
- Pretty Prairie, 38
- Price, 84, 116, 118, 126, 129
- Price Place, 130
- Prices Store, 122
- Pricetown, 82, 88
- Pride, 41, 43, 44, 88, 116
- Priest, 11, 23
- Prim, 122
- Primrose, 4, 23, 36, 66, 68, 101, 104, 116, 129
- Prince Chapel, 59
- Prince Frederick, 47
- Prince George, 122
- Princess Ann, 47
- Princessville, 73
- Princeton, 8, 11, 14, 19, 23, 26, 29, 32, 36, 38, 43, 50, 53, 56, 59, 60, 63, 68, 69, 71, 73, 82, 95, 106, 112, 116, 126, 129
- Princeville, 24
- Prince William, 32
- Prior, 23
- Prismatic, 59
- Prison Farm, 66
- Progress, 32, 59, 95, 102, 116, 122
- Prohibition City, 63
- Promise, 95, 108, 112
- Promise City, 36
- Promised Land, 8, 102, 106
- Promontory, 118
- Pronto, 3, 69, 75
- Prospect, 3, 11, 14, 16, 29, 38, 43, 44, 47, 53, 59, 69, 73, 82, 88, 95, 102, 112, 116, 122, 129
- Prospect Grove, 63
- Prospect Hill, 50, 82

- Prospect Plains, 73
- Prospect Point, 73
- Prosper, 56, 82, 84, 116, 119
- Prosperine, 63
- Prosperity, 8, 19, 23, 32, 63, 102, 106, 112, 126
- Prospertown, 73
- Protection, 38
- Protem, 63
- Providence, 3, 19, 32, 47, 56, 59, 63, 82, 88, 103(2), 104, 106, 112, 116, 118, 124, 126
- Provo, 8, 108
- Prunedale, 11
- Prussia, 36
- Public Fork, 122
- Puddle Town, 16
- Pueblo, 32, 40, 69
- Puerto Rico, 116
- Pulaski, 8, 23, 29, 32, 36, 53, 59, 63, 88, 93, 101, 112, 129
- Pull Tight, 3
- Pumpkin, 116
- Pumpkin Bend, 8
- Pumpkin Center, 3, 11, 32, 43, 47, 59, 63, 82, 93, 108, 112, 122
- Pumpkin Hill, 79
- Pumpkin Hollow, 79
- Pumpkin Hook, 79
- Pumpkintown, 82, 106, 126
- Pump Springs, 8
- Punity, 88
- Punkin Center, 5, 14, 38, 43, 63, 116
- Punkin Corner, 26
- Punxsutawney, 102
- Purchase, 79
- Purchase Line, 102
- Pure Air, 63
- Purgatory, 44
- Puritan, 14
- Purple Sage, 130
- Pursglove, 126
- Pushmataha, 3
- Putney, 118

- Putty Hill, 47
- Puzzletown, 102
- Pyramid, 29, 69
- Pyramid Corners, 93
- Pyro, 88

-Q-

- Quackenkill, 79
- Quaddick, 16
- Quail, 11, 116, 122
- Quail Hollow, 82, 106
- Quail Ridge, 82
- Quail Roost, 82
- Quail Run, 47
- Quail Valley, 11, 59
- Quaker, 29, 32, 38, 63, 102
- Quaker City, 71, 88, 102
- Quaker Gap, 82
- Quaker Gardens, 73
- Quaker Heights, 17
- Quaker Hill, 16, 17, 79
- Quaker Meadow, 11
- Quaker Settlement, 79
- Quakertown, 16, 17, 32, 53, 73, 102
- Quality, 11, 23
- Quantico, 122
- Quapaw, 93
- Quarantine, 106
- Quarry, 36, 88, 116
- Quarryville, 16, 17, 73, 102
- Quartz, 66, 95
- Quartzburg, 26
- Quartz Hill, 11
- Quartz Mountain, 69, 95
- Quartzite, 5
- Quartzville, 14
- Quay, 59
- Quebec, 16, 43, 66, 82, 116, 122
- Quebec Junction, 71
- Quebeck, 112
- Quecreek, 102

- Queen, 66, 75, 102
- Queen Ann, 47
- Queen City, 11, 63, 69, 102, 116
- Queens, 75
- Queensland, 23
- Queens Point, 66
- Queens Run, 102
- Queensville, 32
- Queen Valley, 5
- Quercus Grove, 32
- Quick, 36, 43, 68, 126
- Quick City, 63
- Quick Crossroads, 106
- Quicksand, 116
- Quicks Bend, 102
- Quicktown, 102
- Quiet Dell, 102, 126
- Quietus, 66
- Quiggleville, 102
- Quincy, 29, 50, 59, 63
- Quinebaug, 16
- Quitman, 23, 116
- Quonochontaug, 104
- Quote, 63

-R-

- Rabbit Bay, 53
- Rabbit Bluff, 112
- Rabbit Corner, 82
- Rabbit Hill, 23
- Rabbit Town, 3, 47
- Rabbittown, 3
- Rabbityard, 3
- Raccoon, 32
- Raccoon Bend, 116
- Racetrack, 66, 116
- Racine, 36, 56, 63, 102, 127
- Racket, 63
- Radar, 63
- Radar Base, 116
- Radcliffe, 36

- Radersburg, 64
- Radiant, 122
- Radio Springs, 23
- Radioville, 32
- Radium, 14, 38, 56, 116
- Radium Springs, 75
- Rafter, 112
- Raft River, 26
- Ragged Mountain, 14
- Ragtown, 69, 126
- Railroad, 102
- Rail Road Flat, 11
- Rainbow, 3, 11, 16, 66, 88, 95, 116, 118
- Rainbow Bend, 38, 53
- Rainbow City, 3
- Rainbow Falls, 19, 106
- Rainbow Island, 8
- Rainbow Mines, 5
- Rainbow Spring, 12
- Rainbow Springs, 82
- Rainbow Valley, 5
- Rainbow Wells, 12
- Rain Rock, 88
- Rains, 106
- Rainsville, 32, 75
- Raintown, 32
- Raiser City, 69
- Raisin, 116
- Raisin Center, 53
- Raisin City, 12
- Rake, 36
- Raleigh, 23, 29, 32, 36, 59, 80, 84
- Rally Hill, 8
- Ralph, 3, 8, 47, 53, 93, 108, 126
- Ralphs, 17
- Ralston, 84
- Ramp, 126
- Ramtown, 73
- Range, 14, 88, 93, 95, 112
- Ranger, 23, 32, 82
- Ranier, 95, 124
- Ransom, 38, 56
- Ransom City, 84

- Rapelje, 66
- Rapid City, 53, 108
- Rapid River, 53
- Rapids, 66
- Rapids City, 29, 69
- Rapture, 32
- Rare Metals, 5
- Rash, 3
- Raspberry, 8
- Raspberry Creek, 69
- Rat, 63
- Ratio, 8
- Ratler, 116
- Ratliff, 59
- Raton, 74
- Rattan, 93, 116
- Rattle Run, 53
- Rattlesnake, 66, 75
- Rattlesnake Gap, 116
- Raven Creek, 102
- Raven Rock, 73
- Raven Rocks, 126
- Ravine, 59
- Rawhide, 12, 59, 69, 122
- Ray, 53, 84, 88, 116
- Raytown, 23, 63, 102
- R Corner, 124
- Reading, 38
- Reagan, 32, 93, 112, 116
- Rebecca, 23, 26
- Rebecca Plantation, 43
- Rebel City, 82
- Rebel Creek, 69
- Reclamation Village, 26
- Recluse, 130
- Recovery, 23
- Red Apple, 12
- Red Apple Orchard, 122
- Red Bank, 3, 8, 12, 72, 73, 102, 106
- Red Banks, 59, 129
- Redbanks, 12
- Red Barn, 102
- Redbay, 19
- Red Bay, 3

- Red Bird, 63, 130
- Redbird, 8, 68, 88, 93, 102, 126
- Red Bluff, 8, 12, 23, 75, 106, 116
- Redbone Crossroads, 23
- Red Branch, 116
- Red Bridge, 50, 102
- Red Brush, 82
- Red Bud, 29
- Redbud, 3, 23
- Redbush, 88
- Red Butte, 69, 130
- Red Cedar, 129
- Red Chute, 43
- Red Clay, 23
- Red Cliff, 14
- Red Cloud, 68
- Red Creek, 126
- Redcrest, 12
- Red Cross, 82, 102
- Redcross, 82
- Red Desert, 130
- Red Diamond, 88
- Red Dog, 12
- Red Eagle, 66
- Red Elm, 108
- Redeye, 122
- Redfern, 108
- Redfield, 8
- Red Fish, 43
- Red Gate, 116
- Red Gum, 43
- Red Head, 19
- Redhill, 59
- Red Hill, 3, 8, 12, 23, 47, 59, 73, 75, 82, 102, 106, 112, 116
- Red Hot, 102
- Redhouse, 47
- Red House, 69, 82, 126
- Red Jacket, 126
- Red Lake, 5, 56, 116
- Red Lake Falls, 56
- Redland, 19
- Redlands, 12, 14
- Red Lane, 130
- Red Leaf, 8
- Red Level, 3, 19, 116
- Red Lick, 59
- Red Line, 36
- Red Lion, 14, 17, 73, 102
- Red Lodge, 66
- Redman, 12, 36, 53
- Red Mesa, 5
- Red Mill, 73, 75, 102
- Red Mountain, 14
- Red Mud, 116
- Red Oak, 3, 8, 29, 36, 43, 53, 63, 82, 88, 93, 102, 116
- Redoak, 43
- Red Oak Corner, 106
- Red Oak Grove, 73
- Red Oak Hollow, 122
- Red Onion, 61, 63
- Red Owl, 108
- Red Point, 47, 63, 118
- Redridge, 53
- Red River, 75, 88, 106, 129
- Red River City, 116
- Red River Hot Springs, 26
- Redrock, 75
- Red Rock, 3, 5, 8, 12, 23, 56, 75, 93, 102, 116, 129
- Red Rock Corner, 44
- Red Rock Junction, 26
- Red Rock Point, 66
- Red Run, 102
- Red Scaffold, 108
- Red Schoolhouse Corner, 102
- Red Shirt, 108
- Red Spring, 127
- Red Springs, 3, 82, 116
- Red Star, 3, 8, 106
- Red Stone, 75
- Redstone, 14, 53, 66, 71, 75
- Redstone Arsenal, 3
- Red Top, 12, 56, 59, 63, 66, 69, 116
- Reduction, 102
- Redvale, 14
- Red Valley, 73

- Red Village, 119
- Red Walnut, 112
- Red Wash, 118
- Redwater, 59, 116
- Redway, 12
- Red Willow, 68
- Red Wine, 23
- Redwing, 8, 38
- Redwood, 59, 95, 116
- Redwood City, 12
- Redwood Corral, 12
- Redwood Grove, 12
- Redwoods, 12
- Redwood Valley, 12
- Reed, 93, 102
- Reed City, 53
- Reed Point, 66
- Reeds, 44, 63
- Reedtown, 88
- Reform, 3, 8, 59, 63, 88
- Refuge, 3, 59, 116, 122
- Regal, 56, 63, 124
- Register, 23
- Regret, 112
- Relay, 19, 23
- Reliance, 102, 108, 112, 116, 122, 124, 130
- Relief, 12, 82, 124
- Rembrant, 102
- Remote, 95
- Remus, 59
- Rendezvous, 8, 130
- Renfro, 63
- Reno, 23, 26, 29, 32, 38, 53, 56, 69, 108
- Replete, 127
- Republic, 36, 38, 53, 63, 88, 102, 124, 127
- Republican, 82
- Republican City, 68
- Republican Grove, 122
- Rescue, 12, 53, 63
- Reservation, 69
- Reserve, 38, 66, 75, 129
- Rest, 38, 112
- Rest Haven, 23
- Retreat, 12, 23, 43, 73, 82, 106, 116, 129
- Retrop, 93
- Return, 106
- Revenge, 88
- Revere, 50, 63, 84, 102, 124, 127
- Reverse, 26
- Revive, 59
- Reward, 12
- Rhineland, 63
- Rhode Island, 3, 40, 49, 78, 102, 103, 113, 116
- Rhododendron, 95
- Rice, 12, 29, 56, 116
- Rice City, 104
- Rice Creek, 19, 53
- Rice Hill, 95
- Rice Hope, 106
- Rice Lake, 56
- Rice Square, 50
- Ricetown, 106
- Riceville, 8, 32, 36, 43, 59
- Rich, 8, 12, 112
- Rich Fountain, 63
- Rich Hill, 63, 82, 88
- Richlnd Center, 127
- Richmond, 12, 29, 32, 36, 38, 43, 44, 50, 53, 56, 59, 63, 71, 88, 93, 95, 102, 104, 106, 108, 116, 118, 119(2), 129
- Rich Patch Mines, 122
- Rich Valley, 56, 88, 102
- Richville, 53, 66
- Ricketts, 36, 102
- Riddle, 3, 26, 32, 82, 95
- Riddle Hill, 29
- Rideout, 19
- Rider, 84
- Ridge, 3, 12, 43, 53, 56, 66, 116
- Ridgedale, 26
- Ridge Spring, 106
- Ridgetop, 112
- Ridgeview, 108

- Ridgeville, 32
- Ridgeway, 36, 82, 95
- Ridgewood, 16, 73
- Rifle, 14
- Rift, 127
- Rig, 127
- Right, 112
- Rim Junction, 71
- Rim Rock, 5
- Rimrock, 12, 66, 124
- Rim Rock Colony, 66
- Ring, 95, 129
- Ringer, 38
- Ring Gold, 116
- Ringing Hill, 102
- Ring Neck, 29
- Ring Place, 75
- Ringtail Pine, 95
- Ripley, 3, 12, 23, 29, 32, 44, 47, 53, 59, 63, 66, 69, 79, 88, 93, 112, 127
- Ripon, 128
- Ripple, 95, 102
- Ripplebrook, 95
- Rip Rap, 122
- Rising, 84
- Rising City, 66, 68
- Rising Corner, 16
- Rising Fawn, 23
- Rising River, 26, 95
- Rising Star, 116
- Risingsun, 88
- Rising Sun, 17, 29, 32, 36, 47, 59, 66, 129
- Ritz, 26
- Ritzville, 124
- Riverbank, 12
- River Bend, 3, 14, 43
- Riverbend, 12, 66
- River Corners, 88
- Riverdale, 53, 84(2)
- River Edge, 73
- River Falls, 106, 129
- River Glen, 16
- River Hill, 116
- River Mill, 75
- River Oaks, 12
- River Pines, 12
- River Point, 56
- River Raisin, 53
- River Ridge, 3, 32
- River Ridge Run, 82
- River Rouge, 53
- Rivers End, 23, 44
- Riverside, 12, 17, 19, 23, 26, 32, 36, 38, 63, 66, 68, 69, 73, 75, 82, 84, 95, 102, 108, 116, 119, 122, 127, 129, 130
- Riverside Park, 12
- Riverstream, 29
- Riversville, 16
- Rivertown, 23
- River Vale, 32
- Rivervale, 8
- River Valley, 56
- River View, 104
- Riverview, 14, 17, 53, 59, 63, 66, 68, 130
- Riverwood, 32
- Roach, 19, 63, 68, 116, 127
- Roachtown, 29
- Roads, 63
- Roads End, 12, 95
- Roanoke, 29, 32, 43, 63, 88, 121
- Roaring Creek, 82
- Roaring River, 82
- Roaring Springs, 112, 116
- Robbers Creek, 12
- Robbers Roost, 5
- Robbins Neck, 106
- Robert, 12, 43
- Roberts, 44, 47, 59, 66, 95, 127, 129
- Robertson, 36, 112, 116, 130
- Robertsville, 16, 73
- Robin, 26
- Robinhood, 44
- Robins, 36
- Robinwood, 59

- Rochester, 12, 29, 32, 36, 50, 53, 56, 63, 66, 69, 71, 88, 102, 116, 119, 124
- Rock, 8, 29, 38, 43, 50, 63, 88, 127
- Rockaway Beach, 26
- Rock Bluff, 19, 106
- Rock Branch, 23
- Rockbridge, 29, 63, 88
- Rock Bridge, 112
- Rock Cabin, 75
- Rock Castle, 127
- Rock City, 3, 11, 29, 112
- Rock Cliff, 127
- Rock Creek, 3, 11, 19, 29, 32, 36, 38, 56, 59, 63, 82, 88, 93, 95, 116, 130
- Rock Creek Park, 14
- Rock Elm, 129
- Rockfall, 16
- Rock Falls, 29, 36, 129
- Rock Fence, 3
- Rockfield, 32
- Rockfish, 82
- Rockford, 29, 32, 36, 63
- Rock Grove, 29
- Rock Haven, 12
- Rockhill, 59
- Rock Hill, 8, 19, 23, 32, 43, 59, 88, 106, 112, 116, 122
- Rock House, 69, 112, 116
- Rockhouse, 8
- Rock Island, 29, 93, 112, 116, 124
- Rockland, 17, 26, 38, 53
- Rockledge, 19, 23
- Rock Point, 5, 95
- Rockport, 29, 50, 73
- Rock Port, 63
- Rock Rapids, 36
- Rock Ridge, 19
- Rockridge, 23, 127
- Rock River, 130
- Rock Run, 47
- Rock Spring, 23, 88
- Rocksprings, 19
- Rock Springs, 3, 63, 66, 75, 112, 116, 130
- Rocks Village, 50
- Rockton, 29
- Rocktown, 73
- Rockvale, 14, 66
- Rock Valley, 36, 50
- Rockview, 53
- Rockville, 16, 23, 32, 36, 47, 50, 56, 63, 68, 95, 118
- Rockwood, 44, 73
- Rocky, 93
- Rocky, 14
- Rocky Bar, 26
- Rocky Bottom, 106
- Rocky Boy, 66
- Rocky Brancy, 43
- Rocky Brook, 104
- Rocky Comfort, 8
- Rocky Creek, 23
- Rocky Face, 23
- Rocky Ford, 14, 23, 32, 38, 93, 95, 108, 112
- Rocky Fork, 112
- Rocky Glen, 16
- Rocky Hammock Landing, 23
- Rocky Head, 3
- Rocky Hill, 8, 16, 50, 59
- Rockyhock, 82
- Rocky Mound, 8, 116
- Rocky Mount, 3, 23, 43, 59, 63
- Rocky Mountain, 93
- Rocky Mt, 122
- Rocky Plains, 23
- Rockypoint, 130
- Rocky Point, 5, 19, 59, 95, 104, 124
- Rocky Ridge, 47, 63, 88, 124
- Rocky River, 82, 89, 106
- Rocky Springs, 47, 59, 82, 112
- Rodeo, 12, 75
- Roe, 8, 14, 112
- Roeville, 19
- Rogers, 91
- Rogue Elk, 95
- Rogue River, 95
- Rohrer, 29

- Roll, 32, 93
- Rolla, 38
- Roller, 47
- Rolling Fork, 59
- Rolling Ground, 129
- Rollingstone, 56
- Rolling Stone, 102
- Roman, 122
- Romance, 8, 63, 127, 129
- Rome, 3, 23, 29, 32, 36, 38, 44, 59, 63, 79, 89, 95, 102, 106, 112, 129
- Rome City, 8, 32
- Romeo, 14
- Ronceverte, 127
- Rookstool Corner, 26
- Roosevelt, 56, 63, 73, 93, 116, 118, 124
- Roosevelt City, 73
- Roosterville, 23, 50, 63
- Roots, 53, 95
- Rorer, 127
- Rose, 38, 68, 93
- Roseau, 56
- Roseberry, 26
- Rosebloom, 59
- Rosebud, 3, 5, 23, 29, 32, 59, 63, 66, 69, 75, 82, 108, 116, 127
- Roseburg, 53
- Rosebush, 53
- Rose City, 8, 53, 56
- Rose Creek, 56, 69
- Rosedale, 12, 14, 19, 23, 32, 43, 53, 59, 68, 73, 89, 93, 95
- Rosefield, 43
- Roseglen, 84
- Rose Hill, 23, 29, 36, 38, 43, 59, 63, 82, 112, 122
- Rose Lake, 26
- Roseland, 19, 32, 38, 43, 73
- Rosemont, 73
- Rosepine, 43
- Rose Place, 12
- Rose Springs, 124
- Rose Valley, 69, 124

- Roseville, 8, 12, 17, 29, 53, 56, 73, 82, 84, 122
- Rose Well, 5
- Rosewood, 19, 63, 89, 116
- Roslyn, 102, 107
- Rosseau, 89
- Roswell, 74
- Rotterdam, 79
- Rough and Ready, 12, 79, 102
- Rough Edge, 59
- Rough Rock, 5
- Roulette, 102
- Roundaway, 59
- Round Bottom, 89, 127
- Round Butte, 66
- Round Grove, 32, 63
- Roundhead, 89
- Round Head, 102
- Roundhill, 3, 82
- Round Hill, 8, 69, 122
- Round Knob, 29
- Round Lake, 56, 59
- Round Mountain, 12, 44, 69, 116
- Round O, 106
- Round Oak, 23
- Round Peak, 82
- Round Pond, 8, 112
- Round Prairie, 29, 56, 66, 95, 116
- Round Rock, 5, 116
- Rounds Place, 68
- Round Spring, 63
- Roundtop, 23, 102
- Round Top, 104,112
- Roundup, 66,116
- Roundup Junction, 14
- Round Valley, 12, 68
- Rouseau, 56
- Rousseau, 53, 108
- Rover, 8, 23
- Rowan, 36, 82
- Rowan Bay, 4
- Royal, 8, 19, 23, 36, 68
- Royal City, 124
- Royal Oak, 47, 63

- Royal Pines, 43
- Royalton, 29, 32, 56, 89, 129
- Royalty, 116
- Rubicon, 26
- Ruby, 26, 29, 43, 66, 129
- Ruby City, 82
- Ruby Falls, 112
- Ruby Hill, 69
- Ruby Valley, 69
- Rudeville, 73
- Ruff, 124
- Rugby, 14, 84
- Rule, 8, 116
- Rumble, 127
- Rum Junction, 127
- Rumpus Ridge, 108
- Running Deer, 122
- Running Springs, 12
- Running Water, 108
- Rural, 3, 32, 95, 129
- Rural Hill, 59
- Rural Shade, 116
- Rural Valley, 102
- Rush, 89
- Rush City, 56
- Rush Hill, 63
- Rushing, 8
- Rushmore, 56, 89
- Rush River, 56
- Rushsylvania, 89
- Ruso, 84
- Russell, 3, 8, 12, 14, 19, 23, 29, 36, 37, 38, 50, 56, 59, 71, 84, 89, 93, 102, 129
- Russell Crossing, 44
- Russell Springs, ,38
- Russellville, 23, 29, 32, 36, 43, 50, 53, 59, 60, 63, 82, 89, 93, 102, 106, 112, 116, 119, 127
- Russia, 73, 79, 89
- Russian Village, 24
- Russiaville, 32
- Rust, 29, 53
- Rustic, 14

- Ruth, 8, 12, 53, 59, 82, 122, 124
- Ruthsburg, 47
- Ruthton, 56
- Rutland, 119
- Ryan, 90
- Rye, 14, 71, 116, 124
- Ryegrass Junction, 130
- Rye Patch, 69
- Rye Valley, 95

-S-

- Sabine Pass, 116
- Sable, 59
- Sabre City, 12
- Sac City, 36
- Sacramento, 29, 68, 75
- Saddle, 5, 8, 12
- Saddle Brook, 73
- Saddle Butte, 66
- Saddle River, 73
- Saddlestring, 130
- Saddletree, 82
- Safe, 63
- Sag Bridge, 29
- Sage, 8, 69, 130
- Sage Creek Colony, 66
- Sage Hen, 12
- Sageland, 12
- Saginaw, 8, 23, 56, 63, 124
- Sailor, 95
- Sailor Springs, 29
- Sailors Rest, 112
- Saint George, 19
- Saint Helen, 124
- Saint Louis, 12, 43, 53, 119, 122
- Saint Marys, 38
- Saint Nicholas, 19
- Sale City, 23
- Sale Creek, 112
- Salem, 16
- Salem Four Corners, 16

- Sales Corner, 122
- Sales Place, 130
- Salesville, 8
- Salina, 93
- Saline, 8, 29, 43, 53, 63, 116, 118
- Saline City, 63
- Salineville, 89
- Salisbury, 70
- Salmon, 26, 95
- Salmonberry, 95
- Salmon Brook, 16
- Salmon Creek, 124
- Salmon Prairie, 66
- Salt Chuck, 4
- Salt Creek, 12, 14, 95, 130
- Salter, 38
- Salters, 106
- Salters Depot, 106
- Salt Flat, 116
- Salt Fork, 93
- Saltillo, 89
- Salt Lake, 24, 75
- Salt Lake City, 85, 117(2), 118
- Salt River, 63
- Salt Rock, 127
- Salt Springs, 19, 63
- Salt Sulphur Springs, 127
- Saltwell, 127
- Salt Well, 3
- Salt Wells, 69, 130
- Salty, 116
- Salvia, 12
- Salyer, 12
- Salyersville, 104, 129
- Sam Houston, 116
- Samoa, 12
- Sample, 14
- Sampson, 19
- Sampson City, 19
- Sam Rayburn, 116
- Sam Sing Village, 24
- Samson, 3
- San Andreas, 12
- San Antonio, 14, 19, 63, 69, 75, 113(2), 116
- Sanatorium, 59
- Sand, 116
- Sandals, 63
- Sand Bay, 129
- Sand Bend, 23
- Sandbluff, 93
- Sand Creek, 38, 53, 93, 129
- Sand Cut, 19
- Sand Draw, 130
- Sand Hill, 17, 19, 23, 63, 127
- Sand Hills, 73
- Sand Hollow, 26, 95
- San Diego, 116
- Sandisfield, 49
- Sand Lake, 53
- Sand Mountain, 3
- Sand Pass, 69
- Sandpoint, 26
- Sand Point, 4, 26
- Sandridge, 68
- Sand Ridge, 8, 29, 32
- Sand River, 53
- Sandrock, 129
- Sand Rock, 3
- Sands, 12, 29, 75
- Sand Slough, 6
- Sand Spring, 47
- Sand Springs, 5, 36, 66, 69, 75
- Sandstone, 53, 56, 127
- Sand Switch, 112
- Sandtown, 8, 17, 23, 73
- Sandusky, 29, 53, 116, 127
- Sandwich, 29, 44, 50, 71
- Sandwich Center, 71
- Sandy, 8, 23
- Sandy Beach, 32
- Sandy Bend, 8
- Sandy Bottom, 23, 47, 82
- Sandy Creek, 44
- Sandy Hill, 43, 59
- Sandy Hills, 19

- Sandy Hook, 16, 32, 47, 59, 63, 73, 102, 112, 129
- Sandy Land, 8
- Sandy Nook, 32
- Sandy Point, 19, 23, 44
- Sandy Ridge, 59, 73, 82
- Sandy River Plantation, 44
- Sandy Spring, 47
- Sandy Springs, 23
- Sandytown, 32
- Sandyville, 36
- San Francisco, 3, 12, 14, 75, 120
- San Gabriel, 9, 12
- San Jose, 29
- San Juan, 69, 116
- San Leandro, 12
- Santa, 26
- Santa Claus, 5, 23, 30, 32
- Santa Fe, 19, 32, 36, 63, 74, 89, 93, 112
- Santa Monica, 9
- Santiago, 36, 63
- Sapphire Village, 66
- Sapulpa, 93
- Sarah, 23
- Sarasota Springs, 12
- Saratoga Springs, 84
- Sarepta, 43
- Sargeant, 56
- Sargent, 12, 19, 23, 63, 68, 116
- Sargent Place, 95
- Sargents, 14, 89
- Sargentville, 44
- Sassafras, 32, 47, 122, 127
- Sassafras Ridge, 61
- Satin, 116
- Saturn, 32
- Sault Ste Marie, 53
- Sautee, 23
- Savage, 29, 56, 59, 66, 102, 116
- Savages Crossroads, 82
- Savanna, 29, 93
- Savannah, 20, 36, 59, 63, 82, 89, 112
- Savannah Place, 17

- Savercool Place, 12
- Savoy, 43
- Sawdust, 19, 23, 112
- Sawmill, 5
- Sawmill Corner, 122
- Sawmill Flat, 12
- Sawmills, 82
- Sawpit, 14
- Sawtooth City, 26
- Scab Hill, 102
- Scales, 12
- Scales Mound, 29
- Scalp Level, 102
- Scandinavia, 129
- Scant City, 3
- Scarlet, 23, 127
- Scarville, 36
- Scary, 127
- Scenic, 108, 124
- Scenic Hills, 23
- Scenic Oaks, 116
- Schenectady, 75, 79
- School Hill, 129
- Schoolview, 17
- School Village, 24
- Schubert, 102
- Science Hill, 89
- Scircleville, 32
- Scissors, 116
- Scissors Crossing, 12
- Scituate, 44, 50
- Scotch Bonnet, 73
- Scotch Grove, 82
- Scotch Hill, 102, 127
- Scotch Hollow, 102
- Scotch Plains, 73
- Scotch Ridge, 89
- Scotchtown, 79
- Scotia, 68
- Scotland, 3, 8, 12, 16, 19, 23, 29, 44, 47, 50, 59, 71, 89, 102, 108, 116, 122
- Scotland Beach, 47
- Scotland Neck, 82

- Scott, 8, 23, 32, 36, 38, 43, 59, 71, 89, 93, 102, 106, 112, 116
- Scottsville, 38, 43, 63, 119
- Scrabble, 122, 127
- Scranton, 8, 12, 36, 38, 69, 82, 84, 96, 106, 116
- Scraper Springs, 69
- Scrap Town Crossroads, 17
- Scratch Ankle, 3
- Screamer, 3, 112
- Screamersville, 122
- Scuffletown, 23, 122
- Sea Acre, 124
- Seaboard, 82
- Seabree, 26
- Sea Breeze, 74
- Sea Bright, 74
- Seabright, 12
- Seaburg, 26
- Seacliff, 12
- Seaforth, 56
- Sea Girt, 74
- Seal Beach, 12
- Seal Rock, 95, 124
- Searchlight, 69
- Seaside, 19, 95, 106
- Seattle, 68
- Seawall, 44
- Sebree, 63
- Seclusion, 116
- Second Cliff, 50
- Second Crossing, 116
- Second Mesa, 5
- Secret, 69
- Secretary, 47
- Secret Town, 12
- Section, 3
- Security, 14, 43, 47
- Sedan, 36, 38, 56, 63, 66, 68, 75, 89, 93, 127
- Seehorn, 29
- Seekonk, 50
- Seewhy, 53
- Selection, 36

- Self, 8
- Self Creek, 59
- Sellers Store, 8
- Sells, 23
- Selma, 12, 14, 32, 38, 53, 63, 95
- Seminary, 122
- Senate, 116
- Senate Grove, 63
- Senior, 89, 116
- Sensation, 8
- Sentinel, 93
- Sentinel Butte, 84
- Sequatchie, 112
- Sequoia Grove, 112
- Sequoyah, 93
- Sergeant, 102
- Sergeant Bluff, 36
- Sergeantsville, 74
- Service, 59
- Service Creek, 95
- Sessions, 59
- Settlement, 8, 69
- Setters, 26
- Seven, 112
- Seven Bridges, 82
- Seven Corners, 122
- Seven Fountains, 122
- Seven Heart Crossing, 116
- Seven Hickories, 17
- Seven Hills, 82, 89
- Seven Knobs, 116
- Seven Lakes, 14, 75, 82
- Seven L Crossing, 116
- Seven Mile, 89, 106
- Sevenmile, 5
- Sevenmile Corner, 84, 93, 108, 116
- Seven Oaks, 12, 47, 93, 106, 116
- Seven Paths, 82
- Seven Pines, 3, 12, 116
- Seven Points, 102, 116
- Seven Rivers, 75
- Seven Springs, 19, 32, 59, 75, 82, 102
- Seven Stars, 74, 102
- Seventeen, 89

- Seventeen Mile Crossing, 116
- Seven Trees, 12
- Seven Troughs, 69
- Seventysix, 63
- Seven Valleys, 102
- Severance, 14, 38
- Seviereville, 110
- Seville, 19, 23
- Shacktown, 82
- Shade, 63, 89
- Shadehill, 108
- Shade Valley, 102
- Shadeville, 19
- Shadow, 124
- Shadow Hills, 12
- Shadowland, 116
- Shadow Shuttle, 102
- Shady, 8, 19, 43, 95
- Shady Banks, 32
- Shady Beach, 29
- Shady Bend, 38
- Shady Bower, 47
- Shady Brook, 38, 44, 75, 127
- Shady Corner Curve, 79
- Shady Cove, 95
- Shady Dale, 23
- Shady Glen, 12
- Shady Grove, 3, 8, 17, 19, 23, 36, 43, 59, 63, 93, 112, 116, 122, 127
- Shady Harbor, 16
- Shady Nook, 44
- Shady Oak, 36, 59
- Shady Oaks, 47
- Shady Point, 93
- Shady Rest, 19, 112
- Shady Shores, 53
- Shadyside, 127
- Shady Side, 47
- Shady Spring, 127
- Shake Rag, 23, 59
- Shakerag, 29
- Shakerhill, 50
- Shaker Village, 45, 50, 71
- Shakespeare, 75

- Shaketowne, 63
- Shale City, 95
- Shallow Water, 38
- Shamrock, 14, 19, 29, 38, 43, 63, 69, 79, 93, 102, 116, 127, 129
- Shamrock Lake, 32
- Shanghai, 82, 127
- Shanghi City, 29
- Shanks, 127
- Shankstown, 59
- Shantytown, 63, 129
- Shanty Town, 56, 69
- Shark, 8
- Sharp, 63
- Sharpeye, 89
- Sharp Place, 112
- Sharp Point, 82
- Sharpsburg, 23, 29, 36, 47, 59, 63, 82, 89, 102
- Sharpsville, 32
- Sharp Top, 23
- Sharptown, 47
- Shawnee, 89, 91
- Shaytown, 74,102
- Shea, 112
- Sheds, 79
- Sheephorn, 14
- Sheep Landing, 45
- Sheepranch, 12
- Sheepscott, 45
- Sheepshead, 12, 69
- Sheep Springs, 75
- Sheep Town, 122
- Shelby, 3, 32, 36, 53, 66, 68, 80, 82, 108, 129
- Shelbyville, 8, 17, 29, 32, 53, 63, 112, 116
- Shell, 130
- Shell Bluff, 19, 23
- Shell Lake, 8, 129
- Shell Pile, 74
- Shell Rock, 36
- Shenandoah, 36, 102, 122
- Shepardsville, 53

- Shepherd, 32, 53, 59, 66
- Shepherdstown, 89
- Sherwood Forest, 17, 23, 59, 82
- Sheybogan, 112
- Sheyenne, 84
- Shine, 82
- Shiner, 116
- Shingletown, 12
- Shin Hollow, 79
- Shining Rock, 112
- Shin Pond, 45
- Shiny Town, 19
- Ship Bottom, 74
- Ship Rock, 75
- Shiprock, 130
- Shipshewana, 32
- Shirley, 8
- Shivwits, 118
- Shoal, 63
- Shoal Creek, 23
- Shoals, 23, 32, 82, 93
- Shock, 127
- Shoe, 82
- Shoemaker, 75
- Shongaloo, 43
- Shoofly, 82
- Shook, 38, 63
- Shooting Creek, 82
- Shores, 69
- Short, 59, 93, 116
- Short Bend, 63
- Shorter, 3
- Short Gap, 127
- Shortly, 17
- Shoulder, 12
- Shoulderbone, 23
- Shovel Lake, 56
- Show Low, 5
- Shreveport, 41
- Shrewsbury, 50
- Shrub, 12
- Shucktown, 59
- Shutersville, 59
- Shy Corner, 45

- Siam, 36
- Siberia, 12
- Sibley, 43(2)
- Sicily, 89
- Sicily Island, 43
- Sickleville, 74
- Side Lake, 56
- Sideview, 112
- Sidney, 8, 29, 32, 36, 45, 53, 63, 66, 68, 79, 89, 116
- Sierra City, 12
- Sierraville, 12
- Sierra Vista, 5
- Sierra Way, 69
- Sightly, 124
- Signal, 59, 63
- Signal Hill, 12, 29
- Signal Mountain, 112
- Sign Pine, 82
- Sign Post, 122
- Sikeston, 63
- Siler City, 77
- Silica, 56
- Silk Hope, 23, 82
- Silk Mills, 23
- Silo, 93
- Silt, 14
- Silver, 106, 116
- Silver Acres, 75
- Silverado, 12
- Silver Beach, 26, 124
- Silverbow, 69
- Silver Bow, 66
- Silver City, 12, 23, 26, 36, 53, 59, 66, 69, 75, 93, 118
- Silver Cliff, 14, 26
- Silver Creek, 5, 23, 56, 59, 63, 68, 79, 89, 102, 124, 129
- Silver Crown, 130
- Silverdale, 14, 38, 56
- Silver Falls City, 95
- Silver Gate, 66
- Silver Heights, 14
- Silver Hill, 8, 23, 50, 127

- Silver Lake, 32, 36, 38, 50, 56, 63, 71, 95, 102, 124
- Silverleaf, 63, 84
- Silver Mine, 63
- Silver Palm, 19
- Silver Peak, 69
- Silver Pines, 23
- Silver Plume, 14
- Silver Point, 32
- Silver Reef, 118
- Silver Ridge, 45
- Silver Rock, 47
- Silver Run, 47, 59
- Silverside, 17
- Silver Spring, 104
- Silver Springs, 3, 14, 19, 63, 69, 74, 79, 82
- Silver Springs Shores, 19
- Silver Spruce, 14
- Silver Star, 66
- Silverstone, 82
- Silverstreet, 106
- Silverthrone, 14
- Silvertip, 4
- Silverton, 14, 26
- Silvertown, 23
- Silver Valley, 82
- Silverwood, 32, 53
- Silver Zone, 69
- Simpson, 3, 8, 14, 23, 29, 32, 38, 43, 63, 69, 82, 95
- Simpson Corners, 45
- Sincerity, 127
- Singer, 43, 47
- Singerly, 122
- Singers Glen, 122
- Singersville, 102
- Singing Springs, 12
- Singleshot, 66
- Sink Creek, 19
- Sinking Spring, 89, 102
- Sinks, 95
- Sioux City, 36, 68
- Siren, 129

- Sister Bay, 129
- Sisters, 95
- Sistersville, 102, 127
- Six, 127
- Six Corners, 89
- Sixers, 95
- Sixes,
- Six Forks, 17, 82
- Six Hill, 127
- Six Lakes, 53
- Six Mile, 3, 23, 36, 89, 106
- Sixmile Bend, 19
- Sixmile Creek, 19
- Sixmile Crossing, 116
- Six Mile Falls, 45
- Six Mile Gate, 75
- Sixmile Point, 118
- Six Point, 116
- Six Points, 74, 89
- Sixprong, 124
- Sixteen, 36, 66
- Sixteen Acres, 50
- Sixteen Mile Crossing, 116
- Six Towns, 59
- Sixty Six, 106
- Six Way, 3
- Skeleton Creek, 26
- Skelton, 32
- Skiddy, 38
- Skinner, 63
- Skinners, 14
- Skinquarter, 122
- Skit, 89
- Skookumchuck, 124
- Skowhegan, 44
- Skullbone, 112
- Skull Creek, 130
- Skull Spring, 95
- Skull Valley, 5, 12
- Skunk River, 36
- Skunks Corner, 79
- Sky Ball, 3
- Skyforest, 11
- Skygusty, 127

- Sky High, 12
- Skyhigh, 12
- Skyland, 50
- Skylight, 8
- Skyline, 56, 59, 66, 127
- Skytop, 12, 102
- Sky Valley, 12, 23
- Sky Village, 14
- Skyway, 14
- Slab, 127
- Slab City, 71, 129
- Slab Crossing, 66
- Slabtown, 47, 63, 74, 89, 102, 116, 127, 129
- Slacks, 43
- Slacks Corner, 26
- Slapneck, 53
- Slapout, 3, 93
- Slate, 127
- Slate Creek, 26
- Slate Run, 102
- Slate Spring, 59
- Slate Valley, 102
- Slaughter, 43
- Slaughtersville, 93
- Sledge, 3, 57, 59
- Sleeper, 63
- Sleepy Eye, 56
- Sleepy Hollow, 12, 79, 124, 130
- Sleepytown, 11
- Sleepy Valley, 12
- Slick, 93
- Slicker, 8
- Slicklizzard, 3
- Slickpoo, 26
- Slick Rock, 14
- Slide, 112, 116
- Slim Butte, 108
- Slippery Rock, 102
- Smacker, 93
- Smackover, 8
- Small, 26, 82, 116
- Smalltown, 50
- Smarts Corner, 45

- Smartville, 12
- Smelter Hill, 66
- Smelter Town, 5
- Smeltertown, 14
- Smelterville, 26
- Smileyberg, 38
- Smith-Lee, 93
- Smithland, 8, 32, 36, 43, 102, 112, 116
- Smithton, 100
- Smock, 89, 95
- Smoke Corner, 32
- Smoke Hole, 127
- Smokehouse, 26
- Smokeless, 127
- Smoke Rise, 3, 74
- Smoke Signal, 5
- Smoketown, 89, 102
- Smoky Hollow, 63
- Smugglers Notch, 119
- Smuteye, 3
- Smyrna, 20
- Snake, 95
- Snake Creek, 93, 108
- Snake Nation, 23
- Snake River, 124
- Snapfinger, 23
- Snapping Shoals, 23
- Snark, 95
- Snoosville Corner, 95
- Snow, 8, 63, 93
- Snowball, 8
- Snowball Gap, 14
- Snow Bend, 12
- Snow Camp, 82
- Snow Corner, 45
- Snow Creek, 12
- Snow Flake, 127
- Snowflake, 5, 12, 122
- Snow Hill, 3, 8, 19, 32, 47, 82, 112, 116, 112, 127
- Snow Hill Falls, 102
- Snow Lake, 8
- Snowmass, 14

- Snowmass Village, 14
- Snows Corner, 19, 129
- Snow Settlement, 45
- Snowshoe, 53, 127
- Snow Shoe, 102
- Snowslip, 66
- Snows Mill, 23
- Snow Springs, 23
- Snow Town, 106
- Snowville, 53, 89, 118
- Snow Water Springs, 14
- Soap Lake, 124
- Soapstick, 23
- Soapweed, 12
- Social Circle, 23
- Social Hill, 8
- Social Plains, 82
- Social Town, 3
- Society Hill, 3, 47, 59, 106
- Sod, 127
- Soda, 66
- Soda Bay, 12
- Soda Hill, 82
- Soda Springs, 12, 26, 66, 95, 116
- Sodaville, 95
- Soda Well, 130
- Soddy Daisy, 112
- Sodium, 130
- Sodom, 45, 79
- Soldier, 26, 36, 38
- Soldier Camp, 5
- Soldier Creek, 108
- Soldier Pond, 45
- Soldiers Grove, 129
- Soldier Summit, 118
- Solitude, 32, 43, 118, 122
- Solo, 63, 82, 112
- Somber, 36
- Somerset, 3, 12, 14, 29, 32, 38, 43, 47, 50, 53, 68, 74, 82, 89, 96, 102, 116, 122, 129
- Somerset Junction, 45
- Sooner, 93
- Soo Nipi, 71
- Sopchoppy, 19
- Soso, 59
- Soul City, 82
- Sourdough, 66
- Sour Lake, 116
- South, 3
- South Alamo, 113
- South Bend, 32, 68, 124
- South Carolina, 6, 40, 104
- South Carrollton, 63
- South Dakota, 40, 106
- South Dayton, 79
- South Egg Harbor, 74
- Southern Klondike, 69
- South Fulton, 112
- South Lancaster, 50
- South Lincoln, 50
- South Logan, 89
- South Lyon, 53
- South of the Border, 106
- South Orange, 74
- South Park, 29
- South Pass City, 130
- South Point, 116
- South Thompson, 23
- Southward, 23
- South West City, 63
- Sovereign, 127
- Spade, 116
- Spades, 32
- Spain, 23, 108
- Spangle, 124
- Spanish Flat, 12
- Spanish Ranch, 12
- Spanish Springs, 70
- Spanish Town, 26
- Spanish Valley, 118
- Spanish Village, 14
- Sparkill, 79
- Sparkling Springs, 122
- Sparks, 14, 38, 68, 70, 93, 95
- Sparrow, 63
- Sparrow Bush, 79
- Sparta, 23, 109

- Speaker, 53
- Speaks, 116
- Spear, 66
- Spearmint, 118
- Spears, 75
- Spearville, 38
- Speck, 112
- Speck Oaks, 129
- Speed, 3, 32, 38, 63, 82, 127
- Speedtown, 59
- Speedway, 127
- Speedwell, 74, 82, 102, 112
- Spencer, 14, 26, 29, 32, 36, 38, 43, 50, 53, 89, 93, 108, 112, 127, 129, 130
- Spencer Store, 3
- Sphinx, 66
- Spiceland, 32
- Spiderweb, 106
- Spies, 82
- Spike Buck, 14
- Splinter, 59
- Split Hill, 45
- Split Rock, 102, 129
- Split Rock Junction, 66
- Split Silk, 23
- Spokane, 63, 89, 108
- Spooner, 23
- Spot, 112
- Spotsylvania, 122
- Spotsylvania Courthouse, 122
- Spotted Horse, 130
- Spotted Robe, 66
- Spout Springs, 82, 112
- Spray, 19, 95
- Spraytown, 32
- Spring, 38, 116
- Spring Arbor, 53
- Spring Bluff, 23, 63
- Spring Branch, 23, 36, 106
- Springbrook, 36
- Spring Brook, 102
- Spring City, 70
- Spring Cottage, 59
- Spring Creek, 8, 19, 43, 56, 59, 63, 70, 82, 84, 93, 102, 108, 116, 122
- Spring Creek Junction, 66
- Springfield, 3, 8, 14, 19, 23, 26, 27, 29, 32, 43, 45, 50, 53, 56, 59, 63, 68, 71, 89, 95, 102, 106, 112, 116, 122, 127, 129
- Spring Forest, 63
- Spring Fork, 63
- Spring Fountain, 36
- Spring Gap, 47, 127
- Spring Garden, 12, 29, 63, 102
- Spring Green, 129
- Spring Grove, 29, 32, 36, 56, 63, 89, 104, 108
- Spring Gulch, 66
- Spring Gully, 105
- Springhill, 43, 63, 66, 93
- Spring Hill, 3, 8, 16, 17, 19, 29, 36, 38, 43, 56, 59, 102, 106, 112, 116, 122
- Spring Lake, 32, 43, 45, 53, 56, 104
- Spring Mill, 74, 89
- Spring Mills, 74, 102
- Spring Place, 23
- Spring Prairie, 129
- Spring Ridge, 43, 59
- Springs, 66
- Springtime, 66
- Springtown, 32, 63, 66, 74
- Springvale, 56
- Spring Valley, 3, 12, 17, 29, 36, 47, 56, 74, 89, 95, 116, 122, 124, 129, 130
- Springview, 68
- Springville, 12, 19, 32, 36, 38, 43, 59
- Springwater, 36, 95
- Spruce, 14, 53, 56, 63, 70, 102, 127, 129
- Spruce Center, 56
- Spruce Corner, 50
- Spruce Creek, 102
- Sprucedale, 14
- Spruce Hill, 102

- Sprucemont, 7
- Spruce Pine, 3, 82, 112
- Spruce Valley, 127
- Sprucewood, 14
- Spry, 118
- Spuds, 19
- Spurior Place, 68
- Spur Lake, 75
- Squabbletown, 12
- Square Butte, 66
- Square Corner, 102
- Square Lake, 45
- Squaretop, 93
- Squaw Valley, 12
- Squirrel, 26
- Squirrel Flat, 112
- Squirrel Hill, 102
- Squirrels Corners, 79
- Squirrel Town, 89
- Stacey, 66, 82
- Stacy, 8, 12, 56, 82, 112, 116
- Stacy Crossroads, 119
- Stacyville, 45
- Stacyville Junction, 36
- Stag Creek, 116
- Stage, 14
- Stage Bridge,
- Stagecoach, 70, 116
- Stage Coach Woods, 3
- Stairtown, 116
- Stallion Springs, 12
- Stamp, 3
- Stampede, 84, 124
- Stamper, 59
- Stamps, 8, 116
- Standard, 3, 43, 47, 59, 124
- Standard City, 29
- Standard Umpstead, 8
- Standing Rock, 75
- Standing Stone, 102
- Stanford, 8, 12, 26, 29, 32, 66
- St Annie, 63

- Stanton, 3, 12, 17, 19, 36, 38, 43, 53, 56, 59, 63, 68, 74, 84, 95, 102, 112, 116, 129
- Staples, 43, 56
- Stapletown, 63
- Star, 8, 26, 43, 53, 68, 82, 93, 116, 127
- Starboard, 45
- Starbuck, 56, 124
- Starbucktown, 89
- Star City, 32, 53, 70, 127
- Star Corner, 108
- Star Cross, 74
- Starfield, 63
- Star Hill, 17
- Stark, 38, 53, 66, 71
- Starkville, 59
- Starkweather, 84
- Star Lake, 56
- Starlight, 102
- Star Point, 23
- Star Prairie, 129
- Star Tannery, 122
- Start, 43
- Startup, 124
- Star Valley, 5
- Starvation Heights, 95
- State Bridge, 14
- State Center, 36
- State College, 102
- State Farm, 106
- State Levee, 59
- State Line, 3, 8, 26, 32, 43, 56, 59, 79, 102, 112, 124, 129
- Stateline, 12, 70
- State Line City, 32, 71, 116
- Staten Island, 75, 76, 79
- State Park, 106
- State Road, 45, 89
- Static, 112
- Station 15, 89, 102
- St Augustine, 17
- Staunton, 119, 121, 122
- Stavebolt, 95

- Stay, 43
- St Bernice, 32
- St Catherine, 59, 63
- St Charles, 8, 14, 23, 26, 29, 36, 43, 47, 53, 56, 63, 68, 89, 106, 108, 122
- St Croix, 32
- St David, 29, 45(2)
- St Davids Church, 122
- Steam, 12
- Steamboat, 5, 14, 70, 95
- Steamboat Landing, 106
- Steamboat Rock, 26, 36
- Steamboat Springs, 14
- Steam Corner, 32
- St Edward, 68
- Steel, 59
- Steel City, 29
- Steel Creek, 82
- Steelhead, 12
- Steel Point, 89
- Steep Falls, 45
- Steep Landing, 45
- St Elizabeth, 63
- Stellar, 116
- Stephen, 56, 59
- Stephen Creek, 116
- Stephens, 23, 59, 63
- Stephensburg, 74
- Stephens City, 122
- Stephens Fort, 122
- Stephenson, 53
- Stephens Point,
- Stephensville, 23
- Stephenville, 43, 59
- Steptoe, 70, 124
- Sterling, 16, 23, 26, 36, 38, 43, 50, 59, 63, 66, 68, 82, 84, 89, 93, 102, 118, 122
- Sterling Center, 56
- Sterling Hill, 16
- Sterling Place, 14
- Sterling Spring, 8
- Sterling Springs, 8
- Stetson, 26, 45
- Stetson Corner, 16
- Steubenville, 89
- Steve Forks, 66
- Stevens, 12, 26, 36, 59, 95, 102, 108, 116, 119
- Stevensburg, 122
- Stevens Corner, 45
- Stevens Crossing, 23
- Stevensdale, 43
- Stevenson, 16, 56
- Stevens Point, 129
- Stevenstown, 129
- Stevens Village, 4
- Stevensville, 45, 53, 66, 129
- Stewartville, 54
- St George, 17, 29, 45, 56, 63, 84, 102, 106, 118, 127
- St Georges, 17, 47
- Still, 84
- Still Creek, 102
- Stillhouse Springs, 63
- Stillmeadows, 47
- Still Pond, 47
- Still River, 50
- Still Valley, 74
- Stillwater, 8, 56, 66, 70, 71, 74, 89, 93, 102, 104, 124
- Stillwell, 93
- Stiltz, 102
- Stinking Bay, 8
- Stinking Creek, 112
- St Joe, 8
- St Joseph, 60(2)
- St Louis, 23, 53, 59, 60,9 3
- St Louis Crossing, 32
- St Louis Heights, 24
- St Louisville, 89
- St Margarets, 47
- St Mary, 66, 68
- St Marys, 32, 36, 38, 63
- St Marys City, 47
- St Matthews, 106
- St Nicholas, 53, 56
- Stockade, 19

- Stockbridge, 63
- Stockholm, 45, 56, 74, 79, 108, 129
- Stocks, 23
- Stokesville, 18
- Stomp Springs, 106
- Stone, 12, 26, 32, 66, 89, 95, 112
- Stonebluff, 32, 93
- Stone Bridge, 108
- Stone Cabin, 70
- Stone City, 38
- Stone Creek, 89
- Stonefort, 29
- Stone Hill, 63
- Stonehill, 66
- Stone House, 70
- Stonehouse, 70
- Stone Lake, 106
- Stone Mill, 74
- Stone Mountain, 23
- Stone Place, 12
- Stones Crossing, 32
- Stone Station, 106
- Stonetown, 74
- Stoneville, 82, 89
- Stonewall, 8, 14, 23, 59, 93
- Stoney Point, 23, 43, 93
- Stony Bottom, 127
- Stony Creek, 32, 53, 82
- Stony Ford, 16
- Stony Fork, 82
- Stony Hill, 63
- Stony Knob, 82
- Stony Point, 43, 53, 82, 93, 122
- Stony Ridge, 89
- Stop, 8, 23
- Storck, 122
- Store Village, 24
- Storm Lake, 36
- Storms, 89
- Story, 66, 68, 93, 130
- Story City, 36
- Stout, 59, 116
- Stovepipe, 12
- Stovepipe Wells, 12
- Stow, 50, 89
- St Paul, 53, 54, 56, 68, 89, 95
- Straight, 93
- Straight Mountain, 3
- Strain, 116
- Strange Creek, 127
- Stranger, 116
- Strasburg, 29, 53, 83, 84, 89, 122
- Strassburg, 14
- Stratford Hall, 122
- Stratosphere Bowl, 108
- Straw, 66
- Strawberry, 3, 5, 8, 12, 38, 70, 95, 106
- Strawberry Hill, 70
- Strawberry Plains, 112
- Strawberry Point, 36
- Strawberry Ridge, 82, 102
- Strawberry Spring, 93
- Strawberry Valley, 12
- Strawbridge, 129
- Strawtown, 32
- Strayhorse, 5
- Street, 47
- Stringer, 59
- Stringtown, 8, 29, 32, 36, 47, 53, 59, 64, 89, 93, 112, 116, 122, 124, 127
- Strong, 5, 8, 45, 59, 118
- Strong City, 38, 93
- Stronghold, 45
- Structure, 116
- Strum, 129
- St Stephen, 47, 106
- St Stephens, 68, 82, 130
- Stubenville, 32
- Stump Creek, 102
- Stumptoe, 8
- Stumptown, 47, 82, 116, 127
- Stump Town, 66
- Sturges, 64
- Sturgis, 8, 53, 59, 93, 108
- Stuttgart, 8
- Styra, 61
- Sublette, 14, 29, 38, 64, 75

- Sublime, 116
- Sublimity, 95
- Success, 8, 59, 64, 89, 93, 122
- Sucker, 26
- Suckerville, 45
- Sudan, 102, 116
- Sudden, 12
- Sue, 127
- Sue City, 64
- Sugar, 14, 116
- Sugar Bush, 129
- Sugar Bush Knolls, 89
- Sugar City, 14, 26
- Sugarcreek, 89, 102
- Sugar Creek, 3, 23, 32, 36, 43, 64, 89, 93
- Sugarfield, 12
- Sugar Grove, 29, 53, 82, 89, 102, 112, 129
- Sugar Hill, 23, 45, 59, 71, 102, 112
- Sugar Hollow, 112
- Sugar Island, 29, 129
- Sugarite, 75
- Sugar Junction, 14
- Sugar Lake, 64
- Sugarland, 47
- Sugar Land, 116
- Sugar Loaf, 53
- Sugarloaf, 14, 56
- Sugarloaf Shores, 19
- Sugarmill Woods, 19
- Sugar Pine, 12
- Sugar Rapids, 53
- Sugar Ridge, 82, 89
- Sugar Run, 102
- Sugartown, 23, 43
- Sugar Town, 82
- Sugartree, 64
- Sugar Tree, 112
- Sugar Tree Ridge, 89
- Sugar Valley, 23, 116, 127
- Sugarville, 3
- Sulphur, 32, 43, 70, 93, 108, 116, 124
- Sulphura, 112
- Sulphur City, 8, 127
- Sulphurgrove, 89
- Sulphur Rock, 8
- Sulphur Spring, 32
- Sulphur Springs, 3, 8, 32, 36, 75, 79, 82, 89, 95, 102, 112
- Sumac, 23
- Sumach, 64
- Summer, 116
- Summer City, 112
- Summerdream, 122
- Summerduck, 122
- Summerfield, 43
- Summer Harbor, 45
- Summerhaven, 5
- Summer Hill, 29
- Summer Home, 12
- Summers, 127
- Summertown, 12, 23
- Summerville, 23, 29, 43, 64, 95, 108
- Summit, 3, 4, 5, 8, 12, 29, 32, 36, 38, 43, 50, 53, 56, 59, 64, 66, 70, 74, 75, 82, 89, 95, 102, 104, 112, 118, 119, 124, 127
- Summit Bridge, 17
- Summit City, 53, 64
- Summit Grove, 32
- Summit Hill, 23
- Summit Valley, 66
- Summitville, 14, 32, 89
- Sumter, 68
- Sun, 43, 79, 127
- Sunbeach, 124
- Sunbeam, 14, 26, 29, 122
- Sunbelt, 26
- Sunbright, 112, 122
- Sunburg, 56
- Sunburst, 66, 82
- Sunbury, 23, 29, 39, 97
- Sun City, 5, 12, 19, 38
- Suncrest, 3, 12
- Sundad, 5, 12
- Sundance, 66, 130
- Sundial, 127

- Sundown, 64, 70, 116
- Sun Down, 32
- Sunfield, 29, 53
- Sunflower, 35, 38, 59, 102, 127
- Sun Garden, 19
- Sun Hill, 23, 127
- Sunizona, 5
- Sunkist, 12, 59, 93
- Sunland, 12
- Sunlight, 3, 64, 66, 127
- Sunny Brae, 79
- Sunny Brook, 106
- Sunnybrook, 12, 47
- Sunnydell, 26
- Sunny Hill, 43, 124
- Sunny Home, 3
- Sunnyland, 29
- Sunny Point, 122
- Sunny Shores, 124
- Sunny Side, 23, 75, 106, 112, 116, 122
- Sunnyside, 4, 5, 8, 12, 14, 19, 23, 26, 29, 50, 53, 64, 66, 70, 74, 79, 89, 95, 102, 112, 118, 124, 129
- Sunnyslope, 12, 26, 95, 124
- Sunny South, 3
- Sunnyvale, 12, 82
- Sunnyview, 108
- Sunny View, 82
- Sun Prairie, 66, 129
- Sunray, 116
- Sunrise, 5, 8, 12, 56, 59, 64, 75, 89, 93, 102, 112, 122, 124, 127, 130
- Sunrise Beach, 32, 124
- Sunrise Hill, 130
- Sunrise Vista, 12
- Sun River, 66
- Sunset, 5, 8, 12, 19, 43, 45, 59, 64, 75, 93, 95, 106, 112, 116, 118, 124, 129
- Sunset Beach, 19, 24, 95, 124, 127
- Sunset City, 14
- Sunset Corner, 93
- Sunset Corners, 19

- Sunset Harbor, 19
- Sunset Hills, 82
- Sunset Park, 38
- Sunset Point, 19
- Sunset Valley, 102
- Sunset View, 47
- Sunset Village, 23, 122
- Sunshine, 3, 4, 5, 8, 14, 36, 43, 45, 47, 75, 82, 102, 116, 124, 130
- Sunshine Beach, 19, 53
- Sunshine Camp, 70
- Sunshine Valley, 75
- Sun Springs, 38
- Sunsweet, 12, 23, 93
- Sun Tree,
- Suntree, 5
- Sunvalley, 70
- Sun Valley, 5, 19, 26, 75, 75, 82, 95, 102,1 27
- Sunview, 5, 32, 47
- Superior, 5, 14, 36, 43, 53, 66, 68, 89, 95, 127, 129, 130
- Superior Bottom, 127
- Suppersville, 38
- Supply, 8, 82, 122
- Supreme, 43
- Surf, 12
- Surf City, 74, 82
- Surfside, 12, 19
- Surprise, 5, 68, 112
- Surprise Hill, 122
- Surprise Station, 11
- Surprise Valley, 124
- Surrey, 84
- Surry Ridge, 47
- Susan Beach Corner, 17
- Susanna, 64
- Susanville, 11, 95
- Susie, 124
- Sutherland, 36, 64, 81, 82, 118, 122, 129
- Sutherland Crossroads, 9
- Sutton, 707
- Suwanee, 23

- Suwannee, 19
- Suwannee Springs, 19
- Suwannee Valley, 19
- Swallow Hill, 17
- Swallows Nest, 14
- Swamp Angel, 38
- Swampers, 43
- Swamproot, 102
- Swampscott, 50
- Swan, 32, 36, 95
- Swanburg, 56
- Swan Corner, 50
- Swan Creek, 29, 47, 53
- Swan Falls, 26
- Swanlake, 26
- Swan Lake, 9, 59, 68, 108
- Swannsylvania, 112
- Swan Pond, 127
- Swan River, 56
- Swans Island, 45
- Swantown, 124
- Swan Valley, 26
- Swanville, 56
- Swastika, 79, 95
- Swede Heaven, 124
- Swede Hill, 102, 124
- Sweden, 9, 23, 45, 64, 102, 106
- Swedenburg, 68
- Swedenhome, 68
- Swedentown, 95
- Swedesboro, 74
- Sweet, 26
- Sweet Air, 47
- Sweet Briar, 17, 84
- Sweetbriar, 12
- Sweet Corner, 50
- Sweetgrass, 66
- Sweetgum, 82, 112
- Sweet Gum, 23, 32
- Sweetheart City, 129
- Sweet Hollow Ford, 64
- Sweet Home, 3, 9, 43, 95, 116
- Sweethome, 9
- Sweet Lake, 43
- Sweetland, 12
- Sweet Lips, 112
- Sweet Springs, 64, 127
- Sweetser, 32
- Sweet Valley, 102
- Sweetville, 43
- Sweet Water, 3
- Sweetwater, 5, 19, 26, 29, 64, 68, 70, 74, 75, 82, 84, 93, 102, 106, 112, 116
- Sweetwater Crossing, 130
- Sweetwater Station, 130
- Swift, 56, 64, 116, 124
- Swiftcurrent, 66
- Swift Falls, 56
- Swift Ford, 3
- Swiftown, 59
- Swift River, 50
- Swift Run, 122
- Swift Trail Junction, 5
- Swiftwater, 59, 71, 102
- Swindleville, 43
- Swinesburg, 74
- Swisher, 36
- Swiss, 64, 82
- Swiss Alps, 116
- Swisshome, 95
- Switch Back, 122
- Switzerland, 19, 106
- Switzerland Village, 14
- Swords, 23, 43
- Sycamore, 3, 5, 9, 17, 19, 29, 32, 64, 89, 93, 102, 106, 112, 116, 122, 127
- Sycamore Corner, 32
- Sycamore Flat, 12
- Sycamore Spring, 9, 112
- Sycamore Springs, 12
- Sylaucuga, 1
- Sylvanite, 66
- Syndicate, 32
- Syracuse, 32, 38, 64, 68
- Syria, 122

-T-

- Table Bluff, 12
- Table Grove, 29
- Table Rock, 64, 68, 95, 127, 130
- Tacoma, 14, 45, 89, 123, 124
- Tad, 127
- Taft, 93
- Tahoe, 26
- Tails Creek, 23
- Talc, 66
- Talent, 95
- Talking Rock, 23
- Tall Pines, 106
- Tall Timbers, 47
- Tall Trees, 9
- Tallyho, 102, 127
- Tampa, 19, 38
- Tampa Bay, 17
- Tampico, 27, 29, 124
- Tangent, 95
- Tangerine, 19
- Tango, 127
- Tanks, 95
- Tannenbaum, 9
- Tanner, 3, 124
- Tanner Springs, 5
- Tannery, 47
- Tan Oak Park, 12
- Taps, 64
- Tarbox Corner, 104
- Tar Corner, 82
- Tar Heel, 82
- Tariffville, 16
- Tarpon, 19
- Tarpon Springs, 20
- Tar River, 82
- Tarzan, 116
- Tarzana, 12
- Tater Peeler, 112
- Taterville, 43
- Tavern, 64
- Tax, 9
- Taxahaw, 106

- Tax Crossroads, 23
- Taylor, 3, 4, 5, 9, 12, 20, 26, 29, 36, 43, 47, 53, 59, 64, 68, 70, 79, 84, 93, 102, 116, 118, 122, 129
- Taylor Corner, 32
- Taylor Corner Gin, 93
- Taylor Corners, 16
- Taylor Crossing, 12
- Taylor Hill, 29
- Taylor Ridge, 29
- Taylors, 32
- Taylors Bridge, 17
- Taylors Corner, 17
- Taylors Falls, 56
- Taylors Mill, 23
- Taylors Mills, 74
- Taylor Springs, 29, 75
- Taylorsville, 12, 23, 32, 36, 47, 59, 89, 112, 116, 118
- Taylortown, 17, 43, 74, 82, 89
- Taylorville, 26, 29, 32
- Tchula, 59
- Tea, 64, 108
- Teaberry, 127
- Teakettle Junction, 12
- Teal, 64
- Teaneck, 74
- Teapot Dome, 53
- Teaticket, 50
- Teegarden, 32
- Teepee Creek, 26
- Teeterville, 53
- Telegraph, 116
- Telegraph City, 12
- Telegraph Hill, 26
- Telegraph Spring, 122
- Telephone, 116
- Telescope, 102
- Tell, 116, 129
- Tell City, 32
- Temperance, 23, 53
- Temperanceville, 9, 89
- Temperence Hill, 59, 106
- Tempest, 70

- Temple, 84
- Tenafly, 74
- Ten Degree, 45
- Ten Hills, 50
- Tenkiller, 93
- Tenmile, 43, 64, 95, 130
- Ten Mile, 36, 59, 102, 106
- Tenmile Corner, 56
- Tenmile Crossing, 116
- Tenmile Post, 4
- Ten Mile Run, 74
- Tennant, 12, 36
- Tennessee, 9, 29, 56, 80, 99, 108, 109
- Tennessee City, 112
- Tennessee Colony, 116
- Tennessee Ridge, 112
- Tennis, 38, 108
- Ten Sleep, 130
- Tenstrike, 56
- Tent, 8, 17
- Tent City, 12
- Tenth Legion, 122
- Terrace, 116
- Terra Cotta, 38
- Terre Haute, 30, 64, 89
- Testo, 106
- Teton Village, 130
- Texarcana, 9, 116
- Texas, 3(2), 23, 32, 47, 59, 70, 74(2), 79, 89, 90, 92, 102, 112, 113, 114, 119
- Texas Bend, 64
- Texas City, 29, 116
- Texas Corner, 102
- Texas Corners, 53
- Texas Creek, 14
- Texas Valley, 79
- Texasville, 3
- Texhoma, 93, 116
- Texico, 29, 75
- Thankful, 82
- Thayer, 29, 36, 53, 68
- The Basin, 9
- The Bend, 89

- The Bottle, 3
- The Burg, 29
- The Cedars, 12, 16, 26
- The City, 12
- The Crossing, 12
- The Cross Roads, 122
- The Dalles, 95
- The Diamonds, 64
- The Eastern, 89
- The Forks, 12, 45
- The Four Corners, 119
- The Gap, 5
- The Green, 50
- The Grove, 116
- The Harbor, 4
- The Holy City, 93
- The Jackpines, 53
- The Landing, 45
- Themopolis, 130
- The Oaks, 12, 47
- Theososia, 64
- The Pinery, 14
- The Pines, 9, 12, 45
- The Plains, 122
- The Point, 89
- The Quarry, 9
- Thermal, 12
- Thermal City, 82
- The Rock, 23
- The Springs, 50
- The Street, 50
- The Timbers, 17
- The Village, 3, 93
- The Willows, 12
- The X, 50
- Thick, 112
- Thicket, 116
- Thief River Falls, 56
- Third Cliff, 50
- Thirteen Forks, 23
- Thirteen Points Landing, 43
- Thirty, 36
- Thirty Four Corner, 64
- Thirtymile, 95

- Thistle, 118
- Thistledown, 14
- Thompson, 3, 9, 12, 16, 20, 29, 36, 45, 47, 53, 59, 64, 68, 70, 79, 84, 89, 95, 102, 118, 124, 129
- Thompson Beach, 74
- Thompsonburg,
- Thompson Corner, 24, 45, 71, 93, 106
- Thompson Crossroad, 23
- Thompson Crossroads, 112
- Thompson Falls, 66
- Thompson Grove, 116
- Thompson Mill, 112
- Thompson No 1, 102
- Thompson Place, 12, 124
- Thompson Ridge, 79
- Thompsons, 116
- Thompsons Corner, 47, 79
- Thompsons Crossing, 79
- Thompsons Lake, 79
- Thompsons Mill, 23
- Thompsons Mills, 102
- Thompsons Point, 119
- Thompson Springs, 118
- Thompsons Station, 112
- Thompsons Store, 112
- Thompsontown, 47, 74
- Thompson Valley, 122
- Thompsonville, 16, 17, 23, 29, 38, 50, 53, 59, 79, 116, 118, 129
- Thoreau, 75(2)
- Thorn, 59
- Thornberry, 116
- Thorn Hill, 112, 116
- Thorn Hollow, 95
- Thorofare, 74
- Thousand Oaks, 12, 64
- Thousand Palms, 12
- Thousand Springs, 70
- Thralls Prairie, 64
- Thrasher, 59
- Threadville, 59
- Three-Way Corner, 93
- Three-Way Corner, 5

- Three Arch Bay, 12
- Three Bar, 70
- Three Bridges, 74
- Three Brothers, 9
- Three Churches, 127
- Three Churches Corner, 53
- Three Creek, 26
- Three Creeks, 9
- Three Crossing, 12
- Three Forks, 3, 5, 14, 23, 26(2), 66, 82, 89, 95, 112, 118, 127, 130
- Three Lakes, 53
- Three Leagues, 116
- Three Locks, 89
- Three Lynx, 95
- Three Mile, 82, 102
- Threemile Corner, 26, 122
- Threemile Crossing, 26
- Three Notch, 3
- Three Oaks, 20, 53, 116
- Three Pines, 118
- Three Points, 12, 23, 112
- Three Rivers, 12, 53, 59, 75, 95, 116
- Three Rocks, 12,95
- Three Seasons, 17
- Three Springs, 95
- Three Square, 122
- Three States, 9, 29, 64, 116
- Three Streams, 45
- Three Trees, 106
- Three V Crossing, 84
- Three Way, 5, 8, 9
- Threeway, 122
- Thrift, 116, 124
- Thrush, 64
- Thunderbird, 75
- Thunderbolt, 23
- Thunder Butte, 108
- Thunder Hawk, 108
- Thursday, 127
- Ti, 93
- Ticaboo, 118
- Tickfaw, 43
- Ticktown, 122

- Tide, 43
- Tidewater, 20
- Tidings, 23
- Tie Plant, 59
- Tie Siding, 130
- Tiger, 23, 93, 124
- Tiger Bay, 20
- Tiger Lily, 12
- Tigertown, 116
- Tigerville, 106, 108
- Tightsqueeze, 122
- Tightwad, 64
- Tigris, 64
- Timber, 64, 95
- Timber Creek, 68
- Timber Grove, 47, 95
- Timber Lake, 108
- Timberland, 129
- Timberlane, 59
- Timberlost, 53
- Timber Ridge, 29, 47, 122
- Timbuctoo, 74
- Timbuktoo, 12
- Timbuktu, 95
- Time, 29, 102
- Timewell, 29
- Tin City, 4
- Tin Cup, 14, 112
- Tingle, 75
- Tingley, 36, 102
- Tin House, 5
- Tinkertown, 50
- Tinkerville, 71
- Tinmouth, 119
- Tin Top, 79, 116
- Tin Town, 64
- Tiny, 122
- Tiny Town, 14
- Tioga, 36, 53, 84, 95, 102, 113, 116, 127, 129
- Tip, 93
- Tipp City, 89
- Tippecanoe, 32, 70, 89, 102
- Tipperary, 36, 64
- Tipperary Corner, 26
- Tiptop, 122
- Tip Top, 106
- Titanic, 93
- Toad Lake, 56
- Toadtown, 12
- Toadville, 3
- Toadvine, 3
- Toast, 82
- Tobacco, 66
- Tobacco Patch Landing, 20
- Tobaccoville, 82, 122
- Todd, 4, 43, 64, 68, 82, 93, 102, 116
- Todd Town, 112
- Togo, 59
- Tokio, 84
- Toledo, 9, 23, 29, 32, 36, 38, 64, 82, 89, 95, 116, 120, 124
- Tollgate, 47, 95
- Toll Gate Corner, 79
- Tollhouse, 12
- Tomahawk, 9, 83, 108, 127, 129
- Tomahawk Bluff, 29
- Tomboy, 14
- Tombstone, 5
- Tom Corwin, 89
- Tompkinsville, 47
- Toms Brook, 122
- Tongue Point Village, 95
- Tonto Village, 5
- Tool, 116
- Toonerville, 23
- Top, 102
- Top-of-the-World, 5
- Topaz, 9, 12, 26, 53, 64
- Topeka, 29, 32, 59
- Topeka East, 47
- Tophill, 95
- Topnot, 83, 122
- Top of the World, 12, 75
- Top O'Deep, 66
- Topsy, 43, 64
- Torch, 64
- Torch Lake, 53

- Tornado, 127
- Toronto, 29, 36, 38, 64, 89, 108, 116, 127
- Torpedo, 93, 102
- Torreys, 26
- Torreys Landing, 23
- Toto, 32
- Touchstone, 59
- Tower, 53, 56
- Tower City, 84
- Town, 26
- Town Creek, 3, 47
- Townhall, 68
- Town Hall, 50
- Town Hill, 16, 33, 45
- Town Line, 79
- Town of Pines, 33
- Town Plot Hill, 16
- Townsend, 64
- Townville, 106
- Tractor, 38
- Tracy, 56
- Trade, 3, 112
- Trade City, 102
- Trade River, 129
- Traders Hill, 23
- Trading Post, 38
- Trail, 56, 66, 93, 95
- Trail City, 108
- Trails End, 33
- Trailtown, 20
- Trainer, 127
- Tramway, 26
- Tranquility, 12, 74, 89, 112
- Transylvania, 43
- Transfer, 102
- Trap Corner, 45
- Trapper, 14
- Travelers Rest, 3, 106
- Traverse, 56
- Traverse City, 53
- Treasure, 14
- Treasure Island, 20
- Treasureton, 26

- Treaty, 33
- Tree of Knowledge Corner, 50
- Trees, 43
- Tree Spring, 33
- Tree Top, 83
- Treetops, 47
- Tremont, 57
- Trenton, 23, 33, 53, 64, 68, 83, 84, 89, 106, 118, 129
- Trestle Creek, 26
- Trestle Ford, 93
- Tri-City, 95
- Triadelphia, 89, 127
- Triangle, 26, 83, 95, 116, 122
- Tribune, 70, 116
- Trickem, 3
- Trident, 9
- Trigg, 9, 112
- Trimble, 3, 14, 23, 29, 64, 89, 112, 122
- Trimountain, 53
- Trinidad, 14, 116,1 24
- Trio, 3, 106, 116
- Triple Divide, 66
- Triple Springs, 83
- Triplet, 122
- Triplets Corners, 59
- Tripoli, 36, 79, 129
- Tripoli Mill, 71
- Triumph, 26, 29, 89, 102
- Trolleys, 127
- Trooper, 102
- Trophy Club, 116
- Tropic, 118
- Trots Hills, 50
- Trotters, 84
- Troublesome, 14
- Trout, 26, 43, 68, 95, 127
- Trout Creek, 95, 116, 118
- Troutdale, 14, 45
- Trout Lake, 53, 124
- Trout Springs, 75
- Troutville, 47
- Trow Grove, 27, 29

- Troy, 66, 71, 79, 83, 108, 119, 122, 127, 129
- Truce, 116
- Truck, 47
- Truckers, 23
- True, 116, 127
- True Blue, 122
- Truly, 66
- Truman, 129
- Trumbull, 16
- Trump, 14
- Truth or Consequences, 74, 75
- Tryme, 122
- Tryon, 68
- Tuba City, 5
- Tuckahoe, 79
- Tucson, 4, 89
- Tug Hollow, 104
- Tulip, 9, 43, 64, 116, 122
- Tulip Hill, 47
- Tulips, 124
- Tullahassee, 93
- Tulsa, 90, 91(2), 95
- Tumbling Shoals, 9
- Tumtum, 124
- Tumwater, 124
- Tuna, 102
- Tungsten, 14, 66
- Tunnel, 89
- Tunnel Camp, 70
- Tunnel City, 129
- Tunnelhill, 102
- Tunnel Hill, 23, 29, 89
- Tunnel Springs, 3
- Tupelo, 57, 59, 93
- Turkey, 9, 83, 89, 116, 127
- Turkey Cobble, 16
- Turkey Creek, 9, 20, 33, 43, 59
- Turkey Foot, 20, 122
- Turkeyfoot, 102
- Turkey Foot Corner, 89
- Turkey Ford, 83, 93
- Turkey Knob, 127
- Turkey Pond, 106
- Turkey Ridge, 64, 108
- Turkey River, 36
- Turkey Scratch, 9
- Turnback, 64
- Turnip, 9
- Turnkey, 17
- Turnpike, 26, 59, 112
- Turquoise, 75
- Turret, 14
- Turtle, 53, 64
- Turtle Creek, 127
- Turtle Lake, 43, 66, 84
- Turtle River, 56
- Tuscumbia, 1,3
- Tuskegee, 60
- Tuxedo, 47, 83, 116
- Twain, 12, 70
- Tweedie, 124
- Twelve Corners, 45, 53, 129
- Twelvemile, 64, 106
- Twelve Mile, 33
- Twelvemile Corner, 14, 29
- Twelve Oaks, 59, 112
- Twentymile, 20
- Twentymile Bend, 20
- Twentynine Palms, 12
- Twentythree, 9
- Twig, 56
- Twilight, 127
- Twin, 3, 59, 124
- Twin Beaches, 26
- Twin Bridges, 9, 12, 66
- Twin Brook, 45
- Twin Brooks, 108
- Twin Buttes, 84
- Twin Cedars, 14
- Twin City, 23
- Twin Creek, 9, 66
- Twin Creeks, 12
- Twin Crossing, 14
- Twin Falls, 5, 26
- Twin Flat, 70
- Twin Forks, 14, 26
- Twin Grove, 56, 129

- Twin Groves, 130
- Twin Lake, 53
- Twin Lakes, 12, 16, 53, 56, 59
- Twinlow, 26
- Twin Mills, 14
- Twin Mountain, 71
- Twin Mountains, 116
- Twin Oaks, 12, 17, 43, 83, 93
- Twin Pines, 12
- Twin Rocks, 95
- Twin Sisters, 116
- Twin Springs, 26, 36, 64
- Twin Spruce, 14
- Twin Town, 129
- Twin Valley, 56
- Twisp, 124
- Twist, 9
- Two Bridges, 74
- Two Chestnut, 112
- Two Creeks, 129
- Two Dot, 66
- Two Eggs, 20
- Two F Crossing, 116
- Two Forks, 26
- Two Grey Hills, 75
- Two Guns, 5
- Two Harbors, 56
- Two Inlets, 56
- Twomile, 95
- Two Mile, 9
- Two Rivers, 12, 74, 124, 129
- Two Strike, 108
- Tyler, 3, 9, 20, 38, 47, 56, 59, 64, 71, 93, 102, 116, 124
- Ty Ty, 23

-U-

- U-No, 83
- Ucon, 95
- Ucross, 130
- Ulm, 66, 130

- Ulysses, 26, 68, 102
- Umbria, 89
- Umpire, 9, 64
- Umpqua, 95
- Una, 14, 106
- Unalaska, 4
- Uncertain, 116
- Uncle Sam, 43
- Uncompahgre, 14
- Undercliff Junction, 74
- Une, 129
- Uneeda, 127
- Uneedus, 43
- Unicorn, 47
- Uniform, 3
- Union, 9, 14, 20, 23, 29, 36, 43, 45, 53, 59, 64, 68, 70, 74, 83, 95, 106, 116, 124, 127
- Union Bridge, 47
- Union Burg, 36
- Union Camp, 112
- Union Center, 33, 36
- Union City, 12, 16, 23, 33, 53, 74, 93, 102, 112
- Union Corner, 127
- Union Creek, 95
- Union Cross, 83
- Union Furnace, 89
- Union Gap, 124
- Union Grove, 3, 74, 83, 129
- Union Hill, 3, 9, 12, 23, 29, 43, 50, 56, 59, 74, 83, 102
- Union Hope, 83
- Union Mills, 12, 33, 36, 47, 74, 83
- Union Point, 23, 43, 83, 95
- Union Ridge, 127
- Union Springs, 43
- Union Star, 64
- Union Station, 89
- Union Town, 29
- Uniontown, 9, 29, 33, 38, 47, 59, 64, 74, 89, 127
- Union Valley, 93, 102

- Unionville, 16, 23, 29, 33, 36, 43, 47, 53, 64, 89, 122
- Union Wharf, 71
- Uniopolis, 89
- Unique, 36
- Unity, 29, 45, 47, 59, 71, 89, 93, 95, 112, 129
- Universal, 33, 102
- University, 29
- University City, 64
- University Place, 124
- Uno, 9, 89, 122
- Upco, 43
- Upland, 33, 38, 43
- Upper Crossing, 26
- Upper Dam, 45
- Upper Fruitland, 75
- Upper Green,
- Upper Lake, 12
- Upper Pig Pen, 83
- Upper Pocosin, 122
- Upper Pyramid, 70
- Upper Shaker Village, 71
- Upper Soda, 95
- Upper Sunnyside, 118
- Upper Town, 12, 70
- Upper Village, 71
- Upper Wheatfields, 5
- Upright, 122
- Up the Grove Beach, 20
- Upward, 83
- Urbana, 29, 33, 36, 47
- Useful, 64
- Usher, 20
- Ustick, 29
- Utah, 29, 33, 112, 117
- Utah Junction, 14
- Utahville, 102
- Utica, 79
- Utility, 43
- Utopia, 20, 38, 95, 116
- Uttertown, 74
- Uvalde, 116
- Uxbridge, 50

-V-

- Vacation Beach, 12
- Vail, 74
- Valdez, 4, 14
- Valencia, 66, 75, 102
- Valentine, 5, 9, 33, 43, 66, 68, 106, 116
- Valley, 68, 74, 89, 108, 124, 130
- Valley Center, 38
- Valley City, 29, 64, 83, 84,8 9
- Valley Creek, 116
- Valley Falls, 38, 106
- Valley Forge, 64
- Valley Head, 3
- Valley Ranch, 12
- Valley Ridge, 9
- Valley Spring, 116
- Valley Springs, 9, 12
- Valley Stream, 47
- Valleytown, 66
- Valley View, 9, 17, 23, 29, 64, 70, 89, 116
- Valley Wells, 116
- Valparaiso, 20, 33, 68
- Value, 59
- Van Buren, 6, 9, 33, 36, 45, 59, 64, 79, 89, 102
- Vancleve, 59
- Van Cleve, 64
- Vancouver, 124
- Vandalia, 29, 33, 36, 53, 64, 66, 127
- Vandrbilt, 53
- Vanderbilt Hill, 4
- Vanilla, 102
- Vatican, 43
- Vein Mountain, 83
- Venango, 38, 68, 102
- Venice, 20, 64, 68, 89, 102, 118, 124
- Venus, 9, 20, 64, 68, 116
- Verbena, 3, 116

- Veribest, 23, 116
- Vermillion, 29
- Vermont, 29, 40, 118
- Vernon, 16
- Vernon Center, 16
- Vernon Rockville, 16
- Versailles, 16, 29, 33, 64, 79, 89, 112
- Verse, 130
- Vesuvius, 122
- Veteran, 70, 130
- Veto, 59, 89, 127
- Vicksburg, 20
- Victor, 108
- Victory, 93, 112, 119
- Victory Hill, 50
- Vidalia, 59
- Vienna, 3, 23, 29, 33, 43, 44, 45, 47, 53, 64, 74, 79, 89, 108, 116, 127
- Vienna Woods, 122
- View, 23, 26, 116
- Viewpoint, 3
- Vigil, 14
- Viking, 56
- Village Five, 24
- Village Four, 24
- Village Hill, 16
- Village Number 1,3
- Village of Four Seasons, 64
- Village Six, 24
- Village Thirteen, 24
- Village Two, 24
- Villanova, 59
- Vincennes, 33, 36
- Vine Creek, 38
- Vinegar Bend, 3
- Vinegar Hill, 47
- Vine Hill, 3, 12
- Vineland, 3, 14, 56
- Vineyard, 102, 116
- Vineyard Crossroads, 23
- Viney Grove, 9
- Vinita, 90
- Vinnie Ha Ha, 129

- Viola, 9, 14, 17, 26, 29, 36, 38, 56, 64, 70, 127, 129, 130
- Violet, 64, 116, 127
- Violet Hill, 9
- Violin, 108
- Virgin, 118
- Virginia, 26, 29, 40(2), 48, 56, 64, 68, 79, 81, 84, 85, 95, 104, 108, 109, 119(2), 120(2), 124(2)
- Virginia City, 66, 70, 75
- Virginiatown, 12
- Virginville, 127
- Virtue, 112
- Viscose City, 122
- Vista, 36, 64, 66, 70, 75, 124
- Vistallas, 95(2)
- Vixen, 43
- Vocation, 3, 130
- Volcano, 12, 24, 70
- Volcanoville, 12
- Volt, 66
- Voltage, 95, 124
- Volunteer, 83, 108
- Vowell, 59
- Voyage, 64
- Vulcan, 14, 53, 127
- Vya, 70

-W-

- Waco, 23, 59, 68, 116
- Wading River, 74
- Wagon Mound, 75
- Wagontire, 95
- Wagon Wheel, 20, 23
- Wagon Wheel Gap, 14
- Wahoo, 68, 127
- Waikiki, 24
- Waite, 45
- Waits, 124
- Wake Forest, 83
- Wakemup, 56

- Wales, 50, 84, 129
- Walet, 43
- Walhalla, 84, 106
- Walkinghood, 38
- Wall, 107, 108, 116
- Walla Walla, 29, 124
- Wall City, 66
- Wallhill, 59
- Wallkill, 79
- Wall Lake, 33, 34, 36, 43, 56
- Walls, 93
- Wall Street, 64
- Wallstreet, 14
- Walnut, 9, 12, 29, 33, 36, 38, 47, 59, 64, 68, 83, 102, 127
- Walnut Bottom, 102, 127
- Walnut City, 36
- Walnut Corner, 9
- Walnut Corners, 33
- Walnut Cove, 83
- Walnut Creek, 12, 59, 83, 89
- Walnut Grove, 5, 9, 12, 23, 29, 33, 36, 56, 59, 64, 89, 102, 106, 112, 116, 122, 124, 127
- Walnut Grove Corner, 9
- Walnut Hill, 3, 9, 17, 20, 29, 43, 45, 50
- Walnut Log, 112
- Walnut Point, 53, 122
- Walnut Prairie, 29
- Walnut Ridge, 9, 17, 33, 47, 116
- Walnut Shade, 64, 112
- Walnut Springs, 9, 116
- Walnut Valley, 74
- Walpole, 50
- Walton, 68
- Wamego, 37
- Wanamaker, 64
- War, 127
- Warden, 43, 124
- War Eagle, 9
- Warehouse Point, 16
- Warfield, 23, 127
- Warfieldsburg, 47

- Warm Beach, 124
- Warm Creek, 70
- Warm Farm, 70
- Warm Lake, 26
- Warm Mineral Springs, 20
- Warm River, 26
- Warm Springs, 9, 23, 66, 70, 95, 122
- Warren, 16, 26, 29, 33, 45, 47, 50, 53, 56, 64, 66, 71, 74, 84, 89, 93, 95, 102, 104, 116, 119, 124
- Warren Glen, 74
- Warrior, 3
- Warroad, 56
- Warsaw, 3, 23, 29, 33, 56, 59, 64, 79, 83, 84, 89, 102, 106, 116, 122
- Wartburg, 112
- Washer, 116
- Washington, 3, 4, 5, 9, 12, 14, 16, 23, 29, 33, 36, 38, 43, 45, 50, 53, 59, 64, 68, 68, 70, 71, 74, 83, 89, 93, 102, 104, 106, 116, 118, 119, 122, 123, 127, 130
- Washington Camp, 5
- Washington Court House, 89
- Washington, D.C., 45, 46, 114, 121, 124
- Washington Depot, 16
- Washington Hall, 89
- Washington Harbor, 124
- Washington Park, 74
- Washington Prairie, 36
- Washington Square, 102
- Washington Valley, 74
- Washingtonville, 74, 89
- Wasp, 127
- Watch Hill, 104
- Water, 75
- Waterbury, 15
- Waterfall, 122
- Waterflow, 75
- Waterloo, 34
- Wateroak, 3
- Waterproof, 43
- Waters, 53

- Watersmeet, 53
- Watersville, 36, 47
- Watertown, 16, 20, 50, 53, 56, 108, 130
- Water Valley, 29, 59, 112, 116
- Watervalley, 9
- Water Village, 71
- Waterville, 38, 50, 56, 119, 124
- Waterville Valley, 71
- Waterwitch, 74
- Watonga, 90
- Waukesha, 128
- Wauneta, 14
- Wausau, 68
- Wax, 23
- Way, 59, 89
- Wayback, 23
- Waycross, 23
- Wayland, 26, 29, 36, 49, 50, 53, 56, 64, 95
- Wayne, 45, 68, 89, 93, 130
- Wayside, 23, 38, 50, 59, 83
- Wealthy, 116
- Weathers, 3, 9, 93
- Weaver, 14, 23, 29, 33, 38, 84, 127
- Weavers, 89
- Weavers Corners, 89
- Weaverville, 12
- Webfoot, 95
- Webster, 29, 33, 36, 38, 45, 47, 50, 53, 56, 59, 68, 71, 79, 83, 84, 89, 102, 108, 112, 116, 127
- Weckerly Park, 79
- Weed, 12, 66, 75
- Weedpatch, 12
- Weeds Point, 12
- Weeks, 9, 93, 106
- Weekstown, 74
- Weeping Water, 68
- Wee Town, 68
- Weiner, 9
- Welcome, 9, 20, 43, 47, 56, 70, 79, 83, 89, 106, 116, 122, 124
- Welcome Corners, 53

- Welcome Hill, 23
- Weld, 45
- Welfare, 116
- Well Spring, 112
- Wellsville, 79
- Wenona, 23, 47
- Wenona Beach, 53
- Wenonah, 3, 29, 74, 127
- West, 59, 112, 127
- West Allis, 128
- Westborough, 49
- West Branch, 33, 36
- Westby, 84
- West Carson, 12
- West Egg Harbor, 74
- Western, 56, 68
- Westernport, 46
- West Glasgow, 64
- West Juneau, 4
- West Keystone, 64
- West Liberty, 9, 29, 33, 36, 47, 64, 89, 102, 127
- West New York, 74
- West Philadelphia, 83
- West Pittston, 98
- West Plains, 61, 64
- West Thompson, 16
- West Thumb, 130
- West Valley City, 118
- West Virginia, 40(2), 56, 80, 85, 119(2), 124
- Wetmore, 38, 53
- Whalebone, 83
- Wham, 43
- What Cheer, 36
- Wheat Basin, 66
- Wheatfield, 33
- Wheatfields, 5
- Wheatgrass, 118
- Wheatland, 12, 33, 36, 53, 64, 84, 95, 116, 122, 127, 130(2)
- Wheat Ridge, 14
- Wheat Swamp, 83
- Wheel, 112

- Wheeless, 93
- Wheeling, 29, 33, 64
- Wheelwright, 50
- Whetstone, 5, 106
- Whig Hill, 102
- Whig Lane, 74
- Whigville, 16
- Whipples, 50
- Whippoorwill, 93
- Whipporwill Hills, 83
- Whipsaw Saddle, 26
- Whipstick, 16
- Whirlwind, 127
- Whiskey Dick, 95
- Whisp, 9
- Whispering Pines, 5, 12, 23, 47
- Whispering Springs, 9
- Whisper Walk, 20
- Whistler, 59
- Whistleville, 9, 23
- White, 23, 53, 66, 70, 102, 108
- White Apple, 59
- White Beach, 20
- White Bead, 93
- White Bear, 64
- White Bird, 26
- White Bluff, 9, 23, 59
- Whitebread, 93
- Whitebreast, 36
- White Butte, 108
- White Cap, 59
- White Caps, 70
- White Castle, 43
- White City, 23, 29, 38, 50, 53, 64, 66, 112, 116, 130
- Whiteclay, 68
- White Cliffs, 9
- White Cloud, 33, 36, 38, 53, 64
- White Cone, 5
- Whitecorn, 64
- White Deer, 102, 116
- White Eagle, 56, 93
- White Earth, 84
- White Eye, 4

- Whiteface, 56, 71
- Whitefish, 66
- Whitefish Point, 53
- White Fox, 89
- White Hall, 17, 23, 30, 43, 47, 50, 106, 127
- Whitehall, 9, 43, 53, 104, 106
- Whitehall Crossroads, 17
- White Hawk, 56
- Whitehawk, 12
- White Hearth, 30
- Whitehill, 95
- White Hill, 83, 112
- White Hills, 43
- White Hollow, 112
- White Horn, 112
- Whitehorn, 12, 14
- White Horse, 74
- Whitehorse, 75, 108
- White Horse Village, 118
- White House, 47, 59, 64, 102, 112
- Whitehouse, 3, 20, 47, 74, 83, 89, 112, 116
- White House Springs, 3
- White Kitchen, 43
- White Lake, 108, 130
- White Lakes, 75
- Whitelaw, 38
- White Mesa, 118
- White Mound, 116
- White Mountain, 4
- Whiteoak, 3, 33, 89
- White Oak, 3, 9, 23, 30, 36, 47, 53, 59, 64, 83, 89, 93, 102, 106, 112, 116, 122, 127, 130
- White Oak Bluff, 9
- White Oak Bottom, 74
- White Oak Corner, 45
- White Oak Forest, 112
- White Oak Landing, 20
- White Oaks, 50, 75
- White Oak Springs, 116, 127
- White Owl, 108
- White Pass, 124

- White Path, 23
- White Pigeon, 53
- White Pine, 53, 66, 95, 102, 112
- Whitepine, 14
- White Plains, 3, 23, 59, 79, 83, 106
- White Pond, 106
- Whiteriver, 5
- White River, 12, 70, 108, 130
- White River City, 14
- Whiterock, 83
- White Rock, 9, 30, 38, 47, 53, 56, 64, 70, 75, 106, 108, 112, 116
- White Rose, 33
- Whitesand, 59
- White Sands, 75
- Whitesburg, 23, 102
- White Shed, 116
- White Shield, 84
- Whiteside, 38
- White Signal, 75
- White Spot, 12
- White Springs, 20, 102
- White Star, 53
- White Stone, 106
- Whitestone, 23
- White Sulphur, 23
- White Sulphur Springs, 23, 33, 43, 66, 127
- Whitesville, 23, 43
- White Swan, 124
- Whitetail, 66, 75
- White Valley, 50
- Whitewash, 30
- Whitewater, 14, 33, 38, 64, 66, 75, 95, 130
- White Willow, 56
- White Wolf, 12
- White Woman Creek, 38
- Whitley, 43
- Why, 5
- Whynot, 59, 83
- Wichita, 36, 37, 38
- Wick, 127
- Wickliffe, 33, 43, 89, 122

- Widdowfield, 130
- Widdowville, 89
- Widen, 127
- Wide Ruins, 5
- Widowville,
- Wigwam, 102
- Wilburton, 91
- Wildcat, 43, 118, 127, 130
- Wild Cat, 14
- Wildcat Corner, 122
- Wildcat Point, 93
- Wild Cherry, 9
- Wilderness, 64, 122, 124
- Wildflower, 12
- Wild Goose, 124
- Wildhorse, 93
- Wild Horse, 14, 116
- Wild Meadow, 127
- Wild Rice, 84
- Wildrose, 12, 84
- Wilds, 56
- Wildwood, 12, 20, 23, 30, 43, 53, 56, 59, 64, 71, 74, 95, 112, 116, 118
- Wiley, 14, 23, 53, 122 ,127, 130
- Wilkes Barre, 99
- Will-O-The-Wisp, 14
- William, 127
- William Mountain, 127
- William Penn, 116
- Williams, 38
- Williamsburg, 3, 14, 17, 20, 30, 33, 36, 38, 45, 47, 50, 53, 59, 64, 66, 75, 83, 89, 95, 102, 112, 122, 127
- Williams Gulf, 9
- Williamson, 23
- Williamstown, 3, 33, 36, 38, 50, 64, 74, 89, 119
- Williamsville, 17, 50, 59
- Willoughby, 89
- Willow, 9, 30, 53, 83, 93
- Willow Beach, 5
- Willow Bend, 127
- Willow Branch, 33
- Willowbrook, 30

- Willow Brook, 12, 64
- Willow Chute, 43
- Willow City, 84, 116
- Willowcreek, 95
- Willow Creek, 12, 56, 75, 130
- Willow Creek Crossing, 12
- Willowdale, 38, 50
- Willowdell, 86
- Willow Forks, 95
- Willow Grove, 17, 47, 70, 74, 102, 112, 116, 122
- Willow Hill, 30, 102
- Willow Island, 68, 127
- Willow Lake, 108
- Willow Mountain, 75
- Willow Oak, 20
- Willow Point, 12, 70, 119
- Willow Ridge, 83
- Willow River, 56
- Willow Run, 17
- Willows, 12, 59
- Willow Springs, 3, 5, 12, 30, 64, 75, 83, 95, 102, 116, 130
- Willowtown, 70
- Willow Valley, 12, 33
- Willow View, 93
- Wilmington, 16, 30, 56, 80(2), 83
- Wilson, 16, 33, 38, 43, 47, 53, 56, 64, 70, 71, 83, 93, 102, 116, 124, 127, 130, 130
- Wilsonburg, 127
- Wilson City, 64
- Wilson Corner, 12
- Wilson Creek, 70, 124
- Wilson Crossroads, 106
- Wilsondale, 127
- Wilson Grove, 12
- Wilson Hill, 112
- Wilson Junction, 14
- Wilson Mill, 47
- Wilsons Corner, 102
- Wilsons Creek, 64
- Wilson Springs, 122
- Wilson Station, 112
- Wilsontown, 127
- Wilsonville, 16, 23, 30, 68, 83, 102
- Wilson's Mills, 83
- Wimbledon, 84
- Wimp, 12
- Winchester, 12, 16, 23, 26, 30, 33, 36, 39, 47, 50, 64, 70, 71, 89, 93, 95, 110, 112, 116, 120, 122, 124, 130
- Wind Blow, 83
- Winder, 23
- Windfall, 33
- Window Rock, 5
- Wind River, 130(2)
- Wind Rock, 95
- Windsor, 122
- Windsor Castle, 102
- Windy City, 112
- Windy Curve, 64
- Windy Gap, 26, 83
- Windy Hill, 116
- Windyville, 64
- Winesap, 112
- Wing, 9, 84
- Winifred, 39, 66
- Wink, 116
- Winnebago, 56
- Winnemucca, 70
- Winner, 56, 64, 108
- Winona, 5, 26, 39, 53, 56, 59, 64, 71, 89, 95, 106, 116, 124,1 27
- Winona Springs, 9
- Winslow, 5, 9, 30, 33, 45, 64, 68, 95, 112
- Winslow West, 5
- Winston, 47, 64, 66, 75, 95, 122, 124
- Winston-Salem, 80, 83
- Winstonville, 59
- Winter, 56, 127, 130
- Winter Beach, 20
- Winterboro, 3
- Winter Garden, 20
- Winter Gardens, 12
- Wintergreen 83
- Winter Harbor, 45

- Winter Haven, 20, 116
- Winterhaven, 12
- Winter Hill, 50
- Winter Park, 14, 20
- Winters, 12
- Wintersburg, 5
- Winterseat, 106
- Winterset, 34, 36, 89
- Winter Springs, 20
- Wintersville, 64
- Winterville, 23, 45, 59, 83, 95, 106
- Winterville, 23, 45, 59, 83, 95, 122
- Wire Bridge, 23
- Wisconsin, 40, 127
- Wisconsin Dells, 130
- Wisconsin Rapids, 130
- Wisdom, 66
- Wise, 36, 53, 106, 116, 122, 125
- Wise River, 66
- Witch Creek, 12
- Witch Hazel, 95
- Wolf, 12, 36, 39, 130(2)
- Wolf Bayou, 9
- Wolf City, 116
- Wolf Creek, 3, 30, 39, 66, 89, 95, 108, 112, 130
- Wolf Crossing, 53
- Wolfe, 56, 64, 93, 127, 130
- Wolf Lake, 30, 53, 56
- Wolflake, 33
- Wolf Lodge, 26
- Wolf Mountain, 83
- Wolf Pen, 89, 127
- Wolfpen, 89
- Wolf Point, 66
- Wolf Prairie, 66
- Wolf Run, 127
- Wolfs Corner, 102
- Wolf Springs, 3, 59
- Wolfsville, 47
- Wolf Trap, 122
- Wolquarry, 9
- Wolverine, 26, 53, 95, 112
- Wonder, 95

- Wood-Ridge, 74
- Wood, 26, 64, 70, 108
- Woodbridge, 16
- Woodbridge Corner, 45
- Woodchoppertown, 102
- Woodcliff, 2, 68
- Wooddale, 17
- Wooddlawn, 39
- Woodenhawk, 17
- Wooden Hills, 9
- Wooden Shoe Village, 53
- Woodford, 12, 30, 93, 106, 1 19, 122, 130
- Wood Hill, 64
- Wood Lake, 68
- Woodland, 12, 17, 26, 30, 56, 59
- Woodland Hills, 9
- Woodlandville, 64
- Woodlawn, 64
- Woodleaf, 12
- Wood Place, 66
- Woodridge, 64
- Wood River, 68
- Woodrow, 83
- Woods, 39, 53, 93, 95
- Woods Corner, 104
- Woods Haven, 17
- Woodshaven, 17
- Woodside, 12, 30, 66
- Wood Springs, 5, 59
- Woodstick, 16
- Woodsville, 71
- Wood Trap, 5
- Wood Village, 95
- Woodville, 12, 16, 20, 23, 30, 64, 66
- Woodyard, 30
- Woody Creek, 14
- Wool Market, 59
- Woolstock, 34, 36
- Worcester, 48, 64, 119
- Workman, 106
- Workmans Circle Camp, 50
- Workmore, 23
- Worms, 68

- Wounded Knee, 108
- Wren, 3, 36, 59, 89, 95
- Wrens, 23
- Wyandott, 51
- Wyanoke, 9
- Wynantskill, 79
- Wynona, 93
- Wynot, 68
- Wyoming, 17, 30, 36, 53, 56, 60, 61, 68, 74, 79, 102, 104, 118, 127, 130(2)
- Wyoming City, 127

-X-

- X-Prairie, 59
- Xenia, 14, 30, 36,3 9
- Xenophon, 112

-Y-

- Yaak, 66
- Yaddo, 79
- Yakima, 124
- Yakt, 66
- Yampa, 14
- Yankee, 75
- Yankee Blade, 70
- Yankee Orchards, 50
- Yankee Run, 39
- Yankeetown, 20, 33, 56, 112, 122
- Yankee Town, 33
- Yaphank, 79
- Yarmony, 14
- Yarn Mill, 106
- Yarrow, 64
- Yazoo, 59
- Yazoo City, 59
- Y City, 9
- Yeehaw, 20
- Yell, 112

- Yelling Settlement, 3
- Yellowbanks, 33
- Yellow Banks, 9, 30
- Yellow Bayou, 9, 43
- Yellow Bluff, 20
- Yellow Creek, 30, 83
- Yellowdirt, 23
- Yellow Gap, 83
- Yellow Hammer Mill, 5
- Yellowhorse Ford, 108
- Yellow House, 102
- Yellowjacket, 26
- Yellow Jacket, 14
- Yellow Pine, 3, 26, 43
- Yellow River, 36
- Yellow Spring, 102
- Yellow Springs, 89, 112
- Yellowstone, 130
- Yellow sulphur, 122
- Yellowtown, 89
- Yellow Water, 20
- Yellville, 5, 9
- Yelping Hill, 15, 16
- Ynot, 66
- Yoeman, 33
- Yoemans, 23, 36
- Yonkers, 23, 79
- Yorba Linda, 12
- York, 5, 23, 26, 30, 68, 84
- Yorktown, 33
- Yorktown Post Office, 84
- Yosemite Forks, 12
- Yosemite Village, 12
- You Bet, 12
- Young America, 33, 56, 130
- Youngers Store, 122
- Youngstown, 12, 30, 33
- Youth, 23
- Ypsilanti, 23, 53, 84
- Yreka, 12
- Yucatan, 56
- Yucatan Landing, 43
- Yucca, 3
- Yucca Grove, 12

- Yucca Inn, 12
- Yucca Valley, 12
- Yukon, 9, 64, 93, 102, 112
- Yukon Saddle, 66
- Yuma, 14, 53

-Z-

- Zachary, 43
- Zanesville, 30, 33, 86, 89
- Zap, 66, 84
- Zee, 43
- Zeeland, 53, 84
- Zell, 108
- Zemp, 106
- Zenith, 39, 84, 112, 124
- Zenith Heights, 53
- Zenners, 102

- Zeno, 102
- Zerbe, 102
- Zerby, 102
- Zero, 59,66
- Zig, 64
- Zigzag, 95
- Zim, 56
- Zinc, 9
- Zincville, 93
- Zip City, 3
- Zipperlandville, 116
- Zook, 39
- Zuck, 89
- Zugg, 43
- Zulu, 33
- Zumbro Falls, 56
- Zurich, 12, 39, 66
- Zylks, 43
- Zzyzx, 12

INDEX OF INTERESTING NAMES IN KENTUCKY

-A-

- Aaron, 167
- Aberdeen, 157
- Abigail, 235
- Access, 160
- Acorn, 235
- Acton, 241
- Adaburg, 229
- Adair, 183
- Adams, 205

- Add, 216
- Adele, 224
- Adeline, 205
- Aden, 160
- Adolphus, 145
- Aetnaville, 229
- Aflex, 233
- Agawam, 165
- Ages, 185
- Agnes, 210
- Airedale, 205

- Airport Gardens, 232
- Albany, 166
- Alberta, 186
- Albia, 235
- Alexandria, 159(2), 198
- Alhambra, 235
- Aliceton, 153
- Allais, 232
- Allegheny Mine, 233
- Allegre, 242
- Allen, 176
- Almo, 158
- Alpha, 167
- Alphoretta, 176
- Alpine, 235
- Alta, 229
- Alton, 145
- Altro, 154
- Alum Springs, 153
- Alvin, 176
- Amandaville, 168
- Amba, 176,176
- Amelia, 202
- Ammie, 166
- Amos, 145
- Anchorage, 195
- Anco, 199
- Anderson, 210, 242
- Anderson City, 145
- Anna, 245
- Anna Lynn, 178
- Anneta, 181
- Annville, 191
- Ano, 235
- Anthoston, 188
- Antioch, 145, 186, 247
- Anton, 190
- Apex, 163
- Apple Grove, 146
- Arat, 168
- Arch, 184
- Argentum, 183
- Argillite, 183
- Argo, 233

- Argyle, 161
- Arista, 241
- Arjay, 148
- Ark, 148
- Arkansas, 176
- Arkle, 203
- Arlington, 159, 213
- Arrow, 233
- Arthurmabel, 214
- Artville, 221
- Arvel, 205
- Ary, 232
- Asa, 197
- Ashbrook, 145
- Ashcamp, 233
- Asher, 206
- Ashers Fork, 166
- Ashland, 151(2), 236
- Ashville, 195
- Askew, 163
- Aspen Grove, 159
- Asphalt, 170
- Atchison, 241
- Athens, 174
- Atlanta, 203, 204
- Atoka, 153
- Attilla, 203
- Auburn,
- Augusta, 153(2), 216
- Ault, 171
- Aurora, 215
- Austerlitz, 150
- Austin, 146
- Auxier, 176
- Avawam, 232
- Avon, 174
- Awe, 208

-B-

- Bachelors Rest, 231
- Back, 221
- Badger, 241

- Bagdad, 239(2)
- Bailey Creek, 185
- Baileys Switch, 203
- Bald Eagle, 147
- Bald Hill, 175
- Baldrock, 204
- Ballard, 145, 221
- Ballardsville, 230
- Balls Fork, 201
- Balltown, 228
- Baltimore, 181
- Bancroft, 195, 227
- Bandana, 146
- Bangor, 237
- Bank Lick, 198
- Banks, 207
- Banner, 176(2)
- Baptist, 247
- Baralto, 174
- Barbourville, 202, 203(2)
- Bards Hill, 227
- Bardstown, 227, 234, 236
- Bardwell, 159
- Barefoot, 228
- Bark Camp, 247
- Barlow, 146
- Barnrock, 197
- Barnyard, 203
- Barren River, 245
- Barrier, 246
- Barterville, 228
- Bascorn, 171
- Basil, 144
- Basin Spring, 155
- Baskett, 188
- Bass, 161
- Bath, 202
- Battle, 245
- Battle Run, 175
- Battletown, 221
- Bayou, 209
- Beagle, 159
- Bear Branch, 206
- Bear Fork, 233

- Beartown, 171
- Bearville, 199
- Bear Wallow, 187
- Bearwallow, 224, 245
- Beatyville, 205
- Beauty, 216
- Beaver, 176
- Beaver Bottom, 233
- Beaver Creek, 233
- Beaver Dam, 228, 229
- Beaver Junction, 176
- Beaverlick, 149
- Beckley, 195
- Becks Store,
- Beda, 229
- Bedford, 243
- Bee, 187
- Beech, 154
- Beech Bottom, 161
- Beechburg, 175
- Beech Creek, 227
- Beech Grove, 156, 160, 220
- Beechland, 195, 210, 221
- Beechmont, 227
- Beechville, 223
- Beechwood, 195, 230
- Beechy, 183
- Beefhide, 207, 233
- Bee Lick, 235
- Bee Spring, 170
- Beetle, 160
- Bel Air, 165
- Belcher, 233
- Belfry, 233
- Bell City, 171, 181
- Bellcraft, 207
- Bellefonte, 183
- Belle Point, 205
- Belleview, 149
- Bellevue, 149, 198
- Bell Farm, 220
- Bells Run, 229
- Belltown, 215
- Bellview, 189

- Bellville, 246
- Bellwood, 228
- Belton, 227
- Ben Bow, 205
- Bengal, 241
- Benham, 185(2)
- Benito, 185
- Bent, 235
- Benton, 215(2)
- Berea, 212, 213
- Berkley, 159
- Berlin, 153
- Bernice, 166
- Berry, 186
- Berry Store, 146
- Berrytown, 195
- Bertha Station, 203
- Bertrum Mountain, 246
- Bethanna, 214
- Bethany, 195, 247
- Bethel, 147, 196
- Bethelridge, 161
- Bethesda, 246
- Bethlehem, 189
- Betsey, 246
- Betsy Layne, 176(2)
- Betty, 200
- Beulah, 189, 190
- Beulah Heights, 220
- Beverly, 148, 163
- Beverly Hills, 153
- Bevier, 227
- Biddle, 238
- Big Bone, 149
- Big Branch, 207, 233
- Big Card, 233
- Big Creek, 166
- Big Eddy, 177
- Big Fork, 206
- Bighill, 213
- Big Laurel, 185
- Big Rock, 206
- Big Sandy, 151
- Big Spring, 155

- Bigstone, 171
- Big Windy, 187
- Big Woods, 221
- Billows, 204, 236
- Bimble, 203
- Birdie, 145
- Birdsville, 209
- Birmingham, 215
- Black Bottom, 185
- Black Creek, 234
- Blackey, 202, 207
- Black Gnat, 182, 241
- Black Gold, 170
- Black Hawk, 157, 242
- Black Jack, 189, 240
- Blackmont, 148
- Black Mountain, 185
- Black Rock, 181
- Blacks Crossroads, 150
- Black Snake, 148
- Blackwater, 204, 221
- Blairs Mills, 224
- Blanche, 148
- Blandville, 146
- Blaze, 224
- Bliss, 144
- Bloomfield, 228(2)
- Bloss, 236
- Blowing Springs, 182, 187
- Bloyd, 182
- Bluebank, 175
- Blueberry Hill, 174
- Blue Diamond, 232
- Blue Gap,
- Blue Grass, 213
- Blue Grass No 3, 232
- Blue Heron, 220
- Bluehole, 166
- Blue John, 233, 235
- Blue Level, 245
- Blue Lick, 209
- Blue Moon, 176(2)
- Blue River, 176
- Blue Spring, 242

- Bluestone, 237
- Bluff Boom, 182
- Bluff City, 188
- Bluff Spring, 163
- Blythe, 223
- Board Tree, 233
- Boat,
- Boaz, 181
- Bobs Creek, 185
- Bobtown, 213, 233, 235
- Bogie, 172
- Bohon, 222
- Boiling Spring, 245
- Bonanza, 176
- Bond, 191
- Bondville, 222
- Boneyville, 209
- Bonita, 247
- Bonny, 224
- Bonnyman, 232
- Boone, 236
- Boone Furnace, 160
- Boonesboro, 213
- Booneville, 230
- Boons Camp, 197
- Booth, 184, 247
- Boreing, 204
- Boston, 157, 170, 195, 228, 231
- Botto, 166
- Bottom Fork, 207
- Boundary Oak, 203
- Bourbon, 233, 235
- Bourbon Springs, 228
- Bow, 168
- Bowling Green, 156, 192, 210, 244, 245
- Bowlingtown, 232
- Boxville, 243
- Boyd, 186
- Bracht, 198
- Bradley, 214
- Brady, 237
- Brandenburg, 220
- Brandy Lick, 208
- Brandywine Creek, 217
- Brazil, 191
- Breckinridge, 186
- Breeding, 144
- Bremen, 225
- Briartown, 245
- Bridgeville, 153
- Brien, 215
- Briensburg, 215
- Brightshade, 166
- Brightside,
- Brinkley, 202
- Britmart, 242
- Broad Bottom, 233
- Broadhead, 236
- Broadway, 170
- Brock, 204
- Bromo, 236
- Brooklyn, 157, 196
- Brooksville, 153(2)
- Browder, 227
- Browns Crossroads, 167
- Brownsville, 170
- Brown Town, 227
- Bruin, 171
- Brush Grove, 245
- Brushy Fork, 171
- Brutus, 166
- Bryan, 238
- Bryants Store, 203
- Buchanan, 205
- Buckeye, 180
- Buck Grove, 221
- Buckhorn, 232
- Buckingham, 176
- Buena Vista, 180, 186, 208, 215
- Buffalo, 203, 242
- Buffalo Fork, 210
- Bug, 167
- Buggytown, 213
- Bugtussle, 223
- Bulan, 232
- Bull Creek, 176
- Bullitsville, 149

- Bullitt, 155
- Bummer, 236
- Bunker Hill, 150
- Burg, 224
- Burgin, 222
- Burkesville, 167(2), 219
- Burlington, 148,149
- Burna, 209
- Burnetta, 233
- Burning Fork, 214
- Burning Springs, 166
- Burnside, 234, 237
- Burnwell, 233
- Burr, 236
- Bush, 204
- Bushong, 223
- Bushtown, 222
- Busy, 232
- Butchertown, 161
- Butler, 231
- Butlersville, 145
- Butterfly, 232
- Buttonsberry, 220
- Bybee, 213
- Bypro, 176(2)

-C-

- Cabot, 183
- Cadiz, 218, 242
- Cains Store, 235
- Cairo, 188
- Calaboose, 247
- Caldwell, 231
- Caledonia, 242
- Calf Creek, 216
- Calhoun, 220
- California, 159
- Callaway, 148, 203
- Calloway Crossing, 172
- Calvary, 215
- Calvert City, 215
- Calvin, 148

- Camargo, 224
- Camelia, 219
- Campbellsville, 241(2)
- Camp Creek, 233
- Camp Grounds, 204
- Camp Pleasant, 177
- Camp Springs, 159
- Campton, 247
- Canada, 233
- Canby, 230
- Cane Creek, 204
- Cane Valley, 144
- Caney, 224
- Caney Creek, 200
- Caney Mound, 243
- Cannel City, 224
- Cannon, 203
- Cannons Point, 155
- Canoe, 154
- Canton, 242
- Cantown, 161
- Canyon Falls, 205
- Carbondale, 190
- Carbon Glow, 207
- Carcassonne, 207
- Cardinal, 148, 203
- Cardwell, 245
- Carl, 163
- Carlisle, 222, 228(2)
- Carmack, 211
- Carpenter, 247
- Carr Creek, 200
- Carrie, 202
- Carrollton, 159
- Carson, 160
- Carter, 160
- Cartersville, 180
- Cary,
- Casey, 148, 157
- Cash, 187
- Castle, 216
- Catalpa, 205
- Cat Creek, 234
- Catherine, 238

- Catlettsburg, 150
- Catnip, 196
- Cave City, 146(2)
- Cave Hill, 245
- Cave Ridge, 223
- Cave Spring, 155, 210
- Cave Springs, 210
- Cawood, 185(2)
- Cecil, 219
- Cecilia, 184
- Cedar Bluff, 157
- Cedarcrest, 246
- Cedarcrest,
- Cedar Flat, 221
- Cedar Flats, 223
- Cedar Grove, 156, 235, 242
- Cedar Knob, 167, 246
- Cedar Point, 230, 242
- Cedar Spring, 170
- Cedar Springs, 145
- Cedarville, 233
- Center, 223
- Centerfield, 230
- Center Point, 223
- Centertown, 229
- Centerville, 150, 157, 174
- Central City, 225, 226
- Ceralvo, 229
- Cerulean, 242
- Chad, 186
- Chalybeate, 170
- Chance, 144
- Chandlers Chapel, 210
- Chapel Hill, 145
- Chaplin, 228
- Charleston, 190
- Charley, 205
- Charters, 208
- Cherokee, 205
- Cherry, 158
- Cherry Grove, 180
- Chestnut, 197
- Chestnutburg, 166
- Chestnut Gap, 231

- Chestnut Grove, 239
- Chevrolet, 186
- Chevy Chase, 174
- Chicken Bristle, 209
- Chilton, 161
- Christianburg, 239
- Christine, 144
- Christy, 237
- Church, 181
- Church Hill, 163
- Cimota City, 219
- Cinda, 206
- Cisco, 214
- Clabber Bottom, 238
- Clare, 145
- Clarence, 235
- Clarks Corner, 223
- Clarkson, 181
- Clay, 246
- Clay City, 234
- Clay Fork, 171
- Claysville, 186
- Clay Village, 239
- Clear Creek Furnace, 147
- Clear Creek Springs, 148
- Clear Springs, 181
- Cleaton, 227
- Cleopatra, 220
- Clermont, 156(2)
- Cliff, 176
- Cliffside, 151
- Clifty, 242
- Climax, 236
- Clinton, 189
- Clintonville, 150
- Clio, 247
- Closplint, 186
- Cloud Crossing, 215
- Clover, 186
- Clover Bottom, 191
- Cloverdale, 151
- Cloverport, 155(2)
- Clovertown, 186
- Cloyds Landing, 168

- Clutts, 186
- Co-Operative, 220
- Coal Run Village, 233
- Coalton, 151
- Cobblers Knob, 155
- Cobhill, 172
- Cody, 200
- Coe, 223
- Cofer, 223
- Cogswell, 237
- Coiltown, 190
- Coin, 233, 235
- Coldiron, 186
- Cold Spring, 159
- Cold Springs, 160, 221
- Coldstream, 195
- Coldwater, 158
- College Hill, 213
- Colts, 186
- Columbia, 144
- Columbiatown, 233
- Columbus, 174, 189(2), 192
- Comargo, 220
- Combs, 232
- Comer, 220
- Commissary Corner, 149
- Concord, 175, 181, 208(2), 219, 231, 235
- Confederate, 211
- Confluence, 206
- Conrad, 235
- Consolation, 239
- Constance, 149
- Constantine, 155
- Cooksville, 181
- Cooktown, 146
- Cool Springs, 229
- Cooperstown, 210
- Coral Hill, 146
- Coraville, 188
- Corbin, 147, 203, 247
- Cordell, 205
- Cordova, 180
- Corinth, 180, 210
- Cork, 223
- Corn Creek, 243
- Cornelius, 191
- Corners, 155
- Cornishville, 222
- Corydon, 188(2), 190, 247
- Costelow, 210
- Cote Brilliant, 159
- Cottageville, 208
- Cottle, 224
- Cottonburg, 213
- Covington, 149, 159, 197(2), 198
- Cow Creek, 172
- Cowcreek, 231
- Cow Valley,
- Coxs Creek, 228
- Crab Orchard, 179, 208, 209(2), 230
- Crafts Colly, 207
- Craintown, 153
- Crane Nest, 203
- Cranetown, 238
- Cranks, 184, 186
- Craycraft, 144
- Creekmore, 220
- Creekville, 166, 206
- Creelsboro, 237
- Cressy, 172
- Crest, 184
- Crestwood, 229, 230
- Crittenden, 180
- Croakers, 245
- Crockett, 148, 224
- Crockettsville, 154
- Crocus, 144
- Cromona, 207
- Crooked Creek, 233
- Cropper, 239
- Crossland, 158
- Crossroad, 210
- Cross Road, 211
- Crow, 234
- Crowcreek,
- Crown, 207
- Crowtown, 157

- Crow Valley, 213
- Cruise, 204
- Crum, 208
- Crummies, 184, 186
- Crystal, 172, 205
- Crystal Falls,
- Cuba, 181
- Cubage, 148
- Cub Run, 187
- Cull, 230
- Cumberland, 186
- Cumberland City, 167
- Cupio, 156
- Curdsville, 170
- Curlew, 243
- Currentsville, 150
- Curtis, 223
- Custer, 155
- Cutshin, 186, 206
- Cutuno, 214
- Cuzick, 213
- Cyclone, 223
- Cynthiana, 186(2)
- Cyrus, 214

-D-

- Dada, 176
- Daisy, 232
- Dal, 247
- Dale, 214
- Dalesburg, 154, 175
- Dan, 221, 229
- Dana, 176
- Daniel Boone, 190
- Danville, 148, 151, 152(2), 153(2), 157, 179, 198, 230
- Darnell, 242
- Darthoe, 204
- Datha, 191
- Davella, 216
- David, 176(2)
- Davisburg, 148

- Davis Hill, 153
- Dawson Springs, 190(2)
- Day, 207
- Daysboro, 247
- Daysville, 242
- Dayton, 159(2)
- Deane, 207
- Decide, 167
- Decoy, 200
- Deep Creek, 222
- Deephole, 205
- Deer Lick, 166, 210
- Defeated Creek, 207
- Defiance, 232
- Defries, 187
- Dekoven, 243
- Delaware, 170
- Delia, 180
- Delphia, 232
- Delta, 246
- Delvinta, 205
- Dema, 176, 202
- Democrat, 207(2)
- Demplytown, 230
- Denmark, 238
- Dennis, 210
- Dent, 238
- Denver, 197
- Depoy, 226(2)
- Derby, 246
- Desda, 167
- Dewdrop, 171
- Diablock, 232
- Diamond, 246
- Diamond Springs, 210
- Dice, 232
- Dimple, 157
- Dingus, 224
- Dishman Springs, 203
- Disputant, 236
- Divide, 186, 206
- Dixie, 188, 214, 247
- Dixie Plantation, 174
- Dixon, 246

- Dixon Town, 196
- Dizney, 186
- Dock, 176
- Doe Creek, 172
- Dogcreek, 187
- Dogtown, 215
- Dog Trot, 221
- Dog Walk, 209
- Dogwalk, 229
- Dogwood, 163, 181
- Doorway, 232
- Dorema, 233
- Dorena, 235
- Dorton, 233
- Do Stop, 181
- Dot, 210
- Double Culvert, 238
- Douglas, 233
- Douglas Hill, 195
- Douglas Town, 168
- Dover, 217
- Draffin, 233
- Drakesboro, 226(2)
- Drew, 202
- Drift, 176
- Dripping Spring, 170
- Drip Rock, 172, 191
- Drum, 233, 235
- Dry Creek, 202
- Drydock, 145
- Dry Fork, 146, 233
- Dryhill, 206
- Dry Ridge, 180
- Dublin, 181
- Dubre, 168
- Duckers, 247
- Duckrun, 247
- Duco, 214
- Duff, 181
- Dukedom, 180, 181
- Dukes, 183
- Duluth, 213
- Dundee, 229
- Dunmore, 227

- Dwale, 176
- Dwarf, 232

-E-

- Eagle Hill, 230
- Eagle Station, 160
- Earlington, 190(2)
- Earls, 227
- East Bardstown, 228
- East Cairo, 146
- East Diamond, 190
- Easterday, 160
- Eastern, 176
- East Fork, 223
- East Jenkins, 207
- East Pineville, 148
- East Point, 176,197
- East Union, 228
- Eastview, 184
- Ebenezer, 222, 223, 227
- Ebon, 224
- Echo, 223
- Eddyville, 210, 211(2)
- Eden, 157
- Edgewater, 233
- Edgewood, 148, 198
- Edmonton, 222
- Edna, 214
- Edsel, 171
- Edwards, 210
- Egypt, 191
- Eighty Eight, 146
- Ekron, 221
- Elba, 220
- Elfie, 157
- Eli, 238
- Elihu, 233, 235
- Elizabeth Station, 150
- Elizabethtown, 183, 184(2), 220, 221
- Elizaville, 175(2)
- Elk Creek, 240
- Elkfork, 224

- Elk Horn, 241
- Elkhorn City, 233(2)
- Elkin, 165
- Elko, 170
- Elkton, 241, 242(2)
- Ella, 144
- Ellen, 205
- Elliottville, 237
- Elmburg, 239
- Elmendorf, 174
- Elmrock, 200
- Elmville, 177
- Elmwood, 246
- Elna, 197
- Elsie, 214
- Elsmere, 198
- Elva, 215, 219
- Emanuel, 203
- Emberton, 223
- Eminence, 189
- Emma, 176
- Emmalena, 202
- Empire, 163
- Endee, 231
- English, 160
- Ennis, 227
- Enoch, 205
- Eolia, 207
- Equality, 229
- Era, 163
- Ermine, 207
- Erose, 203
- Escondia, 150
- Essie, 206
- Estesburg, 235
- Estill, 176
- Esto, 238
- Etna, 235
- Etty, 233
- Eudora, 187
- Eunice, 144
- Euterpe, 188
- Evanston, 154
- Eve, 182

- Eveleigh, 181
- Evelyn, 172, 205
- Ever, 214
- Evergreen, 177, 205
- Eversole, 231
- Evona, 161
- Ewing, 175(2)
- Ewington, 224
- Exie, 182
- Ezel, 224

-F-

- Fair Acres, 221
- Fairbanks, 181(2), 230
- Fairdealing, 215
- Fairfield, 228
- Fairland, 167
- Fairplay, 144
- Fairview, 145, 151, 157, 163, 170, 175, 198, 211(2), 247
- Fairview Hill, 160
- Falcon, 214
- Falling Branch, 181
- Fall Rock, 166
- Fallsburg, 233
- Falls of Rough, 155, 181
- Falmouth, 231(2)
- Fancy Farm, 180, 181
- Farmdale, 177
- Farmers, 237
- Farmers Mill, 186
- Farmersville, 157
- Farmville, 175
- Faye, 170, 171
- Faywood, 247
- Feathersburg, 144
- Federal, 233
- Fedscreek, 233
- Feliciana, 181
- Felty, 166
- Ferguson, 235
- Fern Creek, 195

- Ferndale, 148
- Fernleaf, 217
- Ferrell, 233
- Fiddle Bow, 190
- Fidelio,
- Fidelity, 220
- Field, 148
- Fies, 190
- Fillmore, 159, 205
- Fincastle, 205
- Finchville, 239
- Firebrick, 208
- Fisher, 155
- Fisherville, 195
- Fiskburg, 198
- Fisty, 201
- Five Forks, 205
- Fivemile, 154
- Five Points, 158
- Fixer, 205
- Flag Fork, 177
- Flag Spring, 159
- Flat, 247
- Flat Fork, 214
- Flatgap, 197
- Flat Lick, 203
- Flat Rock, 157, 157, 220, 221, 236, 240
- Flatwood, 144
- Flatwoods, 151(2), 182(2), 183, 233
- Flat Woods, 166
- Fleet, 145
- Fleming, 207
- Fleming-Neon, 207
- Flemingsburg, 174, 175(2)
- Flemingsburg Junction, 175
- Flint, 207
- Flint Hill, 184
- Flint Springs, 229
- Flintville, 154
- Flippin, 223
- Floral, 183
- Florence, 149(2)
- Florress, 224

- Flossie, 246
- Floyd, 235
- Floydsburg, 230
- Fogertown, 166
- Fonthill, 238
- Foraker, 214
- Forerst Hill, 219
- Forest Hills, 198, 233
- Forest Springs, 145
- Forestville, 187
- Forkland, 153
- Forks of Elkhorn, 177
- Forkton, 223
- Fort Campbell North, 162, 163
- Fort Knox, (Nelson County) 228
- Fort Mitchell, 198
- Fort Spring, 174
- Fort Wright, 198
- Fount, 203
- Fountain Run, 223
- Four Corners, 180, 184
- Fourmile, 148
- Four Oaks, 231
- Fourseam, 232
- Fox, 172
- Fox Chase, 156
- Fox Creek, 145
- Foxport, 175
- Foxtown, 191
- Fragrant, 181
- Frakes, 148
- Frances, 167
- Francisville, 149
- Frankfort, 164, 165, 167, 170, 171, 174, 177(2), 179(2), 182, 192(2), 212, 221, 236, 238, 239, 247
- Franklin, 239, 240
- Fredonia, 157
- Fredville, 214
- Freeburn, 233
- Freedom, 146, 238
- Freemont,
- Freetown, 223
- Free Union, 246

- Fremont, 219
- Frenchburg, 221
- Fresh Meadows, 186
- Frew, 206
- Friendship, 157
- Frisby, 246
- Fritz, 214
- Frogtown, 174, 215
- Frogue, 168
- Frost, 183
- Frozen Creek, 154
- Fruit Hill, 163
- Fry, 182
- Fryer, 157
- Fulgham, 189
- Fulton, 178(2)
- Funston, 220
- Furnace, 172
- Fusonia, 232
- Future City, 219

-G-

- Gadberry, 144
- Gage, 146
- Gainesville, 145
- Galdia, 214
- Gallup, 205
- Galveston, 1769(2)
- Gamaliel, 223
- Gandertown, 215
- Gapcreek, 246
- Gap in Knob, 156
- Gapville, 214
- Gardenside, 174
- Garden Village, 233
- Gardner, 166
- Gardnersville, 231
- Garfield, 155
- Garrard, 166
- Garrett, 200, 221
- Garrison, 208
- Gascon, 223

- Gasper, 210
- Gates, 237
- Geddes, 240
- Gee, 145
- Geneva, 188, 209
- Georges Creek, 205
- Georgetown, 186, 217, 238(2)
- Germantown, 153
- German Town, 195
- Gertrude, 153
- Gest, 189
- Gethsemane, 228
- Gifford, 214
- Gilbertsville, 215
- Gilmore, 247
- Gilpin, 161
- Gimlet, 171
- Ginseng, 203
- Girdler, 203
- Girkin, 245
- Glade, 215
- Glasgow, 146, 237
- Gleanings, 203
- Glenarm, 230
- Glo, 176
- Globe, 160
- Goddard, 175
- Goforth, 231
- Goldbug, 247
- Gold City, 240
- Golden Ash, 186
- Golden Pond, 242
- Golo, 181
- Gomez, 171
- Goodluck, 223
- Goodman, 233
- Goodnight, 146
- Goodwater, 235
- Goody, 233
- Goose Creek, 166, 195
- Goose Rock, 166
- Gordon, 207
- Gordon Ford, 224
- Gordonsville, 210

- Gordonville, 210
- Goshen 230
- Grab, 182
- Grace, 166
- Gracey, 163
- Grade, 235
- Graham, 227
- Grand Rivers, 209, 215
- Grandview, 170, 223
- Grannie, 247
- Grant, 198
- Grapevine, 190
- Grassland, 151, 170
- Grassy, 206
- Grassy Creek, 224
- Grassy Lick, 224
- Gratz, 230
- Gravel Switch, 215
- Gray, 203
- Grayfox, 214
- Gray Hawk, 191
- Grayson, 160
- Grayson Springs, 181
- Greasy Creek, 233
- Greeley, 205
- Green, 171
- Green Acres, 153, 215
- Greenacres, 211
- Greenbriar, 215, 228
- Greencastle, 245
- Greendale, 174
- Green Grove, 168
- Greenhaven, 230
- Green Hill, 191
- Greenhill, 245
- Greenmount, 204
- Green Road, 203
- Greensburg, 182
- Greenup, 183
- Greenville, 220, 224, 225, 226
- Greenwood, 220, 231, 245
- Gregory, 246
- Gregoryville, 160
- Grove, 247

- Grove Center, 243
- Guage, 154
- Guffie, 220
- Gulnare, 233
- Gum Grove, 243
- Gum Sulphur, 236
- Gum Tree, 223
- Gunlock, 214
- Gus, 227
- Guthrie, 242(2)
- Guy, 245
- Gypsy, 214

-H-

- Habit, 170
- Hadensville, 242
- Hail, 235
- Hailwell, 189
- Halfway, 145, 146
- Halifax, 145
- Hall, 196, 202
- Hallie, 207
- Halls Store, 210
- Halo, 176
- Hamin, 237
- Hamlin, 158
- Hammacksville, 242
- Hammond, 203
- Hamner, 243
- Handshoe, 201(2)
- Handyville, 170
- Hanging Rock, 181
- Hannah, 205
- Happy, 232
- Happy Acre, 238
- Happy Landing, 213
- Happy Top, 172, 234
- Harbell, 148
- Hardburly, 232
- Hardcastle, 245
- Hardin, 215
- Harding, 243

- Hardinsburg, 154, 155(2)
- Hardin Springs, 184
- Hardmoney, 219
- Hardshell, 154
- Hardy, 233
- Hardyville, 146
- Hare, 204, 206
- Harlan, 184, 185(2)
- Harlan Crossroads, 223
- Harlan Gas, 186
- Harmony, 230
- Harmony Village, 230
- Harold, 176(2)
- Harper, 214
- Harper Crossroads, 157
- Harper Ford, 157
- Harpers, 147
- Harpers Ferry, 189
- Harps Hill, 227
- Harris, 208
- Harrisonville, 239
- Harrodsburg, 213, 222(2)
- Hartford, 228
- Hatfield, 233
- Hawesville, 183(2)
- Hays, 245
- Hays Crossing, 237
- Hazard, 198, 232
- Hazel, 157, 158, 243
- Hazel Green, 247
- Hazel Patch, 204
- Head of Grassy, 208
- Head of Linefork, 208
- Headquarters, 228
- Heater, 209
- Heath, 219
- Hebron, 149
- Heidelberg, 205
- Helechawa, 247
- Helena, 217
- Hell for Certain, 206(2)
- Hellier, 233
- Helm, 238
- Hemp Ridge, 239

- Henderson, 187, 188(2), 189, 234
- Henrietta, 197
- Henry Clay, 233
- Herd, 191
- Herman Valley, 243
- Hi-Acres, 174
- Hiatt, 236
- Hibernia, 241
- Hickman, 177
- Hickory, 181
- Hickory Corner, 181
- Hickory Flat, 240
- Hickory Grove, 145, 220, 224
- Hickory Hill, 195
- Hicksville, 181
- Hico, 158
- High Bridge, 196(2)
- High Falls, 247
- Highgrove, 228
- High Hickory, 187
- High Knob, 191
- Highland, 240
- Highland Springs, 146
- High Plains, 155
- High Plains Corner, 155
- High Point, 219
- Highsplint, 186
- Hightop, 204
- Highview, 229
- Highway, 167
- Hi Hat, 176
- Hilda, 237
- Hillgrove, 221
- Hillsdale,
- Hillside, 227, 240
- Hill Top, 175, 220, 221
- Hilltop, 180, 210
- Hillview, 170
- Hilo, 186
- Himyar, 203
- Hindman, 198(2), 199(2), 200(2), 201(2), 202(2)
- Hippo, 176
- Hittville, 235

- Hodgenville, 203
- Holbrook, 180
- Holiday Ford, 230
- Holland, 145
- Holliday, 224
- Hollow Bill, 210
- Hollybush, 202
- Hollyhill, 220
- Hollywood, 174
- Holy Cross, 215
- Honey Acre, 161
- Honeybee, 220
- Honey Fork, 233
- Honey Grove, 163
- Hooker, 166
- Hooktown, 228
- Hootentown, 165
- Hope, 147, 224
- Hopewell, 204
- Hopkinsville, 161, 162(2), 163(2)
- Horn Back Mill, 155
- Horntown, 238
- Horse Branch, 229
- Horse Cave, 186, 187
- Horse Creek, 151, 166, 204, 242(2)
- Horsemail, 157
- Hot Spot, 176, 208
- Houston, 154
- Hubble, 209
- Hueys Corner, 149
- Huff, 170
- Humble, 238
- Hummel, 236
- Hunnewell, 183
- Hunter, 176
- Hunters, 228
- Hunters Hollow, 156
- Hunter Town, 247
- Huntsville, 157
- Hurricane, 233
- Hurricane Hills, 228
- Hutch, 148
- Hyden, 206(2)
- Hydro, 245

- Hylton, 233

-I-

- Ibex, 171
- Ice, 208
- Ida, 167, 215
- Idamay, 205
- Independence, 198
- Index, 224
- Indian Creek, 233
- Indian Fields, 165
- Indian Hills, 177
- Indian Lake, 183
- Indian Valley, 181
- Inez, 216
- Ingleside, 146
- Inroad, 144
- Iola, 215
- Irad, 205
- Irma, 167
- Iron Hill, 160
- Iron Mound, 172
- Ironville, 151
- Irvine, 171, 172
- Island, 220
- Island City, 231
- Iuka, 209
- Ivan, 202
- Iverdale, 148
- Ivis, 202
- Ivor, 231
- Ivy Grove, 148
- Ivyton, 214

-J-

- Jabez, 238
- Jackson, 154(2), 198, 200, 222, 236
- Jacksonville, 150, 239
- Jackstown, 150
- Jamboree, 233

- Jamestown, 237
- Jarvis Store, 203
- Jason, 206, 242
- Jeff, 232
- Jeffersontown, 195
- Jeffersonville, 224
- Jeffrey, 223
- Jellico, 247
- Jenkins, 208
- Jeptha, 224
- Jeremiah, 208
- Jericho, 180, 189, 203, 224, 238
- Jerico, 210
- Jerusalem Ridge, 229
- Jessamine, 196
- Jetson, 157
- Jewel City, 190
- Jimhill, 232
- Jimtown, 150, 174, 245, 246
- Jingo, 229
- Jinks, 172
- Job, 216
- Joe Branch, 216, 247
- Joe Fork, 205
- Johnetta, 236
- Johns Run, 160
- Jolly, 246
- Jonancy, 233
- Joppa, 144
- Jordan, 178
- Josephine, 238
- Joy, 209
- Judio, 168
- Judy, 224, 234
- Jugville, 181
- Julip, 247
- Jumbo, 209
- Junction City, 153
- Junte, 239
- Justice, 210
- Justiceville, 233

-K-

- Kaliope, 206
- Kansas, 181
- Katharyn, 156
- Kathryn, 155
- Kties Creek, 166
- Kayjay, 203
- Keavy, 204
- Keene, 196
- Keenland, 195
- Kellacy, 224
- Kelly, 163
- Kennebec, 177
- Kennedy, 163
- Keno, 235
- Kensington, 149
- Kenton, 198
- Kerney, 214
- Kettle, 168
- Kettlecamp, 233
- Kettle Island, 148
- Kevil, 146
- Kewanee, 233
- Keysburg, 210
- Kidder, 246
- Kidds Store, 161
- Kiddville, 165
- King, 203
- Kingbee, 233, 235
- Kingdom Come, 208, 232
- Kings Creek, 208
- Kings Mountain, 209
- Kinniconick, 208
- Kino, 146
- Kirbyton, 159
- Kite, 201, 202
- Klondike, 224
- Klondyke, 145
- Knifely, 144
- Knightsburg, 227
- Knob Lick, 223
- Knoxfork, 203
- Knoxville, 231
- Kodak, 232

- Koon, 211
- Korea, 221
- Kosmosdale, 156, 195
- Kraft, 184
- Krebs, 219
- Krypton, 232
- Kuttawa, 211(2)
- Kyrock, 170

-L-

- Labascus, 161
- La Center, 146
- Lacey, 214
- Lacie, 189
- Lackey, 176(2)
- Laden, 186
- La Grange, 229
- Lair, 186
- Lake, 204
- Lake City, 209
- Lake Louisvilla, 230
- Lakeville, 214
- Lamasco, 211
- Lamb, 198, 223
- Lamont, 232
- Lancaster, 179(2)
- Lancer, 176
- L and E Junction, 165
- Landsaw, 247
- Langnau, 204
- Langstaff, 160
- Larkslane, 201
- Larue, 166
- Laura, 216(2)
- Laurel, 205
- Laurel Creek, 166
- Laurel Grove, 221
- Lawrenceburg, 145(2)
- Lawrenceville, 180
- Leafdale, 203
- Leatha, 214
- Leatherwood, 232

- Lebanon, 198, 214(2), 215
- Lebanon Junction, 156
- Ledocio, 205
- Lee, 156
- Lee City, 247
- Leeco, 205
- Leisure, 224
- Leitchfield, 181
- Lemon, 220
- Lenore, 228
- Lenoxburg, 153
- Lerose, 231
- Leslie, 168
- Letcher, 208
- Letitia, 183
- Levee, 224
- Level Green, 236
- Levi, 166, 231
- Levias, 167
- Lewisburg, 217
- Lewisport, 183
- Lexie, 247
- Lexington, 147, 149, 152, 153, 172, 173(2), 174(2), 221, 222, 236, 247
- Liberty, 161, 221, 242, 246, 247
- Lick Branch, 224
- Lickburg, 214
- Lick Creek, 233
- Lick Fork, 237
- Licking River, 224
- Lickskillet, 210, 221
- Lida, 204
- Liggett, 186
- Ligon, 176(2)
- Lilac, 181
- Lily, 204
- Limaburg, 149
- Limestone, 160
- Limestone Springs, 156
- Limeville, 183
- Limp, 184
- Lincoln, 166
- Lincoln Ridge, 239
- Linefork, 208

- Liro, 230
- Littcarr, 201
- Little, 154
- Little Barren, 182
- Little Colly, 208
- Little Cypress, 215
- Little Dixie, 233
- Little Floyd County, 233
- Little Georgetown, 174
- Little Hickman, 196
- Little Mount, 240
- Little Needmore, 153
- Little Rock, 150
- Little Sandy, 171
- Little Tar Springs, 183
- Little Texas, 174
- Littleton, 166
- Little Valley, 190
- Littleville, 219
- Little Zion, 246
- Livermore, 220
- Livia, 170
- Livingston, 236
- Lloyd, 183
- Load, 183
- Loam, 191
- Lockport, 189
- Locust, 160, 175, 238
- Locust Branch, 172
- Locust Grove, 165, 231
- Locust Hill, 155
- Logana, 196
- Logansport, 157
- Logantown, 209
- Logville, 214
- Lola, 209
- Lombard, 234
- London, 204
- Lone, 205
- Lone Oak, 181, 219, 234
- Lone Star, 187
- Long Bottom, 238
- Long Fork, 233
- Long Ridge, 168, 230

- Long Run, 195
- Long View, 184
- Lookout, 233
- Loradale, 174
- Lost City, 210
- Lost Creek, 154, 224
- Lost River, 245
- Lot, 247
- Lothair, 232
- Lotus, 156
- Louellen, 186
- Louisa, 204, 205
- Louisville, 145, 161, 168, 174, 187, 191(2), 192, 193(2), 194(2), 195(2), 207, 211, 216, 220(2), 233, 236(2), 240
- Love, 157
- Lovely, 216
- Loving, 245
- Low, 186
- Lower Buffalo, 205
- Lower Burning Fork, 214
- Lower Gilmore, 247
- Lower Spencer, 224
- Lowes, 181
- Low Gap, 144, 246
- Lucile, 171
- Lucky, 247
- Lucky Stop, 196, 224
- Luzerne, 227
- Lykins, 214
- Lynch, 185, 186
- Lynch Town, 172
- Lynn, 182, 183
- Lynn Camp, 204
- Lynn City, 227
- Lynnville, 181
- Lyons, 203

-M-

- Macedonia, 154, 163, 191
- Maceo, 170

- Madisonville, 190(2)
- Madrid, 155
- Magee Springs, 159
- Maggard, 214
- Maggie, 242
- Magnolia, 203
- Majestic, 233
- Major, 231
- Malaga, 247
- Mallie, 202
- Malone, 224
- Manchester, 165(2), 166(2)
- Manila, 197
- Manitou, 190
- Manse, 180
- Manuel, 232
- Maple, 241
- Maple Grove, 242
- Maple Mount, 170
- Maples Corner, 221
- Maplesville, 204
- Marcellus, 180
- Mare Creek, 176
- Mariba, 221
- Marion, 167
- Mark, 233
- Marrowbone, 168, 233
- Marshall, 215, 217
- Marshallville, 214
- Martha, 205
- Marthas Mills, 175
- Martin, 176(2)
- Martwick, 227
- Mary, 247
- Mary Alice, 186
- Marydale, 149
- Marydell, 204
- Mary Helen, 186
- Mashfork, 214
- Mashville,
- Mason, 180
- Massac, 219
- Matanzas, 229
- Matthew, 224

- Mattoon, 167
- Maud, 245
- Mavo, 222
- Maxine, 203
- Maxwell, 170
- May, 202
- Mayfield, 180(2), 181
- Mayflower, 233
- Mayking, 208
- Mayo, 222
- Maysville, 147, 153, 216(2), 217
- Maytown, 224
- Maywood, 209
- Mazie, 205
- McCreary, 180
- McKee, 191
- Meadow Creek, 247
- Means, 221
- Meathouse, 233
- Melbourne, 159, 198
- Meldrum, 148
- Melvin, 176
- Mentor, 159
- Mercer, 227
- Meredith, 181
- Merrimac, 241
- Merry Oaks, 146
- Mershons, 204
- Meshack, 223
- Mexico, 167
- Mid, 214
- Midas, 176
- Middleburg, 161
- Middlesboro, 148(2)
- Middletown, 195, 213, 238
- Midland, 147, 227
- Midway, 157, 158, 167, 221, 247
- Mikegrady, 233
- Mildred, 191
- Mill Creek, 217
- Miller, 178
- Millersburg, 150
- Million, 213
- Millport, 227

- Millseat, 151
- Mill Springs, 214, 246
- Millstone, 208
- Milltown, 144, 228
- Milo, 216
- Mima, 224
- Minefork, 214
- Minerva, 216
- Mining City, 157
- Minnie, 176
- Minor, 237
- Minorsville, 238
- Miracle, 148, 209
- Mistletoe, 231
- Mize, 224
- Moct, 154
- Modoc, 168
- Mog, 227
- Monica,
- Monitor, 243
- Monkeys Eyebrow, 146
- Monroe, 187
- Montago, 232(2)
- Monterey, 150, 230
- Montgomery, 242
- Monticello, 174, 219, 220, 246(2)
- Montpelier, 144
- Mook, 155
- Moon, 224
- Moore, 161
- Moores Ferry, 147
- Moorman, 227
- Morehead, 227, 236
- Morgan, 231
- Morganfield, 243(2)
- Morgans Creek, 205
- Morgantown, 156(2)
- Morning Glory, 228
- Morning View, 198
- Morris Creek, 234
- Morris Fork, 154
- Mortons Gap, 190
- Moscow, 178, 189
- Mossy Bottom, 233

- Motley, 245
- Mount Aerial, 145
- Mountain Ash, 247
- Mountain Top, 160
- Mountain Valley, 154
- Mount Carmel, 175, 190
- Mount Eden, 240
- Mount Gilead, 182, 217
- Mount Hermon, 223
- Mount Lebanon, 196
- Mount Olive, 161, 205
- Mount Olivet, 235
- Mount Pisgah, 215, 246
- Mount Pleasant, 243
- Mount Sterling, 221, 223(2)
- Mount Vernon, 155, 235
- Mount Victory, 235
- Mount Washington, 155(2), 156
- Mount Zion, 145, 180
- Mousie, 201
- Mouthcard, 233
- Moxley, 230
- Mozelle, 206
- Mt Auburn, 231
- Mt Beulah, 187
- Mt Carmel, 175
- Mt Eden, 239
- Mt Gilead, 217
- Mt Olive, 205
- Mt Pleasant, 229
- Mt Savage, 160
- Mt Sterling,
- Mt Union, 145
- Mt Zion, 180, 235
- Mud Camp, 168
- Muddy Ford, 238
- Mud Lick, 223
- Mud Lick, 147, 223
- Mulberry, 239
- Muldraugh, 220
- Mummie, 191
- Munfordville, 186, 187
- Munk, 179
- Murl, 246

- Murphyfork, 224
- Murray, 157, 158(2), 181
- Music, 160
- Myra, 233
- Mystic, 155

-N-

- Nada, 234
- Nampa, 233
- Nancy, 235
- Naomi, 235
- Napier, 206
- Naples, 183
- Napoleon, 179
- Narrows, 229
- Narvel, 167
- Nash, 170
- Natlee, 230
- Nazareth, 228
- Neafus, 181
- Neatsville, 144
- Neave, 153
- Nebo, 190, 227
- Ned, 154
- Needmore, 146, 153, 157, 157, 205, 230
- Nell, 144
- Nelson, 227, 247
- Nelsonville, 228
- Neon, 208
- Neosheo, 240
- Nerinx, 215
- Nero, 197
- Netty, 214
- Nevada, 222
- New, 230
- Newbern, 209
- New Camp, 233
- New Castle, 189
- New Columbus, 230
- New Concord, 158
- New Cypress, 189, 227

- Newfound, 166
- Newfoundland, 170, 171
- New Haven, 227, 228
- New Hope, 228
- New Liberty, 223, 230
- New Market, 215
- Newport, 158(2), 159(2)
- New Providence, 158
- New Salem, 167
- Newtown, 238
- New York, 146
- New Zion, 238
- Niagara, 188(2)
- Nicholasville, 195
- Nichols, 189
- Nigh, 233
- Nihizertown, 174
- Nina, 180, 196
- Ninevah, 145, 240
- Ninteen, 229
- Nippa, 197
- Noble, 154
- Nobob, 146
- No Creek, 229
- Noctor, 154
- Node, 223
- Noetown, 148
- Nolin, 184
- Nonesuch, 247
- Nonnel, 227
- Nora, 167
- Normal, 151, 158
- Normandy, 240
- North Corbin, 204(2)
- Northern, 176
- Northfield, 195
- North Irvine, 172
- North Middletown, 150
- North Millersburg, 150
- North Pleasureville, 189
- Northtown, 187
- Nortonville, 190
- Nuckols, 220
- Number One, 246

- Nunn, 167

-O-

- Oakbrook, 149
- Oakdale, 154, 219
- Oak Forest, 145
- Oak Grove, 163, 229
- Oak Hill, 190, 224, 235
- Oakla, 147
- Oakland, 245
- Oak Level, 215
- Oakley, 204
- Oak Ridge, 170, 170, 198, 208
- Oaks, 148, 219, 229
- Oakville, 186, 210
- Odds, 197
- Oddville,
- Offutt, 197
- Ogle, 166
- Oil Center, 235
- Oil City, 146
- Oil Springs, 197
- Oil Valley, 246
- Oklahoma, 170
- Okolona, 195
- Old Christianburg, 239
- Old Cypress, 189
- Old Flat Lick, 203
- Oldham, 230
- Old Landing, 205
- Old Lombard, 234
- Old Olga, 238
- Old Orchard, 205
- Old Pine Grove, 165
- Old Stephensburg, 184
- Oldtown, 183
- Old Washington, 217
- Olga, 238
- Olin, 191
- Olive, 215
- Olive Branch, 175, 239
- Olive Hill, 160(2)

- Ollie, 170
- Olympia, 147
- Olympia Springs, 147
- Omaha, 202
- Omega, 235
- Oneida, 165, 166
- Ono, 238
- Oolite, 221
- Ophir, 224
- Oppy, 216
- Orangeburg, 217
- Orchard Grass Hills, 230
- Ordinary, 171
- Oregon, 222
- Orinoco, 233
- Oriole, 190
- Orkney, 176
- Orlando, 236
- Oscaloosa, 208
- Oscar, 146
- Otia, 223
- Ottawa, 236
- Otter Pond, 157
- Ottusville, 177
- Outwood, 163
- Ova, 214
- Oven Fork, 208
- Overda, 205
- Owensboro, 168, 169(2), 216, 230
- Owenton, 230
- Owingsville, 147(2), 221
- Owsley, 233
- Oxford, 238
- Oz, 220
- Ozark, 144

-P-

- Packard, 247(2)
- Pactolus, 160
- Paducah, 150, 175, 192, 217, 218(2), 219(2)
- Paint Creek, 196, 234

- Paint Lick, 180, 213
- Paintsville, 196(2)
- Palisades, 211
- Panama, 224
- Panhandle, 154
- Panola, 213
- Pansy, 186
- Panther, 170
- Paradise, 227
- Paragon, 237
- Paramount, 148
- Paris, 149, 150, 179, 222, 243
- Park, 146(2)
- Park City, 146
- Park Lake, 230
- Parrot, 191
- Partridge, 208
- Pascal, 187
- Pathfork, 186
- Patsey, 172
- Paw Paw, 233
- Peach Grove, 231
- Peach Orchard, 205
- Peak, 238
- Pea Ridge, 172, 175, 242
- Pearl, 148, 247
- Peasticks, 148
- Pebble, 148
- Pebworth, 231(2)
- Pecks Creek, 234
- Peedee, 163
- Peeled Oak, 148
- Pee Vee, 190
- Peewee Valley, 229
- Pendleton, 189
- Penile, 195
- Penny, 158,233
- Penrod, 227
- Peoples, 191
- Permon, 203
- Perryville, 151, 177, 184, 232
- Persimmon, 223
- Persimmon Grove, 159
- Petra, 153

- Petri, 183
- Petroleum, 145, 240
- Petros, 245
- Peytons Store, 161
- Philpot, 170
- Phyllis, 233
- Pickett, 144
- Picnic, 144
- Pierce, 182
- Pig, 170
- Pigeon, 233
- Pigeonroost, 166
- Pigeon Roost, 233
- Pike View, 187
- Pikeville, 232, 233(2)
- Pilgrim, 216
- Pilot, 172
- Pilot Oak, 181
- Pilot View, 165
- Pinchem, 242
- Pinckneyville, 209
- Pine Grove, 161, 165, 204, 221
- Pine Hill, 236
- Pine Knob, 181
- Pine Knot, 220
- Pine Mountain, 186, 228
- Piner, 198
- Pine Ridge, 247
- Pine Top, 202
- Pineville, 148
- Piney Grove, 235
- Pink, 196
- Pinnacle, 205
- Pinson, 233
- Pinsonfork, 233
- Pioneer, 232
- Pippa Passes, 200, 201
- Piqua, 235
- Pisgah, 247
- Piso, 233
- Pittsburg, 148, 204
- Pitts Point, 156
- Plank, 166
- Plano, 245

- Plato, 235
- Pleasant Green Hill, 163
- Pleasant Grove, 245
- Pleasant Hill, 157, 158, 163, 222, 231
- Pleasant Home, 230
- Pleasant Ridge, 229
- Pleasant Valley, 228, 233
- Pleasant View, 247
- Pleasure Ridge Park, 195
- Pleasureville, 175, 239
- Plum, 150
- Plummers Landing, 175
- Plummers Mill, 175
- Plum Springs, 245
- Plum Springs,
- Plumville, 217
- Plutarch, 214
- Poindexter, 186
- Pointer, 235
- Point Pleasant, 229
- Polly, 208
- Pomeroyton, 221
- Pomp, 224
- Ponderosa, 181
- Pongo, 236
- Pope, 145
- Poplar, 160
- Poplar Corner, 215
- Poplar Flat, 208
- Poplar Grove, 175, 179, 220, 230
- Poplar Highlands, 183
- Poplar Level, 156
- Poplar Plains, 175
- Poplarville, 235
- Portland, 193, 195, 231
- Port Royal, 189
- Possum Trot, 215
- Post, 181
- Potters Fork, 208
- Poverty, 220
- Powderly, 226(2)
- Powder Mill, 187
- Powell, 172
- Powell Valley, 234

- Powersburg, 246
- Pratt, 246
- Preachersville, 209
- Preece, 216
- Premier, 148
- Premium, 208
- Press, 154
- Prestonsburg, 160, 176, 198, 216, 236
- Prestonville, 160
- Price, 176(2)
- Prices Mill, 240
- Pricetown, 161
- Pride, 243
- Primrose, 205
- Prince, 176
- Princess, 151
- Princeton, 157, 167
- Printer, 176
- Privett, 191
- Prospect, 195
- Prosperity, 170
- Protemus, 158
- Providence, 167, 196, 203, 240, 243, 246
- Provo, 157
- Pruden, 148
- Public, 235
- Pueblo, 246
- Pulaski, 235
- Pumpkin Center, 157
- Puncheon, 201, 214
- Pyramid, 176
- Pyrus, 144

-Q-

- Quail, 236
- Quality, 157
- Queendale, 166
- Queens, 208
- Quicksand, 154
- Quincy, 208

-R-

- Rabbit Hash, 149(2)
- Rabbit Ridge, 190
- Rabbit Town, 165
- Raccoon, 233
- Raceland, 151, 183
- Ragland, 219
- Rain, 203, 247
- Raleigh, 243
- Ralph, 229
- Ransom, 233
- Rapids, 240
- Raven, 202
- Ravenna, 171, 172
- Ray, 205
- Raydure, 223
- Raywick, 215
- Razorblade, 207
- Ready, 181
- Rebelsville, 221
- Red Ash, 247
- Redbird, 247
- Redbud, 186
- Red Bush, 148
- Redbush, 197
- Red Cross, 146
- Redfox, 202
- Red Hill, 145, 170, 184
- Redhouse, 213
- Red Lick, 223
- Redwine, 224
- Reed, 188
- Region, 157
- Relief, 197, 224
- Render, 229
- Renfro Valley, 218, 235, 236
- Repton, 167
- Republic, 233
- Rex, 187
- Rhoda, 170
- Rhodelia, 221
- Ribbon, 238

- Ribolt, 208
- Ricetown,
- Riceville, 197
- Richland, 190
- Richmond, 211(2), 219
- Rich Pond, 245
- Richwood, 149
- Ridgetop, 156
- Ricetown, 231
- Ridgeway, 186
- Rightangle, 165
- Right Fork, 224
- Right Middle Fork, 214
- Ringgold, 235
- Ringos Mills, 175
- Rio, 187
- Rio Vista, 186
- Ritchie, 201
- Rivals, 240
- River, 197
- River Bluff, 230
- River Ridge, 186
- Riverside, 245
- Riverview, 183, 219
- Roachville, 182
- Road Fork, 233
- Roanoke, 203
- Roaring Spring, 242
- Roberta, 221
- Robinsville, 213
- Rob Roy, 229
- Rochester, 156, 157
- Rockbridge, 223
- Rockcastle, 242
- Rock Creek, 181
- Rockdale, 230
- Rock Haven, 221
- Rockholds, 247
- Rockhouse, 224, 233
- Rock Lick, 154
- Rockport, 229
- Rock Springs, 153, 188
- Rockville, 237
- Rockybranch, 246

- Rocky Hill, 146, 170
- Rodburn, 237
- Rome, 170
- Romine, 241
- Roosevelt, 154
- Roper, 181
- Roscoe, 171
- Rosebud, 187
- Rose Crossroads, 238
- Rosefork, 247
- Rose Hill, 222
- Rose Terrace, 184
- Rosetta, 155
- Roseville, 146, 183
- Rosewood, 226, 227
- Rosine, 228, 229
- Rough and Tough, 177
- Roundhill, 170
- Round Hill, 213
- Roundstone, 236
- Rousseau, 154
- Rowdy, 232
- Rowena, 238
- Roxana, 208
- Royal, 181
- Royalton, 214
- Ruddels Mill, 150, 179
- Rugless, 208
- Ruin, 170, 171
- Rural, 233
- Rush, 151, 160
- Russell, 151, 183
- Russell Corner, 230
- Russell Springs, 237
- Russellville, 154, 209, 210(2)
- Ruth, 157, 235
- Ruthton, 213
- Rye, 247

-S-

- Sacramento, 220
- Sadieville, 238

- Saint Elmo, 163
- Salem, 209, 224, 238, 243
- Salmons, 240
- Saloma, 241
- Salt Gum, 203
- Salt Lick, 146, 148
- Salt River, 156
- Salvisa, 222
- Salyersville, 213(2), 214(2)
- Samaria, 183
- Sample, 155
- Sampson, 186
- Samuels, 228
- Sandgap, 191
- Sand Hill, 172, 186, 208, 245
- Sand Lick, 238
- Sand Springs, 191, 236
- Sandy, 227
- Sandy Furnace, 151
- Sandy Gap, 235
- Sandy Hook, 171(2)
- Santa Fe, 153
- Sarah, 171
- Saratoga, 211
- Sardis, 217, 235
- Sassafras, 199, 202
- Sassafras Ridge, 178
- Sasser, 204
- Savage, 167
- Savage Branch, 151
- Savoy, 247
- Savoyard, 223
- Sawyer, 220
- Scale, 215
- Schochoh, 210
- Schweizer, 240
- Science Hill, 235
- Scottown, 229
- Scottsville, 144, 145, 229
- Scranton, 221
- Scuddy, 232
- Scuffletown, 155, 156, 188
- Scythia, 170
- Seaville, 222, 245

- Sebree, 246
- Select, 229
- Seminary, 167
- Seminary Village, 195
- Semiway, 220
- Senterville, 233
- Se Ree, 155
- Sergent, 208
- Settle, 144, 145
- Seven Corners, 184
- Seven Gums, 243
- Seventy Six, 167
- Shade, 172
- Shady Grove, 157, 167, 171, 215, 219, 2323
- Sandy Hook, 171
- Shady Nook, 186
- Shakertown, 222
- Sharondale, 233
- Sharon Grove, 242
- Sharpsburg, 147(2), 148
- Sharpsville, 245
- Shawhan, 150
- Shawneeland, 195
- Shelbiana, 233
- Shelby City, 153
- Shelbyville, 239
- Shepherdsville, 155, 156(2)
- Shepherdtown, 166
- Shetland, 247
- Shiff, 239
- Shiloh, 158
- Shipley, 167
- Shoal, 206
- Shopville, 235
- Shoreacres, 247
- Short Creek, 181
- Short Mountain, 246
- Short Town, 186
- Shoulderblade, 154
- Sideview, 224
- Sideway, 171
- Sidney, 233
- Siler, 203

- Silica, 160
- Siloam, 183
- Silver City, 157
- Silver Creek, 213
- Silver Grove, 159, 198
- Silverhill, 224
- Simpson, 155
- Sinai, 145
- Sinking Fork, 163
- Sinks, 236
- Sip, 197
- Sirocco, 221
- Sixth Vein, 190
- Sizerock, 206
- Skilesville, 227
- Skillman, 183
- Skinnersburg, 238
- Skullbuster, 239
- Skylight, 230
- Skyline, 208
- Slabtown, 189
- Slade, 234
- Slat, 246
- Slate Lick, 213
- Slaughters, 246
- Slemp, 232
- Slick Rock, 146
- Slickway, 177
- Sligo, 189,243
- Smilax, 206
- Smile, 237
- Smithboro, 202
- Smithland, 209
- Smith Town, 220
- Smyrna, 195
- Snap, 181
- Snow, 167
- Snow Hill, 239
- Soft Shell, 201
- Soldier, 160
- Solitude, 155, 156
- Somerset, 234, 235
- Somo, 217
- Sonora, 184

- Sophi, 160
- Sourwood, 191
- South, 181
- South Buffalo, 203
- South Campbellsville, 241
- South Carrollton, 227
- South Columbus, 189
- Southdown, 208
- South Fork, 209, 231, 234
- Southfork, 231
- South Highland, 181
- South Irvine, 172
- South Marshall, 215
- South Shore, 183
- South Union, 210, 210
- Southville, 239
- Spa, 210
- Spanglin, 171
- Sparksville, 144
- Sparrow, 145
- Spears, 174
- Speck, 144, 241
- Speedwell, 213
- Speight, 233
- Spice Knob, 170
- Spider, 202
- Spiro, 236
- Sprout, 228
- Spout Springs, 172
- Spring Creek, 166
- Springdale, 217
- Springfield, 245
- Spring Grove, 243
- Spring Hill, 189
- Springhill, 245
- Spring Lick, 182
- Spring Station, 247
- Sprout, 228
- Sprout Springs, 234
- Spruce Pine, 206
- Sprule, 203
- Spurrier, 182, 184
- Squib, 235
- Squiresville, 230

- Stab, 235
- Stacy, 232
- Stacy Fork, 224
- Stamping Ground, 238
- Standing Rock, 247
- Stanford, 208
- Stanton, 234(2), 234
- Stanville, 176, 177
- Stark, 171
- State Line, 178
- State Valley, 148
- Static, 167, 246
- Station Camp, 172
- Stay, 231
- St Charles, 190
- Steamport Landing, 246
- Stella, 158
- Stephens, 171
- Stephensburg, 184
- Stephensport, 155
- Stepstone, 224
- St Helens, 205
- Stillwater, 247
- Stinking Creek, 203
- St Joseph, 215
- St Mary, 215
- Stockholm, 170
- Stone, 180, 233
- Stonequarry, 221
- Stonewall, 153, 238
- Stoney Fork, 148
- Stoney Point, 153
- Stony Point, 150
- Stoops, 224
- Stopover, 233
- Straight Creek, 148, 224
- Straw, 170
- Stringtown, 145, 149, 175, 180, 205, 213, 214, 222, 227, 233
- Stroll, 221
- Strunk, 220
- Stump, 172
- Sturgeon, 231
- Sturgis, 167, 243

- St Vincent, 243
- Sublett, 214
- Sublimity City, 204
- Sudith, 221
- Sugar Grove, 157, 209
- Sugar Hill, 235
- Sugartit, 149
- Sulphur, 189
- Sulphur Lick, 223
- Sulphur Springs, 229, 243
- Sulphur Well, 223
- Sulphur Wells, 196
- Summer Shade, 223
- Summersville, 182
- Summit, 151, 184, 205
- Sumpter, 246
- Sunfish, 170
- Sunny Acres, 198
- Sunnybrook, 246
- Sunny Corner, 183
- Sunnydale, 229
- Sunnyside, 245
- Sunrise, 186
- Sunset, 175
- Sunshine, 183, 186
- Susan Creek, 167
- Susie, 246
- Sutherland, 170
- Suwanee, 211
- Swallowfield, 177
- Swamp Branch, 197
- Swan Lake, 203
- Swanpond, 203
- Sweeden, 170
- Sweet Lick, 172
- Sweet Owen, 230
- Switzer, 177
- Sycamore, 195, 233
- Sycamore Flat, 238
- Sylvandell, 186
- Symbol, 204

-T-

- Tabernacle, 242
- Tablow, 222, 245
- Tacky Town, 186
- Taffy, 229
- Taft, 231
- Talcum, 202
- Talley, 203
- Tanbark, 168
- Tanner, 203
- Tannery, 208
- Tarascon, 189
- Tar Fork, 155
- Tar Hill, 182
- Tarkiln, 224
- Tatham Springs, 245
- Taulbee, 154
- Taylorsport, 149
- Taylors Store, 158
- Taylorsville, 240
- Teaberry, 177
- Teddy, 161
- Tejay, 148
- Temperance, 240
- Temple Hill, 146
- Ten Spot, 186
- Teresita, 230
- Terrapin, 222
- Texas, 245
- Texola, 172
- Thealka, 197
- The Bluff, 157, 167
- Thelma, 197
- The Ridge, 171
- The Rocks, 243
- Thompson, 165
- Thompsonville, 245
- Thousandsticks, 206
- Three Forks, 180, 245
- Threeforks, 216
- Threelinks, 191, 236
- Three Point, 186
- Three Springs, 187, 245
- Tidal Wave, 247

- Tiline, 209
- Tillie, 208
- Tina, 202
- Tiny Town, 242
- Tiptop, 214
- Tiptop Station, 184
- Tolu, 167
- Tomahawk, 216
- Tompkinsville, 223
- Tom Ray, 233
- Tonieville, 203
- Toonerville, 233
- Topmost, 202
- Torchlight, 205
- Torrent, 247
- Totz, 186
- Touristville, 246
- Tram, 177
- Travellers Rest, 231
- Trenton, 242
- Tress Shop, 242
- Tribune, 167
- Tri City, 181, 182
- Trigg Furnace, 242
- Trimble, 235
- Trimble Bend, 221
- Trinity, 205, 208
- Triplett, 237
- Trisler, 229
- Trixie, 166
- Trosper, 203
- Trout, 243
- Troy, 247
- Tuck, 170
- Tunnel Hill, 188
- Tunnel Hills, 184
- Turin, 231
- Turkey, 154
- Turkey Creek, 233
- Turkey Foot, 191, 238
- Turkeytown, 209
- Tutor Key, 197
- Tway, 186
- Twentysix, 224

- Twila, 186
- Tyewhoppity, 242
- Tyner, 191
- Typo, 232

-U-

- Ulvah, 208
- Ulysses, 205
- Union, 149
- Union City, 170, 213
- Union Hall, 172
- Union Mills, 196
- Union Ridge, 227
- Union Star, 155
- Uniontown, 243
- Unity, 151
- Uno, 187(2)
- Upchurch, 167
- Upper Blue Licks, 228
- Upper Bruce, 208
- Upper Elk, 233
- Upper Gilmore, 247
- Upper Laurel Fork, 206
- Upper Spencer, 224
- Upton, 203
- Urban, 166
- Utility, 183

-V-

- Vada, 205
- Valerie, 247
- Valley Hill, 245
- Valley Oak, 235
- Valley Station, 195
- Valley View, 213
- Vanarsdell, 222
- Van Buren, 145
- Vanceburg, 208
- Van Cleave, 158
- Vancleve, 154

- Vandetta, 190
- Van Lear, 196, 197
- Varilla, 148
- Varney, 233
- Venus, 186
- Versailles, 247(2)
- Vest, 202
- Vicco, 232(2)
- Vicksburg, 209
- Victoria, 190
- Victory, 204
- View, 167
- Villa Hills, 197
- Vine, 166
- Vine Grove, 184
- Vineyard, 157, 196
- Viola, 181
- Viper, 232(2)
- Virden, 234
- Virgie, 233
- Virginia, 246
- Visalia, 198
- Volga, 197
- Vortex, 247
- Vox, 204

-W-

- Wabd, 236
- Waco, 213
- Waddy, 239
- Wagersville, 172
- Wago, 167
- Wait, 246
- Waldo, 214
- Wales, 233
- Walker, 203
- Wallins Creek, 186
- Wallonia, 242
- Wallsend, 148
- Walltown, 161
- Walnut Flat, 209
- Walnut Gap, 172

- Walnut Grove, 145, 215, 235, 243
- Walnut Hill, 145, 174
- Waltersville, 234
- Walton, 149
- Waltz, 237
- Wanamaker, 246
- Waneta, 191
- Warbranch, 206
- War Creek, 154
- Warfield, 216
- Warren, 203
- Warsaw, 178(2)
- Washington, 217
- Wasioto, 148
- Waterford, 240
- Watergap, 177
- Waterloo, 149
- Water Valley, 181
- Waterview, 168
- Wax, 182, 187
- Wayland, 176, 177
- Wayside, 145
- Webster, 155
- Weed, 144
- Weedonia, 217
- Weeksbury, 177
- Weir, 227
- Welcome, 157
- Wellhope, 236
- Wendover, 206
- Westbend, 234
- West City, 182
- West Covington, 198
- West Fairview, 151
- West Future City, 219
- West Irvine, 172(2)
- West Liberty, 224, 236
- West Louisville, 170
- West Lovely, 216
- West Paducah, 218, 219
- Westplains, 181
- West Point, 184(2)
- Westport, 230
- West Prestonsburg, 177

- West Van Lear, 197
- West Viola, 181
- Wheatcroft, 246
- Wheatley, 230
- Wheel, 181
- Wheelersburg, 214
- Wheel Rim, 224
- Wheelwright, 176, 177
- Whetstone, 168, 235
- Whick, 154
- Whippoorwill, 210
- White Ash, 205
- White City, 188, 203
- White Hall, 165, 212(2), 213
- Whitehouse, 197
- White Oak, 180, 224
- White Oak Junction, 220
- White Plains, 190
- White Rose, 241
- White Run, 229
- Whites, 213
- Whitesburg, 198,206, 207(2)
- White Sulphur, 157, 238
- White Tower, 198
- White Villa, 198
- Whitewood, 182
- Whitley City, 219, 220
- Whittle, 238
- Whoopflarea, 231
- Wiborg, 220
- Wickliffe, 145, 146, 147
- Wicks Well, 190
- Widecreek, 154
- Wilbur, 205
- Wild Cat, 166
- Wilder, 159, 172
- Wildie, 236
- Wildwood, 195
- Wilhelmina, 242
- Willailla, 236
- Williambsburg, 247
- Williams Store, 210
- Williamstown, 180
- Williba, 205
- Willow, 153, 205
- Willow Grove, 153
- Willow Shade, 223
- Willowtown, 241
- Willow Tree, 172
- Wilmore, 195
- Wilsonville, 240
- Winchester, 158, 164(2), 165(2), 213, 224
- Wind Cave, 191
- Windsor, 161
- Windy, 246
- Windy Hill, 229
- Windyville, 170
- Winesap, 187
- Winford, 159
- Winifred, 197
- Winslow, 151
- Winston, 172
- Winston Park, 198
- Wiscoal, 202
- Wisdom, 223
- Wisemantown, 172
- Wises Landing, 243
- Wiswell, 158
- Wolf, 160
- Wolf Creek, 154, 221
- Wolf Lick, 210
- Wolf Pen, 247
- Wolfpit, 233
- Wolverine, 154
- Wonder, 177
- Wonnie, 214
- Woodbine, 203, 247
- Woodburn, 245
- Woodbury, 156
- Woodlake, 177
- Woodlawn, 228
- Woodman, 233
- Woods, 177, 186
- Woodsbend, 224
- Woodside, 170, 233
- Woodstock, 235
- Woodville, 219

- Woollum, 203
- Worthville, 160
- Wrigley, 224
- Wyoming, 148

-Y-

- Yamacraw, 220
- Yamallton, 174
- Yeaddiss, 206
- Yellow Creek, 148
- Yellow Mountain, 202
- Yellow Rock, 205
- Yerkes, 232
- Yesse, 145
- Yocum, 224
- Yoder, 240

- Yorktown, 233
- Yosemite, 161
- Yuba, 243
- Yuma, 241

-Z-

- Zachariah, 205, 247
- Zag, 224
- Zekes Point, 191
- Zelda, 205
- Zion, 188, 242
- Zion Hill, 238, 247
- Zion Station, 180
- Zoe, 205
- Zoneton, 156
- Zula, 246

INDEX OF PERSONS

-A-

Hank Aaron, 1
Bud Abbott, 72, 184
Norm Abram, 103
Roy Acuff, 109
John Adair, 144, 222
Abigail Adams, 33, 244
Green Adams, 203
John Adams, Jr., 48, 49, 50, 209
John Quincy Adams, 49, 50, 165, 243, 244
Samuel Adams, 48, 49
Silas Adams, 161
Thomas Adams, 76
"Uncle Billy" Adams, 213
Robert Aitken, 99
David "Stringbean" Akeman, 188
Henry Akin, 237
Alabama, 218

Eddie Albert, 29, 83
Louisa Mae Alcott, 98, 101
Alfalfa (Carl Switzer), 29
Horatio Alger, 48
Mohammud Ali, 194, 195
Colonel John Allen, 144
Martin Van Allen, 176
Sandy Allen, 27
Tim Allen, 103
Thomas Allin, 187
Jason Amburgey,
Don Ameche, 127
Dr. David Amos, 157
Betty Anderson (Elinor Donahue), 123
Bill Anderson, 104
Eddie Anderson (*Rochester*) 11
Lew Anderson (*Clarabell*), 35
Lucien Anderson, 180
Sgt. Pepper Anderson (Angie Dickinson), 83

Richard Anderson, Jr., 145
Simeon H. Anderson, 179
Sparky Anderson, 107
Landaff Watson Andrews, 175
Andrews Sisters, 54, 128
Santa Anna, 76
Susan B Anthony, 49
Jesse Applegate, 40
Eddie Arcaro, 86
Harold Arlin, 97
Louis Armstrong, 41, 42, 194, 197
Desi Arnaz, 77
James Arness, 54, 194
Nanie Harper Arnett, 214
Benedict Arnold, 15, 244
Eddie Arnold, 111
Chester A. Arthur, 118
Adele Astaire, 67
Fred Astaire, 67(2), 68
Charles "Speedy" Atkins, 218
Chet Atkins, 109, 218, 226
Casey Atwood, 225
John James Audubon, 187
Prince William Augustus, 255
Gene Autry, 41(2),86, 92, 113, 116
Frankie Avalon, 98

-B-

Burt Bacharach, 59
Jim Backus, 54, 87
Parley Baer (*Mayor Stoner* on *Andy Griffith*) 117, 118
James Anthony Bailey, 51
Absalom Baird, 245
Harvey Ball, 48
Lucille Ball, 37, 77, 79
Bland Ballard, 145
Phil Balsley, 119
David Banner, 176
Simon Barber, 166
David Bard, 227
William Bard, 227
Bob Barker, 13, 123
Alben W. Barkley, 181, 218, 243

Samuel Kimbrough Barlow, 228
Frances Barnes, 172
P.T. Barnum, 15
Gene Barry, 77
Ethel Barrymore, 98
John Barrymore, 98, 77
Lionel Barrymore, 98
Josiah Bartlett, 70
Clara Barton, 50
W. Ralph Basham, 169
Count Basie, 72
Francis Bavier, 77
Beach Boys, 41
L. L. Bean, 43
Roy Bean, 216
Butch Beard, 155
Daniel Carter Beard, 198
Joe Beard, 229
Percy Beard, 155
Ralph Beard, 155
Ned Beatty, 193
Hugh Beaumont (*Ward Cleaver*), 38
Harriet Beecher, 216
Henry Ward Beecher, 15(2)
Joshua Fry Bell, 148
William Bendix, 77
Edgar Bergen, 27,127
Polly Bergen, 109
Milton Berle, 27, 79
Bea Benaderet, 37
Yogi Berra, 59
Steve Beshear, 190(2)
James Best, 226
Carl Betz (*Dr. Alex Stone*), 98
Jack Bibb, 177
Bernie Bickerstaff, 185
Greg Biffle, 225
Bigfoot, 185,218
Billy the Kid, 1
Larry Bird, 30, 31
James Dixon Black, 202
Luke P. Blackburn, 211(2)
Tom Blackburn, 74
Elizabeth Blackwell, 76
Joe Blanton, 170
Claude Bloch, 156

Dan Blocker (*Hoss* or *Eric*), 113, 114
Blondie (Arthur Lake), 203
William Bobbitt, 235
Napoleon Bonaparte, 5
Ward Bond, 67
Andrew Rechmond Boone, 180
Daniel Boone, 33, 99, 148(2), 150, 152, 157, 164, 187, 196, 197, 203, 208, 212, 227, 237, 241
Debbie Boone, 153, 217
Hannah Boone, 152
James Boone, 237
Nathan Boone, 33
Pat Boone, 19
John Wilkes Booth, 46
Shirley Booth, 77
The Big Bopper, 83, 116
Gutzon Borglum, 25
Al Borland (Richard Karn), 103
Boswell Sisters, 85
Jim Bowie, 210
Charles Bowman, 30
Eliza Steward Boyd, 130
Linn Boyd, 150
William Boyd (*Hopalong Cassidy*), 86
John Boyle, 151
Bozo the Clown (Willard Scott), 121
William Bracken, 153
John Bradley, 128
Milton Bradley, 44
Omar Bradley, 60
William O. Bradley, 179, 214
Braxton Bragg, 192
Thomas E. Bramlette, 167, 168(2)
Carter Braxton, 120
Edward Thompson "Ned" Breathitt, 163, 189
John Breathitt, 153, 154, 236
John C. Breckinridge, 152, 154, 171, 174
Thom Bresh, 227
Teresa Brewer, 89
David Brinkley, 64, 80, 83
Hezekiah Briscoe, 247
Benjamin Bristow, 242
Helen Broderick, 98
David Brooks, 153

Foster Brooks, 193
Garth Brooks, 90
B. Gratz Brown, 230
Sgt. Ed Brown (Don Galloway) 153
James Brown, 105
John Y. Brown Jr., 190
Les Brown, 86
W. Earl Brown, 158
William Wells Brown, 174
Robert Browning, 200, 201
The Browns, 41
Paul "Bear" Bryant, 6, 163
Edgar Buchanan, (*Uncle Joe*), 62
James Buchanan, 96, 152, 174
Pearl S. Buck, 125
Buffalo Bob Smith, 78
David Dunbar Buick, 51
Alexander Bullitt, 155
Dagwood Bumstead (Arthur Lake), 203
Archie Bunker (Carrol O'Connor), 77
Martin Van Buren, 196
Anne Burford, 130
Sam Burk, 167
Carol Burnette, 113, 116
Ambrose Burnside, 234
Aaron Burr, 168
Lonnie Burr, 159
George H. W. Bush, 49, 50, 67, 229
George W. Bush, 15, 67
Sam Bush, 244
William Bush, 164
Richard Butler, 156
Simon Butler, 197
Phobee Button, 236
Pat Buttram (*Mr. Haney*), 1
Jean Byron, 219

-C-

John Caldwell, 157
Richard Callaway, 157
Cab Calloway, 105
Marquis Calmes, 247
Potilla Calvert, 215
Adam Campbell, 240

Andrew Campbell, 240
Glen Campbell, 6, 227
John Campbell, 158
Otis Campbell (Hal Morris), 53
William Campbell, 224
John Cannon, 183
Al Capone, 192
John Griffin Carlisle, 159
Kittie Carlisle, 105
Richardson Carlson (*Herb Philbrick*), 54
Hoagie Carmichael, 20, 30
Michael Carneal, 218
Andrew Carnegie, 196
Art Carney, 79
Charles Carroll, 45, 159
Julian Carroll, 218
Johnny Carson, 33
Kit Carson, 212
Carter family, 109
Jimmy Carter, 20, 21
Joanna Carter, 185
Lynda Carter, 4
William Grayson Carter, 160
Hoss Cartwright (Dan Blocker), 113
George Washington Carver, 60
Moses Carver, 60
James Casey, 68
William Casey, 161
Johnny Cash, 6, 160, 120, 121, 218, 240
June Carter Cash, 240
Butch Cassidy, 117
Hopalong Cassidy (William Boyd) 86
Alexander Catlett, 150
Harry M. Caudill, 207
Steve Cauthen, 149
Clyde Cessna, 34
Albert "Happy" Chandler, 165, 166, 188, 189, 247
Ben Chandler, 247
Lon Chaney Jr., 90, 92
Lon Chaney Sr., 13
Charlie Chaplin, 230
Ray Chapman, 228
Rex Chapman, 169
Nick Charles (William Powell), 64
Nora Charles (Myrna Loy), 64

Samuel Chase, 45
Steven Curtis Chapman, 218
Ray Charles, 20,21
John Cheap, 182
Joel Cheek, 168(2)
Chubby Checker, 105
Dick Cheney, 67
Chief Crazy Horse, 107
Samuel Canning Childs, 242
Herman Chittison, 175
Joie Chitwood, 65
Jesus Christ, 9
Tom Christerson, 226
William Christian, 161
Walter Chrysler, 37
Jerry Clairborne, 163
Ellie Mae Clampett (Donna Douglas), 41
Clarabell (Lew Anderson), 35
Clarabell (Bob Keeshan), 79
Abraham Clark, 72
Billy C. Clark, 151
Dick Clark, 79,105
George Rogers Clark, 108, 120, 145, 157, 163, 191, 197, 208
James Clark, 145, 164, 165
Lewis and Clark, 83, 93
Roy Clark, 122
William Clark, 191, 217
George Clarke, 198
Cassius Marcellus Clay, 165, 194, 212(2)
Cassius Marcellus Clay Jr., 194
Green Clay, 165
Henry Clay, 151, 165(2), 171, 173, 191, 212
Laura Clay, 212
Ward Cleaver (Hugh Beaumont),
Samuel Clemens (Mark Twain), 62, 165
Earl C. Clements, 243
Grover Cleveland, 1, 72, 162, 163, 205
Montgomery Clift, 219
Patsy Cline, 41, 120, 229
DeWitt Clinton, 166
William "Bill" Clinton, 6, 229, 232
George Clooney, 153(2), 174
Rosemary Clooney, 153, 216, 217
George Clymer, 98

William "Buffalo Bill" Cody, 27, 33, 35, 130
James Lowry Cogar, 222
Sheriff Boy Coffee (*Bonanza)* 52
George M. Cohan, 103
Nat King Cole, 1, 128
Brad Coleman, 225
Martha Layne Collins, 190, 239
Roscoe P. Coltrane (James Best), 226
Christopher Columbus, 144
Anderson Combs, 199
Bert T. Combs, 165, 166, 189
Earl Combs, 231
Sarah Walter Combs, 166
Perry Como, 98, 100, 193
Tara Conner, 238
William Conrad, 194
Tim Conway, 89
James Cook, 98
Calvin Coolidge, 118
Gary Cooper, 64,65
Gordon Cooper, 91
Jackie Cooper (*Our Gang Comedy)*, 11
John Sherman Cooper, 235, 243
Ellen Corby, 127
Manton Cornett, 202
Jon Corzine, 71
Bill Cosby, 98, 101
Howard Cosell, 80
Lou Costello, 72(2), 73, 184
Costello Twins, 161
Tim Couch, 206
Dave Cowens, 159
Hattie Cox, 200
Leander Cox, 175
Wally Cox (*Mr. Peepers)*, 51
C. W. Craig, 149
Elijah Craig, 238(2)
Floyd Cramer, 41, 218
Bob Crane, 15
Broderick Crawford, 98
Lester Crawford, 98
Nellie Crawford (Madame Sul-Te-Wan), 193
Chief Crazy Horse, 107
John Jordan Crittenden, 167, 171

Davy Crockett, 109, 111
Walter Cronkite, 60
Bing Crosby, 124, 128, 217
Powel Crosley Jr., 86
John Crow, 152
J. D. Crowe, 171
William J. Crowe Jr., 229
Bill Cullen, 110
Lee Cummings, 204
Robert Cummings, 60, 62
Ken Curtis (*Festus Haggen)*, 14
General George Custer, 27, 88, 184
Billy Ray Cyrus, 151, 182, 183
Kevin Cyrus, 183
Miley Cyrus, 182, 183

-D-

Condy Dabney, 185
Louis Dampier, 190
Robert Damron, 233
Walker Daniel, 152
Charles Darrow, 98
Joseph Hamilton Daviess, 168
Jefferson Davis, 162, 173, 192(2), 193, 240, 242
Jim Davis, 30
Joan Davis, 54
Roger Davis, 245
Sammy Davis Jr., 77
Doris Day, 86, 87
"Dizzy" Dean, 6
Edward Deeds, 87
Don DeFore (*Hazel)*, 35
John De Lorean, 51
William Demarest, (*Uncle Charley)*, 56
Jack Dempsey, 13
John Denver, 74
Kassie DePavia, 243
Johnny Depp, 169
Jackie DeShannon, 157, 158
Joseph Desha, 217
Hernando DeSoto,
Andy Devine (*Jingles)*, 5
Lou DeWitt, 119, 120

Little Jimmy Dickens, 125
Angie Dickinson, 83
Walter Diemer, 97
Phyllis Diller, 88
Matt Dillon (James Arness), 54, 194
James and Martha Dinsmore, 149
Dion, 78
Archibald Dixon, 246
Arthur Dixon, 207
William Henry Dixon, 196
Jimmy Dodd, 87
Horace Dodge,
John Dodge, 51
Bob Dole, 37
Fats Domino, 41, 105
Elinor Donahue (*Father Knows Best*),
123, 124
Billy Donovan, 196
Howdy Doody (Buffalo Bob Smith), 78
Dudley Dooright, 194
Jimmy Dorsey, 41, 102, 110
Tommy Dorsey, 41, 72, 102, 110
Donna Douglas (*Ellie Mae Clampett*), 41
Banjamin Dowell, 166
Denny Doyle, 237
Patrick Duffy, 64
James B. Duke, 157, 162
Patty Duke Show (Jean Byron), 219
Peyton Duke, 198, 201
Sanford Duncan, 239, 240
Irene Dunn, 194
E. I. du Pont, 16
Jimmy Durante, 77

-E-

Amelia Earhart, 37
Dale Earnheardt Jr., 219
Wyatt Earp, 36, 228
Roger Ebert, 172
Buddy Ebsen, 27, 28
Nelson Eddy, 103
Thomas Alva Edison, 86, 97, 192, 194
John Edmonson, 170
Ralph Edwards (*This Is Your Life*), 13, 74

Wayne Edwards, 156
Dwight D. Eisenhower, 23, 114
Mamie Eisenhower, 33
Jack Elam, 5
William Ellery, 103
Duke Ellington, 124
John Milton Elliott, 170
Stu Erwin, (*The Stu Erwin Show*) 12
Faith Esham, 208
James Estill, 171
Dale Evans, 86,116
Everly Brothers, 41(2), 158
Ike Everly, 226, 227
Don Everly, 226
Phil Everly, 226
Tom Ewell, 169

-F-

F-Troop, 21
Shelley Fabares, 9
Fabian, 99, 105
David Crockett Fannin, 224
Peter Fannin, 224
Richie Farmer, 166
Philo Farnsworth, 117
Charles Farrell (*My Little Margie*), 50
John Gregg Fee, 153, 212
Freddy Fender, 41
Edward Ferguson, 235
Gabriel Ferrer, 153
Jose' Ferrer, 153, 217
George Ferris, 96
John Field, 144
Marshall Field, 48
W. C. Fields, 98, 101
Barney Fife (Don Knotts), 125, 127
Eddie Fisher, 99
Ella Fitzgerald, 105, 121, 122
F. Scott Fitzgerald, 192
Lester Flatt, 80, 109, 205, 229
Frank Fleer, 97
John Fleming, 174
Ernie Fletcher, 211, 223
Myron Floren, 107

John Floyd, 175
William Floyd, 77
Henry Fonda, 67
June Foray (voice of Chatty Kathy), 50
Hugh Forbes, 223
Gerald Ford, 67(2)
Henry Ford, 51
John Baptiste Ford, 153
Tennessee Ernie Ford, 109, 111, 227
Travis Ford, 190
Wendell H. Ford, 166, 169
Stephen Foster, 99, 153
Pete Fountain, 218
Fontaine Fox, 193
Nathan Bedford Forrest, 180
John Fox Jr., 150
Connie Francis, 73
David L. Francis, 176
George Francis, 202
Stephen Frank, 177
Benjamin Franklin, 49, 96, 98, 177, 209, 239
John Franklin, 201
William Frawley (*Fred Mertz*), 35
Alan Freed, 85
Heather French, 153, 216
William Frost, 213
Woodie Fryman, 175
Robert Fulton, 177, 209
Annette Funicello, 9, 79
Alan Funt, 197

-G-

Clark Gable, 87
Abner Gaines, 149
Paul "Showtime" Gaffney, 185
Albert Gallatin, 178
Don Galloway, 153
Officer Bill Gannon (*Dragnet*), 51
Judy Garland, 52
James Garner, 90
James Garrard, 179
Pat Garrett, 1, 77
Greer Garson, 113

Crystal Gayle, 196(2)
George (the servant), 241
Lonesome George, 27
Elbridge Gerry, 48
The Great Gildersleve (Harold Peary), 12
Dizzy Gillespie, 105
Haven Gillespie, 197
Mickey Gilley, 41
Edna Gladney, 113
Jackie Gleason, 77(2), 78, 121
George Gobel, 27
Arthur Godfrey, 121
William Goebel, 177
Bobby Goldsboro, 18
Barry Goldwater, 4
Benny Goodman, 41, 83, 110, 194
Howard and Vestal Goodman, 190
Julian Goodman, 146
B. F. Goodrich, 84
Mark Gottfried, 237
Mike Gottfried, 237
Robert Goulet, 49
Sue Grafton, 194
William Gragg, 235
Billy Graham, 80
Aunt Granny, 110
Earl Grant, 91
John Grant, 180
Joshua Grant, 161
Kirby Grant (*Sky King*), 65
Samuel Grant, 180
Squire Grant, 180
General Ulysses S. Grant, 88(2), 189, 192, 217
Benjamin F. Graves, 180
Peter Graves (*Fury*), 54, 55
John Gray, 241
Trey Grayson, 166, 197
William Grayson, 181
Horace Greeley, 70
David Green, 169
Jeff Green, 169
Nathaniel Greene, 182, 224, 225
Christopher Greenup, 182
Noble Jones Gregory, 181
William Vores Gregory, 181

Zane Grey, 86
Francis Dennis Griffin, 194
Merv Griffin, 151
Andy Griffith, 80, 125
D. W. Griffith, 230
Marsha Griffith, 237
William Grigsby, 202
John Grisham, 6
Button Guinette, 20
Don Gullet, 182

-H-

Cliff Hagan, 169
Festus Haggen (Ken Curtis), 14
Nathan Hale, 15
Bill Haley, 41, 52
Joe B. Hall, 186
Lyman Hall, 20
Tom T. Hall, 127, 160
Mordecai Ham, 144
Levi Hampton, 151
Lionel Hampton, 194
John Hancock, 48, 49, 50, 183
W. C. Handy, 1, 187
Fielding Hanks, 224
Nancy Hanks, 125, 183
John Hardin, 183
William Hardin, 154
James Hardy, 146
Oliver Hardy (*Laurel and Hardy*), 21,22
John Marshall Harlan, 152
John Marshall Harlan II, 152
Silas Harlan, 184
Rev. A. C. Harlowe, 213
Larnell Harris, 153
Benjamin Harrison, 31, 120, 186
Benjamin Harrison V, 186
Cynthia and Anna Harrison, 186
Robert Harrison, 186
James Harrod, 184, 222
John Hart, 72
Harold Hatcher, 176
William Henry Harrison, 119, 186, 230, 239, 243

James Harrod, 222
Nathaniel G. T. Hart, 186
Paul Harvey, 91
Clem Haskins, 241
Devil Anse Hatfield, 125
Hatfield-McCoy 233(2)
Alvin Hawkins, 147
Hoyt Hawkins, 218
Gabby Hayes, 79
Anderson Hays, 198
Hazel (Don DeFore), 21
Sherman Helmsley, 101
Sally Hemings, 174
Florence Henderson, 31
Richard Henderson, 187
Patrick Henry, 120(2), 161, 188
Steve Henry, 169
Jim Henson, 57
Josiah Henson, 168
Katherine Hepburn, 16
William Herndon, 182
Josehp Hewes, 80
William Hewlett, 51
Thomas Heyward, 104
Paschal Hickman, 189
Wild Bill Hickok, 27, 37, 60
Mildred and Patti Hill, 195
Clifton Hilleglass, 66
John Kenneth Hilliard, 103
James P. Hindman, 198, 201
Duncan Hines, 244, 245
Earl "Fatha" Hines, 101, 105
Al Hirt, 41, 218
Don Ho, 24
Doc Holliday, 228
Sterling Holloway, 21
Buddy Holly, 83, 115, 218, 226
Daniel Henry Holmes, 197
Joseph Holt, 154
Darla Hood, 92
John Bell Hood, 147
William Hooper, 80
Herbert Hoover, 33,36
Hopalong Casidy (William Boyd), 88
Johns Hopkins, 46
Samuel Hopkins, 161, 187, 189

Stephen Hopkins, 103
Thelma Hopkins, 194
Francis Hopkinson, 72
Hop Sing (Sen Yung),
Capttin Richard Hornberger, 172
Paul Hornung, 194
Chief Crazy Horse, 107
Hoss (Dan Blocker), 113, 114
John Houchins, 170
Hot Lips Houlihan, 172
Whitney Houston, 117
Clint Howard, 90
Rebecca Lynn Howard, 214
Ron Howard, 90, 92
Theodore Roosevelt Mason Howard, 158
Carroll Hubbard, 158, 181
John Wesley Hunt, 173
Samuel Huntington, 15
Chet Huntley, 64, 65
Andrew Hynes, 184

-I-

Lee Iacoca, 100
Mike Ilitch, 51
Charles Ingalls (Michael Landon), 79
Steve Inskeep, 237
Dan Issel, 190

-J-

Andrew Jackson, 105, 109, 191, 216, 222, 237
Frank James, 60
Harry James, 72
Jesse James, 60, 210, 227
Calamity Jane, 60
Ann Jarvis, 96
Thomas Jefferson, 119, 120, 174, 178, 189, 191, 209, 227
Waylon Jennings, 160
Jingles (Andy Devine), 5
Little Joe (Michael Landon), 79
Uncle Joe (Edgar Buchanan*)*, 62

Elton John, 41
Andrew Johnson, 80, 109
George W. Johnson, 210
Lyndon B. Johnson, 1, 4, 166
Richard Johnson, 193, 196
Robert Johnson, 178, 238
Sarah Johnston, 184
Clabe Jones, 198
Curt Jones, 218
George Jones, 160
Grandpa Jones, 112, 188
Kennedy Jones, 226, 227
Larry Jones, 244
Lee S. Jones, 211
Lelia Jones, U.S. Army nurse, 172
Shirley Jones, 98, 100
"Wah Wah" Jones, 185
Scott Joplin, 113
Naomi Judd, 151
Wynonna Judd, 151

-K-

Duke Kahanamoku, 24
Captain Kangaroo (Bob Keeshan), 79
Boris Karloff, 60
Richard Karn, 103
Cesar Kaskel, 217
Chatty Kathy (June Foray),
Danny Kaye, 77, 217
Sammy Kaye, 41
Bil Keane, 99
Buster Keaton, 37, 38
Bob Keeshan (*Captain Kangaroo*), 79
Toby Keith, 90
Helen Keller, 1
Will Keith Kellogg, 51
Emmett Kelly, 38
Gene Kelly, 98
Grace Kelly, 101
Walter T. Kelly, 181
Dr. Dave Kelsey (Bob Crane), 15
Evel Kenievel, 65
John F. Kennedy, 49, 165, 235
Tom Kennedy, 196

Simon Kenton, 150, 197
Charles Kettering, 87, 88
Francis Scott Key, 46, 47
Marshall Key, 216
Otis Key, 210
Stan Key, 158
Billy the Kid, 1, 77
George Kimble, 237
Bradley Kincaid, 188
B. B. King, 57
Coretta Scott King, 170
Elhanah King, 207
Mac King, 163
Martin Luther King Jr., 21, 70
Sky King (Kirby Grant), 65
Durward Kirby, 197
Stuart Kirby, 169
Eartha Kitt, 105
Jack Klugman, 98
Arthur Kneibler, 128
Bob Knight, 186
James Proctor Knott, 198(2)
Don Knotts, 125, 126
Henry Knox, 108, 202
Sebastian Kresge, 99
Gene Krupa, 41, 194
Dennis Kucinich, 87
Nancy Kulp, 101
Charles Kurtsinger, 156

-L-

Alexander Lackey, 176
Alan Ladd, 6
Lafayette, 172, 247
Ruby Laffoon, 30, 190
Arthur Lake, 203
Louis L'Amour, 83
Jane Lampton, 165
Michael Landon, 79
Henry Lane, 147
Frances Langford, 127
John LaRue, 203
La Salle, 65
Stan Laurel, 21

James Lawrence, 204, 231
Betsy Layne, 176
Cawood Ledford, 185(2)
Brenda Lee, 21, 41, 158, 218
Francis Lightfoot Lee, 120
Henry "Light Horse Harry" Lee, 181, 205, 245
Peggy Lee, 83, 84
Robert E. Lee, 120, 122, 181, 183, 193, 205, 240
David Leitch, 181
Jack Lemon, 48
"Meadowlark" Lemon, 80, 185
Ponce de Leon, 17
Preston H. Leslie, 167, 168, 205
Robert P. Letcher, 179, 206
Lewis and Clark, 83, 93
Francis Lewis, 77
Jerry Lewis, 73
Jerry Lee Lewis, 41
Meriwether Lewis, 191, 208
Liberace, 128
Charles Yancy Ligon, 176
Abraham Lincoln, 6, 27, 30, 40, 46, 48, 80, 90, 124, 125, 154, 161, 167, 168(2), 174, 182, 183(2), 184, 191, 192(2), 203, 208, 210, 212, 213, 217, 224, 227, 242, 243, 245
Benjamin Lincoln, 208
Captain Abraham Lincoln, 245
Mary Todd Lincoln, 173, 174, 203, 241, 242
Nancy Hanks Lincoln, 184
Mordecai Lincoln, 245
Sarah Lincoln, 183
Thomas Lincoln, 125, 167, 168, 183, 184
George Lindsey (*Goober*), 1
Isaac Lindsey, 235
Sonny Liston, 6
Philip Livingston, 77
Robert R. Livingston, 209
Alice Lloyd, 200
John Uri Lloyd, 149
Benjamin Logan, 208, 209(2)
The Lone Range (Clayton Moore), 28
Brice Long, 163

Henry Wadsworth Longfellow, 44
King Louis XIV, 40
Princess Louisa, 255
Patty Loveless, 196, 233
Thomas Lowe, 183
Myrna Loy, 64
Allen Ludden, 128
Elcaney Lykins, 224
Malone Lykins, 224
Thomas Lynch, 104, 185
Paul Lynde, 88
Loretta Lynn, 111, 160, 196(2)
Crittenden Lyon, 210

-M-

Marian MacDougall, 98
Ted Mack, 14
Fred MacMurray, 28
George Madison, 212
James Madison, 119, 190, 193, 211, 212, 216, 240, 243
Carl Magee, 90
Beriah Magoffin, 192(2), 213, 238
Larry Mahoney, 160
Lee Majors, 51
Henry Mancini, 87
Rose Marie, 78
Francis Marion, 167, 214
John Marriott, 117
Olive Marsh, 200
John Marshall, 215
Clay Martin, 201
Dean Martin, 89, 90, 193, 194, 197
John Preston Martin, 216
Mark Martin, 6
Wink Martindale, 110
Lee Marvin, 219
Marx Brothers, 77, 78
George Mason, 216
Bat Masterson, 36
Jerry Mathers (*Leave It to Beaver*), 36
Johnny Mathis, 115
Don Mattingly, 30
Victor Mature, 193

Cicero Maxwell, 183
Willie Mayes, 80
Jeremy Mayfield, 169
Frederick Maytag, 27
General Douglas McArthur, 6
Charlie McCarthy, 27, 127
Paul McCartney, 226, 229
Virgil McCracken, 217
James Bennet McCreary, 219
Hattie McDaniel, 37
Jeanette McDonald, 103
Ronald McDonald (Willard Scott), 121
Marion McDougall (*Mrs. Gurney*), 51, 98
Dr. Ephraim McDowell, 80, 152
George McFarland (*Spanky*), 114
Thomas McKearn, 16
Andrew McKee, 145
Dallas McKennon, 94
Alney McLean, 220
McNeil Family, 161
Butterfly McQueen (*Prissy* and *Beulah*), 19
James Meade, 220
Richard Hickman Menefee, 147, 221
Lori Menshouse, 236
Hugh Mercer, 221(2)
Johnny Mercer, 221
Fred Mertz (William Frawley), 37, 38
Thomas Metcalfe, 222
Arthur Middleton, 104
Glenn Miller, 33, 35, 41
John Miller, 212
Samuel Freeman Miller, 212
Mills Brothers, 86
Milliken Family, 242
Mary Louise Milliken, 242
Billy Mills, 107
Elsie Mitchell, 94
Kerri Mitchell, 203
Margaret Mitchell, 20
Tom Monaghan, 51
Bill Monroe, 80, 109, 205, 228, 229, 244
James Monroe, 119, 223, 239
Maria Monroe, 223
Marilyn Monroe, 169
Eddie Montgomery, 152

John Michael Montgomery, 152(2)
Richard Montgomery, 223
Dwight L. Moody, 48
Clayton Moore (*The Lone Ranger*), 28
Garry Moore, 46, 197
George Moore, 244
Robert Moore, 244
Wild Bill Moore, 85
Lester "Roadhog" Moran, 120
Agnes Morehead, 219
James T. Morehead, 236
Daniel Morgan, 224, 243
Garrett Morgan, 150
Harry Morgan, 51
John Hunt Morgan, 184, 214, 242
Orlena Combs Morgan, 200
Thomas Hunt Morgan, 173
Hal Morris (*Otis Campbell*), 53
Lewis Morris, 77
Robert Morris, 98
Edward P. Morrow, 235
"Jelly Roll" Morton, 41
John Morton, 98
Moses, 46
John Peter Gabriel Muhlenberg, 224
Richard Jones Munford, 186
Audie Murphy, 115
John L. Murray, 157

-N-

Jim Nabors (*Gomer Pyle*), 1
Joe Namath, 100
Charles Napier, 144
Clarence Nash, 90
Francis Nash, 109
Carrie Nation, 179
Patricia Neal, 247
Harriet Nelson, 35, 151
Teri Nelson, 151
Thomas "Scotch Tom" Nelson, 227
Thomas Nelson Jr., 227
Ozzie Nelson, 73, 151
Ricky Nelson, 41, 158
Thomas Nelson, 120

Bob Newhart, 29
Christopher Newport, 158
Tommy Newsom, 218
Wayne Newton, 121
George Nicholas, 228
Pat Nixon, 68
Richard Nixon, 12, 25, 64, 67, 68, 197
Chuck Norris, 90
Trixie Norton (Joyce Randolph), 51
Louis B. Nunn, 146
Aaron Nussbaum, 27

-O-

Annie Oakley, 33, 86
Warren Oates, 226
Barack Obama, 24, 165
Carroll O'Connor, 77
Sandra Day O'Connor, 114
William Oldham, 229
Ransom E. Olds, 87
Frederick Law Olmstead, 156
Merlin Olsen, 117
Roy Orbison, 218
Radar O'Reilly, 35
Tony Orlando and Dawn, 194
Osborne Brothers, 206
Sonny Osborne, 229
Donnie Osmond, 117
Marie Osmond, 117
Abraham Owen, 168, 230
Thomas Dye Owings, 147
William Owsley, 179, 230
Ozzie and Harriet, 117

-P-

William Paca, 45
David Packard, 51
Chief Paduke, 217(2)
Patti Page, 91, 92
Robert Treat Paine, 45
Peggy Parish, 105
Fes Parker, 94, 115

Dolly Parton, 61, 110
Shirley Partridge (Shirley Jones), 98
Samuel Patterson, 237
George S. Patton, 9, 221
Paul Patton, 205
Les Paul, 109, 128
George Peabody, 50
Minnie Pearl, 110
Harold Peary, (*The Great Gildersleve*), 12
Mr. Peepers (Wally Cox), 51
John Pelphrey, 196
John Patrick Pelfrey, 197
Edmund Pendleton, 231
Penn family, 152(2)
John Penn, 80
William Penn, 95
J. C. Penney, 60
Carl C. Perkins, 199
Carl D. Perkins, 199
Edwin Perkins, 66
Marlin Perkins, 60
Oliver Hazard Perry, 104, 204, 231
Peter, Paul, and Mary, 194
Katherine Petit, 198
Herb Philbrick (Richard Carlson), 54
Frank Philips, 89
Franklin Pierce, 70
Zebulon Montgomery Pike Jr., 232
John Pillsbury, 70
Scottie Pippen, 6
Poage (family), 150, 151
Pogo Possum, 20
John K. Polk, 80, 109, 152
Leonidas Polk, 192
Cole Porter, 30, 32
C. W. Post, 51
Col. Sherman Potter (Harry Morgan), 51
Annie Potts, 240
Terence Powderly, 226
Colon Powell, 229
Dick Powell, 6
Lazarus W. Powell, 233, 234
William Prescott, 49, 244
Elvis Presley, 41(2), 57, 59, 110, 158, 218, 226, 229

John Preston, 176
Emory R. Price, 176
Vincent Price, 60
Charlie Pride, 57, 59, 125
Kazimierz Pulaski, 234(2)
Israel Putnam, 244
Ernie Pyle, 30

-Q-

William Quantrill, 240

-R-

Mose Rager, 226, 227
Cedric Rainwater (Howard Watts), 229
Dottie Rambo, 190
Venus Ramey, 151
Frank Ramsey, 190
JonBenet Ramsey, 125
Patsy Ramsey, 125
Tony Randall, 51, 91
Boots Randolph, 218
Joyce Randolph, 51, 52
Jon Rauch, 236
Patricia Lee Ramey, 196, 233
Martha Raye, 64
George Read, 16
Ronald Reagan, 27, 49, 229
Vinnie Ream, 90
Jeffrey Reddick, 154
Orville Redenbacher, 30
Frank Redford, 146
Donna Reed, 34, 35
Stanley Forman Reed, 216
George Reeves (*Superman*), 34, 36
Jim Reeves, 41
Don Reid, 119
Harold Reid, 119
Don Reno, 229
Deborah Renshaw, 244
Mary Lou Retton, 125(2)
Paul Revere, 49
Condoleeza Rice, 1

Charlie Rich, 6
Little Richard, 21, 41
Jody Richards, 244
Kevin Richardson, 174
Tom Rickman, 215
Chester A. Riley (Jackie Gleason), 77
The Life of Riley, 21, 77
LeAnn Rimes, 57
Abbie Ritchie, 201
Crockett Ritchie, 201
Jean Ritchie, 232
Margaret Ritchie, 201
Marty Robbins, 5
Jimmie Roberts, 190
Pernell Roberts, 23, 113
Dale Robertson, 91
George Robertson, 235
Brooks Robinson, 6
Jackie Robinson, 21
James F. Robinson, 213, 238
Sugar Ray Robinson, 21
Rochester (Eddie Anderson), 11
Rocky and Bullwinkle Show, 197
Jimmie Rodgers, 109,123
Caesar Rodney, 16
Edmund P. Rogers, 222
Fred Rogers, 98
Ginger Rogers, 62
Hal Rogers, 246
Roy Rogers, 86
Will Rogers, 89, 92
Linda Ronstadt, 4
Mickey Rooney, 77, 78
Franklin D. Roosevelt, 24, 77
Theodore Roosevelt, 1, 56, 77
Brian Rose, 244
Leo Rosenberg, 97
Joe Rosenthal, 175
Julius Rosenwald, 27
Betsy Ross, 96, 97, 99
George Ross, 98
Nellie Tayloe Ross, 61
John Rowan, 236(2)
Paul Marvin Rudolph, 242
Vernon Carver Rudolph, 218
Adolph Rupp, 37, 38, 185, 186

Benjamin Rush, 98
Henry Russell, 237
William Russell, 209, 237
William Russell III, 209
Babe Ruth, 77, 231
Kelly Rutherford, 184
Edward Rutledge, 104
Wiley Rutledge, 155
Perry Ryan, 155

-S-

Albert Sabin, 86
Eva Marie Saint, 219
Pat Sajak, 151
Soupy Sales, 80
La Salle, 40
Samuel Salyer, 213
Colonel Harland Sanders, 204, 239
Bob Sargent, 219
Diane Sawyer, 146
Henry Scalf, 198
Kenny Schrader, 219, 225
Charles Schultz, 55
John Scopes, 218
Arthur Scott, 97
Charles Scott, 164(2), 238(2)
Willard Scott, 121
Earl Scruggs, 80, 109, 205, 229
Steven Seagal, 219
Edmund Sears, 49
Richard Warren Sears, 54
E. G. Sebree, 246
Doc Severinsen, 94, 218
William Shannon, 239
Philip Sharp, 231
Anna Nelson Shelby, 213
Isaac Shelby, 148, 213, 239(2)
Alan Shepard, 70
Adam Shepherd, 155
Henry Shepherd, 200
Roger Sherman, 15, 209
William Tecumseh Sherman, 20
Dina Shore, 110, 112
Cincinnatus Shyrock, 174

Gideon Shyrock, 174, 177
Molly Simms, 158
Phil Simms, 215
John Simpson, 239
Frank Sinatra, 72, 73, 197
Ricky Skaggs, 171, 205
Red Skelton, 33, 86
Gustavis Slaughter, 246
Moneta Sleet Jr., 170
Elizabeth Slone, 201
Sarah Slone, 201
Buffalo Bob Smith, 78
Burnard Smith, 201
Charles Shaler Smith, 196
Charles "One Handed Charlie" Smith, 150
Daniel Morgan Smith, 156
Dean Smith, 186
Elinor Smith, 125
James Smith, 98
Jeremiah and Thomas Smith, 202
Kate Smith, 120, 122
Margaret Chase Smith, 44
Tubby Smith, 47
William and Millie Smith, 202
George Snyder, 150
Franklin Sousley, 175
Ann Southern, 83
Red Sovine, 125
Spanky (George McFarland), 114
REO Speedwagon, 218
Spier Spencer, 240
Steven Spielberg, 86
Spillman family, 158
Charles Haddon Spurgeon, 48
Ralph Stanley, 121, 171, 205
Robert E. Stanley, 176
Rick Stansbury, 220
Harry Dean Stanton, 172
John Stark, 113
Statler Brothers, 119, 120, 121, 122
Woody Stephens, 234
Adlai Stevenson Sr., 162
John White Stevenson, 197
James Stewart, 98, 101, 246
Martha Stewart, 72

Tony Stewart, 219
Richard Stockton, 71, 72
Dr. Alex Stone (Carl Betz), 98
May Stone, 198
Thomas Stone, 45
Mayor Stoner (Parley Baer), 117
The Rolling Stones, 41
Three Stooges, 77
Gale Storm, 114
Harriet Beecher Stowe, 15, 168, 179
George Straight, 197
Stringbean (David Akeman), 112, 229
Jesse Stuart, 182
Frank Albert Stubblefield, 158
Nathan Stubblefield, 158
David D. Sublett, 214
Sullivan brothers, 34
Billy Sunday, 34
Superman, 21, 34, 36
Eddie Sutton, 37, 196
Jimmy Swaggart, 41
John Cameron Swayze, 64
Carl Switzer (*Alfalfa*), 29

-T-

William Howard Taft, 85
Aunt Bea Taylor (Francis Bavier), 77
Elizabeth Taylor, 219
George Taylor, 98
James Taylor, 158
John Taylor, 119
Opie Taylor, 90
Richard Taylor, 240
Tim Taylor (Tim Allen), 103
Sarah Knox Taylor, 162, 193, 240
William S. Taylor, 156
Zachary Taylor, 119, 162, 193, 240
Ray Teal (*Sheriff Roy Coffee* on *Bonanza*), 52
Tecumseh, 209
Walt Terrell, 237
Danny Thomas, 52
Dave Thomas, 204
George Thomas, 214

Hardin Thomas, 184
Helen Thomas, 165
Willis Thomas, 185
George William Thompson, 236
John Thompson, 159
Henry David Thoreau, 49
Matthew Thornton, 70
Jim Thorpe, 93
Emma Thurman, 200
John Todd, 241, 242
Lee Trover Todd, 190(2)
Daniel D. Tompkins, 223
Spencer Tracy, 127
Mary Travers, 194
Merle Travis, 109, 226(2), 227
Stephen Trigg, 242
Lawrence Trimble, 175
Robert Trimble, 165, 242
Trixie Norton (*The Honeymooners*), 52
Anderson Shipp Truman, 61
Harry Randall Truman, 125
Harry S. Truman, 6, 61, 128, 181
John Trumbull, 209
Harriet Tubman, 46
Cal Turner Sr., 145
Ike Turner, 85
Ted Turner, 20
Mark Twain (Samuel Clemens), 62, 165
Conway Twitty, 57

-U-

Uncle Charlie (William Demarest), 56
Uncle Joe (Edgar Buchanan), 62
Thomas Rust Underwood, 163

-V-

Richie Valens, 83
Rudy Vallee, 119
Dick Van Dyke, 64
Jerry Van Dyke, 7
Vivian Vance (*Ethyl Mertz*), 37, 38
Nick Varner, 169

Jim Varney, 174
Billy Vaughn, 146
Bobby Vee, 83
Steven M. Vest, 172
John Vickers, 220
Bob Vila, 103
Fred Moore Vinson, 205
Bobby Vinton, 98

-W-

Porter Wagoner, 61, 64, 110
Ellie Walker (Elinor Donahue), 123
Marcy Walker, 218
Dr. Thomas Walker, 148, 203, 204, 235, 255(2)
William Walker, 215
Fats Waller, 86
Ray Walston, 41
Amba Walters, 176
George Walton, 20
Sam Walton, 91
Darrell Waltrip, 169
Michael Waltrip, 169
John Wanamaker, 99
Joseph Warren, 244
Robert Penn Warren, 242
Chad Warrix, 154
Booker T. Washington, 121
George Washington, 45, 71, 85, 105, 119, 123, 150, 160, 165, 181, 182, 191, 202, 204, 209, 221(2), 223, 235, 238(2), 245, 247
Mary Washington, 221
Harry Lee Waterfield, 189
Ethel Waters, 175
Clarence Wayland Watson, 176
Ruth Watson, 200
Howard Watts (Cedric Rainwater), 229
Anthony "Mad Anthony" Wayne, 245
John Wayne, 34, 36, 67, 194, 219
Jacob Weatherholt, 154
Charlie Weaver, 89
Clara Marie Ramey Webb, 196
Jim Webb, 207

Daniel Webster, 70, 246
Lawrence Welk, 83,107
Orson Welles, 128
Harvey Weskit (Tony Randall), 91
Irving Wheatcroft, 246
Greenville P. Wheeler, 214
Jere H. Wheelwright, 176
William Whipple, 70
Betty White, 29
Daugherty White, 206
Vanna White, 105
Gustav Whitehead, 15
Wayne Edward "Ed" Whitfield, 163
William Whitley, 208, 209, 219, 246, 247
Christopher Antoine Whitney, 163
Eli Whitney, 49
Jackie "Keith" Whitney, 171
Charles Wickliffe, 145
Harlow Wilcox, 92
Terry Wilcutt, 210
Laura Ingles Wilder, 54, 63
Andy Williams,34, 36, 41, 117(2)
Hank Williams, 1
Roger Williams, 103
William Williams, 15
James Willis, 157
Charles Wilson, 99
James Wilson, 98
Mary S. Wilson, 188
Teddy Wilson, 194
Woodrow Wilson, 119
Scott Wimmer, 225
Oprah Winfrey, 57
Ed Winn, 101
Winnie the Pooh, 21
Chubby Wise, 229
Grant Withers, 117
John Witherspoon, 72
Oliver Wolcott, 15
Nathaniel Wolfe, 247
Bartholomew and Martha Ann Wood, 161
John Wooden, 30
William Woodford, 247
Silas Woodson, 203
Woody Woodpecker, 94

Chuck Woolery, 151, 236
James Woolridge, 237
Ernest P. Worrell (Jim Varney), 174
Frank Lloyd Wright, 127
Orville Wright, 60
William Wrigley, Jr., 99
Private Henry Wyatt, 79
Jane Wyatt (*Father Knows Best*), 73
Tammy Wynette, 57
George Wynn, 235
George Wythe, 120

-Y-

Henry Yates, 178
Trisha Yearwood, 90
Dwight Yoakam, 233
Billy Yocum, 224
Sgt. Alvin C. York, 110, 112
Loretta Young, 117
Solomon Young, 61

-Z-

Led Zeppelin, 41
Ron Ziegler, 197
Fuzzy Zoeller, 31

Made in the USA
Lexington, KY
02 December 2010